Faulkner and Love

William Faulkner in Paris, fall 1925, photographed by his friend
William C. Odiorne. Odiorne took a series of photographs of
Faulkner in Paris; this is probably the one Faulkner sent to Estelle in
Shanghai. (Courtesy of Jill Faulkner Summers)

Faulkner and Love

The Women Who Shaped His Art

Judith L. Sensibar

YALE UNIVERSITY PRESS   NEW HAVEN & LONDON

Designed by James J. Johnson and set in Monotype Baskerville and Bulmer types by
Technologies 'N Typography.

Printed in the United States of America.

Library of Congress Cataloging-in-Publication Data

Sensibar, Judith L. (Judith Levin), 1941–

    Faulkner and love : the women who shaped his art / Judith L. Sensibar.

      p.   cm.

    Includes bibliographical references (p.) and index.

    ISBN 978-0-300-11503-1 (alk. paper)

  1. Faulkner, William, 1897–1962—Family. 2. Faulkner, William, 1897–1962—Childhood and
youth.   3. Novelists, American—20th century—Family relationships.   4. Women in literature.
5. Oxford (Miss.)—Social life and customs.   I. Title.

    PS3511.A86Z96647 2008

    813'.52—dc22

[B]   2008040283

A catalogue record for this book is available from the British Library.

This paper meets the requirements of ANSI/NISO Z39.48–1992 (Permanence of Paper).

10 9 8 7 6 5 4 3 2 1

To David

In memory of Jill Faulkner Summers
24 June 1933–21 April 2008

It's much more fun to try to write about women because I think women are marvelous, they're wonderful, and I know very little about them, and so I just—it's much more fun to try to write about women than about men—more difficult, yes.

—Faulkner, 1957

Contents

List of Illustrations   ix

Preface   xii

Acknowledgments   xviii

General Introduction   1

Part 1. William Faulkner and Caroline "Callie" Barr

INTRODUCTION   19

1. Caroline Barr in Black and White Voices   25
2. Caroline Barr's Origins   34
3. Negotiating the "Mammy" Tradition:
   Callie Barr as "Second Mother"   56
4. Callie Barr and Maud Falkner   66
5. Caroline Barr and Faulkner's Poetics: *Go Down, Moses*   89
6. Family Secrets: "Mississippi"   111

Part 2. Faulkner's Mother, Maud Butler Falkner

INTRODUCTION   129

7. Maud's Mysterious Ancestry   139
8. Willie Falkner's Childhood World, 1896–1907   161
9. From Honor Roll to Truancy, 1907–1914   186

10. Choosing Roles and Role Models   197
11. Learning to Speak with His Eyes   205
12. Reading Faulkner's "Mothers"   221

Parts 3, 4, and 5. William Faulkner and Estelle Oldham

INTRODUCTION   237

Part 3. Estelle and Billy, 1903–1914

13. Estelle Oldham's Mississippi Frontier Family   249
14. Kosciusko Childhood, Southern Belledom,
    and Estelle's Fictional Memoir, 1897–1903   264
15. Billy Falkner and Estelle Oldham, Oxford, 1903–1914   289

Part 4. First Loves, First "Marriages," 1914–1926

16. Shifting Alliances, 1914–1918   309
17. The Oldham-Franklin Wedding, April 1918   323
18. Marriage in the "Crossroads of the Pacific," June–September 1918   336
19. An Army Wife, Schofield Barracks, Hawaii,
    September 1918–May 1919   348
20. Stolen Interludes, 1919 and 1921   359
21. The Marketing of Estelle and Her Rebellion   387

Part 5. The Emergence of a Mature Novelist

22. Estelle's Shanghai Sojourn, 1922–1924   407
23. Collaborating with Estelle, Oxford, 1924–1925   424
24. Faulkner's Other Collaboration, New Orleans, 1924 and 1925   441
25. *The Sound and the Fury* and Its Aftermath, 1925–1933   456
26. Faulkner's Suppressed Tributes to Estelle, 1933–1935   481

List of Abbreviations   501

Notes   504

Select Bibliography   569

Index   581

Illustrations

Book frontispiece	William Faulkner in Paris, fall 1925, photographed by William C. Odiorne.	ii
Frontispiece to Part 1	Caroline "Callie" Barr's gravestone, 1940.	18
1.1	Barr family genealogy.	26
2.1	The road Callie Barr walked from Rowan Oak to her daughters' homes in Hipps Hollow, Miss.	36
2.2	Map of the Barr family's postwar migration from South Carolina to Arkansas and Mississippi.	41
2.3	The Barr-Rudd family graveyard on Blackjack Road, near Sardis.	43
2.4	Caroline Barr and Dean Falkner, c. 1909.	44
2.5	Site of James Rudd's one-room schoolhouse.	52
3.1	Map of Oxford, Mississippi.	58
3.2	Two Southern rural jook joints, c. 1930.	59
4.1	Painting and detail of cabin genre scene by Maud Butler Falkner.	68
4.2	Six generations of Falkner-Faulkners painted by Maud Butler Falkner in the 1940s and 1950s.	69
4.3	*Life* photo (1941) showing Mourning painting of Maud's mother, Lelia Dean Swift (Butler), and her grandmother Mahalah Pullen Swift (c. 1857).	70
4.4	Two portraits by Maud, c. 1941: *Preacher Green Liggens* and *Dulcie*	71
4.5	Caroline Barr holding Dean Falkner Wells, 1936.	72
4.6 and 4.7 (details)	Maud's portrait of Caroline Barr, c. 1941.	73, 74

6.1	Callie Barr's cabin behind Rowan Oak, 2002.	112
6.2	Faulkner's photo of Callie Barr and Jill Faulkner, summer 1939.	122
Frontispiece to Part 2	Studio photo of Maud Butler, 1896.	128
Introduction.1	Maud Butler Falkner's gravestone.	134
7.1	Mourning painting, after Maud's extensive revisions, post-1941.	138
7.2	Lelia Swift Butler and her young daughter, Maud Butler.	142
7.3	Swift-Butler-Fa(u)lkner genealogy.	146
7.4	Wedding photos of Maud Butler and Murry Falkner, 1896.	159
8.1	"William Falkner, age 2 years, 8 months."	160
8.2	Maud and Mary Holland (Auntee).	162
8.3	Oldham-Fa(u)lkner family genealogy.	168
10.1	Faulkner posing in various Royal Canadian Air Force outfits, c. 1918–20.	200
11.1	Faulkner's self-portrait as "Kodak negative," 1918.	207
11.2	Faulkner's illustration of the "fallen" Marietta; Aubrey Beardsley's illustration for Oscar Wilde's *Salome*.	214
11.3	Faulkner's "virgin" Marietta; Estelle's engagement portrait, April 1918.	215
11.4	Pierrot and Marietta, the fatal dance scene; Estelle Franklin with her son, Malcolm, c. 1927.	216
11.5	Faulkner posing as a young dandy, 1918.	219
12.1	Faulkner's photo of Caroline Barr, summer 1939.	232
Frontispiece to Part 3	Estelle Oldham Franklin and her daughter Victoria ("Cho-Cho") Franklin, summer 1921.	236
13.1	Allen-Oldham genealogy.	256
13.2	Estelle's maternal grandparents' house in Kosciusko, Miss.; the "cottage" Lem and Lida Oldham rented from Miss Vic and Judge Henry C. Niles.	258
14.1	Baby picture of Estelle Oldham, 1897.	265
14.2	Estelle, at age six or seven, and her sister, Victoria ("Tochie").	267
15.1	Studio portrait of Estelle Oldham, summer 1913.	290
15.2	Yearbook photo of Estelle Oldham at Mary Baldwin Seminary, 1914.	297
15.3	Estelle Oldham with friends, c. 1914.	300
15.4	Estelle's father, Major Lemuel Earle Oldham, c. 1912.	304

17.1	Estelle's first husband, Cornell Franklin, 1918.	325
17.2	Cornell Franklin's "Southern mansion" in Shanghai, 1935.	327
17.3	Photo of Estelle Oldham, 1913.	329
18.1	Estelle Franklin's U.S. Citizen's Identification Card of July 1918.	343
19.1	Uncle Malcolm Franklin and relatives disembarking from the *USAT Sheridan*, Honolulu, Hawaii, 1920.	357
22.1	Passport photos of Estelle Franklin and her daughter Cho-Cho, 8 December 1921.	408
22.2	The Franklin cottage in Shanghai; Estelle, Cho-Cho, and Cho-Cho's nurse in their garden, c. 1922–23.	410
24.1	William Spratling's line drawing of Faulkner and himself, New Orleans, 1926.	452
26.1	Proof sheet of Faulkner's five photos of "Caddy Compson," 1935: "Caught without dialogue by a camera."	492
26.2	First frame: "A beautiful and tragic little girl."	494
26.3	Second frame: "We watched the muddy bottom of her drawers."	495
26.4	Third frame: "And scattered my precious dolls."	496
26.5	Fourth frame: "Caddy was all wet and muddy behind."	497
26.6	Fifth frame: "All knowing must begin and end with that fierce hotbreathing, paused and stooping wet figure that smelled like trees."	499

Preface

This book is about William Faulkner and the three most important women in his life: his mother, Maud Butler Falkner (1871–1960), the black woman who raised him, Caroline "Callie" Barr (c. 1833–1940), and his wife, Estelle Oldham Faulkner (1897–1972).

"Pappy liked the ladies," confirms the author's only child, Jill Faulkner Summers (1933–2008). Not only did he like them, but they were the people with whom he chose to live his life. In writing about Faulkner and these three generations of North Mississippi women, and in the process showing how these relationships shaped his poetics, I open up a fresh perspective on Faulkner the man and on his art. Why another book on Faulkner's life and art? We have Joseph Blotner's original and essential chronological biographies; the critical biographies by Judith Wittenberg, David Minter, Stephen Oates, Frederick Karl, Richard Gray, and Jay Parini; and the revisionist historical accounts of Joel Williamson and Don Doyle. Despite these works and the remarkable transformations in Faulkner studies effected by cultural studies, new historicism, and most significantly, feminist theory and criticism over the past twenty-five years, portrayals of Faulkner and his world lack a vital human dimension; the Faulkner women appear as caricatures or shadow figures. There is an underlying assumption still working in Faulkner studies that results in a portrayal conforming to the popular and essentially romantic stereotype of the Great (White Male) American Writer. Insistence on this myth is one reason why, until the publication of my *Origins of Faulkner's Art* (1984), Faulkner's very unromantic but fascinating ten-year self-apprenticeship to poetry was ignored; the myth requires no hint of effeteness and an instantaneous transformation to Genius. In Faulkner biography, the driven, lonely, misunderstood artist is judged, ultimately, a magnificent Failure—a man consumed by two fatal obsessions—alcohol and his life-long commitment and "disastrous" and "doomed" marriage to a helpless hysteric.

There is some truth in all myths, but this picture is not accurate or complete. Furthermore, this interpretation demeans both Faulkner and his wife. We need to try for greater accuracy, for if we misread Faulkner's erotic attachments, we misread the ways they shape his psychological and aesthetic literary strategies and affiliations. The myth also insists that the most significant positive influences on Faulkner's creative development were white Southern men. Because Faulkner's ne'er-do-well father, Murry, was not one of these, attention centers on a host of other dead and living father surrogates. In contrast, the highly articulate, imaginative, and creative living women with whom Faulkner was first surrounded and later chose to surround himself are simultaneously distorted and marginalized.

Faulkner writes about the erotics of relationships—love and desire in all its myriad and strange manifestations. His works center on the powers exerted by genealogy, kinship, history, and memory. Yet we know little about these women in his life. They are excluded through flattening accomplished by gender and racial stereotyping, which produces parody and caricature. This is a kind of critical minstrelsy that alternates between sentimentalizing and demonizing.

My book seeks a more balanced approach, for, by so limiting our view, we have missed a large subject in the expansive field of the human scene that Faulkner inhabited and transmuted into art. In writing Maud Falkner, Callie Barr, and Estelle Oldham back into Faulkner's life, I now want to fill out the canvas. In doing so, I take my lead from Faulkner's art. There, family, community, and erotic relationships are central and women and men, black and white, are portrayed, with greater and lesser success, as subjects, not objects. I focus on Faulkner and these women in relation to each other and to the Southern culture in which they all lived. When Faulkner was writing, he closed out the world. But he did not live an isolated life. Although Rowan Oak, the Faulkners' house in Oxford, is large enough that the writer could have had a quiet, upstairs bedroom for his study, he chose instead a light and airy ground-floor room adjacent to the front door and opposite the living room, with doorways to both the front hall and what was originally the gallery, or porch. The Faulkners' daughter, Jill Summers, explains: "My friends and I almost always came through as a matter of course and the colored people who worked for us never hesitated to beat on the door to ask him for something. When he was at the typewriter, he was just playing. The only time they didn't disturb him was when he was asleep on the couch. There was no such thing as the library ever being off-limits. I spent much of my childhood reading on the couch while he was working. I could even talk at him, make comments and such; but I wasn't supposed to ask direct questions, and I wasn't to expect an answer. When Pappy was really concentrating, he didn't hear anything anyway. Nothing could bother him."[1]

Faulkner writes with great sensitivity about how his men and women fail and, more rarely, succeed in love. He is preoccupied with the imbricated politics of sexuality and race. How art and life intersect to form and inform this central aspect of an imaginative vision steeped in history and memory is my subject. This narrative includes far more of his career than I could address in *Origins*. Because my emphasis there was to demonstrate the role of his poetry as a vital and constant generative agent in Faulkner's fiction, I only touched on the delicate transactions between art and life suggested by the intriguing biographical information that surfaced in initial interviews with Jill Faulkner Summers and other women he loved. I have now expanded my scope to include research in Southern and feminist history and culture; interviews with relatives and friends of Callie Barr, Maud Falkner, and Estelle Faulkner and with other men and women from the Faulkners' and their daughter's generations; and further discussions with Jill Summers.

These materials, augmented by new biographical data, neglected archival materials and public documents, private Faulkner and Oldham family letters, papers, and other unpublished primary-source materials, have confirmed the rich reality of Faulkner's relations with these three crucial women. Reconfigured historical and cultural contexts further enriched by the perspectives of my informants provide an unfamiliar view of Faulkner's inner life and creative process.

The biographical, critical, and historical groundwork for my book has been laid by others and encompasses several disciplines; the exploration of and debate about the nature of sexuality in Faulkner's fictional men and women still has far to go. The larger question of the origins of Faulkner's perceptions of the relation of creativity to sexuality has similarly received little attention. Despite the growing literature on Faulkner and gender, Faulkner and race, lesbian Faulkner, gay Faulkner, Faulkner's women characters, and Faulkner and "the feminine," no one has yet attempted to relate fiction to fact—to the history and politics of sexuality in his actual world. Nor is there a description and analysis of these politics as they were experienced and taught by the three generations of black and white women among whom Faulkner lived his entire life.

In looking at Faulkner's relationships with these three women and at the roles family and societal relationships played in the development of his creative imagination, I seek to identify and examine determining conditions of possibility in their lives. Maud's and Estelle's families were the first settlers of their respective towns in the 1830s and 1840s. In the mid-1860s, Caroline Barr walked from her ex-owner's South Carolina rice plantation to Arkansas and then back to Mississippi in search of work and safety. She was part of that still unwritten first black migration in this country. Like Faulkner's fictional narratives, the overlapping historical periods in which my book is set are conceived as interactions among structures, processes, and people. While these structures and processes mold Caroline, Maud, Estelle, and William, my four subjects, in turn, shape them. This constant interaction of forces creates the drama of their lives, one that nourishes the core fantasies and poetics of Faulkner's fiction.

Methodology

Although verifiable facts are the backbone of critical biography, all biography is necessarily speculative. But there are difficulties in writing the histories of women who had no public life, kept no surviving journals and very few letters, owned no property, moved constantly, and, as in Callie Barr's case, could not write. Callie Barr's Oxford relatives had a photograph album and scrapbook that a "friend" borrowed and later sold to a collector. This was the family's only written record. According to her granddaughter, Jill, when Maud died, in 1960, many of the papers in her house "just disappeared." Victoria Johnson reported that her own mother, Victoria ("Cho-Cho"), who was Estelle's daughter from her first marriage, burned all her mother's papers. In the mid-1950s, Estelle's parents' home was razed, and most of its contents thrown in the trash. She had lived there until her first marriage, to Cornell Franklin in 1918, and had returned to it in 1926, when her husband kicked her out of their house in Shanghai. In it were letters she had written during her marriage to Franklin and some documents recording its dissolution. There may as well have been other letters and more of her fiction. It is where she lived until her marriage to Faulkner, in June of 1929. Shortly after her final return from Shanghai, Estelle herself burned the manuscript of the one novel she is known to have written. Shortly after she and Faulkner married, she apparently stopped writing fiction. She never wrote again until after her husband's death, in 1962, when she made a few revisions on two of her extant short stories. Fortunately, her first husband's heirs had kept some letters, photographs, and documents relating to Estelle's first marriage and divorce, along with a few letters of Estelle's mother, Lida Oldham, and her maternal grandmother, Victoria ("Miss Vic") Niles. These and public records, especially social columns of the local newspapers in Mississippi, Honolulu, and Shanghai, school and college transcripts and catalogues, Federated Women's Club notes, ships' manifests, court records, census records, slave schedules, and gravestones, make up the written records of Callie Barr, Maud Falkner, and Estelle Oldham.

For these reasons, the memories of family members and of the men, women, and children of various generations who knew William, Caroline, Maud, and Estelle have been one of my primary sources of information. I have traveled throughout the South and elsewhere in the States to work in local and national archives and to interview and reinterview these men and women. Memory is often flawed, and, as the long-overdue official revision of Sally Hemings and Thomas Jefferson's relationship demonstrates, there is institutional gender and racial bias against facts kept in circulation through oral history, particularly facts that threaten the status quo. It is no coincidence that for close to two hundred years white male historians suppressed or discounted Jefferson's African American ancestors' oral histories and the kinship claims in the 1873 memoir of Madison Hemings (the son of Jefferson and Hemings). Nor is it coincidence that this discounted history was first put into mass circulation by Fawn Brodie, a woman whose work all prominent Jefferson historians ridiculed, or that another woman, Annette Gordon-Reed, an African American legal historian, wrote the first fully documented account (also ridiculed), or that a third woman, Winifred Bennett, an "amateur historian," instigated the DNA testing that finally resulted in final acceptance of what, until fall 1998, was only oral history.[2] It is especially ironic that the coauthor of the first official revisionist account, published in the prestigious journal *Nature* (5 November 1998), was Joseph J. Ellis, the prominent Jefferson historian who, in 1996, won the National Book Award for a book that flatly denied the existence of Jefferson's black family.[3] Even in the twenty-first century, the black family of the segregationist Strom Thurmond kept themselves hidden until his recent death, when his biracial daughter, Essie Mae Washington-Williams, published her memoir (2005).

Another limitation on the written record is also cultural. Most white Southern women of Maud's and Estelle's generations were taught not to write down anything unladylike. As part of their Victorian education into Southern womanhood, they were trained in a code of conduct that confined unruly stories to the realm of oral history. "The things that ought to be told are not told," commented Bessie Sumners, a childhood friend of Estelle's. Then to illustrate her point that oral histories contain the stories that are never written down she told the following story. Mrs. Calvin Brown, whose mother was a good friend of Maud Falkner's, was shocked when

Bessie's husband asked if he could tape-record her. She said, "Why do you think I'm telling you and Bessie these stories? If you put these in print, I'd be run out of town." Then she went on: "I'm telling you all because you got children. I want these to stay alive but I can't put them in print."[4]

In interviewing Callie Barr's family, I have tried to be guided by Paul D's warning in Toni Morrison's *Beloved:* "Nothing more dangerous than a white school teacher" (266). To date no one had interviewed any of the Barr relatives and descendants. I knew when I began my research that a black interviewer would get a different story than would a white interviewer—if a white interviewer got anything at all. I hired Patricia Tingle, an African American graduate student in the Southern Studies Program at the University of Mississippi, to help me. When she first interviewed Caroline Barr's relatives, Rachel McGee and her daughter, Mildred Quarles, they told Tingle they'd never tell a white person "anything." Although Tingle explained to all those she interviewed that she was working as a researcher for me, she said they assumed that because she was black, I was black, too. This was deceit, perhaps even exploitation. After all, even though I have worked from taped and transcribed interviews and discussed the interviews with Patricia Tingle for further clarification, who is speaking for whom? The bottom line was that if someone didn't begin this work, the Callie Barr "Mammy" myths narrated by the Faulkner family and honed by Faulkner's biographers would stay intact. I felt it was worth taking the risk in order to begin the job of writing Callie Barr back into Faulkner's life for what it could reveal about her sustaining impact on his imagination.

Rewriting Faulkner's life by radically altering its context, as I have, by writing in his life-long relations with this *community* of three generations of black and white women, alters the ways we read his art. I stress the word *community* because even when critics do refer to Faulkner's mother or Callie Barr or his wife or daughter, it is never in terms of a living web of ongoing intrapsychic and psychosocial dynamics. Faulkner makes the point repeatedly in his fiction that this was a community, and he insists in "Mississippi," his avowedly quasi-autobiographical essay, that as a small boy this was his earliest community: "at four and five and six [when] his world was still a female world and he had heard nothing else that he could remember" ("Mississippi," 17).

Acknowledgments

Faulkner and Love began in an attic. One steamy August afternoon, looking for any papers belonging to Estelle Oldham Faulkner in Jill Summers's attic, I found an old brown Best & Co. box labeled "Mama's Papers." In it was a manila envelope containing typescripts of three stories, two with her mother's bylines, "E.O. / Oxford Mississippi" and "E. Oldham-Franklin [Franklin crossed out in ink] / Oxford, Mississippi." The third, set in Shanghai, was marked with holograph edits in what looked like both Estelle's and Faulkner's hand. The idea of conceptualizing Faulkner's creative development as a web and series of imaginative collaborations, grounded in evidence from my earlier work on the origins of Faulkner's art, began to assume a solid form.

Jill Summers, William and Estelle Faulkner's daughter and executor, wanted this story told. Her fairness, courage, and sense of history have made that possible. *Faulkner and Love* is not about her, but her voice informs my narrative. In Jill's infancy, her parents, her grandmother Maud, and Caroline Barr composed her world. All remained close to her the rest of their lives. She recognized and understood the strengths and weaknesses of her parents and their marriage; she appreciated what each gave to and took from the other. From Jill directly and through her introductions, certain rare privileges of research were extended that enabled me to draw on materials previously unavailable. I am grateful for her permission to quote extensively from her father's published and unpublished works, including letters, drawings, and photographs, from her mother's short stories, and from other Faulkner and Oldham family papers and to publish examples of her grandmother Maud's paintings.

Estelle's granddaughter, Victoria Fielden Johnson, and stepgrandson,

Cornell Franklin, Jr., offered valuable insights and observations and permission to publish from their collections of Oldham-Franklin papers, documents, and photographs.

Caroline Barr's family, most particularly Rachel McGee, Dora Lewis, Mildred Quarles, Chief Deputy Sheriff (retired) James Rudd, and other members of the Barr family and community were instrumental in providing their family's history and perspectives on both Caroline Barr and the Faulkners. Their interest and cooperation made possible the telling of Callie Barr's story from her family's and community's hitherto silenced perspective. I am especially grateful to Mildred Quarles, who took me to the Barr family graveyard outside of Oxford, where Callie Barr is *not* buried, and to James Rudd, who showed me the homesites, churchyard, and burying grounds of at least two of Callie Barr's daughters, Fanny Ivory and Millie Holman, and their descendants.

For their memories and their time, I thank the friends, acquaintances, and other relations and descendants of the Oldham, Franklin, and Faulkner families living around the world—from small towns in Mississippi to Hawaii and China. Their contributions to the intertwined Faulkner, Butler, and Oldham stories are acknowledged in my notes.

I am especially grateful to Ann C. Abadie, Assistant Director of the Center for the Study of Southern Culture at the University of Mississippi, who offered wise advice and suggested many useful leads and introductions. I also thank Mary Emma Graham, former chair of the university's African American Studies Program, for suggesting her student Patricia Tingle, who first interviewed Callie Barr's family and community and acted as my liaison. I also thank those associated with the Center who assisted in my research: Mary Hartwell Howorth, Lisa Howorth, Katie Drayne, and Amy C. Evans, in particular.

This book is built from material evidence and information delivered to it through networks of people. Courthouse clerks throughout Mississippi, Honolulu, and Shanghai helped locate crucial documents, as did librarians in the Faulkner collections at the Harry Ransom Humanities Research Center, University of Texas, the University of Virginia, Southeast Missouri State University, and the University of Mississippi Library in Oxford. I also thank librarians at the Mississippi University for Women and the Public Library in Columbus, Mississippi, and the Mary Baldwin College Library in Staunton, Virginia, and the unfailingly resourceful librarians at many small Southern public libraries who, in addition, often introduced me to local historians and community members who were related to or had known the Barr, Oldham, and Fa(u)lkner families.

This biography was completed with the assistance of research grants and fellowships from the National Endowment for the Humanities, the American Council of Learned Societies, and a research fellowship at the Chicago Institute for Psychoanalysis. Time to write was provided by an NEH Senior Fellowship, an ACLS Fellowship, and two residency fellowships at the Virginia Foundation for the Humanities. I also wish to thank my lawyer, Nancy Wechsler, for her wise council. Several research assistants over the years located materials, checked sources, and lent their advanced computer skills to keeping my Macs running and preparing artwork for publication: Robert Zackowski, Elizabeth Ebert, Jonathan Enfield, Ajay Bhatt, Adam Kissel, Monica Iyer, Caitlin Parton, and Ted Pennings.

At Yale University Press, Lara Heimert read, sent out to readers, and contracted for *Faulkner and Love* when it was far from finished. John Kulka then shepherded it through to final readers. Jonathan Brent, Editorial Director, has lent his enthusiastic support, and I thank him for his efforts on its behalf. I am especially indebted to Karen Gangel, my thorough, efficient, and patient manuscript editor, and to my production editor, Margaret Otzel. Any errors are my own.

My readers for Yale University Press were generous with their time and expertise. The length and complicated subject of this book called for much more than is ordinarily asked of a reader. They gave sound advice and correction.

In researching and writing this book, I have been sustained and emboldened by the friendship, knowledge, and searching questions of a great many colleagues. Wayne C. Booth, David Bevington, Thomas C. Moser, and Judith Bryant Wittenberg read and queried the earliest versions of various chapters on Estelle Oldham and Faulkner. Thadious Davis and Linda Wagner-Martin offered years of steady encouragement while reading and querying me on early and late book drafts. I learned much from extended conversations with Susan V. Donaldson and Deborah McDowell during two semesters at the Virginia Foundation for the Humanities; Deborah, Susan Donaldson, Susan McCabe, Jennifer DeVere Brody, Sharon Patricia Holland, and Minrose C. Gwin read later versions of chapters and helped me clarify my ideas and prose. I thank all for their friendship, good humor, terrific breakfasts and dinners, and their belief in *Faulkner and Love*.

Don Kartiganer's invitations to several annual Faulkner and Yoknatpatawpha conferences in Oxford, Mississippi, offered a chance to present work in progress, parts of which were later revised and integrated into various book chapters. My students at Arizona State University and friends and colleagues at other universities have all given generously of their time, advice, and expertise.

Besides colleagues who read chapters and sections at various stages, I am grateful to other scholars in my own and related fields whose work enriched mine—M. Thomas Inge, Charles Joyner, Joe Urgo, Anne Goodwyn Jones, Susan Snell, Eric Sundquist, James G. Watson, Diane Roberts, Peter Conn, James Clifford, Grace Elizabeth Hale, James M. McPherson, and many more whose contributions I acknowledge in my notes.

Finally I wish to thank my common readers—longtime friends and teachers whose observations and questions often led me to see what I really wanted to say: Eleanor Himmelfarb, Hilda Lass, Judith Raphael, Debby and Harvey Strauss, Jacqueline Kieff, Yvonne Lange. Mark Levey helped me to recover my voice. And David, who believed when I doubted, who was always there, even when I wasn't, and who, over more than four decades, has read for me again and again.

General Introduction

U NLIKE THE NOVELS of most of his high Modernist counterparts, Faulkner's greatest works—*The Sound and the Fury, As I Lay Dying, Light in August, Absalom, Absalom!, Go Down, Moses*—are about families, generations of Mississippi families, and, perhaps most of all, they are about marriage, in its most inclusive sense. In current critical terms we would say that the politics of racialized desire are central to Faulkner's imaginative vision. So, it is surprising that those politics in his life and family history remain untraced. We have little sense of the relation of Faulkner the Southerner, the son, lover, friend, husband, or parent to the tortured marriages and love affairs in his fiction. Biographical assessments of Faulkner and his actual world tell a great deal about the family patriarch, Colonel William C. Falkner, who died years before William's birth, but little about Callie Barr, Maud Falkner, and Estelle Oldham. These three generations of North Mississippi women were *alive* when Faulkner was and were at least as important as Colonel Falkner; they and their communities are heard across the entire spectrum of his imaginative domain. Looked at together with the men and women to whom they are joined, they can teach us much that is fresh and new about the art and craft of Faulkner's fiction.

Archival work, interviews, and new primary-source materials have further confirmed the rich reality of Faulkner's relations with the three crucial women I focus on. These different perspectives provide an unfamiliar view of the artist's inner life and his creative process. This view suggests strongly that while his relations with both men and women naturally formed and informed his vision of sexuality, his fictions of love and desire, his relations with the women in and outside of his family, rather than his connections with a tenuous and questionable masculine ideal, shaped both his understanding of what it meant to love and his vision of what an artist and a man could be.

Caroline ("Callie") Barr, the black ex-slave who raised the artist from infancy and later cared for the Faulkners' daughter, Jill, lived "with" him in the old shotgun cabin behind his antebellum house until her death, in 1940. In past Faulkner biography and criticism, Callie's only family is the Falkner brothers, who called themselves "her white children." My reconstruction of *her* story, her post–Civil War migration from South Carolina to Mississippi, supplemented with interviews of members of her *own*, black family, substitutes reality and dimension for the "Mammy" tales of previous biographies.

Who was this articulate and bossy African American woman who two generations of her employers' children claim ran Maud's and then Estelle's households? Her stories "spell-bound" three generations of Falkner children. How do Faulkner's competing and conflicted identifications with his dark and light "mothers," Callie and Maud, fuel his imaging of psychic fragmentation, of desire, and of identity itself as fluid and tenuous? What do the compulsively reiterated tropes of repulsion, shame, and desire, portrayed as seeing but not touching, or as touching only when coated with dirt or mud, or as "negro-rank smell," have to do with the politics of race and sex in Faulkner's fiction? Jill says that "the women Pappy most loved and admired were Granny, Mammy Callie, and Aunt Bama."[1] Callie was central to Maud's household, but of her relationship with Maud and, later, Estelle, we know little. Nothing is written about Callie's own family, though her daughters lived within a day's walk of Oxford and she had great nieces in Freedman Town with whose mother she pieced her last wedding-ring quilt. In her community she was loved and feared. In some ways she was as much an outsider as Faulkner would choose to be in his. Faulkner's Modernist novels' tropes of loss have their genesis in his education into race by his black and white mothers. These originary human connections, connections he *never* abandoned, inform the politics of race and gender in his greatest fiction. Yet little or nothing is known about them.

We can caricature Faulkner's mother, Maud Butler Falkner, as the little old lady in size three Buster Browns, but that fails to illuminate. She was certainly controlling and probably "tough as shoe leather" and "mean as a snake." However, these and other descriptions don't touch on the extent and nature of her intelligence, her creative sensibilities, her iconoclasm, or her quiet but withering wit. Nor do they explain the devotion of her sons and women friends. She was reserved, "austere," say some, but she was full of life. Interviews reveal an intricate and tightly knit group of women with whom she played bridge, went driving (she preferred to drive—not be driven), and attended the movies, which she loved, and the Memphis dog races. She was passionate about her children and about literature. Her literary tastes were as eclectic as her famous son's: she read everything from the classics to murder mysteries. When her young children were confined by measles to a darkened room, she read to them, lying beneath one of their beds with a lamp. In the year before she died, Maud's library borrowings included Tolstoy, Dostoyevsky, Chekov, and Turgenev. Her "library courier" reported that she confided to him that her current "bedtime" favorite was *The Caine Mutiny*.[2] Her daughter-in-law Louise Meadow said Maud was reading *Lady Chatterley's Lover* in the bathtub when she had her final stroke.[3]

Maud also loved to paint. Some of her late paintings still survive. How did her imaginative and very visual perceptions of reality transmute to Faulkner's art? Both Maud and Callie passed on their strengths and weaknesses, passions and prejudices, to young Willie, as his mother first called him. Together but apart, they educated him into his culture's Jim Crow codes of white Southern masculinity and femininity. So did his father and paternal grandfather. Alcohol played a prominent role in that education. Despite Maud's and Callie's deep apprehension and disapproval, Faulkner began tippling before he was in his teens. Drinking as a trope for faux masculinity is embedded in his fiction. There, it also serves as an anodyne for unbearable loss that cannot be mourned and a metaphor for total disorientation, paralysis, psychic numbness, and boundary dissolution.

Faulkner's and Estelle's families had known each other since at least the 1870s: the two children became friends at age six. The Murry Falkners and Lem Oldhams moved to Oxford and onto the same street within a year of each other, and by 1908, if not earlier, the three oldest Falkner boys, their cousin Sallie Murry Wilkins, and the two Oldham girls began "running over" those "streets all night" together and "living only in the present."[4] From early adolescence until at least 1929, Willie (later called Billy and Bill) shared his writing with Estelle. From 1918 to 1924, while living in American colonial enclaves in Hawaii and Shanghai, Estelle began to write fiction that was, in part, her response to and revision of themes central to the poetry Billy read to her and gave her during those years. Yet, unlike his poetry, her stories embraced realism and social critique. Although she was no Zelda Fitzgerald, her unpublished short tales are competently crafted, humorous, sad, and particularly insightful on the Jim Crow world of the pre- and postwar South and the casual racism of American Colonials in Shanghai during the 1920s. When she first returned to Oxford with them in late 1924, they became the basis for the continuation of an imaginative collaboration with Faulkner that led to his own sudden and remarkable artistic breakthrough in early 1925. Like her mother-in-law, Estelle was also a visual artist. She had taken lessons in the early twenties while living in Shanghai and continued painting until her marriage to Faulkner in 1929. In 1962, after his death, she began painting again. In fascinating contrast to her mother-in-law's professed realism, Estelle's paintings were surreal and impressionistic transformations of reality.

Unlike Maud's and Callie's materially austere lives, Estelle Oldham's world was rich in all variety of outward show. Shortly after her family moved to Oxford in October 1903, they rented a large two-story house on South Street. Two years later, Estelle's father, Lem, bought a much more showy Victorian home on the corner of South and Fillmore, just two blocks away from Willie's grandfather's "Big Place." It was a house built for socializing, with a wrap-around porch, lovely gardens, and later, a tennis court. The Oldhams were social snobs who claimed American ancestry as far back as the *Mayflower*, a snobbery Estelle mocked in an autobiographical short story she wrote in the 1920s.[5] Lem Oldham owed his position as clerk of the federal court of North Mississippi to his step-father-in-law, the well-known Republican judge Henry C. Niles. Republicans were anathema in Oxford, and while Judge Niles transcended the "stench" of Reconstruction associated with that party in Mississippi, his son-in-law did not. Unlike his father-in-law, Lem Oldham was a terrible businessman and was thus primarily dependent on the Republican Party for his income. The family's social snobbery was often sniffed at in Oxford. It is a constant refrain among the women who knew the family that Lida Oldham "pushed Estelle." Jill says, "I think that all of Nanny's children were a disappointment to her—her only son dying in the flu epidemic, and the pretty daughter [Victoria] who married well and then promptly died. And Ma-ma—whom they thought they'd married off—and then she made a botch of it. And then Aunt Dot [Dorothy Oldham] just generally making a botch of life. That didn't please Nanny at all. Those children just didn't do what they should have done. Nanny was very easy-going as far as I was concerned. But I think she was extremely hard on her own children. There was not much love lost between Nanny, Aunt Dot, and Ma-ma."

Lida Oldham worked by indirection: "Nanny had the delightful habit that seems to run in the family—of talking about people when they were in the room. For example, Aunt Dot would be in the room and Nanny would start discussing her in definitely uncomplimentary terms like, 'Isn't Dorothy's hair-do terrible?' or something unkind like that. She did that all the time to both Ma-ma and Aunt Dot. But she never said anything mean or ugly to them directly. It was just as though they were not there."[6] Her mother could not complain about Estelle's looks because her daughter was always immaculately groomed. So instead she'd criticize her for her house-keeping or for not being a dutiful daughter.

Lemuel Oldham was equally controlling in his own quiet way. He determined that "Estelle would marry well—to a family that could trace every ancestor back a long time. In Mississippi particularly, family is important. And when Ma-ma was twelve or thirteen, Granddaddy and Nanny started scouting the eligible families and decided which direction they intended Ma-ma to go. Marrying Cornell Franklin was strictly an arrangement between Granddaddy and Mr. Franklin."[7]

Faulkner chose to be an outsider. He had strong support from his mother. In different ways, Estelle's parents were outsiders too. And they were not as wealthy as they seemed. Estelle spent nearly ten years in a lonely, demanding, and unsatisfying marriage to her first husband, Cornell Franklin. Financial, cultural, and familial constraints compelled her to stay married until Cornell wanted a divorce. Then, with no independent income or family support, she attempted to support herself. She had begun writing fiction, perhaps as early as nine years before her divorce. Evidence indicates that she intended to sell it. Her extant short stories are as good as much of the women's magazine fiction being published at the time. Estelle was also an exquisite seamstress and loved this work. She often designed her own and her daughters' clothes, sewing without patterns. At least twice, in the 1930s and 1940s, she adopted the profession of one of her own fictional protagonists, organizing showings of her gowns and using as models students at Ole Miss and friends from Oxford and Memphis.[8]

Aside from their iconoclasm, Estelle and Maud seem totally unalike. Yet, apparently, Faulkner needed both. He was neither naïve nor young when he and Estelle married in 1929. Despite much talk of divorce by both, the marriage lasted. We have read about Faulkner's infidelities, Estelle's hysteria, and her drug dependency. Viewing her as Disease and Faulkner as Myth, we have effectively silenced both. Estelle is much more than a spoiled Southern Belle, a part she played to the hilt when necessary. "Mama played up the 'clinging-vine' 'Southern Belle' business when required, but she was really the least clinging person I've almost ever known," observes the Faulkners' daughter.[9] Estelle's life tells a great deal about her husband's life and art.

In reconstructing these women's lives and reading Faulkner's life and art into the rich political, cultural, and emotional landscape their biographies provide, I focus on three historical and biographical issues that directly inform Faulkner's thematics and poetics. The first is Willie's and Estelle's earliest experiences with the black and white women who mothered them, in what Anne Firor Scott, and others, have shown was a patriarchal but matrifocal world governed by apparently rigid racial and sexual hierarchies and boundaries. Within their own families, however, these boundaries were extraordinarily fluid. Both Estelle's and Faulkner's imaginative representations of racial and sexual relations reflect and comment on this conflicted cultural discourse. Faulkner reveals an important part of its essence in an early screen memory representing his "two mothers." He recalls himself as a three-year-old homesick child being carried through the night between two women who simultaneously attract and repel him. One is dark, warm, and sensual: "she must have carried me." The other is blond, cold, and "aloof," but "she was holding the lamp."[10]

This remarkable conflation of race and sexuality is a core fantasy that fuels his imaginative visions of desire and loss from his early, handmade and self-illustrated dream-play, *The Marionettes* (1920), to *Go Down, Moses* (1942) and beyond. Often in his fiction, a tortured and torturing pierrotique male lover merges these two images in one woman (as Joe Christmas does with Joanna Burden in *Light in August*). In *Absalom, Absalom!* Faulkner invents four generations of black and white brothers and sisters (races are literally split and merged) to continue his fictive exploration into the meanings of and relations between racism, gender, desire, and sexuality. Because this splitting or doubling is a constant source of creative tension in his poetry and fiction, it is worth looking at its extra-literary origins. From whom did he learn to split and why? What are the implications in a culture where white men and women say again and again that their black nurse "was my real mother"? Faulkner's changing relations with the women in his family and other women in his life are reflected in the increasing complexity, dexterity, and brilliance with which he gives imaginative form to these questions. My chapters on Caroline Barr and *Go Down, Moses*, the novel Faulkner dedicated to her, explore these questions, as do those on Faulkner's and Estelle's childhood and adult imaginative collaborations, which culminate with his second great creative breakthrough, *The Sound and the Fury*. New evidence reveals that both *Go Down, Moses* and Faulkner's first great novel have a history and afterlife that also tries to capture, contain, and explain that loss. Throughout *Faulkner and Love*, I trace a pattern of multiple splittings that he imposed on all the women he loved. Most vividly, Estelle was both "black" and "white," while their daughter was alternately "Jill" and "Bill."

The sense of impotence—the inability to create that Faulkner's earliest poetic personae experience—has been explained as his creative response to the loss of Estelle Oldham in April 1918, when she married Cornell Franklin and moved with him to Hawaii. Although that loss was doubtless a precipitating event, we must look further back to understand both the formal and psychological implications of his ultimately triumphant fictional blurring and merging of racialized gender distinctions, and the consummate ease with which he handles his polymorphous characters. Supportive as they were, his two "mothers"—one black and one white—seem to have been a source of his fears of artistic impotence. In a family headed and supported by Faulkner's inarticulate and hard-drinking father, these two women, Maud and Caroline, controlled the word and, between them, taught the young artist the power of language to cut or caress. They also had little use for the grown men in their lives. Homophobia and Southern codes of masculinity also worked against Faulkner's choice of art as a vocation. In Oxford, only women and men like Stark Young and Ben Wasson (both of whom were gay and had left Mississippi) attempted to be artists. In this context it is important to remember that Faulkner was the South's first great novelist and that art in the South, particularly, was a sissified occupation. He really had no significant male models: the *living* storytellers and the visual artists in his family were all women.

My second historical and biographical issue is the cultural and psychological role of alcohol in Estelle's and Faulkner's actual and imaginative worlds, particularly its function in initiating and defining white Southern masculinity, segregating the social lives of men and women, educating its white children into the codes of Jim Crow, and in inuring them to sexual and racial violence and child abuse. There is a relationship between alcoholism and Faulkner's tropes of suicidal and homicidal violence, of sadism, psychic numbness, and total dissolution of identity. We need to understand why, in both Faulkner's and Estelle's fiction, there are so many scenes of adolescents being forced by their elders to drink.[11] We can then begin to understand his and Estelle's addiction as, in part, a cultural disease and a legacy of slavery.

Of equal importance in exploring the relationships among creativity, sexuality, and alcoholism is Faulkner's recurring trope of Estelle Oldham as the Fatal Dancer. Discussion of the Dancer includes Pierrot, her besotted partner. The most interesting of his poems and poem sequences center on these two central images of late romanticism, symbolism, and early Modernism. However, Faulkner's original attraction to them did not stem merely from their literary ancestry. Rather, these highly charged symbols of desire draw their emotional power from the artist's reality. I suggest that he chose them, or they chose him, because they mirrored central aspects of his relations with women, but especially with Estelle Oldham. She once said that although she never recognized any of Faulkner's characters as herself, she had noted that her husband's more savage inventions often displayed some of her worst qualities. This frank and insightful remark is characteristic of the woman who has emerged from my research.

That Estelle Oldham was the seductive and exhibitionistic Dancer, and Faulkner the voyeuristic and often sadistic Watcher, is well documented. She was quintessentially theatrical and her theatricality played directly into Faulkner's. In his poetry and fiction, the dance (literal and figurative), often coupled with alcohol, is always threatening. Pierrot and his fictional successors silence and literally still the Dancer in order to hear their own "silent music." In Faulkner's fiction, such dances are always racialized and often end in literal or psychological murder. One has only to recall Faulkner's jazzy collagelike dance scenes in *Soldiers' Pay*, or Red's, Popeye's and Temple Drake's, or Joe Christmas's and Joanna Burden's, or Quentin's and Caddy's, or Quentin's and Dirty Natalie's carefully choreographed dances of shame, hatred, and desire to recognize the incipient power of this early vision.

The third issue is the relation between what I call collaborative fantasy, Faulkner's creativity, and his raced and gendered self-representations. The historic difficulties and repercussions of defining oneself as an artist in Mississippi in the first third of the twentieth century were transmuted into art in Faulkner's fiction and in Estelle's unpublished short stories. But each paid a price for tampering with cultural mythologies: Estelle for rejecting the Southern mystique of the "ice maiden" and attempting to alter her image as the Southern Belle; Faulkner for tearing at the myths of Southern Manhood and white supremacy epitomized in his self-naming as "black man" and poet. What pleasures and dangers did Estelle and Faulkner share as they experimented with self-representation in life and fiction in ways that either flouted cultural structures governing race and gender or revealed their hypocrisy?

Faulkner did not draw clear boundaries between his art and his life; masking and theater define and shape his erotic relationships and his art. In his poetry and fiction, masking as well as racial and gender transformations constantly attend the consciousness of characters who ask, in one way or another, "Who am I?" In *The Marionettes*, Faulkner's 1920 dream-play, Pierrot woos Marietta in the guise of his shade, and, as I have shown in *Origins*, Faulkner's drawings of his heroine bear an uncanny resemblance to photographs of Estelle Oldham, photographs taken shortly before and early in her marriage to her first husband, Cornell Franklin. Thus masking and theater figure prominently in one of Faulkner's earliest imaginative productions, which was, in part, a reworking of his already long relationship with Estelle Oldham. It is well known that Faulkner delighted in role-playing in his life as in his art. What is not common knowledge is that his wife joined him, that the two had acted together since childhood and shared equally in an attendant love for costume, and that their private theater remained central to their marriage. It is this aspect of their relationship that I want to introduce here, because theater played a role in all of his relationships and because it illustrates vividly one of the many ways Faulkner's marriage, contrary to popular conceptions, fueled his creativity. Let me first sketch the outlines of that popular conception.

In Faulkner biography, Estelle Oldham is, to use one of Faulkner's favorite poetic adjectives, an "opaque" but negative and somewhat pitiful figure. By all accounts, including Faulkner's own, she is the millstone around the great author's neck. Coming to him as used goods, she merely repeated the role she had played with her first husband before they divorced in 1929.[12] Faulkner's letter to his editor Hal Smith asking to borrow five hundred dollars to finance his marriage establishes the basis for this interpretation. In it, he claims dramatically that he is marrying because

> [I] both want to and have to. THIS PART IS CONFIDENTIAL. UTTERLY. For my honor and the sanity—I believe life— of a woman. This is not bunk; neither am I being sucked in. We grew up together and I don't think she could fool me in this way; that is, make me believe that her mental condition, her nerves, are this far gone. And no question of pregna[n]cy: that would hardly move me: no one can face his own bastard with more equanimity than I, having had some practice. Neither is it a matter of a promise on my part; we have known one another long enough to pay no attention to our promises. It's a situation which I engendered and permitted to ripen which has become unbearable, and I am tired of running from devilment I bring about. This sounds a little insane, but I'm not in any shape to write letters now. I'll explain it better when I see you.[13]

Note here the stagy quality of Faulkner's cleverly balanced rhetoric, his piling up of negatives, his hyperbolic exaggeration as, like one of his most famous characters, Rosa Coldfield, he denies only to suggest and claims to accept blame only to shift charges of manipulation to his lover. I include this letter because it conveys in Faulkner's own words the accepted version of why he and Estelle Oldham married and why, despite affairs with which he taunted her, they remained married. Here is a typical description of Oldham's state of mind shortly before her marriage to Faulkner: "[Faulkner's] stalling and uncertainty [about whether to marry her] threw Estelle into a panic. Unless he married her, how could she go on living— she, a 32-year-old divorcee with two children? A failure in the eyes of her family and friends, worse than that to the town at large? Without him she felt she had nothing, was nothing. For the sake of her sanity, of her life, he must marry her. She had no one else to turn to. Her nerves were gone, her mind, too. He was her last hope."[14]

Here, as in all other biographies, she appears as the Southern Belle gone bad—a caricature of failure, helplessness, and hysteria. In fact, the role of Southern Belle was one Estelle assumed with apparent ease, when it suited her purposes. Her daughter notes that she used it as "a protective screen, very much like Pappy used his 'I'm just a dirt farmer' role."[15] Note that Faulkner is also stereotyped, as a dutiful son and an honorable Southern gentleman: "Estelle's frantic helplessness appealed to his sense of honor. . . . Here was a chance to prove to his father and Major Oldham . . . that he was a *man*, not a wastrel."[16] Such biographical fictions distort our perceptions of Faulkner the person and Faulkner the artist. The author has, for example, a history of *seldom* concerning himself with others' opinions. That he would allow one of the most important decisions of his life to be dictated by the opinions of two men he neither admired nor respected seems far-fetched at best. But, perhaps most disturbingly, this portrait insists that—again, according to this biography—"there was a wall of irreconcilable difference between Faulkner and Estelle which made real intimacy impossible."[17] Such a view persists in spite of the *facts* of a virtual lifetime of mutual attachment that began when Willie and Estelle were six or seven years old, was continued throughout Estelle's eleven-year marriage to her first husband, and concluded with the Faulkners' own thirty-three-year marriage. The deletion of all erotic and affectionate material from surviving letters Faulkner wrote his wife from Hollywood and New York in the 1930s and early 1940s in the published *Selected Letters* reinforces such interpretations, especially in the light of Meta Carpenter's memoir of her affair with Faulkner during just those years. To suggest that Faulkner spent his life with a woman with whom he had no real relationship debases both partners.

But in virtually every portrayal of Estelle, her hysteria, her alcoholism, her narcissism, her profligacy, her exhibitionism, and her stupidity are her most commonly noted qualities. There is more to her than that.

Our interpretation of his letter to Hal Smith changes if, rather than allowing ourselves to be seduced by its histrionics, we remember its intent— to get a loan, an advance on *The Sound and the Fury*. Faulkner will write many of these letters to his various editors in the course of his life. In all of them he presents himself similarly.[18] Our interpretation also changes if we look for the letter's fictional parallels and read it as part rhetorical ploy and part practice arena for Faulkner's fictions of love and desire. For besides being rhetorically convincing, this letter is a shorthand version of some of the most redundant and powerful images of desire in his novels. Like Joe Christmas in *Light in August* or Jack Houston in *The Hamlet*, Faulkner, too, is tired of "running" from his own devilment. Like Houston and his wife, Estelle Oldham and he have known each other forever.

In *The Hamlet* Faulkner elaborates on this fiction. There, Houston says of his desire, "It seemed to him that it had been in his life always, even between those five years between his birth and hers; . . . that he himself had not begun to exist until she was born, the two of them chained irrevocably from that hour and onward forever." Like many of Faulkner's tortured men, Joe Christmas's and Houston's organizing fantasy, or fiction of love, fuses infancy and childhood with adult erotic desire: the woman he marries has been in his life before he was born. Houston wants it all. But because this fusion is incestuous, and therefore forbidden, his conscious response must be to fight it. He sees himself chained "not by love but by implacable constancy and invincible repudiation—on the one hand, that steadfast and undismayable will to alter and improve and remake; on the other, that furious resistance" (206).

Theater springing from the tension of yoking antitheses was as important to the structure of Faulkner's love affairs as it was to the formal concerns of his poetry and fiction. One thinks of him in Hollywood in the 1930s insisting to his twenty-eight-year-old lover, Meta Carpenter, that she wear hair ribbons like a teenager, as well as of Meta's and other women's comments that he was more passionate in letters than he ever was in the flesh. Or of the nasty and transparent fiction he, Ben Wasson, and Meta Carpenter performed for Estelle the summer of 1936, when Meta went to dinner at the Faulkners' Hollywood apartment as Ben Wasson's date.[19] There are dozens of examples; a brief reminiscence, "Faulkner: A Flirtation," in the *New York Times Magazine* in 1987, provides a nice vignette of the writer flirting with a young admirer. In this instance, he assumes the guise of Januarius Jones, one of his earliest self-parodies.[20] The *Times* essay aptly illustrates Faulkner's habit of almost immediately imposing his own fictional frame upon any potentially romantic relationship. During the ten years he wrote poetry almost exclusively, his most favored persona was Pierrot, the quintessential masker. Cyrano de Bergerac, who wooed his true love in the guise of another man's voice, was another of his favorite characters. Throughout his life he cribbed from Cyrano to woo a series of women, including Helen Baird in the 1920s and Joan Williams and Jean Stein in the 1950s.[21] In short, when we read Faulkner's 1929 letter to his editor in the dual contexts of his erotic and aesthetic life, its meaning changes. The letter's fictional drama and the practical function of that drama are revealed.

The Faulkners' daughter, Jill, describes growing up in a household in which masks were the order of the day:

> Living with Ma-ma and Pappy was like living on a stage-set. Everybody was playing a role. You never knew who was being what today. They played roles to each other and, largely, I was left out of it. There was always lots of storming up and down the stairs and threats on my mother's part to slash her wrists. She really liked playing tragic parts. They both enjoyed it, and even I got to know it was not for real. But it was pretty exciting. The only time I touched base, you know, hit the ground in the real world, was when I went to school. When I walked back through the gates at Rowan Oak, it was like Alice going down the rabbit hole. I never knew exactly what would be at the end of the hole when I reached my front porch. . . . Pappy always—it would be hard for me to say that I could look at him at one point and say, "this is who he really is," because, almost always, he was playing a part. When I was young, it gave me a feeling of unreality. I never knew whether I was real to them.[22]

As it had been in Estelle's and Willie's childhood games, costume was part of this theater. When she grew older, Jill could often predict the tone and theme of the evening's performance when she saw what her mother was wearing as she came down to dinner:

> When Ma-ma was getting ready to really have a major scene, she wore major clothes for it. . . . If we were going to have a real confrontation— you know, "My life is wasted, I've been abused"—then it would usually be something really elegant. If it were going to be a fairly smooth, uneventful evening, it would just be an ordinary, decent type of dress. And then, if it were going to be a "Aren't we all happy together in this nice little threesome here in the country" sort of thing it would—there was just a difference in her dress that would fit that too. Life was never dull at Rowan Oak. Pappy did the same thing. He liked to play the country squire but he also liked to play the good ole' boy with all the men from the fishing camp or the hunting camp and he changed his clothes and his accent accordingly. To a certain extent Ma-ma was the same way.
>
> So often what was said was said for effect, and so often the position that was taken was taken for effect. It didn't really reflect anyone's true feelings on the matter. What I'm really trying to say is that people had roles. Everyone had—they were standing back and watching themselves play this particular part.[23]

She also notes that both her parents "enjoyed making grand gestures" and that "they had a life of gestures together."[24]

Theater was not reserved for special occasions, however, and often entered into the daily routine. A friend of Jill's loved to visit Rowan Oak because it was so much more interesting than any other home in town. "It was the atmosphere—I always felt like they sort of—it was like a play, maybe." Even a family meal at Rowan Oak was a performance:

> Well, to me Mrs. Faulkner—she was not the greatest housekeeper, but she had a lot of flair. I mean you could have the simplest food but it would be served up buffet on silver platters. It was just great. Nobody's mother actually cooked. But she could cook when she wanted to. She was very inventive, very artistic with whatever she did—cooking, gardening, sewing—she made beautiful clothes. It was a household that was so entirely different from anything I knew. I enjoyed going down there so much. It was just highly entertaining.

Jill's friend makes the following comparison:

> At our house, we ate in the dining room only for Sunday dinner and when company came. Well, the Faulkners always ate in the dining room—except for in the winter when everything was frozen as we didn't have any central heating. But, no matter how simple the meal was, it was very elaborately served. Mr. Faulkner was at one end and the plates were stacked and he served the dinner—he served the meal and everything, always. And even if it were bacon, lettuce, and tomato sandwiches, it would all be on silver trays with the lettuce beautifully arranged. I thought it was the greatest. I think they all enjoyed it.

Faulkner's daughter's comments about her parents reveal more similarities in her parents' likes and dislikes than differences: "My parents went out of their way to make my friends feel welcomed, and they always enjoyed them. They both tried to be careful that none of my friends saw them drinking. There were exceptions like the time when Pappy ruined my birthday."[25]

Estelle also told Jill and her friends stories she invented based on characters in Hawaiian folklore. Jill says: "Ma-ma would weave fantastic tales around them which we would mix in with our own remake of whatever movie was playing at the matinee that week. Our main props, besides our ponies, were the trees and grapevines in the garden at Rowan Oak. We'd do a lot of climbing and swinging."[26] Besides making up tales for her daughter, Estelle wrote some fiction of her own. In fact in the late 1920s, Faulkner sent Scribner's a coauthored story (originally Estelle's), which they rejected.[27] There is also Estelle's fictionalized memoir, "Dr. Wohlenski." Deliberately autobiographical, it tells much about her feelings when, as an almost seven-year-old girl, she was just about to move from Kosciusko to Oxford. In this story, she already privileges the imagination and sees herself as, therefore, different. After offering her good-night prayers, she is admonished for asking God to "deliver me from playmates. Grown-ups—white and colored—were far superior company" (22). One reason she prefers grown-ups is that they tell stories. These details about Estelle Oldham call into question biographers' portrayals of her as a totally dependent lightweight whose greatest concerns were her clothes and her reputation in the community. Her daughter explains, "Ma-ma would try to please people she cared about or for a reason. But she really didn't care about public opinion."[28]

Estelle Faulkner is supposed to have craved a more active social life. Perhaps she did. Yet her daughter says, "She wasn't interested in the activities of the other ladies' clubs and bridge. She loved to fiddle around the garden. She wasn't doing the gardening herself, but she was out there supervising and cutting flowers. I don't think there was ever a problem with boredom as far as Ma-ma was concerned—not at the beginning of her life or at the end either. It was not a question of 'what I am going to do with myself for the next hour because there's nothing I don't have to do.' Time was something she enjoyed."[29] As for Estelle's supposed neediness, again her daughter's comments suggest a kind of self-sufficiency, independence, and strong sense of selfhood that is at odds with current biographical assessments:

> She was ready to listen, always wanted to help. But if I didn't come with a specific problem, she was perfectly willing to let me fend for myself. She wasn't intrusive, but also she was very wrapped up in her own self and her own thoughts. I was more important to her than anything else other than Pappy. At the same time, she herself was very important to herself. I realized early—and it probably saved me too—that I was not of primary importance to either one of them. You know, some people tend to forget that there is a "me." They are *always* concerned with other people. But she wasn't. It's probably one of the reasons she and Pappy stayed together.[30]

To a newspaper reporter years after Faulkner's death, in 1962, Estelle remarked, "I have never been bored in my life—lonely, maybe, but never bored."[31] Along with her collaboration in Faulkner's "games," evidence shows that her self-knowledge and self-sufficiency compelled his respect.

Although Rowan Oak may have been fun to visit, living there was complicated. When it became too much, Jill could go to the cabin where, first, Caroline Barr and, later, other black women who cared for her lived: "It was sometimes a happier place to be. There was no feeling of tension there. It was the difference between sitting under a nice cool shade tree and sitting on top of a volcano."[32] That dangerous tension their daughter experienced sustained and enlivened the Faulkners' marriage, a point Summers makes herself: "Ma-ma and Pappy were two very different and difficult people trying to coexist. They walked on tight-wires around each other, and I walked an equally tight wire around the two of them. But I think they both enjoyed it. I think *I* was the only one who felt uncomfortable. . . . There was always the feeling that something was getting ready to happen. I'm trying to think if there was ever any time when life was simply there. There wasn't. There were always undercurrents and just a feeling of tension. There's no other way to describe it."[33] Jill's description of their marriage sounds eerily similar to her father's fictional portrayals of obsession and desire, particularly in *Sanctuary* and *Light in August.*

Further elaborating, she contrasts her mother's two husbands:

Judge Franklin was a delightful man, but pretty pedestrian. He had money, he liked the things that money provided—polo ponies and steeple-chase horses. But, despite all the places he'd been and things he'd done, he was really pretty dull and predictable. I think *that,* as much as anything, caused the problems between them, because Ma-ma didn't care for the pedestrian aspects of any life. I think that because she enjoyed living, to some degree, in a fantasy world. Because she didn't like the pedestrian aspects of any life or thing, she completely enjoyed the sort of life she had with Pappy even though it was difficult. I'm not sure Pappy would have stayed married to anyone else. He married an idea; he didn't marry a person.

Ma-ma was very good and so was Pappy—if something was distasteful or wasn't quite as it should be, they could simply not see it. I think moving into Rowan Oak to begin with was something of a lark. It was a romantic adventure and both of them liked that. For example if there was no electricity, they'd say "Oh, isn't candlelight nice." There is no running water; a bottle of wine on ice is better than water coming out of a tap. That's what I'm trying to say about their fantasy world. And remember, everyone had help.[34]

To say that the Faulkners' marriage translated directly into his fiction (that it was an instance—to use his own words—of sublimating the actual to the apocryphal) is simplistic. But their daughter's observations on why her parents stayed married, despite much talk on both sides of divorce and desertion, give one a sense that it was a stimulating relationship for both partners.[35] In many respects, Faulkner very consciously used the tension and theater in his marriage for imaginative experimenting. His marriage and love affairs, even his relationship with his daughter, functioned somewhat like his role-playing.

Exploring further the tension she experienced, Jill Summers says, "Mama herself was not a tense, uptight person. I think a lot of people got the impression that she was a little high-strung and tense. I don't really think she was. I think that the tension that I'm talking about was between her and Pappy, and in a situation where the two of them were involved. But I don't think that she, herself, was tense. It may, in part, have been a way of their maintaining in their marriage the illusion of unattainability that seemed to have been so important to Pappy."[36] And, I might add, to Estelle.

If we misread the intentions of the fictions of love and desire that Faulkner and Estelle created in their lives, we risk misreading the fictions of love and desire in Faulkner's art.

My book is about the family of perhaps our greatest American novelist, the first to come out of the South. The dynamics of family relations in a Jim Crow society fractured by racism and sexism and its enduring legacy of slavery; the problems of culturally sanctioned addiction; the place of the artist in our culture; the difficulties of achieving a clear sense of self in such a world are the issues on which I focus. In many ways Faulkner's life is a Type for The American Artist. Perhaps this is why the myth to which I referred earlier is so compelling. Relinquishing this one-dimensional myth, however, and attending instead to those dimensions it obscured, changes and enlarges our understanding of Faulkner's tremendous achievement and of the peculiar place of the artist in our culture. To clarify the significance, complexity, and richness of Faulkner's originary and enduring relations with Caroline, Maud, and Estelle, and suggest their relevance to the crucial concerns of Faulkner's fiction, releases fresh perceptions of his art.

PART 1

William Faulkner and Caroline "Callie" Barr

"MAMMY"—*Her white children bless her.*
—FAULKNER, 1940

Caroline Barr's gravestone, erected and with an inscription by William Faulkner, 1940. St. Peter's Cemetery, the "colored section," Oxford, Miss. (Photo: Amy C. Evans)

My idea is, a tombstone in a public cemetery is set up as a true part of the record of a community. It must state fact, or nothing.
　　　　　—Faulkner, concerning his mother Maud's gravestone

O N THE SQUARE, FLAT, unadorned, gray granite tombstone that marks Caroline Barr's grave in the old "colored" section of St. Peter's, Oxford's main cemetery, William Faulkner had carved, "CALLIE BARR CLARK / 1840–1940."

He knew her given name but marked her with the familiar diminutive; he knew her death date but did not give it; if he knew her real birth date, he chose not to reveal it here. According to Barr's relatives, he was wrong about her last name. I begin with her gravestone, ordinarily a source of vital factual information, in order to alert you to the paucity of correct facts about Caroline Barr and the attendant difficulty of finding her real story. There is a long history of scholarly neglect concerning the black women of Callie Barr's generation, the last to become adults under slavery.

Other than her gravestone, there are no official records for Caroline Barr. She cannot be found in any pre–Civil War slave schedule or post–Civil War census in any of the places her relatives or members of Faulkner's family report that she lived, but then, from the time of her birth she moved constantly. In the 1840s, her owner may have sent the young child from Nottoway County, Virginia, to South Carolina. She was probably one of the more than a million slaves who either were sold or were part of forced migrations into the Deep South and West during the domestic slave-trading period (1790–1860).[1] Freed sometime between 1863, when Union troops first occupied South Carolina, and 1865, she and at least *some* of what was left of her family, traveled in stages and by the round-about way of Arkansas to northern Mississippi. They seem to have survived by sharecropping or tenant farming, but because they were terrorized by the Ku Klux Klan and didn't prosper, they moved on.[2] Like the vast majority of newly freed

African Americans in the postbellum rural South, they found it almost impossible to make a living in what historians now refer to as a system of "neo-slavery."[3]

Sometime in the late 1880s, when her children were grown, Caroline Barr may have given up the idea of ever making a living from the land. Leaving at least two of her daughters in the cotton country east of Batesville, Mississippi, she headed on alone northeast to Ripley, Mississippi, some fifty miles northeast of Oxford. There she began working as a house servant for members of the Falkner family.[4] When William was born, in 1897, she became the baby's nurse or, in Faulkner's and his generation's words, his "Mammy." Her tombstone maintains that she retained that role until her death in 1940.

Until now, the only published accounts of Callie Barr are based on the impressions of white people: members of Faulkner's family—his brothers and mother—and members of Oxford's white community. I have used past accounts of whites and added new ones. But, to provide a more complete picture, I have also included information from interviews with members of Callie Barr's own family, a family whose voices have not been included in this narrative. Dora Lewis and Rachel McGee, Barr's great-nieces; Mildred Quarles, one of Rachel's daughters; and James Rudd, Barr's great-great grandson, agreed to speak to my research assistant, Patricia Tingle, a fellow Mississippian. Their insights, the facts they could provide, and their stories about their family change and enlarge our understanding of Callie Barr's character and life and of the doors to other worlds she opened for young Willie Faulkner. Callie Barr taught him uncolored love; from her he learned the courage to plumb the terrible psychic and cultural consequences of denying and being ashamed of that love. His fiction gives imaginative form to a shame he felt and a loss he mourned all his life.

In the 1920s and 1930s, Barr also cared for Estelle Faulkner's son, Malcolm Franklin, and the Faulkners' daughter, Jill. Malcolm's brief memoir and my interviews with Jill Summers added more new facts and insights about Callie's relationships with her charges and with the two Faulkner women for whom she worked, Faulkner's mother, Maud, and later, from 1929 until Barr died, his wife, Estelle. Unfortunately, the facts remain sparse and fragmentary; stories sometimes conflict. As a result I have had to speculate more than I would have liked. This is only a beginning. I hope that the richness of this new material will spur others to present a fuller and more accurate profile of this woman whom Faulkner rightfully saw as remarkable.

Callie Barr has held a minor place in all Faulkner biography and in critical discussions of his work. Following the lead of Faulkner's brothers, biographers and literary critics portray her as a stereotypic "mammy" figure. They also write that the constant stream of stories she told influenced him. But what these were and why they had that power was not explored by scholars who had access to the living record. Equally important, what it might mean to Faulkner's readers to think of Callie Barr as a formative influence on the artist's imaginative vision and how that might alter the ways we read his work, has not been considered. Faulkner urges us to do this explicitly in two of the few avowedly autobiographical texts he ever wrote—his eulogy for Caroline Barr in 1940 and what may be read as his final elegy for her, "Mississippi," a quasi-autobiographical essay (1954). Faulkner's constant retelling of the story of a Southern white boy's (for it is almost always a boy) psychologically violent education into race and racism is a defining moment in the boy's quest for identity and white Southern Manhood. In that moment when he begins to act white, he always has to demean and to cut himself off physically and emotionally from the black mother who nursed him and the black child with whom he ate, slept, and played. This moment marks him for life. He never recovers from his transformation, this moment when, by denying his black family in order to define himself as white, he experiences himself as permanently cut off from love.

In his imagination, where Faulkner really lived, Callie Barr commanded lots of space. Much of his work that dramatizes and anatomizes the terrible and continuing legacy of slavery testifies to the depth of his imaginative engagement with how racism has mis-shaped white Southern identity. Faulkner's fiction constantly writes and rewrites memorials to his own, his family's, and his culture's complex relationship with Callie Barr and her worlds, particularly the cost of creating their whiteness by insisting, along with the sheriff's deputy in Faulkner's "Pantaloon in Black," that black people "just ain't human."

Called "Aunt Callie" or "Moma Callie" by her own family, and "Mammy" by successive generations of Faulkners, what kind of person was Caroline Barr, the high-cheek-boned, large-eyed, swift, but spare-speaking woman with the heart-shaped face and blue-black skin whose small frame resembled Maud Falkner's except for its color? Like the famous white child she raised, taught, and lived with all her life, Callie Barr wore many masks. What did Willie learn from them?[5] How did her relationships with her real family and the one that the Falkner brothers write she called "mah white family" affect the young William Faulkner? What is her diaspora story, and why is it a study in conflicting information?

In many ways, the multiple and contradictory images that emerge to compose Faulkner's two "mothers" mirror the myths and realities of black and white Southern Womanhood that were the lessons of his childhood. Along with the stories these women told him of the "Great Insurrection," they were, Faulkner wrote, "the most important thing the white child knew at that time since at four and five and six his world was still a female world" ("Mississippi," 17).

Like most intelligent people, Callie Barr is a study in seeming inconsistencies. She made the black field-workers stand outside the Faulkners' kitchen door and insisted that Estelle Faulkner dress "like a lady." But, when they were children, she regularly took Billy and his younger brothers and, decades later, his daughter, with her to her favorite niece's home and jook joint on the outskirts of Freedman Town, Oxford's "colored" section. Pursuing these lines of inquiry writes into history a very different woman with a very different relationship to William Faulkner than the "Mammy" of prior accounts.

These first six chapters focus on the Faulkner family's three-generational relationship with Caroline Barr. Her storytelling was so powerful that, according to Faulkner's brother John, "[it] twined her whole life with ours."[6] Yet, amazingly, neither his nor his brother Jack's memoir bears out this claim.

What about this twining? How was Willie Falkner's forced *un*-twining the defining moment in his traumatic fall into the knowledge of race? How did this Southern white boy's fall, whose psychological damage his fiction obsessively replays in perhaps the most painful scenes of untwining and of its white subjects' attendant feelings of rage, shame, and repressed grief in white American literature, shape and define his modernist poetics of racialized loss?

How did his childhood travels into the world of Callie Barr's family, one he and his three younger brothers visited regularly, also shape these poetics?

I am interested in Faulkner's subversive, personal, and therefore more coded figures of loss—how his own racial unconscious figures the threat of the loss of his artistic imagination, which, for Faulkner, is the loss of Self. "*'Wait,' she said. . . . 'Don't you go up there, Rosa.' That was how she said it . . . to her of all who knew me I was no child. 'Rosa?' I cried. 'To me? To my face?' Then she touched me, and then I did stop dead . . . at that black arresting and untumorous hand on my white woman's flesh*" (*AA*, 111). This visceral, cinematic moment vividly articulates the racial transgressions embodied in the slave Clytie Sutpen's four outrageous acts—commanding, naming, infantilizing, and touching her white aunt Rosa Coldfield. Who is supposed to be in charge of naming and touching in the American scenes that Faulkner's fiction invokes? What sacred Southern codes and laws is the "black" daughter of her white master, Thomas Sutpen, violating here? Who taught these codes to William Faulkner? From whom did he learn the desire and skill to subvert them? Who taught him to perform his color, and that race could be either and sometimes both performative and performance? From whom did he learn the reciprocal nature of black-white racial identity and the inextricable relation between race and sex? Who first made him reel back in horror and grief and shame at the incredible toll that performative "whiteness" and "blackness" would exact? In short, how was Faulkner's *experiential* education into race and sex first embodied? Whose touches and voices, whose narratives for survival, whose social worlds gave to the "peculiar" realities and myths of black and white relations in the Jim Crow South an urgency, sensuality, and materiality that Faulkner's imagination would transmute into what Toni Morrison speaks of as "a past that was not available in history, which is what art and fiction can do but sometimes history refuses to do." Whose intelligence and perceptions, whose words, skin, body, kisses, embraces, anger, pain, and love gave Faulkner what Morrison calls "a gaze that was different . . . a refusal-to-look-away approach" that, like this scene between Clytie and Rosa, never loses its shock?[7] These are some of the questions the following chapters on William Faulkner's upbringing by and lifelong attachment to Caroline Barr try to answer.

1

Caroline Barr in Black and White Voices
Miss Callie, Aunt Callie, Aunt Carrie,
Great-Great Grandma Callie, Mammy Callie

I N 1897, ONE YEAR AFTER *Plessy v. Ferguson* legalized racial segregation and Jim Crowism was accepted as constitutional, William Faulkner was born in New Albany, Mississippi.[1] Caroline Barr began caring for the baby, known as Willie, either at his birth or in 1898, shortly after the Falkners moved from New Albany to Ripley, William's great-grandfather's hometown. Then sixty-five years old, which to Willie "seemed already older than God," Caroline had grown to maturity and borne children as a slave and then had lived through Reconstruction and its failure ("Mississippi," 16). Freed in 1865, she did not work again in the homes of whites until her daughters, who had been born free, were grown. When she did, it was far from their home in the Sardis area of Mississippi.

Barr's daughters and at least one of her nieces, this first generation of freeborn Barrs, were independent and enterprising. At a time when 90 percent of the country's rural African American population worked as sharecroppers or tenant farmers, her daughters' families would eventually own the cotton fields near Batesville they had once sharecropped.[2] Her brother Ed Barr's daughter, Molly Barr, bore and raised eleven children of her own; she also became one of Oxford's few black businesswomen. So famous, or infamous (depending on the sources), did Molly Barr become that in the late 1980s the town of Oxford built and named a road after her. When Callie Barr moved from Ripley to Oxford with the Falkners in late September 1902, Molly Barr was the niece she often visited, with the Falkner boys in tow.

Callie Barr and the Falkner Women: History of a Relationship

A racially composite matriarchy composed of Maud's mother, Lelia Butler, Maud, and Callie began living together and sharing the care of Maud's

1.1. Caroline Barr Genealogy

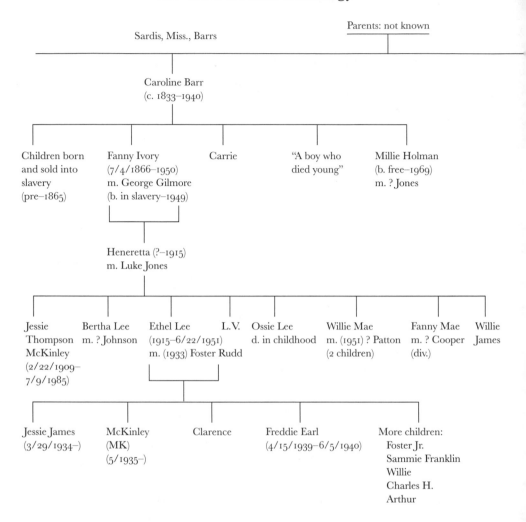

Source: Compiled from census materials, gravestones, and interviews with the Barr family.
Note: Callie Barr's probable origins: Lower Guinea ("Rice") Coast, Africa; Nottoway County, Va.;
Barr's Landing, Lower All Saints Parish, Georgetown District, S.C.

and her husband Murry's three little boys before the Falkners moved to Oxford.[3] Jill remembers Callie often prefacing remarks with "'When we lived in Ripley' or 'when I came from Ripley with the boys.' I remember her mentioning the Barrs briefly, saying she came from Carolina with the Barrs, is the image I have."[4] She thinks Callie had been "a house servant of Pappy's grandfather's before Pappy was born."[5] Jill's father confirms this,

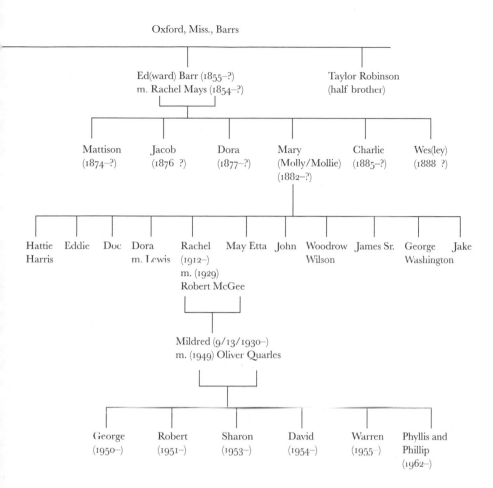

Oxford, Miss., Barrs

Ed(ward) Barr (1855–?)
m. Rachel Mays (1854–?)

Taylor Robinson
(half brother)

Mattison (1874–?) | Jacob (1876 ?) | Dora (1877–?) | Mary (Molly/Mollie) (1882–?) | Charlie (1885–?) | Wes(ley) (1888 ?)

Hattie Harris | Eddie | Doc | Dora m. Lewis | Rachel (1912–) m. (1929) Robert McGee | May Etta | John | Woodrow Wilson | James Sr. | George Washington | Jake

Mildred (9/13/1930–)
m. (1949) Oliver Quarles

George (1950–) | Robert (1951–) | Sharon (1953–) | David (1954–) | Warren (1955–) | Phyllis and Phillip (1962–)

writing that "she did not enter [the Falkner] household until my father's children began to arrive." From then on "she was present day and night, in the house with us while I and my brothers were in our successive infancy."[6] Callie may have come to Ripley by way of Pontotoc, a town directly south of Ripley and slightly southeast of Oxford. Rachel McGee and her daughter say that "they [Callie Barr, her children, and her brothers, Ed Barr and Taylor Robinson] all came from Pontotoc."[7] In one account Faulkner writes that Callie "was born a slave, on the plantation of Samuel Barr, in Pontotoc County" and later "came to this county [Lafayette] and to Samuel Barr's brother near the end of the Civil War."[8] Neither census nor tax records confirm Callie's presence in any of these places.

Caroline Barr and Faulkner's maternal grandmother, Lelia Butler, belonged to the same generation.[9] Historically speaking, both were frontier women, both had had hard lives, both had done their share of farm work and of traveling in search of a better living, and neither seemed to have much use for the grown men who had entered and left their lives. But one was born a slave: she may also have lost husbands or lovers to the auction block; according to her great-great grandson, she had seen her own children sold.[10] She spent the majority of her life caring for white families' children, first as a slave and later as a free woman.

By 1907, the year Maud's fourth and last child, Dean Swift, was born, both Lelia, for whom Maud named Dean (Lelia was a Swift), and Maud's mother-in-law, to whom Maud was very close, had died of cancer. Between helping to care for her two mothers and her own children and coping with a difficult and probably unexpected and unwanted pregnancy and her husband's apparently permanent unhappiness, Maud had had a traumatic two years. During this time her emotional dependence on Callie increased as her own mother, suffering intense pain that only morphine could ease, faded. Callie, who had by then worked for the Falkners for ten years, became the eldest in Maud and Murry's household. John Faulkner speculates that "Mammy, in a strong measure" replaced both grandmothers: "Perhaps in a stronger measure than they, for Mammy was never adverse to scolding and had a good deal sharper tongue. I can remember her making any one of the three of us to 'hump it' when we were a little slow in minding her."[11] Whether Maud confided in Callie, we'll never know. Like Caroline Barr in her community, Maud Falkner was known as a very "close" and private woman. Nonetheless, working day and night for the Falkners made Callie privy to family secrets that, as Susan Tucker notes, "could not be hidden within the private home." With her, as with so many black women of her time and place, "such secrets were safe because of racial etiquette that ensured that what went on in a white home would never be mentioned by a black to another white."[12] (At least not another white adult. Children were a different matter.)

The white home Callie Barr first entered in New Albany, Mississippi, in 1897 was perhaps more emotionally volatile than most. She became part of the Falkner household during one of the most difficult periods in Maud's long and often rocky marriage. Between November 1896, when Maud Butler and the tall, handsome, and quick-tempered Murry Falkner married in Oxford, and the fall of 1902, she had borne three sons and lived in three towns. In 1902, her husband, who had a reputation for heavy drinking and quick fists, had been summarily removed from his job by his equally hard-drinking and overbearing father, J. W. T. Falkner. Murry's involvement with the family railroad was to be the only work he would ever enjoy.[13] His father, a successful criminal lawyer and entrepreneur, then ordered his son (who had never finished college) to Oxford and put him in nominal charge of one of his several businesses. Murry hated his new work and hated being bossed around, but he had three children to support and a wife who refused to head to Texas to make a fresh start, like so many Mississippians, including her future daughter-in-law's family, the Oldhams. During the years his children grew from babies to young adults, Murry allowed his father to shift him from one unsatisfying job to another, offering only passive resistance.[14] He did minimal work and he drank.

Compounding Murry Falkner's problems was his wife's mother, Lelia Butler. A fervent Baptist and daughter of two of Oxford's founding families, the Swifts and the Pullens, she had joined the household shortly after Murry lost his railroad job. She brought with her painting supplies, Jeremy Taylor's *Rules and Exercises of Holy Dying* (1850 reprint), Frederick G. Wright's *The Logic of Christian Evidences* (1893), and T. C. Blake's *History and Defense of the Cumberland Presbyterian Church* (1880).[15] Besides objecting to alcohol on religious and pragmatic grounds, Lelia disliked Murry, whose freeness with guns and fists reminded her of the husband who'd deserted her and their teenaged children in 1887, when she was in her mid-thirties.[16] Before Maud and Murry moved to Oxford, Lelia addressed letters to her daughter as "Mrs. Maud Butler."

We know from Faulkner's daughter and Barr's relatives that Callie also disapproved of Murry's drinking. She could no more curb it than could Maud or Lelia, but the job of coping with him while drunk was among the many intimacies shared by the black and white women whom the four Falkner boys had been taught to think of as their first and second mothers.[17] A generation later and long after his death, Jill learned that her grandfather Murry was an alcoholic, "because all the colored people talked about it. I think his drinking was pretty spectacular. I mean that it was worth comment. When he drank, everybody knew about it. He was a rip-roarer, a pretty exciting drunk and also, I think, a mean one. I've never been told that, exactly, but Mammy Callie alluded to it—that Mr. Murry was bad news when he had been drinking."[18]

Murry died in 1932, a year before Jill was born; her impressions of him are formed by what she learned from Callie Barr, whose teaching methods are revealed in Jill's account. She taught by telling stories. Sometimes these were about confusing or frightening but ever-present taboo subjects that the children's parents never mentioned, like drinking and sex: "Mammy Callie was the only person who ever talked to me about him. Mostly, she talked about how difficult he was. When I'd done something I shouldn't have, she'd say I was exactly like my grandfather. If I were stubborn about eating, for example. He would not eat vegetables. That was very unusual for a Southerner. Well, he drank a lot, and one time, after he'd been to Byhalia, the doctor said he had to start eating them. His answer to that was to demand that Mammy Callie bring him a leaf of lettuce every morning before he'd get out of bed. He'd wash it down with a shot of whiskey, which she'd also bring."[19]

Callie's story makes a joke out of the grandfather's drinking, but it also instructs Jill in how not to grow up like him. Even more important for understanding Faulkner's childhood and Callie's role in his education, Callie's story characterizes Murry in the same infantilized terms whites typically reserved for blacks. Callie has, as Ralph Ellison would say, "changed the joke and slipped the yoke." Here, instead of a black servant, it is Murry, the white master, who, though an adult, is only half a person, a person of a race (and gender) that remained a child. Callie treats him as a "boy" or "uncle"—not as a man.[20] Such shrewd reversals were a constant in the stories Callie told the young Willie and his brothers. As Faulkner's own, often piercing stories about race reveal, the implications of her tales were not lost on him. But what he envisioned in his fiction and what he would or could do in his life did not necessarily coincide.

From the time he was a small child, Faulkner saw that his father's drinking engaged the attentions of both his mother and Callie Barr. From his grandfather and father, he learned that drinking could be used to dull emotional pain, attract a certain kind of care, and avoid responsibilities.[21] The response Murry Falkner got from his two mothers may explain one reason why the grown Faulkner repeated his father's self-destructive and childlike behavior with his mother and Callie. Only as a child had he not felt guilt and shame for wanting the emotional warmth Callie gave him. Drunk, he could reclaim that childhood state, just like his father and grandfather.

Although Jill says that, long after Callie's death, she was told that Callie was the only person who could stop her father's binges, the record shows—and she remembers—that no one could. Callie's relatives report that even in the late 1930s, when Faulkner drove Callie to their house on the outskirts of Freedman Town to visit, he'd take along a jug of white lightning and go off in the woods to drink. When he'd return to the Mc-Gees', Callie would reprimand him; "he'd weep and promise to stop and she'd say, if he stayed this late [in the woods] again, 'I goin' to come and get you.' And he'd get in his old high-wheel car and him and her—she was so little you couldn't hardly see her—down the road they go."[22]

These stories are significant because they help explain Maud's and Callie's relationship to each other and to the man and the children they both spent five decades of their lives caring for. All the Falkner boys experienced their joint mothering as a twinning and a twining, but Willie was the only one to use his experience of being cared for by a black and a white mother to create some of the most revealing and painful fictional renderings of how racism permeates, binds, yet, ultimately, destroys every relationship it touches.

He was also one of the few Modernist writers to push beyond the macho mystique of alcohol to explore its role in the class, racial, and sexual politics of Southern culture and history. He was the only writer to translate its effects on the mind into a unique poetics of modern identity, one that destabilizes time and space and dissolves the boundaries and traditional distinctions between exterior and interior reality.

By the time he was sixteen, Faulkner was probably already, by medical definitions, an alcoholic. At twenty-three, when he still was trying to become a poet, Faulkner first used alcohol as a trope for the divided and disintegrating self. *The Marionettes* (1920), his symbolist dream-play, is its protagonist's alcohol-induced dream about his double, whom he imagines as another, freer self. By early 1925, owing in part to Faulkner's reading of Estelle Oldham's unpublished short story "A Crossing," her fictionalized response to and revision of his play, his aesthetics of alcohol had become de-idealized. His first novel, *Soldiers' Pay* (1926), reflects this. Its opening scene draws on what Estelle's story had revealed to him about how parents or surrogate parents can use alcohol to destroy their children and make them conform to their will. In the novels that follow, *The Sound and the Fury* and *Sanctuary*, alcohol is the weapon of choice of those in charge, like the Compson children's father and uncle and all of Temple Drake's would-be and actual rapists. Characters as dissimilar as Benjy Compson and Temple Drake are force-fed bootleg liquor in scenes that portray the ways the strong literally force alcohol on the weak to obliterate their identity or selfhood by disorienting them so that they lose their grasp on reality.

Forcing liquor on young boys appears to have been a rite of passage in Faulkner's family. Although Faulkner never told such a story about himself, except to say that before he'd reached his teens he was regularly downing his grandfather's "heeltaps," his brother John's son, Jimmy Faulkner, remembers his induction at fourteen: "That was bad. John and Brother Will were drinking out at the farm. They were drinking straight whiskey—corn whiskey—out of a tin cup. I was going from the house down to the barn to catch a horse and go riding. I walked past them and Brother Will called out and said: 'You're old enough now to have your first drink, and we want you to have your first drink with us.' I said 'All right.' So they had this tin cup, poured whiskey in it and said, 'Here.'" Jimmy had seen his father and uncle drinking, so he, too, drank the whole cup of "200-proof" alcohol at once. "I couldn't breathe. . . . It burned my stomach." Jimmy could barely drag himself home and once there, he couldn't even crawl into bed. His mother was furious and called Maud. But the family punished Jimmy and his father: "This caused a split in the family: nobody would talk to John or me." Only Maud tried to protect the child from any more of his uncle's jokes: "Nanny [Maud] wouldn't let me come down to Brother Will's house by myself."[23]

By 1936, Faulkner had fully worked out and integrated the trope of alcoholism into his modernist poetics. In *Absalom, Absalom!* young Thomas Sutpen's father's alcoholic haze spreads like a disease to his impressionable youngest son. It enfolds and disorients the ten-year-old child in the first temporal stage of his dislocating "fall" from innocence to knowledge. This stage is figured literally in his family's journey from the "unraced and unclassed" country of the child's birth in the mountains of West Virginia, "where the land belonged to anybody and everybody," down into his "rebirth" in the Tidewater Basin of large-scale plantation slavery. As the boy drives their wagon filled with his brothers and sisters, their few belongings, and his father "snoring with alcohol," then waits outside an endless stream of taverns "for the father to drink himself insensible," and drives on "to a sort of dreamy and destinationless locomotion after they had got the old man out of whatever shed or outhouse or barn or ditch and loaded him into the cart again," his mind becomes a mirror of his father's and a metaphor for his own dissolving but as yet unraced and unclassed self. Like a drunk, he loses all sense of direction and time: "So he knew neither where he had come from nor where he was nor why." He even loses his memory: "He became confused about his age and was never able to straighten it out again" (*AA*, 179, 182, 184).

In the Tidewater, this boy who has lost his mother, his home, his country, even his age (eerily familiar tropes associated with the deliberate destruction of a slave's identity in American slave narratives) suffers a violent rebirth; he emerges inscribed with race and class. Here the land and people are "all divided and fixed and neat because of what color their skins happened to be and what they happened to own." In this world he "had hardly heard of . . . until he fell into it," he first sees slavery, the system where "a certain few men . . . had the power of life and death and barter and sale over others." In an ominous prefiguring of the drinking scenes preceding his own murder some thirty years later by his outraged and abused servant, the boy, Sutpen, observes that these slave owners also "had living human men to perform the endless repetitive personal offices such as pouring the very whiskey from the jug and putting the glass into his hand" (*AA*, 179, 180).

Not until four years later, when Faulkner began writing what became his first elegy for Callie Barr after her death, in 1940, would he explicitly connect a Southern white boy's loss of his black "mother" to a grown man's need to destroy anyone he might possibly love, including himself. Not until then did that loss become his controlling metaphor for loss of self.

2

Caroline Barr's Origins
A Speculative Reconstruction

My daddy was a lion, my moma was a tigah,
But people all say I'm an old Guinea niggah.
                              —Callie Barr

S OMETIMES SHE'D SAY instead, 'a blue-gum niggah' or 'Gullah niggah.' I have a vague memory of someone who was kin to Mammy, someone I used to see with her. Her gums were purplish looking. She and Mammy had the same color skin—very dark, a dull black, not a shiny black. She had a relative called Aunt Blue-Gum or Aunt Tempe, who used to visit sometimes." Concerning what Callie told her about her life as a slave, Jill remembers very little. "She'd talk about when she was a house-slave on a rice plantation in the low-country. I don't remember her ever saying much more about being a slave. But she told me a lot of ghost stories and animal stories—about animals with human traits. She used to try to teach me Gullah."[1]

Jill was not yet seven when Caroline Barr died. This rhyme, Jill's memories, the brief account by her half-brother, Malcolm, in his memoir, *Bitterweeds*, and the accounts of Faulkner's brothers and Callie's relatives are among the few, often fragmented and contradictory clues to Caroline's origins and her life before she joined the Falkner household. Within the Faulkner family, there are two apparently differing versions. Both Malcolm and Jill say that Caroline came from South Carolina with her own, black family after Emancipation. Faulkner's stepson wrote that Faulkner told him Callie "was born in slavery in South Carolina" on a plantation owned by the Barr family.[2] Faulkner's two brothers' versions claim that she came to Mississippi from some unknown state as the slave of a Colonel Barr before the Civil War and that when Oxford was invaded, he moved with his slaves to Pontotoc, which is just southeast of Oxford. After the war he returned to Oxford, and Callie came with him as a paid servant.[3]

Although there are no written records to support either account, both

may be partly correct. There are South Carolina Barrs recorded in Pontotoc as early as the 1860 census. Among them is a Colonel Alex Barr of
Oxford, who died in 1899, and whose brother, Samuel Barr, lived in Pontotoc. As far as is known, these Barrs came from the Abbeville District, on the
western edge of South Carolina. But no Barr slave named Caroline is listed
in any South Carolina slave schedule, and no servant named Caroline is
recorded in the Pontotoc census, which argues against Callie's coming with
them as a slave from South Carolina. Possibly when she reached Pontotoc
on her own, or Oxford, she did work for Colonel Barr's family, who might
well have been relatives of the Barrs who were her original owners and
who lived not *in* but *next* to the Georgetown District. Traditional sources
are useless in tracing her history, for several reasons: Callie was once a slave;
she moved a great deal; what we know of her private nature suggests she
was not the kind of person to be willingly counted in a census; and she was
illiterate and never owned any property.

These are the known facts: she or her family may have been from the
Guinea coast of Africa; in any event, she could speak a Gullah dialect or
knew some Gullah words, stories, and sayings; she may have been born in
Nottoway County, Virginia, and then sold South or have been transported
South to the Carolinas by her original owner during the early period of the
domestic slave trade; she was small and small-boned, and her skin was a
deep blue-black; she was opinionated and passionate; she had a wry wit
and told compelling stories but could not read or write; she was strong both
physically and mentally and remained mentally acute until her death at
107; she quilted and crocheted for pleasure; in Mississippi, she worked in
both vegetable and cotton fields with her own family, which, when she died,
included at least two daughters, two brothers, and their descendants. She
told the Faulkners that as a slave she had never been a field laborer; she appeared to enforce social hierarchies learned in slavery, yet she introduced
two generations of Faulkner children to a relative of whom the grown
Faulkners would have disapproved. She seems to have kept her family life
separate from the lives of the adult Faulkners: she maintained her ties with
her children's families, even when it meant traveling long distances, often
on foot, to see daughters with whom she quarreled constantly.

Her great-great grandson, James Rudd, who when interviewed for this
book was Chief Deputy Sheriff in Batesville, was six years old in 1940,
when his great-great grandmother died. He tells of her walking from Oxford "out to our house, out there around Sardis Dam," near Sardis, to visit
her daughters, Fanny Ivory, Millie Holman, and, perhaps before Rudd was
born, another daughter named Carrie: "I can remember seeing her and
what she looked like. I can remember her being a little old small lady wear-

2.1. The road Callie Barr walked from Rowan Oak to her
daughters' homes in Hipps Hollow, near Sardis, Miss.
(Photo: Amy C. Evans)

ing a little white looking torn looking sack looking—we used to call them flour sack looking—hat, bonnet on her head, just barely can remember. And I do remember after that. She walked from Oxford down to our house once, out here 'round the (Sardis) dam."[4]

On the pre–Civil War census rolls for the Georgetown District of South Carolina, where Faulkner told his stepson, Malcolm, that Callie's life began, slaves are listed as a number.[5] Like the bales of rice and, later, cotton that they were brought to this country to plant and harvest, they are property—without name, age, sex, or origin. Surviving records kept by individual planters provide more information, but Callie's name is not among them.[6]

Brief as it is, Malcolm's account of Callie's slave childhood and postwar migration to the Arkansas bank of the Mississippi River is more detailed than all other oral or written accounts. She is described "as quite a young woman" who had "married a Barr slave" from the rich rice plantations of the long-settled South Carolina inland river ways and seacoast. It also gives her an autonomy consistent with other facts we know about her, something lacking in the Faulkner brothers' accounts.[7] From a historical perspective it is indicative of her uniqueness. Her choice to migrate from South Carolina to Mississippi marks her as exceptional, since the vast majority of freed slaves stayed "in the vicinity of their enslavement."[8] Most important, it is *her* account (or, rather, Malcolm's transcription) of *her* oral history. As he writes, "In the afternoons I would go out and sit listening to the tales she had to tell me." Malcolm describes her narratives of her family's "migration to the West after the war," tales about their trip from South Carolina to Arkansas, as "hair-raising." There is no mention of her making this migration with her former owner. Rather, he writes that "Mammy Callie and her husband, with a number of children [crossed and] re-crossed the Mississippi looking for a new home."[9] The account by Faulkner's brother John of the Barr family's constant fears of the Ku Klux Klan—"Every Negro got his family in the house before dark and shut and barred the doors and windows"—suggests that the black Barrs were on their own in the alien Mississippi Delta.[10]

Callie's age is also disputed. If she was only sixteen when she was freed, as John Faulkner reports, her "family" might have been part of a group of Barr ex-slaves who left South Carolina together.[11] She may have begun her second and free family sometime during this migration, a journey made in stages and stretching, perhaps, over a period as long as thirty years. Taking into consideration the territory she covered and the places Malcolm reports her having lived along the way, she may well not have reached Ripley and Pontotoc County until the early 1890s. But John's dating makes Callie only ninety at her death, a figure contradicted by Callie herself. Like Callie's family members, both Malcolm and Jill say that Callie joined the Murry Falkners in New Albany when Faulkner was born, that she moved with them to Ripley shortly afterward, and that she traveled with them to Oxford in 1902 when Murry's father relieved him of his railroad job, forcing them to move again. Jill remembers Callie often prefacing remarks with "When *we* came from Ripley."

Faulkner's daughter also gives Callie Barr's birth date as earlier than other sources. Her dating is based on what Callie told her. On Jill's fifth birthday, in 1938, Callie said that she was 105 years old, indicating her birth year as 1833 rather than 1849, a more likely date for a woman who had some of her children "sold into slavery," as Sheriff Rudd reports.[12] Jill elaborates: "Mammy Callie and I were sitting together outside in the yard and Mammy had just killed a snake with her peach-wood switch. She hated snakes so much. And she said, 'Look how long it takes to die.' And I guess she must have been thinking about herself because then she told me, 'Today,' she said, 'you are five years younger than I am—less 100.'"[13] Jill's father adds further confirmation in his essay "Mississippi," where he describes Callie as more than a hundred years old, still quite lucid, and possessed of a prodigious memory; "she who had forgotten nothing" ("Mississippi," 40). Two other facts lend credence to the 1833 date. Callie told Malcolm and Jill that her mother had told her she "was born the night the stars fell."[14] Huge meteor showers occurred in both 1833 and 1866.[15] Other evidence comes from Faulkner and is cast as a fictional fact in the novel he began writing within a week of Barr's death and dedicated to her. In *Go Down, Moses*, the month and year the stars fell and the 1833 date is the birthday of Tomey's Turl (the slave of Carothers McCaslin, whom Thadious Davis names the "figure of transgression and hybridity at the center" of what I have called Faulkner's very problematic first elegy to Barr.[16] According to Carothers McCaslin's ledgers, Tomey's Turl, who is McCaslin's son, grandson, and slave because his mother was also McCaslin's slave and daughter, was born and his mother "dide in Child bed June 1833 . . . Yr stars fell" (*GDM*, 257). Possibly she was born on the slave ship carrying her mother to America and the phenomenon occurred at sea. As such she would have been imported illegally, for the last legal slave importations occurred in 1810.[17] Thus, Faulkner's habit of autobiographical encoding here makes Tomey's Turl and Callie either twins or doubles. In many ways Callie Barr was also the "figure of transgression and hybridity at the center" of Faulkner's imagination.

According to Malcolm, Callie, like the McCaslin slaves, also came from "Callina" (*GDM*, 254, 266). She called the plantation where she was enslaved in South Carolina (one of several her master owned) Barr's Landing. Although Malcolm says she came from Georgetown, the historian Charles Joyner claims there is no mention of Barrs or Barr's Landing in that parish's very extensive records.[18] It's possible that Callie belonged to one of the many branches of the Barr family in Williamsburg, the parish just west of Georgetown whose trading center was Georgetown.[19] Much poorer than its neighboring parish, it was populated largely by subsistence farmers whose principal crops were cotton, tobacco, and indigo.[20] Williamsburg is also the site of one of the oldest slave settlements in North America. In Williamsburg, Callie and her immediate family may well have been her master's only slaves, whereas in Georgetown she might have been one of a thousand.[21]

Although she lived in spectacularly beautiful country, her childhood as a slave left little time for play. As Jacqueline Jones and others have written, "The quest for an 'efficient' agricultural work force led slave owners to downplay gender differences" among their slaves. Thus "most women spent a good deal of their lives plowing, hoeing, and picking cotton. In the fields the notion of a distinctive 'women's work' vanished as slave holders realized that 'women can do plowing very well & full well with the hoes and are equal to men at picking.'"[22]

Such heavy work with man-sized tools must have been especially hard on Callie because she was so small. Jones writes that although "hoeing was backbreaking labor, . . . the versatility of the tool and its importance . . . meant that female hands used it a good part of the year." This all-purpose hoe, used throughout the South, was "hammered out of pig-iron [and] broad like a shovel." Such "'slave-time hoes' withstood most forms of abuse." The tool "also served as pick, spade, and gravedigger: 'Dey make 'em heavy so dey fall hard, but de bigges' trouble was liftin' dem up.'"[23]

On a subsistence farm or a large plantation there is little likelihood that Callie (despite her later claims to the Faulkners) escaped such work by being assigned only house chores. According to Eugene Genovese, as few as 5 percent of antebellum adult slaves "served in the elite corps of house servants trained for specific duties."[24] In many cases, before and after spending up to fourteen hours a day in the fields, slaves also did household chores.

It was there that children, particularly, were employed. As in the fields, until puberty, gender had little effect on task assignments. Jones describes typical chores that filled a slave child's life, the life Caroline Barr led before she left Barr's Landing and headed west to what she hoped was freedom. "Between the ages of six and twelve," children were responsible for filling wood boxes, lighting, and keeping lit, morning and evening fires in all the bedrooms; cleaning the house, making beds, "washing and ironing clothes, parching coffee, polishing shoes, stoking fires" during the night; fetching food and water from the smokehouse and well; preparing and serving three meals a day, even passing "the salt and pepper on command," washing dishes; brushing away flies and fanning their owners; and caring for white infants. As Jones notes, it was "no wonder that Mary Ella Grandberry, a slave child grown old, 'disremember[ed] ever playin' lack chilluns do to-day.'"[25]

The only memory fragment of Callie Barr's childhood that we are left is a story she told Faulkner's brother John. Predictably it portrays her at work, not play. It also argues for her belonging to a large plantation rather than a small farmer. Candle making, a children's task, was supervised by an elderly black woman who was probably assigned to supervise slave children who were too young to work in the fields. Callie called her "Ol Mistus." Sitting in a semicircle around a huge kitchen fireplace, each child held a heavy, awkward candle mold that had twelve cane joints attached to a wooden frame. After inserting wicks in every joint, the children then held up their molds so that tallow could be poured in. Children had to have strong and steady hands to avoid being burned by the boiling fat. If they misbehaved, Ol Mistus, who smoked a long-stemmed pipe, would lean over from the center where she sat and rap the offender on his or her head. Yet the urge to play is hard to kill; children would tease each other by sneaking water in their neighbors' molds. When hot tallow hit the water, a steaming geyser shot toward the cook-cabin ceiling.[26] How no one was scalded is not part of John's account. It's hard to understand why, of all the stories Callie told him, John chose to tell this one. Perhaps he liked it because it shows his "Mammy" acting like an ordinary child, making it possible for him to imagine her slave child's life as not so bad.

Malcolm Franklin reports that, like the few other white families living in this part of South Carolina, Callie's masters, the Barrs, also owned several other plantations.[27] More African slaves were brought to South Carolina than to any other part of the North American mainland. In the 1850 "census" for Georgetown County, blacks outnumbered whites by 60 to 1. Some Georgetown planters owned as many as 1,000 slaves. In contrast, the same 1850 census for Mississippi, where plantations were relatively small, and cotton, not rice, was the principal crop, showed a ratio of 1.3 blacks to every white.

Like most other freed African Americans who left their owners and their states, Callie headed west and south instead of north.[28] Physically intact but economically destroyed, Georgetown County experienced a massive postwar exodus of blacks and whites. The middle-class sons and

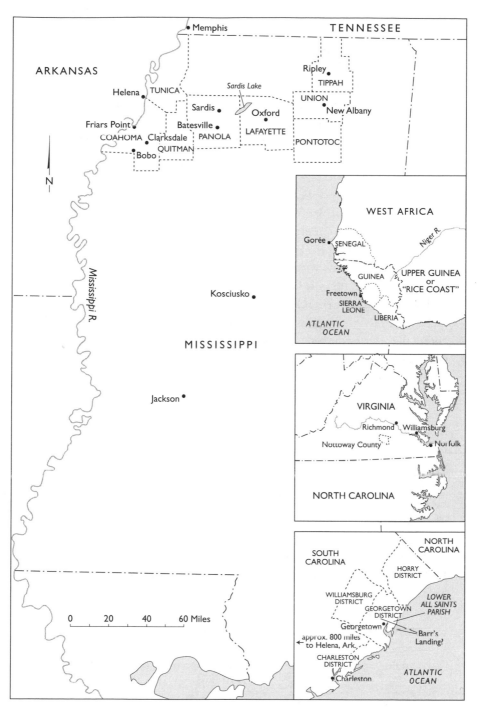

2.2. Towns in Mississippi and Arkansas that Callie Barr and her family lived
in or traveled through after they migrated from South Carolina at the end of
the Civil War. The three insets show (1) Callie Barr's family origins on the
Guinea Coast of Africa; (2) Nottoway County, Va., where she worked as a
slave prior to being sold "down river"; and (3) the probable site of Barr's
Landing, a rice plantation in the Georgetown District of South Carolina.
(Map drawn by Bill Nelson)

daughters of the original rice millionaires couldn't earn a living at home. Many headed for California, following the same roads, train-track beds, and rivers as their ex-slaves.

White families probably rode in wagons and on horseback. Black families walked. Callie's walked almost eight hundred miles—across their own state and through north central Georgia, Alabama, and Mississippi—before reaching the muddy banks of the Mississippi River near the Mississippi-Tennessee border (fig. 2.2, the Barrs' probable route).

There is no way of knowing how long it took Callie Barr's family to reach the Mississippi. We don't know if it was months or years. But, according to Malcolm's memoir, they camped on the great river's edge at Friar's Point, Mississippi, and then crossed the river to Helena, Arkansas. Perhaps the muddied swirlings of the largest body of water they'd come upon since leaving South Carolina reminded them of their slave "home" and of just how unsweet it had been. Perhaps it was their sense of safety on the far side of the Mississippi that made them stop in Arkansas when, after taking the ferry or one of many privately owned boats at Friar's Point, they landed at Helena's busy waterfront docks. More likely, their reasons were pragmatic. For the numerous South Carolinians, black and white, who poured into Helena in the two decades after the Civil War, this thriving river town, one of many billed as the "Gateway to the West," offered the promise of employment.[29] Its topography and agriculture are very similar to those in Williamsburg, South Carolina. Its swampy inland riverbanks and river ways and its surrounding cotton fields would have seemed familiar to Callie and her family. But because it was a Delta town and an important western gateway, Helena was wealthier and more industrialized than any place she had known in South Carolina.

The Barrs sojourned near Helena for an unknown number of years, making their living by sharecropping or tenant farming on one of the many Delta cotton plantations whose fields began just behind the string of gentle hills called Crowley's Ridge, where the town is built. According to the six pages on Callie Barr in Malcolm's memoir, they spent several years trying to farm there but, after a series of crop failures, headed back east.

Recrossing the Mississippi in high water, Callie and her family were swept slightly downstream. Once they went ashore, they walked almost twenty-five miles inland through the Delta before reaching Clarksdale, the nearest town, which lies in the midst of acres and acres of cotton plantations and is now famous as a cradle of the blues. According to what Callie told Malcolm, they then worked on a Colonel Bo's cotton plantation near Clarksdale. When they left Clarksdale (Malcolm's memoir is silent on why they left), they headed slightly north and then east to the Batesville-Sardis

2.3. The St. Peter Missionary Baptist Church cemetery on Blackjack Road, Hipps Hollow, near Sardis, Miss. This is where Callie Barr's daughters and their descendants are buried. (Photo: Amy C. Evans)

area, where at least Callie and her freeborn daughters, Fanny and Millie (and, possibly, Carrie) settled. Perhaps other Barr relatives kept heading farther east, through Oxford and then on to Pontotoc. Callie's Oxford relatives say that she had immediate family there. Assuming that Callie was born in 1833, as she told Faulkner's daughter, she would have been thirty-two in 1865. Her eldest daughter, Fanny, told her great grandson James Rudd that she—Fanny—was born that year "on the 4th of July of the year after the surrender." But Rudd also says that when Fanny died, her sister Millie Holman began claiming that date as *her* birthday. So it is hard to know whether Fanny was speaking figuratively or factually. Sheriff Rudd showed me the tree in the Hipps Hollow cemetery on Blackjack Road beneath which lie the unmarked graves of both daughters.[30]

Aunt Callie Barr of Oxford, Mississippi

There is an undated snapshot (c. 1909) of Callie Barr in her early seventies and William's youngest brother, Dean Falkner, at about two years of age. The photographer was probably Maud or Willie.[31] Dean stands with legs spread apart, balancing somewhat uncertainly, as if he was just beginning

2.4. Callie Barr, c. 1909, with Faulkner's youngest brother, Dean (b. 15 August 1907). This unusual photo may well have been taken by Maud or Willie. (Courtesy of HRC)

to walk. Callie is behind him, stooping slightly, her hands reaching toward or resting ever so slightly on his shoulders to catch him should he start to fall. Like her charge, she is dressed to be photographed. Her dark checked calico dress, white apron, and white head rag are the clothes she wore on Sunday mornings when she took the Falkner boys with her to visit with Rachel's mother, Molly Barr, when Rachel was a child.[32]

Callie's gaze is on Dean so that only her downcast, highlighted lids covering her large eyes are visible. Light flooding in from a side window also splashes upon her forehead, high cheek bones, nose, and upper lip. The still, masklike quality in her expression is impossible to read. It is hard to know whether her hovering hands and almost beatific expression signal attentiveness and adoration or an elderly woman just doing her job. The only other details we see are her large, slender hands (which are brought into relief by the light as she reaches for Dean's shoulders), and Dean's white hat, face, and jacket. The relative largeness of her hands further emphasizes what a small woman she was.

Mildred Quarles, Molly Barr's granddaughter (see fig. 1.1, Barr genealogy), says that Callie was more circumspect than other women in her family. "Aunt Callie was a very close person. [She] wasn't outspoken like Mama or me or none of us." She explains that there were very few people Callie spent time with in Oxford: "As far as Aunt Callie visiting folks round here in town, that wasn't her style." Rather she went out to Molly Barr's house and, later, to Mildred's mother's. She also made trips to Batesville: "Every once in awhile she would go back down there, down on the beach by Sardis Bay. That where her daughters lived."[33] On her way west on route 6, she might visit Earl Wortham at his blacksmith shop; she had known Earl and the sister who lived with him since childhood.

Besides her advanced age, Callie's long work hours limited her visiting with other black families. Evelyn Golliday, Earl Wortham's daughter, says Callie stopped by during watermelon season because her father grew fine ones. Ms. Golliday says, "My father use to raise huge watermelons and she liked watermelon and he would always have her to come (at least once a year anyway) by the time the watermelons was ripe and he'd cut this large watermelon and give her half of it and she would eat that half and set there and talk awhile." She adds, "Father seemed to have thought a lot of her 'cause he make sure when his watermelon were ready that he would send and get Aunt Callie. And she'd walk here. Occasionally she would come visit my aunt [too] because they both worked somewhere close together."[34]

Wortham (b. 1888) and his sister were the same ages as Callie's grandchildren in Sardis. They had known her since her arrival in Oxford with the Murry Falkners in September 1902. Wortham told a white male interviewer (from Oxford) that "we didn't call her Callie Barr. . . . [We] called her Callie Watermelon. She'd eat so many watermelons. She never did get enough, I don't believe." He also said he had no idea how old he was: "I was born way back yonder on an old plantation, you know, and we didn't get any schooling and so we just could never tell our age."[35] In contrast, his daughter knows exactly when her father was born and told Pat Tingle that "we called her Callie or Aunt Callie. My father, he was born in 1888—he was just a boy under her." When asked if Callie came from Pontotoc with a Colonel Barr, she said, "I hear my father say, I thought he said she came here with the Falkners."[36]

Eleven years older than Willie, Earl Wortham also knew the Falkner boys because he worked in their father's ill-fated livery stable before establishing himself as an independent blacksmith west of town on the road to Batesville. Ms. Golliday corrected Tingle when she said she had read in Earl Wortham's interview that Callie visited the Worthams on her day off: "She was not off 'cause I don't think she had any days off. . . . Back there the maids would fix breakfast and dinner and when she get through with all the dinner dishes, on a day maybe when she didn't have to wash, she'd walk out to our house. And then when she got through with the watermelon she'd set there and chat awhile and then she would walk back to her job and it would be time for her to prepare supper. That's the way they did in those days. I think she had a little house somewhere on the [Falkner] place."[37]

Both Callie's descendants and Malcolm and Jill remember Callie's quickness with a switch on both children and snakes. Jill recalled: "I remember Malcolm and Jimmy and Chooky being switched by Mammy Callie, but I was pretty good around her and I never got switched." Jill and her half brother both say Callie hated snakes, many of which lived under the house. Jill said that "with one flick" of her switch "she'd break its back and then beat it to a bloody pulp. She was notorious for that snake-killing. Whatever was left of the carcass, she'd hang it up on the fence—either to make it rain, or make it stop raining. She used to tell stories about a stinging snake. I used to spend all my time looking for snakes to ask her if it were the stinging snake."[38]

Besides being expert at turning the other cheek, Faulkner's character Dilsey, whom Maud and many others insist "is Callie Barr," was an ardent churchgoer. According to Jill, Callie could "quote whole swatches of the Bible and Shakespeare" and belonged to the Second Baptist Church in Oxford, the black church where her second funeral service was held before she was buried in the "colored section" of the Oxford cemetery; nonetheless, Jill claimed, Callie was not much of a churchgoer. Rachel explained that "back in them days you didn't hardly get to go to church," because even on Sundays she, and other women who cared for white people's children, "worked in the mornings."[39]

Instead, on Sundays, according to Rachel, Callie visited with Molly Barr, her family, and friends:

> She'd go 'round and visit on Sunday mornings with those little boys, that's what they'd do. And she carried a bag with quilt pieces in it and she'd sit and visit and cut 'em up. She loved to paice quilts. I remember her making a double-wedding ring quilt for someone's wedding.
>
> She had to take care of those kids because their father was always drunk. She'd come out every Sunday morning, about nine o'clock—the church bells would rang, all the church bells would rang, and we could look up and see Callie and Dean and William be coming. Now, I wasn't born then but my moma tell me this: William would be gone to the woods with his tablet and pencil.[40]

Rachel's daughter adds that in the 1930s Jill used to come with Callie too, once "she got up some size."[41] And Jill confirms:

> I remember going to Rachel's. Mammy Callie was quite a walker. She walked all over and I walked with her. We'd go through Bailey's Woods to her house. It must have been before my first trip to California (late June 1936). I was pretty sturdy on my feet at a young age because I recall the first time I ran away—I was not much more than three. I was having my hair washed, which I hated. They must have left me sitting alone for a moment in the tin washtub out back, and I took off for the woods, covered with soap but no clothes. It took most of the day to find me and I got thoroughly spanked by Pappy. Later, when we got back from California and Mammy Callie was too old to walk [that far], Pappy would drive us out to Rachel's.[42]

Rachel's daughter, Mildred, who is a little older than Jill, also remembers these visits, but not with pleasure: "They drove her up in them old model car, to Molly Barr's. When I seen that little midget drove out there in that car, I didn't want to be nowhere close. I use to call her a devil 'cause she was mean: [imitating her] 'Git on away from round here. Chillen dont suppose to listen.' She could pick up something—if she say she was going to hit you, she would hit you."[43]

Jill concurs, insisting that both her mother and the other "colored people" who worked for her parents "stood in awe of" and were "terrified" by Callie's commanding presence. She also says she got the impression from the latter, and from what she overheard, that "Mammy was a bit of a witch. It had something to do with her ancestry—something that ran on the female side of the family. I think it was voodoo, not a witch. In summer there

were voodoo meetings in the woods around Oxford. I don't remember being part of it but I remember sitting with her in her cabin and listening
to the drums." She also remembers "Mammy telling tales about what was
happening in the woods. That's probably why it seemed so real."[44] Shortly
before Faulkner died, he told a visitor that "once the Negroes used to have
these parties where you could hear the drumming all night long in the distance. They called them 'picnics.' But no white person ever went near them
and we didn't know what went on." He added that he thought "the younger Negroes now are ashamed of all that. It's the same in the churches.
They used to have trombones and banjos at the services. From outside you
could hear the music and it was fine. Now they have to imitate the white
folks' services." Jill's cousin, Jimmy Faulkner, who is ten years older than
she and has lived in Oxford all his life, says that until the late 1960s older
"black people still talked to each other on drums at night. We'd sit outside
on summer nights and listen to them. . . . When the drums got the air vi-
brating, you could hear them for miles." He also claims that the drums had
hypnotic powers: "People would hear them, get up, and walk straight as a
plum-line to those drums, through barbed-wire fences, briar thickets, anything—to the source of the drum beat."[45] Voodoo is widespread in the
South and is not confined by either geographical or racial boundaries.
Hortence Powdermaker's sociological study *After Freedom* found that one
voodoo doctor in Indianola, Mississippi, had 1,422 white clients, roughly
one-third of his practice.[46] Although none of Callie Barr's relatives were
asked, none volunteered that she practiced voodoo. However, her great-
great grandson's descriptions of her and her daughters and nieces foreground them as commanding women whom their communities and their
families respected, loved, and feared.

Callie Barr and Her Sardis Daughters

In her role as "Mammy Callie" in front of Jill and Jill's father, Callie may
have acted superior to the black field hands who worked around Rowan
Oak or at Greenville—what Faulkner calls in his ledgers "The Falkner
Brothers' Farm." But according to Malcolm Franklin's narrative of Callie's
life in Mississippi before she began working for the Falkners, she and her
family were employed on a cotton plantation near Clarksdale. Her great-
great grandson says of Callie's daughters that both "Millie and Ma Fanny
were raised on the farm," and he remembers his great grandmother Fanny
and great aunt Millie picking cotton for his "daddy" on their joint farm
near Sardis, east of Batesville, when both were well into their seventies.[47]
Callie herself did farm work with her family in Oxford once the Falkner

boys were grown. Rachel McGee, Callie's great niece, was twenty-seven when Callie died. She says that in the 1920s Callie sharecropped with her mother. This would have been before Faulkner and Estelle married, in 1929. In 1930 Callie came to Rowan Oak to care for the Franklin children, Malcolm and Cho-Cho, and later Jill, who was born in 1933. Rachel remembers Callie doing field work: "Callie used to work and pick vegetables for my mother. She was picking with my mother on the Moore place. That's when she didn't have them children and she was still staying with the [Maud and Murry] Falkners."[48]

Callie would have been familiar with farm work from childhood because most slaves, whether their primary job was in the field or the house, needed to keep vegetable gardens to supplement their owner's rations.[49] It is likely that when their father told the Falkner boys that their "Mammy had run off again with some man," she had actually gone to help her daughters' families get in their crops.

Despite the Faulkner brothers' claims, Callie Barr's family also doubt that she ever married.[50] Rachel says, "I ain't knowed of Aunt Callie was married. And I been knowing her all my life and I am seventy-six years old. And I ain't never knowed of a husband."[51] Nor did James Rudd ever hear Callie's daughters say anything about a father.[52] Perhaps being owned once was enough for her. In contrast to her mother, Callie's oldest freeborn daughter, Fanny, was married twice; but she, too, was a woman who spoke her mind in her own community and her great grandson's observation that he thought "the men in Mama Fanny's life was kinna frighten of her" might apply to her mother as well.[53]

Rachel suggests another reason why Callie may never have married. As she does, she provides limbs and branches of the Barr family tree and explains why such knowledge was essential to slave families and to the first generation of ex-slaves. In a society where a black woman might be bred to many men and where slave masters often sold parts of families, one way to try to prevent incest was to know who your mother was and who your half brothers and half sisters were—to know, as Rachel puts it, "the mother-half." She explains that Ed Barr was Callie's brother and Molly Barr's (Rachel's mother's) and Wes Barr's father. "Ed Barr, he come from Pontotoc. All these people is from Pontotoc. Ed Barr my grandaddy." She never uses the word *slavery*. Instead, she says, "back in them day I ain't never seen a husband. Never been told of one. But you see, in them day they were half— you understand what I'm talking about? Now, Ed Barr was her brother, Taylor Robinson was her brother. I know when they wasn't full by their names." Her daughter, Mildred Quarles, elaborates: "But they [their elders like Callie and her brothers, Ed and Taylor who had been slaves] never said nothing about that. They didn't talk about it—'you know, that's my half-brother now.' Taylor Robinson was her half-brother and Ed Barr was her brother but she never said they were half or full or nothing. But they had different names. You *know* what I'm talking about."[54] Therefore, Callie's first four "husbands," if they existed, may well have been slaves too. According to Estelle's son, Malcolm Franklin, Callie "married a Barr slave."[55] But the only thing James Rudd remembers his great-great grandmother telling about her life as a slave is "her saying she had some more children that were sold into slavery, enslaved. But I don't know any of their names, nothing."[56] As Callie's great-great grandson says, this history of Diaspora is lost.

James, his great grandmother Fanny's favorite—"I was her heart"—notes the strong physical and personality resemblances between Callie Barr and her freeborn daughters, Fanny Ivory and Millie Holman.[57] They were small, fierce, and outspoken; they were also sought after because they were fun and good-looking:

> All of the women in that family was small, very small. None of them more than 120 pounds. Mama Fanny was real, real dark. My Mama never weighted over 115 in her life. My great grandmother, Fanny Ivory Jones, she was married twice, was Callie Barr's daughter. I remember Callie's other daughter Millie Holman, too, as she stayed with us some. Me and Millie was real close. She looked a little different. All of the women [in our family] were very, very dark but she was brown. Her hair was longer. Millie was a good-looking black thing as I can remember as a little boy. She still was a cute old woman; got around real good and stuff up until she died. She used to tear down here. She was full of fun. She had that hair hanging down and them boys—run them crazy and she never looked at a one of them. They [Fanny and Millie] all talked about how they use to tease the boys. But they was high tempered. They were mean. Ma [Fanny] and Molly—all of them.
>
> My grandmother died when my mother was small but Mama Fanny lived until 1949 or '50, shortly after I started high school. My parents said she spoiled me. I never got to live with her, but I was always close. I was closer to her than any other of my brothers. I was her favorite.[58]

Some forty years after the fact, Rudd zestfully recalls his great-aunt's and great grandmother's "high tempers":

> And Millie and Ma Fanny would fight. I mean I see them just physical, just go at it even though, you know, I'm talking about after I was a big boy. Big enough in there trying to stop them. I seen them. They would hang up just over nothing. I remember one day Millie told Fanny, "Ma Fanny"—Millie

was the type, sure enough she would fight in a minute. Told her, "That a lie, Fanny, and that a fighting lie, and if you feel mistreated, come on."

They used to—Millie and Ma Fanny—we were raised on a farm. We rented our own farm from a white farmer, Mr. Woods. I was born on the Woods place. They would pick cotton by the hundred for my daddy. Every day they would pick cotton. I've seen them get to fighting in the field, one picking off the other's row: "You quit picking on my row, Fanny, you did!" And they would hang up. We are talking *old women*. They were *old* then. My God, Ma Fanny—let's say she was born in 1865. You know she was what? Eighty-five! All those women were small, very dark, hard-looking women, but they would fight any body, any color, any size. And they all talked about how they used to tease the boys. The sisters [Fanny and Millie] were referred to as the "fighting Joneses." Mama Fanny was married a second time to a Jones and so was Millie.[59]

Thinking associatively as he reconstructs a history of these quarrel-some, independent, and sometimes fierce Barr woman, he tells another story about his much loved great grandmother, Callie's daughter Fanny Ivory. His maternal grandmother died when his mother was just a child. Thus his great grandmother Fanny brought up his own mother and became, for all practical purposes, his mother's mother and his grandmother. Fanny Ivory died "in the spring of [19]50, the year I started high school." From his story about his great grandmother, Fanny Ivory, he passes back again to his great-great grandmother. His associations recall fragments of both the story and personality of Fanny's mother. His story takes place in 1940, the year Callie died.

I remember once when I was in the first or second grade, I had a teacher—she got sick and 'cause she didn't want to close down the school, she sent her husband to teach. I decided I didn't want him teaching me so I stomped out of the room. I threw a piece of brick back into the school room and then ran home. Just as I got close to home, I started to cry. When Mama Fanny saw me—I can still see her in my mind—she had on a long white dress with a white apron, and she lifted them above her ankles and she started running toward me screaming, "What happen, Baby? What happen?" I told her, "The teacher threw a rock at me." And then she went to the school. She was mad. She ran that man out of the school. He told her, "Aunt Fanny, that boy is lying." She just got madder. She said, "Dog-footed!"—that was her curse word—"Nobody calls my baby a lie." He got out of her way, too, 'cause he knew she would get him.

He told my parents or it got back to them somehow. Anyway, they came and got me. Said Mama Fanny was spoiling me. Mama Fanny got so mad, she stopped talking to my parents for about two months. Said my Mama

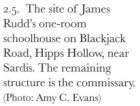

2.5. The site of James Rudd's one-room schoolhouse on Blackjack Road, Hipps Hollow, near Sardis. The remaining structure is the commissary. (Photo: Amy C. Evans)

was letting my father tell her what to do. She still came to our house to see me, but it was a long time before she said anything to my folks.[60]

His is a stunning portrait or re-memory that illustrates how these women demanded space for their children's and their own individuality when they perceived they were being threatened by institutions and community. Moving on from his tale of his great grandmother's unquestioning defense of him from both familial and communal authorities, James Rudd recalls an earlier family quarrel, this one between Mama Fanny and her mother, Callie Barr: "I remember her and my great-great grandma Callie, they couldn't stay together very long. They couldn't get along." He elaborates, "I have heard my mother say many times, they just couldn't get along. I remember my mother saying, 'She [Callie] come down, gonna spend the night, get mad at Ma Fanny and leave in the middle of the night, going home.'" When asked why he thought Fanny and her sister lived near Sardis while their mother lived in Oxford he says again, "I have heard my mother say many times, they just couldn't get along." As he continues, he enlarges his portrait of Callie Barr, her daughters, and the family as a unit. In doing so, he weaves in his commentary on how they dealt with being black and being women. He concludes, "Everybody, black and white, knew that these women would fight a snake. They didn't care what color you were or how big you were or *what* you were. If you made them mad, they would get you. . . . Maybe that's why Fanny and Callie didn't get along. They were both so mean."[61]

Sheriff Rudd's relatives in Oxford tell similar stories about Caroline Barr's bossiness and stubbornness. Mildred Quarles explains that when they were children, the family lived in what was then deserted countryside out beyond Freedman Town. "And my Daddy was a fellow, if he got the hot foot and he felt like going to Ohio, to the rest of the family, he would do it. So that left my mother and myself together. So that why my mother had an ice pick stuck up over the bed." Rachel picks up her daughter's story here; she explains that when her husband was home, he also worked nights and "I had an ice pick stuck in the wall, you know 'cause I didn't know who come in on me and I can't shoot no gun." One night "I never will forget," recounts Rachel, as a preface to her story, Callie came by and stayed with them. "Aunt Callie had been over to my mother's and she made it as far as my house and she decided to spend the night with me. So I got out my bed and let her have it, you know. And she said, 'What's this ice pick stuck in this wall?' I told her I put it there for protection. She said, 'Why, you ought not to stick an ice pick. Get that thing out of the wall!' Because she believe in shooting a gun and anything else. She was tough. But I ain't gonna shoot no gun. And Aunt Callie, she always kept a knife in her pocket, a penknife. And I mean, she'd get you with it too. Oh, Aunt Callie was something. And I mean, she was bossy. She would tell you what to do and you had to do it, too, baby." Mildred adds, "She was always talking about it, her knife."[62]

To readers unfamiliar with the history of the post-Reconstruction, Jim Crow South, Callie's and her niece's fears of attack may seem excessive, Callie's daughters' violence and their reputations as fighters may seem exaggerated, and their surviving male progeny's obvious pride in their behavior may seem odd. But considering the place and time the South during and after slavery—their concern was legitimate and their response healthy. In Mississippi, during years of casual and legalized racial violence, almost three hundred black men were lynched by white Mississippi mobs in just two decades, from 1889 to 1909.[63] Callie Barr taught Fanny and Millie, the daughters she didn't lose to slavery, how to survive Reconstruction and its dangerous aftermath. Perhaps part of that teaching was to ensure that they never worked as white families' mammies, which they never did. Like Janie's grandmother in Zora Neale Hurston's novel *Their Eyes Were Watching*

God, Callie wanted to be sure her free daughters were really free. But what gave them independence may have become a source of deep disagreement between the daughters and their mother.

Callie's fierceness frightened Molly Barr's granddaughter.[64] But her concern with night riders needs to be viewed in the context of the gratuitous violence to which black women were often subjected and in terms of the kinds of everyday verbal and physical violence and abuse that blacks experienced in the South in general. Especially significant was the rise of what Joel Williamson calls "racial radicalism . . . a racial extremism that has, perhaps, never been equaled in the American experience." Williamson notes that Governor James K. Vardaman of Mississippi, whom the Falkner family helped elect, was praised in both the Northern and Southern press for saying that "the Negro was 'one-third more criminal in 1890 than he was in 1880,' and that black male assault on white women was especially high. 'You can scarcely pick up a newspaper whose pages are not blackened with the account of an unmentionable crime committed by a negro brute, . . . a manifestation of the negro's aspiration for social equality.'" Williamson also writes that in 1897, the year Faulkner was born, the first woman senator (from Georgia) gave a speech urging white men to "do their duty. '. . . if it takes lynching to protect woman's dearest possession from drunken, ravening human beasts, then I say lynch a thousand a week if it becomes necessary.'" Many white Southern men leapt to do her bidding. Williamson notes that "in the twenty years from 1889 to 1909, at least 293 blacks were lynched" in Mississippi alone.[65] Between 1889 and 1909 there were at least 2,000 lynchings in the South in general.[66]

Williamson points out that "William Faulkner spent the formative years of his life in the very midst of this radical racist hysteria."[67] In 1908, when he was eleven years old, he was part of a crowd of two thousand who watched as Oxford's white elders mobbed and lynched Nelse Patton, a black bootlegger accused of raping and killing a local white woman. At its end, Patton's naked, bullet-ridden body hung from a tree a couple of blocks from Willie Falkner's home. The boy had to square this with the sexual relations between whites and blacks in his own family, where, if the custom of the time and place were inverted, it was white "brutes" who were committing "unmentionable crimes" with black women. He heard stories from both family members and schoolmates about his maternal grandfather running off with a black lover and his paternal grandfather's weekly afternoon visits to his black mistress.[68]

In Faulkner's short story "That Evening Sun," the easy potential for exploitation present in such relationships is observed and denied by the Compson children as part of their education into racism. They see Nancy

Manningoe, their laundress who also fills in as cook and "Mammy" when Dilsey is sick, kicked in the mouth and beaten by the deacon of the Baptist church for asking to be paid for her sexual services: "When you going to pay me, white man? It's been three times now since you paid me a cent——." When the sheriff then hauls *her* off to jail, in spite of what they've just seen and heard, the Compson kids think it's because she's "drunk," not, as she tells them later, because "I ain't nothing but a nigger." They are also present when her lover says bitterly, "I cant hang around white man's kitchen, but white man can hang around mine. White man can come in my house, but I cant stop him. When white man want to come in my house, I aint got no house" ("That Evening Sun," *CS*, 291, 290, 292, 293). As all the Falkner brothers but little Willie had learned by the age of five, they know better than to hear him. Willie heard because of what he had learned about life from Callie Barr.

Callie's great-great grandson's descriptions of the Barr women's feistiness, their tempers, their sharp tongues, and their reputations as women no one messed with, and corroborating stories about Callie from the McGees, suggest some of the reasons why William Faulkner was so drawn to Caroline Barr, what he learned from her, and why the irresolvably painful issues their relationship raised remained such a dominating presence in his imagination.

3

Negotiating the "Mammy" Tradition
Callie Barr as "Second Mother"

I N THE LATE 1940s, the Southern writer and activist Lillian Smith
wrote that a Southern white child's education into race marks its violent passage from child to adult. Central to this education is the tissue
of lies about what a black person is, lies that center necessarily on the person whom the child most loves, the black woman who has cared for him
or her since before memory began. Smith states it succinctly: the most bitter lesson her white parents taught her was "that my old nurse . . . was
not worthy of the passionate love I felt for her but must be given instead a
half-smiled-at-affection similar to that which one feels for one's dog. . . . I
learned to cheapen with tears and sentimental talk of 'my old mammy' one
of the profound relationships of my life."[1] The nexus of these lies is myths
about blacks' ungovernable sexuality. The Falkner brothers' stories about
Callie's sexual proclivities fall in this category. John Faulkner claims that
"she was married five times but none of them took. She'd been married
four times when she came to us." She then married once more to a man
who took her off to Arkansas and "mistreated her." Murry Falkner sent
one of his livery stable drivers to her rescue and "she never again left Oxford or us."[2] His older brother has a racier memory: "When we were children, she would suddenly take off with some man she had run across in
one way or another." Her running took her to Tennessee, Arkansas, and
the Mississippi Delta. Yet Jack Falkner also wrote that Callie had grown
children who "lived in the western section of the county, her original home,
and they would visit her from time to time."[3] Like his brother, he claims his
father always rescued their "mammy" and returned her to "her white
children."[4]

These compulsively retold stories are then codified as fact in Joseph

Blotner's authorized biography, where he repeats and embroiders them, enshrining the Jezebel characterization by adding that Callie Barr "had borne the name of four different husbands . . . had a salty vocabulary and a taste for men"![5] There is some irony in the brothers' image of the ineffectual Murry Falkner as a "white knight" who transforms or reforms Callie Barr from Jezebel to Aunt Jemima and restores her to her rightful place in her white family, where, besides her other duties, she can coddle him through his habitual drunks. More likely, in their hyperbolic fixating on Callie's imagined sex life, the Falkner brothers were engaging in the racial stereotyping they had been taught. Not surprisingly, their memoirs say nothing about their own grandfathers' extramarital miscegenation. Nor do they acknowledge the existence of other members of Callie's family, the family she probably went to visit when, according to Jack Falkner, she had run off again with some man.

Crossing with Callie Barr into Freedman Town

James Snead observed that, in *The Sound and the Fury*, the mute Benjy is the only white person to cross the "linguistic and racial fence" into Nigger Hollow and Dilsey's church.[6] In fact, in Faulkner's South, the women that white children called "my second mother" often brought them across that fence when they were small, into a world at once separate from and at odds with their white lives. Crossing the "racial fence" figures prominently in both Faulkner's and his daughter's childhoods, as it does in much white Southern fiction (and many memoirs), including Faulkner's and an unpublished story of Estelle's. But Maud Falkner's assertions aside, Callie Barr was no Dilsey and the Faulkner children's exposure to Callie Barr's world was richer than the Compson children's to Dilsey's. If the Falkner boys saw the inside of a black church (and Faulkner's fiction suggests they did), they also saw a lot more, including the inside of Molly Barr's jook joint.

Today, Molly Barr Road marks Oxford's northern margins. It parallels and then crosses the railroad tracks in Freedman Town, its oldest black section.[7] Built in the 1980s to provide an access to the Ole Miss Campus that avoided downtown traffic, the road was named, according to Herman Taylor, one of Faulkner's many local white memoirists, "for a Negro woman who had owned some property through which the new road passed." Taylor doesn't mention that this woman, Molly Barr (b. 1882), was related to Callie Barr or that she also owned a roadhouse, or jook joint, where black people came from miles around to make music, dance, play the dozens, drink, and gamble. Instead he says that in the 1920s and 1930s there was a grocery store at an intersection there named "Three Way" that sold boot-

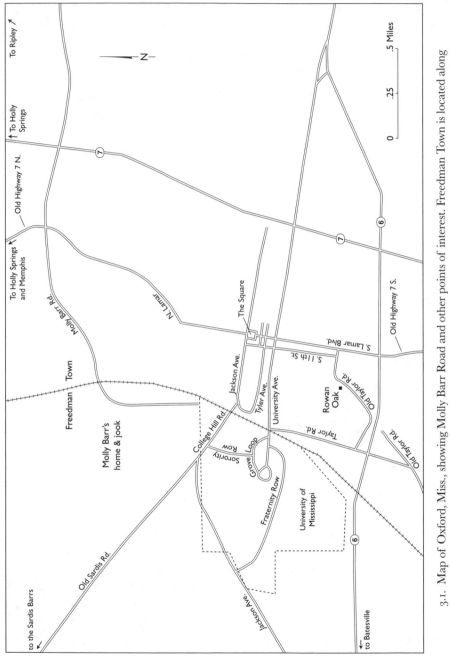

3.1. Map of Oxford, Miss., showing Molly Barr Road and other points of interest. Freedman Town is located along the railroad, northwest of the square. (Adapted from a map of Oxford from the Oxford-Lafayette Chamber of Commerce, 1981. Map drawn by Bill Nelson)

3.2. Classic Southern rural jook
joints, c. 1930.
(WPA photos: Courtesy of the
Library of Congress)

leg whiskey.[8] According to her family and others in Oxford's black community, Molly Barr was also a midwife.[9] She used her earnings to purchase
that land, a highly unusual occurrence in Jim Crow Mississippi. Her two
strictly cash businesses also enabled her to loan money to local blacks, perhaps with less collateral and at better terms than Oxford's white-owned
banks and local farm commissaries, such as the one Faulkner opened at
Greenfield Farm in 1938, which charged a minimum of 8 percent at a time
when the prime rate was 1.5 percent.[10]

In both her personal and business life, Molly Barr was the antithesis of
the "chaste, disciplined, and servile labor force—an ideal imposed by white

employers and embraced by the black middle class reformers intent on mollifying white animosity and racial prejudice."[11] "'Jook'" was, as Zora Neale Hurston wrote in 1934, "the word for a Negro pleasure house." Throughout the rural post-Reconstruction South and in its cities' black ghettoes as well, jooks provided a haven and center where modern black music and dance were created. Hurston wrote that "musically speaking, the Jook is the most important place in America. For in its smelly, shoddy confines has been born the secular music known as the blues, and on blues has been founded jazz. The singing and playing in the true Negro style is called 'jooking.'"[12] Jooks were also one of the few public places where, for an evening anyway, black working-class people could elude the punishing and exclusionary Jim Crow social codes and laws and celebrate their bodies and their voices. In these nightclubs, which often doubled (like Molly Barr's) as their owners' houses, modern black popular culture was invented and celebrated.[13]

Since the age of the Puritans, dancing has been a hot button for enforcers of public morality, particularly in times of social and political unrest. With the failure of Reconstruction, white employers especially objected to "black women domestic workers" frequenting jooks or other public dancing halls, "because they feared that the dance halls bred social contagion that would infect their homes." Citing articles in various turn-of-the-century Atlanta papers, Tera Hunter writes that "some child-nurses were accused of sneaking into the 'dives' with white children during the day, exposing the little ones to immorality and vice." Both white employers and many black ministers and members of the black middle class argued that the "'unholy passions' provoked by dancing and the aggressive behavior of [black] women" posed a serious threat to the community at large by encouraging sexual promiscuity.[14]

Molly Barr may or may not have sung and danced in her jook, but from what their relatives say, she and Callie Barr's Sardis daughters had characters and reputations like those of the many smart, mouthy, dark black women immortalized in the blues. Hurston also claimed that authentic black theater originated in the jooks, dramas "based on Jook situations, with women, fighting and drinking," and making love. In such theater, "the girl who could hoist a jook song from her belly and lam it against the front door . . . was the lead, even if she were black as the images of Hell." Even though songs might seem to prefer "yaller" women and mock "nappy headed" black women—"They say that she is evil. That she sleeps with her fists doubled up and ready for action"—they also claim that the "'Blacker de berry, sweeter de juice.' To be sure the black gal is still in power, men are still cutting and shooting their way to her pillow. To the queen of the

Jook!"[15] Such women were the antithesis of the Victorian ideal of Southern Womanhood. Yet Callie Barr, who insisted that Faulkner's wife adhere
to those ideals, made no such demands of her niece. And, on the rare evening when she was free of the Falkner family, she, too, probably enjoyed
herself at her niece's jook joint.

Molly Barr's reputation as a woman who spoke her mind is legendary
in the black community and among her descendants.[16] Her grand-nephew,
James Rudd, says admiringly, "Molly was Hell! Uh, ah, Molly was tough."
He elaborates: "That woman had the nastiest mouth I have ever heard.
She could say words that nobody ever heard. You could hear her before
you got to her house. You could hear her." He adds that when his brothers
and he were children, "my father didn't want us there much." Unlike his
great-great grandmother Callie, Rudd says that Molly Barr was "a pretty
good size woman," a factor that may have contributed to her business success. She is also rumored to have been a bootlegger and gambler, activities
in keeping with the owner of a jook joint. Molly's daughter, Rachel Mc-
Gee, remembers her great aunt Callie's temperament as more like Molly's
than any of her mother's own children. Although John Faulkner remembers Callie Barr taking the three older brothers to play in the woods just
outside of Oxford's town limits, he writes nothing about these walks, including a visit to Molly Barr's.

We learn from Callie Barr's close friendship with her niece that, at least
by age six, the age Faulkner's fictional children fall painfully into their
knowledge of race and sex, the acutely impressionable and observant Willie was crossing regularly into an exclusively black community where he
was exposed to a view of black life radically different from the one he
learned in the "big house." Perhaps most important, he was exposed to a
black aesthetic that, as Thadious Davis was the first to point out, is intricately and inextricably bound to his poetics. This aesthetic is grounded in
Faulkner's very early experiential knowledge of black music, especially the
blues and jazz.[17] It was the only music Faulkner *chose* to listen to; he actively
disliked any other.[18] Second, Faulkner and his brothers entered a community and a home where a black woman was first in command, not "second," as his brother John wrote, where blacks did not "go around to the
back" and where the woman he called "Mammy" all his life did not need
to act a white definition of "black." In Freedman Town the Barr family did
not become, as Faulkner would later write of the Deacon in *The Sound and
the Fury,* "that self he had long since taught himself to wear in the world's
eye" (64). Third, in taking Willie with her to Molly Barr's, Callie revealed
to him a space where black families worked for themselves rather than for
white families and where a black businesswoman was a mother to her own

children, not a white child's mammy. Faulkner was never able to explore the psychological and cultural dimensions of that space in his fiction. But entering this world with a black woman he loved at an age when he could still remember a time when he had loved her uncritically did lead to art that does critique the roles black people played in white Southern homes and communities.

Watching Barr's transformations as she moved between these two worlds first taught him that race, like culture, was performative and that its performance changed in response to place and audience. Such knowledge would inspire stories that begin to dissect the hypocrisy of racism and show how whites of every class use racism to maintain the Jim Crow status quo. In "That Evening Sun," the five-year-old Jason Compson, frightened yet fascinated by the family laundress's fear that she'll be killed because "I aint nothing but a nigger," keeps insisting to anyone who will answer him, "I ain't a nigger. . . . Am I?" Throughout the story, Jason is watching how his parents and community treat Nancy in order to sort out who he is by determining what he is not (*CS*, 289–309, passim).

For young Willie such watching led initially to partial insights like the one he will give Quentin Compson in 1928: "I learned that the best way to take all people, black or white, is to take them for what they think they are, then leave them alone. That was when I realized that a nigger is not a person so much as a form of behavior; a sort of obverse reflection of the white people he lives among" (*TSAF*, 55). Faulkner's earliest experiences with Callie Barr account for his lifelong preoccupation with the fluidity of identity and with deceptive theatricality or performance as a means for both inventing and preserving a private primary identity or selfhood.

Exposing this impressionable white child to her world also alerted him to how hard white people, including himself, fought to maintain the fictive wall between whiteness and blackness. This consuming subject of so much of his fiction is most tragically articulated in *Light in August* (1931), where it is played out upon the body of Joe Christmas. Trying to explain the white townspeople's rage at Joe, a man says, "He never acted like either a nigger or a white man. That was it. That was what made folks so mad" (*LIA*, 350). In a culture where gender and race are the only markers of identity, indeterminacy must be killed. This is why Hightower and Joanna Burden are also killed. In bringing young "Memmy," as she called Faulkner, to Molly's jook-home, Callie exposed the child to the possibility of indeterminacy ("Mississippi," *ESPL*, 40). With her he entered a world where masks of black servitude dropped and where sexuality was an accepted part of daily life. By loving her niece, a black woman who prospered despite ignoring Victorian ideals of femininity that were irrelevant to her life, Callie Barr taught young Willie what he would need to know to imagine a complex, sympathetic, and empathic portrait like that of Nancy in "That Evening Sun."[19] She may also have alerted him to the shortcomings of those white ideals, shortcomings, and hypocrisies that his fiction often critiques.

In Freedman Town today, Molly Barr's daughter and Caroline Barr's oldest living relative, Rachel McGee, and Rachel's daughter, Mildred Quarles, call Caroline Aunt Callie or Aunt Carrie. Some twenty-three miles west of Oxford, out by the Sardis Reservoir near Batesville, where Caroline's daughters, Millie Holman, Fanny Ivory (and Carrie?), lived and farmed cotton, her great-great grandson, James Rudd, who was six years old when she died, calls her Great-Great Grandma Callie.[20] Other members of Oxford's black community called her Aunt Callie or Miss Callie.

The Faulkner family called and call her Mammy. Jack Falkner explains that "the 'Mammys' of that time were women who . . . became second mothers to white children."[21] His brother John writes that "we were her 'white children.'"[22] Yet both brothers grew up to be unapologetic segregationists, who, like their mother, Maud, believed absolutely in racial inequality. The brothers' accounts of Callie Barr's relationship with their family are colored by their own racism captured exquisitely in Jack's remarks about Faulkner's position on racial inequality: "I have read statements by some who professed to believe that Bill considered the white and black races to be equal. He never said anything in my presence to indicate any such conviction."[23]

Callie Barr lived two lives—one with the Falkners, whom the brothers say she called "mah white family," and one with her own family, about whom they chose to remember very little, if anything. What roles did these second mothers play in Jim Crow Mississippi's white middle-class families like the Falkners, and Estelle Faulkner's family, the Oldhams?[24] In his 1940 eulogy for Callie Barr, Faulkner said that she had known him since birth and formed his earliest memories. Like many artists, he often inserted private jokes and puns into his works. Many relate to either his family or himself. The latter often comment either on his writing or on him as professional tale-spinner. How closely he identified the origins of his creativity with Callie and with the concept of racial identity as a construction and performance that is essential to that creativity is first suggested in *Mosquitoes* (1927), his second published novel, where he portrays artistic genius as black. Gordon, a sculptor, has white skin but the eighteen-year-old naïf, Pat, who recognizes his talent asks, "Why are you so black?" She elaborates, "'Not your hair and beard. I like your red hair and beard. But you. You are black. I mean . . .' her voice fell and he suggested Soul? 'I don't know what that is,' she stated quietly." Faulkner's autobiographical intent becomes explicit toward the end of *Mosquitoes* in an exchange between Pat and Jenny about another artist. Jenny begins:

> "I got to talking to a funny man. A little kind of black man—"
>
> "A nigger?"
>
> "No. He was a white man, except he was awful sunburned and kind of shabby dressed—no necktie and hat. Say, he said some funny things to me. . . . He said he was a liar by profession, and he made good money at it. . . . I think he was crazy. Not dangerous: just crazy. . . . [His name was] Faulkner." (*MOS,* 25, 144–45)

Faulkner often spoke of writing as lying and robbing to invent the truth. Spilling the "secrets of [his] profession" to his mother in a letter in which he also announced that he had begun his first novel, Faulkner wrote that "what really happens, you know, never makes a good yarn. You have to get an impulse from somewhere and then embroider it."[25]

Like many Southerners of their generation, Faulkner's brothers saw no discrepancy between their insistence on the biological inferiority of blacks and their insistence on their mammy's primacy as a moral force and the source of their brother's imaginative inspiration. Jack writes that "like our mother," Callie Barr was "big in will power and a sense of right and wrong. It was understood that, while Mother always had the last say, we were never to disobey Mammy Callie." Callie's subordination to Maud, her powerlessness, is contained in Jack's subordinate clause. Every male Falkner narrative stresses Mammy's quickness with a whip, her sexual promiscuity, and her total and abject devotion. Jack writes of "her everlasting devotion and loyalty" to her white family.[26] In a scene similar to those in the dozens of "Mammy" memorials published in the *Confederate Journal,* the official monthly magazine of the Sons and Daughters of the Confederacy, John recalls the "long winter days" that Mammy spent "on her old black knees . . . playing marbles with me and letting me win. . . . I never remember her complaining. I only remember her there when I needed her."[27] In the Falkner brothers' loving, sentimentalized, and condescending accounts, she appears alternately, but with no conscious contradiction, as a "shepherdess," as an "avenging angel" whose "black wing saved us many a hurt," and as a sexually freewheeling wanderer. In short, Jack and John paint Callie as two age-worn stereotypes for black women: Mammy (or Aunt Jemima) and Jezebel. In these accounts, her family is barely mentioned. This flattened portrait of Caroline Barr that has been memorialized in Faulkner biography erases much of the evidence of her transformative effect on William Faulkner's imagination.

Many white Americans are still deeply attached to this strange image of African American women. What is the connection between this myth and those of white Southern Man- and Womanhood, a connection that so much of Faulkner's fiction mercilessly interrogates? How did this image of Callie Barr that the Falkner boys learned from their parents and community affect Willie as a young child? These questions are worth asking, in that they are a constant in everything Faulkner ever wrote about race and sex, most specifically the racing and sexing of Southern white children's childhoods—from Benjy, Quentin, Caddy, and Jason Compson, to Joanna Burden and Joe Christmas, to the Sutpen children, to Roth Edmonds and beyond. Doing so requires paying more attention to the relationship between the Falkner boys' two mothers, Caroline Barr and Maud Falkner.

4

Callie Barr and Maud Falkner
"Twin Sistered to the Fell Darkness"

WHITE SOUTHERNERS' memorial tributes to their African American mammies, which appeared regularly in the *Confederate Veteran,* always stress their fidelity to (white) racial hierarchies and their total availability to their white employers.[1] "Mammy next to mother, was the children's best friend." She was "second only to their mother," and "her faithful heart beat like an echo of 'her white folks.' She belonged to them and they to her." But the narratives that follow confirm only the first part of that clause: "In her strong arms every white child was laid at birth. . . . On her breasts childish sorrows sobbed themselves out, and her broad lap was the most comfortable shelter against all the evils of the world."[2] Her body belongs to the white family, especially their children; a second womb. Maud and her sons John and Jack spoke and wrote about Callie Barr in similar terms. As Maud's granddaughter Dean Wells says, Maud and her two sons, like most Southerners of that generation, were outspoken racists. For Maud, one of Callie Barr's virtues was that "she knew her place."[3] But, as the legal history of Mississippi and Faulkner's fiction make abundantly clear, knowing one's place, whether one is black or white, and staying in it are not simple matters.[4] And trying to keep oneself and others in their places takes immense vigilance.

Art, like the imagination, is a subversive space. In both, subversiveness is not always intentional. Generally a culture's art reflects the inherent slipperiness of these categories. Maud Falkner's paintings do just this; as such they contribute to our understanding of the complex relationship between Faulkner's two mothers and its influence on the child's education into race and sex.

Although Maud's mother, Lelia, had been an artist who also taught painting and china painting and specialized "in the art of coloring photographs," her daughter apparently did not begin to paint seriously until the late 1930s.[5] She saw herself as a realist. Her subjects were primarily still lifes (many of which are competent academic copies of Old Masters), idealized family portraits, "negro cabin scenes," and a few portraits of members of Oxford's black community who worked for her. Her paintings are fascinating because, like her son's fiction, they illustrate both racial vigilance and its failure. It would be silly to suggest that Maud's extant work, executed in the 1940s, shaped Faulkner's intensely visual and anti-narrative aesthetic—a chronological impossibility. However, her paintings embody a sensibility—conscious and unconscious—that Faulkner had lived with from birth. As the archival evidence shows, the first language that he learned was visual.

Although most of her cabin genre paintings are nostalgic and sentimental, a few are satirical. An example of the latter is an interior scene with a tattered FDR poster pinned to the wall and a black matriarch's face painted to look like a caricature of Eleanor Roosevelt. Most often, though, they conform to the genre, at least at first glance.

This plantation summer lawn scene celebrates, in C. Vann Woodward's famous phrase, the "moonlight and magnolia" version of the Old South. Black service is its subject (see fig. 4.1). A "mammy" dressed in white apron and cap and cradling a white baby centers Maud's composition. A brood of angelic-looking golden-haired white children, one black child, a black-and-white dog, and a ginger cat play around her. In the background looms the "big house" flanked by two more black folks, a woman carrying a tray of cool drinks for the children and a gardener mowing their lawn. Yet, the detail reveals that even here Maud fails to suppress rupture. She has used shades of green to highlight the three figures performing black service. Also with greens, she camouflages the two small black and white boys playing together—the figure grouping that Maud foregrounds spatially. Beneath this camouflage she paints the boys' paradoxical and unspeakable relationship. The white boy's position appears dominant. Yet Maud has locked their hands together. Like Faulkner's many black and white fictional couples, they are "joined by that hand and arm which held us, like a fierce, rigid umbilical cord" (AA, 112).

Just as Maud's cabin genre scenes are often nostalgic evocations of the pre–Civil War South, so her portraits of six generations of her own family idealize and mythologize that same past. Here she has painted four generations of Falkner-Faulkner patriarchs as quintessential images of Southern Manhood and two generations more of angelic, blond, rosy white children. Yet, unlike even her cabin scenes, their flat, scrubbed and shiny

4.1. Cabin genre scene and detail by Maud Falkner, n.d.
(Courtesy of Jill Faulkner Summers)

surfaces, the frozen, monumental faces, repel rupture. Their subject is white mastery.

Most unique as a demonstration of Maud's insistent idealization of her white subjects is an anonymous "Mourning Portrait" of Maud's mother, Lelia Dean Swift (as a child), and Maud's maternal grandmother, Mahalah Pullen Swift. Maud revised this painting in two stages, the first by 1941 and the second sometime after (see figs. 4.3 and 7.1). First, according to her granddaughter, Jill, she substituted a Bible for the original iconic skull

4.2. Six generations of Falkners-Faulkners painted by Maud Falkner in the 1940s
and 1950s. (*left to right, top to bottom*), Colonel William Clark Falkner, William
Faulkner's great grandfather (1825–89); John Wesley Thompson ("J. W. T.") Falkner
(1848–1922), Faulkner's paternal grandfather; Murry Cuthbert Falkner (1870–1932),
Faulkner's father; William Faulkner (1897–1962); the Faulkners' daughter, Jill
Faulkner Summers (1933–2008); Paul D. ("Tad") Summers (1956-), Jill's oldest child.
Courtesy of Jill Faulkner Summers. Photos of Colonel William Clark Falkner and William
Faulkner: Amy C. Evans)

4.3. Maud's first revision of the anonymous Mourning painting of Lelia Dean
Swift, Maud's mother, and Mahalah Pullen Swift, Maud's grandmother,
originally painted c. 1857. Pictured are Maud and her son John.
(From LIFE, January 1941. Courtesy of the Walter Sanders Estate/LIFE Magazine.
Photo: © Walter Sanders)

4.4. Portraits by Maud Falkner: *Preacher Green Liggens* (*left*) and *Dulcie*.
(Courtesy of Jill Faulkner Summers.
Photo of *Preacher Green Liggens:* Amy C. Evans)

Mahalah held. In her second revision (see Chap. 7, frontispiece) she erased the anonymous painter's realistic portrayal of her haggard and grieving pioneer grandmother and mother seen here and replaced them with an idealized vision of white Southern Womanhood. In this final revision, Maud's now plumped up, bland, and smiling grandmother and mother are fitting company for her Faulkner family portraits.

Maud's three extant portraits of black people, however, bear no relation to the flattened figures in the majority of her cabin scenes or family portraits (see Maud's portrait of Callie Barr, figs. 4.6, 4.7). They are neither the caricature nor stereotype that characterize these other paintings. It's as if in choosing to confront head-on Preacher Green Liggens, Dulcie, and Callie Barr, these three African Americans who worked for her, in immersing herself in the art of understanding how to represent the play of light on their features so as to master the difficult technique of painting their darker skins, she opened herself to studying and experiencing the emotional content of her subjects' expressions.

Maud's emotional response is recorded on these canvases; she has painted individuals, not types. Her seeing takes these paintings beyond the

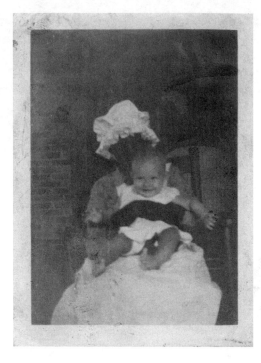

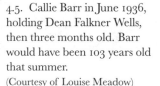

4.5. Callie Barr in June 1936, holding Dean Falkner Wells, then three months old. Barr would have been 103 years old that summer.
(Courtesy of Louise Meadow)

accepted parameters of racist stereotyping; her paintings of Dulcie, Preacher Green Liggens, and Callie Barr convey a sense of lived lives. One might argue that this is because in these portraits, her involvement with technique dominates. But that explanation fails because, in the context of their genres, both her academic copies of Old Masters and her cabin paintings are equally concerned with technique and detail. Her portraits of her black employees, like her son's fiction, are imaginative expressions of her conflicted attitudes toward racist practices, conflicts that find imaginative expression in her paintings but that she seems to have repressed in daily life. Her art suggests that in educating her artist son—and her long relationship with Callie Barr, including her portrait of her, was part of that education—she unknowingly taught him to question the codes in which she consciously believed.

In the 1950s, when a student asked Maud about her portrait of Caroline Barr, she identified her as "'Mammy Callie, the Dilsey of *The Sound and the Fury* and of the short story, 'That Evening Sun.'" She then provided her version of Callie Barr's and the Falkner family's relationship, claiming, in a rush of post–Civil War nostalgia, that "'Mammy was in the Falkner family for three generations, kind of passed on from one generation to another.'"[6]

4.6. Maud's painting of Caroline Barr, done from a photograph,
c. 1941, following Barr's death, and three details of the portrait.
(Courtesy of Jill Faulkner Summers)

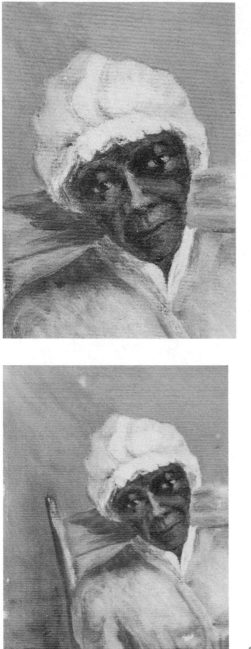

4.7. Details of fig. 4.6.

But next Maud offered a very different and more private glimpse of her relationship with Callie, saying, "She used to come up here and sit with me to keep me company. In her old rocker, just like in my picture."[7] (Compare fig. 4.5, a stock mammy–white child photograph of Callie holding Dean Falkner Wells, to fig. 4.6, Maud's painting of Callie Barr, along with details.) The photograph illustrates the "Legend of the old South" relationship Maud describes when she speaks of Callie being handed down from generation to generation. This kind of photograph, a Southern genre in itself, which includes formal family portraits in which the white family is flanked by its black servants, depicts Callie as servant for a Faulkner child.[8]

In contrast, Maud's painting is not about a mammy figure; no white child is included in the composition, nor is there any hint of caricature or condescension. Callie the person is its subject, not a compliant, self-effacing ex-slave who served as part of her white masters' inheritance, a faithful servant who could just be passed around. The portrait feels deeply personal. Maud told her granddaughter, Jill, that she had painted it from a photograph (now lost) the year after Callie died.[9] Callie appears here as a contemplative and sympathetic listener, someone with ideas and stories of her own, someone who, as Maud wistfully noted, was a good companion. Her painting gives Callie a stature and subjectivity that Maud denies her when she describes her role as mammy to three generations of Faulkners. It's a stature that she may not consciously acknowledge. The Callie in this painting contrasts sharply to Maud's portrayals of mammy figures and other black stereotypes in her cabin scenes.

Maud's portrait conveys the expressiveness of Callie's face; she looks directly at the viewer. Her thin, unsmiling mouth, the deep lines in her cheeks, confirm and accentuate the sadness and suffering reflected in her eyes, a sadness that may reflect the painter's own as she paints the dead woman who, in her words, kept her company for almost all of her adult life. Callie's humanity is perhaps a reality that Maud could acknowledge only in her art. As if wishing her alive again, Maud has painted a somewhat younger Callie. Her eyes in this portrait and her long, slim fingers are like those of Callie in the 1909 photograph of her with Maud's last child, Dean (see fig. 2.4). She has chosen not to paint the swollen rheumatoid hands seen in the photographs Faulkner took of Callie and of Callie with Jill the summer of 1939, a few months before her death (see Chap. 12). Maud has paid great attention to Callie's skin tones and to the textures of her dress and cap and the wooden rocker in which she sits. The success of Maud's likeness is confirmed when one compares this painting with the 1909 photograph.

Maud demonstrates a similar technical and emotional attentiveness in her two other extant portraits of black people. *Dulcie* and *Preacher Green Liggens* are much more carefully painted and imaginatively compelling than any she painted of her own family, which seem lifeless and almost perfunctory.

Long after Callie's death, Maud Falkner still kept two rocking chairs, which she rotated according to the seasons. In winter, she set them in her living room on either side of the fireplace or in her bedroom facing the windows.[10] In summer, she would move them onto her front porch. The standard-size rocker was hers; the almost child-size one, with a cane seat, was Callie's. Both John and his brother Jack conclude their family memoirs with images of empty rocking chairs and a mother's work of art left unfinished at the time of her death. In Jack's memoir, it's his white mother Maud's uncompleted painting. Yet Callie is there, too, as a liminal figure. In Faulkner's, which he wrote before Maud died, the art is a quilt that his black mother, Callie, had been piecing with his little daughter ("Mississippi," 40).

Maud Falkner died in 1960, twenty years after Callie Barr and two years before Faulkner. After his mother's funeral, Jack returned to her house: "There was her easel with an unfinished oil painting upon it; there were her books, pamphlets, and newspapers in orderly array, family paintings and photographs on the walls and tables, and close beside her bed Mammy's small and ancient, but still sturdy rocking chair."[11] In Jack's informal eulogy for his two mothers, he transforms Callie into Maud's caretaker as well, one who sits by her bedside, comforting her. It is a sad and poignant image of the limits racism places on Jack's ability to imagine the relationship between the women he called his two mothers. Or, perhaps, the world in which they lived made that, in fact, the nature of their emotional ties. Jack's memoir, his ordering of his own life, is framed by Maud's and Callie's joint mothering. He begins with an elegiacal description of the partnership of Maud and Callie Barr and ends with this equally elegiacal description in which he links their partnership in mothering—even in death. "And I thought of how Mother, in common with the rest of us, never ceased to remember Mammy. Now both were gone forever; only the rocking chair remained."[12] Yet, throughout his memoir, although he claims to idolize Callie (as Mammy), his idealization is itself a form of control, as is his insistence that because of her skin color, she is naturally childlike, ignorant, primitive, bestial, and dumb.

In the memoirs that John and Jack wrote after Faulkner's death, both brothers express discomfort with what they saw as his integrationist position.[13] Maud Falkner, too, remained firmly opposed to what she called "this integrationist business." Interviewed in the early 1950s by a northern student, she said that most black people in Oxford "don't want equality, they want to trample us down." In contrast to the tramplers, Maud felt that Callie Barr preferred the status quo: "We all loved her. But I'll tell you one thing, she always wanted you to know she was a nigrah."[14] When speaking to her Yankee interviewer, Maud chooses the derogatory "nigrah" instead of "Negro" to make her point clear. Her portrait of Callie tells us more. Maud's reasoning and attitudes were typical of her time, place, and personal circumstances; they protected her from intimacy, memory, and perhaps, most particularly, her own fears of "blackness." For she was the daughter of a father who was so in love with a black woman that he ran off with her, absconding with the town's money and deserting his white family when Maud was a teenager. She was also the wife of the ne'er-do-well alcoholic whose own father kept a black mistress right in town.[15] Faulkner's fiction is filled with white Southerners who live in fear of being identified as culturally and morally black and whose lives are paralyzed and destroyed by this obsession. I think particularly of Mrs. Compson in *The Sound and the Fury*, trying to shame her daughter, Caddy, with her own worst fears by telling her that she is not *acting* white: *"Why wont you bring him to the house Caddy? Why must you do like nigger women do in the pasture the ditches the dark woods hot hidden furious in the dark woods."* Where, even as she tries to frame and shame Caddy, her own erotic attachment to "darkness" bubbles up from her unconscious and runs away with her sentence, revealing her own wish to revel like her "black" daughter, "hot hidden furious in the dark woods" (*TSAF,* 59). I think also of Thomas Sutpen and his son, Henry, in *Absalom, Absalom!*, and of Miss Rosa Coldfield, whose confrontation with Clytie Sutpen articulates and dramatizes Faulkner's own mother's worst fears. But *Go Down, Moses* is, in some ways, Faulkner's most eloquent and emotionally draining portrait of white folks' fear and black folks' speaking truth.

Unlike his mother's framed portraits, Faulkner's fictional frames are often ironized to reveal the innate instability of all kinds of social constructions and to show their role in maintaining, first, slavery and, then, Jim Crow cultures. I suggest that he learned how to frame from both his black and white mothers. But from observing the complicated relationship *between* his black mother and his white mother and from passing with Callie into her black world he also learned that these frames were permeable; they could seep and leak and, sometimes, even dissolve. Furthermore, his travels into the homes of Callie's family demonstrated to him the craft of acting multiple roles, which he emulated to forge and then preserve his identity and selfhood. This skill first manifested itself during his ten-year self-apprenticeship to poetry, though he practiced it all his life. It manifests in his fascination with tropes of transformation and performativity, with life lived as a kind of high-wire theater. Recall Jill uneasily watching her parents' sometimes nightly theater, and think of the consummately and consciously theatrical scenes between Joe Christmas and Joanna Burden; Rosa Coldfield and Clytie Sutpen; Quentin and Caddie Compson; Temple Drake and Popeye, which are some of the greatest moments in Faulkner's fiction. In such scenes his characters are always watching themselves and one another playing a role, or multilayered roles.

Like his brother Jack, Faulkner wanted to imagine his two mothers as a cohesive, intimate unit. He wrote that even during Callie Barr's last four years, when "nobody knowing anymore exactly how many more years than a hundred she was but not mixed up, she: who had forgotten nothing" would walk from her half of the little servant-house in Rowan Oak's back yard, "all the way in to town to sit with his, the middleaging's, mother, talking, he liked to think, of the old days of his father and himself and the three younger brothers, the two of them two women who together had never weighed two hundred pounds in a house roaring with five men: though they probably didn't since women, unlike men, have learned how to live uncomplicated by that sort of sentimentality" ("Mississippi," 40, 42). Faulkner's daughter, Jill, sees Callie Barr as "one of the more important people in his life, particularly when he was growing up because Granny [Faulkner's mother] was hardly affectionate. She was a very austere lady."[16] She contributes to her father's joint cameo of his two mothers:

> She didn't seem to associate much with the colored community during the time I remember. But remember, she was pretty old then. The most she ever did was go with me to Granny's or take me to visit Rachel. In her time off she would work with her plants and flowers. Then we'd walk up to Granny's [from Rowan Oak on the Old Taylor Road to the corner of University and South Lamar]. We'd visit awhile and then sit on the steps that go down to the curb from Granny's yard, and watch the traffic. Then we'd walk up Lamar to the Square and she'd wait for me outside the drug store while I got an ice cream cone from "Hoot" Roan, the soda-jerk.
>
> I think she did like Granny—they were so much alike. They had a kind of armed truce because they were both so strong-minded and opinionated and didn't like anyone to tell them anything.[17]

In her position as the Falkner family's revered and ancient Mammy, Callie might have opinions about the Faulkner children's upbringing and sit and rock with Maud on her porch, but she waited outside the drug store for Maud's granddaughter and had no ice cream, even though it was one of her favorite foods, because only whites were served at the drugstore counter. In the Jim Crow South of Callie Barr's lifetime and Faulkner's and his daughter's childhoods, "Blacks and whites could not touch the same Bibles in courtrooms, could not sit next to one another on streetcars even as prisoners riding to the stockade, could not patronize the same restaurants, parks," churches, schools, or libraries.[18]

Jill then contrasts Callie's and Maud's relationship to Callie's and her mother's: "I'm not sure she had any fondness for Mama but I think Mama was genuinely fond of Mammy Callie. But that's just a feeling; I may be wrong. Also I think Mama was really a little bit afraid of Mammy Callie. In her last years, Mammy really had only two duties besides me. She took care of her turkeys and her guineas and she did what she called 'dressing the beds'—making them. But Mammy's idea of making the bed was to strip it completely and start over again from scratch. I can remember Mama fussing about this because she, from time to time, liked to stay in bed late in the morning and drink coffee, read, and what have you. Mammy would stand right in the door until she got up. She'd be in bed and as soon as Mammy got up the stairs and stood in the door, Mama got up. I can remember that."[19]

Callie's concern for Jill might also have motivated her to force Estelle to get up. "From time to time" may have been when Estelle was dealing with a hangover. Perhaps Estelle was also "a little bit afraid" of Callie because she knew, and she knew that Callie knew that her drinking harmed Jill. Jill also remembers Callie insisting that her mother conform to her standards for a Southern Lady's attire: "Mammy was a formidable little lady. As long as [she] was alive, Mama never wore slacks or pants of any sort. As soon as Mammy Callie died, she started wearing slacks when she was [working] in the garden. I don't know if I heard Pappy say something, or somebody said something to the effect that the reason she'd never worn them was because Mammy had said, 'Ladies don't do that.' There was just something about the way Mama treated Mammy Callie."[20]

Lula Law was the best girlhood friend of Cho-Cho Franklin, Estelle's other daughter. Lula was fourteen the summer of 1934, when she first visited the Faulkners. In her memory, Estelle and Callie seem to have a much more cordial and equable relationship than that described by Jill. She, too, recalls paying her respects to Callie Barr: "That summer was my first visit to Rowan Oak. When I arrived, Mammy Callie and Miss Estelle were out in the back making blackberry jelly. They were working over a little brick oven that was outside between the house and Mammy Callie's cabin. They were cooking in one of those old iron skillets with legs. It seems to me that I saw that same scene again and again in the following summers when I'd come to visit Cho-Cho. It was my impression that she was doing it that old-fashioned way to accommodate Mammy Callie whom I remember as a little old lady in a headrag constantly smoking her pipe. Whenever I'd arrive at Rowan Oak, the first thing we'd do was go to visit her. Then when I'd leave, I'd always go say good-by. She didn't talk very much, to me anyway. But Malcolm spent hours with her."[21]

Like Faulkner's Elnora, in "There Was a Queen," or Estelle Faulkner's "Mammy," Nolia Cottrell, in "Dr. Wohlenski," the fictionalized memoir she wrote about her early childhood, Callie is remembered by the little white girls who knew her as an elderly woman who enforced strict codes of conduct for white Southern Womanhood, which, like those of Faulkner's and Estelle's fictional mammies, distinguished "quality" from "trash."[22] Estelle's Nolia is more typical of the mammies in conventional postbellum plantation novels as she speaks in the voice of Southern patriarchy to the outspoken, ill-mannered little white girl named Estelle. The little girl's inventor, however, creates ambiguity in her story by making the fictional Estelle's relationship with an elderly black male servant one of her escape routes from stifling conventions.

In contrast, in "There Was a Queen," Faulkner lodges ambiguity in the mammy figure itself: Elnora's voice is difficult to pin down. Like Nolia, does she unquestioningly enforce the antebellum standards for behavior that kept post–Civil War white women as well black servants in their places? Or, is she using those standards to mask her attempts to assert her own authority? Or, is she doing a bit of both? Jill says she isn't sure Callie Barr "had any fondness for Mama, but I think Mama was genuinely fond of Mammy Callie." By way of explanation she adds, "I don't think Mama did everything Mammy Callie told her to. That may have been a source of trouble."[23] As in these stories that Jill tells about subtle clashes of will between her mother and Callie and implies about the relationship between Maud and Callie in characterizing it as an "armed truce," the question is unanswerable. But Callie's friendship with her niece, the independent, and unconventional Molly Barr, suggests that she embraced a more realistic and relevant set of standards for the black women in her family than for the white women and children she served. In Callie's care, the child, Willie, was exposed to Callie's dual standards to make what he could of their puzzling contradictions. Ultimately his observations of the contradictions they exposed became a basis for his incisive and often searing critiques of this particular manifestation of the white South's prevailing passion for its own mythical past. That Estelle, too, was exposed, and that she wrote fictional accounts of these ambiguities when Billy Faulkner was still identifying himself primarily as a poet, is also significant for understanding the centrality of Faulkner's relationships with all these women and their relations with each other to his imaginative development.

As a small child, Faulkner became a careful and acute observer. These stories about Caroline, Maud, and Estelle, told in black and white voices, suggest that Faulkner first learned that race had different meanings in different spaces and that masking was essential to both black and white racial and gender performance from watching his second mother switching roles and lifting and dropping her mask as she moved back and forth between her two worlds—Oxford and Freedman Town. He watched her with her "white family" and he watched her when she took him with her to her black family. And he listened to her words and observed her body language. In his fiction he transformed those lessons into dramatizations and meditations about race and the white American psyche that, as Thadious Davis writes, "forever changed the landscape of modern American writing."[24] His painful education into race by his two mothers results in fiction that continually explores white children's responses to a similarly confusing and painful education. (But, as Faulkner's black critics were the first to observe, it offers only fleeting glimpses of black children's and adults' responses.)[25] Davis points out that Faulkner's great achievement was to create "characters who are consciously white, racialized as white, and he depicted the construction of whiteness within Southern, and by extension, American society. This treatment of white people within the normalizing, universalizing elision of racial identity, but with the complexity of the burden of racial subjectivity, is an extraordinary achievement, unequaled in the first half of the twentieth century and unparalleled in the second."[26]

In 1936, four years before Callie died, Maud's second granddaughter, Dean Falkner Wells, was born. The baby and her newly widowed mother lived at Maud's for at least the next three years. According to Faulkner's brother Jack (imitating Callie's speech), Callie walked down from Rowan Oak "to Mother's nearly every day to 'look atter de baby.'" When Jack visited Oxford the summer that Dean was three, "Mother, Mammy, and I sat on the front porch, Mammy in her rocking chair with the newest Falkner [a three-year-old toddler] in her arms."[27] Still walking to her mistress's house, the ancient ex-slave, now less than five feet tall, is rocking another Falkner child—still being "passed on," still choosing to be passed on (see fig. 4.5). Jill captures the paradox of Caroline Barr's position in her white family and one way she dealt with it: "There was very little warmth in Granny [Maud Falkner] I think that Mammy Callie took *her* place in Pappy's life. Mammy had been his mother, his nurse, his teacher, and everything else for so long. [She] was the only person in the world who's ever called Pappy a nickname, that I know. She may have been the one who gave me the name

'Missy' because she always called me that and I imagine Pappy took it from her. She had names for everybody, including my grandfather Murry, for whom she cared little."[28]

Although Jill may be idealizing here, one point is clear: for her father, as for her, Callie Barr was also the warm and tender mother and teacher, the one who, in naming him, held fast not only to the child he once was but perhaps also to the illusory dominance his childhood name gave her. According to Faulkner and his brother John, Caroline Barr called all three generations of Falkners she cared for *only* by their given names or by names she had made up for them.[29] Faulkner's was "Memmy," which, he explains "was as close as his brothers could come to 'William'" when they were little ("Mississippi," 40). But I am struck by the phonetic similarity of "Memmy" and "Mammy." I wonder if Faulkner himself clung to the name that kept alive his memory of his preracialized childhood self. This self was unashamed of passionately loving and identifying with the dark, articulate, strong-willed woman who offered him both structure (her "teaching") and what he felt was unconditional love in his often frightening ("roaring"), angry, unpredictable, and chaotic household. This twinned name evoked a time before he would rage at having to deny his passion and the shame and grief his denial caused him.

In *Go Down, Moses*, the novel Faulkner dedicated to Barr, he invokes her loss again in the passionate love of a young black man, Rider, for Manny, his wife of six months. Manny, "whom he had known all his life," dies suddenly. We do not know why. To try to keep from feeling his grief and rage, Rider embarks on a suicidal quest that, among other things, exposes the systemic racism in his community. Its white members respond by lynching him. They punish his demands for equality and deny the reality of his grief by asserting that "'they ain't human. They look like a man and they walk on their hind legs like a man, and they talk and you can understand them and you think they are understanding you, at least now and then. But when it comes to the normal human feelings and sentiments of human beings, they might as well be a damn herd of wild buffaloes'" (*GDM,* 150, 149). The community's white members can no more allow that blacks "have normal human feelings and sentiments" than it can allow its white children to maintain normal feelings of love and desire for their black second mothers and their families. Here the writer (Rider?) has changed the color of his grieving persona and his relationship to the loved black woman, Manny (Mammy?), who is killed by the white community. As I trace the effects of this primary love relationship on Faulkner's racialized imagination in the following chapters, we will see the fictional fruits it bore.

Like Clytie Sutpen in *Absalom, Absalom!,* Faulkner's most fully realized black and mixed-race characters imitate or expand on Callie's naming system for the Falkner family to assert agency and to tip the racial playing field. By using only the given names or nicknames of their grown masters or employers, they attempt to slip out of their assigned roles of "Mammies" or "Uncle Toms." In *Go Down, Moses,* for example, a white child, Roth Edmonds, is learning how to be a racist. The grown Roth mystifies the origins of racism by claiming not to know how he learned, but the reader sees the boy Roth learning (like his creator) by listening, feeling, and watching. Among his first lessons are the rules of naming and their materialized extension, touching.

Although both Faulkner's and Roth's childhoods occurred in the Jim Crow South of the first decades of the twentieth century, not the South of slavery, they still learned the same rules for keeping blacks "in their place" that Rosa Coldfield in *Absalom, Absalom!* was taught. When Roth sees his father's mixed-race servant Lucas Beauchamp violating these rules, he is puzzled and (like Rosa) furious. "He listened as Lucas referred to his father as Mr. Edmonds, never as Mr. Zack; he watched him avoid having to address the white man directly by any name at all with a calculation so coldly and constantly alert, a finesse so deliberate and unflagging, that for a time he could not tell if even his father knew that the negro was refusing to call him mister. At last he spoke to his father about it" (*GDM,* 111).[30]

Unlike Roth Edmonds or Rosa Coldfield, if the grown Falkners objected to either kind of touching, of violating a racial barrier, they never consciously admitted it. But nonetheless, all of them assert dominance and mastery over Callie and over their childhood feelings for her in their literary portraits of her. In his memoir, for example, John writes that "she called us by our first names . . . a habit she never relinquished." Then he adds, "Nor did we notice it or take it amiss."[31] John's assertion is self-contradictory: you can't take amiss what you choose not to notice. Although John's aim is to empty Callie's naming of its power, his words backfire. By telling about her naming at all, he elevates it to history. In their memoirs, the Falkner brothers, like Faulkner's biographers, skate back and forth between idealizing, sentimentalizing, and caricaturing Caroline Barr.[32]

The Faulkners' daughter, Jill, provides further insight to the emotional need Caroline Barr once filled in the Falkner brothers' lives. Speaking of her father's regard for Callie Barr, she notes further similarities between Callie and Maud: "Not only in disposition, but also in looks. Mammy Callie meant the most to him. She was independent, positive, and self-sufficient. Physically, they reminded me of each other. . . . They were all small. Mammy Callie was the biggest. They were both wiry, tough little ladies."[33]

Jill remembers Callie as the bigger, even though her grandmother,

Maud, was actually taller. Perhaps for her, Callie was bigger in those first seven years of her life *because* she offered a stability, warmth, and comfort that were not forthcoming from either her grandmothers or her mother. "When I was troubled," she said, "I turned to the colored people. I went to the cabin."[34] Before she was old enough to go to school, Jill was mostly alone. As she points out, her half sister, Cho-Cho, married when Jill was three. Her half-brother, Malcolm, was ten years older than she and although he spent a great deal of time at the Faulkners', he really lived down on South Street with his Oldham grandparents. But, she says, "I had all the colored people. And I had Mammy Callie who was basically my mother. When things got really bad, or really exciting, I could go down to the cabin. I lived as much down there as I did in the house."[35] Jill, too, associates physical and emotional intimacy with Callie, not with her white mother. As she says of Estelle, "Sensual would not be a word I would apply to Ma-ma. She was too fastidious to really be sensual, at least in my feelings about it. You know, my conception of someone who is either sensuous or sensual is—allows a little license. You know, a little . . . not blousy, that's not the word I want. But a little—laxity, ease." She struggles to get the focus clear and then adds, "Fastidious. That's the best word I can think of. And I would have thought in the general concept of things, she would probably have been a fairly cold person."[36]

She becomes more explicit when she returns to her relationship with her grandmother, Maud: "Well, I would spend the night with Granny, oh probably once every week to ten days, and we would paint together and we would do things together. But she was never physically demonstrative. I don't ever remember her . . . I mean I always kissed her good-by—even I don't *ever* remember her hugging me or anything like that. I just . . . I don't think there was a great deal of warmth in her nature. And I could be wrong; I imagine an awful lot of it was beaten out by Murry."[37] Jill's memories of her mother and grandmother portray their emotional range as limited by the constrictions placed on whiteness, most particularly white Southern Womanhood. In contrast, Callie "was basically my mother."[38]

Like the black male house slaves and servants who guard their white masters' front doors in Faulkner's *Absalom, Absalom!* and "Barn Burning," Faulkner's daughter also remembers Callie Barr as "a terrible snob: she used to tell me about South Carolina and about the Gullah people. She claimed she had lived on a rice plantation, but she *always* maintained that she had *never* been anything but 'a house niggah.' She wanted nothing to do with what she called 'field niggahs.' The people who worked outside on our place would come to the back door and she'd make them stand outside."[39]

The Barr family members and Southern historians of the South Carolina rice plantations provide a somewhat different portrait, one that makes sense when we recognize the similarities between Callie's class prejudice and the classism practiced by Southern rural blacks in Zora Neale Hurston's contemporaneous novels. It is no less hierarchical than the class consciousness of Southern whites. But why, then, if she was such a snob, would she also favor her niece, Molly Barr, the jook joint owner who, according to her great nephew, "was the cursingest woman I ever heard in my life!" Perhaps the snobbery she practiced at the Faulkners' was just another facet of her "Mammy" mask. The point is that Callie Barr made her own rules, ones that were sometimes at odds and sometimes in keeping with general practice. Her apparent lack of concern for the opinions of others was another trait that cemented her relations with Maud. It was one that was practiced with a vengeance by Maud's iconoclastic son, Bill Faulkner, who "lived unconventionally, openly." According to his daughter, Oxford's disapproval of her father was based "not so much on what he did as the fact that he didn't care what people said." She adds that "Oxford was probably full of more reprehensible things than anything Pappy ever said, did, or wrote about. But the fact that he didn't care what people thought and just went his own way was what caused problems."[40]

Callie Barr's Tales

"She would tell her stories and we would stay close and listen. This twined her whole life with ours." John briefly describes pastoral woods walks with Callie where the four little brothers hunted birds' eggs for their collections—"bird-nesting," she called it: "She taught us to take one egg from a nest with a spoon so the mother bird would not desert the rest of the eggs because our hands had touched them."[41] Besides teaching them to recognize different birds, Callie taught the Falkner brothers much about the forest, where they seemed to have spent a good deal of time. Each fall they'd gather hickory nuts and walnuts together and then return to Callie's cabin, where, on cold fall and winter days, she built a roaring fire. There, according to Jack Falkner's idyllic account, cracking their nuts and sucking on large peppermint sticks their mother had provided, "we would eat and talk the rest of the day." Callie told them "endless tales of small animals and big wars." Jack writes that "here as I recall it, Bill began telling tales of his own, and they were good ones too. Some of them even stopped Mammy, and she was a past master." He also insists that "surely from her came many of Bill's writings about events in Lafayette County, especially those dealing with whites and blacks."[42] Other than a ghost story that is a defanged tale for white children of a night when Ku Klux Klan "ghosts" visited Callie and her family, and the candle-making story, neither brother's memoir includes any of Callie's stories.[43] For an uncensored perspective, we have to turn to Faulkner's terrifying fictional inventions of white children's visits to their black caretaker's cabin, most memorably in "That Evening Sun" and *Go Down, Moses*, where the subject is often the white children's education-initiation into racism.

Twenty-five years later, Callie continued to tell stories to the next generation of Faulkner children. Malcolm describes listening, "sometimes with Billy," who "would come and sit on the wood pile," to her "tales about the war," "her migration West," and "her years in Arkansas [which] made it obvious that this was not the promised land." She also told tales he calls "utterly absurd," that is, folktales. One of the two he records, one she also told Jill, is about the "stinging snake. It would go to a tree, sting the tree, and twelve hours later, the tree would wilt and die."[44] Jill remembers that the stinging snake stories had many variations or episodes, like another animal series her father used to tell her about a wily squirrel named Virgil Jones, a character whose basic narrative she thinks he learned from Callie Barr. "That's why she was so fascinating to me; she wasn't that busy and she'd just let me follow her around." As soon as Jill could walk, she used to trail after Callie in the yard at Rowan Oak as she tended to her guineas and turkeys: "Of course turkeys and guineas are both stupid—so while we were getting them out of the various and sundry troubles they managed to get into, she'd tell me stories. She wasn't histrionic—it was the interest of the story itself. She told a good, rambling sort of story. It sort of picked up where it left off the last time. I think there was probably a certain amount of truth in these tales, and then a lot of embroidery. That's where the first of the Virgil Jones stories came from. Then Pappy took them over. Animals with human traits figured very prominently in her stories. She was entertaining, vastly entertaining, and sometimes the stories she told were funny. But her wit was different from Granny's."[45]

Callie as Moral Arbiter

In his eulogy for Caroline Barr, which conforms, in many ways, to the white sermons delivered over generations of Southern black women who served as "real" or "second" mothers to generations of Southern white children, while their own children were cared for by grandparents, aunts, or older siblings, Faulkner said that Callie Barr "remained one of my earliest recollections, not only as a person but as a fount of authority over my conduct and of security for my physical welfare, and of active and constant affection and love." He also asserted her importance as a moral force: "She was an active and constant precept for decent behavior. From her I learned to tell the truth, to refrain from waste, to be considerate of the weak, and respectful to age."[46] Faulkner's eulogy was a public statement made by a then famous Southern white novelist and crafted with his awareness of a tradition of "Mammy Memorials" and his knowledge that it would be broadcast to his readers throughout the world.

Jill offers a less lofty but clearer and more heartrending sense of Callie's moral force and the emotional needs she filled. What *she* says is much closer to Faulkner's myriad fictional renderings of the original bonds between a white Southern child and the black family who cared for him or her. Bearing in mind the similarity between father's and daughter's childhoods—the constant presence of a web of deceptions and silences in a household where one or both parents drinks—the stability Callie's "security," her "active . . . affection and love," and her "truth" offered—made a considerable difference in first Willie's and then in Jill's life.

As a child, Jill would frequently go to Callie's cabin. After Callie died, Narcissus McKewen and, later, her husband, Andrew Price, came to live in the same cabin and care for her. For Jill, both Callie and Narcissus were the black women who acted as mothers when she needed the attention she couldn't get at home: "They always had time for my particular problems. My particular problems seemed as big to them as they did to me. My problems didn't seem that big to Mama. She [like Maud, when Faulkner was a child] had problems of her own, and mine were of lesser importance. So far as Mammy Callie, or Narcissus were concerned, my problems were the biggest thing in the world."[47]

Jill explains an essential aspect of the safety Callie offered:

When Mama or Pappy, particularly Pappy talked about the truth—with him it sounded like something up there. When you're seven or eight years old and you're told in very abstract terms, "this is good, this is bad," it makes it awfully hard to understand it. That's the time when you want someone to say, "No! That's wrong. You were bad." You don't want to have to deal in terms you don't really understand anyway. When Mammy Callie talked about the truth, and she talked about truth quite a bit, honesty and everything else. It was something like here. When she talked about truth, she was talking about being truthful, telling the truth. When Pappy talked about truth, he talked about this great, grand abstraction that we all had to live up to. You didn't have to live up to Mammy Callie's truth; you just had to do it. There was a difference. That sort of thing doesn't worry a child. It's concrete. But living up to Pappy's ideas of truth and beauty, and everything else, because he was very fond of pulling Keats into the conversation—you know, Truth is Beauty, Beauty, Truth.[48]

Jill expands on the differences in her education concerning the meaning of "truth" as taught by her father and by Callie Barr: "I remember him telling me once when I was real young that the one thing I was never to do was to lie. When you tell someone of that age that this is the one thing they are never to do, particularly when truth is a very variable thing at that age—well, I went for some time fully convinced that a bolt of lightning was going to come out of the ground and strike me dead if I lied, and I wasn't really sure what lying was. I didn't really know what he was talking about. It didn't seem as though there really was a truth. That haunted me for years." She never dared to ask her father what he meant by telling the truth, "not even till the day he died, I never did." But throughout her childhood, she continued to try to figure it out for herself: "After several years I realized the lightning bolt was not going to strike if I slipped up somewhere. I probably developed a really good feeling for lying in the course of it. When you're not really sure what the truth is to begin with, you're always tempted to test it a little bit to see whether this is lying or that's lying." That both her parents were constantly involved in their own deceptions and their role-playing with each other made it even harder to determine what a lie was: "I sort of had to determine on my own what truth and lies were. And when you get right down to it, I'm not sure today what they are. What is the fine line between being absolutely, brutally honest and destroying people right and left, particularly when I grew up in a situation where everybody lied. The colored people felt that truth was only dealing with someone else's lie, and anything you told to a white face was fine. So it was really a strange set of circumstance." Jill's memory of the role played by her father as opposed to that played by Callie Barr in her moral education enacts a much more conflicted and painful rhetoric of avowal and disavowal than her uncles'. She sees the "strange" contradictions and resolves them, finally, by asserting another truth, one that held for her father's childhood as well: that she "grew up in a situation where everybody lied."[49] This situation is part of the legacy of slavery that Faulkner's fiction explores.

Seeing Caroline Barr as a real person instead of a stereotype and understanding what she brought to William Faulkner's childhood that actually did entwine his imagination would be just an interesting story if he had not transformed what he experienced in this relationship into some of the finest fiction of the twentieth century. This new understanding gives us a much more complex and complete appreciation of what he accomplished in *Go Down, Moses* and "Mississippi," each in their own way, meditations on and elegies for this African American woman "who raised me." The next two chapters explore this new terrain.

5

Caroline Barr and Faulkner's Poetics
Go Down, Moses

> Go down, Moses, way down in Egypt land,
> Tell old Pharaoh to let my people go.
> Oppressed so hard they could not stand,
> Let my people go.
> > —African American spiritual

LOSS IS A MAJOR theme in all of Faulkner's art. It is one of the most significant organizing tropes of his poetics, shaping the content, form, tone, and texture of his best writing. Loss as in "Things fall apart; the Center cannot hold; / Mere anarchy is loosed upon the world" is the trope of high literary Modernism to which his European and American critics link Faulkner.[1] Loss, as in "The South lost the Civil War," was also, in Faulkner's lifetime, a (white) Southern preoccupation. And although many Faulknerian characters are similarly preoccupied, that loss is not Faulkner's subject. He is unique in that his fiction, taken as a whole, comprises an aesthetics of racialized loss that is rooted in his lifelong relationship with Caroline Barr.

This chapter and the one following explore that aesthetic and its implications in the context of Faulkner's two elegies for Caroline Barr: *Go Down, Moses*, which he dedicated to her, and his late quasi-autobiographical essay, "Mississippi" (1954). He wrote these elegies for Callie Barr and himself, to lament her loss and to try to explain what it meant to him. Yet, Faulkner's primary concern is white subjectivity and consciousness. In contrast to his eulogy for Caroline Barr, *Go Down, Moses* mourns not her literal death but rather *his* "murder" of his own black family when he was just a child. In "Mississippi," Faulkner portrays himself, "the middleaged," as trying to live up to those precepts his 1940 eulogy claimed Callie Barr had taught him. In traditional elegies, the mourner reaches some resolution. Not so in Faulkner's.

In rare moments when he spoke or wrote about his writing process, Faulkner always stated that his initial inspiration was a "symbolical" image, "a mental picture," or what Henry James called an "impression." For the most part, Faulkner left no record describing that mental picture, but in several crucial instances he did. There is a remarkable sameness to these images: most often they are racialized and they are always about loss. Both in writing and in interviews Faulkner consistently said that what inspired *The Sound and the Fury* (1929) was a mental picture of "Caddy climbing the pear tree to look in the window at her grandmother's funeral while Quentin and Jason and Benjy and the negroes looked up at the muddy seat of her drawers."[2] Here, on Caddy's body, her "shame" and her brothers' "loss" are already coded black.

He began forming his mental picture for *Go Down, Moses* (1942) within hours of Callie Barr's death, as he wrote her eulogy. The Southern myths and realities he invoked in those three short paragraphs and, later, entered almost unaltered into *Go Down, Moses* pervade the lives of the Southern white boys and men that it's about, even when Faulkner masks them as black. His eulogy is central to the argument of this novel. It is part of what transforms *Go Down, Moses* into his first elegy for this black woman, one that mourns a loss he could never consciously acknowledge.

Racialized maternal loss and its devastating effects on identity formation are the ghosts that haunt the psyches of Faulkner's white fictional children and adults. This is a fact that *Go Down, Moses* never lets readers forget. I am using maternal loss here to signify both the loss of the black "mother" *and* the whole constellation of familial relations that are also destroyed when the white child accepts his education into racism. By "racialized" I mean complicated by racist components.[3] Literary and cultural critics typically read Faulknerian themes of loss as a kind of high Modernist ennui and alienation, emptied of any specific cultural content. Although theories of psychosocial and psychosexual development have explained a great deal about identity formation, they are, generally, ahistorical and ignore race.[4]

Faulkner was born one year after *Plessy v. Ferguson* and the same year the Supreme Court approved Mississippi's plan to deprive its black citizens of their voting rights. He was raised, lived, and wrote in the Jim Crow South. And he insisted that his art was that life: "It is himself that the Southerner" invents and reinvents; it is himself "which the writer unconsciously writes into every line and phrase" (*TSAF,* 229).[5]

Faulkner's fictional constructions of childhood loss are shaped and colored by the prevailing myths of the pre–Civil War South and the realities of Jim Crow that controlled children's earliest and most intimate relationships. Racialized maternal loss marks defining moments in his fictional characters' movements toward or away from self-definition. Like many white Southern middle-class children of his time and place, the writer was raised by two women he called his mother, one white and one black.[6] The artist's infancy began, he claimed in his fictionalized autobiographical essay, at the breast of a daughter or granddaughter of Caroline Barr, the black woman he called "Mammy" all his life ("Mississippi," 17). Although Caroline could not literally have nursed him, Faulkner here preserves psychological verisimilitude by making his wet nurse Barr's daughter or granddaughter. Like many other white Southern memoirists of his and earlier generations, he recounts his infancy as twinned and racially intermingled— he and another boy, Callie Barr's infant grandson or great grandson "born in the same week with the white child . . . suckled at the same black breast and sleeping and eating together."[7] This relationship is grounded on the most intimate physical and emotional touching and exchange.

Yet, by the time he was three, he already knew what another Southerner, Lillian Smith, called the "bleak rituals of keeping Negroes in their place."[8] He had learned to simultaneously denigrate and sentimentalize the human relationship he valued most. My discussion of *Go Down, Moses* as the culmination of Faulkner's fictional exploration of this loss will focus on its second and third sections, "The Fire and the Hearth" and "Pantaloon in Black."

Go Down, Moses: Writing Loss in a Racialized Culture

As was Faulkner's, my path to the intermingling of memory, desire, and the trope of racialized loss in this novel is through the persona of the writer's poetic apprenticeship. I begin with these observations. The novel's third section is called "Pantaloon in Black." Twenty years after Faulkner had abandoned his first persona, Pierrot—the dominant voice of his long self-apprenticeship to poetry—he (in what many consider the culminating moment in his career as a novelist) explicitly invokes the language of his literary childhood.[9] In "Pantaloon" he resurrects these haunted and haunting commedia figures from his difficult and protracted years as a would be poet to create a suicidally grieving black millworker from Yoknapatawpha County. The structural conception of *Go Down, Moses* also harks back as Faulkner realizes in prose the elliptical and lyrical form of his early poem sequences.

Why, in a novel about loss, shame, rage, and mourning, does Faulkner return to this ghost from his own imaginative life and figure him as black? What do his choices signal about the power of memory and, in particular, the power of the childhood memory of interracial love, in the deeply conflicted and racially charged cultural terrain of his own North Mississippi between 1865 and 1940 and in a novel set in that same time and place? What does the language of these memories say about the pervasive need for a certain kind of masking?

In asking these questions I seek a fuller understanding of a crucial moment in Faulkner's five-decades-long imaginative engagement with the forces and fields of cultural intermingling and of cross-racial embrace and exploitation that are the structural and emotional matrix of his best fiction. Such questions can help to unearth the complex negotiations behind one of Faulkner's most self-revealing texts. I see his perception and representation of black and white racial cultures as permanently interdependent and therefore constantly threatened by and subject to destabilization. This destabilization is figured in a series of uniquely experimental novels whose forms themselves constantly threaten to implode. The form of *Go Down, Moses*, which treats this representation and interdependency most directly, is the most threatening.

In reading "The Fire and the Hearth" and "Pantaloon" chapters of *Go Down, Moses*, through the rich political, emotional, and cultural landscape of Faulkner's life and art, I want first to suggest an organic connection between their role in *Go Down, Moses* and Faulkner's earliest recorded racially figured memory. I will show how he invokes this memory and mines its benign surface and its narrative gaps and repressions to write scenes of the racialized maternal loss that are the crucible of these sections of *Go Down, Moses* and of his most compelling fiction. I suggest that knowledge of the historical, cultural, and familial context of the artist's childhood offers a richer understanding of the meaning of themes of loss and mourning in his art.

Lillian Smith writes of her education into racism: "Neither the Negro nor sex was often discussed at length in our home. We were given no formal instruction in these difficult matters but we learned our lessons well. We learned the intricate system of taboos, of renunciations . . . of manners, voice modulations, words, and feelings along with our prayers, our toilet habits, and our games."[10] Central to this education was learning that the "respect" she felt for the black woman who cared for her, "the tenderness, the love, was a childish thing which every normal child outgrows, that such love begins with one's toys and is discarded with them" and "that I must outgrow these feelings."[11] Other white Southern fiction, memoirs, journals, and letters written about or during the period between 1870 and 1950 echo Smith's experience, with greater or lesser degrees of self-consciousness and understanding.[12]

Other than "Mississippi," Faulkner wrote no memoirs or journals and very few intimate letters. But his fifty-year imaginative and passionate engagement with these issues gives us what Toni Morrison has called "an artistic articulation" of this country's "past that was not available in history, which is what art and fiction can do but sometimes history refuses to do."[13]

Faulkner's Screen Memory of Racialized Maternal Loss

In 1925, just months after completing his first novel, Faulkner recorded his only known and earliest racially figured memory. His fictional reconstructions and analyses of this memory reveal that it is about a maternal loss that he is forbidden to acknowledge. Writing home from Paris to his favorite great-aunt Bama McClean in September 1925, he says he is looking forward to the arrival of a relative his mother's age: "I will be awfully glad to see Vannye again. The last time I remember seeing her was when I was 3, I suppose. I had gone to spend the night with Aunt Willie and I was suddenly taken with one of those spells of loneliness and nameless sorrow that children suffer, for what or because of what they do not know. And Vannye and Natalie [her daughters] brought me home, with a kerosene lamp. I remember how Vannye's hair looked in the light—like honey. Vannye was impersonal; quite aloof: she was holding the lamp. Natalie was quick and dark. She was touching me. She must have carried me (*SL*, 20)."[14]

We know something about Faulkner's actual experience with his two mothers from his brothers' memoirs and from his daughter, Jill. She observes that although her father's mother was physically aloof, "Mammy Callie" acted as "his mother, his nurse, his teacher, and everything else."[15] Her thoughts repeat the emotional divisions in Faulkner's screen memory. Vannye holds the light, which, in the fictional scenes I'll presently discuss, represents the power of whiteness. Yet, she remains aloof. Natalie, the dark sister, provides intimacy. But if she provides pleasure or comfort, Faulkner cannot acknowledge it.

The term *screen memory* is used to designate early childhood memories that on the surface appear mundane, so mundane that it seems strange that they are so vividly remembered. Freud proposes that this kind of remembering is not an actual memory but a screen for an emotionally dangerous memory. This explains its benign surface. However, when its author probes or analyses it, which is what Faulkner does in fictional scenes derived from such a childhood experience, he exposes and explains its intensely conflicted and disturbing content.[16]

The screen, or indifferent, images here would be Faulkner's two white aunts. How could he have *any* memory, let alone such a desolate memory, of someone whom he saw only once in his life, at age three? Who is she, really? Why is there such a visually and sensually sharp dichotomy between the two sisters? Faulkner's fiction suggests that these women, a "dark" and a "light" sister, displace the "objectionable" memory of his two mothers and perhaps an even more objectionable memory of a time when he made no distinction between them or between himself and them.

More clues to the memory's repressed content lie in the illogic of its narrative and in its vivid, racially coded tactile and visual elements. It seems logically narrated. But closer attention reveals that its narrative is full of holes and contradictions. For example, although he writes that "I will be awfully glad to see Vannye again," the memory that follows is so fraught with anxiety that we can't imagine why.

What makes the tactile and visual elements Faulkner assigns the two sisters racially coded? First, one is figured as "white / light" while the other is "dark." Further, when colors are coupled with the emotional affects Faulkner attaches to them, and to all his fictional representations of white and black feminine, it's clear that Vannye is white and Natalie is black. The fiction that Faulkner will make of this screen memory also suggests that both become competing self-representations.

In Faulkner's screen memory, there's also an interesting reversal. The possibility of pleasure seems at first to emanate from the white sister: "I remember how Vannye's hair looked in the light—like honey." She looks edible and sweet to the tongue, like milk and honey. We expect her to be warm and enveloping in her response to the little boy's intense suffering, his "loneliness and nameless sorrow." Instead the narrative ruptures a second time. Faulkner's next brutally abrupt sentence is completely unexpected: "Vannye was impersonal; quite aloof: she was holding the lamp." No further explanation is offered by the next and final sentences, where the subject shifts to Natalie. Besides the marked difference in affect, Faulkner's grammar changes dramatically. He shifts from complex to simple, childlike sentences as he moves from outside to inside his narrative to remember the black mother who nursed him and whom he wished to be inside of: "Natalie was quick and dark. She was touching me. She must have carried me." Here he also moves from being the illuminated object of an aloof and impersonal gaze to becoming the subject of a sensuous and sensual embrace. In his fiction, the passionate and disturbing matter that fills these gaps is always, at some level, about what it means to have and to identify simultaneously with both a black mother and a white mother (or feminine?) but to be barred from emotional and physical closeness with either by the written and unwritten racial and sexual codes of his culture. Both the triangulation and the split and doubling aspects of Faulkner's intrapsychic relations with Maud and Callie Barr appear reflected in this screen memory of two sisters, one dark and one light.[17] In his fiction he often returned to this memory as he invented the racialized world of black and white mothers, lovers, sisters, brothers, and fathers that people his novels.[18]

Even if, as Freud theorizes, Faulkner's memory represents a condensation and displacement of later racial knowledge, his memory suggests that the earliest conflict he experienced manifested as tension caused by the demand on him to split his love between these two "mothers."[19] This tension was aggravated by his "shame" and "grief" at knowing that the one who responded to and encouraged his own sensual responses and whom he apparently most desired—to "touch"—was degraded and rendered taboo simply by the color of her skin.[20] His education into race and racism demanded that he reject the warm black "mother" he passionately loved. In an early poem, his rage-filled image for and solution to this demand is a "dismembered breast" (*TM,* 6). Thus, in his screen memory, his "loneliness and nameless sorrow" is for a desire that can never be named, let alone satisfied. Faulkner's fascination with and remarkable insights concerning the permeability of his culture's racial and gender constructions suggest as much.

Faulkner's imagination continually mines the repressed content of this core or organizing fantasy, drawing upon it for the increasingly rich and complex fantasies that figure the troubled conjunctions of race and sexuality throughout his fiction. But before discussing one of the roles this fantasy plays in *Go Down, Moses* I want to establish its genealogy by discussing its figuration in some earlier novels.

Faulkner's Early Fictional Reconstructions of His Racialized Screen Memory

In some of Faulkner's most powerful scenes of loss and mourning coupled with savage aggression, he mines this screen memory of wishing to be held by the quick, dark sister-mother; yet he is terrified that such surrender will make him black and feminine too. In these reconstructions, characters are frozen by the light of whiteness—the strict surveillance system of institutionalized racism.

In *The Sound and the Fury,* Faulkner draws on this memory to create Quentin's white and black constructions of female sexuality, most specifically the "dirty," "black," and "friendly" little Italian girl in the "Land of the kike home of the wop" (79) whom he calls "sister" and who reminds him of a childhood sexual initiation with another Other "in the high sweet emptiness" of his father's barn, a place hidden from the prying eyes of his real sister, her white counterpart. Quentin calls this other a "dirty girl."

Naming her Natalie, the same name as the dark aunt in his screen memory, Faulkner invokes his own first memory of being touched and held by a dark woman under the light (sight?) or direction of a honey-haired but aloof white woman:

> *There? Touching her*
> *Not there*
> *There? not raining hard but we couldn't hear anything but the roof and if it was my*
> *blood or her blood. . . .*
>   *Did Caddy go away did she go to the house you cant see the barn from our*
> *house.*

Here the forbidden, dangerous, disgusting, yet deeply erotic quality of blackness is made explicit as Quentin elides images of sweetness, touch, secretiveness, darkness, and dirtiness with sexual excitement and the mingling and merging of his (understood white) body and blood with "dirty" Natalie's:

> *It's like dancing sitting down did you ever dance sitting down did you ever dance sitting*
> *down? We could hear the rain, a rat in the crib, the empty barn vacant with horses. How*
> *do you hold to dance do you hold like this*
>   *Oh*
> *I used to hold like this you thought I wasn't strong enough didn't you*
> *Oh Oh Oh Oh*
> *I hold to use like this I mean did you hear what I said I said*
> *oh oh oh oh* (*TSAF,* 85)[21]

Here, the gradual loosening and then disintegration of syntax and the merging of the two voices figure the disintegration of body boundaries. It lasts only a moment. Quentin cuts off his fantasy and yanks himself into the bleak and sterile present where "the road went on, still and empty, the sun slanting more and more," where, turning his gaze outward to the dark and dirty and sweet little Italian girl, he still grasps for the tattered remnants of memory and desire: "Her stiff little pigtails were bound at the tips with bits of crimson cloth. A corner of the wrapping flapped a little as she walked, the nose of the loaf naked" (85, 86).

Quentin's fear of the white female gaze, his agony, his inability to permit himself to satisfy his desire, his need to punish this "blackness" in himself derives from his equation, learned from his racist biological parents, that to feel erotic pleasure is to, indeed, be black.[22] Faulkner himself will achieve such a transformation—in a highly coded form—in *Go Down, Moses.* But because this transformation, like the early idealizing love that fuels it, is taboo, it must always be punished. To be black, as Quentin's fantasies so vividly illustrate—"trampling my shadow's bones into the concrete with hard heels"—is to enter "the dungeon [which] was Mother herself," to "not be" (*TSAF*, 109, 110). Quentin's fear and his mirroring desire operate at both oedipal and pre-oedipal levels. But it is his fear of, mixed with forbidden desire for, not castration but annihilation, if he gives into his wish to enter this inviting yet suffocating prison of blackness—that is, his racialized pre-oedipal fear—that causes him to kill himself. Quentin's real fear is that if he gives in to his desire to enter into and to merge with his black mother / Natalie—in short, the feminine conceived as sexual, as black—he will erase his white self.

Faulkner's screen memory also figures prominently in *Light in August*, his novel about three Southern men and a woman whose obsessions with their families' and culture's mad beliefs about the meaning of race destroy them. Joe Christmas does not know whether he is white or black. Invoking the language of Faulkner's screen memory he thinks that "it was loneliness he was trying to escape and not himself" (*LIA*, 226). One night, desperate for food, he sneaks into a white woman's darkened house: "he seemed to flow into the dark kitchen: a shadow returning . . . to the allmother of obscurity and darkness." But the sweet smells of the "allmother's" black food (field peas cooked in molasses) provoke an anguished childhood memory of food denied him by a punitive white foster father: "*How can he be so nothungry and I smelling my mouth and tongue weeping the hot salt of waiting my eyes tasting the hot steam from the dish*" (230). Memory becomes cold reality as "the door opened and the woman entered. . . . She . . . carried a candle, holding it high, so that its light fell upon her face." In its "soft light" she looks young and vulnerable. But her voice and manner shatter this illusion: "'If it is just food you want, you will find that,' she said in a voice calm, a little deep, quite cold" (231). As in Faulkner's screen memory, Joe's crying need to "enter the allmother of obscurity and darkness," to feed from the black food, is cut off by white law—the punishing father, the white light and the cold, manlike voice of the white mother.

Memory, Desire, and the Racialized Poetics of *Go Down, Moses*

Faulkner subjects this memory's repressed content to ever deeper analysis as he draws upon it throughout his writing life. But its fullest meaning is realized in *Go Down, Moses*, where identification with, desire for, and fear of the feminine are irremediably linked with race, gender, and the maternal in every male character's quest for identity and selfhood. *Go Down, Moses* is Faulkner's last great novel about loss and mourning. Set like his other novels, in the racially charged cultural terrain of his own North Mississippi, it is about the power of the memory of a love that a racist society cannot tolerate, a love for everything that blackness first signified to its white children. Still seeking for words to explore and articulate the secrets of his treasured screen memory, Faulkner gives the experience of abandoning and demeaning his black mother to another white boy, named Roth. The boy's white mother is assuredly "aloof" as she dies bearing her only child. Faulkner begins by sketching Roth's life *before* he learns his culture's cruel lessons of racial difference. At first Roth identifies completely with his black mother and her family. The shift Faulkner makes into the camouflage of fiction gives him license to articulate clearly the child's idealizing identification: "Even before he was out of infancy, the two houses had become *interchangeable:* himself and his [black] foster-brother sleeping on the *same* pallet in the white man's house or in the *same* bed in the negro's and eating of the *same* food at the *same* table in either, actually preferring the negro house, the hearth on which even in summer a little fire always burned, *centering the life in it, to his own.*" Roth assumes that all children's earliest identification is with a black mother and that everyone has *"the first of remembering projected upon a single woman whose skin was likewise dark. One day he knew, without wondering or remembering when or how he had learned that either, that the black woman was not his mother, and did not regret it; he knew that his own mother was dead and did not grieve"* (GDM, 107, my italics).

Because Roth's white mother died at his birth, his black mother, Molly Beauchamp, is the only mother he has ever known. Yet although he describes his mirroring relationship with her, he claims to feel no regret when he learns that Molly is not really his mother. Faulkner clarifies the psychic form that denial takes. To identify not only with the feminine but with the black feminine is so shameful and so taboo that the feeling part of the self has to be killed. That loss, because one is never permitted to mourn for it, is felt always as a loss. He then describes the child's conscious fall into race and his subsequent attempt to dismember his black mother so that he can be sure he is white.

At first Roth experiences his black and white families as "interchangeable" and the "same." Molly literally *is* his mother. He does not know race. He prefers her house to his father's because he associates it with emotional and physical warmth—with the safety of unconditional love. In stark contrast, the narrator describes the white boy's legacy of Southern racism abstractly and naturalizes it—as the "old curse of his fathers" and the "old haughty ancestral pride" that "stemmed not from courage and honor but from wrong and shame" (GDM, 107).

One night when Roth is seven, he suddenly refuses to sleep at the house where his life is "centered" or to share a bed or pallet with his "foster-brother," Henry. In the morning, he sees that the pallet where he had forced Henry to sleep alone, is empty. He feels "grief he could not explain" and "shame he would not admit." A month later he returns to his black family's house and announces, "trembling a little, lordly, peremptory: "I'm going to eat supper with you all tonight." Molly is impassive but appears infinitely agreeable: "'Course you is,' she said. 'I'll cook you a chicken.'" But when she calls him in to the table where in the past they have all eaten together, he suddenly sees that Lucas, Molly's husband, "was not there and there was just one chair, one plate, his glass of milk beside it, the platter heaped with untouched chicken, and even as he sprang back, gasping, for an instant blind as the room rushed and swam, Henry was turning toward the door to go out of it." Projecting his own "shame" at what he has done on to his foster-brother, Roth lashes out at Henry: "'Are you ashamed to eat when I eat?' he cried. Henry paused, turning his head a little to speak in the voice slow and without heat: 'I aint shamed of nobody,' he said peacefully. 'Not even me'" (GDM, 109, 110).

Molly, as Faulkner's white mother would say, "knows her place." Taking it now, because Roth has assigned her to it, she shocks the white child into the enormity of his loss by presenting it to him at a primal level—feeding and touching. The single place setting and the platter heaped with untouched chicken also mark his self-imposed and permanent exclusion from his black family. Roth panics. Momentarily he is blinded and can't breathe; like the young Thomas Sutpen in his fall into race, Roth loses all sense of time and space as he sees his identity with and ties to his black family disintegrate before him.

The narrator concludes, "So he entered his heritage. He ate its bitter fruit" (GDM, 110). The violence of Roth's fear and his rage at the shame and emptiness he feels is imaged here, as it was for Joe Christmas in Light in August, as food made by a black "allmother"/lover, which he cannot eat. He has indeed dismembered the breast. In the process he has also dismembered himself. Roth is permanently damaged. He will spend his life compulsively repeating that first loss, which he was not permitted to feel. That is one reason why, as a grown man, he abandons his "black" lover (who is also a cousin) and their infant son. He has been taught that is the only way he can be a White Man. Yet Roth's lover demonstrates the falseness of part of this definition when she tells their uncle, "I would have made a man of him. He's not a man yet. You spoiled him" (343). "Spoil" here means teaching him to be a racist. Racism spoils anyone, negating the possibility of becoming a man (or woman).

But Faulkner in *Go Down, Moses* is also a man of his time. He never tells how Henry is damaged, although perhaps we hear his creator's fervent wish in Henry's corrective reply to Roth, given "peacefully" and "without heat."[23]

In "Pantaloon in Black," where the authorial voice dons a commedia mask from his literary childhood to slip inside a mythically endowed young man with skin the same blue-black color as that of his recently dead black "Mammy," his erotic desire is momentarily unmediated by fear and disgust. Faulkner constantly rivets the reader's gaze on Rider's idealized and eroticized body: "the mounting sun sweat-glinted steel-blue on the midnight-colored bunch and slip of muscles" (*GDM*, 140). But because Faulkner ultimately can't imagine erotic desire as anything other than taboo and always identifies it with blackness and the feminine in this racialized culture, he has to destroy his black mask, Rider.

"'Mammys' . . . Became Second Mothers to White Children"

We now know something about the nature of Faulkner's earliest experiences with the black and white women who mothered him in a world governed by apparently rigid sexual and racial hierarchies and boundaries.[24] So we can assume, with some assurance, that he was aware that, within his own family, the racial boundaries between white men and black women appeared extraordinarily permeable. Certainly we see that paradoxical rigidity and permeability refracted in much of Faulkner's fiction, including *Go Down, Moses*. Like prior generations of white Southerners, the Faulkners assumed exclusive ownership of Callie Barr. The inscription Faulkner had carved on Barr's grave—"MAMMY / Her white children / bless her"—was used by white masters and, later, employers on the gravestones of thousands of black women throughout the South. For all of them, such epitaphs staked out their white children's exclusive ownership, even in death and even in the black cemetery. But such claims, which erase black kinship ties as they appropriate their black servants' bodies, also reveal the dehumanization that ownership of other human beings necessitates. This dehumanization is a constant and constantly conflicted subject of Faulkner's fictional texts, as it is in his brothers' memoirs.

This and the question of Faulkner's own "place" in relation to Caroline Barr is the masked and encoded subject of "Pantaloon in Black," as it is, less opaquely, elsewhere. In "Pantaloon in Black," donning the mask of blackface (the pantaloon, Rider), Faulkner further explores the meaning of that loss. But his exploration throughout this novel and throughout the record of *his writing* of this novel, as always, is fraught with an ambivalence often articulated as blatant racism.

"The Old Matriarch Who Raised Me": Callie Barr's Death and the Birth of *Go Down, Moses*

Explaining why he was late in returning the galleys for *The Hamlet,* Faulkner wrote Robert Haas, his editor at Random House, that on the last day of January 1940, Caroline Barr, "the old matriarch who raised me died suddenly from a stroke" and "so I have had little of heart or time either for work."[25] Yet besides continuing to fictionalize her life, he had already begun fictionalizing her death in what would become *Go Down, Moses,* the book that, in some ways, is his most intimate and startling report on the degree to which the underlying instability and permeability of the codes and conventions that dominated his public and private discourse on race were reflected in, fueled, and structured his imaginative vision.[26]

Faulkner responded to Haas's sympathy note and enclosure two days after receiving it. The latter was probably the *New York Times* account of the eulogy he had written and delivered to Callie Barr's family and friends at a gathering he and Estelle held in their parlor. Following that event there was a black funeral service for Barr at what was then called the Negro Baptist Church in Oxford and burial ceremonies later that afternoon in the black section of St. Peter's Cemetery. He sent Haas the now-polished version of Barr's eulogy, parts of which he later used verbatim in the then-unwritten third section of "The Fire and the Hearth."[27] In an accompanying note he wrote, "This is what I said and when I got it on paper afterward, it turned out to be pretty good prose."[28]

In a moment I will discuss Barr's eulogy more fully because the literal space in which it was delivered—the Faulkners' parlor—the inspiration for its composition and its later use, and the small ambivalences masked by the conventional rhetoric of the white master's eulogy to his faithful servant, brought here into the realm of art by virtue of its particular author, serve as part of the foundation for my argument: that *Go Down, Moses* offers the clearest genealogy of its author's own racial unconscious. This and the cumulative evidence drawn from all of Faulkner's art argues for Faulkner's lifelong relationship with Caroline Barr as central to his poetics. The novel's elliptical shape is a return to and a repetition of Faulkner's earliest narrative experiments, his poem sequences of the teens and early twenties. A narrative gap encloses its keelson, "Pantaloon in Black," the section / chapter that just won't fit, where Faulkner brings to formal fruition a coded poetics he has been developing since the beginning of his writing career to articulate his vision of the racial politics of his North Mississippi culture. In this deliberately decentered and apparently unconnected third section of the novel he returns, as he has in a more guarded fashion throughout his fictional career, to his talismanic earliest narrative persona, Pierrot / Pantaloon, to house the form and give shape to what Eric Lott calls the "white racial unconscious" and to explore its origins in his own split maternal. This maternal is composed of all the paradoxes and contradictions that mark both the black "Mammy" figure and the Southern (white) Lady.[29] This dual mothering produces the black-white commedia trickster figure, which Faulkner adopts as his first narrative persona and which he resurrects in "Pantaloon in Black."

Much of Faulkner's white racial unconscious springs from his doubly mothered childhood.[30] One of these was a mother that cultural conventions prevented him from ever fully acknowledging.[31] Often they required that she be demeaned. In contrast to Faulkner's eulogy for Caroline Barr, a public act that conformed to those conventions, *Go Down, Moses,* a fiction, is both an act of true mourning and, in rare, unguarded moments, of the liberation that true mourning brings. The mask of art permits Faulkner to articulate those conventions and explore the history of his complicity in them and the confusions, desire, hatred, shame, and pain they cause. The masks and theater generated by those conventions are vividly represented in Rider's mourning as, echoing phrases from an early Faulkner poem, he tries to write and merge with his dead Mannie, making "his own prints" in the dust where she had walked each week, "setting the period now as he strode on . . . his body breasting the air her body had vacated, his eyes touching the objects . . . her eyes had lost" (*GDM,* 133). They are equally present in the homosocial and homoerotic world of the hunt where another encoded version of his African American mother, the half-Choctaw, half-black Sam Fathers, mothers the white boy. The boy experiences the warmth of Sam's body, "the two of them wrapped in the damp, warm, negro-rank quilt while the wilderness closed behind his entrance" creating a womblike "fluid circumambience, drowsing, earless, almost lightless" so that it seemed to the boy that "at the age of ten he was witnessing his own birth" (187). Only Rider's aching desire is expressed in his futile attempts to merge with his dead wife. In contrast, desire in Faulkner's white men and boys, expressed in the moment of their merging with a black body, is always freighted with disgust.

In terms of its form, this novel does not cohere in any formal high Modernist sense; rather, it deliberately does not cohere and "Pantaloon in Black" tells why. Furthermore, the section warns that the only way the novel *will* cohere is in its systematic revelations about the ways race is figured and about how those figurations work to split communities apart. John Limon argues that in "Pantaloon in Black," "Faulkner has formed a text in the image of a Southern Negro and invited us to join an interpretive community on the model of Yoknapatawpha County."[32] I would suggest, rather, that like the actors and white audiences of black minstrel shows, with which he was familiar, Faulkner has formed a text, Rider the Pantaloon, in the image of his own racial unconscious, the Rider / writer who mourns over the grave of his beloved Mannie / Mammy, "a grave marked off without order about the barren plot by shards of pottery and broken bottles and old brick and other objects insignificant to sight but actually of a profound meaning and fatal to touch, which no white man could have read."[33] And this is precisely the point. The problem with this novel is that Faulkner does not want to read what he is writing. As Ralph Ellison, from whom some of Lott's argument derives, explains: "The mask was the thing (the 'thing' in more ways than one) and its function was to veil the humanity of Negroes thus reduced to a sign, and to repress the white audience's awareness of its moral identification with its own acts and with the human ambiguities pushed behind the mask. . . . When the white man steps behind the mask of the trickster his freedom is circumscribed by the fear that he is not simply miming a personification of his disorder and chaos but that he will become in fact that which he intends to symbolize; that he will be trapped somewhere in the mystery of hell (for there is a mystery in the whiteness of blackness, the innocence of evil and the evil of innocence . . .) and thus lose that freedom which . . . he would recognize as the white man's alone."[34]

This circumscription of the white trickster reveals itself in the next note Faulkner wrote Haas in May 1940, five months after Caroline Barr's death: "Do you want to consider a collection of short stories, most of them from magazines since 33 or 34, perhaps one or two unpublished yet? Could get it together in a month. Also, Ober has four stories about niggers, I can build onto them, write some more, make a book like THE UNVANQUISHED, could get it together in six months perhaps" (*SL*, 124). Among these four was "Pantaloon in Black," which Faulkner had sent to his agent in March, less than two months after Barr's death.[35] Masking his emotional involvement and yet revealing the dual consciousness with which he approached his project in the apparently demeaning and self-demeaning racist epithet describing it to his Eastern publisher, Faulkner was already well into his private eulogy. Yet, I wonder, are the "niggers" to whom he refers here only in his stories, or is Faulkner including himself as well? Up against the authority of his (Northern) New York publisher, is he dropping into blackface here for reasons similar to those he attributed to Lucas Beauchamp, who "without changing the inflection of his voice and apparently without effort or even design . . . became not Negro but nigger, not secret so much as impenetrable, not servile and not effacing, but enveloping himself in an aura of timeless and stupid impassivity almost like a smell" (*GDM*, 50)? Faulkner needed money desperately. Earlier, in April, he had written Haas that he'd have to postpone work on what had now, in his mind, become a novel "since the *chapters* which I have written and tried to sell as short stories have not sold."[36]

It turned out to be a difficult year. As usual, he was strapped for funds: "I'm so busy borrowing money from Random House," he wrote his agent at the end of May, that "I dont even have time to write" (*SL*, 125).[37] Yet by November, in the ten months since Callie Barr's death, he had completed all of *Go Down, Moses* but "The Bear." He took off to the Delta for his annual hunting trip with the usual crowd. There, perhaps reliving Rider's vain attempt to dull thinking and feeling with bootleg liquor, he nearly died of acute alcohol poisoning.[38] But perhaps also, his drinking and hunting served as a violent but private and wordless negation of the romanticized role he had given them—the lie "the boy" spoke in "The Bear," which, like the other hunts in this novel, proposes that what makes a white man is not a relationship but the ritual killing of a black man or his surrogate, while simultaneously perpetuating a romantic myth that men in the Edenic wilderness are beyond racism: "There was always a bottle present, so that it would seem to him that those fine fierce instants of heart and brain and courage and wiliness and speed were concentrated and distilled into that brown liquor which not women, not boys and children, but only hunters drank, drinking not of the blood they spilled but some condensation of the wild immortal spirit, drinking it moderately, humbly even" (*GDM*, 184). Drinking moderately was the last thing Faulkner ever did. The context, Eucharist metaphor, and color of the blood here suggest that brotherhood, too, is colored; that the hunters are white, and the sacrificed Christ figure, another black man.[39]

Not until May 1941 do his letters mention *Go Down, Moses* again. Now he omitted the racist epithet. In the intervening months his project had blossomed and paid off; he had sold short story versions of everything but "The Bear," increasing his confidence in the interest of his subject. Although still anxious about marketability, he was no longer defensive: "Last year I mentioned a volume, collected short stories, general theme being relationship between white and negro races here. . . . Do present conditions warrant such a book? That is, do you want to publish such a book, and will it do enough to ease the financial situation between us for me to get at it?

. . . I do not want to gamble the time and effort of getting this mss. in shape unless it will really benefit me."[40]

In January 1942, two years after Caroline Barr's death, Faulkner sent Haas the dedication for his tenth novel:

> TO MAMMY
> CAROLINE BARR
> Mississippi
> [1840–1940]
> Who was born in slavery and who
> gave to my family a fidelity without
> stint or calculation of recompense
> and to my childhood an immeasur-
> able devotion and love (*SL*, 148)

Her gravestone, which Faulkner ordered, read "CALLIE BARR CLARK / 1840–1940 / "MAMMY" / Her white children bless her." His book epigraph, drawn from his eulogy, removed the inaccurate Clark but inserted another mis-naming. Now "Mammy" appears as Barr's given name. When Faulkner's nephew wrote asking what he'd like carved on Maud's grave-stone, he replied: "My idea is, a tombstone in a public cemetery is set up as a part of a true record of a community. It must state fact, or nothing." He added that "if such factual information as dates etc. are to be kept se-cret, the tombstone is no longer a part of the record of a place and a fam-ily, but a private memento of grief, and should be kept in a private home" (*SL*, 454). In a sense, Callie's gravestone was a record of the facts—from Faulkner's Southern white community's perspective. But was it the truth that, as he never tired of saying, is different from fact? And if so, whose truth was it?

By the end of March 1942, *Go Down, Moses* was in the bookstores and Faulkner told Haas, with the characteristic understatement he had reserved for good work, both his own and that of others since the early twenties, that the book was "all right. It will pull its weight" (*SL*, 149). As his letters tell, Faulkner's financial situation was the major external exigency driving the production of this novel. Was there a market out there? he had asked his publisher when he first proposed it. The novel's dedication, Faulkner's pub-lic statement about his feelings for Barr, falls within and so perpetuates the convention of white masters' eulogies for faithful black slaves (and later, servants). Narratively, as a framing device, it functions as an introduction to and extension of its fictions. In this sense, the inscription closes down his novel before it even begins. Is it, too, a mask? One that signals its author's inability to escape the constructions of his racialized culture?[41]

Let us go back to this novel's beginnings, and also return to Faulkner's original, or rather, not so original, eulogy and the space and circumstances under which it was delivered and received.

Caroline has known me all my life. It was my privilege to see her out of hers. After my father's death, to Mammy I came to represent the head of that family to which she had given a half a century of fidelity and devotion. But the relation between us never became that of master and servant. She still remained one of my earliest recollections, not only as a person, but as a fount of authority over my conduct and of security for my physical welfare, and of active and constant affection and love. She was an active and constant precept for decent behavior. From her I learned to tell the truth, to refrain from waste, to be considerate of the weak and respectful to age. I saw fidelity to a family which was not hers, devotion and love for people she had not borne.

She was born in bondage with a dark skin and most of her early maturity passed in a dark and tragic time for the land of her birth. She went through vicissitudes which she had not caused; she assumed cares and griefs which were not even her cares and griefs. She was paid wages for this, but pay is still just money. And she never received very much of that, so she never laid up anything of this world's goods. Yet she accepted that too without cavil or calculation or complaint, so that by that very failure she earned the gratitude and affection of the family she had conferred fidelity and devotion upon, and gained the grief and regret of the aliens who loved and lost her.

She was born and lived and served, and died and now is mourned; if there is a heaven, she has gone there.[42]

Faulkner delivered this eulogy at a service he held for Caroline Barr's family, but their presence in his speech (where Faulkner uses the word *family* or its equivalents five times) is noted only by its absence. The only family he mentions is his own. Underpinning Faulkner's image of Barr is the formulaic characterization in the Mammy memorials printed in the *Confederate Veteran* of the ex-slave turned faithful servant as Christ figure. The dominant image is of Barr's selfless service. Faulkner's description of her place in his family gives the lie to his claim that they were never "master and servant." She existed not for herself or her black family but in order to serve her white family.

Barr's relatives were grateful for some of Faulkner's efforts. Her greatniece, Rachel McGee, recalls that bitter cold and snowy day and Faulkner's generosity: "When she died, he called me and I got my sister [Dora] and we went 'cross the Bailey Woods (we call it Bailey Woods), from South Eighth Street that is hitting Bailey Woods—we went 'cross there and the snow was on the ground. It was cold—ice and stuff. We went 'cross the field and Mr. Faulkner told us he would furnish *everything* and we called Bankhead [Funeral Home]. And they took care Aunt Callie and I had her bonnet made in Clyde Bolden [shop]. They furnished *everything* and I mean it. It wasn't no poor person stuff you know." She pauses then, hesitating. Her next sentence explodes on the tape in a rush of indignation: "And *then* he had the funeral in the living room! In his *living room!* And I think he had the Community Choir of Oxford. I think they call that choir to come down and sing and *then* he let us brought her to the Baptist Church. He come with it [the body]. His and Miss Estelle had the funeral and carried her on out there and buried her."[43]

Faulkner's biographers interpret this moment as indicative of the author's love and respect, a moment of great honor for Caroline Barr. From the Faulkners' perspective, it was. Barr's relatives see differently, however. They believe that had he really meant to honor Barr, he should have given his eulogy in *their* church or family home. They felt that he was taking over and that "even at the bitter end, he couldn't let go of her, couldn't let her be with her family."[44] When asked why no one said anything, Mrs. McGee explained that they felt Faulkner should have realized what he was doing, that they shouldn't have needed to tell him. What she didn't say was that in 1940 it would have been unheard of to "say anything." In a later interview, Mrs. McGee's daughter, Mildred Quarles, amplifying her mother's account, explained: "It was awful that he had it in his parlor. William said he was gonna have it at his house and they had her [Callie Barr] in his parlor! You know, white folk call it parlor. In his parlor! My mother and Aunt Dora told me some things you don't do. And my mother and all of them told me about William speaking over Aunt Callie. One aunt, she said 'Hell, he drunk. He don't know any better than to have it in the parlor.'"[45]

Equally important, they felt that Faulkner showed an indifference to "local black rituals that have to do with burying your relatives." John Faulkner's description of his brother's role in Barr's funeral further validates her family's belief that the Faulkners felt they owned Callie Barr and their sense of being erased: "Bill had Mammy's frail body moved to the funeral home, selected her casket and when she was ready, had her moved to his own house, where she lay on his hearth for a day and a night and a part of the next day, until time for her burial. Bill selected her grave site in the colored portion of our cemetery and her friends, both white and colored, assembled at Bill's for her funeral."[46]At no place does John mention Barr's family. One would expect that John's description of his mother Maud's death, which follows his account of Callie Barr's, would be equally detailed. He gives it one sentence: "She died at eighty-nine."[47]

In *Go Down, Moses* Faulkner returns to Callie's eulogy in several instances. Each time he draws from it, he shifts from critique and rupture into sentimentality. Thus, from a rhetorical and narrative perspective, invoking her eulogy is a reactionary move.

A good example is the flashback scene in "The Fire and the Hearth," where Molly punishes the seven-year-old Roth by giving him just what he demands when he suddenly begins treating the black family who has raised him "as a subject race." Yet immediately following this powerful critique are the grown Edmonds's ruminations, in the present, where he contemplates "the breaking up after forty-five years the home of the woman who had been the only mother" he ever knew. Edmonds's recital of Molly's qualities reads like a catalogue of the positive conventional character traits white Southerners claimed for their "mammies." One cannot read it ironically because both Roth and the narrator sentimentalize and stereotype Molly throughout this section. The language with which Faulkner introduces it is that of Callie Barr's eulogy. Molly becomes once more "the only mother he, Edmonds, ever knew, . . . who had surrounded him always with care for his physical body and for his spirit too, teaching him his manners, behavior—to be gentle with his inferiors, honorable with his equals, generous to the weak and considerate of the aged, courteous, truthful and brave to all—who had given him, the motherless, without stint or expectation of reward that constant and abiding devotion and love which existed nowhere else in this world for him" (*GDM*, 113–14).

With this set piece Faulkner succeeds in throwing into serious question what lessons Molly had ever been able to teach Roth Edmonds about honor, courtesy, and simple human decency. Roth's behavior throughout *Go Down, Moses* only reinforces the empty rhetoric of these claims. But here, having made them, he physically transforms Molly into a static, doll-like figure: "She sat . . . motionless . . . her tiny gnarled hands immobile again on the white apron, the shrunken and tragic mask touched here and there into highlight by the fire" (115). As Edmonds says, "Then it was as if it had never happened at all" (109).

Sentimentalism simultaneously exalts and murders. It operates here in the same two-pronged manner that it functions in the songs associated with minstrel shows, songs that have a remarkably long afterlife in pieces like Al Jolson's rendition of "Mammy" in *The Jazz Singer*.[48] What Eric Lott calls the "vogue of the dear departed," Ann Douglas established as a "cornerstone of sentimentalism . . . the Christian exaltation of the powerless," as a way of justifying and naturalizing slavery. Such eulogizing was always the death of an other—dead women and dead male and female slaves. Lott reads the repetition of this theme in nineteenth-century blackface minstrelsy "as a form of racial and sexual aggression, that is, metaphorical murder." Its purpose was to bury the "whole lamented business of slavery" by eliminating "black people themselves."[49] In *Go Down, Moses* invocations by white male characters of Callie Barr's eulogy ("the social configuration of the elegized black woman") function similarly. They close down the narrative.

However, Rider's mourning in "Pantaloon in Black" has the opposite effect. To create Rider, Faulkner invokes what seems at first an equally stultifying convention, his earliest persona, an alienated *pierrotiste*, to enact a story of mourning that denies the efficacy of eulogy. Coding Rider as his originary poetic voice, he fuses his identity with his character's.[50] Faulkner, the becoming artist, and Rider, the becoming man and mythmaker, are one. The Mannie whom Rider mourns is both his mother and his tabooed lover; Caroline Barr and the self he fears the loss of in losing her as well as the self he fears to acknowledge.[51] She is indeed a ghost. Thus the linguistic play in Mannie's dually gendered name, which for Faulkner would have also encoded (enfolded?) Callie Barr's nickname for him—"Memmy" (pronounced "Me-me"); thus Rider's constant attempts to "touch" and merge with her traces—her footprints in the road, her dust, her shadow, her shade.[52]

Here Faulkner seems to be suggesting that his imaginative impulses and vision spring, in part, from his identification with his "Mammy" as, in this highly coded way, he momentarily moves, through Rider, into a zone of feeling and experience where no one else can follow. This is why only blacks can read the memorials on Mannie's grave and why no one in Rider's community, either black or white (except the ghost of Mannie), can understand him. Rider deliberately marginalizes and ultimately obliterates himself from the text. In doing so, he succeeds in merging with his Mannie and he creates a powerful myth—this story of his grief—that his community will never forget.[53]

Rider's (the writer's) rage and grief at Mannie's (his Mammy's and thus his own, "Memmy's") death is beyond his control. No language can express it; therefore his body speaks. Mourning the lost maternal, all his senses take command to speak an image of the body in pain and conflict. When he tries to eat, to nurture himself with food she once cooked for him, he gags: "The congealed and lifeless mass seemed to bounce on contact with his lips . . . peas and spoon spattered and rang upon the plate; his chair crashed backward and he was standing, feeling the muscles of his jaw beginning to drag his mouth open, tugging upward the top half of his head. But he stopped that too before it became sound, *holding himself* again while he rapidly scraped the food from his plate" (*GDM*, 137–38, my italics). As he did with young Roth Edmonds, Faulkner figures the death of his male protagonist's black mother / lover at its most primal level; that is how it felt to cut himself off from the black woman who had been, as Edmonds repeats almost like an incantation, "the only mother he ever knew" and "fed him from her own breast" (97, 106, 107, 113, 126).[54] Here Rider's body acts out the violence of his emptiness. Manny is not there to hold him; he can only hold himself. In one of the most powerful scenes of loss and mourning he ever wrote, Faulkner draws again upon his screen memory of being held by the quick, dark sister but still feeling so terribly alone, kept aloof by the light of the white sister, the whiteness of racism.

The white community lynches Rider because he breaks out of the myths they invented to contain him. In doing so, he creates his own myth, one that violates his Jim Crow culture's racial laws and codes. He moves from wearing a mask of servility and deference to being a lawmaker. He remakes himself, not as the long-suffering and selfless Christ figure (the "good" black servant memorialized by Roth Edmonds and in other Mammy memorials) but as an avenging and righteous Old Testament God figure and as a black man who is deeply in love.[55] Like his creator, Rider is, first and foremost, a myth-breaker and remaker. In effect, in "Pantaloon in Black" Faulkner is figuring as black both artistic marginalization and the passion that fuels art, or mythmaking. Its sources stream in part from an identification he can never acknowledge, which is why blackness in Faulkner's fictional world is freighted with such hatred, such shame, such grief, and such desire.

I doubt whether Faulkner consciously recognized the richly generative role his relationship with Caroline Barr and the world she showed him played in his creativity. However, it is clear that in plumbing his very complicated and culturally determined loss of her that occurred when he was just a child, he found his life's work. His relationship with his black "mother" is a key to his racialized poetics. Admitting it into our readings of his texts revises and enlarges the meaning of loss in Faulkner's fiction.

6

Family Secrets

"Mississippi"

E ARLY IN HIS childhood Faulkner transformed his forbidden and therefore unmourned love for Callie Barr into a core memory. Lodged in his unconscious it served as the "figure of transgression and hybridity at the center" of the writer's imaginative life. His fiction claims the world she opened to him as central to his creativity. Consistently he adopts "blackness" as an artistic persona—from "Faulkner," the "crazy," "little kind of black man" who "said he was a liar by profession" in *Mosquitoes*, to the rebel and mythmaker Rider, in *Go Down, Moses* (*MOS*, 144–45). His poetics of racialized loss, deeply eroticized and defined always by "rage," "shame," and "grief"—none of which his Southern white men and boys are permitted to feel—draws its pathos and energy from his early forced denial of the black maternal personified in Caroline Barr.

In "Mississippi" (1954), this late, avowedly autobiographical essay, which *Holiday* magazine commissioned and which Faulkner completed in March 1953, one year before the Supreme Court decision on *Brown v. Board of Education*, he makes a last attempt to lay to rest the ghost of the black mother he may not mourn.[1] This time his mode is confession. This essay, Faulkner's final elegy for Caroline Barr, is a slippery, perplexing read: part political polemic condemning racism, part demeaning sentimentalism toward the black people who worked for the Falkner family, part autobiography, part fiction. Once more, but less guardedly, he writes the story of the killing of his love for Callie Barr and her family. But this time there's a striking difference.

"Mississippi" as Autobiography, Or Lying to Tell the Truth

Faulkner first signaled his fictional-autobiographical intentions for "Mississippi" in a letter to Bob Haas at Random House: "I am thinking about

6.1. Callie Barr's cabin behind the Faulkners' house in Oxford. There are no extant photographs of the cabin as it was when Barr lived there in the 1930s. (Photo: Amy C. Evans, 2002)

writing my memoirs. That is, it will be a book in the shape of a biography but actually about half fiction, chapters resembling essays about dogs and horses and family niggers and kin, chapters based on actual happenings but 'improved' where fiction would help [this phrase recalls his 1925 letter to Maud from New Orleans in which he describes his writing process], which will probably be short stories. I would like to use some photographs. Maybe some of my own drawings. It would probably run about novel length, it will ramble some but mostly be confined between Rowan Oak, my home in town here, and the farm, Greenfield."

Structurally, this plan is the artist at his most inventive, imagining a unique hybrid mixed-media, mixed-genre form for his own modernist "biography." Once more, he is breaking all molds. At the very least, it would have been a marvelous experiment. There is no record of Haas's reply. But according to Joseph Blotner, "Mississippi" was the end result.[2]

Although the form he proposes is radical, Faulkner's use of the epithet "family niggers" (as in his first letters proposing the novel that became *Go Down, Moses*) appears to signal his reactionary stance in the current national discussion on race relations and his commitment to preserving plantation mythology. Ostensibly a travel piece for *Holiday*'s well-to-do readers, "Mississippi" has a narrative structure that's a mix of magnolia-scented travelogue, Old South memoir, and tall tales, all dripping with nostalgia. Yet throughout, he creates a tension or contradiction that he never resolves. Constantly, he jars his folksy Southern gentleman's account of his family's slave-holding origins, his idyllic childhood, his adolescence, and his present "middleaging" with a severe social and economic critique of slavery's legacy—the daily racism that keeps black Mississippians in their place. Thus politically, this essay is also a hybrid, a composite of the thoughts of two people who cannot hear each other. Its racial politics veer constantly between reactionary and revolutionary. Although he sketches his family's history and his own life against a sometimes trenchant analysis of race, class, and caste in Mississippi, from the first white settlers' invasion of Chickasaw and Chocktaw lands to his own unsettled present, he portrays his family's relations with their black employees as the stuff of a plantation novel. In short, the essay is radical in its general and abstract pronouncements about racial inequality but reactionary in its telling of the story of Faulkner's childhood and adulthood, which, in this essay, is the story of his relationship with Caroline Barr and her family.

One explanation might be as follows. In imagining "Mississippi," Faulkner's problem in 1953, one year before the Supreme Court ended de jure segregation in public spaces, was complicated. By this time in his career, four years after winning the Nobel Prize, he had taken on the role of Public Man, serving as Good Will ambassador for the State Department at home and abroad. This essay in *Holiday* offered him a means to extend that role by providing a national forum. If he wanted to make a strong case in "Mississippi" for radical reform, he had to show his readers how it was—to set out the facts of life in Mississippi past and present in their most extreme form. His method in this memoir is to offer himself and his family history as a case study of "benign" white middle-class racism and classism. What better example could he offer than his new persona, this "sixty-year-old smiling public man"?[3] In keeping with his Modernist aesthetic, he does not make this connection for his readers; he leaves them to make it for themselves. This is an appealing argument; it allows liberal readers to claim Faulkner as a liberal Southerner of his generation and culture. But its portrayal of the Falkner family's "happy darkies" assures conservatives that the status quo is still firmly entrenched. However, for this explanation to wash, we would need to be able to read ironically Faulkner's embrace here of some of the most trite and abhorrent images of the Old South mythology. Yet he does not appear to be ironic: his essay's dissonance remains jarring because it insists on the "truth" of these myths.

Unless. We need to watch the various masks and myths the narrator of "Mississippi" assumes as he picks his way through his avowedly semiauto-biographical minefield. Why is there such a striking similarity between the McCaslin family history and the fictions Faulkner invents here about his own family? Is there a hidden family history that some of the most blatant "fictions" or lies in this essay might be revealing?

The question of truth in memoir writing is no longer contested. Yet in this genre, as in the novel, Faulkner pushes the limits. He invents just where he claims to be most factual, in his account of Callie Barr's connections with the Falkner family. Contrary to Faulkner's assertions here, she was no Falkner ex-slave "who had declined to leave" at the war's end; none of her "descendants" worked for the Falkners; her family's last name was not Falkner; William Faulkner was not "born in the same week" as one of her great grandsons or grandsons ("even she did not remember"); nor were "both bearing the same (the white child's grandsire's) name, suckled at the same black breast and sleeping and eating together and playing together" (17). So why is he claiming Caroline Barr's family as both slaves and kin? Why is he claiming as his own his fictional Roth Edmonds's miscegenated genealogy and twinned birthing into a world where his earliest and most basic needs, physical touching, love, and food, are provided by a black mother and shared with a black brother? Is fiction disguising fact, the family secret that like Roth's great grandfather, Faulkner's own great grandfather, Colonel William C. Falkner, had at least one child with one of his female slaves, a wife and children he never publicly acknowledged? Is the essay's veiled purpose to confess the existence of the white Falkners' slave and ex-slave relatives, Faulkner's great grandfather's common-law wife and their offspring? That there were and are such Falkners was not general public knowledge until 1993, when the historian Joel Williamson published the strong circumstantial evidence in his revisionist *William Faulkner and Southern History*. My sense is that all of his life Faulkner was writing around and about this secret, which with each fictional rendering becomes more and more exposed. One can track its presence from his earliest work, but here I will just remind you of its progressively more explicit articulations in *Light in August*, *Absalom, Absalom!*, and *Go Down, Moses*.

"Something Is Wrong with Me": Intimations of Mortality

At the end of March 1953, Faulkner gave the completed typescript of his essay "Mississippi" to his agent Harold Ober. Faulkner's hospitalization record and all accounts of his emotional and physical state in 1952 and 1953, the period during which he conceived and wrote "Mississippi," describe a man coming unglued.[4]

He had had a terrible autumn and winter punctuated by a series of binges and blackouts—what he called "collapses"—during which he cycled in and out of various hospitals and sanitariums in Paris, Mississippi, Tennessee, and New York. His file at the Gartly-Ramsay Psychiatric Hospital in Memphis diagnosed him as "a chronic and acute alcoholic."[5] Between September and mid-November 1952 Faulkner's drinking caused his first convulsive seizures and blackouts; he had been hospitalized three times for acute alcoholism, twice in Mississippi and a third time in New York. In February 1953 he was hospitalized twice more. For the first time in his life he had sought and received psychiatric care. In letters sent during these months, Faulkner writes that he thinks he is losing his mind. He often felt he could no longer write. To friends and business associates he complained of having "run dry," of being "tired of writing," and of finding writing "more and more difficult" (*SL*, 344, 345). In July 1952 he wrote to Saxe Commins, his Random House editor, that "I have done no work in a year," that "I am really sick, I think. Cant sleep too well, nervous, idle," and that he looked "forward only with boredom to the next sunrise." A month later he wrote, "I feel rotten, no life much" (*LDB*, 2, 79, 80). On 18 September 1952, his drinking caused his first recorded convulsive seizure. Estelle took him to the Gartly-Ramsay Hospital, where eight days later and despite having had a second seizure, he insisted on being released. He could not stop drinking.

In early October 1952, Estelle telephoned Saxe Commins, who had worked with him for more than thirty years. Faulkner was incoherent. She begged Commins to come from Princeton to Oxford. He arrived late on the night of 7 October. The next morning, in a letter to Bob Haas and Bennett Cerf at Random House, Commins reported that before his arrival he had thought Estelle's and Malcolm's accounts of Faulkner's past six weeks were "slightly exaggerated but my first glimpse of Bill made me realize how accurately they had reported on his condition. He was lying on the couch in the drawing room in a stupor. His face is covered with bruises and contusions. His pajamas had slipped down and I could see how battered his body is. He greeted me mumblingly and incoherently, saying, 'I need you. Get me beer!'" Commins went on to describe a terrible night of dealing with Faulkner's "moaning and pleading for drink." His report continued: "The fact is that Bill has deteriorated shockingly both in body and mind. He can neither take care of himself in the most elementary way or think with any coherence at all. This may be only evidence of his condition in a state of acute alcoholism. But I believe this goes much deeper and is real disintegration."[6] By the next day they were able to move Faulkner to the Gartly-Ramsay Hospital. It was his second trip in less than a month.[7]

Yet by mid-November he had recovered sufficiently to leave Oxford for New York. There he was again hospitalized at Westhill Sanitarium in Riverdale and given six electroshock treatments to try to help him quit drinking and to relieve his depression. His doctor, "a European trained psychoanalyst" named Eric Mosse, found Faulkner's posttreatment behavior unusual. Unlike most patients after electroshock therapy, he was "neither hostile nor disoriented. Instead he was gentle; he put his arms around the doctor." Mosse thought Faulkner "had a great need for affection and he put his own arms around the patient to return the warmth." Blotner's account indicates that Mosse, like Faulkner's many male friends whom he had pressed into service as nurses over the past thirty years, was charmed by him. His patient took little interest in food. So Mosse changed his regular schedule to make his daily trips from his Manhattan office to Westhill coincide with Faulkner's lunch hour. At one point Mosse asked, "'Will you eat if I feed you?' the patient said he would and he did.'"[8] This sad and eerie scene in which Faulkner begs like a small child to be held and repeats with Mosse his father's behavior with Caroline Barr, when he was recovering from a binge, was one Faulkner had repeated with increasing frequency over the past twenty years.

The second neurologist and psychiatrist, Bernard Wortis, who saw him for nine sessions shortly after he had completed "Mississippi," and was again hospitalized, thought that Faulkner "had such an intense emotional responsiveness, such receptiveness for others and their problems, that life must be very painful for him. Obviously, his alcoholism was a narcotizing device to make it almost bearable for him."[9] He also noted that Faulkner did not permit his face to register the emotions he was speaking about: "this responsiveness never overflowed into facial expression" and "his mustache helped to conceal emotions," serving as a mask.[10] When Wortis asked Faulkner about his mother, he was met with "stony silence." He speculated that "he had not had enough love" from her. Right diagnosis, wrong mother. Wortis's observations, Faulkner's behavior towards Mosse, and the functions alcohol plays in Faulkner's poetics of racialized loss all suggest that the deepest and most personal pain he sought to dull was his fall into race. A fall marked indelibly by his killing of his earliest love for Caroline Barr.

His letters from this period continue to express his concerns about his physical health. In February 1953 he wrote that he had had at least "three spells of complete forgetting," blackouts that he ascribed to "a possible skull injury" from repeated falls from his horse. "I would not know what had happened until I would wake up in a hospital." He neglects to add that his hospitalizations always included detoxification, or attempts at it. Tests he had that March in New York, where he was again hospitalized and cared for by Wortis, Chair of the Department of Neurology and Psychiatry at the New York University Medical School, revealed "no skull injury," only that "a lobe or part of my brain is hypersensitive to intoxication," which he said his doctor defined as "any form of mental unease, which produces less resistance to the alcohol" (*SL*, 437). Faulkner was scared. He wrote that "something is wrong with me. . . . My nature has changed." Although he does not say so directly, he suggests that his doctors have confirmed his worst fear: alcohol had begun to destroy his brain. We have only Faulkner's account of his doctor's advice, which was that "he did not tell me to stop drinking completely, though he said that if the report had been on him, he would stop for 3 or 4 months and then have another test. He said that my brain is still normal, but it is near the borderline of abnormality. Which I knew myself; this behavior is not like me" (*SL*, 347).

The amazing thing is that, in spite of himself, Faulkner kept writing. For Faulkner, to write was to feel, to live, to love. But to love was, always, to feel loss. Like Rider, in "Pantaloon in Black," no matter how much he keeps drinking to stop feeling the death of his love, "Hit look lack Ah just cant quit thinking. Look lack Ah just cant quit" (*GDM*, 154). On 29 September 1952, less than a week after his return from ten days at Gartley-Ramsay, he responded to a query from Ober, saying that although he still felt "pretty bad," he was "interested in the Mississippi piece" and that he'd think about it and "write either it or you later" (*SL*, 341). In late February 1953, a month before giving "Mississippi" to Ober, he finished another elegiacal piece. Its subject was Sherwood Anderson, who had nurtured Faulkner's first novel, much as Callie Barr had cared for his infant self, and whom he had repaid with a vicious review published shortly before Anderson recommended *Soldiers' Pay* to his own publisher.[11] This new essay was the closest Faulkner ever came to reparation. That he wrote both confessional essays seriatim adds weight to the idea that his fears that he was failing spurred him to confess—via his fiction of making Callie a Falkner—the fact of his great-grandfather's unacknowledged black family.

"Mississippi" makes sense only if read as a memoir that is simultaneously Faulkner's final elegy for and confession to Caroline Barr. Barr gave this Southern white boy an alternative education into race that initiated and encouraged his much deeper and sustained critique of not only what Patricia Yaeger calls "epic" racism but also the "everyday" racism that saturated his actual and, later, his apocryphal worlds.[12] In "Mississippi"

Faulkner demonstrates that the two are inextricable. It is unfashionable to assert a relationship between an artist's moral life and his art, but "Mississippi" demands it. The writer's peculiar twining of fact and fiction in this essay makes a powerful statement about the impress of Caroline Barr and her family on his sense of his own family's responsibility for America's legacy of racial injustice.

"Mississippi" as Elegy and Confession

"Mississippi" needs to be read not as Faulkner's "legendary" account of his self-transformation into "famous novelist," a tale that only touches on racism, but as he wrote it—his troubled, final elegy for Caroline Barr, a last attempt to repudiate his culture's and his own racism and so come to terms with his disavowed love.[13] The genealogy of his racial unconscious is embedded in *Go Down, Moses*. The genealogy of his racial consciousness is found in "Mississippi."

"Mississippi" is about racism. More specifically, it is the story of the racing of the artist's imagination, and it begins and ends with Caroline Barr. Faulkner wrote this essay some thirteen years after *Go Down, Moses*. His emotional state at the time is as relevant as that which precipitated *Go Down, Moses*. Barr's death and his writing of her eulogy triggered the latter; fear for the death of his imagination drove "Mississippi." In his novel about the white and black McCaslins he pushed to its furthest limits his lifelong exploration of the psychological cost of Southern white men's education into racism. Doing so, he had also imagined African American women, men, and boys who, in a very limited way, spoke back, which suggested he might even have begun to allow himself to think of them as *acting*, not just acted *upon*. Faulkner's most daring fictional leap there was to invent Rider, who (as the writer) freed him to imagine a black person's subjectivity that he could sustain for more than a few scenes or sentences. But by the time he wrote "Mississippi" he appears to have lost that ability, or his aims had shifted to even more private concerns. The protagonist of this essay is more like Roth Edmonds, who, because he is forbidden to mourn his childhood black family, re-creates it with a second black family of his own making, which he also abjures. Or like Roth's uncle, the "impotent" Ike McCaslin, the "old man" of the final chapters of *Go Down, Moses*, who, when it comes to accepting his "black" relatives as family, doesn't "remember anything [he] ever knew or felt or even heard about love" (346). The essay enacts Faulkner's amnesia even as he continues to grieve for his loss of the black maternal and to preach, in the abstract, against the injustices brought to his attention by his lifelong relationship with Caroline Barr.

In "Mississippi" Faulkner borrows his romantic premise about his relationship with his Southern heritage from Quentin Compson of *Absalom, Absalom!*: "loving it even while hating some of it" (36, 38, 39, 42–43). His memoir serves as the basis for his analysis of his own love-hate relationship with the South, exemplified in his relationship with his "mammy," Caroline. He frames his essay with two events: Barr's entrance into his life and her death. The frame of her presence and absence embraces his telling of his own life. Other than himself, she is the only even partially developed character in his household. His daughter, Jill, and his mother and wife, neither of whom are named and whom he mentions only as they relate to Caroline Barr, are the only white "kin" Faulkner mentions more than in passing. This frame of Callie's presence and absence encloses one of the strongest nonfictional statements he ever made about the evils of racism and his own implication in that system. His social and economic analysis of racism's roots, begun prior to introducing Callie Barr ("Mississippi," 17), leads up to and away from this climactic rhetorical moment. And yet almost every instance of critique is either introduced or followed by one of what seems a willed blindness and regression.

His first fiction about Barr, for example, obliterates her actual diaspora story (which reveals her fiercely independent character) in order to transform her into a faithful old "befo' de war niggah" who shares "her white family's" hatred of the Yankees and longs for the good old days of slavery. In a massive act of narrative appropriation, Faulkner claims her as one of the family's "old house slaves." The real Caroline Barr had left her white owners and made sure that her freeborn daughters lived nowhere near the white family for whom she worked. Faulkner's fictional Caroline loves her white owners so much that although she has been "free these many years . . . declined to leave" (16). Her huge, extended family also lives with and serves the Falkners.

Some thirty-five years later, the author's childhood is overseen by these "indomitable unsurrendered old women holding together still, . . . a few of the old house slaves: women too who . . . refused to give up the old ways and forget the old anguishes" (16). Yet he also writes that he hates the racism this refusal to give up the old ways has perpetrated: "he hated the intolerance and injustice: the lynching of Negroes not for the crimes they committed but because their skins were black . . . the inequality: the poor schools they had then when they had any, the hovels they had to live in unless they wanted to live outdoors: who could worship the white man's God but not in the white man's church; pay taxes in the white man's courthouse but couldn't vote in it or for it; working by the white man's clock but having to take his pay by the white man's counting . . . ; the bigotry which could send to Washington some of the senators and congressmen we sent there and which could erect in a town no bigger than Jefferson five separate denominations of churches but set aside not one square foot of ground where children could play and old people could sit and watch them" (37–38).

Ike McCaslin calls his grandfather's ledgers "that chronicle which was a whole land in miniature, which multiplied and compounded was the entire South" (*GDM,* 280). In "Mississippi," thinly masking fact as fiction, Faulkner tacitly acknowledges his own white family's complicitness in that chronicle. Characteristically and much like the white McCaslins, he does so in moves that show him simultaneously clinging to and demeaning the biracial Falkners.

As he tells it in "Mississippi," Faulkner, like Roth Edmonds, is taught to be a racist at an early age. His description of this learning process explains why racism is endemic in the Jim Crow South. Drawing a parallel between his own past and America of the early 1950s he writes that "children played . . . just as now, . . . they still played, aped in miniature, what they had been exposed to, heard or seen or been moved by most" (16). For the young Willie this turns out to be a game, another ritual of mastery in which white always rules black as he and his "twinned brother" play the War over and over again "in miniature" (17). He claims that already "at four and five and six," he had learned the power of his white skin: "because he was white arrogating to himself the right to be the Confederate General—Pemberton or Johnston or Forrest—twice to the black child's once, else, lacking that once in three, the black one would not play at all" (17). It is a small moment, this portrayal of the white boy's enactment of his knowledge of his "right" to be unjust to the black child who shares his last name and whom he portrays as his figurative twin. It is only a game, but Faulkner introduces this moment by telling his readers that the games children play are representations of their lived reality. The reality of Jim Crow. Through her "grandson," Caroline "Falkner" is part of this moment, as Faulkner recreates the peculiar Southern family romance that haunted his white Southern childhood and his greatest fiction.

The long middle section of "Mississippi" is given over to Faulkner's autobiography, during which he travels around Mississippi. As he travels and ages, he transforms the land and its famous river into a character that serves as the backdrop for his description of his growth to "middleaging" and his analysis of the state's racist and classist politics and economics. He notes the origins of post–Civil War white rural working-class prejudice in its "bitter hatred and fear and economic rivalry of the Negroes who farmed little farms no larger than and adjacent to their own, because the Negro, remembering when he had not been free at all, was therefore capable of valuing what he had of it enough to struggle to retain even that little and had taught himself how to do more with less" (13). He writes that poor whites' hatred and jealousy sent them "in droves into the Ku Klux Klan" (19) and into the towns where they "could escape from the land into the little grubby side street stores where [they] could live not beside the Negro but on him by marking up on the inferior meat and meal and molasses the price which he, the Negro, could not even always read" (13). Faulkner does not need to explain why the majority of rural black people in Mississippi in the 1950s still could not read or why they would not be owning a store whites would patronize. That is the reality of Jim Crow.

In "Mississippi," Faulkner intimates that the McCaslin genealogy mirrored his own family's. In the two scenes that compose his portrayal of Callie Barr's final months, he makes another revealing revision. Up to this point in his narrative, Barr's presence, compromised in both instances by Faulkner's mythologizing, brackets passages in which he condemns the racism driving that mythology. In the first of the scenes with Callie Barr that conclude his essay, his critique turns further inward. Its subject is his own racialized aesthetic and a series of related tropes that mark its unresolvable tensions.

On a summer day in the late 1930s, Callie Barr, "nobody knowing anymore exactly how many more years than a hundred she was," sits by her cabin hearth sewing with the Faulkners' five-year-old daughter, Jill. As in Molly's and Lucas's cabin and Rider's and Manny's cabin, the fire in Callie's hearth burns summer and winter alike. The mingled smells of smoldering wood ashes and the burning sugar oozing from roasting sweet potatoes fills the dark little room where she has lived in the decade since Faulkner and Estelle became Rowan Oak's owners. She is teaching Jill how to piece a quilt. According to Faulkner's narrative, it will be the last quilt Callie Barr ever makes: "the five-year-old white child in a miniature rocking chair at one side . . . and the aged Negress, not a great deal larger, in her chair at the other, the basket bright with scraps and fragments of cloth between them and in that dim light in which the middleaged himself could not have read his own name without his glasses, the two of them with infinitesimal and tedious and patient stitches annealing the bright stars and squares and diamonds into another pattern to be folded away among the cedar shavings in the trunk" ("Mississippi," 40).

"Twin sistered to the fell darkness," the white child and the elderly black woman, who, she says, retrospectively, "was basically my mother," work harmoniously in that dim light with scraps and fragments of cloth to

6.2. Faulkner's photograph of Callie Barr and Jill Faulkner, 1939.
(Courtesy of Jill Faulkner Summers)

create a patterned whole. Only the young white girl and the old black woman can see to work in this light. Faulkner's lesser, raced, and racist sight excludes him.

For the first and only time, in this scene of Callie and his daughter quilting, Faulkner transforms what has been for his fictional white boys and men a redolent and racially charged image of desire masked as disgust into something lovely and magical.[14] The rag fragments shimmer with the magic of creativity and desire, magic all prior fiction suppressed with images of dirt and revulsion. Yet, in this scene of Callie and his daughter touching, he abjures the rank smell of disavowal. Describing the quilt Callie and his daughter are piecing, he reveals its beauty and its magic: that imagination—so much shaped by his forbidden love for her, was magical. He seems to be portraying a time in his daughter's life when love was not colored—when, as his fictions describing this period constantly reiterate, white children did not differentiate between black and white because they had not yet been taught in brutal initiation rituals that they were *not,* as he repeats over and over again, "the same." Imagining this scene between Callie and Jill he can again experience what was forbidden to him by his fall into race. Only through her can he see the quilt's beauty in the scene of collaboration that occurs in a dim light from which his constricted, racialized vision excludes him.

In Barr's deathbed scene, which also concludes his essay, Faulkner reduces her once again to a caricature of a faithful black servant. In mock heroic language, a typical rhetorical device in such contexts, he reports Callie Barr's "valedictory": "Miss Hestelle, when them niggers lays me out, I want you to make me a fresh clean cap and apron to lay in" (42). Always white identified, always the faithful servant, Callie delivers her farewell: her last wish is to be buried in "fresh clean" serving clothes supplied by her white mistress.

Yet that brief firelit moment summarizing (from Faulkner's white perspective) Callie Barr's life's work serves, as well, as a synecdoche for his own life's work and its process. Whenever he was asked about his writing process, Faulkner consistently responded that his initial stimulation was "an image, a very moving image."[15] Moving because all his image fragments taken together comprise a constellation of images, each of which signifies forbidden and, so, demeaned desire for someone or something figured as black. Examples Faulkner gave in interviews include "A Rose for Emily," which he said "came from a picture of the strand of hair on the pillow," and *Light in August*, which "began with Lena Grove, the idea of the young girl with nothing, pregnant, determined to find her sweetheart."[16] But the image fragment for *The Sound and the Fury,* "the book I feel tenderest to-

wards" and which he wrote "to rid myself of the dream which would continue to anguish me," was the one he most often talked of and the only one
he wrote about (*TSAF,* 232, 233).[17] Faulkner's inspiration came in "an image, a picture to me, a very moving one which was symbolized by the
muddy bottom of [Caddy's] drawers."[18] This dream image—the "mud-
stained drawers" of the "doomed little girl and the shame they symbolized
and prophesied"—became the book "I couldn't leave alone and I never
could tell it right" (*TSAF,* 231, 233). Why that was, why this image is also
crucial to Faulkner's imaginative play with Estelle and how he continued,
in both life and art, to tease out his dream of anguish is the subject of much
of the rest of this book.

Caddy's muddy underpants are just one of the many rag fragments
that make up the quilt from which Faulkner fashions his own quilt of
masked love and desire for the love he'd consigned to garbage.[19] When
pieced together, these fragments, Faulkner's "bright stars and squares and
diamonds," form a trope of racialized loss that tell the story of the terrible
rituals that mark Southern white children's education into race in the Jim
Crow South that was Faulkner's world. These fragments, reeking with a
need to touch and be enfolded in every forbidden sensate and infantile experience—the "ragged and filthy," quilts "impregnated with the unmistakable odor of negroes" (*FITD,* 389); the "damp, warm, negro-rank quilt"
(*GDM,* 187); Quentin's little Italian girl, a "dirty child," with her "moist and
dirty" skin," her "dirty dress," and ragged red hair ribbons; another black-
figured "sister," the "shadow" he cannot shake, with the "flying black
glance" and "moist dirt ridged into her flesh" and her "fingers, damp and
hot like worms" (*TSAF,* 79, 80, 82)—negate the apparent harmony of this
moment in "Mississippi." These are the fetishized feminine darknesses that
Faulkner's hysterical and alienated white boys wrap around themselves to
try to keep from emotionally freezing, to try to stave off paralysis and an-
neal a hopelessly fragmented self. But they celebrate the centrality of Callie
Barr to Faulkner's imaginative vision.

Later that summer, as he tells it here, Caroline Barr suffered her first
stroke. Faulkner writes that although she appeared to recover, "it was as if
she knew" she would soon die "because she never touched the last unfinished quilt again. Presently it had vanished, no one knew where, and as the
cold came and the shortening days she began to spend more and more
time in the house, not her cabin but the big house" (42). Faulkner leaves us
with a mystery: he never speculates about why or how the quilt vanished.
Such magic is too dangerous.

On Saturday evening, 27 January 1940, just before supper, Callie Barr was sitting in her rocker by the kitchen fireplace when she had her second and fatal stroke.[20]

Charles Bon assembled evidence of the secret of his white father, Thomas Sutpen, and wrote it out in his letter to his sister and lover, Judith. Judith Sutpen assembled the evidence of the Sutpen family secret and wrote it out on the gravestones in the Sutpen family plot; Carothers McCaslin wrote his in his ledgers; Joel Williamson found evidence of Colonel William C. Falkner's black family on Mrs. Emeline Lacy Falkner's gravestone and in interviews with her surviving relatives; Faulkner confirms it in this last elegy and confession for Caroline Barr.[21]

As Patricia Tingle was concluding her first interview with Caroline Barr's great-great grandson, James Rudd, he began asking her some questions about her background and education. She told him she was working on her doctorate in African American Studies and that she was especially interested in oral history:

> *Tingle:* I'm interested in oral history so I have been doing quite a bit of this kind of thing.
> *Rudd:* You got yourself a hard subject right there.
> *Tingle:* Oral history?
> *Rudd:* God, but it takes patience.
> *Tingle:* Yea, it takes a lot of patience.
> *Rudd:* It's like piecing a quilt. You ever piece a quilt?
> *Tingle:* Yeh. My grandmother and my great-grandmother taught me.[22]

PART 2

Faulkner's Mother, Maud Butler Falkner

Dear Miss Lady

— FAULKNER

Studio photograph of Maud Butler, 1896.
(Courtesy of Jill Faulkner Summers)

T HESE NEXT CHAPTERS foreground Faulkner's relationship with
his mother, Maud. My division of Parts 1 and 2 of this narrative,
between Callie Barr and Maud Butler Falkner, is to some extent
arbitrary. They are "joined," as Yoknapatawpha's poetess laureate says,
"like a fierce rigid umbilical cord, twin sistered to the fell darkness that produced" them (AA, 112). By this, Rosa Coldfield means that she, Clytie, and
Judith are haunted by the central paradox of their common history: the
intensely charged physical intimacy of the vestiges of what was once a slave
economy together with the racism that is slavery's legacy. They are haunted
by their shared conception, Clytie's literal and Judith's and Rosa's figurative, in that most intimate space of all, the raped womb of the black mother.
Maud's and Callie's shared household in all its permutations, so common
in Faulkner's Deep South, also haunts his fiction. As Maud appeared in
Callie Barr's story, so Callie is a presence in Maud's.

Just as Faulkner's attachment to Callie Barr included her black family
and community and was regulated by the unspoken and spoken rules and
codes of his white family and their world, so his relationship to his biological mother played out in the same realm. We have seen how his imaginative vision fed on his lifelong relationship with Callie Barr and what I have
called the black maternal. In turning to Maud, I will explore further the
actual composition of a white Southern maternal to better understand its
figuration and role in the formation of Faulkner's aesthetic vision. Although
both Maud and Callie are real people, in Faulkner's imaginary world and
in his consciousness they become the two originary figures of his maternal
imaginary.

Maud Falkner was so slight, one of her friends said, that "she was a miniature kind of person." It seemed to irritate and wryly amuse her that salespeople always showed her children's clothes. An interviewer noted that despite her small size(!) she appeared "very alert and intelligent with very perceiving eyes, not unlike Faulkner's." Her granddaughter Dean said Maud's eyes were "snapping dark brown, almost black, just like William Faulkner." A hapless Memphis reporter wrote that she was "a doll-like, pert little woman," which, according to Dean, infuriated her. Born in 1936, when Maud was sixty-five, Dean recalled, "My first memory of Nanny is of smells: a smell like powdery lilacs. She kept sachet like that in her drawers. But then she also smelled of paints. She had a wizened, wrinkled face and good strong hands."[1]

Maud's parenting and support of her eldest son's choice to become an artist needs to be viewed in its various contexts. (Historical, biographical, and thematic contexts are highlighted in Chapters 7, 8, and 9; the basis of Faulkner's aesthetic vision in the symbols and processes of the Southern white maternal in Chapters 10, 11, and 12.)

Faulkner's relationship with Maud necessarily includes significant members of his white family. Many have written about his various attitudes toward and indebtedness to his male ancestors. In their narratives of origins, the writer's genius derives from his great grandfather, Colonel William C. Falkner, who wrote a best-selling melodrama, a travel book, and a long ballad loosely based on his exploits in the Mexican-American War. We are urged to pass over "the complex issue of Faulkner's response to the women who inhabited his life and the images of womanhood," marriage, and parenting "they engendered." We are told that while "women inhabited that life, certainly, most of the time they inhabited its edges: nothing was more important to Faulkner than his work."[2] Yes. Faulkner's work was his life, but the three women at the center of that "woman world" of his first ten years (1897–1907) modeled this work life for him. Their contributions to his imaginative development were primary and central. That his great grandfather had been a published writer was important; however, he died long before Willie was born. Until the boy was almost ten, he was in the daily presence of and being taught to express himself imaginatively by two practicing visual artists: his mother, Maud, and his grandmother Lelia Butler.

Faulkner's work was also the part of his affective life that he seldom spoke about. The primal subject of his many fictional bedroom battles, often represented as a fatal dance, as if such conventions could contain their violence, is the erotics of what is forbidden: interracial, incestuous, and homosexual sex or coupling. Faulkner's complex and always evolving portrayals of these battles are layered to articulate the multiple lines of conflict fought out in white Southern homes and in Southern culture at large. His figurations of a racialized sexuality come not from the sexually and racially sanitized Southern myths surrounding the long-dead colonel but from the stories of his white forefathers' betrayals: of the colonel's shadow family, of Faulkner's paternal grandfather's black mistress, of his maternal grandfather's escape from Oxford with a black lover. Almost always Faulkner conceptualizes and images these figurations as violent struggles both sought after and fought against—often across a bed and pallet—that site of the forbidden.[3]

They also came out of Faulkner's childhood experience. Like the children of many Southern slaveholding and post-Reconstruction white families, he had a personal history rife with examples of white men (and women) exercising over black men and women what Faulkner named "the power deeded them by virtue of the color of their skin" ("Mississippi," 17). In his poetry and fiction, he continually returned to that defining moment in his childhood, characterized in his novels variously as a sense of "loneliness," "hopeless despair," "nameless grief," and finally, in Go Down, Moses, "rage" and "shame," of being forced by his white mother's culture to tear himself from the black. His initial attempts to find imaginative expression for this subject began with a single and final drawing in The Marionettes (1920), his first self-illustrated and published book. Tellingly, this drawing has no text, underscoring the significance of the visual. Painting, drawing, and even photography were the exclusive languages of the women in his family, Maud, and her mother, Lelia.

Like his racialized aesthetic, such stories—his "family romances"— may also have been fueled by the arguments "little Willie" witnessed between his towering and sometimes physically violent father and his tiny but verbally violent mother. Maud and her son spoke with the same voice. Murry called Willie "Snake Lips," commenting on the shape and cleverness of his mouth, which was like his mother's. To Murry, who never spoke much himself and imposed daily silence on his entire family while he ate his dinner, his oldest son's increasing commitment to vocations that his culture and the important men in his family labeled feminine—drawing, painting, and writing poetry and fiction—further aligned Willie with his mother and other female ancestors. What this alignment meant to Faulkner's imaginative and psychological development and how he articulated it, first in his drawings and poetry and later in both actual and fictional photographs and in his fiction's theatrical, filmic, and photographic tropes, leads to a new understanding of what I call his visual aesthetic.

Maud had a deep and abiding impact on her eldest son's imaginative life. To understand its ramifications requires knowing something about her and her relations to her family and community over time. In the Falkner family's early years in Oxford (1902–7), when her mother and mother-in-law were living, Maud was intellectually and socially active. She joined the Women's Book Club, which included her mother-in-law and her best friend and sister-in-law Mary Holland Wilkins ("Auntee"). There the mother of three little boys began writing on politics and literature. Her contributions to club programs suggest she was thinking about women's roles. In March 1903, she read "an original poem," a response to the club's discussion topic, "What is the happiest period of a woman's life?" That May she gave a paper whose subject was also women.[4] In addition to her reading and club work in those years, she returned to pastels and painting, something she had not done since her college art classes.[5]

Maud and Auntee had been close friends long before Maud's marriage. That friendship, characterized by almost daily contact for nearly fifty years, lasted until Auntee's death, in 1946. Maud was also very close to Auntee's daughter, Sallie Murry Williams. Together the three went to the movies at Oxford's only theater, often several times a week. Maud drove them to the dog races in Memphis, a sport that bored her but that her niece loved. Another lifetime friendship was with Maud's niece, Sallie Falkner Burns. Their mutual respect and affection is documented in letters Maud wrote to her in the 1950s.

In his extended adolescence (1914–25), Faulkner the would-be poet was stuck in other poets' voices. The chapters on his parents' marriage and his childhood in his white family document how Maud encouraged Willie to grow from imitator and impostor into his own authentic voice. They provide her with a past and explore further the life of her mind as revealed in her paintings and her letters to Sallie Falkner Burns.

In Oxford, Maud Butler's immediate family consisted only of her mother and her older brother, Sherwood Tate. But when she married into the much larger Falkner family, she brought with her a history of trauma that was ignored by biographers, until Joel Williamson brought attention to what for Maud must have been its most painful and shameful part. Between her tenth and sixteenth year, her father had subjected his family to a series of humiliating betrayals culminating in felony, miscegenation (which in Mississippi was illegal), and desertion. We know where the Falkners came from and who they were. We now know a good deal about Maud's father's family, the Butlers. But Williamson says almost nothing about Maud's mother's family, the Swifts, a history included here because of its relevance to understanding what she brought to her marriage, Callie Barr, her community and, most important, her eldest son.

Maud has been seen as a loner with few interests other than her four sons and, in later life, her painting. This is somewhat misleading. She was reserved and could be introverted and solitary, but she also maintained close lifelong friendships. She loved bridge and played regularly with other Oxford women. Some time after her husband died, the series of young, single, professional women whom she also befriended and who came to board with her included Christine Drake, Katharine Andrews, and Frances Ward, who became bridge partners and admirers of a woman they saw as independent and self-contained, with a quiet and occasionally withering wit. "She spoke almost in epigrams," observed Katharine Andrews.[6] Frances Ward bought many paintings Maud began to make, beginning in 1940. Maud also had a clear sense of who and what she was. She supported her son in his bid to be different from what Southern and Oxford conventions allowed. Furthermore, from 1918 through 1925, Faulkner's letters home indicate that she convinced her husband to join her.

Maud's personality and behavior were, in part, responses to others and to the current conditions under which she was living. Although many people, including Maud's granddaughter Jill, felt she could be remote and cold, Maud was not always so reserved. Jill also thought her grandmother, though never physically demonstrative, was like Jill's father in that she loved Jill more when she was a child than when she was grown.[7] She was perhaps most standoffish with family members whom she saw as, in any way, threatening her sons' love for her. The only daughter-in-law Maud seems to have treated as much loved was Louise Meadow, who married Dean, Maud's youngest son, and was widowed within three months. Louise and her daughter, Dean, named after her father who died four months before her birth, felt Maud was warm and loving. Yet, before their marriage, Maud's youngest son had told his wife-to-be, "You know, Louise, that Bill and mother will always come first." Louise claimed that "it didn't faze me," but she never had time to find out.[8]

Whatever disappointments, meanness, and vanquished dreams Maud's father, Charlie Butler, and her husband, Murry Falkner, had dealt her in her childhood and marriage were recompensed fourfold in the devotion and involvement all of her sons maintained with her throughout her long life. According to Faulkner, shortly before she died she told him that one of her concerns was that she might meet Murry in the afterlife. "Will I have to see him?" she asked. "Not if you don't want to," he assured her. "That's good. I never did like him," she replied.[9] This story may well be apocryphal—following convention, their sons buried Maud beside the husband she so disliked—but it tells a lot about her eldest son's sense of his relationship to both parents. Unlike the elaborate and proprietary epitaph Faulkner placed on Callie Barr's gravestone, his white mother's epitaph gives only

Maud Falkner's gravestone in Saint Peter's Cemetery,
Oxford, Miss., with Faulkner's inscription.
(Photo: Amy C. Evans)

her dates (1871–1960) and identifies her simply as "wife of Murry C. Falkner." Perhaps her sons felt their father's ownership was enough, or they felt no need to idealize and sentimentalize the mother whom Southern codes of white supremacy permitted them to love and respect. Or perhaps their feelings about their mother exceeded the boundaries of language.

Faulkner is reported to have visited his mother daily when he was in Oxford, which was most of his adult life. His brothers followed his example. According to Louise Meadow and others, from the 1930s to the 1950s the grown Falkner brothers' patterns did not vary much regarding time spent alone with their mother. "She knew Bill was coming every afternoon if he was here, and he did." Ella Somerville often saw Faulkner and "Miss Maud on her verandah, he in one rocker and she in the other, rocking out of phase with each other by the hour."[10] In the 1950s, when the Faulkners were living near Jill's family in Charlottesville, Maud, anticipating a visit, wrote Sallie Burns that "Billy's back in Virginia until April when he comes home to sit on the front porch with me every evening."[11]

As with Caroline Barr, Maud's lifelong relationship and influence on her eldest son's creative processes was profound. Maud and Lelia taught by example. Faulkner learned the languages of the visual arts along with his spoken language. And in exploring Faulkner's imaginative engagement with them, as with Callie Barr, these chapters treat not just Maud and

Faulkner in isolation but the constellation that includes family and friends and the Jim Crow culture of the North Mississippi town in which Maud and Callie and their respective extended families raised the four Falkner brothers. The legacies of slavery present in the post-Reconstruction South deformed the affective lives of both Maud's and her oldest son's generations. Maud and Lelia introduced him to other languages for probing that deformity.

Methodology

Despite Joseph Blotner's indispensable biography, little is really known about Maud Falkner—as daughter, mother, wife, or woman in her own right. He never interviewed her. Because she was educated, and highly literate and literary, and because she was white, we expect to find the usual documentary evidence. By all accounts, Maud was a private person. Hers was a specific kind of privacy developed in response to the two men with whom she lived—her father and then her husband. Maud grew up in a household filled with secrets made necessary by her father's constant social indiscretions and brushes with the law. She then married a man who was a mean drunk. Like so many of Faulkner's fictional fathers, he often had to be found and led home by his eldest son. As an adult, Maud maintained a household that was equally, if not more, secretive than the one in which she was reared. Thus, Maud's life, and particularly her relationship with her oldest son, is in some ways as difficult to reconstruct as Callie Barr's, though for different reasons.

There are few extant personal papers. Family members who were willing to share their knowledge and memories of Maud—particularly Jill Faulkner Summers and Louise Meadow—had no letters or other documents. Louise had given her letters, photographs, and other Falkner family papers she possessed to her daughter, Dean Faulkner Wells. Jill says that when Maud died, in 1960, her cousin Dean "came and cleaned out Granny's house." Any papers in Dean's possession were not available to me. At an early stage in my research, Dean allowed me to see and photograph some of her grandmother's paintings. But when she learned that my book was about her uncle, her grandmother, *and* Callie Barr, she refused any further access, saying, "I'm not doing anything for a book about some old black Mammy."[12] Dean's and Jill's cousin, Murry Cuthbert II ("Chooky") Faulkner, showed me one or two of Maud's cabin scenes, what he called his grandmother's "nigger pictures," which he had stored in his attic.[13] He did not respond to my requests for permission to reproduce them for this book. Like the fictional photographs in Faulkner's novels (see Chap. 12), most of

Maud's paintings of black people are missing from this book. Their absence represents another instance of the power of racism to occlude history and memory.

For the most part, interviewees had known Maud only in the last twenty years of her life, long after her sons were grown. Dean Faulkner Wells's master's thesis on Maud elaborates on information Dean offered in an interview in the 1980s. Although Maud saved 145 letters and postcards that Faulkner wrote to her and his father between 1918 and 1925, no one kept her side of that correspondence. Her spoken voice is captured in the few newspaper and magazine interviews she gave in the 1950s, when the press realized that, even though she would not grant interviews to talk about her famous son, she was happy to discuss her painting. Her intelligence and humor are preserved there, in stories and memories recounted by her relatives and women friends, and in her letters to Sallie Falkner Burns.

Besides information from other biographies and archival materials, there is one other source: Maud's art. Although hers is not great or even very good painting, it offers insight into her inner life and her artistic and cultural vision. During her last twenty years, Maud spent a good part of every day painting. Unlike her daughter-in-law Estelle, Maud had never liked cooking and had no interest in food or formal entertaining.[14] Although her design for the last house she and her husband lived in (on Lamar) included a dining room, once she began painting again, she set up her easel in that room. She never wore a smock or used a palette, claiming that the latter "just gets in the way." Instead she painted directly from the paint tube, mixing her pigments right on her canvas.[15] She wanted that physical, tactile closeness to her medium. Discussing her work habits in an interview, Maud said that "after breakfast 'if I feel like painting, I leave the dishes and go at it. If the spirit is moving, I paint right on through dinner. But once I get tired, I just walk out and leave it.'" This notion of imagination as a gift echoes in Faulkner's response to being asked about his work habits: "I write when the spirit moves me and the spirit moves me every single day." According to the reporter, "She seemed disconsolate" the day he interviewed her, for, "as she expressed it, 'I've been unable to do a lick of work for two weeks.'"[16] Her obituary reports that she completed some six hundred paintings between 1941 and her death, in 1960.[17] Few are extant.

Although she took an art course or two when she was enrolled in the technical program at the Mississippi State College for Women (MSCW, now the Mississippi University for Women) and, according to her own account, spent two weeks in a WPA-sponsored art course offered locally in 1940, she was not a "trained artist." Hers was what is now called "outsider art," although for the most part, it was not very outside. Her subjects were fairly traditional for Southern women of her generation and background: the kinds of paintings noted in Chapter 4, as well as the more commercially viable engraved wedding announcements, which she colored and decorated; and figurines made from a bought mold, which she hand-painted. Maud's paintings of the 1940s did not shape Faulkner's visual aesthetic. Yet, as we saw earlier, her portraits of black and white men and women and her cabin scenes, like her eldest son's fiction, illustrate both racial vigilance and its failure. As such they contribute to our understanding of Faulkner's triadic relationship with his two mothers and the role it played in his moral and aesthetic education. This education formed the bedrock of his racialized aesthetic.

From both Lelia and Maud, Faulkner learned at an early age that a photographic image could be easily altered. Since before his birth, his grandmother had given lessons in the "art of painting" or "coloring" photographs "to order."[18] Maud had given her son a box camera before he was a teenager, and throughout his life he remained fascinated by photography, photographs, and the technical process by which they were produced. Perhaps watching his grandmother and mother at their work led to his own manipulation of this process. Their upsetting of the premodern expectation that photographs record the truth also made him aware that photographs, like paintings, can lie, and that, like any art form, a photograph is a subjective version of the truth. This understanding would lead him to the Modernist visual aesthetic that is central to his contribution to Modernism. As the next chapters show, this aesthetic was formed at the knees of his mother and maternal grandmother, both of whom had a passionate attachment to the visual.

7.1. Maud's extensive and final revision of anonymous Mourning
painting of Lelia Dean Swift and Mahalah Pullen Swift. Maud
made these final revisions sometime after 1941.
(Courtesy of Jill Faulkner Summers)

7

Maud's Mysterious Ancestry
Wild Butlers and Wandering Swifts

> Lelia's background and ancestry remain mysteries. All we really know of
> her beginnings is that she was there in Oxford on July 31, 1868, to take
> out a license to marry Charlie Butler.
> —Joel Williamson

AULKNER'S FICTION TEEMS with wandering women. In his first
novel, *Soldiers' Pay*, Margaret Powers, a woman who marries men but
loves women, rides the rails from North to South. In the final frame
of her, she's on a train again, this time heading West—willfully homeless,
without destination, still fiercely desirous, still unattached. Lena Grove, in
Light in August, is Faulkner's most famous wandering woman. Unmarried
but pregnant, she sets off from Tennessee, supposedly in search of her
child's father. But at the novel's conclusion, like Margaret, she, too, is still
happily on the road, now with babe in arms. In *Go Down, Moses*, Faulkner's
last great work, Roth Edmonds's unnamed, mixed-race lover (also his
cousin) roams fearlessly into the rigidly gendered territory of Yoknapatawpha's Big Woods to call out the names of other outlawed desires and
call shame upon the hypocrites who forbid them. These women are descendants of such powerful American myths as the road heroine and the
traveling blues woman. They are also Faulkner's unique Southern rural incarnation of one of high Modernism's iconic figures, the flâneur. As in the
works of Gertrude Stein, H. D., Nella Larsen, and Virginia Woolf, the
flâneur, who in Baudelaire, Henry James, or T. S. Eliot is gendered male, is
often an irresolutely sexed and raced fallen woman, or—as Quentin Compson and his father obsess—"notvirgin." Figuratively, then, Faulkner's Southern flâneuse, a flagrant violation of gender and racial boundaries, even
when she is a white Southern Belle like Caddie Compson, is coded black.
Like Stein's most marvelous flâneuse, Melanctha, and Larsen's Claire Ken-

dry, many of Faulkner's wandering women are also literally or figuratively biracial.

Faulkner's flâneuse is a fictional representation of a historical reality manifest in the writer's own familial past as well as in American culture. Faulkner's maternal grandmother, Lelia Dean Swift, and Lelia's parents were among those wanderers who, beginning in the 1830s, sought to occupy and settle the vast tracts of government-confiscated Indian lands that stretched to the south and west. Lelia was born in Oxford, Mississippi, but from the time she was nine years old until her return to Oxford and marriage, in 1868, she was on the road. Twenty years later, when her husband, Charlie Butler, left them, she and her sixteen-year-old daughter, Maud, took to the road once more. Lelia did not settle permanently again until 1902, when Maud and her family moved from Ripley to Oxford and she joined her daughter's household.

Faulkner's work consistently stresses the psychologically and educationally crucial role such indomitable women played in creating the memories and shaping the imaginations of his parents' and his own generation. As he explains in "Mississippi," these women, most specifically his grandmothers, his mother, and Callie Barr, provided his earliest understanding of how his world worked. The children learned their lessons well. Even "the games they played, aped in miniature" the stories they had been "exposed to, heard or seen or been moved by most" (16).

Family lore portrays Lelia as the defiant artist-daughter of a Baptist father who deemed all artwork blasphemous, a mother who initially refused to recognize her only daughter's marriage, and a grandmother who spent her days sculpting, painting, or giving art lessons in a variety of mediums. Yet she took time to teach her oldest grandchild Willie to draw and paint and to carve dolls for her grandchildren, and, when playing with them in the Falkners' yard, entered freely into the neighborhood children's games.

A vivid presence in her Willie's life for his first nine and a half years, she, and to a somewhat lesser extent Maud, remain ciphers. Lelia's origins are unknown. Her marriage to Charles E. Butler on 2 August 1868, recorded in the Lafayette County Courthouse, is the earliest documentation of her existence.[1] In North Mississippi, as in most of the South, family history is a valued possession. For many white Southerners—especially those of Lelia's or Maud's generations—it connected to and defined them in terms of the South's glorious, mythologized past, as epitomized in cavalier and plantation legends. Both the Falkner and Oldham family-origin stories participate in these myths—the Falkners descend from a Scots Highlands clan, whereas the Oldham-Allen ancestors either arrived on the *Mayflower* or could trace their lineage to the Swiss baron de Graffenried, founder of New Bern and scion of North Carolina royalty. Mississippi invents, records, treasures, and guards its white ancestry; even in the smallest towns, a room in the public library is always given over to genealogy. There, lining the walls, stand detailed books of grave markers, including graveyard maps compiled by the county's white citizens. Local historical societies spend decades jointly writing and publishing their county histories. Yet oddly, there is no mention of Lelia's family in the Lafayette County histories.

According to all current accounts, in 1868, at age nineteen, Lelia Dean Swift "abrupted" into Oxford as suddenly and as apparently devoid of kin and acquaintances as her grandson's fictional Thomas Sutpen. Her marriage that year to Charlie Butler, the sixth and last child of Charles and Berlina Butler, one of the town's founding and still prominent families, also has no history. She appeared. They married. The only record of her birth is on her gravestone, which lies in her husband's family plot.[2] Even her parents' birthplaces—Mississippi, Tennessee, and Arkansas have all been given by different sources—are unknown.[3]

There is one surviving photograph of Lelia and her young daughter, Maud; the unsigned and undated Mourning portrait painted of Lelia and her mother, Mahalah Pullen Swift (see frontispiece, this Chap.);[4] and a still life probably painted by Lelia. This photograph, the portrait, Lelia's still life, her neighbors' and grandchildren's brief memories, and notices in the local papers where she advertised her skills as artist and teacher are all that document her committed and highly disciplined imaginative life, one her famous grandson would emulate.[5] Like hers, his began in rebellion and was dedicated to art.[6]

Faulkner studies has been slow to ask the kinds of paradigm-shifting questions that feminist historians, beginning with Anne Firor Scott (1970), have been fruitfully pursuing for over three decades. Even Faulkner's mother had no past until 1993, when Joel Williamson, in a chapter called "The Butlers," provided the first written account of her *paternal* history. He confined her maternal history to the epigraph with which I began this chapter. As Williamson writes about Maud, "The history behind Maud Butler appeared to be barely worth mentioning, especially in comparison with that of old Colonel Falkner and his son, John Wesley Thompson Falkner."[7] Why do these women's stories matter? The more pertinent question is, rather, why don't they matter at least as much as the one, always foregrounded, of the artist's great grandfather? Unlike the Colonel's brief foray into literature, which he abandoned for the law and entrepreneurship, Lelia's practice of her art was a lifetime pursuit. Unlike Colonel W. C. Falkner, who died seven years before Faulkner's birth, Lelia, both artist and

7.2. Lelia Swift Butler (*left*) and her daughter, Maud Butler
(later Falkner). (Courtesy of Jill Faulkner Summers)

grandmother, was a daily presence and an early model. She visited her
daughter's family often until they moved to Oxford, and then lived with
them until her death five years later. By then Willie Falkner had soaked in
her passions and prejudices, her hates and fears. And, it appears, he had
learned her work habits: her ability to lose herself in her art. He also knew
her stories; like Quentin Compson, "His childhood was full of them, his
very body was an empty hall echoing with sonorous defeated names, he
was not a being, an entity, he was a commonwealth" (*AA,* 7). When he was
asked once where he got his characters, Faulkner replied, "I listen to the
voices." His maternal grandmother's voice was among them.[8]

Lelia Butler's Story

The Falkner family members tell two essentially similar versions of the
young Lelia's circumvention of her father's commands forbidding her to be
an artist. In both, when her father, "a Baptist of the hard-shell variety"
who "thought that any creation which came out of thin air, like painting,
was the work of the devil," catches his daughter painting pictures, he con-
fiscates her paints and tells her "never to touch them again." Lelia's probably somewhat apocryphal response was to save up and buy more materials.

She then had one of her father's slaves row her out to the middle of a nearby lake, where she could paint and "no one could tell what she was doing."[9] A lake is shown on a topographical map of the last farm Lelia's father purchased in Drew County, Marion Township, Arkansas, which lends credence to the story. The map also supports the evidence, as I have reconstructed it from public documents, that Lelia was born in Oxford, the last late child of the Butlers' fellow congregants, the farmer and slave-owner John Tate and his wife, Mahalah Pullen Swift. In another version of this tale, Lelia hides beneath her parents' house. Stories of her father's attempts to prevent her from painting are coupled with later tales of deprivation and unfulfilled promise.[10] Jack Falkner wrote that his mother, Maud, had told him that "shortly after the war, some northern art society," noting her mother's talent, had offered to send Lelia to Italy to study, but that "Damuddy [Lelia] had declined."[11] No evidence can be found to support this story.

John, however, tells another tale that suggests where Lelia's grandson might have inherited his powers of concentration. Again, according to Falkner family lore, at one point between Maud's semesters at the Mississippi Industrial Institute and College in Columbus, she and Lelia lived in Texarkana. One morning Maud left for work while Lelia began washing their dishes. John writes that when his mother came home for dinner at noon, "there was Damuddy sitting at the sink making the statue of the little Negro boy. No dinner was ready and the breakfast dishes hadn't been washed." His grandmother had started to wash them but instead was distracted and fascinated by the creative possibilities latent in the melting soap bar. So she "simply sat down and began making the statue. She hadn't moved since Mother left that morning" (*MBB*, 124). Although the story may be a stretch, its intent is clear—to present a working artist, even though her medium was kitchen soap. Willie also heard Lelia's tale of making whiteness by carving a black boy from a soap bar. The sculpture's liminal presence is there in Faulkner's recurring tropes of washing the bodies of blackened white children like Caddy Compson and Thomas Sutpen's outcast octoroon grandson.

Jack's first memory of Damuddy is of her "busy at her easel."[12] Rose Rowland, who was a little older than Willie and often played with the Falkner brothers on South Street when their grandmother was living, portrays her in a way that reveals the difference between her and most grandparents of Faulkner's contemporaries. According to Rose, "Damuddy was a wonderful person" who spent much time with her grandchildren. She didn't just sit and watch them but entered into their games, "playing with us and showing us how to build little villages of sticks, rocks, and other odds and ends. . . . We even built stockades by driving sticks in the ground around the little huts, which had roofs made of grass. We hunted for pretty pieces of broken glass, pebbles, stones. We built walks, streets, churches, and stores." Rose was swept up in the imaginary worlds created jointly by grandmother and grandson: "Both William and his grandmother were good at improvising and using the materials at hand. At the time I didn't fully realize that this was what they were doing. It all seemed so realistic to us. William was the leader in these little projects. He had his grandmother's artistic talents for making things, and his imagination was obvious even then."[13]

Two women who boarded with Maud in the 1930s, when they first moved to Oxford, said that "Miss Maud felt that Faulkner's talent as a creative person comes from the Butler, not the Falkner side." A contemporary of Maud's, explaining how Lelia as a suddenly single mother had supported Maud, said that "Mrs. Butler was very sensitive to beauty. She painted sets for local plays; she made hats; she did anything she could turn her hands to to support her daughter." She also saw to it that Maud got an education that would make it easier for her to be economically independent if she chose. At a time and in a place where very few white women even finished high school, Lelia, a single parent with no professional training, managed to earn enough to help send her daughter to the only college for (white) women in Mississippi.[14]

I include these stories about Lelia Butler because William Faulkner's maternal grandmother also saw herself and was seen by her daughter, Maud, and Maud's sons as a woman who was different *because* she was an artist. Lelia died of uterine cancer in the summer of 1907, at the age of fifty-eight, when Willie was nine and a half, Jack seven, and John five and a half.[15] She had been a compelling daily presence in the Falkner household for the first nine years of Willie's life.

Maud's and Lelia's Ancestry

Who were Lelia's parents and siblings? How did she come to marry the fun-loving Charlie Butler, who became the infamous felon, miscegenist, and deadbeat dad? Why has even the story of the breakup of her marriage—which includes both theft and the violation of the most sacred white Southern racial-sexual taboo—only recently been told?[16] Perhaps his sudden and scandalous disappearance in 1887 made Charlie's past a forbidden subject in the Butler family. Why would Lelia's daughter, Maud, and her grandson Willie know nothing about Lelia's own family, the Swifts? Why, particularly in these circumstances, which are at least as lurid and fascinating as the Colonel's story and as representative of life on the Southern frontier, have the histories of Faulkner's mother and grandmother been considered inconsequential by his critics and biographers?

Lelia Dean Swift Butler's gravestone, in Oxford's St. Peter's Cemetery, gives her dates as 5 March 1849 to 1 June 1907. Yet, not until 1880 does the Lafayette County census list her. There she appears as "Lelia," "keeping house" and "wife of C(harles) E. Butler, Police." She is thirty, and her husband thirty-one. The ages of Lelia's and Charlie's children, Sherwood Tate (20 May 1869–2 June 1930) and Maud (27 November 1871–16 October 1960), are given as eleven and eight.

The spirited young woman Charlie Butler married did not appear out of nowhere. Furthermore, she and Charlie were hardly strangers. The Butlers and Swifts and other Swift relations had known one another since the mid-1830s, when both families came to Lafayette County to buy land and settle on the Mississippi frontier. The land they all bought from the federal government had belonged to the Chickasaw Nation. Charlie's parents, Berlina and Charles G., like Lelia's, came originally from North Carolina; both the Swifts and Butlers first attended the Cumberland Presbyterian Church in Oxford; the Butlers and Mahalah Swift's parents, the Pullens, were neighbors; in 1836 George Pullen served on the first Police Court, while Charlie's father served as the county's first sheriff; Charlie's and Lelia's fathers both had helped lay out the county's lines as well as a road to the county line. Both Charlie and Lelia were born in Oxford within a year of each other. In short, when Charlie Butler married Lelia Swift, he was marrying a hometown girl, even though she had moved with her parents to Drew County, Arkansas, some nine or ten years before and had only recently returned to Oxford following the deaths of her father, in 1865, and her mother, in 1867 (see fig 7.3).

How do we know Lelia was the daughter of *these* Swifts? John R., the Swifts' fourth son, became a newspaper editor and the family biographer.[17] In a brief sketch for the 1890 Arkansas volume from Goodspeed, he gives his parents' migratory history and their death dates.[18] A search for Swifts in the 1840 and 1850 Lafayette County census and in the County Deed Books turns up, among others, the family of a John *Tate* Swift and his wife, Mahalah A.[19] Lelia named her first child Sherwood Tate. It would have been customary for her to name him after her recently deceased father, which is what she did. (Sherwood was for Berlina Butler's father, Sherwood House.) Yet, Lelia does not appear to be listed as one of John Tate and Mahalah Swift's children on the 1850 Lafayette County census. As was common, however, the census taker made many errors. Mahalah Swift appears as Maha, a grown child's gender is reversed, and the ages of three Swift chil-

7.3. Swift-Butler-Fa(u)lkner Genealogy

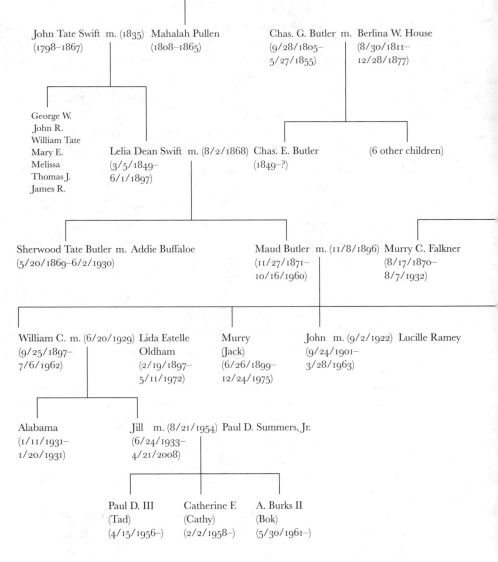

George Pullen m. Dolly ?

John Tate Swift m. (1835) Mahalah Pullen
(1798–1867)   (1808–1865)

Chas. G. Butler m. Berlina W. House
(9/28/1805–   (8/30/1811–
5/27/1855)   12/28/1877)

George W.
John R.
William Tate
Mary E.   Lelia Dean Swift m. (8/2/1868) Chas. E. Butler   (6 other children)
Melissa   (3/5/1849–   (1849–?)
Thomas J.   6/1/1897)
James R.

Sherwood Tate Butler m. Addie Buffaloe   Maud Butler m. (11/8/1896) Murry C. Falkner
(5/20/1869–6/2/1930)   (11/27/1871–   (8/17/1870–
                                                10/16/1960)   8/7/1932)

William C. m. (6/20/1929) Lida Estelle   Murry   John m. (9/2/1922) Lucille Ramey
(9/25/1897–   Oldham   (Jack)   (9/24/1901–
7/6/1962)   (2/19/1897–   (6/26/1899–   3/28/1963)
                          5/11/1972)   12/24/1975)

Alabama   Jill m. (8/21/1954) Paul D. Summers, Jr.
(1/11/1931–   (6/24/1933–
1/20/1931)   4/21/2008)

Paul D. III   Catherine F.   A. Burks II
(Tad)   (Cathy)   (Bok)
(4/15/1956–)   (2/2/1958–)   (5/30/1961–)

Source: Swift-Butler genealogy compiled from the 1850 census for Lafayette County, Mississippi: the 1860 census for Drew County, Arkansas; land deeds; and other archival sources. Falkner genealogy compiled and adapted from Williamson, *William Faulkner*, 64–67, 514. Faulkner genealogy compiled and adapted from Sensibar, *Origins* and interviews.

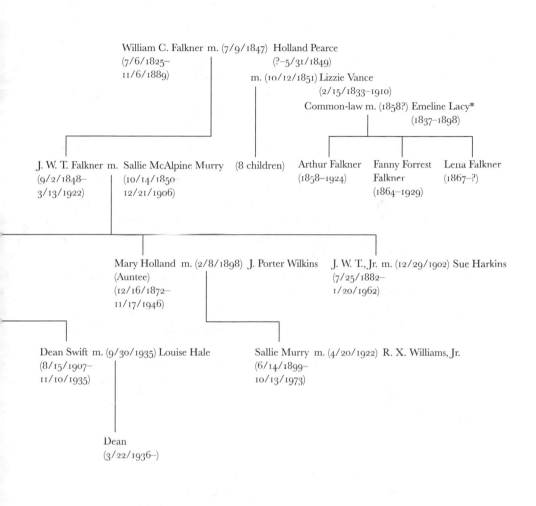

William C. Falkner m. (7/9/1847) Holland Pearce
(7/6/1825–   (?–5/31/1849)
11/6/1889)
                    m. (10/12/1851) Lizzie Vance
                                (2/15/1833–1910)
                    Common-law m. (1858?) Emeline Lacy*
                                            (1837–1898)

J. W. T. Falkner m. Sallie McAlpine Murry   (8 children)   Arthur Falkner   Fanny Forrest   Lena Falkner
(9/2/1848–   (10/14/1850–   (1858–1924)   Falkner   (1867–?)
3/13/1922)   12/21/1906)   (1864–1929)

Mary Holland m. (2/8/1898) J. Porter Wilkins   J. W. T., Jr. m. (12/29/1902) Sue Harkins
(Auntee)   (7/25/1882–
(12/16/1872–   1/20/1962)
11/17/1946)

Dean Swift m. (9/30/1935) Louise Hale   Sallie Murry m. (4/20/1922) R. X. Williams, Jr.
(8/15/1907–   (6/14/1899–
11/10/1935)   10/13/1973)

Dean
(3/22/1936–)

*In September 1858, Col. W. C. Falkner bought Emeline Lacy and her three children, Delia (1853–1918), Hellen (1854–1940), and the unborn Arthur, for $900.00. Williamson, 64–67, 514.

dren are given as twenty years old. The Swifts' youngest children are named as "Selar," a girl aged three, and James, a boy aged one. Yet James is listed as thirteen years old on the 1860 census. It appears that the census taker also confused the genders and ages of the two youngest children and that Selar, or Lelar—the S's and L's are indistinguishable—was actually the Swifts' one-year-old baby girl, Lelia Dean Swift. Pooling other information from John R.'s biography in Goodspeed's *Biographical and Historical Memoirs: Southern Arkansas* with facts gleaned from government documents provides at least a sketch of the kind of family Lelia grew up in and of her life before she and Charlie Butler married.

John R. describes his parents' lifelong search for profitable farmland.[20] The Swifts and Mahalah's parents, the George Pullens (or Pullians or Pulliams), were originally from North Carolina. Since the 1820s, these farming families had been migrating steadily south and west. By 1836 they had arrived in Oxford, shortly after the Butlers. Thus, unlike the Falkners, who did not move to Oxford until 1885, Maud's grandparents on *both* sides were among Oxford's original white settlers.

Mahalah Pullen (1808–65) and John Tate Swift (1798–1867) were both born in North Carolina. Sometime in the early 1800s, both families left North Carolina for Georgia, where they settled in Morgan County on farmland some fifty miles southeast of Atlanta. In 1820, when Mahalah was twelve and her husband-to-be was twenty-two, the Pullens and Swifts were still living there. But by 1830, John Tate and Mahalah had married and, with their first three children, had moved to Newton County, just to the west. There, in 1833, Mahalah bore John R., their fourth child. As he wrote for Goodspeed, he was the last of the Swifts' eight living children to be born in Georgia.

By 1835, the Swifts had pulled up stakes again for Oxford, Mississippi, now with five children, plus Mahalah's parents and four slaves. In Oxford they purchased land made available by the U.S. Government's final removal of the Chickasaw Nation from its homeland.[21] Both the Swift and Butler families served on the county's first governing board. In 1838 John Tate Swift appears on the town's first tax roll as the owner of 250 acres of farmland near the edge of town.[22] The 1842 Combination Tax Roll is extremely useful, because it places individuals in neighborhood order. From it we learn that besides serving together on the town's supervisory board, the Butlers and Pullens, Lelia's maternal grandparents, lived only fourteen houses apart. By 1843, the Swifts had moved next door to Lelia's Pullen grandparents.[23] These facts, plus their earlier church connection, make it reasonable to say that Lelia and little Charlie Butler, both late and youngest children of large families, probably had known each other and played together from early childhood.

Faulkner's grandmother came of age in a place and at a time in American history when living off stolen land and human chattel was a legally sanctioned way of life for the majority of the South's white families. Although they never owned huge tracts of land and hundreds of slaves, as did Lafayette County's richest planters, Lelia's parents were slaveholders, cotton growers, and farmers. Lelia was a plantation owner's daughter, even though the Swift plantation was small.[24] From Callie Barr, Willie had learned something about what it meant to be a slave; from Lelia he learned what it meant to be a master. As he writes so graphically in "Mississippi," one of the earliest lessons embedded in his grandmother's stories, and the tales her brother John had told her of fighting at Bull Run and Shiloh, was the God-given or natural right of white masters.[25]

Like many slaveholders who used religion to justify their personal, political, and economic racist practices, Lelia's parents were deeply religious. Cumberland Presbyterians were much closer to Primitive (popularly called "hard-shell") Baptists in that they held that anyone who was "called" could preach.[26] By 1842, Berlina Butler had left Cumberland to become one of the founders and charter members of Oxford's first Baptist Church, but the Swifts remained members of the Cumberland congregation.[27]

Throughout the 1840s and early 1850s, John Tate Swift had continued to buy farmland in Lafayette County. Lelia's father increased his slaveholdings steadily from five slaves of taxable age in 1840, to eight in 1850, to seventeen in 1855, and at least twenty-one in 1858, two years before the family probably moved from Oxford to Drew County, Arkansas.[28]

The mystery is why, at this time in their lives, they moved to a much more backward, poorer, and undeveloped part of the country. By 1860, John and Mahalah were sixty-two and fifty-two, quite old to begin homesteading again. Yet in this period, just before the Civil War, Arkansas showed "rapid economic growth. Taxable property increased from $42,900,080 in 1852 to $99,872,248 in 1858," with most of the increase occurring toward the end of this period: "Between 1856 and 1858 taxable property increased by almost half. Population between 1835 and 1860 had a more than eightfold increase, from 51,000 to 435,000. Between 1858–60, it increased by 100,000."[29] Traveling in Arkansas around 1857–58 to buy land, John Tate would have been part of this population and cotton boom.

Nevertheless, what happened next to John Tate and Mahalah Swift in Arkansas appears to have been disaster. In 1861 John was sued for a debt of sixteen hundred dollars. The debt holder was William Olivar, the man from whom he'd bought his Arkansas land in 1859. The profit he'd made by selling his land in Oxford in 1861 was not sufficient to cover this debt. The amount he owed on his Arkansas farm was half the price of the tract listed in the original contract, which suggests that he had paid for the land by note and had defaulted. Court records show that he failed to defend himself in that suit and a judgment was issued against him. If he hadn't paid within a reasonable period, his creditor could have seized and sold his tract at public auction. This would account for the disposal of Swift's property without a deed recorded under his name. Swift's absence from the tax rolls after 1862 strengthens the supposition that somehow he lost his land. If he had lost his farm for debt during the Civil War, he would have been forced to sell his remaining assets—his slaves and livestock. During wartime this might have been almost impossible.

Their son, John R., mentions none of this in his optimistic family sketch. But he does report that his father and mother died in Mississippi. There is no record of their deaths in Lafayette County. Somehow, their eighteen-year-old daughter, Lelia, seems to have returned alone.

The idea of her traveling from Arkansas to Mississippi, carrying little or nothing of her past but an oil portrait of her mother and herself, is as touching and comic as Faulkner's road images of her probable fictional namesake, the wandering Lena Grove. Perhaps fond memories of Charlie Butler spurred Lelia's return. Perhaps after her parents' financial failure and deaths, she wanted to be sure that she married into a family that would provide economic stability in her adult life. What better choice than the youngest son of her family's old Oxford friends, Charles and Berlina Butler? Even with the loss of the Butler Hotel, which occupying troops had burned to the ground in 1864, only days before the fall of Atlanta, the Butlers were still among the town's richest families. Furthermore, they were clearly town people. After her experience as a planter's daughter, she had no interest in farming, an occupation she knew was fraught with risk. Besides, for a would-be artist, town life offered more possibilities to market her skills.

As the daughter of a small slaveholder and planter, William's maternal grandmother might at first appear to share the same background as Faulkner's fictional white Southern landed ladies who lived through the Civil War. In reality, she lived a much more precarious existence in a family whose defining characteristic is that they were always on the move. The bare bones of Lelia's parents' biographical profile indicate that from the time of their marriage (c. 1830) to their deaths they had bought, worked, and sold farms and slaves in no fewer than three states and five counties. Unlike her grandson's fictional Southern planters' ladies, whose outwardly stable and timeless existences ended abruptly in the chaos and defeat of the Civil War, Lelia came of age in a household whose father was possessed by wanderlust. Any stability she had known on her father's small plantation just outside Oxford ended when she was nine or ten and her family packed up and left for the Arkansas frontier. That at eighteen she had no interest in continuing frontier life seems clear from the choice she made to return to Oxford rather than join the families of any of her elder siblings, even though at least two of her brothers had opted for town life over farming and were then living and working in Kingsland, one of Arkansas's larger towns.[30]

The Butler Family

Charlie Butler, Maud's father, was the sixth and youngest child of Charles G., Oxford's first sheriff, surveyor, and innkeeper, and his wife, Berlina House Butler. At his birth, Berlina was thirty-eight and his father was forty-three. Eighteen years separated Charlie from his eldest brother, William R., and eight from his parents' second youngest child, Martha K. In 1855, when Charlie was seven, his father died and Berlina continued to run their inn.[31]

Berlina proved an accomplished businesswoman. By 1860, she had doubled the appraised value of the hotel. At his death her husband's estate had been valued at $21,341.55. In the 1860 census, her holdings were $40,000 in real estate and $10,000 in personal property. She now also owned twelve slaves, six of whom were female.[32] Between them, Berlina and her eldest sons, William and Henry, owned $95,000 in property. Berlina's wealth alone was equal to Colonel W. C. Falkner's. With that of her two sons added, her family's worth was double that of the Falkners and far in excess of the Swifts.

Until the Butler Hotel was torched in 1864, it and the family farm continued to prosper.[33] In August 1864, when Union soldiers burned the Oxford town square, which included the hotel, the Butlers lost most of their fortune.[34] Charlie was sixteen years old. In December 1865, Berlina sold the hotel land and other property around the square for only twenty-eight hundred dollars. Henry had died in the war but her eldest son, William, began rebuilding privately and publicly. Like his father, he was a member of the City Council as an alderman and, like John Tate Swift earlier, William built and repaired Oxford's streets. In November of the following year, Berlina felt solvent enough to send Charlie to Ole Miss in accordance with the wishes in his father's will. But college held no allure for him; he stayed only a year. In 1867, Berlina continued divesting herself of her property, selling off "nine prime residential lots" on South Street for eighteen hundred dollars. In February 1868, William died suddenly and Charlie became the oldest living male Butler.

On August 2 of that year, Charlie and Lelia married in Oxford, with the Reverend Whitehead officiating.[35] Charlie was almost the same age as J. W. T. Falkner, the man who became William Faulkner's paternal grandfather, the only one he knew. Besides their age, his maternal and paternal grandfathers had one passion in common, namely, a kind of relationship their grandson would frequently return to in his fiction. Both men married white women but took black women as lovers, and both made little or no effort to conceal their behavior from their families. As one elderly Oxford lady noted dryly, "I grew up with the Falkners and the Oldhams, and William's other grandfather, J. W. T. Falkner, had a Negro woman, too. My father's porter at the store [Neilson's] was the husband of this woman. William's Aunt Holland [J. W. T.'s daughter, "Auntee"] used to say when she was driving her father's buggy and the horse would stop in front of this woman's house, 'It makes me so damn mad. The horse always wants to stop whenever he gets to this place!' After I got grown up, they told me why."[36] Knowing that her daughter had married a man whose father, though well to do, was no more committed to his marriage than her own husband had been would have added to Lelia's concerns for Maud and must have broken Lelia's heart. There is no evidence that Faulkner knew of these betrayals, which were customary but illegal.[37] He never would have spoken of them because, like his attachment to Callie Barr, such things were unspeakable. His fiction is devoted to that unspeakability and its dreadful emotional and physical toll.

Wandering Lelia and Wild Charlie

Lelia and Charlie's marriage was not a success. No personal testimony, diaries, or letters survive, but court records, church records, newspapers, and other public documents reveal that the house in which Faulkner's mother, Maud, grew up was filled with anxiety, disappointment, betrayals, and probably physical abuse. Charlie Butler, though clearly popular with Oxford's voters (its white male population), lived on the edge. Throughout his marriage, he was in constant and, ultimately, serious trouble with both secular and religious authorities. In late 1887, he robbed the city of funds he had been elected to collect and administer and then walked out on his wife, his eighteen-year-old son, and his sixteen-year-old daughter, leaving them without income. By then he had also been thrown out of the First Baptist Church, and he had shot a man but had been acquitted of murder.

By the time he disappeared from Oxford, he had openly flouted the town's racial, religious, social, and legal codes. Even by frontier standards—Oxford was a frontier town when his parents migrated there from North Carolina via Tennessee in the 1830s—Charlie's behavior, like that of William Faulkner's paternal great-grandfather, grandfather, and father, was extreme. Thus, William Faulkner inherited from the fathers of both his mother and father a history of and penchant for physical and psychological violence, as well as for miscegenous marital discord. From other family members he inherited a legacy of ancestors who could write and paint.

Charlie did not follow his parents' and staid older brothers' example. Brought up in the family inn, Charlie was early introduced to and enamored of gambling, public dancing, and other entertainments offered to the inn's guests. Other than a brief stint in a confectionery business that failed, Charlie's livelihood was his sheriff's job and associated duties, for which he was paid the comfortable salary of twelve hundred dollars per year.[38] What little is known about him personally suggests that he was charming, smart, and efficient, but that he was also dishonest, short-tempered, and used to getting his way. He was well liked among the men who ran Oxford, who elected him town marshal six times. But until his first election in 1876, a job he held for the next eleven years, he seems to have been unsuccessful at making a living.[39] Although he and Lelia married in 1868, they are not listed anywhere in the 1870 Mississippi census, suggesting that they, like many other Mississippians, may have initially gone west to seek their fortune.

However, since both Maud and Sherwood Tate were born in Mississippi, it is also possible that during the first three years of their marriage the Butlers either lived in rooming houses or boarded with various relatives.[40] In any case, the First Baptist Church records indicate that by 1871 they had returned to Oxford for good.[41] In 1872, Charlie's mother turned over three lots of ten acres, each worth $1,500, as his share of his father's estate.[42] He must have sold them almost immediately and spent the proceeds on consumables, because he does not show up on the county tax rolls until 1874, where he is listed as a merchandiser, being part owner of the confectionery business, but apparently owning no land. His principal taxable possessions are a horse and carriage, a pistol, and a watch, all totaling $107.00.[43] By 1875 Charlie's short-lived business had failed, and he was borrowing money to support his wife and two children, aged five and three. Not until his election as marshal of Oxford one year later did his family begin to have a steady and sufficient income.[44]

After she and Charlie married, Lelia became pregnant almost immediately. Their son, Sherwood Tate, was born a little more than nine months later, on 20 May 1869. Lelia bore Maud two and a half years after that, on 27 November 1871.[45] That these were their only children in an era of large families is not sufficient to conclude that the Butlers' marriage was unhappy. Other evidence, however, suggests that Charlie was not much of a husband or parent. When he deserted Lelia and her children after twenty years of marriage, he humiliated them in the most public manner and devastated them economically. In December 1887, one of the coldest in Oxford's history, Charlie Butler disappeared, along with town money and, according to town gossip, an "octoroon" woman who had worked for the Jacob Thompsons, one of the wealthiest planter families in northeastern Mississippi.[46] Some say "he joined a Negro woman in Chicago," but all agree that afterwards "Lelia supported herself and her daughter in Oxford by various means, including at one point, a small hat shop."[47] That Charlie left his family in dire financial straits, as dire as Miss Emily's in Faulkner's "A Rose for Emily," is indicated by a bill of sale for the Butlers' house recorded in February 1888, two months after Charlie's disappearance. In 1880, to secure a debt he never paid, Charlie deeded his family's house to a Mr. B. Roach. On 30 January 1888, fearing he would never be paid, Roach advertised Lelia's and her children's house as for sale. At this point, according to the deed, "Harry Carothers and others contributed the purchase price of said land as a gift to Mrs. L. D. Butler and her children," with the proviso that if Lelia "at any time hereafter to resumes her marital situation with C. E. Butler she shall thereby forego all her interest in said property to Maud and Sherwood Butler."[48] This is a remarkable transaction, for it demonstrates the lengths to which the town went to care for the wife and children of a man who had stiffed them and violated his wife's "sacred honor." Had Lelia and Charlie not been the descendants of Oxford's founders, would Carothers and other residents have moved so swiftly to rescue Lelia and her children? The terms of the deed may also indicate the town patriarchs' wish to maintain control over what they had given Lelia, and their lack of trust in her judgment. Or perhaps their intent was to protect her property from Charlie, should he ever return.

Nor was this the end of public humiliation for Lelia and her children. Less than a month later, on 5 April, a notice signed by Oxford's new sheriff appeared in the *Oxford Eagle* and was posted on the courthouse doors. It advertised the auction of the rest of Charlie Butler's assets. This notice read in part: "I will on Monday 7 April 1888 at the courthouse door in Oxford . . . expose to sale at public outcry to the highest bidder all the rights, interest, and claim of the defendant C. E. Butler has in and to the following" assets.[49] Finally, on 21 June the City Board met with Charlie's bondsmen and reached a settlement concerning the "deficit in the town funds."[50]

Yet well into October, notices from individuals suing the Butler estate appeared regularly in the Oxford papers.[51] A further humiliation was the family's sudden poverty. Overnight, and for the second time in her life, Lelia became almost totally dependent on the kindness of others.

Even now, people disappear all the time in this country; in the late nineteenth century it was a much simpler matter. There is no extant record of Charlie's life once he left Oxford, nor of his death or burial. Maud apparently never spoke of her father to her children. She did, however, once tell her daughter-in-law Louise that her father did not think girls needed formal schooling. In an escalation of her mother's story about defying *her* father, Maud added that when her father still lived with them, she needed to hide under the latticework of their porch to read or do homework.

Why did he leave as he did? Charlie Butler's difficulties with authority and in his marriage began long before late 1887, when, in his sixth term as town marshal, he skipped town. There is no record that explains why Maud's father didn't last long at Ole Miss, but the meetings of the town board and the Baptist church records provide evidence of his difficulties in conforming to either secular or religious rules. As town marshal he was, in effect, Oxford's general manager. One of his duties was to collect taxes and pay out wages for work done for the county. In 1880 and 1881 his books failed to balance.[52] The amounts missing were not great and the board was lenient; Butler's parents and his wife's parents were among Oxford's founding families; as Oxford's "tax collector, purchasing agent, engineer, disbursing officer, and general manager for a host of other town functions," he was efficient; and he was well liked by the people who counted.[53] Similar problems occurred in 1883. In 1881 he also seems to have been unaccountably away from Oxford a great deal, so much so that in January 1882 the board passed an ordinance forbidding the marshal to leave town without the mayor's approval.[54]

Then, in the spring of 1883, a volatile side of Charlie's character became part of the public record. In front of a large crowd on the town square, he shot and killed the editor and owner of the *Oxford Eagle*, Sam Thompson, when he resisted arrest for public drunkenness and obscenity.[55] This was far from the first time Butler had arrested Thompson on such charges; furthermore, Thompson was due in court the next day to answer a much more serious charge: abducting and debauching a minor.[56] Under the circumstances, Charlie's deadly response was unnecessary and cruel. In light of his own marital behavior and subsequent crimes, his merciless treatment of Thompson, who was drunk and unarmed, seems inexplicable. Yet Oxford's was a frontier culture and Charlie was the town's elected sheriff: "The end result was that a jury acquitted Butler of all charges."[57]

Another of Charlie's difficulties began in church. During the course of his marriage his run-ins with church elders had steadily escalated. Records of the First Baptist Church document what can be read as a story of continual marital discord from 1871 on. The Butler family's church ties were long and strong. Besides being founders and active members since at least the 1840s, Charlie's parents had donated the land on which the church was built, at the corner of North 13th and Madison Ave.[58] He had grown up and was active in this church, which Lelia also joined in June 1873, some five years after her return to Oxford and marriage and after the births of her children. Yet, the more committed Lelia (and their children) became to Charlie's church, beginning with her baptism in June 1873, the more Charlie challenged and violated church law.[59] In 1871, he was in such good standing that he was chosen as one of three delegates to represent his congregation at the annual meeting of the Baptist Association. But by January 1874, six months after his wife's baptism, the elders were meeting to discipline him. Charged with attending *and* dancing at a hotel Christmas ball in December, Charlie defended himself by saying that "he did not feel he was doing any harm by the act but if he had given any offense to the Church . . . he hoped to be forgiven." The elders were satisfied, "granted that he be not guilty of the offense any more."[60]

Lelia, however, was a different matter. Once aware that her husband's extramarital activities were the talk of her newly adopted congregation and the subject of possible disciplinary action, she may not have felt so forgiving. No more incidents are recorded in the extant church records until almost nine years later, but these subsequent charges indicate that Charlie continued to pursue banned pleasures—namely, gambling and public dancing. It may be coincidence that his next serious break with the church occurred two weeks before ten-year-old Maud's baptism. On 1 July 1882, he resigned his deaconship.[61] Thus, for the second time, Charlie cast a pall over what should have been a joyful religious ceremony and family occasion. Worse, he publicly shamed his family, in particular little Maud. Her lack of involvement with organized religion in later years and her son's deep probing of the crippling psychological effects of organized religion on the minds of children, most memorably in *Light in August*, may find their initial inspiration in the childhood experiences of Faulkner's mother, which, without speaking explicitly of her father's role, Maud passed on to her children.

The next year was frightening for the Butler household. Sherwood and Maud, then fourteen and twelve, were probably part of the large crowd in the square who watched their father kill the *Eagle*'s editor early that May. In any case, whether they saw it or not, they heard eyewitness reports from classmates and read about it in the papers. This, apparently, was the last straw for Charlie's church elders. By 23 September 1883, some five months after he had killed Thompson and been indicted for manslaughter, the elders finally signaled that they had had enough. No mention is made of the manslaughter charges, perhaps because Charlie had not yet been tried. Instead they cited lesser crimes, resolving that "whereas Brother Charles E. Butler has by his own admission repeatedly played cards for money in palpable violation of the law of the land and the law of God, and whereas furthermore it is his wish that his name be erased from the Church roll— Resolved therefore, that he be and is hereby excluded from the membership of the church."[62]

In summary, the church records, though cursory, reveal that in the fifteen years that Lelia and Charlie Butler had been married, Lelia and her children had become increasingly committed to their religion and involved in church affairs, whereas Charlie became increasingly alienated. Instead of bringing them together, their church became the arena where Charlie acted out and his family was publicly exposed to his dissatisfaction and unhappiness with his roles as faithful congregant, husband, and father.

Then, in December 1887, four years after his expulsion from the Baptist church, Charlie Butler disappeared. It was a terrible time. Maud's later reaction was to erase her father from the family: "My mother rarely spoke of her ancestors and stated to me once that she did not know what became of her father after he quit the family and had no desire to ascertain the facts," her son Jack (Murry) wrote.[63] She spent the next nine years alternating between work and school in order to help put herself through a three-year business degree program in Columbus at the state's only college for women, the Mississippi Industrial Institute and College, founded "for the Education of White Girls of Mississippi" (later, Mississippi State College for Women). There she received both a liberal arts and technical education. Maud was eighteen when she registered for the business program in the fall of 1889; she completed her second year in 1891–92 and her third in 1894–95. According to the catalog, "In the 3rd year the amount of required work is lessened in order that students who desire it may have the opportunity for special work in Industrial Arts." Since requirements were stiff and had to be met for promotion, Maud's registration for this special program in the third year of her attendance suggests that she had completed the first two years successfully.[64] Before Maud entered college, her mother had supported them both. From then on, Maud helped support her mother and herself.

During these same years, Lelia, either alone or with Maud, seems to have taken to the road again. Although the Butlers did not sell their house until 1893 (and only with the town's permission), newspaper notices from as early as 1891 indicate that Lelia had been living elsewhere since at least then. However, she made extended visits to Oxford. They are reported to have lived in Tennessee, Mississippi, Arkansas, and Texas.[65]

Maud and Her Mother

In 1896 Maud married Murry Falkner. That she married relatively late could suggest that her life with a father like Charlie made her leery—but not leery enough. Her choice of Murry seems almost uncanny given the marked similarities between her husband and father. Lelia saw those similarities and vehemently opposed Maud's choice.[66] Maud, like most daughters, ignored her. Auntee (Mary Holland), Murry's sister and Maud's best friend, helped his case. It may have been Maud's affection for Auntee and her future mother-in-law that opened her to Murry's advances. It may have been that she was tired of moving wherever she could find work and relatives. Perhaps like many children, she sought to repeat in her marriage a traumatic parental relationship. It may also have been that she was optimistic and in love.

At just under six feet, with blue eyes and blond wavy hair, twenty-six-year-old Murry was a presence, although a fairly silent one. In the fall of 1896, when Maud paid Auntee an extended visit at J. W. T.'s "Big House," as it was called, she saw an affluent family. There was one drawback: Murry drank a great deal. The quick and violent temper he displayed when drunk was common knowledge. Five years before his marriage to Maud, he had nearly been killed in a feud involving a girlfriend's quarrel with her seamstress.[67] But in Oxford, as in most of the South, hard drinking and fighting for "honor" were indulged as badges of white Southern Manhood. Murry's most serious flaw, his deep dependence on his father, was something Maud could not have anticipated. When they were courting, even though he worked for one of the family enterprises, he was not even living in Oxford. Before 1902, when J. W. T. arbitrarily pulled the rug out from under his eldest son (see Chap. 8), Maud probably had no idea of her husband's emotional fragility.

Even if she had, she could not have helped him. When, in a desperate attempt to free himself from his father, Murry suggested that the family pick up and head west, he ran up against the wall of Maud's own emotional wounds, the fears and insecurities stemming from her father's desertion, which had resulted in the itinerant and economically precarious life she and her mother had led. Growing up with a father like Charlie Butler, Maud had learned how to ignore, or at least pretend to ignore, the public

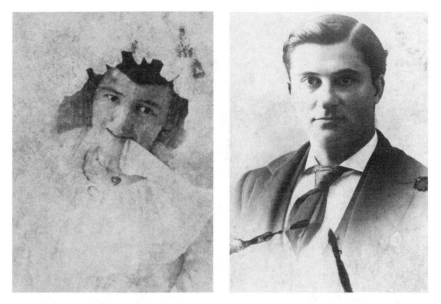

7.4. Wedding photos of Maud Butler and Murry Falkner, 1896.
(Courtesy of Jill Faulkner Summers)

embarrassment that her father's behavior caused her. As an adult, she, like her eldest son, had a reputation for caring very little about what people thought of her.

But such uncaring came at a price. Faulkner's fiction does not exaggerate the violence with which the small Southern town's voice marginalizes and silences community members who are confrontational in their nonconformity. Describing the county's population as "stable—made up of the descendants of first settlers," with many families going back six or seven generations, the local historian of a small Mississippi town notes that "such stability has, I think, allowed a gradual development of habits of life and thought that a frequently changing people would not permit."[68] All the Falkner-Faulkner women—the writer's maternal grandmother, his mother, and his wife—were, at various times, objects of this communal violence. Unlike Estelle Oldham's mother, Lida Allen, the Faulkner women—Lelia, Maud, and Estelle, as well as Caroline Barr, who raised him—refused to conform to such habits.

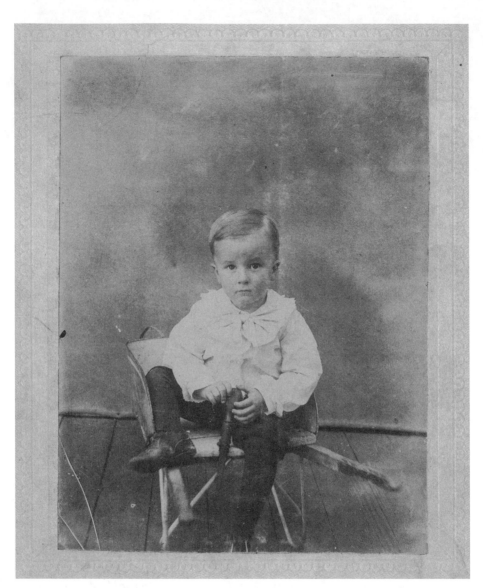

8.1. Photo of "William Falkner, 2 years 8 months," captioned by Maud and
taken by either Lelia or Maud in the Falkners' house.
(Courtesy of Jill Faulkner Summers)

8

Willie Falkner's Childhood World, 1896–1907
Oxford, New Albany, Ripley, Oxford

OST CHILDREN REFLECT on and react to the intellectual, emotional, and psychological climates into which they are born and raised. Their subjectivity, their identities, are influenced by them. Faulkner was no exception. This chapter re-creates the volatile emotional and psychological currents flowing in the bitterly racialized political, domestic, and social worlds into which he was born and in which he lived, worlds further complicated by a family history of three generations of alcoholism. In doing this, it outlines the shifting dynamics in Faulkner's white family between 1896 and 1907. It begins with the players in his parents' household, during the prelude to Willie's childhood and adolescent years. The chapter focuses on Willie's relationship with Maud, but always in the context of the black and white mothers who cared for him from birth and the white husbands and fathers in the Jim Crow community in which all these people lived. We have seen how Callie Barr shaped Faulkner's identity and aesthetic. How did his parents' and his community's faith in the belief system of White Supremacy—for it was a belief system, not merely an ideology—further influence his identity and aesthetic?[1]

The three principal women in the early years of the Falkners' marriage were Maud's mother, Lelia; Maud's mother-in-law, Sallie Murry Falkner; and Maud's sister-in-law, Auntee. Maud and her sister-in-law remained neighbors and close friends all their lives. In fact, Maud had married Murry Falkner in part because of her admiration and love for his mother, Sallie Murry, and his sister, Auntee, who was just a year younger than she. In 1896, the year of their marriage, Maud spent the summer in Oxford visiting the Falkners. A charming interior snapshot of Maud and Auntee, taken sometime before Maud's marriage, shows them having a

8.2. Maud Butler and her best friend, Auntee (Murry Falkner's sister),
c. 1896. (Courtesy of Jill Faulkner Summers)

spirited and apparently amusing discussion. With their matching upswept hairdos, similar profiles, and equally tiny figures, they could easily be mistaken for sisters.

In the photograph, Auntee leans towards Maud, who, smiling enigmatically, listens to whatever Auntee is emphasizing with her pointed finger. In this relationship Maud seems to have been the observer while Auntee was the doer. Maud was the quiet one who silenced many thoughts and feelings that her sister-in-law expressed with ease.

As for Auntee, her friends and relatives remember her as "a fiery little woman who had a fuse as short as her father's and brother Murry's." A nephew said that his "Uncle John said that Auntee had such a temper that if she had been a man someone would have shot her before she was twenty-one."[2] Faulkner said that "when Auntee dies and goes to heaven, either she or God will have to get out."[3] Whereas Maud was physically timid, Auntee's daughter, Sallie Murry Williams, claimed that her mother "didn't know what fright was." Unlike Maud, Auntee was a fine horsewoman. When Maud's grown sons introduced her to barnstorming in the early thirties, unlike Maud, she was equally enthusiastic about taking to the air. Like Maud, but more overtly, Auntee was also something of an iconoclast. Challenging Victorian dress codes, she was one of the first women in Oxford to wear divided riding skirts and, like her daughter, was known for saying exactly what she thought.

While Maud and Auntee remained best friends until Auntee's death, their positions in the community and their domestic lives were very different. Auntee married two years after Maud, but her husband died shortly afterward, leaving her with only one child. Instead of remarrying, Auntee moved back in with her parents and, after her mother's death, in 1906, took over her father's household until his death, in 1922. She never remarried. Her position of relative economic privilege, as the widowed only daughter of one of the richer men in Oxford, gave her freedoms Maud never enjoyed and made her relatively impregnable to public censure. Unlike Maud and her boys, Auntee and the younger Sallie Murry were neither pitied nor shamed nor held responsible for J. W. T.'s making a drunken fool of himself. That had been his wife's problem—just as his son Murry became Maud's.

In the elder Sallie Murry Falkner, Maud found a compassionate woman and an intellectual equal who cared about books and ideas. One of the founding members and leaders of Oxford's Women's Book Club, Maud's mother-in-law provided her with a model and a community of women who valued their minds as well as their housework. Shortly after the Falkners moved back to Oxford from Ripley in September 1902, Maud joined the Women's Book Club, where she remained an active member until her mother died in 1907. At that point, she had lost both mothers within six months and with them an intellectual and emotional support system that had sustained her during the family's first five years in Oxford.

The men in these women's lives served both as additional bonds among them and as separate influences on Willie. Coping with these men offered the women the opportunity to provide additional support for one another. Whether Maud ever sought Sallie Murry's, Lelia's, or Auntee's advice in coping with Murry is not known. We do know that Maud and Willie benefited from Sallie Murry Falkner's empathy and support.

Maud's niece thought that "it was from this grandmother and not from the Falkners that Willie got his compassion and concern for others' welfare."[4] Her Book Club's memoriam for her enumerated Sallie Murry's values as friend and club member, especially "her frank and generous character, and ready sympathy." She always gave "her time and her best efforts to the work [of the club], showing both extensive research and originality of thought. Her varied intellectual gifts, strong mentality, and steadfast loyalty" as friend and "homemaker" had endeared her to the other women.

Like Maud's mother, she was sustained by her religious faith, "which grew even brighter to the end."[5]

Another Falkner guest in the summer of Maud and Murry's courtship was Sallie Murry's older sister, Elizabeth (Lizzie) Murry Burns, a librarian who had come to take six weeks of courses at the university. For every letter Lizzie wrote to Sallie Falkner Burns, her fourteen-year-old daughter at home in Ripley, Maud did an accompanying drawing.[6] Although Sallie Burns was eleven years younger than Maud, Maud's letters to her during Maud's last decade express an admiration, loyalty, and a range and depth of interest, feeling, and emotional warmth that are absent in other biographers' portrayals of Maud. That same warmth and commitment are equally apparent in her strong and sustaining relationships with these other women in her husband's family.

Like Sallie Murry, Maud had always been an avid and serious reader. The breadth and depth of her reading caused one of her sons to characterize her literary taste as "like a man's." Reading to and teaching each of her four sons to read before they entered first grade engaged them in her love affair with language. She taught them narrative skills as well. John writes that his mother "showed us that words put together the right way could make a story worth the time it took to read it. She kept us supplied with books that matched our age and comprehension."[7]

Of all her children, only Willie would share her passion for literature. *Speaking in pictures*, however, was literally Maud's mother tongue, taught to her by her mother. Expressing herself visually was natural to Maud and a lot less perilous than speech. For as long as her son Jack could remember, she had posted a board above her stove. On it "she had written in red paint in her neat, clear brush strokes, 'Don't Complain—Don't Explain.'"[8]

Until Lelia died, Maud continued to draw and paint and, with her mother, teach this language to her eldest son. Probably even before Willie could talk, mother and grandmother were mirroring for him the advantages, pleasures, and value of speaking with his eyes. One of Maud's early memories is of Willie doing just that. One day shortly after the Falkners had moved to Oxford, Willie burst into the house filled with excitement about the new water wagon the town had bought to lay the dust down on its unpaved streets. When his family failed to understand how the wagon worked from his oral description, he "quickly drew a picture and though he was extremely young, included significant engineering details of its watering system."[9] Learning and practicing this other language had two effects on Willie's behavior, which struck almost anyone who knew him as a child. At an early age he became a silent observer. His older Ripley cousin Sallie Burns remembered him as "an exceptionally silent child who even when he was very young was an observer."[10] Fifteen years older than he, she had known him from birth and saw him, probably daily, until Willie was five and the Falkners moved from Ripley to Oxford.

During the first ten years of Willie's life his grandmother and mother taught him what would become a crucial aspect of his identity as an artist—what I call his pictorial or visual aesthetic. The trope of framing so central to this aesthetic, of composing his seeing in frames and through frames, was a kind of vision he learned from watching his mother and grandmother painting or drawing in the blank white rectangle of paper or canvas. He experienced it himself when he sat with one of them or by himself to fill the paper set before him on the "study table" that Maud placed in the hall of each of the six houses the Falkners lived in between 1902 and 1913.[11]

Maud recognized and praised Willie's talent. If not before, then shortly after the Falkners arrived in Oxford, she began saving his drawings, and later his illustrated stories. "She was very proud of Billy. Whatever he wrote or drew, when he was little, she'd put in a shoe bag." In the 1950s she still kept this juvenilia in the same old cloth shoe bag (now apparently lost) that hung on her closet door.[12] In making these drawings, he may have first experienced the sense of mastery attendant in creating his own ordered world out of the constant moving, tension, conflict, and perpetual chaos caused by his father's drinking and inability to make a decent living.

From observing Lelia teach her students the "art of coloring photographs" and paint photographs to order, Willie learned at an early age that photographs were not necessarily accurate representations of reality. By the time he was fourteen, perhaps even earlier, Willie owned a camera that both he and his mother used.[13] With this visual device Maud encouraged Willie to see in frames, to compose what he saw, and to observe closely the sometimes startling disjunctions between seeing, remembering, believing, and knowing. Years later this knowledge would bloom into fictional moments that in a sentence or two compose the whole texture and feeling of a human being struggling to find order, meaning, and identity in such a world. "Memory believes before knowing remembers. Believes longer than recollects, longer than knowing even wonders" begins the sixty-one-page flashback in *Light in August* that enfolds us in the consciousness of the tragic "shadow" child, Joe Christmas (*LIA,* 119). Seeing and transforming what he saw or imagined into images he could alter, select, and control, images framed by the physical confines of the chalk board or page or photograph frame, marked the initial stages of his visual education.

Faulkner readers know that he was as fascinated by the alchemy of the photographic process as he was by its final result. The metaphorical language of the photograph and photography itself as a figure for exploring and articulating the difference between the actual and the apocryphal, of angles of perception; this, too, was organic to his pictorial aesthetic. He had learned it experientially, in one instance making his little brother John the hapless subject of his experiments with photography and light. When Willie was eight or nine, he got the four-year-old to pose for him. Setting a bowl of gunpowder collected from their father's shotgun shells in front of John, he told him to drop a lighted match into it when he said "Now!" John obeyed and was engulfed in a roaring, smoke-filled light. The smoke cleared to reveal John minus hair and eyebrows. All he remembered of Willie's reaction was his saying, "Well, I'll be damned![14] There is no record of either brother's emotional response to this terrifying and unforgettable event. Yet the power of photographs and of the camera's eye, the artist's eye, to probe, order, disorder, interpret, and most important, catch hidden and forbidden desire in both the viewer and the viewed, is an arresting presence and organizing trope in novels as disparate as *Sanctuary, Light in August,* and *Absalom, Absalom!*.[15]

The process of photography itself—specifically developing negatives— may have first brought to the boy's attention the arbitrariness and interdependence of black and white, the ways, as he writes in those novels, whiteness "resolves" out of blackness and the ways blackness is created by and imposed by whiteness. *Light in August* and *Absalom, Absalom!* depict the process of this arbitrary resolution as brutal initiation rites by which white Southern parents and parental figures instruct and induct their children into a racist culture, determining which are white and which are black. Both novels narrate the tragic results of those attempts to "fix" race.

Faulkner is a viscerally visual writer. As he often pointed out, many of his novels began with a picture, most famously his image of Caddy Compson in *The Sound and the Fury*, the "flash and glare" of that moment when the entire story seemed to "explode" all around him (*TSAF,* 230). Looking back on his conception of that novel, he wrote that he "discovered for the first time one physical ideality which all the novels I had believed good had possessed. This was that the action, the desires of the people all came to a single head . . . in a picture [so explicable] that it could be acted by lay figures and caught without dialogue by a camera."[16] This "physical ideality," his mother tongue, helped lead him to his authentic voice.

What does it mean to write through a visual or pictorial aesthetic? How does it affect one's perception of the world? Faulkner's fiction constantly considers these epistemological questions. Because his Southern culture viewed making art as something only women did, little Willie, in learning this mother tongue and then pursuing it to the exclusion of more manly vocations or avocations, wandered across another boundary, besides the one he crossed when he went with Callie Barr into Freedman Town. Noting his passion for drawing and painting, his grandfather J. W. T. acted quickly to quash such lawless, feminine pursuits in his eldest grandson. Sallie Burns recalled that even as a small child Willie already wanted to be "an artist, a draftsman, and a painter but that his grandfather said that this couldn't be because he didn't want any men painters in the Falkner family. Once when his grandfather's store was being painted Willie offered to help. The workmen gave him a wall section of his own on which he painted a mural so good that the men praised his talent to Willie's grandfather and told him it ought to be encouraged. His grandfather replied he didn't want such artists in his family."[17]

The visual or pictorial aesthetic became organic to Faulkner's stylistics. This legacy, from Maud and Lelia, was as central to Faulkner's identity as an artist and to his poetics as his legacy from Callie Barr. And it was gendered female.

Faulkner's "Fathers"

Determining the origins of Faulkner's creative genius involves not only several generations of women but also four generations of firstborn sons. The wounded-officer pose that Billy Falkner assumed when he limped off the train in Oxford upon his return from service in World War I both replayed his famous great grandfather's homecomings from the 1847 Mexican War and the Civil War and anticipated and eclipsed his wounded brother Jack's return from the battlefields of France in March 1919. Faulkner's imposture thus displaced two important men. In perpetrating this hoax and in changing the spelling of his last name to accord with the original spelling of his great grandfather's name, Faulkner imposed a basic element of his fantasy life on reality: his identification with and assumption of the role of a familial and societal ideal and myth.[18] This myth was a composite made up of Colonel William Clark Falkner and his time—the postbellum and antebellum South. This Civil War hero figure and this particular historical period were as central to Faulkner's childhood fantasies as superhero myths are to those of today's children. The difference is that many of Faulkner's grown relatives and fellow townsmen shared his fantasy and embraced the myth— a fact that made his first pose so easily accepted.[19]

After writing a poem and a novel in the same year, the Colonel abandoned literature to concentrate on the law, land speculation, business, and politics. Unlike his great grandson's fictional heroes and his culture's ruling elite, the Colonel did not make or invest his money in plantations and large

8.3. Oldham-Fa(u)lkner Genealogy

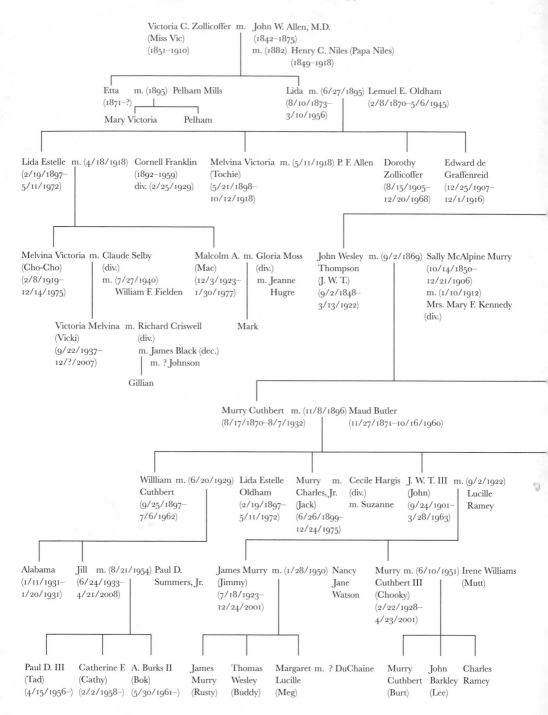

Victoria C. Zollicoffer m. John W. Allen, M.D.
(Miss Vic)   (1842–1875)
(1851–1910)   m. (1882) Henry C. Niles (Papa Niles)
                          (1849–1918)

Etta   m. (1895) Pelham Mills   Lida m. (6/27/1895) Lemuel E. Oldham
(1871–?)   (8/10/1873–   (2/8/1870–5/6/1945)
                                          3/10/1956)
Mary Victoria   Pelham

Lida Estelle m. (4/18/1918) Cornell Franklin   Melvina Victoria m. (5/11/1918) P. F. Allen   Dorothy   Edward de
(2/19/1897–   (1892–1959)   (Tochie)   Zollicoffer   Graffenreid
5/11/1972)   div. (2/25/1929)   (5/21/1898–   (8/15/1905–   (12/25/1907–
                                                 10/12/1918)   12/20/1968)   12/1/1916)

Melvina Victoria m. Claude Selby   Malcolm A. m. Gloria Moss   John Wesley m. (9/2/1869) Sally McAlpine Murry
(Cho-Cho)   (div.)   (Mac)   (div.)   Thompson   (10/14/1850–
(2/8/1919–   m. (7/27/1940)   (12/3/1923–   m. Jeanne   (J. W. T.)   12/21/1906)
12/14/1975)   William F. Fielden 1/30/1977)   Hugre   (9/2/1848–   m. (1/10/1912)
                                                                     3/13/1922)   Mrs. Mary F. Kennedy
Victoria Melvina m. Richard Criswell   Mark   (div.)
(Vicki)   (div.)
(9/22/1937–   m. James Black (dec.)
12/?/2007)   m. ? Johnson

Gillian

                    Murry Cuthbert m. (11/8/1896) Maud Butler
                    (8/17/1870–8/7/1932)   (11/27/1871–10/16/1960)

Willliam m. (6/20/1929) Lida Estelle   Murry   m.   Cecile Hargis   J. W. T. III m. (9/2/1922)
Cuthbert   Oldham   Charles, Jr.   (div.)   (John)   Lucille
(9/25/1897–   (2/19/1897–   (Jack)   m. Suzanne   (9/24/1901–   Ramey
7/6/1962)   5/11/1972)   (6/26/1899–   3/28/1963)
                                        12/24/1975)

Alabama   Jill   m. (8/21/1954) Paul D.   James Murry m. (1/28/1950) Nancy   Murry m. (6/10/1951) Irene Williams
(1/11/1931– (6/24/1933–   Summers, Jr. (Jimmy)   Jane   Cuthbert III   (Mutt)
1/20/1931)   4/21/2008)   (7/18/1923–   Jane   (Chooky)
                                                  12/24/2001)   Watson (2/22/1928–
                                                                                    4/23/2001)

Paul D. III   Catherine F. A. Burks II   James   Thomas   Margaret m. ? DuChaine   Murry   John   Charles
(Tad)   (Cathy)   (Bok)   Murry   Wesley   Lucille   Cuthbert   Barkley   Ramey
(4/15/1956–) (2/2/1958–)   (5/30/1961–) (Rusty)   (Buddy)   (Meg)   (Burt)   (Lee)

Source: Adapted from Sensibar, *Origins;* Blotner, *Faulkner;* Williamson, *William Faulkner;* and revised from archival sources and interviews.

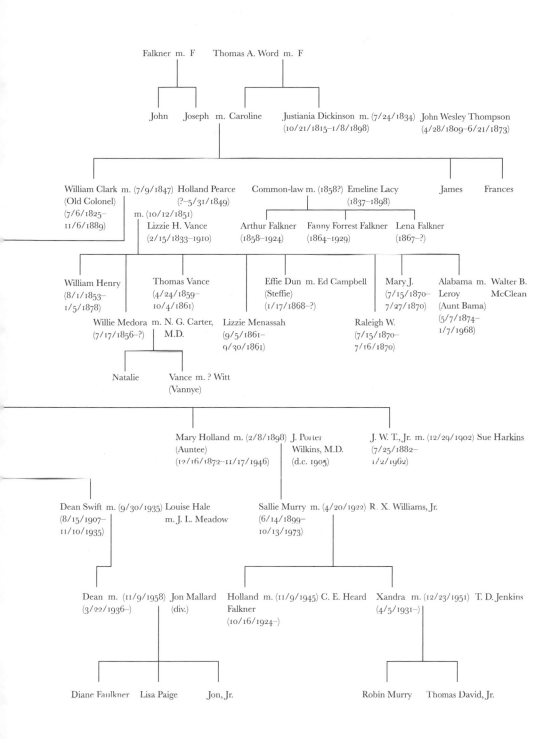

Falkner m. F   Thomas A. Word m. F

John   Joseph m. Caroline   Justiania Dickinson m. (7/24/1834)   John Wesley Thompson
                              (10/21/1815–1/8/1898)   (4/28/1809–6/21/1873)

William Clark m. (7/9/1847) Holland Pearce   Common-law m. (1858?) Emeline Lacy   James   Frances
(Old Colonel)   (?–5/31/1849)   (1837–1898)
(7/6/1825–   m. (10/12/1851)
11/6/1889)   Lizzie H. Vance   Arthur Falkner   Fanny Forrest Falkner   Lena Falkner
                     (2/15/1833–1910)   (1858–1924)   (1864–1929)   (1867–?)

William Henry   Thomas Vance   Effie Dun m. Ed Campbell   Mary J.   Alabama m. Walter B.
(8/1/1853–   (4/24/1859–   (Steffie)   (7/15/1870–   Leroy   McClean
1/5/1878)   10/4/1861)   (1/17/1868–?)   7/27/1870)   (Aunt Bama)
                                                                                       (5/7/1874–
     Willie Medora m. N. G. Carter,   Lizzie Menassah   Raleigh W.   1/7/1968)
     (7/17/1856–?)   M.D.   (9/5/1861–   (7/15/1870–
                                        9/30/1861)   7/16/1870)

          Natalie   Vance m. ? Witt
                       (Vannye)

          Mary Holland m. (2/8/1898) J. Porter   J. W. T., Jr. m. (12/29/1902) Sue Harkins
          (Auntee)   Wilkins, M.D.   (7/25/1882–
          (12/16/1872–11/17/1946) (d.c. 1905)   1/2/1962)

Dean Swift m. (9/30/1935) Louise Hale   Sallie Murry m. (4/20/1922) R. X. Williams, Jr.
(8/15/1907–   m. J. L. Meadow (6/14/1899–
11/10/1935)   10/13/1973)

          Dean m. (11/9/1958) Jon Mallard   Holland m. (11/9/1945) C. E. Heard   Xandra m. (12/23/1951) T. D. Jenkins
          (3/22/1936–)   (div.)   Falkner   (4/5/1931–)
                                             (10/16/1924–)

Diane Faulkner   Lisa Paige   Jon, Jr.   Robin Murry   Thomas David, Jr.

numbers of slaves. He was a town dweller. Yet, though he owned few slaves, like many other slaveholders he used one of his black women to create a shadow family, an assertion of white power and a violation whose dynamics figure so prominently in his great grandson's imagination. Twenty years later, his financial success assured, the Colonel turned again to writing, producing a travel book modeled on Mark Twain's. But he wrote for amusement. Unlike his namesake, the Colonel was primarily a man of action. And although he included fraudulent elements in his early war record and was probably a blockade runner in the last two years of the war, he did fight heroically, if briefly, in the Civil War.[20] Furthermore, as a man of action, he claimed only to play at writing while aggressively pursuing his real work, amassing a modest fortune. His great grandson "played" at being a war hero while pursuing his real work, writing.

When he assumed the identities of a poet and soldier, altering the spelling of his last name, Faulkner symbolically rejected both his father, Murry, and the name associated with all his great grandfather's descendants' accomplishments. He renounced the name, the values, and the achievements associated with the three previous generations of Falkners in order to begin the family again. Faulkner's childhood had been marked by traumatic experiences and a family constellation similar to those of pathological impostors. It suggests that while Billy Falkner consciously chose to become a writer when he was quite young, his choice was marked by a unique conflict: in choosing to write, he also chose not to become the kind of impostor whose only creative achievement is ephemeral impersonation.[21] The evidence of the rejected choice remains in his long years as a poet using other poets' voices and the mask of Pierrot, as well as in the episodes of imposture that in later life appear related to his increasingly severe drinking binges.[22]

Why did Colonel Falkner hover in the lives of the Falkner clan much as the fictional colonels Sartoris, Benbow, and Sutpen ruled their descendants? The Falkners' history offers clues. That history of four generations of fathers and sons became the forcing bed for all of Faulkner's white fictional grandfathers, fathers, and sons (see genealogy, fig. 8.3). Part fact and part myth, it is a history in which intense, thinly disguised father-son rivalry remains the one stable component from generation to generation. When Faulkner the poet pretended to be his great grandfather or his own wounded brother, he was acting out those conflicts. But when, as a novelist, he wrote about the terrible antagonisms dominating the lives of his fictional fathers and sons—the Sartorises, the Benbows, and the Sutpens—he found a creative way of handling these same conflicts. He could now, as he said, fix them on "something like rational truth," translating them into the essential concerns of his art (see Chap. 9).

My account of the Falkner clan, drawn from Blotner, Williamson, and my own earlier work, concentrates on the incidents in these men's lives that best illustrate the anger and jealousy that characterize four generations of Falkner father-son relations. The first incident may be apocryphal, but because the Colonel told it, it is his perception of his relationship with his father and, later, with his adopted father. Thus, it is valid as a measure of his attitude toward father figures.

At fourteen, after a bitter quarrel in which he almost killed his younger brother, the Colonel was beaten so severely by his father that he ran away from home in Tennessee to his maternal aunt and her husband, John Wesley Thompson, in Pontotoc, Mississippi. Colonel Falkner's description of his arrival gives a sense of the boy's state of mind as he tried to track down his self-chosen "father," a man remarkably like the father he'd abandoned in Tennessee. "He came from Memphis on foot, to meet his uncle. . . . He was a poor, sick, ragged, barefoot penniless boy. His cup of sorrow was filled to the brim when he learned that his uncle had left for Aberdeen the day before. He sat down on the hotel steps and wept bitterly, as though his heart would break." Contemporaries claimed that when the Colonel spoke of this childhood episode "he became so affected that utterance failed him, and he had to pause until his emotions had subsided."[23]

The first clear indication of any tension between foster father and son occurred when the Colonel was about twenty years old. Thompson apparently refused to allow William to clerk with him, so Falkner trained at a rival firm.

His legal training came in handy in that the Colonel, like his uncle and like Colonel Sartoris, was jailed several times on murder charges. He also seems to have had difficulty dealing with authority figures, as indicated by his clouded service records in both the Mexican and the Civil War.

Although his relationship with his uncle was uneasy, when the Colonel's first wife died, leaving a baby boy, Colonel Falkner gave the child, John Wesley Thompson Falkner (known as J. W. T.), to the Thompsons to raise as their own. When he remarried shortly thereafter, he did not ask to have his son returned. The official account of this transaction states that Thompson's terms for taking his namesake were that he could keep him and that the Colonel would provide for his financial support. The Colonel did not, however, fulfill his responsibility. Meanwhile, he continued to compete with his foster father, running against him in an election for the state legislature in 1855.[24]

Years later, the Colonel countenanced the murder of his son Henry, the oldest child of his second marriage. Acting on protocol, the cuckold who shot Henry said to the Colonel, "I hate to have to tell you this, but I had to kill Henry." The Colonel answered, "That's alright. I'm afraid I would have had to do it myself anyway."[25] While this story may also be apocryphal, its persistence suggests the public's awareness of the Colonel's great dislike for Henry. The Colonel thus disposed of both his sons.

The young J. W. T. became a lawyer like his father and foster grandfather and was admitted to the Mississippi bar in 1869. Although Thompson had refused his foster son the privilege of practicing with him, he granted it to his foster grandson. Such kind treatment apparently did not make up for the rejection of J. W. T.'s real father, and in turn J. W. T. Falkner's treatment of his eldest son, Murry Cuthbert, Willie Falkner's father, was more cruel, although subtler, than his clear rejection had been.

With behavior characteristic of Falkner fathers toward their sons, J. W. T. Falkner never made life easy for his eldest son. Despite Maud's perpetual childbearing—three children at fifteen-month intervals between September 1897 and September 1901—the first six years of Willie Falkner's parents' marriage were probably their happiest. Murry was working for his father's railroad, a job he loved and had chosen for himself, and the couple lived in New Albany and then Ripley, a healthy distance away from J. W. T.'s perpetual bossing and meddling but close enough to Oxford for regular visits. Murry was also making a good living. By 1900, despite the addition of two children and a third expected shortly, he had bought into the Ripley Drug Company and acquired a farm west of town, where he raised and trained horses and bird dogs, which he showed, even in nearby states. Since starting out as a trainman or engineer, he had been steadily advancing to more and more responsible positions. He worked his way up from fireman to auditor and treasurer by the time his first son was one year old. It seemed that Maud's mother's resistance to their marriage might have been unwarranted, that Murry had inherited his father's ability to make money despite his temper and his drinking.

But J. W. T. retained financial control of the railroad operation and kept its workings to himself. In September 1901 he told Murry the railroad was for sale. By June it was gone. J. W. T. had literally sold it out from under his son. There was not even an employment contract for Murry under the terms of the sale. Not only had his father arbitrarily stripped Murry of his profession, but he also substituted in its stead the operation of a much less prestigious means of transportation, a livery stable. Overnight he demoted his son from the twentieth century to the nineteenth.

It is difficult to believe that the actions of Murry's father contained no conscious element of malice. Financially the sale appears illogical. Although on 24 June 1902, Colonel Falkner's estate received a cash payment of seventy-five thousand dollars for the railroad, the railroad's annual earnings for that year were near thirty-five thousand dollars. Billy's brother John claims in his memoir that prior to the final sale Murry tried unsuccessfully to borrow enough money to buy the railroad from his father. Blotner describes the situation: "Murry Falkner . . . had suffered through two years of college before he was allowed to go to work full time for the railroad. He had advanced from one job to another until he had reached a responsible position. He was 32 years old, with a wife and three small children to support, and now his job was . . . taken away from him. . . . He was an inarticulate man who was not very adept at personal relationships. . . . He was . . . a dutiful son . . . too dutiful to attempt revolt, and certainly too proud to implore."[26] For most of their children's early years and adolescence, the life of the Murry Falkners was that of a downwardly mobile, upper-middle-class, sixth-generation Southern family dominated by the whims of Murry's father, the rich and successful offspring of the mythically proportioned Colonel Falkner. But when Maud and Murry married in 1896, and when Willie was born in September 1897, this had not appeared to be the case.

Baby Years in New Albany and Ripley, 1896–1902

Murry's promotion at his father's railroad and his subsequent move to New Albany at the end of September 1896 prompted him a month later to propose to Maud, who agreed to marry him when he returned to Oxford to visit. They married without fanfare. On 7 November Maud and Murry went for a walk, stopped at the Methodist parsonage, and returned a married couple. The next day they left for New Albany, where Murry had rented a house, and he resumed his duties as the railroad's general passenger agent. Within two months Maud was pregnant. There is no record whether her pregnancies and the children's births were difficult or easy. But even with no complications, caring for three babies fifteen months apart, even with help and even if she was not nursing, would have been an exhausting, almost around-the-clock job. A 1901 studio photograph of her with her third child, John, who was born that September, shows the lined face of a middle-aged woman. She was only thirty.

By 1898 the Falkners had moved to Ripley because Murry had been promoted to be Gulf and Western's auditor and treasurer, in charge of the Traffic and Claims Department.[27] Unlike all the other jobs he was to hold in his life, none of his railroad work was primarily sedentary or involved salesmanship. Much of it required him to be away from home, so that even when Maud's mother began visiting for long stretches to help her care for Willie and then Jack and John, her presence created little friction. Maud had her hands full. Fortunately the two grandmothers, Lelia and Sallie Murry Falkner, came to stay and help at the birth of each of Maud's three sons. Besides, Maud had friends and relations in Ripley, particularly her mother-in-law's large family, the Murrys, and the Ripley branch of the Falkner family. A letter Maud wrote Sallie Burns in the 1950s conveys Maud's nostalgia for the years she lived in Ripley. Returning for a day with a grandson and his wife and "showing them the Ripley we claim, I got so homesick for you—I missed you and could go over the trip taking you there until I got quite low in mind."[28]

However, during her first three boys' earliest years, Maud's primary and constant help with her babies came from Callie Barr. Describing Callie's role to a black minister shortly after her death, Faulkner details the extent of her labor. Although she was already in her late fifties, he writes that she "was present day and night, in the house with us while I and my three brothers were in our successive infancy, then sleeping in her own house in the back yard after we became older. She nursed us in sickness, she went where we went, she fought our battles, she would have sacrificed her life for us if necessary." Yet for these services "she asked for nothing, demanded nothing." Here, as in his other accounts, Faulkner portrays Callie Barr as an all-sacrificing mammy straight out of the moonlight-and-magnolia school of post-Reconstruction Southern myth. His letter's text and subtext exemplify the psychological currents present in the racialized family structure in which Faulkner and his brothers were raised. His letter provides clear evidence for and helps to explain why Faulkner's childhood education into race would be so painful.[29]

Although Faulkner and his brothers claimed Callie as "a companion" to Maud in Maud's old age, and Faulkner wrote to the minister that "she might have been my mother's mother," there is no narrative from Callie and, besides her revealing painting, not much from Maud concerning how she and Callie got along.[30] That Callie stayed until all four Falkner boys were grown and then returned to care for their children and visit with Maud suggests that these two equally reserved, short-tempered, opinionated women were congenial. According to their respective friends and relations, both women had a clear understanding of their own and everyone else's place in a society that was exquisitely attuned to such matters.[31] Both understood how to manipulate the system without appearing to upset the status quo. The memoirs of Faulkner's brothers and Faulkner's own semi-fictionalized accounts of Callie's role in the household and Callie's and Maud's teamwork all suggest that, from the Falkner children's perspective, she held the family together. Again to this same minister Faulkner writes: "She bossed the other servants, she bossed my father, she might have been my mother's mother; she bossed us as children, watched over us; I have seen her defy my father to his face when one of us was about to get some punishment which he certainly deserved. Without ever preaching to us she was a living example to us children of unselfishness and honesty and loyalty and consideration of the weak and respect to age."[32]

Reading beyond Faulkner's sentimental idealizing, what emerges is an appreciation of the alliance between his mother and Callie that protected all the children from their father, who became a poorer and poorer parent after losing his job at the railroad. Over years of shared responsibility, a compatibility was built, perhaps even some level of trust. But it was a one-way street. Callie knew all this white family's secrets, but they knew none of hers. Maud was a racist, and Callie a snob. According to Faulkner's daughter, Callie "was very disdainful of any black person who didn't belong to a white family—that they were trash—that they'd been thrown away. Belonging to a good white family was a status symbol"—perhaps for herself and some others of her generation.[33] Callie's lifelong relations with her own family, who were not domestics, suggests that if these were her rules, she made a lot of exceptions.

The social columns of the New Albany, Ripley, and Oxford papers record births, serious illnesses, and visits of the Butler and Falkner grandparents to their grandchildren. Nothing is known of the tenor of those visits. Lelia was with her daughter before and during all the children's births, and in each instance J. W. T. and Sallie Murry Falkner arrived shortly thereafter. With the arrival of each new child, Lelia's stays lengthened. In 1899 and 1900 she spent time in Ripley both before and after Jack's birth. The Falkner grandparents also paid long visits. In 1901, when Maud was in her third pregnancy, Lelia spent the summer in Ripley and stayed through John's birth in September, the day before Willie's fourth birthday. Less than a week later, Willie and then Jack caught scarlet fever. Sallie Murry joined Lelia and Callie to help out.

To celebrate his oldest grandson's recovery, J. W. T. gave Willie a Shetland pony, a lavish present for a four-year-old, more lavish than anything his father could provide, especially after what J. W. T. did to him in the following months. Although Murry had no interest in college, J. W. T. had forced him to go. He had lasted two years there. Only then had his father grudgingly allowed him to do what he wanted, work on the railroad. Both John's and Jack's memoirs say that their grandfather's decision to sell the railroad devastated their father, but theirs are the only accounts. It is clear, though, that by early 1902 something unusual was going on. A sudden rash of visits from both of Murry's parents occurred during the first six months of 1902. In March Sallie Murry Falkner arrived without her husband. On her return to Oxford she took four-and-a-half-year-old Willie with her.[34] On 24 June the newspapers reported that J. W. T. had sold the Gulf and Western Railroad. Overnight Murry Falkner was jobless. Again, according to Jack and John, Murry Falkner never forgave Maud for denying him the chance to go west once his father had sold the railroad.[35]

For a few months Murry had tried to make it on his own. Then, apparently unable to support his family on what he was earning from his farm or his interest in the Ripley Drug Company, or to find other work without his father's support, he accepted the position managing J. W. T.'s livery business in Oxford. So, on 24 September, the day before Willie's fifth birthday, the Falkner family moved to Oxford, and Lelia joined her daughter's household permanently.[36] Even their first house in Oxford was not their own but the former home of Murry's father—the Brown house on Second South Street, with a lot one block square. It was a large house with fireplaces in every room and was well located: three blocks from the square and an easy walk to the senior Falkners' brand-new home on South Street. The Brown house was the first of five houses and seven moves the family made between 1902 and 1919. As the Falkner fortunes dwindled and Murry's jobs, always in one of J. W. T.'s many ventures, became less lucrative, they moved to less and less distinguished homes.

Murry's response to his demotion was passive and self-destructive. He drifted from job to job and he drank copiously. Regular family trips to a nearby sanatorium, where Billy observed his father being "dried out," would become integral to Faulkner children's childhood.

"A Household of Women": Oxford Childhood, 1902–1905

When fortified with liquor, Murry might abuse his immediate family or pick a fight with someone in Oxford. But as far as is known he never attacked the person primarily responsible for his condition, his powerful and ever-present father. Rather he focused his ire on weaker opponents like his eldest and physically smallest son, "Snake Lips."

Although Murry was unhappy, Maud's activities during their first five years of living in Oxford suggest that the community of sympathetic women with whom she was in daily contact was partly responsible for the appearance that all was well in the Falkner household. They also suggest that the usual view of Maud as withdrawn and antisocial, as a woman who had no interior life or interests apart from her children and sought no other avenues of pleasure or self-fulfillment, is inaccurate. During Willie's first eight or nine years, Maud, with her mother's help, entertained an enriching life apart from her family, one from which they benefited. Invited by her mother-in-law, Maud quickly entered into Oxford's intellectual community for women.[37]

One of its centers was the Women's Book Club. Some sense of the women's commitment to the intellectual circle they created for themselves appears in the minutes for what was to be their last meeting of the season, in June 1903. The seven members present, including Maud, discussed the reasons for absences "which had caused programs not to be given the full justice that their subject deserved." Despite this drawback these "busy housewives and mothers" decided that "the study and interchange of ideas and the social feature had been of lasting benefit and pleasure, so much so, that by unanimous consent," they agreed to continue through the summer, during which they planned to read "our latest American authors."[38]

That July at Maud's house the club discussed *The Speckled Bird* and the life and writings of its Alabama author, the then wildly popular Augusta Jane Evans. At that same meeting the women also discussed Owen Wister's *The Virginian,* which Maud would soon pass on to her boys. The afternoon concluded with Maud's reading of her projection concerning which current authors would be read in the near future. She called it "A Visit to the Cemetery of Books in 1920."[39] Maud remained an active member until sometime during 1906, the year Sallie Murry Falkner died.[40] The last paper she gave was on Sir Walter Scott, and at the last meeting held at her house in February 1906 the club heard a paper on Jane Austen and discussed her novels.

A few titles of papers presented by members and topics of debate gives a sense of the women's interest in feminist issues, literature, and current affairs. One program, "The College Woman," had as its epigraph "No hasty fool of stubborn will/ But prudent, cautious, pliant still." The program included a paper titled "The Effects of Higher Education" and a reading from Tennyson's gently feminist poem *The Princess,* followed by a discussion held under the rubric "The Problems Respecting Women." One can only speculate about the tenor of the women's discussion: clearly there is tension between the competing images of and possibilities for women presented in the day's discussion topics. Maud may well have then read *The Princess* to Willie, for like much of the Victorian literature she gave her sons, it would take on a new life, first in Billy Falkner's poetry and later in his fiction.[41]

The subject of another meeting was "The Decline of Literature for Girls." One member gave a paper called "Has Louisa May Alcott a Successor?" followed by a reading from "a selection on the subject." Club members then discussed the question "Do Girls need a literature of their own or is it wiser to let them read maturer books?" At another meeting, also on "Problems Affecting Women," the club discussed the influence of literary clubs on women's lives. The paper topic at that meeting was "Club Women and Club Life in the South." The consensus of the meeting was that such clubs were invaluable because they served as a forum where "all things are put to question." Besides engaging in feminist issues at home, the club was interested in women from other cultures. In a program on French history and culture, Maud's mother-in-law gave a paper titled "France as Seen Through Josephine." Club members even studied religious issues in their cultural context. In a program on the place of the theater, Sallie Murry, who was the organist and choir master at her Methodist church, wrote an essay on "The Influence of the Church on the Stage." We will never know what of all this Maud shared with her sons, but it is clear that between meetings she and her mother made her household an artistically and intellectually stimulating place for her children.

Meanwhile, besides supervising the household, caring for her husband, and helping to care for her children, Maud was painting, often using her young children as subjects.[42] But after the deaths of Sallie Murry Falkner and Lelia, she resigned from the Women's Book Club and gave up her art. Her fourth and last son was born in August 1907, two months after Lelia's death. With neither her mother nor her mother-in-law for emotional and material support, Maud seems to have been overwhelmed. She withdrew from the community of women to which her mother-in-law had introduced her. She did not paint again for thirty-five years. Like the book club, her artwork had given her an expressive outlet and register of feeling and a medium and space where she could momentarily have an identity apart from her children and family and a respite from the sadness and the chaos caused by Murry's increasingly frequent binges.

At the same time, because she shared her enthusiasms with her children, reading to them, often from books like *The Virginian*, teaching all of them to read, and encouraging them to paint and draw, they too had benefited. But the deaths of Lelia and Sallie Murry affected Maud in a way that caused drastic changes. She lost crucial companions with whom she had shared her artistic and intellectual life. Besides, they had acted as buffers who protected Maud and their grandchildren somewhat from their father's behavior. Lelia, as live-in grandmother, had also provided Maud with extra child care that gave her time to pursue her intellectual and social interests. Although this ended in 1907, for their first four years in Oxford, little Willie and his brothers lived surrounded, taught, protected, and cared for by these three generations of four "indomitable women," including Maud and Callie.

According to Jack Falkner, when the family first returned to Oxford, in 1902, his father's reputation as a wild drinker preceded them.[43] Although he does not say so, stories of his grandfather Butler and his thievery and miscegenation, and of his grandfather Falkner's drinking sprees and affair with a local black woman in a town as small as Oxford—just over eighteen hundred people in 1902—would also have been part of the local gossip greeting the little Falkner brothers. It would make their grandmother and mother wary of returning permanently to the site of the Butler family scandal.

Here, too, Maud's mother-in-law's reputation *apart* from her husband, her model of behavior, was useful to Maud. Besides her club work, Sallie Murry was active in the Methodist church. Although Maud never went to church as an adult, her mother had remained active in the Baptist church. Maud took an ecumenical approach to her children's religious upbringing. She sent them to Sunday school with Lelia as long as her mother taught there, but she had them baptized in their other grandmother's Methodist church.[44]

Sallie Murry's goodness failed to curb her husband's philandering or her husband's and son's drinking. In March 1903, six months after the Falkners' move to Oxford, Murry fought with a local constable and knocked him through the plate-glass window of his brother John's grocery store on the square. This well-publicized public display of violence had repercussions his little boys, particularly his eldest, had to absorb.

The brothers learned to defend themselves. They withdrew. Jack explained their relations with other children: "My brothers and I were by and large, sufficient unto ourselves, in the sense that we had no bosom friends. We were far from being alone with ourselves, though; we played games and hunted with boys our own age and attended many social affairs with girls." They were there but they were not there. They had to keep secrets that any intimate relationship with an outsider might tempt them to reveal. Like so many families of alcoholics, they and their mother created a self-sustaining unit to protect themselves and their father. Jack elaborates, writing that the first time any of the family had been separated was April 1918, when Bill went to stay with his friend Phil Stone in New Haven: "Up until that day . . . our lives, together with those of our parents and brothers, had been as one in a closely knit and self-sustaining family unit." He insists that whatever his brothers did, they did as a unit: "In short, the day-to-day life of one had been the same as that of the other." That life, as he and John tell it, is always descriptive, never analytic, always at the level of doing, never of feeling. Feelings, unless they are pleasant, are absent. Thus Jack writes that he never heard his grandmother Lelia "complain or saw her cry, even during those last terrible months." Nor did he ever see his mother cry, "how-ever close she may have been to it."[45] A woman and a wife and mother who has as her guiding principle "Don't Complain—Don't Explain" sets severe limits on her own and her children's affective lives. Jack's and John's mem-oirs and, most painfully, Faulkner's fiction articulate those limitations.

Faulkner never wrote a memoir, but his letters, even the most intimate and loving ones, are surprisingly flat. As I have written elsewhere, even in letters to various women with whom he attempted or had affairs, he often recycled the same language. It was as if for him, to paraphrase one of his most inadequate fictional lovers, love could exist only in books. Only when he was writing or drinking could he allow himself to feel love and all the joy and utter unashamed and unself-conscious neediness that one who is in love experiences. All the Falkner brothers learned to drink from their father and grandfather and to repress much of their affective life by imitating their mother's and grandmothers' ways of living with and protecting an alcoholic.

At work, Murry's dissatisfaction and frustration continued. In April 1903, his father made him the manager of his newly acquired cottonseed-oil processing plant. By October, J. W. T. continued to steadily expand his holdings by buying the Opera House and a local transfer line with cash he had received for the railroad.[46] Apparently Murry did nothing but resist passively. He invited his cronies in to drink with him at the livery stable and did little work. By August 1905 J. W. T. had made him manager of the Ox-ford Oil Mill Company, which sold coal oil for lamps.[47] It was his third new job in as many years, and he did no better at it than at previous employs. By July 1908 Murry had so mismanaged the business that its stockholders fired him in order "to put the property in good repair and in good manage-ment."[48]

At home, when drunk, Faulkner's father shouted and raged at his mother. In Callie's words, "he was a mean drunk." He was no easier on his children. Jack wrote of his father, "How little I actually came to know him, and perhaps, even less to understand him. He was not an easy man to know." In striking contrast to his mother, "his capacity for affection was limited, but"—he adds protectively—"I'm sure to such extent as it allowed, he loved us all."[49]

Although Faulkner experienced Murry's fathering as deficient at best, the forms of black and white mothering he and his brothers received were rich, varied, and confusing. His grandmother Lelia was constantly making things and involving Willie in her projects, which extended from butter pats she shaped into swans and roses and sold to neighbors and friends, to di-oramas constructed for Oxford's store windows. In September 1904 the *Ox-*

ford Eagle reported that she made "a charming panorama, 'The Presidential Race,' which displays both creative genius and artistic taste. Mrs. Butler's talent is of a high order, and her pictures as well as other artistic endeavors are deserving of the highest praise."[50] Her grandchildren learned their Sunday school lessons orally and visually as Lelia illustrated her narratives with chalkboard drawings. But the strangest object she made was a wooden doll she dressed as a policeman and gave to Willie. His name was Patrick O'Leary, but his uniform was that of Lelia's runaway husband, about whom no one in the family spoke. This doll was perhaps Faulkner's earliest lesson in the subversiveness of art. Art could be created to express a subject and a person whom the family did not talk about.

Willie loved playing with dolls as much as he loved careening around on his pony or playing baseball with the other kids on the block. For companions in his doll play, he had Estelle Oldham, who by 1903 had also moved to Oxford, and his cousin Sallie Murry Wilkins. Both women remembered playing dolls with Faulkner for hours. His cousin said he continued to play with them until he was nine.[51] In his imagination he played with them all his life. First in his poetry and then in his fiction, their lack of control over their lives became a metaphor for a gendered form of helplessness—always feminized and racialized—that he would continue to reinvent and elaborate on throughout his career.

The Making of a White Child in Jim Crow Culture, 1905–1907

In the Jim Crow South, Faulkner's dual mothering was hardly unique. But how it affected his identity, what he did with those effects in his imagination, and how his fictive representations of these effects resonated in the modern collective imagination make it imperative to trace out the history of his education by his white family and community. Faulkner's early screen memory capturing the difference between his black and white mothering suggests that his induction into a racialized worldview occurred while his family still lived in Ripley, although such a dating is uncertain. We know from Faulkner's brother Jack that when they moved to Oxford they were greeted with tales of their father's drinking sprees. He does not say that they were also greeted with tales of both their grandfathers' interracial affairs, but such was probably the case. An important lesson Willie learned from his grandparents' marriages was that his post-Reconstruction grandfathers, like his great grandfather Falkner and other white slaveholders who practiced master-slave sex, sought (or took?) sexual satisfaction not with their "pure," white—which by definition meant sexually anesthetized—middle-class wives, but with black women employed in white people's homes to care for them, their wives, and their children. These grandfathers practiced an "interclass interracial sexuality" that was a legacy of slavery and in which the dynamics of power, as Faulkner's fiction makes abundantly clear, were fairly similar. This was the construct of adult heterosexual sex and sexuality into which Willie Falkner was born and raised. It was a code of conduct reinforced by his community. He learned it at home, in the town square, at school, from books, and at the movies and the theater.

In 1905, the year it was published, Willie's first-grade teacher gave the eight-year-old an inscribed copy of the best-selling novel *The Clansman: An Historical Romance of the Ku Klux Clan,* by Thomas Dixon, Jr. For someone unschooled in white supremacist hyperbole, it is a shocking book. That his teacher would think it an appropriate gift suggests the level of normalization such hyperbole then enjoyed in Oxford. It stands as a vivid temporal marker of his communal and familial indoctrination into the white Southern supremacist belief and value system.

The Clansman, published originally by the New York firm of Doubleday and Page, became, through its film version (1915), one of the most influential racist tracts ever published. Dixon's prefatory note to his readers claims that he writes the "true story of the Ku Klux Klan Conspiracy, which overturned the Reconstruction regime" and "saved the life of a people, [and] forms one of the most dramatic chapters in the history of the Aryan race."[52]

Set primarily in the Piedmont area of South Carolina in the months just following Lincoln's assassination, it depicts a race war between freed slaves, armed and directed by their Northern handlers, and white Southern plantation and professional families, depicted as the "remains of Aryan civilization." In this war "Negro Rule," characterized in a milder passage as "barbarism strangling civilization by brute force," is ultimately overthrown. Its leaders are mutilated and then burned on fiery crosses. But "civilization" is not truly "saved or the South redeemed from shame" until there has been a ritual sacrifice of white Southern Womanhood. The heroine and her mother are raped by "black brutes" and then throw themselves off a cliff to preserve an appearance of unsullied virtue. Thus the Klan saves Southern patriarchy from the "Black Plague of Reconstruction." This novel, whose Northern white villain named Stoneman is ruled by his mulatto mistress, plays to and reinforces all white supremacist racial and sexual fears, desires, and prejudices. Although it asserts that only evil (white) men engage in interracial sex, it supplies its white readers with liberal doses of titillating interracial coupling. Its most riveting pornographic moments occur in scenes between Stoneman and his mistress or between white Southern Ladies and "black barbarians."[53]

When Willie read it to himself, or when his mother read it to him, did he make any connection between his grandfathers' and old Stoneman's affairs with black women? What did he think when *The Clansman*'s Southern gentleman claimed that America was "great because of the genius of the race of pioneer white freemen" and that its "future depends on the purity of this racial stock"? How did he reconcile this with his knowledge of his great grandfather Falkner's shadow family? After reading or hearing read to him passage after passage about "negro[es], exuding [their] nauseating animal odour" and about the "pollution" inherent in "assimilation," how did it make him feel about touch, about hugging and kissing and (as his fiction repeats) eating and sleeping with Callie Barr and the black children with whom he played?[54] How did it further compromise, regulate, and denigrate his love for her and her family? There is no record to tell us other than Faulkner's fiction. It registers in exquisite detail white Southerners' conscious disgust, which fails to mask wishes to recover and cover in the "negro rank quilt" and other equally transparent signs marking their forbidden desire to return to the black maternal. For Faulkner's fictional men and boys the Southern oedipal desire is always to sleep with Mammy.

The subjects that Faulkner's first-grade teacher and his parents considered appropriate reading matter for an eight-year-old included rape, lynching, and portrayals of all black people as "brutes," "apes," "half-child, half animal, the sport of impulse . . . whose speech knows no word of love, whose passions once aroused, are as the fury of the tiger."[55] To know this is to begin to fathom the fury, violence, sexual fear, and rage fueling the racist climate into which Faulkner, his contemporaries, and his parents' generations had been educated. It also provides some sense of the anger, shame, confusion, and fear young children may have felt when they were bombarded with these images in books, in their town squares (where Willie would soon see his first lynching), on their stages, and in films. Within three years Willie saw a dramatization of *The Clansman* at the town's opera house. These were the communally administered brutal and brutalizing rituals and rites of passage that constituted white Southern children's education into race and racism. In teaching their white children to deny black people's humanity and feelings, they also taught them to deny their own humanity.

From early childhood William Faulkner was exposed to the potent combination of two virulent societal diseases, racism and alcoholism. His fiction depicts this mix as psychically lethal. It is possible that by 1905, when Willie entered first grade, he had already learned from Maud not to express any emotion that indicated need or weakness. He would not violate this code until later in life, and then only when he was drunk or in his fiction.

Faulkner passed on to his daughter these rules about containing and suppressing feelings of need, weakness, fear, or unhappiness. When, as a child in Oxford, she was taken by her father to see the film version of *The Phantom of the Opera*, it frightened her, yet when she screamed in terror, "he just moved away from me and left the theater."[56] This incident occurred before Jill had learned how to cope with the loneliness, helplessness, and often fear of being the daughter of parents who when drunk might say and do terrible things: "I spent a lot of nights in the midst of, but still on the fringes of terrible fights. Lots of violence that even if it wasn't physical violence, it was still a violent atmosphere and lots of nights of—as children will when they don't really understand things—thinking they were both dying." Then she explains how she learned to survive: "I felt very alone and very helpless for awhile until I discovered I wasn't helpless. I could cope perfectly well. I don't remember how. It was just all of a sudden I knew that I wasn't helpless, I could cope with whatever happened and [pause] in many ways it's probably made me a not very nice person in many ways because I don't need anybody. You know, once I realized that I didn't need help, and ever since then have never needed anybody for anything. I'm— it's a bad way to be—but I just don't feel like I need to turn to anybody for anything. I can handle it."[57]

Lots of times, the Falkners couldn't handle it. It is not clear exactly when Maud, who brought her children along to teach them an object lesson, began taking their father to the local Keeley Institute, outside of Memphis, to be "cured" of alcoholism, but before Dean's birth, in 1907, the three older boys had been there several times. Jack writes about these trips as if they were a great lark and just part of every Southern child's life: "Our father, in common with a goodly portion of the rest of the male members of our clan, was singularly free of any aversion to the bottle, and this led him, from time to time, to become a guest at the Cure. Mother had to get him there, and on several occasions, Bill, John, and I were taken along too." Dwelling on the joys of riding the train from Oxford to Memphis, he says nothing about the condition his father and the rest of his family must have been in by the time Maud had to commit him.[58]

Leslie E. Keeley, M.D. and LL.D. (1842–1900), was one of the first doctors to treat alcoholism as a disease instead of a vice. He was among the first to note its long history in this country and its epidemic proportions. His psychological and sociological approach to addiction was unique for his time. One of the chief causes of addiction in the Western world, he argued, was the use of addictive substances as cure-alls administered from infancy onward.[59] In his emphasis on the importance of community support, group therapy, and lifetime group support through Keeley Leagues,

he anticipated addiction programs like Alcoholics Anonymous and Ha-
zelden. Keeley had become a millionaire by franchising almost two hundred sanatoriums throughout the United States, Canada, and Europe.[60]

Keeley was also a prolific proselytizer, having written at least fifteen
books on the subject. His most popular, which Maud and her mother-in-
law, who was involved in the temperance movement, probably read, was
The Non-Heredity of Inebriety.[61] Keeley's approach—treating addiction not as
a moral lapse but as a disease needing proper medication just like any
other—may have induced even Murry to read it. Initially it may have given
Maud some hope, since Keeley claimed that his cure rates were close to 50
percent, though his approach did not work for Murry.

9

From Honor Roll to Truancy, 1907–1914
Finding Himself in the Butler-Falkner Legacy

NOT SURPRISINGLY, Willie did exceedingly well in first grade and consequently skipped to third grade at age nine. Until 1908, when he entered fifth grade, he consistently made the honor roll. First grade was marked by *The Clansman*, third grade by the family's loss of both grandmothers and the upheaval that followed. After Lelia's death in June, Maud, now thirty-five and seven months pregnant with her fourth child, moved the family into her father-in-law's house, where they lived for the next three months while their own house was being fumigated and re-painted. Dean, named for Maud's mother, was probably born at his grand-father's. Callie took over his and Maud's care, and the three older Falkner boys began to see her now as replacing their grandmothers, a replacement conveyed to them by a shifting in their mother's and Callie's relationship as Maud became increasingly dependent on her. As Faulkner's brother John recalled, "Mammy, in a strong measure, took their places."[1]

Another replacement may have also been occurring. In first grade Willie and Victoria ("Tochie") Oldham were classmates and fellow honor students. In third grade, he was now in the same classroom with Tochie's sister, Estelle. Estelle notes that at nine, Willie was already "fashion conscious and a fastidious dresser when he chose to be."[2]

This was always a mutual interest—dressing for a role—and may have been part of their shared imaginative life then just as it was in adolescence and after they married. Estelle remembered that a relative had brought the Falkner boys Panama hats that summer, which she called a "Katie" or boater. Willie wore his constantly. She said that because he was so small for his age, it made him look like a miniature man. Perhaps living at his grand-father's, where he observed at close quarters how his grandfather directed his father and constantly compared their successes and failures, encouraged his desire to be seen like his grandfather, not his father. A further source of comparison would have been another of the town's dapper men, Estelle's father, Lem, who was obviously prospering. In the spring of 1905 the Oldhams had moved into a large house diagonally across from J. W. T.'s. Like Willie's grandfather, Lem Oldham was also a natty dresser. His granddaughter claimed that in the summer he wore a white linen suit even when supervising his gardener.

Despite the deaths of Willie's grandmothers, two moves within three months, and the birth of his last brother, his grades for 1907–8 remained stellar. His essays were so remarkable that in fourth grade his teacher accused Maud of writing them for him. Maud was furious and convincing. At year's end Willie made the honor roll again, including an A for deportment.

A contemporary said that although it was the custom for teachers to whip disobedient students, this teacher took it to an extreme: "She was small with an enormous amount of hair piled on her head. She would take the boys out into the hall to whip them. They would bend over and she whipped so hard that her hairpins would fly out—they were heavy hairpins—and they'd ring when they hit the floor. And this enormous coil of hair would come loose and fall clear down her back. Then after the whipping she would have to stoop down and pick up her hairpins and twist her hair back up. We'd be watching her. I cried many a time in that fourth grade feeling so sorry for those boys. I think that's what made him lose interest in school and [eventually] drop out. He just didn't like the whipping. He was a very sensitive person."[3] But apparently he was not so sensitive toward his younger brothers, whom he began enlisting for various "scientific" experiments. One day he convinced his brother John to jump out of a second-story window to test some corn-husk wings Willie had made. Then there was his photography experiment.

While Murry's eldest son continued to excel in school, his own business ventures continued to flounder. In July 1908, at the end of Willie's fourth-grade year, the *Oxford Eagle* reported that Murry had so mismanaged the coal-oil business that its stockholders fired him.[4]

Willie's sensitivity was further tested by his continuing education into the codes and laws of white supremacy. In early September, just weeks before he would enter fifth grade and turn twelve, he was privy to, and probably saw, the mutilation and lynching of a black man. Nelse Patton, who had been caught and arraigned earlier in the day, was dragged from the Oxford jail, shot, castrated, stripped, and hung from a tree on the courthouse square. Seven weeks later Willie got another lesson when a dramatization of *The Clansman* played to a full house in Oxford. The huge production included a cast of forty plus cavalry horses for the scenes in which hooded Clansmen redeemed the South and the honor of their "daughter[s] from the assault of the black brute," from Northern demagogues, and from "ignorant negroes."[5] That October was the last period he made honor roll that year. His radical shift in behavior marked the beginning of his withdrawal from any organized form of education.

Meanwhile at home he continued to read authors Maud had introduced him to. By then these included Conrad, Shakespeare, Balzac, Hugo, Voltaire, and Fielding. Then, in the fall of 1909, twelve-year-old Willie entered sixth grade and promptly began cutting school. Faulkner told a University of Virginia class in the 1950s that he had never liked school and had stopped going "as soon as I got big enough to play hooky and not be caught at it. That was about the sixth grade."[6] According to classmates, he spent all his time writing stories and illustrating them. Some thought him shy and uncommunicative—except through his art: "He never talked. On a rainy day at recess we would gang around and he would entertain us with his drawing. The ones who got close to him could watch him. Then they'd move back and let others come up. He'd often draw trains, the engine with its cowcatcher, the caboose with all the details, smoke pouring out of the chimneys."[7] Estelle remembered that "he'd do anything to get out of school."[8]

Out of school he began spending a great deal of time with his grandfather. "I would sit there on the gallery," Faulkner said, "and a Negro would come and bring grandpappy drinks." If it were a sweet drink like a rum toddy or mint julep, Willie drank the "heeltaps." This was Faulkner's drinking "origins" story, one he often repeated.[9] Perhaps the sweetness was the sixth grader's anodyne for the sweetness destroyed when the culture that gave an eight-year-old *The Clansman* to read shamed and scared him into killing his love for Callie Barr.

While learning to drink like his grandfather (and father), Willie also began imitating his dress. One day he told J. W. T. how much he admired his "fob and that vest." Flattered, his grandfather told him he would buy him the "same thing." According to Faulkner, a couple of Sundays later, when the two went off to church together in their matching outfits, "I was the proudest boy that ever breathed."[10] This was the same grandfather who regularly went on benders that climaxed in public displays of his drunkenness—throwing bricks at plate-glass windows and kicking in doors. Possibly Willie adopted J. W. T.'s drinking and his dress initially as a kind of camouflage, a masculine surface to convince both his father and grandfather to cut him the slack he needed to pursue his real but socially unacceptable desires and identity—to become an artist. Or perhaps he did it to convince himself that despite his passion to be an artist, he really was a man.

Although liked by most of his schoolmates, he was intimate with none.[11] His brother Jack confirmed this. Estelle claimed that he also began withdrawing from group social activities at the Oldhams' around this time. Besides his grandfather, however, another person he chose to be with more, to talk with, and even to imitate was Estelle. Like many adolescents, Willie was preoccupied with his looks. But for this young artist, whose fiction would be defined in part by its passionate exploration of the terrors and pleasures of masking, mirroring, and merging—especially as these relate to those slippery matters of racial-sexual identities—the ability to manipulate his appearance and imitate and emulate others became inseparable from his creative persona. That humans emulate and imitate the objects of their desires and fears is a commonplace. One of the people Faulkner both sought and feared to merge with was Estelle. As an adolescent, he managed his feelings in various imaginative ways. Blotner writes that "there was a kind of dandyism" in Faulkner's adolescent appearance.[12] Faulkner's brother noted that he had "an almost foppish taste in clothes" and that by the time he was working in his grandfather's bank he spent most of his salary on "adorning himself."[13] Like Estelle, Willie had "a graceful slim figure that tight clothes flattered." Not content with a store-bought look, Willie had his mother alter the pants of a dress suit so that "by the time . . . the image in the mirror suited her son, they were close to skin-tight."[14] Like Estelle, he spent excessive amounts on dress clothes and "was very much the fashion plate." Furthermore, Willie's slightness "was augmented by the fact that now, in emulation of Estelle, he took only toast and black coffee for breakfast."[15] The language of Faulkner's brothers and his biographers captures the gender-troubling effect of this pose on others: dandyism, adorning himself, foppish, skin-tight, a fashion-plate. In short, was he a real man?

Another reason for Willie's withdrawal from more physical activities, from group play, and from school at this time may have been his embarrassment and revolt against having to wear what looked like a woman's corset. He was already sensitive about his height—"he hated being small," Estelle said.[16] Corseted, his stiff, doll-like posture and movements further exacerbated his lack of a "manly" physique, especially compared to his father and grandfather, both of whom stood about six feet tall. When Willie was in either the fifth or sixth grade (the precise time is not clear), Maud put him in this mail-order back brace. He had company, since Auntee did the same to Sallie Murry, who said "they hurt like anything." But while she slipped out of hers as often as she could get away with it, oddly, she didn't know whether her cousin did so as well or even what he thought of being forced to wear a corset.[17] Although no biographer ever asked Maud, the reason given for her confining Willie was to correct his posture: the boy had developed a stoop. One of Maud's neighbors and contemporaries said she thought that Willie's hunched shoulders were an outward manifestation of his shame and humiliation at being sent on his own or going with his mother to find his father when he had passed out in some alley or doorway off the courthouse square.

Mrs. Calvin Brown said she always felt sorry for Faulkner as a child because his father was often drunk and he and his mother often had to "cart him home." She remembers that "on cold winter nights they'd go around town looking for him because they feared he was unconscious and might freeze to death in the gutter."[18] Maud couldn't stop her husband's drinking or mitigate the embarrassment it caused her eldest son, but she could erase shame's marker on Willie's back. Perhaps confining him was Maud's effort to assert control over a situation that had long ago spun out of control. She could not keep Willie in school, nor could she keep her husband from what her son Jack described as the Falkner men's "accepted way of life," perpetual benders. "These things—the drinking, the code of personal conduct and philosophy of life—were simply passed on from generation to generation like manners and deportment."[19]

After the first month of fifth grade, in 1908, Faulkner's name appeared only once more on the school's honor roll, in January 1910 of his sixth-grade year. By October, J. W. T. had again showed up Murry. With capital stock of thirty thousand dollars and himself as its only stockholder, he opened the First National Bank of Oxford. His fellow townspeople soon made his newest venture yet another business success, while a few blocks away, Murry's livery stable was turning less and less of a profit. Willie was now in seventh grade and still skipping school.

Moving back and forth between the company of his grandfather and Estelle gave the fourteen-year-old boy access to two antithetical worlds, the former's hypermasculine posturing and the latter's hyperfemininity. Both offered playgrounds for his own role-playing and imaginative expression. He could, in effect, try on different identities. One day he could appear in church as his grandfather's tiny twin, the next he could be the poet dandy with Estelle. Or he could play at being her double.

When he joined other boys' play, he appeared reserved and sometimes hostile. A playmate described Willie: "He didn't seem to enter into many activities" with other boys. "He would roam the woods with us looking for plums, chestnuts, and blackberries. When we piled up leaves to jump in or made sand houses, he would stand by and observe. Maybe he would say, 'Here is a tornado,' and tear everything to pieces."[20]

By the time eighth grade was over, his attendance report listed "Willie, 14" as not even present for the required number of days. Murry may not have been too concerned about Willie's truancy. He had never liked or done well in school himself. Worse, from his perspective, the boy was becoming more and more involved in reading, painting, and writing poetry, hardly manly pursuits. That year Willie read *Moby Dick* and became its passionate advocate, telling his brother Jack he thought it was the best book ever written. Jack was uninterested. That same summer of 1912 Willie attempted but failed to interest another male friend in *Pilgrim's Progress*.

Besides his mother, the only real enthusiast of poetry and fiction was Estelle. When they weren't on the Oldhams' front porch reading or talking, they met at Davidson & Wardlaw's, the combined bookstore and jewelry store on the square, which included a reading area with good light and comfortable seating. They began reading poetry together, and Willie started showing her his own work. One day he gave her two pages of verse he had written and asked which she preferred. With no hesitation Estelle chose the verses that in fact were from "The Song of Solomon." He responded, "You may not be a poetess, but you're a darn good literary critic."[21] Willie's brother John noticed that his brother, who had grown increasingly taciturn in other company, appeared voluble in hers: "With her listening, Bill found he could talk. From then on he spent more and more time down at her house, being with her and talking to her and listening to her play."[22]

In 1912, Murry had a particularly bad year. His finances were seriously compromised, and his father was in no position to bail him out again, having just spent another thirty thousand dollars, this time to extract himself from a brief and stormy second marriage.[23] More people were driving cars, and Murry's livery business, never particularly successful, continued to fail. As his son Jack wrote after Murry's death, his father, unlike Colonel William Falkner, "was not a natural born salesman—of hardware or anything else."[24] Seeking to supplement his income, he had bought another nineteenth-century business on the decline, a coal-oil franchise supplying lamp oil. The Falkners' financial situation worsened. In order to raise enough cash to buy yet a third business, this time a hardware store, the Falkners sold their house and moved to a rental on South Street in March 1912.[25] In mid-August, Maud and Murry Falkner, along with John and Dean, left Oxford on a brief trip. Maud was probably taking her husband on one of their periodic trips to Dr. Keeley's.

That December Maud supervised the family's fifth move since Billie's birth. The Falkner brothers' more observant contemporaries were well aware of the family's financial and domestic difficulties. "Miss Maud had a rough life and they lived ever so many places," said a neighbor and school-mate.[26] According to her granddaughter Dean, Maud's tastes and living habits were "Spartan."[27] But perhaps this was more out of long years of making do with little in order to give her children what she felt they needed. "She wasn't frugal," said her friend Christine Drake; "She never had a lot to be frugal with." When Christine was living with her, Maud bought her-self a second-hand sideboard that she was very pleased with. She explained that her husband "never did invest in a lot of furniture," so that was why she was buying now. Some, including Christine, thought Murry was stingy: "Mr. Murry never turned any money loose for furniture." Christine further commented: "She was very quiet and would just say a few words. She never did lay it all on him but she said then that she never did get to fix up her house because the Falkners spent all of their money on gasoline. That was when she told me she thought 'all the Falkners have octane gas in their veins.'" Several days later Christine noticed the sideboard was gone and asked Maud about it. "She said, 'Well Johnsey [her son John] said he wished he'd have bought it so I just let him have it.'" Maud never had been a "fixey" lady like her stylish sister-in-law, Auntee, but she did like pretty things. "Another time," Christine said, "she asked me to order some glasses with her. They were fruit juice glasses that were a kind of wisteria color. It was late in her life to be buying things like that."[28] But it was also the first time in her life, since before her marriage, that she was making money of her own.

However, that Christmas of 1912 Maud's awareness of the steady downward spiraling of her family's finances and happiness was heightened when she compared her household to her father and sister-in-law's and to her upwardly mobile neighbors, the Oldhams. Neither the Oldham girls nor Sallie Murry ever lacked for clothes or toys. Her friend Marjorie Lewis remembered: "Sallie Murry just had more—a diamond ring when she was a little girl—a modest one—and a Shetland pony. No other girls did. She was indulged. If she came home from school and told her mother some girl had a new hair ribbon, why Auntee would go down and buy Sallie Murry a dozen new ones."[29] Since 1905, when the Oldhams had moved across from J. W. T.'s house, their home had been a social gathering place. Now both Bill, or Billie (as he had become by 1912), and Jack were spending more time there. Lida Oldham encouraged Estelle and Tochie to invite their friends for parties and informal gatherings.[30]

In contrast, the neighborhood children, now teenagers, had long ago stopped visiting the Falkner boys' house, although they often gathered at

Sallie Murry's for parties—which the Oldham girls were not allowed to attend because their parents thought Sallie's guest list too inclusive. There were no parties at the Falkners. When the family did gather for dinner, the mood was often tense. Unable to control his behavior, Murry tried instead to confine and constrict his wife and children. According to one schoolmate, Murry Falkner "ruled those boys pretty rigidly. I know he did William. We thought Mr. Murry was reserved and uncompromising."[31] According to Jack and John, Murry wouldn't even let anyone talk at meals until he had finished eating and placed his napkin down on the table.[32] He also held his wife to a strict schedule. "Dinner was served at . . . Twelve sharp, for if Murry walked in . . . and his meal was not waiting . . . he turned on his heel and left the house. 'In a lifetime,' Maud declared, 'he was never 15 seconds late.'"[33] Although he lacked his grandfather's or his father's ability to make a living, he possessed "their temper and imperiousness."[34] Another contemporary comments, "Mr. Murry was very domineering, just like his father. His father was very pompous, very much the aristocrat in his own opinion. He'd sit out on his porch with his feet on the banisters just surveying the scene." At least once Maud retaliated against Murry's binge drinking by taking "his favorite records—he loved his music—and jump[ing] up and down on them. She told me that [but] I don't think she would like for it to be put in history," said her daughter-in-law Louise.[35]

In the fall of 1913, Billie, just sixteen, experienced another loss, again a woman he loved. Estelle's parents sent her off to a Virginia boarding school for the year. There is no record of how he responded to her absence. Estelle said they wrote to each other and that he often sent her poems and drawings, none of which have survived.[36] She also said that when she was sixteen, she fell in love with him.[37] But over the course of the summer of 1914, Billie Falkner discovered someone else to talk to: Phil Stone, four years older than he, who returned from Yale with a B.A. degree.

In September 1914, having graduated from Mary Baldwin, Estelle registered for classes at the university. Since Billie had not even finished high school, this meant another kind of separation. Estelle was now a coed, while Billie was just a high school boy. Perhaps partly in response, he made sure he wasn't that, either, by not registering for classes that fall. Walking to school in the mornings, Jack and John sometimes saw their older brother coming home from drinking with an older man named Buster Crouch.

Crouch was known to get so drunk he would vomit his false teeth. When they were "in their cups," the two often exchanged hats. Crouch wore a huge cowboy hat that looked even larger on Billie. One morning as his brothers came up to Billie, they taunted their hung-over brother, calling out, "Good morning, Memmy!"—his childhood nickname and the one that only Callie still called him. All he answered was "God dammit!"[38] He may have been a high school boy, but he was acting like a Falkner man.

Faulkner writes about such manhood in "Moonlight," which he said was "about the first short story I ever wrote" and dated from the early 1920s. Only two versions, both drafted after he wrote his first novel and one incomplete, are extant.[39] In the former, Faulkner writes with distanced irony about a movie—a crazed, sixteen-year-old Southern boy who forces himself to drink bootleg whiskey so he'll have the courage to "seduce" his equally movie-crazed girlfriend. His intention is to show that he is a man. The irony is that neither adolescent wants either sex or alcohol. The boy's reasons for needing to seduce "Susan" have nothing to do with his feelings for her but everything to do with his sense (learned from the movies) of how a "real man" should behave. Cribbing lines from Hollywood romances he thinks, "That's all I want . . . I just want to seduce her. I would even marry her afterward, even if I ain't a marrying kind of man." Failure modifies his wish: "All I wanted was just to seduce somebody." Even the smell of whiskey makes him sick, with "his whole being revolting, recoiling." His clumsy attempt to "seduce" Susan frightens them both. What the boy really wants, as he describes it, is the "cool comfortable unlustful kissing of adolescence." Susan's protestations and tears kill even this desire: "He felt nothing at all now." His closing fantasy is of male bonding through alcohol: "He was thinking of himself and Skeet [his confidant] . . . lying on a hill somewhere under the moon with the bottle between them, not even talking" ("Moonlight," *USWF,* 496, 500, 501, 503). Faulkner's portrayal here of the trials of adolescence resonates with Estelle's portrayal in her own short story, "A Crossing," which she brought back with her from Shanghai in 1924.

Maud must have been quietly frantic about her eldest son, but the only surviving evidence is an anecdote she wrote in her Bible and dated "Saturday October 1st, 1914," a week after Billie's seventeenth birthday.[40] In a bleak period it is a memory of a more hopeful time: "Just after his 7th birthday William and Muddie [Lelia, called 'Damuddy' or 'Damuddie'] were studying the Sunday School lesson—In reply to Muddie's question— 'William, what would you rather have than *anything* else?' He answered, after a moment's thought—'I'd rather have honor and do what's right.'" Maud seems to have blamed herself partly for Billie's truancy, but her discussion of that blame shows how aware she was of his genius and also how tender she was toward it. Interviewed in the 1950s, Maud said she "always" thought her oldest son "was different," that he was "just smarter." She noted that he read a great deal as a child and a youth and did well in school at first. But she thought her mother and she had tried too hard to steer him into being a sketcher and painter rather than a scholar, and that through her own interest in painting he was perhaps directed toward it too much. She added that she now realized that what he had wanted most was to be a writer, and quite early had determined to be nothing else. At the same time Maud also suggested that what Billie wanted to learn could not be had in the Oxford school system. She thought he had quit school because "it bored him and because [by the summer of 1914, Phil] Stone had introduced him to the Russian writers," whom he stayed out of school to read.[41] For the next two years, until Stone returned to Yale to study law, he and Faulkner would be inseparable.

Finishing Maud's Story

Meanwhile, by 1917, Murry's hardware store, the most recent business his father had assigned him, was failing. In a last-ditch salvage attempt, Murry moved the store into one of his father's buildings to save rent.[42] Nonetheless the business went under. Murry had put up his house as collateral and lost that too. At this point, according to Sallie Murry, J. W. T. "moved them down to the home place with us. Aunt Maud who wasn't happy with the arrangement, just went out and rented a 2-storey house on Van Buren. They lived there only a short time until Uncle Murry got his job at the university and they moved into the Delta Psi house on campus."[43] The year 1917–18 was also a crisis point in Billie's and Estelle's relationship, for Estelle accepted Cornell Franklin's proposal of marriage. In April 1918, shortly before their wedding, Faulkner left Oxford to visit Phil Stone at Yale. The disintegration of his parents' household would have been one more reason for Faulkner to want to live elsewhere, and Phil was offering him almost free room and board.

Meanwhile, on 1 December 1918, Maud's father-in-law used his political clout to get Murry the job of assistant secretary at Ole Miss.[44] "The Colonel must have decided that he had lost all the money a father could be expected to lose in setting up a middle-aged son in a series of businesses." By all accounts, although this job wasn't terribly demanding, he was very good at it.[45] One of the job's perks was its large house. This was Murry's last job, and only the second one he had ever enjoyed. He was promoted to secretary and retired only when he was forced out by a change in Mississippi's political regimes.

At some point before he died, Murry stopped drinking, and Murry and Maud seem to have come to some kind of accommodation.[46] Yet this turnaround was too late to keep any of the Falkner brothers from becoming alcoholics.[47] Throughout all but the first five years of Faulkner's childhood, his father's depression and alcoholism had shaped the family dynamics and dominated his relationships with his wife and children. These were now an ingrained part of Murry's eldest son's emotional legacy. Murry died in 1932 of a heart attack, ten years after his father, the Colonel. Faulkner said of Murry, "He just gave up. He got tired of living."[48]

In contrast, Maud showed no signs of being tired. Instead, she recovered a part of herself that she had lost in 1907, when her mother and mother-in-law died within six months of each other. She began to paint again, giving visual expression to subjects and feelings that were off-limits for white women of her generation.

10

Choosing Roles and Role Models
Faulkner's Delinquent Fathers

IN ABOUT 1912, at the age of fifteen, Billie Falkner quit school, started drinking, and committed himself to becoming a poet and visual artist. Simultaneously, he began some serious role-playing. As we have seen, his initial poses seem to have sprung from his attachment to two very different people, his grandfather and Estelle Oldham. Until December 1924, he dedicated himself to his poetry and drawing. Then suddenly, within a matter of weeks, he switched from poetry to prose fiction, where he found his genius and his voice. What was the relation of his role-playing, which at times verged on imposture, to his art?

Faulkner's long poetic apprenticeship is promising only in retrospect. Between 1912, when he declared himself an author, and 1925, when he suddenly reinvented himself as a novelist, producing *Soldiers' Pay* in a matter of months, he claimed to be a poet exclusively. We do not know how much of his apprenticeship work Faulkner destroyed, but much remains— in all some three hundred poems and poem fragments and his dream-play.[1] This writing is technically competent but highly imitative and somehow lifeless—as if its language were a kind of double mask—in short, the invention of a literary poseur.

Nonetheless, it is serious apprenticeship work. First, he arduously revised the majority of his poems; sometimes as many as nine drafts survive. Second, he wrote and arranged much of his poetry in sequences that, lacking a commercial publisher and often for private purposes, he illustrated and bound himself. Six of these "books" have survived: *The Lilacs* (1920), *Vision in Spring* (1921), *Helen: A Courtship* and *Mayday* (1926), an early typescript of *The Marble Faun* (c. 1920), and his dream-play, *The Marionettes* (1920). Third, major formal and thematic concerns of Faulkner's poetry are also essential to his fiction. Can we reconcile these apparent contradictions in motivation and dedication?

Looked at in the context of Faulkner's adolescence and young adulthood (1912 to 1925), these contradictions in his work do not seem so surprising. For in his everyday behavior he was also maintaining a series of opposite poses, including those of the Poet-Dandy and the Warrior. In early December 1918 Faulkner, like Donald Mahon, the wounded warrior of *Soldiers' Pay*, returned home from serving in World War I. According to official records of the Royal Canadian Air Force (RCAF), he had renamed himself, claimed his mother's land as Great Britain instead of Oxford, Mississippi, and pretended he had no father.[2] He later explained his name change: "I was secretly ambitious and did not want to ride on grandfather's coattails, and so accepted the U [from Falkner to Faulkner], glad of such an easy way to strike out for myself."[3] He also fabricated his military career. Faulkner's tour of duty in the RCAF amounted to an uncompleted five-month training period in Canada. He never went overseas. In fact he never even flew in a plane.

But when he limped off the train in Oxford he created a different impression, one that was not dispelled until after his death. The real-life cadet Faulkner wore an overseas officer's cap and walked slowly, leaning upon his newly acquired cane. He later claimed he wore a metal plate in his head— to cover a hole made by shrapnel. He also told friends that he drank so much to relieve chronic pain caused by this "head wound." The effect of his pose was immediate and gratifying. Bystanders ignored the other soldiers to cheer the apparently maimed officer and hero. Faulkner's fellow enlistees looked on enviously.

This hoax did not end at the station. Faulkner wore his officer's uniform around town and had an Oxford photographer (perhaps Maud) memorialize his imposture in a series of "official portraits."[4] (Faulkner's fictional voice will make good use of lying or deceptive photographs in his novel *Absalom, Absalom!* and in his early Gothic horror tale, "The Leg.") Throughout the years 1918–25, Faulkner, with the "u," the spelling he adopted permanently when he gave up his dream of becoming a poet, assumed all or parts of his wounded-war-officer imposture as it suited his needs. He alternated this pose with that of a "poet" who consistently assumed in his writing the mask of Pierrot, the impostor par excellence of literary convention.

As I've written elsewhere, his adoption of this mask was not unique. Fellow modernists Conrad Aiken, Wallace Stevens, and T. S. Eliot had all assumed it. In fact Pierrot was so popular in the 1920s that even in Honolulu in 1920, the same year that Faulkner wrote his own Pierrot play, the theater group to which Estelle belonged performed the medieval Pierrot farce, *Master Peter Pathelin.*

The poets' voices Faulkner chose to adopt as his own ranged across the centuries: Shakespeare, Keats, Swinburne, Tennyson, the French Symbolists, Housman and other Georgians, and even early Modernists. His contemporaries—Pound, Eliot, and Aiken—figure prominently in his repertoire. Each poet offered unique imaginative possibilities—a stunning array.

My discussion of Faulkner's self-transformation from poseur to artist begins with this real-life scene of a twenty-two-year-old returning war hero because, throughout his apprenticeship and to a lesser extent throughout his life, Faulkner—like some other artists, though much more flamboyantly—continued to play this and other roles. These roles often verged on, and sometimes were, self-parody. Costume was all-important. In Faulkner's adolescence, his brothers noted what they judged as his effeminate eating and dressing habits—dainty breakfasts, elaborate attention to his dress clothes, his insistence on their being skin-tight. By the early 1920s Faulkner's poet dress was either so outrageously dandified or so slovenly, and his behavior at times so arrogant, that his peers at the University of Mississippi began calling him "Count no 'Count." He also assumed other roles, but the antithetical roles of the androgynous and neurasthenic poet Pierrot and the man of physical action are the most significant: these two poses would deeply affect the nature and the course of Faulkner's creative development as well as the content and moral thrust of his mature fiction.

To pose as a heroic or famous figure is not unusual for a young artist. Biographers have documented many such cases.[5] Walter Jackson Bate's account of Keats donning a laurel wreath is an excellent example, because it shows the difference between an artist for whom imposture is merely an episode and Faulkner, for whom such deception was, in periods of stress, common. Keats's momentary assumption of "Apollo's glories" was followed immediately by feelings of guilt, shame, and self-revulsion.[6] He never repeated his behavior. Faulkner not only repeated his soldier pose but shamelessly reenacted it and preserved it in photographs for posterity. Later, expanding on his experiments with the fluidity of identity (and subjectivity?), he added other poses and elaborated on the first. Obviously, Faulkner was not an impostor. The elaborateness, repetition, and sheer quantity of these episodes anticipate his novelistic treatments of the theme of chameleonlike characters who ultimately commit suicide or allow themselves to be killed because they do not know who they are.

In some ways Faulkner's conduct resembles that of pathological impostors.[7] Like them he appeared to feel no guilt about his activities. In con-

10.1. William Faulkner posing in his various Royal Canadian Air Force outfits. (Courtesy of Jill Faulkner Summers)

trast to Keats, who was embarrassed by his pretense, Faulkner never admitted that his posing was a sham.[8]

According to the literature on impostors (all of which is based on case studies of males), a traumatic event in which a young boy sees his father succumb to either psychic or physical defeat is often a precipitating event in the childhoods of pathological impostors.[9] The trauma lies not so much in the destruction itself as in the parents' inadequate response to it, which leaves the child defenseless. Events alone—certainly not a single incident—

are probably insufficient to explain a lifetime of disease. If the parents' response is healthy, the child's suffering will, most likely, be minimal. But if the parents' response leaves the child emotionally unprotected, so that his father's real devaluation is emphasized, the child may resort to imposture to defend against the terror he feels. Clinicians observe that the situation is made worse if the mother actively aids in her husband's destruction. Maud perhaps contributed to her husband's sense of defeat and helplessness by refusing to allow him to act on his initial reaction—to separate himself physically from his father (as the Colonel had done). Besides vetoing Murry's wish to go West—his last bid for economic and emotional independence—she also humiliated him in front of his children by taking them on trips to the Keeley sanatorium. But perhaps his mother's actions paled to insignificance beside his father's, whose drunkenness shamed him on a regular basis.

Unlike pathological impostors, Faulkner was also producing tangible work. By the autumn of 1920, his anxiety about claiming the dual identity as man and artist moved tentatively toward resolution as he gained the distance needed to begin to give it an artistic rather than a neurotic form. It is apparent that a shift was occurring as, in his life, his impostures varied, moving between the idealized image of white Southern Manhood and a more realistic self-image of the poet-outcast. The beginnings of resolution and a concomitant developmental leap in creative expression mark his next major piece of writing, *The Marionettes*. There, in the characters of the drunken, would-be Pan figures of Pierrot, Pierrot's Shade, and the virgin-femme fatale Marietta, Faulkner begins to explore the darker implications of difficulties merely hinted at in *The Marble Faun*. Faulkner's probings are tentative, and fuller translation does not occur until 1927, when he writes *Flags in the Dust*, "THE book, of which those other things," he said, referring to his poems and two earlier novels, "were but foals."[10] By then he had completed the work necessary to achieve a creative identity separate from his adolescent poses as he gained more access to and control of his fantasy material.

The clearest proof of this is textual. In *Flags in the Dust* Faulkner has begun to hold his great grandfather up for critical and disinterested examination. There he separates the myth from the reality to depict the demise of a white Southern family whose lives are dominated and made impotent by their idealized visions of a past that never was. These visions manifest themselves in an unseen presence: the great grandfather's ghost. Faulkner brings in the ghost in his first chapter: "As usual old man Falls had brought John Sartoris into the room with him. Freed as he was of time, he was a far more definite presence in the room than the two of them cemented by deafness to a dead time. . . . He seemed to stand above them, all around them, with his bearded hawklike face and the bold glamor of his dream" (5). In *Flags* Faulkner sheds his Pierrot mask, transforming it to create Sartoris's great grandsons, the failed twins Bayard and John. These brothers together comprise a composite of a deeply divided self and are Faulkner's first successfully tragic pierrotique figures.

By 1927, when he wrote *Flags*, Faulkner was a long way from the ten-year-old boy who, having sacrificed his black mother to achieve his own whiteness, was already well advanced in his education into white Southern Manhood. The summer he was working on *Flags*, Faulkner wrote his editor that it was "coming fine," adding tellingly that it was "much better than that other stuff" because "I believe that at least I have learned to control the stuff and fix it on something like rational truth."[11] The truth he fixed on was the need to question and critique this concept of manhood and the myths about race and gender that it supported and justified. Thus *Flags* marked the beginning of what would be a major concern of his life's work.

The highly imitative poetry of his youth represented to some degree the work of Faulkner the poet impostor, a public identity he discarded completely after 1925.[12] It was when he was writing this early poetry that he came closest to living out his impostures. The unusual length of his apprenticeship to poetry is explicable if the poetry is considered in some respects to be the work of a poseur. Faulkner's first two novels, *Soldiers' Pay* (1926) and *Mosquitoes* (1927), though not imitative like his poetry, also draw their main characters and settings from the counterfeit worlds of the would-be soldier and the would-be artist. In these novels, he simultaneously satirizes aspects of his impostures and people who have only borrowed identities. His ironic handling of fictional poseurs suggests a new distancing and objectivity about his own poses. However, when he attempts to portray the tragic results of assuming a false identity, he is less successful, producing melodrama in *Soldiers' Pay* and broad satire in *Mosquitoes* rather than tragedy.

Faulkner shows signs of correcting these flaws in his third novel, *Flags in the Dust* (1927). Its setting was modeled on Oxford and its surrounding territory. And it is the first novel that draws directly on Faulkner's family experiences and mythology rather than on the experiences of his soldier and poet impostures. In writing it, he said he first realized that "by sublimating the actual to the apocryphal, I would have complete liberty to use whatever talent I might have to its absolute top. It opened up a goldmine of other people so I created a cosmos of my own."[13]

The original version of *Flags* was judged a failure. Although he was initially stunned by his publisher's response, he was not discouraged. In

1931 Faulkner, acknowledging and reveling in his growing sense of the flu-idity of his own subjectivity and its value to him as an artist, describes an early session with his editor where he is told: "The trouble is . . . that you had about six books in here. You were trying to write them all at once. He showed me what he meant, what he had done [to edit the manuscript] and I realized for the first time that I had done better than I knew and the long work I had to create opened before me and I contemplated those shady but ingenious shapes by reason of whose labor the impulses of my own ego in this actual world without stability, with a lot of humbleness, and I specu-lated on time and death and wondered if I had invented the [teeming] world to which I should give life or if it had invented me, giving me an illu-sion of greatness."[14] Faulkner and his editor were correct. *Flags in the Dust* contained the much edited and renamed third novel, *Sartoris* (1929), plus the seeds of the five great novels that followed. These novels, set like *Flags* in the physical and emotional past of Faulkner's family and culture, mark the high point of his creative achievement and bring to fruition his the-matic concern with the moral and psychological implications of imposture. In them, particularly in *The Sound and the Fury* (1929), *Light in August* (1932), and *Absalom, Absalom!* (1936), he portrays the tragedies of men and women whose commitment to the dead or to loss itself and the concomitant inabil-ity to love the living, including themselves, condemn them to rage, passivity, and impotence. They live only in the past and through others. Their fa-natic devotion to private, untranslatable, repetitive dreams and acts brings spiritual and physical destruction to others. But worst of all, they never ar-rive at even a sense of who they are or might have been. Seeking inspira-tion in the myths and realities of his own history rather than in experiences grafted on by pretending to be what he was not, Faulkner could, as he wrote his fiction, abandon his role as an impostor in real life.

As he portrays characters who fail to establish identities separate from others, inhabiting instead fantasied and glorified pasts, he develops a stylis-tics that vividly portrays this struggle. Faulkner's earliest lessons in mask-ing were learned from Callie Barr and his mother. Similarly, when he later began sharing his reading and early poems with Estelle, he gleaned much about the tropes of transformation from their private theater and from the Swinburne poems he imitated, most importantly "Sapphics" and "Her-maphroditus." American novelists Faulkner read and found fascinating—including Melville, Hawthorne, and James—had also invented fictions whose forms and themes were deeply concerned with the implications of a constantly transforming perception of reality. In Faulkner's own novels such language is associated with characters who are unable to determine who they are and thereby separate themselves from their inherited pasts.

Their struggle to arrive at definitions and their tragic failure are made manifest as these men and women compulsively resort to a series of personas: they imagine themselves and are even seen by others as being alternately or simultaneously male-female, black-white, pregnant-sterile, Satan-Christ, child-adult. Thus, at perhaps the richest period in his career (1928 to 1942), Faulkner's handling of the notion of the impostor in his writing becomes a highly sophisticated and finely integrated aspect of his art.

11

Learning to Speak with His Eyes
Lelia, Maud, and the Origins of Faulkner's Visual Aesthetic

B
Y DECLARING HIMSELF AN ARTIST, Faulkner crossed a cultural divide into feminine pursuits.[1] As he wrote his editor Malcolm Cowley in 1946, "oratory" was the South's "first Art. . . . Apart from that, 'art' was really no manly business. It was the polite painting of china by gentlewomen."[2] A Southern gentleman knew better than to be an artist. "The *forte* of the Old Dominion," wrote a pre–Civil War news editor, "is to be found in the masculine production of her statesmen . . . who have never indulged in works of imagination."[3] Moreover, for all white Southern writers, the difficulty of freeing themselves from a culturally imposed requirement to serve as polemicists for, first, slavery and, then, white supremacy, "to pacify the autocratic voice of [the] ruling classes or established ideas," was especially pronounced.[4] In the antebellum and post-Reconstruction South, there were tremendous pressures on both sexes not to create at all or, at most, to write fiction and poetry reflecting the fantasies of the South's Narcissa Benbows, Ellen Coldfields, and Drusilla Sartorises. Such propaganda, which passed for art, was relegated to women, "in the equation of women, beauty, literature, and irrelevance." Although imaginative realms were off-limits to "real" Southern men—Faulkner's great grandfather dismissed his own writing as a hobby—the three respectable occupations for genteel white women were teaching, sewing, and writing. In fact, the South praised and venerated its women writers, for the most part because they conformed to cultural strictures that guaranteed "a fundamentally nonserious literary tradition."[5]

Such connections among creativity, gender, and the values of late nineteenth- and early twentieth-century Mississippi played significantly in Faulkner's growing sense of himself as an artist. The influence of his early learning of what I have called his second language—from his mother and grandmother—manifests itself in his first books, all of which he made himself. Several of these are composed of both verbal and visual texts. In *The Marionettes,* he interweaves his two languages—verbal and visual—to create a subversive contrapuntal narrative. Yet, for a Southerner of Faulkner's, his parents', and his grandparents' generations, the visual arts, too, were a gendered occupation deemed the exclusive realm of Southern Ladies. This chapter explores how Faulkner responded to this culturally gendered notion of art throughout his career. How did he experiment in expressing what he felt could not be written by counterpointing language first with his drawings and actual photographs, and later with fictional photographs— that is, photographs belonging to characters in his fiction? How were his figurations of filmic and photographic images and techniques, an interest and technique he shared with other Modernist poets and novelists, expressions of his extraordinary and unique visual poetics?

Concomitantly, what are the roles played in all of this by Faulkner's maternal imaginary? His eye's mind had been trained by two of his earliest and most influential teachers, his mother, Maud, and his grandmother Lelia. Maud did not send Willie to school until he was eight. By then he was reading and had been drawing and painting with his grandmother for years, possibly before he could talk. Despite his being a boy, Maud said that she and her mother expected him to become an artist.

The place of the male artist in Southern culture at that time makes the personal genealogy of his visual aesthetic particularly interesting. Faulkner's fiction reveals the inherent fragility of rigid conceptions of gender roles and racial categories. It is immersed in his culture's always historicized and racialized conceptions of masculinity and femininity. He consistently uses photographs, painting, and filmic techniques to figure race, gender, and desire in ways that undermine Jim Crow tenets and assumptions about difference. Particularly at the beginning of his career, the questions of difference he poses with drawings and self-staged autobiographical photographs have to do with the meaning and relation of racialized gender to his chosen vocation.

Seeing Through His Mothers' Eyes: Background

"I look just like a kodak negative now. All brown my self, and my hair is burned rope-color," Billy wrote to Maud from boot camp in Canada in August of 1918. He illustrated this letter with a line drawing of himself as a Kodak negative (fig. 11.1).[6]

Not surprisingly, in Faulkner's early visual experiments, his debt and

II.I. Faulkner's line drawing of himself as a "Kodak negative,"
22 August 1918. (Courtesy of HRC and Jill Faulkner Summers)

attachment to the lived and the imaginative realities of his mother and grandmother reveal themselves most clearly.[7] As Southern women and as artists they were adepts of disguise. John and Jack Faulkner's memoirs show that Maud and Lelia impressed upon all four of Maud's sons a familial, feminine, and artistic tradition of resistance. Maud and Lelia did not make Faulkner into a writer, and their art was not comparable to his. But they did teach him this other language. Training him to observe closely and to speak with his eyes and hands, they communicated their fascination with the wordless arts. He watched them watching others and then transforming their observations into drawings, paintings, photographs, store-window dioramas, soap sculptures, even dolls. Furthermore, as his introduction to visual modernity, he watched his grandmother doctor photographs and teach others her technique. His grandmother's and mother's artwork taught him his earliest lessons in the subjectivity of even ocular perception, the slipperiness of "truth." And they taught this boy child how to mask his subversive activities and use marginalization to his advantage in order to enjoy the forbidden pleasures of serious art.[8]

Although their communities classified them, safely, as amateurs, both Lelia and Maud were, in fact, primitives, or in current terminology, outsider artists.[9] Maud's art sometimes displays the strengths of that origin, an individualism and freedom from convention and tradition that she apparently passed on to Faulkner. Like the art of other primitive painters, hers "derives," as John Berger writes, "from considerable personal experience and, indeed, is often provoked as a result of the profundity or intensity of that experience."[10] Maud's three 1941 portraits of African Americans exemplify this intensity (see figs. 4.4, 4.6, 4.7). Formally they suggest that she enjoyed the challenges presented by flesh tones, ranging from Callie Barr's blue-black skin to the pale tan of Preacher Green Liggens. These paintings are ambitious in that their purpose, unlike that of Maud's more ladylike art—her copies of Old Masters, her still lifes, white portraits, and cabin paintings—is not to decorate a home, glorify ancestors, or confirm racist beliefs about African Americans. In each instance the figure's expression seems intently focused on some inner problem. These human faces are a far cry from the nostalgic "simple darkie" images in her market-oriented works. Because these portraits were the mimetic creations of a mature vision, they also reflect her fully formed perceptions of reality and so may be read as an accurate summation and ordering of how the world seemed to her. Equally important, because primitive or outsider artists are either self-trained or trained in maturity, they have adapted to being marginalized as different or other.[11] This is why so much of this art "was never meant, according to the cultural class [and race] system, to be said."[12] In the 1940s for a white Southern woman to portray her black models' subjectivity, even unconsciously, was not something to be said.

Maud also knew and cared about what would sell. By 1954 she was selling her paintings for between five and fifty dollars, depending on their size. Her cabin scenes were very popular, as were her commissioned portraits. In letters to her niece Sallie Burns, she reports some of her sales: "copies of two Negro pictures to Dr. Elkins of Australia . . . one Negro picture to a lady from Sweden" and a big "portrait of Dr. Mayes . . . to hang in the hospital." And later that year, "Billy took six detailed pictures from my big Negro cabins and gave them to some professors at the University of Virginia." A gallery owner in New Orleans asked for more cabin scenes, "originals of what the man called 'the vanishing South.'"[13] As she wrote Sallie Burns, she was "thrilled" to be making her own money from her art. Consequently, she generally painted conventional subjects and often marketed multiple copies of her more popular paintings. For the wider public, however, the world beyond Oxford to which *Absalom, Absalom!*'s Rosa Coldfield alludes, Maud wanted her art to be seen as different and unclassifiable. A Memphis journalist raised her ire when he compared her to Grandma Moses, and she was even more displeased when Robert Coughlan wrote in *Life* magazine that she was a joiner and an amateur painter: "He said I was a church-goer—I haven't been in a church in ten years, except for funerals. As for my painting, I am not one of these little old Southern ladies who paints porcelain or greeting cards [She did.]. Women come to me to have their china painted or to get greeting cards. I tell them to go somewhere else. I am a picture painter. I sell my paintings; I make money on them."[14] Yet, privately to Sallie Burns, who must have asked for a still life of pansies, she wrote, "I paint whatever anybody wants. Soon as I get my paints from Sears, I'll paint a pansy one for you." Her private remarks also show that she maintained a clear perspective and a sense of humor about the limits of her talent. In another letter to Sallie Burns she wrote that "in the 2 and 1/2 months since September I have painted 26 oils—portraits and such—9 coats of arms, a mess of wedding invitations. I'm convinced Einstein was right when he said if he had to do it over, he would take up plumbing. If I had known I would make a living this late in life, I'd have taken up plumbing instead of a paint-brush." Maud closes, writing in metaphor reminiscent of Faulkner's early poetry and the letters he wrote home to his parents in 1918, that now that the "winter solstice" has passed, "I begin watching for the sun to take a tuck in the hem of evening and stretch the days. I hope to hear from you often 'cause I love you."[15]

She also enjoyed the publicity that she began to receive in the last decade of her life. She wrote Sallie Burns that she was "all excited" because a journalist was going to include her in a nationally syndicated column called "'Geniuses at Work,' and will send me a list of the papers that print it. This really flatters." When Sallie herself asked permission to write an article about Maud's life as a painter, Maud was pleased. She made three restrictions, however: that her age not be given, that her "bairns" not be mentioned, "because I am Maud Falkner and not just the mother of those successful sons," and that the article make no reference to Grandma Moses.

In almost every letter she writes to Sallie Burns, Maud mentions four subjects: family news, her painting, her longing for her niece, and praise for Sallie's independence and professional and personal success. "It's lovely the way you get a zest out of living and having lots of friends. I envy you, Devotedly, Maud," she writes at one point. And, "I'm so glad your life is full and happy—You give so much pleasure to people you are with." She adds wistfully, "I know you have too much culture and training within you to ever get bored. I love you, Maud."[16]

Asked in the 1950s whether she had painted when her children were growing up, Maud said that the only times she could remember "for a thirty-five year span consisted of a few pictures she worked on while standing at the living room mantle with her painting supplies safely above her children's reach."[17] Perhaps in part because she had no time or space or encouragement to paint after her mother's death, Maud was especially supportive of her eldest son's artwork and his very early interest in photography.

Women storytellers and painters were Faulkner's models. Against this backdrop of a Southern tradition of art as a feminine pursuit, I will set his wordless signs, his early drawings, his actual and fictional photographs, and his use of the languages of the visual arts, particularly photography and film, to structure both his narratives of self and his novelistic narratives. These mark the foundation and fruition of his visual aesthetics. It was through this language that ultimately, in *Absalom, Absalom!*, he probed most deeply the two most common but silenced relationships in Southern history, memory, and culture: relations between black and white maternal figures and the often conjoined relations between white Southerners and their shadow wives, sons, and daughters.

Actual and Fictional Photographs

As those who write about photographs and our personal experiences have shown, the photograph encodes the essence of the Modernist and Postmodernist experience of knowing or, rather, not knowing. Some of the multiplicities that make the photograph so powerful are its teasing false reality (in contrast to other frankly interpretive mimetic forms); its use as a device for fragmenting reality, as a tool of aggression, acquisition, and power, as witness or evidence; and its surrealistic ability to freeze time— "The reading of the photograph is always historical"—yet blur the lines between art and life as it demarcates the chasm separating sight from speech.[18] In addition the photograph possesses an often unquestioned ability to testify to "what has been"; an outrageous voyeurism that "makes everyone a tourist in other people's reality and eventually in one's own"; and paradoxically, an ability to do all this without language—to speak with its body or materiality.[19] These are the qualities that make the photograph, particularly the photograph of desire, so compelling to us, to Faulkner, and to his fictional men and women.

But for Faulkner, as his life and use of photographic tropes in his fiction show, the process itself—making a photograph from a negative—was equally compelling. Watching black become white and white become black in the process of transforming a negative into a photograph may well have been the starting point for imagining the unspeakable: that in Mississippi in the 1920s and 1930s, race was a social construction, not a biological fact. The photograph and photographic process are certainly metaphors he uses to foreground racial and gender indeterminacy, most notably in *Light in August*, *Absalom, Absalom!*, and *Go Down, Moses*, his three greatest novels about slavery's legacy. The image of the photograph itself is also central to his Modernist epistemological concerns. Yet, in Faulkner's fiction, where photographs are verbal constructs rather than concrete objects, we never literally see them.

These fictional photographs exert tremendous erotic power in Faulkner's fiction. In "The Leg" (1925), an early, short, supernatural tale, a photograph created by a jealous lover's ghost drives his girlfriend mad, nearly causes his rival's murder, incites the girl's brother to murder, and causes the brother's death. In the first Yoknapatawpha novel, *Flags in the Dust* (written in 1927 and published as *Sartoris* in 1929), Bayard Sartoris burns the photograph of his dead twin brother in a desperate effort to free himself from his obsession with memories of his idolized yet hated dark double. In Faulkner's uncanny doubling and reworking of his most compelling tropes, he will reconfigure and explicitly racialize such moments in *Absalom, Absalom!*, his most photographic and filmic novel. There, the fire set by Clytie, which first frames her and then burns her to death, also kills her white half-brother Henry and, ultimately, causes the death of her (half) aunt Rosa Coldfield. As in a photographic negative, the racial category "white" cannot exist without its "black" double. They "are mutually constitutive as well as always already divided and divisive terms."[20] Rosa confirms this when she is still an adolescent. She first names Clytie to assert her own whiteness: *"Take your hand off me, nigger!"* She tries to deny their kinship with the lie of Southern patriarchy *"which had taught me not only to instinctively fear her and what she was, but to shun the very objects she had touched."* Then *"suddenly,"* in an exquisite moment of recognition, Rosa's *"outrage"* transforms to *"despair"*: She cannot sustain the lie: *"Perhaps I knew even then what I could not, would not, must not believe)—I cried 'And you too? And you too, sister, sister?'"* (*AA*, 112, 113).

Sanctuary and *Absalom, Absalom!* are Faulkner's most stunning invocations of the photograph's multiplicity of meanings and its wordlessness to figure an always racialized desire in ways that reveal the hypocrisy of Southern patriarchy's racial and sexual laws. There it becomes a subversive presence, challenging the boundaries of language and the binarisms comprising definitions of race, sexuality, and gender. In these novels, the force of this image reaches beyond the conventions of the literal photograph.

The epistemological issues double as he uses fictional photographs to question and critique Southern patriarchal ways of seeing, speaking, and acting out forbidden desire. Here *Absalom, Absalom!* is especially relevant. Until he wrote this novel, Faulkner's fiction had tried and generally succeeded in occluding, via caricature, interrelations between black and white maternal figures. (See, for example, the relationship between Quentin's black and white mothers, Dilsey and Caroline, in *The Sound and the Fury*.) In *Absalom, Absalom!* the relations between Judith and her slave half-sister Clytie and between Clytie and Rosa unmask this occlusion. Reading this unmasking, as I will in the next chapter, leads to a new understanding of this novel and of the corresponding importance of Faulkner's two mothers, Callie and Maud, to his maternal imaginary. In *Sanctuary*, Horace Benbow's fantasies of lust, incest, and pedophilia all coalesce as he gazes on a stolen photograph of his nubile young stepdaughter; in *Absalom, Absalom!*. Rosa Coldfield articulates the essence of absence and desire encoded in a photograph of the lover of her niece, Judith. Throughout Faulkner's work, even as late as *The Fable* (1954), fictional photographs are images for epistemological conundrums. They are also sites and sights of the forbidden and therefore unspeakable.

Faulkner consistently uses the fictional photograph to question certain culturally gendered and raced desires and to probe the reasons for their being so. Our not being able to see the photograph—its fictionality—gives it a greater intensity than either straight fantasy or an actual photograph. Faulkner's characters capitalize on the photograph's multiplicity of meanings and its wordlessness to imagine desire and to use it, or fail to use it, to negotiate the prescribed boundaries of their lives.

Artistic Precursors to Faulkner's Fictional Photographs

It is a long way from Faulkner's imitative 1920 dream-play *The Marionettes* to *Sanctuary* and *Absalom, Absalom!* Nevertheless, this play with drawings, which swerve dramatically yet silently from his written text, signals the beginning of his adult revolt as the Southern male artist. In writing, illustrating, binding, and selling four or five copies of *The Marionettes* to his Oxford neighbors and the university community, Faulkner proclaims himself an artist of two mediums. His drawings here are perhaps most provocative, for they say, with concrete visual images, what he cannot say in words.[21] In his later novels, a fictional photograph offers Faulkner's fictional characters a similar chance to free themselves from silence, without imprisoning themselves in language.

It is now a commonplace that his most specific literary and graphic inspiration for *The Marionettes* was the 1894 English translation of Oscar Wilde's *Salome*, which was illustrated by Aubrey Beardsley and which Faulkner owned. Illustrating a play is most unusual: plays are written to be performed—to illustrate themselves. *Salome* is illustrated because Wilde's publisher and Wilde himself knew his English translation would not be performed in public. In fact, the British censors kept it off the boards in England until 1931. Choosing to align himself with *Salome* as a mark of his artistic identity boldly challenged received notions of both the artist and Southern Manhood.

Ever since Wilde's imprisonment for his homosexuality in 1895, *Salome* has been read as a homosexual drama. As early as 1913, essays in psycho-analytic journals had argued for the play's "polymorphous perversity" and identified themes such as "homosexuality, sadism, masochism, castration . . . latent object doubling . . . fetishism, clitoral stimulation" and even "lunar fixation"! Critics also noted that "the sexual power struggle in the text finds its graphic counterpart in the potent illustrative matter."[22] Faulkner could not have chosen a more subversive model. His own text and illustrations are not as sexually explicit and outrageous as *Salome*'s somewhat veiled drama made manifest in Beardsley's frankly homoerotic drawings. Clearly, in adopting *Salome*'s unusual format for his own play and also borrowing from its written text and drawings, Faulkner was suggesting a more than casual affinity with Wilde. By illustrating his play he claimed that what was in it should also not be performed in public. And indeed, despite his active involvement with the campus drama group at this time, *The Marionettes* was not performed. To an audience who knew Faulkner, Maud, and Estelle, *The Marionettes* said and illustrated what should not be said. It was too auto-biographically revealing.

The Marionettes' central protagonist is the young Faulkner's favorite persona, Pierrot, that amoral, often inebriated hero of the nineteenth-century French pantos whom Modernist novelists and poets adopted and rein-vented to serve their own imaginative yearnings. At the opening and throughout *The Marionettes*, Faulkner has drawn him sprawling side-stage "in a drunken sleep," his head resting on a spindly cafe table. There, im-mobilized, insensible, and therefore not morally responsible for his thoughts, he dreams the two dreams that are this play. These uninhibited "fermented" dreams and the drawings that often turn from their text reflect multiple versions of how Pierrot-Faulkner sees and says himself in the world. They may be thought of as his way of (through the scandalous Wilde) appropri-ating his mother(s) tongue. For he also says here, with his drawings of Pier-rot's, his "moon-mad" foster mother's, and the virgin Marietta's minds and bodies, what he dares not say in words.

11.2. Faulkner's "fallen" Marietta (*left*), from Faulkner's *The Marionettes*. Aubrey Beardsley's illustration for Oscar Wilde's *Salome*. (*Marionettes* drawing courtesy of Jill Faulkner Summers)

The text reveals that Pierrot wants to possess his moon mother's magic powers—her "song"—in order to seduce and then abandon a young virgin. The play's final drawing, however, suggests that such coupling will kill Marietta and leave him voiceless, staring solipsistically in a mirror. But only Faulkner's drawing says this. His text never alludes to this illustration, which is the play's "Curtain" image. His silence on this drawing of death and mirror images is so disturbing that it erupts beyond the curtain, denying the closure signaled by this word. In imitating the subject of Beardsley's closing drawing for *Salome*, Faulkner makes further claims on an artistic twinship. Another striking visual-textual-sexual similarity is an illustration of the fallen Marietta sitting front-face and bare-breasted. Her torso, tightly encased in a bejeweled outfit designed to make her bared breasts and navel protrude, looks very much like the poses and costume of Beardsley's *Salome*. Details, like his imitating the design and placement of the jewels between Marietta's breasts, indicate how carefully Faulkner studied his model.

In *The Marionettes*, Faulkner also experiments for the first time with

11.3. The virgin Marietta watched over by the Two Shades (*left*),
from *The Marionettes*. Estelle Oldham at the time of her engagement to
Cornell Franklin, April 1918. (Courtesy of Jill Faulkner Summers)

what will become, in his fiction, a narrative strategy that, like the dissonances between *The Marionettes*'s illustrations and text, negates any objective notion of seeing. A chorus of two "figures" comments throughout on
the play's action, specifically what each one sees. They disagree in matters
small and large, from the weather to whether Marietta's fling with Pierrot
has altered her looks and psyche. They will each "see" a very different
"fallen" Marietta. The Second Figure conceives her as a Salome-like
femme fatale: hard, sadistic, and cold with "gold" hair "bleachened [*sic*]
with blood and passion" and breasts "like ivory crusted jewels for which
men have died, . . . armies have slain one another and brother has murdered brother" (44–45). The First Figure sees her as an innocent child of
nature: "No, her hair is not gold, [it] is like the sun upon a field of wheat
. . . like sunlight combed through maple leaves, and her eyes are . . . like

11.4. Pierrot and Marietta: the fatal dance scene (*left*), from *The Marionettes*.
Estelle Oldham Franklin holding her son, Malcolm, c. 1927.
(Courtesy of Jill Faulkner Summers)

twin pools in which are caught scraps of evening sky." "Yes," responds the
Second Figure, appearing to agree. But then he adds that her eyes are as
dangerous as her other features, for they are "like pools within which one
could drown." No, the First Figure insists, "Her breasts are white roses
asleep upon a pool . . . like two white birds after a long flight." The Figures'
language and their images in these two antithetical blazons seem arty and
forced. Faulkner's Art Deco–Art Nouveau drawings point to the nineteenth
century, not the twentieth. But the epistemological concerns raised about
seeing (perception?), with accompanying counterpointed illustrations of
Marietta, some with roses and some bejeweled, are Modernist (*TM*, 45, 54).

   This and his other drawings, which compose this play's countertext,
also reflect how Faulkner has been stimulated by and has attempted to

merge Lelia's and Maud's imaginative sensibilities with his own. The art of these two women was deliberately realistic. Maud's realistic imaginative perception reveals itself in her paintings and her comments about her own and Faulkner's art. In speaking of the youngest Compson brother in *The Sound and the Fury*, Maud said: "Now, Jason, . . . he talks just like my husband did. My husband had a hardware store uptown at one time. His way of talking was just like Jason's, same words and same style. All those 'you knows.'"[23] Yet her son's childhood exposure to the arts of drawing and photography had taught Billie that both painting and photography could be used to present alternative realities.

He uses this knowledge in composing his play's illustrations. While the fallen Marietta's torso resembles Salome's, the virgin Marietta's face and body bears an uncanny resemblance to contemporary photographs of Estelle Oldham. Not only do Faulkner's drawings of Marietta speak to his text's silences; they also contradict the text. Thus, for example, although Marietta is described as having golden hair (*TM*, 44), Faulkner draws her in her virginal state as a skinny but bosomy flapper, her dark hair cut in a bob. A photograph of Estelle, perhaps even this one taken in 1918, is the only image Billy Faulkner would have had when he was writing *The Marionettes*. The actual Estelle was then living in Honolulu with her first husband (fig. 11.3). Thus his stylized drawings mask autobiographical realism, creating another aspect of the play's hidden psychological tension. Their imitative style screens a deeply serious and disruptive content, Pierrot-Faulkner's desire to be an artist and to become one by using his "moon" mother's magic language to seduce and then abandon the woman who, for the past two years, had been another man's wife. He sings:

> I am Pierrot, and was born
> On a February morn,
> . . . and on my head
> The moon shone, weaving in my head
> A spell . . . (*TM*, 14–15)

On a monthly basis the spell provides him the seductive powers needed to convince young virgins to leave their cloistered gardens to dance and "play at love" with him:

> Every month, when comes the moon
> I leave my musty garret room. (*TM*, 15)

Here Faulkner explicitly feminizes the source of his creativity: not only does it come from his mother, but it also is associated with women's monthly reproductive cycle. Furthermore, he is the seductive dancer.

The physical resemblance between Faulkner's drawings of Marietta and Estelle would have been instantly apparent to the readers and buyers of Billie Faulkner's play—friends and other members of the Oxford community—especially coupled with his portrayal of Marietta's lover as a drink-sodden pierrotiste poet and Marietta as an initially sexually naïf but hot cookie ("I cannot sleep. . . . My bed is heavy and hot with something that fills me with strange desires. Why am I filled with desire for vague, unnamed things because a singing voice disturbed my dreams?" *TM*, 10). Pierrot's moon mother as a white, cold, powerful, and domineering mother might have sparked chuckles about Maud. All this encouraged an autobiographical reading of a play whose archaic and stilted language and stylized, imitative drawings masked fantasies about rich and vital sources of his creativity and his erotic life.

Faulkner's Autobiographical Fictionalized Photos: Self-Portrait as Masquerade

This play is the first known public statement of Faulkner's self-portrait as artist.[24] It is also the first instance of his literally drawing from a photographic image in his imaginative work. We know that since childhood he had been fascinated by photography and had owned a camera. Throughout his life Faulkner used posed photographs to invent sometimes farcical autobiographical narratives. At least once, as we shall see, he posed photographs of others to translate his fiction into the realm of the "real." His earliest known experiments with visual images were self-portraits of himself in masquerade as the wounded officer. By 1918, if not earlier, he had begun what was to be a lifelong manipulation of the camera eye as he played with the power of actual but trick photographs to alter viewers' perceptions by inventing alternative and antithetical selves. In 1918, posing for a series of snapshots of himself as a wounded war hero, Faulkner created a firmly masculine image, an acceptable front or masquerade behind which he could practice his art (see fig. 10.1). In this instance he used photographs to manipulate reality to his advantage, to appear as he wished to be viewed by his family and fellow townspeople.[25]

One photograph Faulkner sent to his mother from his RCAF training camp in Canada showed him posing beside "his plane," which he never flew. Maud, the realist, believed and did a painting of this trick photograph. When, in the 1960s, she agreed to sell this painting, Faulkner forbade her, saying it was "too personal."[26] Apparently he wanted control of his trick photographs. At that point in his life, judging from his letters to

11.5. Faulkner posing as a young
dandy, 1918.
(Courtesy of HRC and Jill Faulkner
Summers)

Malcolm Cowley, he appears to have been embarrassed by this particular
early imposture.[27]

Even in 1918 this military cover was not sufficient for his larger purposes. He needed, as well, to "be" a more subversive self, a manifestation
of and further gesture toward the dandy artist who inspired his unperform-
able dream-play. He had first dressed as a dandy in 1912–13, when he and
Estelle were posing for and imitating each other. At other times, he alternated his flyer and dandy masquerades with the costume of a tramp. Of
this last pose, the only images from the 1920s are people's memories. Just as,
at age twelve, he may have imitated his grandfather's dress and behavior to
distract his grandfather from noticing his definitely "unmanly" passion for
drawing and storytelling, his deliberately outrageous but essentially harm-
less behavior distracted the townspeople's attention from his more disturbing artistic pursuits.

Faulkner's interest in photographs of himself in masquerade suggests that it was an extension of his earliest emotional and aesthetic solutions for exploring a much more fluid notion of identity, one that is often multiple and in flux. His dialogue with this mimetic visual image in one of his earliest imaginative creations, this dream-play, and with his staged wounded-war-hero photographs reveals, in part, why its counterpart in his novels served so well to challenge the culturally prescribed boundaries of the lives of his fictional characters. As I have written elsewhere and as James Watson and others have since expanded upon, Faulkner used drawings, photographs, and, later, fictional photographs and filmic and photographic tropes for a variety of purposes. *The Marionettes* is part of a recurrent pattern of self-presentation in Faulkner's work in which his relation to Estelle is also deeply involved.[28] And, I would add, his conflicted relations with his mother, Maud, and Callie Barr, all core aspects of his sense of who and what he was and wanted to be.

12

Reading Faulkner's "Mothers"
The Maternal Imaginary in *Absalom, Absalom!*

T O MANY PEOPLE OF OXFORD, Faulkner's costumes and behavior made him a joke, but when he was in his teens and early twenties, he felt them a necessity. To give himself space to pursue his art, he assumed a variety of poses. It is no accident, then, that Rosa Coldfield, a mediocre poet like her creator, appears to the twenty-year-old Quentin Compson and his father as a joke as well. Quentin's and other townspeople's descriptions of Rosa frame her in ways that often diminish and caricature. The spinster grotesque they have made of her is an object of pity and laughter. Much of the force of *Absalom, Absalom!* comes from her continual eruption out of that image—her refusal to be conventionally framed. Both Quentin's and his father's aggressively framing language is a form of control. Unlike a proper Southern Lady, Rosa knows and wants to know and tell too many secrets. Besides, she is a superb dramatic narrator, an expert at portraying photographs and other framed and often filmic scenes of forbidden and desired acts. She needs to be confined and silenced.[1]

Rosa has some help. In the opening chapter of *Absalom, Absalom!* three other women's eyes—those of Ellen, Rosa's sister and Sutpen's second wife; Judith, Ellen's daughter; and Clytie, Judith's half sister—carry readers through a series of violent and disjunctive visual images that introduce the wild house(hold) of Thomas Sutpen. Developed, they will become the novel's narrative framework. But Rosa's is the only voice, passing on to Quentin Compson her version of the outrage and mystery of the Sutpen saga.

Rosa Coldfield well understands the role she is supposed to play as Jefferson's penniless and slightly mad piece of "lonely thwarted old female flesh," a role apparently confirmed as we view her through Quentin's eyes in the novel's opening paragraphs. There she sits like a life-sized doll, "bolt upright in the straight hard chair that was so tall for her that her legs hung straight and rigid as if she had iron shinbones and ankles, clear of the floor with that air of impotent and static rage like children's feet" (*AA*, 3). Dehumanized, infantilized, treated as property by her father and as a potential broodmare by her brother-in-law Thomas Sutpen, Rosa Coldfield uses the one title she has garnered because she is so marginalized—poetess laureate of Yoknapatawpha—to move from silence into speech and from object of spectacle to projector of spectacle. Cast by her family and community in the role of fool (foolish child and hysterical old-maid), she becomes the self-conscious fool, thereby taking control of the narrative of the house of Sutpen and releasing it, in all its madness and frenzy, to the world at large.[2]

Like a photograph, whose function in the play and tug of desire she so perfectly understands, Rosa was there and can testify to what has been. She recognizes the underlying instability of the meaning of the photographic image. Thus she knows that the past, too, is subject to reinterpretation. She speaks to open up this past, which is fragmented, dynamic, violent, and disjunctive. Her goal is always to excavate the silenced, hidden history of Thomas Sutpen and use it to construct a narrative that will include the women and children of Thomas Sutpen's shadow families as well as his white family. They are the pieces of their master's flawed design that will not stay in their place. They are the past that is always present, that cannot be disowned or repressed. In a larger context, they represented, in 1936, when Faulkner published this novel, the silenced history of the South.

Quentin does not want to hear Rosa's story. When faced with her oral portraits of the man he calls the "ogre-shape," his "two half-ogre children," and his white wife, Rosa's sister Ellen, "who had conceived to the demon in a kind of nightmare," he still insists that Sutpen's is a typical antebellum Southern gentleman's family. He "seemed to see them, the four of them arranged into the conventional family group of the period, with formal and lifeless decorum, and seen now as the fading and ancient photograph itself would have been seen enlarged and hung on the wall behind and above the voice and of whose presence there the voice's owner was not even aware." Yet the frame he wants to put around the Sutpens, the photograph he wants to see, won't stabilize, won't "fix" to his need to preserve this myth. No sooner does he imagine its formal and lifeless decorum than it becomes "a picture, a group which even to Quentin had a quality strange, contradictory and bizarre; not quite comprehensible, not (even to twenty) quite right" (9). The initial image Quentin frames is bizarre, because he has erased its emotional content, its meaning. The only relationship between the figures is their formal sitting arrangement. Rosa's insistence on finding out who else belonged in that family portrait—his black son and daughter and their respective mothers—becomes the story of *Absalom, Absalom!*.

Faulkner fills this novel with photographic imagery and loads it with theatrical and cinematic scenes that for both Quentin and Mr. Compson are "just incredible. It just does not explain. . . . They are there, yet something is missing; they are like a chemical formula. . . . You bring them together again and again nothing happens: just the words, the symbols, the shapes themselves, shadowy inscrutable and serene"(80). For Quentin's father and the rest, the scenes don't add up, because they refuse to understand the relation of the scenes to their meaning. Rosa's marginalized position as female, artist, and fool paradoxically privileges her intelligence and her voice. She does not know everything, but she knows and understands a great deal more than any fictional listeners or many real readers have given her credit for, because, rather than listening to her, they look at her and listen to her from Quentin's, Mr. Compson's, and other male narrators' perspectives.

Like her creator, Rosa speaks two languages. She also privileges the senses over intellect: *"That,"* she says, *"is the substance of remembering—sense, sight, smell: the muscles which we see and hear and feel—not mind, not thought."* She is especially adept at remembering, imagining, and explaining particular kinds of Faulknerian photographs and filmic moments. She is obsessed by the Sutpen history and mystery of miscegenation. She portrays as much as she does know of it through a series of violent scenes of touch where touch is forbidden. As she explains: *"But let flesh touch with flesh, and watch the fall of all the eggshell shibboleth of caste and color too."* While the town of Jefferson makes her a subject for jump-rope ditties—she herself says, *"Oh yes, I know: 'Rosie Coldfield, lose him, weep him; caught a man but couldn't keep him'"*—she is busy inventing serious art, the story she tells Quentin. Like Faulkner, and many Southern women, she conceals her art making with masks, always insisting that she is only "a Southern gentlewoman" of "very modest character." She appears as a proper lady, producing quantities of polemical art, over one thousand poems—"ode, eulogy, and epitaph"—to fallen Civil War heroes (115, 112, 136, 137, 138, 136, 6, 65). These "beautifully safe and patriotic productions" establish her as the "poetess laureate" of Yoknapatawpha long before she tells Quentin the tale that questions all the Old South values and plantation myths those polemics support.[3] Furthermore, she makes sure that her real art will have national circulation. A pauperized spinster, she may not leave the South, but she tells her story to a young man who is leaving: "'Because you are going away to attend the college at Harvard they tell me,' she said. 'So I dont imagine you will ever come back

here and settle down. . . . So maybe you will enter the literary profession
. . . and maybe someday you will remember this and write about it'" (5).
Rosa cannot escape the confines of her culture. Her genteel poverty, her
ignorance of practical matters, like even how to count money, and her
identity as Southern "gentlefolk(s)" all lock her physically, intellectually, and
psychologically into its codes of conduct. As she constantly reminds Quentin, she is a proper Southern gentlewoman. Yet her voice has been freed
by her outrage at her own brutal initiation into Thomas Sutpen's moral
world. Like the old women Willie Falkner and his childhood peers heard
and overheard, she tells a Southern story deemed unspeakable. She opens
Pandora's box.

At times she gets carried away by her own rhetoric, but for the most
part, she is an astute and compelling narrator. Nowhere is this more evident than in the sadistic, pornographic, and racially charged scene arranged by Thomas Sutpen with which she concludes her story's first seg-
ment. In it, Sutpen is initiating his fourteen-year-old son Henry into being
a slaveholder—a large part of what constitutes Southern Manhood. Part
of this initiation is to watch and then participate in Sutpen's brand of "raree show," which he stages: "Down there in the stable a hollow square of
faces in the lantern light, the white faces on three sides, the black ones on
the fourth, and in the center two of his wild negroes fighting naked." Sutpen holds these shows regularly for his white male neighbors, whom Rosa
describes without irony as "gentlefolks of our own kind" as well as "the
very scum and riffraff who could not have approached the house itself under any other circumstances" (20). In this forced fighting match his naked
slaves fight each other until a winner is declared. Then "perhaps as a matter of sheer deadly forethought toward the retention of supremacy, domination, [Sutpen] would enter the ring with one of the negroes himself"
where he'd "beat" the winning slave (21). Rosa understands the rules of
slavery and tries to read Sutpen by them. But she cannot, because Sutpen
constantly violates the very boundaries he claims are inviolable. The sado-
masochistic ritual she describes is an enactment of something Sutpen keeps
repeating. He believes his power derives from his and his progeny's whiteness, that their blood must be "pure." Yet he cannot keep his hands off
black folk: he continuously mingles his blood with theirs, masking homoerotic desire with these staged beatings while also raping at least one of his
black female slaves.

One night Ellen Sutpen hears her son's screams coming from the stable and rushes to him. The "spectacle," the "grand finale" she sees being
staged specifically for young Henry's edification is "the father of her children standing there naked and panting and bloody to the waist and the

negro just fallen evidently, lying at his feet and bloody too." As she enters, Henry, who has been held forcibly by other slaves, "plunge[d] out from among the negroes who had been holding him, screaming and vomiting," and falls at her feet (21). As Ellen kneels in the "filth" and "dirt" of the stable floor with Henry crying and clinging to her, the only words she says to her husband are, "Where is Judith, Thomas?"

"'Judith?' he said." "Judith?" he repeats. "Isn't she in bed?" Ellen's response indicates the degree to which she, too, accepts Sutpen's horrific initiation of their son into his white manhood as normal: "'Dont lie to me, Thomas,' Ellen said. 'I can understand your bringing Henry here to see this, wanting Henry to see this; I will try to understand it; yes, I will make myself try to understand it. But not Judith, Thomas. Not my baby girl'" (21). Whether or not Sutpen has lied, Judith is there along with her slave half sister, Clytie. Looking up, Rosa says that Ellen saw "the two Sutpen faces this time—once on Judith and once on the negro girl beside her—looking down through the square entrance to the loft" (22). Rosa's narrative suddenly frames for Quentin a portrait of the material evidence of Sutpen's continual violation of that "eggshell shibboleth of caste and color too"—his biracial daughter—"Clytie who in the very pigmentation of her flesh represented that debacle which had brought Judith and me to what we were"—and her white half sister watching him enact another violation—his raree show (112, 126). Through Rosa's narrative of framed, highly visual images, Faulkner creates a scene within a scene in which a woman or girls, not men or boys, are doing the looking and the interpreting. Like Rosa, whom Quentin's father claims had never been "taught to do anything save listen through closed doors," Judith and Clytie, confined though they are, constantly frame images of Sutpen's world that testify to how slavery present and past deforms and destroys from generation to generation. Rosa shows and speaks particularly of white men's rape of their black female slaves: "that debacle which had brought Judith and me to what we were." The images Rosa frames demonstrate repeatedly the permeability and hypocrisy of all the boundaries slavery was meant to enforce.

Sutpen's slave daughter, Clytie, and son, the visibly white but legally black Charles Bon, belie his own fiction of racial purity. As does the biological and emotional relationship between Judith and Clytie. In childhood, the sisters are inseparable. Rosa tells that Clytie "and Judith even slept together, in the same room but with Judith in the bed and she on a pallet on the floor ostensibly. But I have heard how on more than one occasion Ellen has found them both on the pallet, and once in the bed together" (112). Like their father, they are sleeping in the wrong beds. Their love for each other violates all the rules that keep blacks and women of all colors in their places. It spells depths of trouble that Faulkner suggests but either could not or would not—given his gender and time—fully develop. This bed-room scene, set before Judith puts Clytie aside (as all white slavers' children were taught to do), anticipates a later one in which Faulkner tries once more to speak the psychic damage caused by a legal system that mandates that a people—including one's own wife or child or sibling—be less than chattel by virtue of the mix of their blood.

Yet it is Rosa's initial framings in the first twenty-two pages of this novel that provide a prelude for what is to come. For example, the disavowal driving Sutpen's fetishized, bloody coupling with and beating of his male slave will metamorphose, in the next generation, as the triangulated web of incestuous, miscegenous, and homoerotic desire binding his white and black daughters, Judith and Clytie, his white son, Henry, his "put aside" black son, Charles Bon, and his slave daughter who counts so little she doesn't even need to be put aside. Although Henry screamed and vomited that night in the stable at the prospect of being forced to perform like his father, "fighting with a Negro boy of his own age and weight," he ulti-mately digested Sutpen's lessons (95). Henry will kill Charles Bon, whom he loves like a mammy and who does "mammy" him repeatedly. With a signal gesture Faulkner will replay in *Go Down, Moses*, Bon wraps Henry in his own cloak to protect him from the "cold" just moments before Henry, hav-ing learned that his brother is "part negro," renounces his love for Bon (*AA*, 283, 284). Behind every cold law of white Southern patriarchy lies the imagined, always already lost nurturing warmth of the black maternal. Henry kills Bon because, although he can accept incest, he cannot brook his white sister's mixing with Bon's "black blood"; he cannot allow Bon to be *"the nigger that's going to sleep with your sister"* (286).

By the third Sutpen generation, the self-destruction that Sutpen's rac-ism began is almost complete. Charles Bon, like his father, also has a child whose mother is legally black. Like Sutpen, he, too, disowns his "white-colored" child, Charles Etienne Bon (167). Like *his* father's, Charles Eti-enne's body defies his culture's constructs of race and gender. His "ivory skin" confounds his naming as "a negro"; his "body and limbs were almost as light and delicate as a girl's" (167). When he is twelve, his biological mother, Charles Bon's French-speaking "octoroon" morganatic wife, dies. Childless and husbandless themselves, Clytie and Judith, the dark and light sisters, claim and rear their dead half brother's child. In a variation on Faulkner's "nameless loneliness," when he was held between the dark and light sisters-mothers of his early screen memory, Charles Etienne lies in his trundle bed hemmed in on one side by Judith in her bed and on the other by Clytie, who "with a sort of invincible spurious humility slept on a pallet on the floor" (160). Despite the apparent intimacy and physical closeness of this bedroom scene, the child lies "between them unasleep in some hiatus of passive and hopeless despair." Why? What is wrong with this picture? This is what Charles Etienne thinks as he lies there "unsleeping in the darkness between them, feeling them unasleep too, feeling them thinking about him, projecting about him and filling the thunderous solitude of his despair louder than speech could: *You are not up here in this bed with me, where through no fault or willing of your own you should be, and you are not down here on this pallet floor with me, where through no fault nor willing of your own you must and will be, not through any fault or willing of our own.*" The boy is haunted by Judith's and Clytie's voices and gestures, "filling the thunderous solitude of his despair, louder than speech," educating him into race and racism, educating him into their own hatreds and self-hatreds, educating him into their own "yearning" and "antipathy" (160, 161, 160).

Perhaps the most important term here is *projecting.* Faulkner can imagine this scene only from inside a white Southern man's head and skin. He can see a scene that, like so many of his bedroom scenes, is a vivid metaphor for the inseparability of racism, erotic desire, and sexism, but he cannot imagine Charles and Clytie as other than tragic mulattoes. Yet through Charles Etienne he does imagine the loneliness and despair and terrible psychic damage of being educated into race and racism by a black and white mother in this Deep South world. Like the blond sister-aunt of Faulkner's screen memory, Judith treats her nephew "with a cold unbending detached gentleness." Her fear of his touch is such that "her capable hands seemed at the moment of touching his body to lose all warmth and become imbued with cold implacable antipathy" (160). Clytie, "who fed him, thrust food which he himself could discern to be the choicest . . . food prepared for him by deliberate sacrifice, with that curious blend of savageness and pity, yearning and hatred; who dressed and washed him" (a mammy's, not a white mother's tasks), is equally withholding and terrifying. When bathing him she often scrubs his body "with harsh rags and soap, sometimes scrubbing at him with repressed fury as if she were trying to wash the smooth faint olive tinge from his skin as you might watch a child scrubbing at a wall long after the epithet, the chalked insult, has been obliterated" (161).

That simile for his shame that Clytie's white male narrator projects onto her is visually and emotionally powerful, because, within his sentence and through simile, Faulkner reveals its slippage from Clytie to its real owner: a white child. Only a white child would know how to read that epithet. Charles Etienne comes into his full stature as tragic mulatto when he learns that "he was, must be, a Negro" (163). Note the tension embodied in these two phrases. We never know who names him, but the results are cata-strophic. Like his maternal grandmother he is driven mad. In a bitterly ironic twist on his grandfather's raree shows, and his uncle Henry's revul-sion, he constantly instigates racial confrontations in which he is always beaten to a pulp: "It was almost a ritual—the man apparently hunting out situations in order to flaunt and fling" himself (and later his "charcoal col-ored" wife) "in the faces of any and all who would retaliate"; black men "who thought he was a white man and believed it only more strongly when he denied it; white men who, when he said he was a negro, believed that he lied in order to save his skin, or worse: from sheer besotment of sexual per-version." In these fights, similar to those Joe Christmas instigates, Charles Etienne appears impervious "to pain or punishment, neither cursing or panting, but laughing" (167). Here his abjectness is concretized in a literal-ization of his flesh as broken or torn apart, as in those childhood bedroom and bathroom scenes. Here touch literalizes the violence of racist naming, dehumanization, and separation.

Rosa has suffered lifelong emotional deprivation: "I who had learned nothing of love, not even parents' love" (117). Yet she transforms lack to plentitude and ignorance to knowledge with a revelatory and shocking tale of the racism, the child and wife abuse, and the laws against miscegenation that built the South and destroyed it.

Although Rosa's life remains circumscribed (the novel's other narrators nourish the melodramatic belief that she dies because the source of her outrage has been destroyed), she uses fantasies evoked by a photograph of her niece Judith's lover, Charles Bon, to see desire in new ways. Her story then takes on a life of its own. In similar circumstances Horace Benbow in *Sanctuary* will use language to obfuscate; here Rosa uses language to create and illuminate. Evoking Charles Bon for Quentin she says: *I had never seen him (I never saw him. I never even saw him dead. I heard a name, I saw a photograph, I helped to make a grave: and that was all). . . . (I did not love him; how could I? I had never even heard his voice, had only Ellen's word for it that there was such a person) . . . because I had not even seen the photograph then.* (117)

As she talks to Quentin, her inner vision begins to clarify:

> *I dont know even now if I was ever aware that I had seen nothing of his face but that photograph, that shadow, that picture in a young girl's bedroom: a picture casual and framed upon a littered dressing table yet bowered and dressed (or so I thought) with all the maiden and invisible lily roses, because even before I saw the photograph I could have recognized, nay, described, the very face. But I never saw it. I do not even know of my own knowledge that Ellen ever saw it, that Judith ever loved it, that Henry slew it: so who will dispute me when I say, Why did I not invent, create it?* (118)

Rosa has raised the question: Is the existence of the photograph material? That is, if the feelings that it evoked in her and she describes feel true to the listener, isn't that emotional reality more valid than a physical object? And, of course, this is what she is asserting as she then reveals her marvelous invention:

> And I know this: if I were God I would invent out of this seething turmoil we call progress something (a machine perhaps) which would adorn the barren mirror altars of every plain girl who breathes with such as this—which is so little since we want so little— this pictured face. It would not even need a skull behind it; almost anonymous, it would only need vague inference of some walking flesh and blood desired by someone else even if only in some shadow-realm of make-believe. (118)

At first Rosa tells Quentin that she could not have loved Charles Bon because she knew him only from his photograph. But as she describes what Bon's picture connotes, she realizes why his photograph both created and fed her desire. This realization allows her to move on to an elegant and imaginative insight about the kinds of people who crave this kind of desire, what its essence is—absence and illicitness: "*a picture seen by stealth, by creeping (my childhood taught me that instead of love*"—and what lack it fills (118). She never describes what Bon looks like—his features or hair color, his eyes or skin (which she assumes is white). These are facts, and they don't interest Rosa. All she cares about are how and why photographs —images of another reality—work as they do upon the spectator's imagination. Rather than losing herself, like Horace Benbow, in fantasies of illicit and unattainable desire, she frankly acknowledges her wishes to her audience and then uses them and her own experience to abstract and generalize. Her idea is wonderfully playful, amusing, and empathic. Drawn from acute self-observation, hers is also an accurate reading of adolescent sexuality. Retrospectively, the terrible irony of this scene is that Rosa could imagine such desire only because she, like Judith, did not know that Charles Bon (whose initials are the same as Callie Barr's) was legally black.

Unlike the solipsistic Horace, Rosa does not fantasize alone in a dark and empty house. Her intent is to use her feelings to create a story she knows cannot be written in the South, and that perhaps has not been written anywhere. In this story, a woman, not a man, is doing the gazing, and she is looking at and judging a man and his works. Beginning in the opening chapter, each framed still she projects of him, his "house," his deeds, and his progeny, is a further unveiling. For this reason Rosa has to be shut up. It is men who are supposed to be looking at naked women—not the reverse. In an essay on the convention of the female nude in Western painting, John Berger points out that "the principal protagonist is never painted.

He is the spectator in front of the picture and he is presumed to be a man. Everything is addressed to him. . . . It is for him that the figures have assumed their nudity. But he, by definition, is a stranger—with his clothes still on. . . . This picture is made to appeal to his sexuality. It has nothing to do with her sexuality."[4]

Unlike the distanced and "objective" male protagonist, who keeps his clothes on, Rosa has emotionally disrobed. Doing so opens her to analyze this kind of desire. Unlike Horace, she *wants* to communicate because she wants to understand relationships. Her understanding of the photograph's meaning to *her* renders Rosa's telling a success. She achieves a coherence and satisfaction that Horace never experiences. Rosa's tale of the house of Sutpen disrupts because, in its totality, it lays bare the physical and psychological brutality of the racism and sexism that enforce the myths that create (white) Southern Manhood and Womanhood. By telling her tale to Quentin, Rosa breaks her culture's silence.

Both Horace Benbow's and Rosa Coldfield's talismanic use of photographs of desire question, frustrate, and disrupt gendered notions of seeing and sexuality. For each, the photograph is a trope for a thematics of desire that feeds on frustration, absence, incestuous wishes, and voyeurism. But whereas Rosa's intent is (in this instance) to understand and explain desire for herself and her listener, Horace's is opposite. Like her author, Rosa learned at an early age who had the power to name in her world. This is why she wishes she were male so that she could *"have been weaponed and panoplied as a man instead of hollow woman"* (117). She even steals the language of Macbeth and Hamlet. At first Rosa seems to appropriate Judith's photograph of Charles Bon, as Horace stole Little Belle's. But Rosa's aims are antithetical to Horace's. As a lonely, love-starved but passionately interested fourteen-year-old, what she really wants to own is an understanding of her desire. Possessed of that, she does indeed become *"all polymath love's androgynous advocate,"* an artist of visual images (117). With her words, Rosa frames scenes, sets stages, paints pictures, and invents and reads photographs for Quentin—a man—to write down. She never writes down her own story.

As I've noted elsewhere, Rosa succeeds where Horace fails because although she turns what we might call a masculinist gaze upon Judith's photograph of Charles Bon, one that transforms Bon from subject to object, her gaze is, finally, self-conscious. This self-consciousness, her desire to know why she sees the way she does and to analyze her motives and to abstract and learn about this gaze and then to share her knowledge with another, questions all the premises upon which such objectification is based. It changes her and makes us, if we listen to her voice, see her desire in a way that questions the conventions of Rosa's (as well as our own) culture.

Faulkner may be suggesting that because Rosa is doubly marginalized as a woman artist she is better equipped to make that challenge. But her gender alone is no assurance of success, and her success is very limited because, in so many other ways, her behavior meets cultural expectations. Rosa is unlike either her sister, Ellen Sutpen, who retreats into a culturally acceptable madness, or her nieces, or Temple Drake and Little Belle, who, like Horace, know how to use language creatively but, even so, become exemplars of various myths about Southern Womanhood and blackness. In contrast, Rosa takes up one of those myths—the sex-starved, hysterical spinster and lady poet—to camouflage her subversive voice.

Faulkner's portrayals of Rosa's and Horace's desires are complicated and compelling. The roots of their complexity lie deep in his own, always self-conscious conception of himself as an artist in a culture devoid of and hostile to homemade art, a culture so hostile that it had relegated what art it did foster to its women. As a young man claiming to be an artist, Faulkner threatened tightly held convictions about masculinity and femininity and put himself at risk. We see him exploring his anxiety and fear of being silenced or feminized in early poems like "After Fifty Years" and "The Dancer," or *Vision in Spring*, where a young man is imprisoned by the stories, dancing, or music of old and young women. We see his fear more subtly imaged, and better understood, in the three brothers obsessed by Caddy's voice in *The Sound and the Fury* and in the men obsessed by Rosa's in *Absalom, Absalom!*.

Many writers begin as visual artists. Experiments in several media and genres are not unusual. Nor was feminization of American artists limited to the South; one has only to read Emerson or Hawthorne to see the anxiety such labeling produced in nineteenth-century New England. But Faulkner and others have observed that this attitude reached its extreme in the South.[5] What was unusual was his imaginative response. In the first decades of the twentieth century, when he officially began his career as an artist, he cared as much about exploring the visual arts as he did about becoming a poet. Like literature, these also were feminized. Women's and girls' aesthetic values and perceptions, their means for coping in a culture that suppressed and trivialized art, and their privileging of art as a vocation (and in Callie's case also as a didactic tool) were a constant that dated from Faulkner's earliest childhood. His mother and grandmother taught him how to use drawing, painting, and photography to say first with visual images what he could not say with words, how to expect and cope with marginalization as the price of being an artist, and finally how to encode much that he had learned in these fictional photographs in novels that, along with other literary strategies, constantly veer between challenging and colluding

12.1. Faulkner's photo of Caroline Barr, taken the summer before she died.
(Courtesy of Jill Faulkner Summers)

with the Jim Crow heritage to which this region and, to a lesser extent, the rest of United States, was enslaved. Faulkner's imaginative training began in and was supported by this female tradition.

On an overcast afternoon at Rowan Oak in May 1939, a little more than a year before Callie Barr died, Faulkner took a series of photographs of her. Some included his six-and-a-half-year-old daughter, Jill. At least one did not.[6] Like "Mississippi," his last elegy to Barr, these photographs too are elegiac. Like his remarkable Southern poetess laureate, Rosa Coldfield, Faulkner "created," "invented," and used photographs to name, fix, and memorialize someone and something he had both had and never had. Photography and all the other visual arts Maud and Lelia taught him formed the bedrock of his visual aesthetic. Reading *Absalom, Absalom!* as a story that unmasks that relationship between his black and white mothers leads to an understanding and appreciation of the importance of Maud and Callie to his maternal imaginary. Together, Maud and Callie helped produce novels like *Absalom, Absalom!* Another woman, Estelle Oldham, later Estelle Franklin and then Estelle Faulkner, would more and more deeply inhabit his emotional, intellectual, and domestic life as he moved fully into his vocation as a novelist.

William Faulkner and
Estelle Oldham

They don't think we're gonna stick, but it is gonna stick.
— FAULKNER

Estelle Oldham Franklin and her daughter Victoria ("Cho-Cho"),
Oxford, Miss., 1921.
(Courtesy of Jill Faulkner Summers)

William Faulkner and Estelle Oldham

"YOU MAY NOT be a poetess but you're a darn good literary critic," said the fourteen-year-old Billy Falkner to Estelle Oldham when she caught him trying to palm off verses from "The Song of Solomon" as his own.[1] John Faulkner, whose memoir is not sympathetic to Estelle, still claims her continuous intellectual and emotional connection to his brother as primary: it was she who set free his voice. Yet, almost no one writing about Faulkner has suggested that their lifelong relationship was crucial to Faulkner's creativity.[2]

Like Callie Barr and Maud's, Estelle and William's intertwined lives pose hard biographical problems. What access does one have to the inner landscapes of two alcoholics, both children of alcoholic fathers and grandfathers? The disease itself is all about opacity and emotional unavailability. Although most families have secrets, the culture of an alcoholic home is unique, for secrecy and denial pervade its atmosphere. Written source materials are scarce so, as with Maud and Callie, I have drawn primarily on public documents, oral history, and interviews with those who knew Faulkner and Estelle to portray their intertwined life. As with Maud and Callie, few people, including Faulkner's authorized biographer, interviewed Estelle at any length or in any depth. Neither Faulkner nor Estelle kept diaries or journals. Very few intimate or personally revealing letters survive. There are no letters at all from Estelle to Faulkner. Those from Faulkner to her date from the 1930s and 1940s. Written from New York or Hollywood, they are, like his earlier letters to Maud, descriptive, rather than analytical or contemplative, their subject external not internal reality. As with Maud, he writes Estelle about his work. From Hollywood in 1934, when he was drafting treatments for *Sutter's Gold* for Howard Hawks, he gives Estelle an

ting weeks of back-and-forth among him, his agent,
ıen and what he'll be paid. He's hoping to "wangle
ive German camera so that "we can keep a regu-
nd Rowan Oak." He's anxious to be home with
ʾat tyke." He ends by saying that "I am getting
o get home, at the fingernail chewing stage. I
ıothing at all; that's what frets me about this
‿y a penciled P.S. that he'd "done a little work on the
‿ulom, Absalom!] from time to time."[3] The few intimate and loving
sentences that Faulkner included in letters from these years were deleted
from his *Selected Letters*, published five years after Estelle's death and fifteen
years after his own.[4]

Yet, there is one set of documents whose presence and content require
fresh scrutiny of the prevailing Faulkner-Estelle narrative. Sometime between 1921 and 1924, the same years Faulkner was still struggling to find his
voice as a poet, Estelle began writing fiction. She wrote a novel (no longer
extant) and at least six stories. Her stories, in part, an ongoing and long-
term imaginative dialogue with and critique of Faulkner's poetry, reveal
her as a competent writer and observer of the contemporary scene, and, as
Billy Faulkner noted when they were teenagers, a pretty good literary critic.
They also show her exploring themes (absent or deeply masked in Faulkner's
poetry) that in 1925, beginning with his first novel, became vital to his fiction. Finally, in one instance explicitly, the stories tell us much about how
Estelle saw herself (or girls and women like her) and the various relationships and communities that composed her world. These ranged from a six-
year-old girl's conflicts over Southern history and codes of conduct, to racially inflected, gender-bending seductions played out in the other
unremittingly hierarchical communities of Honolulu and Shanghai, where
she had lived with her first husband. She was especially interested in power
plays within erotic relationships and the fluidity of sexual desire and identity.

My story of Estelle and Faulkner will show that Estelle as writer was
critical to Faulkner's creative development. Theirs is not the classic story of
literary influence or collaboration. Coming to him when it did, at the end
of 1924, her fiction literally did give him the means to find his own fiction
writer's voice. For all these reasons I violate the rules of normal biography
and foreground Estelle's stories, that is, her own writer's voice(s), in my narrative of Faulkner and Estelle. Faulkner died in 1962; Estelle died ten years
later. However, since our primary interest is Estelle's effect on Faulkner's
imaginative vision, this account of Estelle and Faulkner ends in 1933, the
year their only surviving child, Jill, was born. For reasons that will become

clear in my final chapter, an unpublished essay Faulkner completed that summer acknowledges Estelle's continuing primacy in his life and art. Some thirteen years later Faulkner vilified this essay as "shit" and begged to buy it back from his publisher so that he could get it out of "danger" by seeing that it was "destroyed."[5] Yet he never did destroy it or its numerous drafts. Why not? What very private value did he give it? How do a series of unpublished photographs he took in 1935 confirm its value?

Unlike the hyperbolic sentimentalizing of Faulkner's relations with Maud and Callie, Estelle's bitchiness, emotional instability, wild spending sprees, and the Faulkners' incompatibility are the principal thematic of all prior Faulkner biographies. "Doom" is the dominant descriptive term for the Faulkner marriage.[6] They share only their addiction. Although Faulkner and Estelle were alcoholics, this disease hardly defined their relationship. The sensitivity of their writing indicates that both had a visceral and intellectual understanding of the complex role alcohol played in their families and in Southern (and Western) culture at large. As we have seen in Faulkner's fiction, and will see in Estelle's, its ubiquitous and always threatening presence haunts their writing.

Also present in Estelle's, and later Faulkner's, fiction, are the little girls or young women who do not play by the rules. In life and in her art, Estelle gave Faulkner models for his rebellious and courageous little girls and young women. More overtly than either Callie or Maud, Estelle broke the rules. Like two of her fictional heroines, she tried "to speak in my own words." Her life and writing helped Faulkner find his voice. The challenge of writing Estelle's biography is to free hers. Her fiction shows Estelle using storytelling to claim subjectivity. She created a fictional "I" or masquerades to speak of matters otherwise off-limits to a proper Southern lady. She needed these disguises to enter a space that was, in her mind and perhaps because of Faulkner, male-defined and -dominated. Whether her fictional voices were also authentic is of less interest than to ask, what were they attempting? What masquerades was Estelle performing with them? What price did she pay and how do the ways in which her masquerades are sexualized and racialized embody that price? Finally, why was Faulkner so drawn to Estelle's "I"? Answering these questions is essential to understanding the shared and entangled space that all three women—Callie, Maud, and Estelle—filled in Faulkner's imaginative vision and why that vision yearned for the presence of all three.

Estelle and her family were such an important part of Faulkner's life that they have already appeared in earlier chapters. Culturally, economically, and intrapsychically, Billy's and Estelle's family histories bear some striking similarities that extend back as far as their great grandparents' generations. Transience, violence, and single-parent households are constants. In each generation the families were held together by independent, educated, and artistically talented Mississippi women who tried to contain the effects of their husbands' alcoholism. The profiles of these Southern frontier families do not conform to any frontier ideal, but census documents indicate that they are probably far more representative.

In terms of their immediate families, Murry and Lemuel ("Lem") were the son and son-in-law, respectively, of domineering, rich, and successful men. Although Lem put more stock in schooling than Murry did, he, too, began as a dreamer and wanderer. Both shared a common desire to escape an overbearing father or father-in-law and the small towns where they grew up. As newlyweds, Lem and Lida Oldham headed for Texas, whereas Maud and Murry Falkner began their life together in New Albany. Lem dreamed of making a fortune on the Texas frontier; Murry embraced a career as railroad man. Both arrived with their young families in Oxford as disappointed men bearing a load of dashed dreams. Each was going to a job provided by either his father or father-in-law.

Their mothers, too, though their personalities and social aspirations were different, had much in common. Lida and Maud, the practical partners in their respective marriages, were college-educated in a time when few women even attended college. The school and college records of three generations of Fa(u)lkner and Oldham women reveal how tenaciously they pursued a higher education at a time and in a culture that discouraged such activities. In addition, Lida had attended the Boston Conservatory of Music, where she continued the study of piano and composition she had begun in college. Early in her marriage she tried to publish her compositions. She also taught piano and passed on her love for music to all three of her daughters, especially Estelle. This was one of the few values she passed on, however. This very proper mother raised a houseful of unruly daughters: her eldest, Estelle, divorced; her second, Victoria ("Tochie"), was pregnant when she married a man of whom her parents disapproved; and Dorothy, in adulthood, wore overalls, drove a pickup truck, ran a roadside bar that also sold bootleg, and lived openly with her female lover in the Oldhams' home.[7]

These are the facts. Seven months older than William Faulkner, Lida Estelle Oldham was born in Bonham, Texas, in February 1897. A lifelong smoker, she died of complications from emphysema in 1972. Like so many other Mississippians, her newly married parents, Lemuel and Lida, had gone west in 1895 to seek their fortune. Yet in less than two years, the Oldhams returned to their hometown, Kosciusko, their Texas dream a bust. For several years they lived with Lida's mother, Victoria Swanson Allen, and stepfather, Judge Henry C. Niles, while Lem struggled to support his growing family. By 1903, Judge Niles was fed up. A respected lawyer and a Republican, he used his political pull to get Lem a clerkship in Oxford. Thus, within the space of a few months, Estelle Oldham and Billy Falkner, the oldest children of two downwardly mobile fathers, arrived in Oxford and settled on the same block. Their families had known each other for two generations, so it was natural that the Falkner and Oldham children became playmates (see Chaps. 13–15).

In keeping with the absence of journals, diaries, or intimate letters, neither Estelle nor Falkner was a confider. However, one of three extant short stories Estelle wrote between 1922 and 1924, while living in Shanghai with her first husband, is a fictionalized intellectual and emotional autobiography of her six-year-old self. Read in the context of what is now known about Estelle's early childhood, before she moved from Kosciusko to Oxford in 1903, "Dr. Wohlenski" is fascinating because it is narrated in part by a little girl whose internal and external world bears striking resemblances to Faulkner's Caddy Compson's. Faulkner read it when she returned to Oxford in December 1924, years before he conceived Caddy. Besides confirming that she had an intellect and used it, "Dr. Wohlenski" is important because of what it tells us about Estelle's understanding of how hard it was to be an independently minded white girl-child in a small Mississippi town at the turn of the century. In particular, and again like Faulkner's much later fiction, it is about the pain and shame of being educated into those inseparable ideologies, racism and Southern Womanhood. For these reasons this story informs my chapter on Estelle's childhood and the chapters on Estelle, Faulkner, and *The Sound and the Fury*.[8]

Estelle wrote other stories that were meaningful to Faulkner. Although he collaborated on revisions and submitted at least one of her stories under their joint byline, and later (under his own name) published it and at least two other stories that were originally Estelle's, none of her fiction was ever published.[9] Apparently, none of her original manuscripts survive. As Joseph Blotner notes, however, there are extant versions of three of the stories that Faulkner is known to have revised or rewritten with Estelle and tried to publish ("Selvage" / "Elly," "Idyll in the Desert," and "A Letter"). There are also typescripts of three other stories, two of which Faulkner also typed for her, probably shortly after she arrived home in December 1924—"Dr. Wohlenski," "A Crossing," and "Star Spangled Banner Stuff."

Billy and Estelle remained close until the fall of 1913, when the Oldhams sent their two eldest daughters to boarding schools. Although neither Faulkner nor Estelle saved the letters marking their first extended separation, all evidence suggests that Billy missed her very much. By the summer of 1914, he had found two substitutes to fill his emptiness: "white lightning" and Phil Stone. Four years older and trained as a lawyer and classicist, Stone became his chief mentor, economic support, and drinking companion for at least the next ten years. Stone's economic support continued until his family lost much of its money in 1928. He introduced Faulkner to both classical literature and the avant-garde, bought and lent him reams of books and "little" magazines, sponsored his first commercially published book of poems, *The Marble Faun,* and (informally) gave him a more valuable intellectual education than any institution would provide. Stone was the first of a long series of very bright men, many of them either bisexual or homosexual, who served, as Stone self-mockingly put it, as Faulkner's "wet nurse" (see Chap. 16).

Although Estelle and Billy (or Billie, as he sometimes spelled it) continued to see each other and he remained a steady visitor at the Oldhams, it became clear to her that the young poet was not about to marry her or any other woman. As Phil Stone's biographer Susan Snell notes, he was married to his work and to Phil Stone.

Yet, despite many offers, Estelle held out until the spring of 1918, when she succumbed to the pull of a lifetime's preparation for her profession— marriage to an eligible suitor. To her parents' delight, she wed Cornell Franklin, a bright young Mississippi lawyer from an old and respectable family. Mamie Franklin (later Hairston) and her son were not well off. Widowed months before Cornell's birth, she made a living as social page editor and writer for the Columbus paper. Cornell had worked his way through college and law school.[10] But his ambitions, his manners, and his excellent connections made him an ideal son-in-law for the Oldhams. As Estelle wrote Lem and Lida eleven years later, after she and Faulkner had eloped, "I wish with all my heart that *this* leave-taking, for you, had been as joyous a one as the other."[11] In 1929, shortly before her second marriage, Estelle told Katherine Andrews, a lifelong friend of hers and Faulkner's, that "I didn't marry who I wanted to the first time, but I will do it the second." "And that," said Andrews, "is when she married William." Years later, speaking to Katherine about her two marriages, Estelle said, "I didn't have the fine clothes and I didn't have a car so long you couldn't see the end when it turned the corner, yet all I regret is that my children [Cho-Cho and Malcolm] are named Franklin."[12]

From 1918 to 1924, the Franklins lived first in Hawaii and then Shanghai. Paradoxically, Estelle's marriage and physical separation from Billy marked the renewal of their dialogue. They carried on this conversation in person and in writing during Estelle's frequent and prolonged trips back to

Oxford between 1919 and 1921, and probably through the mail from 1922 to 1924, when the Franklins lived in Shanghai.

Although Cornell and Estelle did not begin formal divorce proceedings until mid-November 1928, when Cornell filed for divorce in Shanghai, Estelle had left her husband four years earlier. Arriving in Oxford in early December 1924, she stayed almost a year. Then, pressured by both families and Cornell, she returned to Shanghai in late November 1925. Three months later (her marriage a shambles) Estelle and her children returned to Oxford for good. Yet throughout her first marriage and despite becoming an alcoholic, Estelle grew emotionally and intellectually, and her relationship with Faulkner flourished. Like him, she was an observer. Her observations of the sexual, social, and racial politics of colonial life in Honolulu and Shanghai sharpened her understanding of her own Mississippi Jim Crow world and imbued the fiction she began writing once the Franklins settled in Shanghai.

In the late 1960s and early 1970s, Jim Godfrey foxhunted with Jill and her husband in Charlottesville. He was also a student of classical Chinese history and a specialist in ancient Chinese artworks. Eager to talk about Shanghai and China with someone who had lived there in the 1920s, Godfrey became friendly with Estelle during the last four years of her life. He found that "she knew a lot about China" and had been "extremely well educated by her experiences" in the American territories and treaty port. One thing she was "moved by" was that "for the first time in her life she could observe people [colonial expatriates] in a context that in some ways was familiar. Yet she was outside of it and removed." As he described it, "She was very much a product of that colonial expatriate world." At the same time, she could see that world simultaneously from inside and out. And, as with her husband and mother-in-law, the insights of her artist's voice were often at odds with opinions stated in interviews and actual life. As they talked about Shanghai, Estelle emerged as an "energetic, expressive, and insightful woman. She was very, very frail in body but not in mind. She was quite delicate in her way of speaking and engaging and genuinely interested and involved." Godfrey thought she was a "a lonely woman" because "she always seemed to be alone." She wasn't "interested in the hunt crowd chit-chat," but "to me, she was the most interesting person around and invariably I'd be drawn into the library where she usually sat, and I'd spend the rest of the afternoon talking to her."[13]

In the early summer of 1918, the twenty-one-year-old Estelle had left familiar Oxford with her first husband for the unknown "Hawaiian Territory," as it was then called. In December 1924, when she made her return to Oxford and Faulkner, she carried with her the fruits of those difficult years: her two children, her novel (which he would type and submit to his own publisher in early February 1927), and her short stories.[14] Less than six weeks later, Faulkner began his first novel, *Soldiers' Pay*. From early January until he left for a six-month European tour, he was living in New Orleans but making frequent trips home to Oxford and Estelle. That spring in New Orleans, according to his own account, Sherwood Anderson and he walked, talked, and drank together daily, but "in the morning he would be in seclusion working." Anderson's example convinced him that "if that was the life of a writer, that was the life for me." Letters from "Billy" to his mother are the only record of this time. Yet *Soldiers' Pay* gives ample evidence of Faulkner's simultaneous, very different, but equally conflicted and prodigiously profitable collaborations during these breakthrough months—with Anderson in New Orleans and Estelle in Oxford. Estelle's influence was profound and, in its nature, quite distinct from traditional accounts of literary influence like that of Faulkner and Anderson or the Symbolist, decadent, Edwardian, and Modernist poets of Faulkner's poetic apprenticeship years. These latter narratives, particularly the Anderson-Faulkner story, have been told many times. Yet placing Anderson in the context of the creation of Faulkner's maternal imaginary and his racialized aesthetic adds a fascinating dimension to the flowering of his creative genius.[15] Anderson is very much a part of the story of Faulkner, Callie, Maud, and Estelle. The simultaneity of Faulkner's literary collaborations with Anderson and Estelle, similarities in his subsequent cruel demeaning of both, the fact that he worked simultaneously on his elegiac and reparative essays for Callie Barr and Anderson at a time when he feared he would never write again, and Anderson's influence on Faulkner's racialized aesthetic all speak to the importance of this connection (see Chap. 25).

For the next four years, as he had done before and would continue to do after their marriage in 1929, Faulkner gravitated between Estelle and a series of other intense relationships, actual and imagined, with both men and women. Besides Phil Stone and Anderson these included Helen Baird (imaginary), Ben Wasson, Stark Young, Bill Spratling, and William Odiorne. Baird excepted, all these men supported Faulkner monetarily, drank with him, and "nursed" him. For brief periods of time before marrying Estelle, he lived off and on with Spratling (an architect and visual artist) and Odiorne (a photographer).[16] Yet Estelle and Faulkner did marry, and, as Faulkner prophesied, their marriage did "stick."

The problem of realizing her own freedom and selfhood within the confines of Southern Belledom so prized by her parents, her first husband, and those her daughter called the "good people of Oxford" is the main theme of Estelle's life; it occupied center stage in her extended actual and imaginative dialogues with Faulkner.[17] However, Estelle was not and did not see herself as a victim. Katherine Andrews observed that "in some ways she was a timid person." Then she added, "But when Faulkner died and Bennett Cerf [his Random House editor] came down to get all of William's manuscripts, she ordered him out of the house. She said she never had any use for him after that."[18] What some took for timidity, others called reserve: "She wasn't outward but she was real charmin'. She put out, but she was not a person you would confide in," said another Oxford friend.[19] Estelle was adept at using the mantle of Southern Womanhood to protect her privacy. The Faulkners' family doctor in Charlottesville noted that "there was something about her, a reserve, that made one not ask probing questions. She had a capacity to make people feel insecure. She was, at the same time, the epitome of the old-time Southern Lady. I wondered whether it was a deliberate caricature because it was so extreme, so consciously self-parodic."[20] Estelle's daughter observes, "My mother appeared weak and fragile, which she was, physically. But in fact she had great strength of character which my father recognized. She was depressed and often desperate, but she was one tough lady." Faulkner both loved and hated Estelle for the strength that lay beneath her mask of genteel Southern "female" weakness. He once told Jill, "Your mother is like piano wire," a simile bearing layers of meaning in the context of the Faulkners' thirty-three-year marriage and lifelong relationship.[21] He was equally ambivalent about her other masquerades, particularly her racially inflected Southern Belle gone bad (see Chap. 23).

In contrast to Faulkner, Estelle's first husband found nothing pleasing about her independent spirit, except when it served his interests, as in Hawaii during the first three months of their marriage. As a colonial wife in Honolulu and at Schofield Barracks (1918–21) and then in Shanghai (1922–24), she began to write fiction that was original but that also responded to and revised Faulkner's poetry. In Honolulu, in the same year that he wrote his Pierrot dream-play, *The Marionettes*, and belonged to the Ole Miss drama club, Estelle joined the city's avant-garde theater group, which put on a Pierrot play. She also played the lead role in Susan Glaspell's then wildly popular farce *Suppressed Desires*, which spoofed the public craze for popularized Freudian theories, especially those underlying his *Interpretation of Dreams*. Among Estelle's stories is one that, among other things, responds specifically to *The Marionettes*. Both it and another story figure in the genesis (as Faulkner tells it) of *The Sound and the Fury*.

In late October 1926, Faulkner would offer Estelle Franklin another private commemoration. Like those that followed, this one marked the moment of his transformation from poet into novelist. As with other hand-made books he had given her, he dated and dedicated to Estelle *Royal Street*, a handprinted collection of all but one of the eleven short sketches he had published in the January-February 1925 issue of the New Orleans *Double Dealer*. To it, he had added a new sketch called "Hong Li."[22] Re-imagining and amplifying the concluding interior monologues Estelle had written for her Chinese businessman in her Shanghai short story "Star Spangled Banner Stuff," he continued to extend their literary dialogue and pay tribute to the wealth of imaginative material in the fictional narratives Estelle brought him from Shanghai.

From early childhood Estelle and Faulkner were collaborators in fictions deriving from a shared history and memory. Often, as I have mentioned earlier, they would literally act these out. Their daughter recalls times when she'd return from school "and get into the midst of something or other that was not real and I didn't understand it." She calls it "their private drama." As she grew older, she learned that "it was always very fleeting. It didn't last" and that "if I just stuck around long enough, it would change and there would be real people available at some point. But it was part of an on-going thing." She thinks that their theater "was not related to their drinking," noting that "they would play this stuff out against each other all the time" but that "if I needed one or the other of them for something, they came to me, they came back to the real world."[23] Such theatrical and highly eroticized scenes, imagined in photographic, filmic, and theater metaphors, suffuse novels like *The Sound and the Fury*, *Light in August*, *Absalom, Absalom!*, and *The Hamlet*. Early drafts for such scenes may have been played out in the Faulkners' garden, living room, and bedroom. This private drama was part of an imaginative dialogue that fueled Faulkner's creativity throughout their lives together.

PART 3

Estelle and Billy, 1903–1914

The Early Years

You may not be a poetess, but you're a darn good literary critic.

— FAULKNER

13

Estelle Oldham's Mississippi Frontier Family

ON OR SHORTLY AFTER 20 June 1929, in a painful letter to her parents, Estelle announced her marriage to Bill Faulkner, the man she claimed to have loved since she was sixteen.[1]

My Darling Mama and Daddy—

I wish with all my heart that *this* leaving-taking, for you, had been as joyous a one as the other—but circumstance reversed the order—It was I who left home, not with a ghastly fear and abhorrence as before, but with happiness, tinged all about (it is true) with sorrow, but a happiness with the conviction that I'd done at last what was the best and only thing for me to do.

I'm not asking forgiveness, for I wouldn't do that, but I do pray you to try and realize that I honestly love Bill and believe that after all these years, I have at last found peace and understanding in marrying him—

I *want* to be a loving and loyal daughter—I love you both with all my heart, I love *home* dearly and the children love home—they've known no other—*still*, I'm a *woman*, and there are few who don't want a place of their very own.

I have all the faith in the world in having my dream come true—Bill and I both want to live in Oxford where I could see you all every day—

I love you and Daddy above everything on earth except the children—I love and respect Bill—

Please don't shut your hearts and *minds* against me. Let me have my share of the joys all people need for sane, happy lives.

Cho-Cho will be with you when you get this—and will tell you our plans—

I wanted to come too, but I know your hurt is too recent to want to see me—

All my love
Estelle[2]

Handwritten, in an envelope addressed to "Mama and Daddy," the letter was delivered to Lem and Lida Oldham, probably by the ten-year-old Victoria (Cho-Cho) Franklin, Estelle's eldest child. Explaining why she has married Bill and expressing her fear that they will abandon her for doing so, Estelle reveals her fraught relations with her parents and expresses her divided loyalties, giving voice to a woman who remains, despite numerous Faulkner biographies, an enigma. To know the background of the Oldhams' extreme demands on their eldest daughter, and her need to try to meet them, gives needed context to the most compelling relationship in her life, her love affair with and marriage to William Faulkner.

By the time the Oldhams read of the Faulkners' elopement, their daughter, her eight-year-old son, Malcolm, Cho-Cho, and her new husband were well on their way to the home of Estelle's former mother-in-law in the aristocratic river town of Columbus, Mississippi, eighty-five miles northeast of Oxford. Mamie Hairston, the mother of Cornell Franklin, was Estelle's advocate; unlike Estelle's disapproving parents, Mamie faulted her *son*, not her daughter-in-law, for the failure of their marriage. Although Cornell remarried, Mamie always insisted that "Estelle is my only daughter-in-law."[3] Furthermore, Mamie genuinely cared for Estelle. She had spent a good deal of time with her son and daughter-in-law when they were living in Hawaii; it was Mamie, not Estelle's mother, who nursed Estelle and their infant when the Franklins' daughter, Cho-Cho, was born there in February 1919.[4] A writer of sorts herself, she liked Estelle's new husband, too. Until Mamie's death, in 1936, Estelle, Faulkner, and Jill visited her frequently.

After stopping briefly at Mamie's small white cottage, where they left Malcolm and Cho-Cho, Estelle and Faulkner then drove twenty-five miles back toward Oxford to Aberdeen, where they spent their wedding night at the town's only inn. A few days later, they returned to Columbus. There they retrieved the children and with Mamie's housekeeper, Emma, and some borrowed silver—Mamie wanted the newlyweds served, and served with style—they headed for a working vacation at a rented beachfront house on Mississippi's Pascagoula Bay. Three weeks later, as Faulkner continued to correct page proofs of *The Sound and the Fury*, Mamie joined them for a week before returning to Columbus with the two Franklin children.[5]

The Faulkners' marriage began badly. If stories told by Rufus Ward (one of Faulkner's drinking buddies) and the Faulkners' Pascagoula neighbors are to be believed, despite the "love" and "respect" Estelle expressed for her new husband, their honeymoon started with her public humiliation and climaxed in her attempted suicide. (Although her letter says she loves and respects Bill, she never claims that Bill loves her.) Ward said that he and a few other men, mutual friends of his and Faulkner's, were sitting in the Aberdeen Inn having drinks the night Bill and Estelle arrived. After dinner Bill joined them while Estelle went on upstairs to bed. According to Ward, "It got later and later and the bourbon was going down in the bottle. Finally one of the men said, 'Well, Bill, aren't you going to go upstairs to your bride?' And he answered, 'That woman upstairs will be there in the morning but this bourbon won't.' And he just kept on drinking."[6]

Alcohol also figures in the well-known account of Estelle's second "suicide attempt" in the notoriously shallow waters of Pascagoula Bay. According to their neighbor Mrs. Martin Shepherd, the Faulkners had already begun the elaborate theater that their daughter Jill describes as a staple of their marriage. Besides Mamie's borrowed housekeeper and silver, Estelle, like an estranged wife in one of her own short stories, had amassed an elegant wardrobe during her seven years as Cornell's colonial wife and hostess. With these props and a good deal of whiskey, Bill and Estelle staged their evenings alone or with neighbors like the Shepherds. One night as the Shepherds sat on their front porch, Bill, who had been doing some "heavy drinking," raced over shouting for help to save Estelle, who he said had walked out into the bay to "drown herself." Martin Shepherd waded through the shallow water for more than half a block before he caught Estelle "just before the shelf of the beach dropped away at the channel" and dragged her back to shore. They then called Dr. Tom Kells, another friend and neighbor, who gave Estelle a sedative. "In a few days she was better."[7] The Shepherds, at least, believed Estelle was serious. There is precedent to support their claim; Estelle's prior failed suicide attempt took place in Honolulu, probably in February or March 1926, after Cornell had "required" that she leave Shanghai. No one ever asked what Bill Faulkner thought in retrospect. And no one asked Estelle. Jill, her parents' longest and perhaps closest observer, thinks that if her mother had been serious, she would have chosen something "quicker and cleaner" than a half-mile walk through shallow water to the channel. She suggests it was "a pure fake. She would not have walked into the water to kill herself. It was an ugly death. If she were serious, she would have taken poison and then gone and lain down. She didn't like to swim although she could—a tentative but graceful sidestroke—and she didn't like the sun—ladies didn't get sun-burned or tanned. My father enjoyed both. My guess is that she just hated the whole arrangement [in Pascagoula]."[8] Jill's point has some merit. Statistics on suicide show overwhelmingly that people who are intent on killing themselves succeed, generally on the first try. There is a second category of people for whom the attempt is a cry for help.

If she was crying for help, her problem was not other women. Ever since her first marriage in 1918, Bill had written poems and created booklets of poetry for women besides Estelle, namely, Myrtle Ramey and Helen Baird, though neither responded favorably to his literary wooing. Despite Faulkner's affair with Meta Wilde in the mid-1930s, and with Jean Stein, Else Johnson, and Joan Williams in the 1950s, all of which he made sure that she knew about, Bill and Estelle remained married until his death. Like alcohol and their sometimes not so private theater, these brief and always long-distance affairs became a staple of their marriage. Faulkner's literary "love" gifts to Myrtle and Helen, once Estelle had abandoned her first marriage, these accounts of their honeymoon, and his later affairs all suggest that his need for her was as great as his ambivalence about his need for her.

Although some biographers and critics are less censorious toward Estelle than others, all agree that one of the greatest puzzles is what Faulkner saw in her. Research on the Faulkners' lifelong relationship reveals that a good deal of what Faulkner desired and needed was a shared sensibility. Such a sensibility is evident when her letter is read in the context of the one Faulkner had written to his publisher, Hal Smith, shortly before he and Estelle married. His was a similarly theatrical announcement of their impending marriage to someone from whom *he* wanted something: money to finance his marriage. Estelle writes what she does in part because she needs something too: her parents' approval and help. (Cornell will send his three-hundred-dollar monthly child support checks to Estelle's parents, while Malcolm will end up living much of his childhood with them.) Read together, these equally self-dramatizing letters demonstrate that the Faulkners had more in common than a dependency on alcohol, itself a bond whose complex implications in Faulkner's imaginative processes have yet to be explored. A typical assessment of the Faulkners' marriage states that "as a couple, the Faulkners would begin the only habit they would ever really share: drinking themselves into a deadly stupor."[9] That they abused alcohol is well known. That they might have also shared something valuable has never been explored. Yet the fact that theirs was a marriage of minds, emotions, and joint motives as well seems apparent when one reads Estelle's letter to her parents along with Faulkner's to his publisher. Their tandem rhetorical performances show them working *as a team* at this critical moment in their lives to create the best possible conditions for making their marriage a success. They needed the full cooperation of Estelle's parents and the financial support of Faulkner's editor and publisher at his new publishing house, Cape and Smith.[10]

Estelle states her case clearly and with as much rhetorical flourish as her lover lavished on Hal Smith when explaining why he needed an immediate five-hundred-dollar advance. Through her marriage to Cornell Franklin, which she had entered into with "fear and abhorrence," she had sought the Oldhams' joy. Now, eleven years, one marriage, and two children later—seven months after Cornell had filed their final divorce decree in the United States Court for China in Shanghai and a little more than one month since it had been granted—she had married the man of her choice.[11] This time, "with happiness and with the conviction that I'd done at last what was the best and only thing for me to do," she had chosen a husband "I honestly love" and with whom she has "found peace and understanding." Her next paragraphs express both her awareness of her parents' anger and hurt and the anguish of her own conflicting desires. She wants to remain a "loving and loyal daughter," but she also wants them to recognize that she is no longer a child. This Estelle needs adult space, self-respect, and a husband *she* loves: "I'm not asking forgiveness, for I wouldn't do that,"—"*still*, I'm a *woman*, and there are few who don't want a place of their very own" and a husband they "love and respect." She tries to appease them by reminding them that "Bill and I both want to live in Oxford where I could see you all every day"; she then pleads, "Please don't shut your hearts and *minds* against me." Estelle's concern about losing the possibility of her parents' love is as real as her competing and reasonable desire for a sane and happy life. I say possibility because the Oldhams' parenting of their oldest daughter suggests that their love for her was always conditional. They treasured Estelle for what they could get from her, but they did not love her.

In her letter, Estelle begs her parents to "let me have my share of the joys all people need for sane, happy lives." Sanity—both Estelle's and Faulkner's—also figures in Faulkner's letter to Smith. Its tonal register is also high melodrama. He needs an immediate five-hundred-dollar advance because "I am going to be married. Both want to and have to. THIS PART IS CONFIDENTIAL, UTTERLY. For my honor and the snaity [x'd out] sanity—I believe life—of a woman." Perhaps anticipating Smith's skeptical reply he tries to refute it in advance by piling up more melodrama in a series of negatives that climax in ambiguity: "This is not bunk; neither am I being sucked in. We grew up together and I don't think she could fool me in this way; that is, make me believe that her mental condition, her nerves, are this far gone." He then shifts further into the familiar hypermasculine pose he often adopted when talking about women. While he's marrying to protect his "honor," he assures Smith that there's "no question of pregnancy [*sic*]: that would hardly move me: no one can face his own bastard with more equanimity than I, having had some practice." Nor is it a matter of living up to his word: "Neither is it a matter of a promise on my part; we have known one another long enough to pay no attention to our promises." Instead and vaguely, "it's a situation which I engendered and permitted to ripen which has become unbearable, and I'm tired of running from the devilment I bring about." At this point, acknowledging the hysterical tone of his prose he finishes the paragraph: "This sounds a little insane, but I'm not in any shape to write letters now. I'll explain it better when I see you."[12] If, as Faulkner wrote his publisher, he had to marry Estelle because she was suicidal and her nerves were gone, it's not apparent from her letter. Of the two, it's Faulkner's (as he himself observes) that sounds the more insane.

Estelle's letter shows great sensitivity to the possibility of losing her parents, yet she's oblivious to the burden she's putting on her little daughter: "Cho-Cho will be with you when you get this—and will tell you our plans." Estelle's use of Cho-Cho here reenacts her mother's use of her. It also resonates with Jill's portrayal of many aspects of her relationship with both her parents. Interviews with people who knew the Oldhams and with Jill and Cho-Cho's daughter, Victoria Johnson, confirm the accuracy of the parent-daughter dynamics implied in Estelle's letter. According to Victoria, Cho-Cho felt her mother neglected her.[13] Long before Estelle married Faulkner she had learned from her parents to love and be loved in this limited and limiting way.

Further contextualizing of Estelle's letter demonstrates her imaginative grasp of the Oldhams' need to use her for their gratification. An ability to translate such complicated familial psychological relations into fiction was another of Estelle's talents that Faulkner needed, especially during the period in which he was finding his own fictional voice. In early 1925, shortly after her first return from Shanghai with the stories she had written there, Faulkner began publishing his series of prose sketches that he later bound and gave to Estelle. That February he began writing his first novel, *Soldiers' Pay*. Even as late as December 1928, the month he sent his editor at *Scribner's* magazine a story that had been Estelle's originally but that now carried both their bylines, Faulkner had written, "I am quite sure I have no feeling for short stories; that I shall never be able to write them."[14] The damage done by exploitative parents and parent surrogates composes the thematics of all three of Estelle's extant short stories and those that Faulkner rewrote and ultimately published under his own name. In these tales the only empathic parental figures are black servants and other men and women who are figuratively blackened by their outsider status: a New Orleans Creole, a Polish doctor, a Shanghai Jew, a bisexual French dressmaker, a Cambridge-educated Chinese businessman, and a promiscuous, self-supporting aunt. In Faulkner's fiction, too, such parental control and cold manipulation marks almost every parent-child relationship.

When she wrote her elopement letter, Estelle was thirty-two years old. Educated exclusively for the occupation of wife and mother, with no income other than the child-support checks Cornell sent sporadically to her parents, she had chosen as her second husband a man who some Northern and a few Southern book reviewers considered promising. The Oldhams, however, along with the majority of Oxford residents, judged Faulkner, at best, a gifted but arrogant and difficult man, certainly a poor risk as a husband, and, at worst, an irresponsible drunk whom some labeled "Major Oldham's yard boy." As Faulkner once wrote of his fellow townsmen to his Random House editor, "All prophesied I'd never be more than a bum."[15] From a twenty-first-century perspective, it is hard to imagine the courage it took Estelle to marry against her parents' wishes and to write such a letter. The tension between her courage to be different and her apparent desire to be the perfect Southern Belle and dutiful wife and daughter motivates so much of Estelle Oldham's life and illuminates the sources of the Faulkners' mutual attraction and long-term dedication to each other. It is therefore critical to explore the origins of this duality and commitment.

Lem Oldham and Lida Allen: A Love Match, 1895

For Lemuel Earle Oldham (8 February 1870–6 May 1945) and Lida Corrinne Allen (23 August 1873–10 March 1956), their eldest daughter's first marriage was a tremendous financial and social achievement. Cornell Franklin, from Columbus, Mississippi, had a highly respectable ancestry. Although the Oldhams also claimed distinguished forebears, it had been generations since any family member had made anything approaching a fortune.[16] Cornell was not rich, and would not become so until after Estelle and he had separated, but he was smart and had tremendous drive. Upon graduating from law school in 1917 he left North Mississippi, where his prospects of wealth were slight, to seek his fortune in the colonial outposts of the Far East: Honolulu (1916–21) and then Shanghai (1921–44), the "Paris of the East." In marrying Cornell, Estelle had put aside her ambivalence to give her parents what they wanted.

Even though they arranged their eldest daughter's marriage, Lem and Lida had married for love. Neither brought any wealth to their marriage. Their fathers had died when they were very young: Lem's had been murdered in a political brawl; Lida's, a doctor, had died of influenza. Their

13.1. Allen-Oldham Genealogy

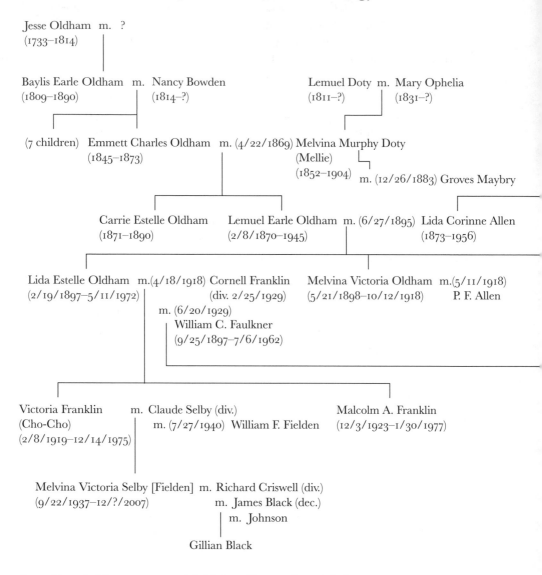

Jesse Oldham   m.   ?
(1733–1814)

Baylis Earle Oldham   m.   Nancy Bowden
(1809–1890)   (1814–?)

Lemuel Doty   m.   Mary Ophelia
(1811–?)   (1831–?)

(7 children)   Emmett Charles Oldham   m. (4/22/1869) Melvina Murphy Doty
                (1845–1873)   (Mellie)
                                                         (1852–1904)   m. (12/26/1883) Groves Maybry

Carrie Estelle Oldham   Lemuel Earle Oldham   m. (6/27/1895)   Lida Corinne Allen
(1871–1890)   (2/8/1870–1945)   (1873–1956)

Lida Estelle Oldham   m.(4/18/1918) Cornell Franklin   Melvina Victoria Oldham   m.(5/11/1918)
(2/19/1897–5/11/1972)   (div. 2/25/1929)   (5/21/1898–10/12/1918)   P. F. Allen
                          m. (6/20/1929)
                            William C. Faulkner
                            (9/25/1897–7/6/1962)

Victoria Franklin   m. Claude Selby (div.)   Malcolm A. Franklin
(Cho-Cho)   m. (7/27/1940) William F. Fielden   (12/3/1923–1/30/1977)
(2/8/1919–12/14/1975)

Melvina Victoria Selby [Fielden] m. Richard Criswell (div.)
(9/22/1937–12/?/2007)   m. James Black (dec.)
                                     m. Johnson

                          Gillian Black

Source: Compiled from census materials, birth certificates, other archival sources, and interviews with family members.

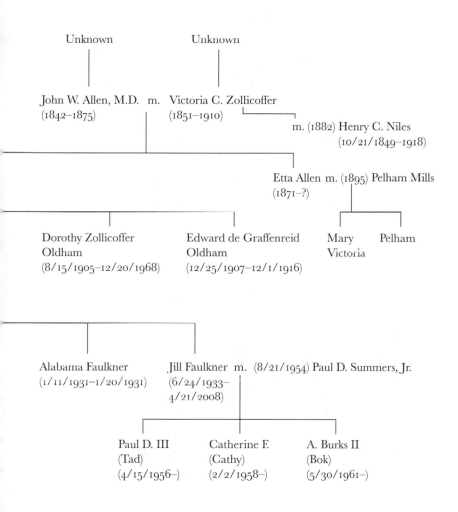

Unknown   Unknown

John W. Allen, M.D.   m.   Victoria C. Zollicoffer
(1842–1875)   (1851–1910)
                                            m. (1882) Henry C. Niles
                                                   (10/21/1849–1918)

                              Etta Allen m. (1895) Pelham Mills
                              (1871–?)

Dorothy Zollicoffer   Edward de Graffenreid   Mary   Pelham
Oldham   Oldham   Victoria
(8/15/1905–12/20/1968)   (12/25/1907–12/1/1916)

Alabama Faulkner   Jill Faulkner m. (8/21/1954) Paul D. Summers, Jr.
(1/11/1931–1/20/1931)   (6/24/1933–
                         4/21/2008)

         Paul D. III   Catherine F.   A. Burks II
         (Tad)   (Cathy)   (Bok)
         (4/15/1956–)   (2/2/1958–)   (5/30/1961–)

13.2. Estelle's maternal grandparents' house (*top*) and the "cottage" Lem and Lida Oldham rented from Miss Vic and Judge Henry C. Niles, Kosciusko, Miss. (Photo: Pauline Barrow)

mothers had later remarried, but Lida's stepfather, the famous judge Henry C. Niles, was unsympathetic to his stepdaughter's precarious finances, and Lem's stepfather, Groves Mabry, was struggling himself. Like their first son-in-law, Estelle's parents had done their own pioneering in an attempt to strike it rich. As newlyweds of a generation earlier who had set out from their economically depressed town of Kosciusko, Mississippi, to North Texas in the summer of 1895, Lem and Lida knew firsthand the hardships of westward expansion. After an embarrassing return to Kosciusko, they were reduced to living in a small cottage on the grounds of the Niles's Big House. The young couple was so poor that Lida's mother, Victoria Swanson Allen Niles ("Miss Vic," as she was called), would secretly return the three dollars of monthly rent that Judge Niles insisted on charging his stepdaughter. Photographs of both homes speak vividly to the disparity between the Oldhams' financial circumstances during the first six years of Estelle's life and those of her maternal grandparents.

The Kosciusko newspaper's account of Lida and Lem's marriage ceremony and of the groom's sunny economic prospects gives no hint of the couple's shaky finances. Miss Vic and her husband, a highly respected lawyer, spared no expense for Lida's wedding, which was *the* event of the season.[17] The bride, "one of the fairest buds that ever adorned Kosciusko society," is also "noted as one of the most accomplished musicians in Mississippi." This was not mere social hype. Lida Allen took her piano playing seriously. Besides formal training in piano, composition, and the teaching of piano in college, she had also taken four semesters of piano and ensemble at the New England Conservatory in 1893–94.[18] As late as 1921 she wrote musical scores that she sent for criticism, with hopes of publishing, to George A. Leighton, a professor of piano, harmony, and counterpoint on the staff of the Cleveland Conservatory of Music and the publisher of *Sinfonian*, a music journal.[19]

Lem's popularity, looks, and intellect equaled his bride's: "The groom is a handsome and rising young merchant of McKinney Texas, being junior partner in the large firm of Mabry, Oldham, and Co., who own stores at Bonham and McKinney," which sold dry goods and clothing. [20] In truth, however, Lem's and his stepfather's firm was short-lived. When he'd married in 1895, he was managing the McKinney store. But by February 1897, the month Estelle was born, that store had apparently closed. Lem and Lida then moved to Bonham, Texas, but their financial situation failed to improve. By July, Lida had returned to Kosciusko with her five-month-old daughter and moved in with her mother and stepfather.[21] Early that September, the papers reported that Lem was "spending a few days in the city."[22] In fact he may have simply stayed, for by December he and D. S. Bachman, a close friend, had bought Henry Herman's "brokerage business," changed its name to Oldham and Bachman, and announced they were going to "conduct a general grocery and produce business."[23]

Lem's partnership with Bachman was no more successful than his venture with his stepfather. By January 1899, news items suggest that, like his stepfather, Lem was trying to make a living as a traveling salesman: "Mr. Lem Oldham spent a few days at home recently."[24] In October 1900 the paper reports his leaving town "on a business trip to New Orleans."[25] In November 1902 the local personal columns report that "Lemuel Oldham is in Mexico this week looking after some mining claims in which he is interested."[26]

What strikes one about the life of Estelle's father during the thirteen-year span from 1890 to 1903, which included the first six years of his eldest daughter's life, is the tremendous amount of wandering involved and the lack of any sense of direction or commitment to professional goals. This seems at odds with his four undergraduate years at the University of Mississippi, from 1885 to 1889. Among the Oldham family papers is a box labeled "Lem Oldham." There, along with a copy of Lem's last will and testament, is a small worn cloth bag containing two engraved medals he won at the university; one dated 8 December 1885 from the Philotechnic Society for Declamation, the other awarded by Professor W. H. MaGruder, 12 June 1886, for Excellence in English. In that same sack are a man's and a woman's rings (both missing stones), a section of gold bracelet, and a child's ring decorated with a slightly chipped chinoiserie bluebird. The contents might be read as a mute testament to his early ambitions and successes and blasted dreams. Lem would make a good living as a political appointee once the Oldhams moved to Oxford. But when he died, in May 1945, the Oldhams were nearly destitute.

A brief item in a 1925 biographical sketch of Lem offers a clue to his seemingly peripatetic behavior prior to 1903, when the Oldhams' lives changed radically.[27] The sketch also reveals that Lem's original ambitions were not at all lawyerly. In 1890, after receiving his M.A. at Ole Miss, he traveled to Poughkeepsie, New York, where he enrolled in a business course at the then famous Eastman College. It was the perfect place for an ambitious would-be mogul to go for instruction.[28]

Although Lem was intensely shy or perhaps, like Estelle, just reserved, he desperately wanted to succeed in business. The retail ventures he engaged in or investigated prior to 1903 make clear that law was the *last* profession he cared about. But it was the one in which, through his father-in-law, he had both training and an entrée. Ironically, while Lem's appointed state and, later, federal legal positions furnished the Oldham family's staple income, he used that to speculate on and finance a continuing series of unsuccessful business ventures. An elderly member of the Niles-Oldham families described the Oldhams and Mabrys as always involved in "financial schemes," adding that despite Lem's legal training, he was never particularly interested in practicing law.[29] His granddaughter Jill Summers says, "Granddaddy didn't have much of a law practice. Yet you never would have known it, to listen to him. He always lived way beyond his means, as though he were an extremely wealthy man. And Nannie [Lida] dealt with the day-to-day. It was she who worried whether there was enough money to do this or that or the other."[30] For many years, Lida had the intelligence, talent, education, and interest necessary to support Lem's dreams and schemes.[31] Perhaps most important, however, she deeply loved her husband, whom she had married despite the Niles family's misgivings.[32] A cousin recalls, "The Oldhams' was certainly a *love* match. Mrs. Oldham was proud of her Lem. But he never had a job until Judge Niles gave him the one in Oxford."[33] This, too, is ironic when considered in the light of the pressure the Oldhams put on Estelle to marry and stay married to Cornell Franklin and, as Estelle's elopement letter indicates, the threats they used to prevent her from marrying Faulkner. But perhaps Lida was also sobered and motivated by her experiences and wanted to save Estelle from repeating her mistake.

Although Lida had come of age in the household of her fairly well-off stepfather, the first nine years of her life had been at least as financially difficult as the first eight years of her marriage. Her father, Dr. John Wilbourn Allen, died in 1875, when Lida was less than two and her sister, Etta, was four. So perhaps also motivating her were childhood memories of the years prior to her mother's remarriage, which overnight lifted the Allen girls from genteel impoverishment to solid upper-middle-class status. In 1882, when Miss Vic married the judge, a widower, she and her two daughters enjoyed the first financial security they had known since her first husband's death.[34] "The Niles were extravagant," recalled a contemporary of Estelle's. "They had horses and the Judge and Miss Vic would go to New Orleans and buy furs and jewelry, and my, did they dress! When he was a young man, Jason would go to New Orleans and buy five hats; they were fancy hats, too."[35] The "imperious" Miss Vic, as some called her, did love her diamonds. And she had an ample bosom upon which she displayed them.

It's also probable that Miss Vic and her adult daughters were estranged; in 1911 when she was dying, neither Etta nor Lida returned to Kosciusko to care for her.[36] If this is so, it suggests a legacy of strained and distant mother-daughter relationships in Estelle's family. Such strain and distancing coupled with startling degrees of manipulation and psychological abuse aptly describes the relationships between white mothers or mother surrogates in Estelle's fiction and in Lida's relationships with her three daughters.

Another legacy of Miss Vic's years of poverty was her insistence that her daughters be taught more than housekeeping skills so that, should they need to, they could support themselves. She therefore sent Lida and Etta to Mississippi's newly opened Industrial Institute and College in Columbus (The State Female College). Both Etta Allen and Carrie Estelle Oldham (Lem's younger sister for whom Estelle was named) are listed in the 1885 catalog as members of the first entering class.[37] Lida graduated from the college's popular two-year Business Course (1887–89). (This was the same program that Faulkner's mother enrolled in three years later.) The extra music program Lida also took was sufficiently rigorous to qualify graduates to teach piano, something that she, like her mother before her, would do.

Lida graduated in 1889, but between then and the fall of 1893 there are no records of her whereabouts. She was probably using her office skills and musical training to earn the money she needed to study more music, for in 1893 she went to Boston where she enrolled for the year at the New England Conservatory of Music as a non-degree student.[38] Both sisters' intellectual interests were serious, wide-ranging, and lifelong. Shortly after graduating from college, Etta was appointed "Mistress of Physics and Chemistry" at the Industrial Institute and College.[39] Although she married a doctor and had children (both compelling reasons not to continue to work outside her home), she continued to teach. Lida's pursuit of advanced musical training, her teaching, and her continuing interest in writing and publishing her music attest to the value of her education. Yet she seems to have discouraged Estelle's obvious aptitude and interest in learning, especially during adolescence. Rather than letting her finish the two-year college preparatory program at Mary Baldwin (1913–14), where she had excelled, she brought their daughter home from Virginia after her first year. Lida was more intent on marrying off Estelle than educating her. Arranging party after party, the Oldhams plunged their sixteen-year-old daughter into Oxford's coed social whirl, which included dating college juniors like Cornell Franklin, whom she would marry four years later. Thus Estelle moved straight from being a child in her parents' home to a marriage her parents had arranged. The results were very sad. She spent the night before her wedding in tears. Just before walking down the aisle on her wedding day, she told Katrina Carter, "I don't know whether I love Cornell, or if I want to marry him.[40] Estelle's need to please her parents, however, coupled with her lack of an education, seriously limited her choices. In contrast, before marrying in 1895, her mother used her college education to buy five years of independence during which she financed her further professional training. That was one reason why, unlike her daughter, she had the luxury of a "love match."

In June of 1895, when Estelle's newlywed parents set off from Kosciusko for the frontier, each brought to the marriage a variety of experiences that had created self-expectations extending well beyond the provincial confines of their sleepy little hometown. Besides their undergraduate educations at Mississippi colleges, both had traveled to the North and had lived and studied in or near the two major centers of American culture and finance, Boston and New York. In retrospect it is ironic to think how those expectations would be lived out in the actual and imaginative life of their eldest daughter. Estelle's frontier experience would take place in the colonies and settlements of American, British, and French adventurers, among young men and women who had gone to seek fame and fortune in one of the richest and, reportedly, most decadent imperialist outposts of the early twentieth century—Shanghai. Estelle's return from that Far Eastern experience would be much more ignominious than her parents' return from Texas. She accepted that ignominy. But by 1929, rather than give in to the constraints and rewards that her family deemed in her best interests, Estelle embarked on a lifetime journey to another frontier, one she would share with William Faulkner.

14

Kosciusko Childhood, Southern Belledom, and Estelle's Fictional Memoir, 1897–1903

> A month later Flem and Eula also departed for Texas (that bourne, Uncle
> Gavin said, in our time for the implicated, the insolvent or the merely
> hopeful), to return the next summer with a girl baby a little larger than
> you would have expected at only three months.
> —Faulkner, *The Town*

WHEN FAULKNER WROTE this sly, private joke impugning his
wife's legitimacy, both of his in-laws were dead, and he was
no longer supporting their insolvency. Contrary to this fictional rendition, Lem and Lida Oldham's daughter was conceived with all
the propriety her parents so esteemed. She was also the first of the Oldhams' four children and the only one born during their ill-fated attempt to
resettle in East Texas. Her name and birth date, recorded in the Oldham-
Doty family Bible in her father's flowery hand, are given as "Lida Estelle
Oldham / Bonham, Fannin County Texas / 19 February 1897, 2:40 A.M.
Friday. It was a rainy night."[1] Her parents named their daughter after her
mother, Lida, and after her father's younger (and only) sister and Lida's
good friend, Carrie Estelle, who had died in Texas seven years earlier while
giving birth to her first child. Newspaper accounts of the wedding of Carrie Estelle, held two days before the Christmas of 1890, confirm that the
Oldham and Falkner families had been friends long before Estelle and Billy
were born. Among the bridesmaids were the Allen sisters, Lida and Etta,
and Murry Falkner's sister, Maud's best friend, Holland ("Auntee").

Carrie's namesake was one of those rare, really beautiful babies. That
spring of 1897, when the weather turned milder and Bonham's muddy
streets (as in Oxford, until 1928, there were no sidewalks) had baked dry,
Lida took her infant daughter for a formal photograph at Charles Foster's
Photo Room, which was just across the square from Mabry & Oldham,

14.1. Estelle Oldham's 1897 baby portrait, taken at Foster Studios, Bonham, Tex. (Courtesy of Jill Faulkner Summers)

Lem's and his stepfather's short-lived dry-goods store. In Foster's sepia-toned photograph, Estelle is propped up with upholstered pillows in the high-backed Victorian wicker chair. Her white lace embroidered dress sets off her large eyes, made larger and brighter by her arched and fully formed eyebrows. With her tiny, up-tipped nose, full, bow-shaped mouth, and dimpled chin, she looks remarkably mature and alert for a three- or four-month-old (fig. 14.1). Estelle inherited her good looks from her father. Soon, she would emulate Lem's love for fine clothes. Because Lem was "the dresser" in the family, it is not surprising that his first full-scale business venture in Texas was a store that advertised "clothing: boots and shoes and stylish millinery; everything in dress goods and trimmings."[2] Since the Oldhams placed great value on their daughters' beauty, their original response to Estelle must have been utter delight. But "Dr. Wohlenski," the fictionalized autobiographical fragment Estelle Oldham wrote about her early childhood, and Estelle's actual relations with her parents suggest that their delight may have been short-lived.

When Lida became pregnant, memories of Carrie's recent death may have prompted more than ordinary anxiety at home in Kosciusko. The family's concern may explain why both Estelle's grandmother and great grandmother made the arduous journey to Bonham, made worse by winter storms and blizzards, to attend her birth. Estelle's birth appears to have been without complications, however, since Lida's mother, the imperious Miss Vic, stayed only a bit longer than a week.[3] Her brief stay may also reflect the cool relationship between Lida and her mother.

Estelle's sister, Melvina Victoria ("Tochie"), named after both grandmothers, would be born about fifteen months later. But by then Estelle's Texas sojourn was over. Like Eula Varner's daughter, Linda Snopes, she spent only the first few months of her life on that frontier. By summer of that year it was clear that Mabry & Oldham was a failure. As much as Lem loved clothes and as bright as he was, he was a poor salesman. That he dressed like a dandy and used arrogance to cover his shyness sealed his failure with Bonham's rough-and-ready customers. So Lem and Lida gave up their dream of striking it rich in the West and returned to Kosciusko in September 1897 to live in the cottage at the back end of her parents' property. Within a month, Lida was pregnant with Tochie. Their last two children were born several years after their fall 1903 move to Oxford.

Although there are photographs of other members of the Niles and Oldham families dating from the 1880s to about 1910, none survive of Lida. There is only one baby picture of Estelle and one photograph of Estelle and Tochie taken shortly before the Oldhams' move to Oxford. Nor are there any extant family diaries or letters from the Oldhams' years in Bonham and Kosciusko. Estelle told neither her daughter, Jill, nor her granddaughter, Victoria, anything about her early childhood. These photographs of Estelle and Tochie and some of the Niles house, which is still standing, and a tiny, one-story wooden building purported to be the cottage Lem and Lida rented from Miss Vic and her husband are the only material evidence, other than brief newspaper articles and tax records, that exists to tell us about the first six years of Estelle's life.

14.2. Studio photo of Estelle and her sister, Victoria ("Tochie"), Kosciusko, Miss., c. 1902–3. (Courtesy of Victoria Fielden Johnson)

Estelle Oldham's Fictionalized Childhood Memoir: "Dr. Wohlenski"

As I have mentioned, however, there is another unusual but important source. Estelle Oldham preserved her fictionalized version of those years in an eleven-thousand-word short-story fragment she called "Dr. Wohlenski," which she wrote some time between 1922 and 1924.[4] (In this chapter only, to avoid confusion, I refer to Estelle, the author, as Oldham, and to Estelle, the character in "Dr. Wohlenski," as Estelle.)

Unlike Oldham's other extant stories, "Dr. Wohlenski" is a mix of fiction and explicit autobiographical narrative. In many instances, the story's facts about Estelle Oldham's family are both specific and accurate. The deliberate correspondence suggests that Oldham wanted the informed reader (most particularly, Faulkner himself) to take her coming-of-age story as a psychologically accurate portrait of herself at age six. Its child narrator, Estelle Oldham, lives in Kosciusko, Mississippi, with her large extended family. Her parents are Lem and Lida Oldham. Estelle has a baby sister, Victoria (nicknamed Tochie), and assorted Niles, Jackson, and Mills relatives, among them the most proper of ladies, Estelle's great-aunt Carrie.[5] The Niles-Oldham household also includes Estelle's other family, the black people who work for her white family. Nolia Cottrell, Estelle's nursemaid, and Nolia's mother, Cinthy, the cook, have real-life counterparts who actually did go to Oxford with the Oldhams.[6] The accuracy of the supposedly fictional information about the daily life of Estelle's family—(their home, occupations, and leisure activities) and about the material culture of its two time frames (Kosciusko just prior to the Civil War and in the early 1900s) is confirmed by other, more traditional sources. One of the story's most interesting themes—Estelle's Jim Crow education into Southern Belledom—is never stated directly, because it concerns feelings that cannot be acknowledged. Her emotional loss of her black nurse and the death of her nurse's less punitive and purely fictional double are the catalysts for all of the conflicts about sexual and racial difference that its rebellious little heroine experiences in the course of her education into Southern Womanhood.

Set during the late fall and winter of 1902–3, the months preceding her real family's move to Oxford, in October 1903, Oldham's narrative is her imaginative re-creation of her white Southern childhood self when, at a vulnerable age, she is faced with a defining loss: her childhood relationship with her black family, symbolized, in part, by the loss of her childhood home.[7] Oldham can speak of this loss only through the death of Dr. Wohlenski, her purely fictional character. Estelle loves him more than anyone, including her parents. Yet, Oldham scripts his death. Making him a ghost frees Estelle to continue loving him.

I suggest that Dr. Wohlenski represents the child Estelle's (and Oldham's) acceptable fictive substitute or screen through whom she can mourn her lost relationship with her black family—what I've called the black maternal. He is one of a series of foreigners (both male and female) who figure prominently in the lives of all of Oldham's female protagonists. In this story about learning the basic lessons of Southern culture, the foreigner also represents a psychological reality. Until Oldham left the South, she didn't grasp the import of those childhood lessons in Southern "propriety," as Estelle's grandfather in this story constantly calls it. Oldham's years in Honolulu and Shanghai—as a foreigner and among foreigners—gave her the distance and experience to form the more critical perspective reflected in both parts of "Dr. Wohlenski."

Another equally important psychological reality is that like the unacceptable love objects in other stories she wrote, this intelligent and creative fictional outsider may also be a figure for exploring and trying to understand her relation to and desire for Bill Faulkner, the self-named "little black man" whom her parents deemed off-limits as a husband in 1918 and for whom Oldham also mourned. In this story Oldham invents a fictional "I," the six-year-old Estelle, who uses her imagination to come to terms with all her losses. She learns this skill, in part, from Dr. Wohlenski, a man of many talents, including storytelling. In his position as outsider and storyteller he provides the little girl with a profession that she adopts. Through writing, she masters her situation.

Within the present time frame of her story—Koskiusko of 1902–3—Oldham's Estelle is emotionally orphaned. Yet, she does not appear to feel grief or anger at any loss or outrage she experiences. Rather, she uses her voice to rebel against becoming "a lady" and instead tries to become like the men in her family: "human—warm and comforting" and "smelling of horses and whiskey and tobacco as did Papa Niles and Dr. Wohlenski." She identifies with the men more so than with the women in her family because she has already begun to realize that to be intellectually alive and connected means to be a man: "I wondered if that was what Papa Niles meant by being 'intellectually compatible.'"[8]

What was Oldham attempting with this "I"? The accuracy of her portrait is less important than the fact that this is the self-image she wanted to project to the audience living in her head when she wrote the story in the early 1920s. It expresses her admiration for and wish to emulate women who can speak and feel for themselves. In short, to be connected: to be warm and human and intellectually active. It also speaks to her recognition of some of the attendant difficulties and resulting opprobrium. Like her other stories, its critique of racial and gender inequities also reveals what she learned about racism and sexism between 1918 and 1924 while living as a foreigner among foreigners in Honolulu and Shanghai.

"Dr. Wohlenski" is important to Oldham and Faulkner's relationship for the crucial role it will play in the making of *The Sound and the Fury*. But here my focus is its value for reconstructing her early childhood as she saw it retrospectively and for revealing the content and quality of her imaginative and political preoccupations when she wrote "Dr. Wohlenski."

The awkward structure of this work—two tangentially related parts—

suggests that Oldham started out intending to write an antebellum plantation romance (like those of Thomas Nelson Page in her grandfather
Niles's library) based on her knowledge of her family's roots in Kosciusko.[9]
Part 1 takes place on her great-uncle's plantation eight miles outside of Kosciusko. However, as she wrote, she must have found both the time frame
and the genre unaccommodating to her paramount interest, Estelle's education into Southern Womanhood or Belledom. Because Part 1 includes
the history of her family's involvement in slavery and their friendship with
Dr. Wohlenski—that section's narrator—and introduces themes concerning Southern codes of conduct that are further developed in Part 2, she
decided to keep it. Part 2, narrated by Estelle in three loosely related
episodes, reveals her desire *to desire* and a particular kind of knowledge and
independence. Her desire pits her against her family's and culture's requirement that she become a Lady.

Briefly, the plot is as follows. In Part 1, set in the office of Estelle's
grandfather on a late fall afternoon in 1902, she listens to Dr. Wohlenski
telling the story of how he first met her great-uncle Felix Jackson and then
spent the night on his plantation around 1860. Part 2, which Estelle narrates in the first person, is set during that same fall afternoon, evening, and
on into the months that follow. Its subject is her unorthodox alliance with
the good doctor and an old black man and what results. Her adventures
are interwoven with rich descriptions of the daily life of her extended family. Although told with humor and irony and in a determinedly upbeat tone,
her story is one in which loss follows loss: first her father announces that
they are moving to Oxford; then her mammy rebukes her for speaking out
instead of "acting like a lady"; then her beloved Dr. Wohlenski dies. The
effects of these losses play out in three loosely related episodes that expand
on themes introduced earlier. In each episode, Estelle's assertions of desire
and agency run contrary to the demands of her community. Her striving
toward an ethical selfhood in a Jim Crow world bent on shaming her into
conforming to its standards of propriety is a touching and astute reading of
the preoccupations of the white South and its literature with "manhood,
womanhood, and their 'proper' [and always racist and racialized] boundaries."[10]

The "foreigner," Dr. Wohlenski, is the only character who makes a significant appearance in both parts of Oldham's story. Oldham opens her
story with a portrayal of the patriarch Felix Jackson, Estelle's slaveholding
ancestor. On florid display are his arrogance, impetuousness, and bad manners—or manners that are all form and no substance. Equally florid is Old-
man's portrayal of the fumes of "potent libations" (four pages describing
rounds and rounds of various before-dinner drinks) pervading this world

Southern slaveholders made. This opening in which Dr. Wohlenski calls Uncle Felix on his "uncouth," "insulting," and "impolite" behavior and one of Jackson's slaves instructs the doctor in master-slave relations—"As you is sho a stanger in a stange land"—alerts readers not to expect any typical "happy darkies" tale about the good old times.[11] Oldham plays Jackson's arrogance and racism against the politeness of Dr. Wohlenski, Jackson's wife, and his servants to show that Southern white men are often the real children in a slave culture, wherein their childishness passes (under Southern codes of gentlemanly conduct) as "honor," "pride," and "propriety." The last, especially, appears frequently in the speeches of Estelle's family patriarchs in Part 2, where it is simultaneously parroted and mocked by family servants and Estelle.

Throughout "Dr. Wohlenski," the tone of this six-year-old's voice, often gently self-mocking and never angry or sad—even as she describes hurtful, violent, and frightening verbal and physical attacks—veils an issue that Oldham's story confronts obliquely: the child's forfeiture and denial of her love for her mammy, Nolia, and the other black people who work for her family to the exigencies of the color line. The consequences of that unacknowledged loss creates what Lillian Smith called the "haunted childhood that belongs to every [white] Southerner." This haunting seeps through this story as the little girl constantly seeks alliances with a substitute and disguised dark other, the warm, direct, and permissive Dr. Wohlenski.[12] Wohlenski seems to signify and mask the loss she pictures but dares not name. Alliances of this kind with an outsider, in which the white girl child is almost always betrayed in some way, recur in all of Oldham's short stories. This loss in her story is, as so much of Faulkner's much later fiction makes painfully clear, the primary attachment that all white Southern children must be taught to denigrate.

Estelle's great-uncle is well schooled in racist practice, which is one reason why he, like her grandfather in the story's second part, is preoccupied with social proprieties yet rude and demeaning toward anyone he considers inferior or different. His little niece has learned this lesson partially, which may be why the mammy, Nolia, speaks only as the voice of the family's patriarch, Grandfather Niles, and why Estelle lacks any negative emotional affect. She does rebel, however, because she has not been as well schooled as her relatives and male ancestors. In contrast to them, she is never rude, demeaning, or cruel to the black people who care for her. She also questions the behavior of her elders and male cousins and tries to protect the black folk who work for her family. For these reasons she is a disturbing presence in an otherwise tranquilly racist post-Reconstruction milieu. As a child being educated by white paternalism into the ideology of Southern

Womanhood and the Jim Crow culture it supports namely, to act, eat, feel, and think "like a lady," "make proper friends," have "suitable playmates," and obey the "proprieties," as its chief spokespersons, her grandfather and Nolia, put it—Estelle is supposed to be racist, asexual, spiritual, morally elevated, and angelic.[13] Most important, she is never to resist the dictates of her male relatives or their spokespersons.[14]

Estelle fails on many counts. She constantly makes trouble as she fights hard not to be socialized into Belledom. She is antisocial, preferring to play alone with her dolls in her tree house, built literally on the border between the domestic spaces of her white and black families; she'd rather curl up with a book in her grandfather's library than play with the other, "boring" little girls in Kosciusko, "with whom I was permitted to associate." Ultimately she aggressively objects to being socialized—"Please God, deliver me from playmates"—and to injustice and abuse of power, exemplified by her grandfather's "tongue-lashing" his black servants. Worst of all, she not only wants to listen to stories she shouldn't hear but tells some embarrassing ones herself, including one about a thieving, "no-count" *Mayflower* ancestor who actually did exist.[15] Finally, allied with a sexy black female ghost and armed with other devices borrowed from Southern Gothic and domestic fiction, she takes revenge on her male cousins' challenge to her storytelling powers, their invasions of her play space, and their destruction of her property (her tree house and dolls). Throughout she constantly makes naive observations that lay bare the daily paradoxes and hypocrisies her genteel family lives by. Ultimately, she does establish a limited legitimacy for her nonconformist voice. This voice's toehold in selfhood is, explicitly, its ability to make those in power believe the stories she tells.

But because she also wants to be considered grown up, she's conflicted. In her early-twentieth-century Southern middle-class family, the bitter lesson she must learn is that a girl cannot be a grown-up; she can only be a Lady. Both her family and her mammy work hard to school her for this role. Her dilemma is that she can be a resistant student. It is a dilemma Oldham continued to contend with during much of her life, even *after* she had apparently given in and adopted a systematically constructed and easily grasped, virtually stereotyped personality for public consumption. Placing the psychic origins of this conflict in her childhood, however, is accurate. Further, as will be discussed in the context of Faulkner's shift into fiction in 1925, its portrait of a little white girl's childhood trauma underlines the story's tremendous value to his own evolving creativity.

Like Faulkner's fictionalized memoir "Mississippi," and for similar reasons, "Dr. Wohlenski" is as valuable for the myths and distortions about Southern history that it perpetuates as for the ones it mocks or subverts. It perpetuates, for example, the myth that before the Civil War all middle-class whites lived on plantations and had lots of slaves, when, in fact, in antebellum Attala County, although cotton was then the main crop, there were no large spreads such as exist in the rice and cotton country of the Mississippi Delta. Instead, yeoman farming (like the farms of the real Jacksons and Oldhams) was the rule.[16]

In general, Oldham's story also perpetuates the image of genial masters, happy slaves, and contented post-Reconstruction servants along with all the contradictions and tensions inherent in those myths. Describing plantation race relations during the Civil War, the child Estelle says, "I do know that the majority of house servants, especially the older ones, stayed behind with full authority to take care of the women and children . . . the whites they *must* have loved."[17] Instances like this reveal tensions in "Dr. Wohlenski" that don't at all conform to typical plantation romance narratives. This assertion about slaves loving their masters, which Oldham dilutes with a conditional, indicates she recognized at some level that a group of people who are literally property can never have "full authority" over their owners, even children. Possibly and despite her education into race and racism, she also recognized that "love" between slaves and masters was an oxymoron or, at most, highly compromised and contingent. When Estelle makes her only visit to the now deserted family plantation, she separates herself clearly from her great-uncle, who is lost in "rose-tinted memories" and spends his time tending its cemetery. Instead she sees its Big House as "crumbling away—brick by brick—windowless and scary. 'Bats and ghosts' I said to myself and turned away quickly. I never went back."[18] She's repelled by white antebellum ghosts—and the plantation mythology they embody—but fascinated by the contemporary ghost stories she hears from her family's black servants. She is also the only white person to see, believe in, and be helped by a ghost they have seen.

It is not just black folk's imaginative creations that Estelle prefers. Throughout "Dr. Wohlenski," Oldham's portrayals of Estelle's relationships with black people or people who are figured as black—including Estelle at her most rebellious—are always linked to her conflicts with white authority. Two of her three revolts against white male authority grow out of her close friendships with adult men who either are black or whose foreignness and inattention to some (white) social codes figure them as black. These episodes form the main plot of the second half of Oldham's story.

The plot of "Dr. Wohlenski" is less interesting than its treatment of narrative voice, because part of what Oldham is doing is establishing the legitimacy of her own writerly voice, her fictional "I." We learn in the first sentence that Part 1 has, in fact, been told to Estelle in the third person by

Dr. Wohlenski. So she hears her family's story from an outsider's perspective. At the beginning of Part 2, when Estelle complains to Dr. Wohlenski that he "left out the exciting part" of the story, his response reflects Oldham's collaboration with Faulkner: "'Well, young lady,' the old doctor smiled indulgently, 'some day I will write a book, with your help, and we will include my omissions, as well as your fancies.'"[19] However, its purpose within this story is to set up for the transfer of narrative voice to Estelle so that she tells the second half of this story. In this very important sense, then, Estelle gains her writerly voice from a man who is figured as black. As will Faulkner several years later, Oldham freights her authorial "I" with contradictory markers that challenge traditional race and gender expectations.

Besides its being about a small Southern girl who seeks to escape Belledom and gain agency through storytelling, Oldham's tale would have appealed to Faulkner because it reveals her perceptions concerning contradictions in her culture's official codes of conduct. For example, even though Estelle's mammy acts traditionally as the enforcer of Southern patriarchy's need for its white women to learn to be acquiescent Ice Maidens, all agents of the child's access to freedom are figured as black. At Estelle's most liberated and rebellious moment, she becomes, in her male cousin's eyes, a conjurer and witch. That is, her cousin identifies *her* as black, an identity Estelle embraces because it invests her with the imaginative powers to revenge herself on him.

Here, Oldham writes about what Toni Morrison calls an "almost completely buried subject" in American literature: "the interdependent working of power, race, and sexuality in a white woman's battle for coherence."[20] Understanding what it means to be white in a racialized culture is predicated on knowing what it means to be black. This fact about the social constructions of race lies at the bottom of every threat to selfhood that Estelle faces. In trying to establish a coherent identity that is at odds with "lady-like behavior," she learns from stories her elders tell and from their behavior that class, race, and gender are the categories by which her parents and community determine who has agency, or power, and who doesn't. Estelle lives in post-Reconstruction Mississippi, where her daily life is filled with huge paradoxes. For example, the black people who work for her grandfather tell her stories and show her sights that her family doesn't want her to hear or see because they reveal racism's daily hypocrisies and contradictions. When she behaves unacceptably, she is figured as black by her grandfather and as (white) "Trash" by Nolia. In her role as classic plantation romance mammy, Nolia transforms the white girl into a Lady by making her visually and socially presentable. Nolia dresses Estelle for her role: "hair smoothed," sash "ironed and retied" so that she can join the grown-ups for dinner in the family dining room. Nolia tells her to "sit up like a lady" instead of lounging in her chair, to take "lady-like bites" of food, even though she's starving, and to present only "a smiling face" to her father.[21] Nolia's scoldings and corrections, designed to transform her charge into a White Lady, are a daily paradox for Estelle. Although she has been told and believes that her family's black servants have been "given full authority for her manners and care," she constantly hears her grandfather speak rudely to them and criticize their care and watches as he treats them like children.[22] As naïve narrator, she calls this paradox to her reader's attention. As author, then, Estelle succeeds in establishing agency for herself by challenging some of her culture's most cherished assumptions. Like her favorite wax doll from New Orleans, Estelle appears neither black nor white (both black and white?).

Once Estelle leaves the office of Judge Papa Niles, the site of white male storytelling, *she* becomes the narrator. As she says at one point, "Papa Niles' chairs don't fit me."[23] Her own story begins when she heads off for the kitchen, the black servants' space. In the white spaces in her grandparents' house—her grandfather's office, the living room, dining room, and nursery—her access to information is censored, her speech is limited, her body is confined, her access to knowledge and even her appetite is restricted by the codes governing a (white) Lady's behavior. In the kitchen and the black servants' quarters—their space—she is fed, groomed, given apparently unlimited access to knowledge and encouraged to use her imagination. She also learns from the "talk" of black men and women who work for her family about the contradictions between the social-racial laws her white elders profess and practice. Moreover, the literal space a black man builds for her—her tree house—gives her a room of her own with a bird's-eye view of her culture's most taboo subject—sex. The favorite doll she plays with in that space is given to her by the outsider, Dr. Wohlenski. The doll, brought from New Orleans, the "Great Southern Babylon" as it was known in antebellum times, represents the most important subject that her education into White Womanhood will repress or deny, sexual desire and miscegenation.[24]

Estelle's story in Part 2 gives an account of her awakening into sexual and racial difference. This awakening marks a significant stage of her education into Southern Womanhood. Her white family and mammy are teaching her that the hallmarks of a girl's education are a willed ignorance regarding all controversy relating to race and sexuality. In all three episodes Estelle's adversaries are white men, boys, or their spokespersons. Each adversary tries to make a lady of her by quelling her curiosity and forcing her to deny her imagination and her desires. Each wants to stop her from speaking a counternarrative. In the first episode Estelle revolts against her grandfather's requirements for ladylike behavior by demanding that God aid her in being antisocial. Her unruly prayer receives a stern reprimand from her mammy. In the second episode Estelle uses her storytelling powers to confront her grandfather directly; in the third she uses them to take revenge on a boy cousin who has destroyed her property, humiliated her, and mocked her imaginative powers. In this last episode, like the octoroon slave, Cassy, in *Uncle Tom's Cabin,* and other Gothic heroines in nineteenth-century domestic fiction, Estelle summons a "black" ghost to wage psychological war on the white boy who has invaded her private space and abused her dolls. Her dolls, as the story makes clear, are an extension of her desiring self.

In her book about representations of race and gender in white women's writings from the 1830s to the beginning of the Civil Rights movement, Diane Roberts, like many others, points out that historically the "knot of fictions surrounding" white representations of black folk is "overwhelmingly erotic. *Blackness* is loaded with sexuality." When a white woman writes about race she is "necessarily a double agent, acting as both 'mistress' in controlling her characters and her plot, and identifying with them."[25] Oldham is no exception. Besides caring for all her physical needs, blacks teach Estelle about or give her access to the irrational and unspeakable—namely, ghosts, desire, and sexuality—and she loves them for it: In "the kitchen . . . I learned a lot about 'white folks' and haunted houses and ghosts. It was from them that I heard about Dr. Wohlenski's 'woman' in New Orleans." "But," she hastens to assure her reader, "that made no impression on me. The 'hants' and ghosts did."[26]

Estelle's story, which climaxes in her wishful vision of a union between herself, Dr. Wohlenski's ghost, and his woman in New Orleans, proves the opposite. Roberts notes that a woman from New Orleans is "one of those white names" for black women that is designed to "divide, categorize, and circumscribe them."[27] It is a coded term meaning a mixed-race mistress and, like "curse" or "bad blood," it signals the transgressive behavior of miscegenation. Among Faulkner's fictional New Orleans women are the wife that Thomas Sutpen "put aside" and the mistress-wife that Shreve and Quentin invent for Charles Bon in *Absalom, Absalom!*. At times, Faulkner himself claimed to be involved in similar alliances, most notably when he used this trope to characterize his relationship with Oldham in 1928. That fall, when he was in New York finishing *The Sound and the Fury,* he told drinking companions about "a woman in New Orleans and the two children she had by him; how some day he would marry her."[28] Always keen to shock his audience, Faulkner knew miscegenation was surefire. Like Estelle in this story, he was also spinning a family romance fantasy about what he perceived as his own socially forbidden desire for the woman who was still, officially, Estelle Franklin. Figuratively, he was telling the truth. By Oxford's standards Oldham *had* blackened her reputation by failing to stay married to her first husband and by other unladylike acts: smoking, drinking, and gambling. Notice how, as Faulkner applies it to the woman he would marry within the next eight months, he also encodes a double standard. That is, he does not encode himself as biracial.

Oldham's story holds to the same standard. Dr. Wohlenski's illicit sex life is figured as black because, as it was in the communities in which she and Faulkner lived, all public discourse about sexuality is represented as a black discourse. One of Oldham's younger female cousins once explained, "Even when my mother and my aunt Lida spoke about someone's being pregnant, they said it in a whisper."[29] Jill says that "so far as my mother was concerned, she never once said a word to me about sex, ever. I could have gotten married knowing nothing. I learned about menstruation from our cook's daughter, whom I played with all the time and who was three or four years older than I."[30] Like her mother, Jill learned about sexuality from her other family, the black people who cared for her. Ironically, her teacher was a girl named Estelle, after Jill's mother.

It makes sense, then, that Estelle's sources of sexual knowledge would also be black folk. Even though their bodies appear emptied of sexual content—they are either ancient like old Malachai, who built Estelle her tree house, or like Nolia, bodiless—the stories they tell her and the toys they make for her or give her lead to knowledge that is explicitly sexual. When Estelle's grandfather finds out that Malachai has soiled his granddaughter's whiteness (purity), that is, "blackened" her by building her a tree house overlooking the servants' privy, he is outraged. In contrast, Dr. Wohlenski just laughs.[31]

Dr. Wohlenski's collusion with black servants in providing Estelle with sexual knowledge is further manifested in his gift of the wax doll from New Orleans. What happens to this doll makes it clear that she symbolizes all the forbidden pleasures and knowledge that Estelle's tutoring in ladylike behavior is supposed to deny her. When her male cousins destroy her tree house and sit her doll in the black servants' outhouse, her grandfather doesn't object, because these young Southern gentlemen are doing the right thing. They are symbolically acting out what they believe will happen to Estelle if she is allowed access to sexual knowledge. Like Faulkner's Caddy Compson's brothers, they just know she will be ruined. She will become even worse than a "New Orleans woman" because she was born "white." From her grandfather's perspective, the boys are enacting Southern Manhood by enforcing Southern Womanhood: they define and protect their cousin's virtue—her whiteness.

Before the night of Estelle's first openly rebellious act, her assertive prayer, all instruction has focused on her table manners, her posture, and her physical neatness. The first time she uses her voice to claim agency by altering her environment to serve her own needs and desires, her black nurse adds silence to her lessons. Unhappy about leaving the town she has known since she was five months old, and about being forced to play with a new group of "proper friends" and "suitable playmates," the six-year-old decides to resist. At evening prayers she spontaneously abandons the usual "'now I lay me.'" Her voice transforms what should be a ladylike, spiritual, and angelic plea into a loud and spirited command: "My need was too urgent and I hoped that my voice was loud enough for God to really hear and be impressed. I told Him that I didn't intend to move to Oxford" and live out her grandfather's expectations—that is, live in a "suitable house" and "make proper friends." Resistant to leaving her black and white families, she concludes, "I told Him, too, to deliver me from playmates."[32]

In Southern plantation romances, mammies scold their white charges when they behave badly; Nolia conforms to type. As guardian of Estelle's white Womanhood, she is appalled at the prayer. "When I had gotten off my knees, Nolia was standing, looking like a thunder cloud. 'God doesn't like to be dictated to, Honey' she said sternly. 'Get on your knees again and ask forgiveness, and for *grace enough to bear like a lady anything that comes your way.* Only Trash think that they can whine to the Almighty—that's why they're Trash—and never got to be anything else'" (my italics). In rebuking Estelle, Nolia invokes the tried if not true binaries of the "plantation ideology of the Old South"—if Estelle chooses to be a religious dissenter instead of "bearing like a lady," then she's (poor white) trash. Estelle tries to argue: "'I wasn't whining, Nolia, I was just telling God how I felt.'" But Nolia quashes her feelings because they are, in her terms, trashy. She then overrides them with the "gospel" of True Womanhood—"bear like a lady anything that comes your way." Estelle appears to comply: "So we knelt again and prayed the familiar 'now I lay me.' Mama and Papa came in to say goodnight. I felt unresentful now, and went to sleep."[33] But there is something odd about this scene—missing pieces. Nolia is totally unsympathetic; she may call Estelle "honey" but she doesn't soften her words by holding the child in her arms. Her scolding seems like a betrayal because Estelle is clearly not expecting it. Yet with no explanation, her resistance and resentment collapse. It is as if Nolia's refusal to validate the child's feelings of loss and abandonment causes her to repress them entirely. But Estelle pays a price for the loss Nolia will not and cannot permit her to acknowledge. She then displaces all her love on to the ghost of Dr. Wohlenski, who, in turn, loved a New Orleans woman. He thus becomes an imaginative representation of the unspeakable love she has been forced to deny.

Estelle's battle to preserve emotionally nourishing relationships, her wishes for personhood rather than personification in her revolt against her earthly and heavenly fathers and their black emissary, is short-lived here.[34] Yet her continued resistance outside of her nursery bedroom to all who are herding her into acting ladylike and her increasing interest in and identification with black people and a foreigner, none of whom espouse her grandfather's "notions of propriety," suggest that *Oldham* recognizes that there is something wrong with the conventional white morality of Nolia and her family.

However, Oldham cannot recognize the blackest and most primal emotional damage that her betrayal of Nolia, which her story reverses to Nolia's betrayal of Estelle, caused her childhood self. This damage seems reflected in Estelle's bland, almost affectless responses to the physical and psychological violence her male cousins subject her to and, perhaps, in the fact of Nolia's absence in the two episodes in which Estelle succeeds at making her voice felt and heard. Estelle knows by this point that her family's black servants cannot speak out for her or for themselves. This may explain why she displaces her love for them on to the dead Dr. Wohlenski, who *could* speak while confining the servants' subversions to spaces that white grown-ups either don't or can't enter: the kitchen, their living quarters, and their imaginations.

Although, Estelle's first attempt to mount a counternarrative fails in the face of Nolia's wrath, she later makes two successful rebellious moves in this story. Both are directed against a specific paternalistic authority, and in both her weapon of choice is storytelling. Her naughty acts and speeches are aided and abetted by the racially and sexually transgressive Dr. Wohlenski. In both episodes Estelle's intent is to preserve continued access to forbidden (that is, sexual) knowledge provided to her by black folk. She will not give it up because this knowledge gives her—as we see in both instances—an informed and therefore disruptive and powerful voice.

The first of these two episodes is a direct attack on Estelle's access to sexual knowledge and her rights to a place she identifies exclusively with imaginative, solitary play—"my favorite place to be alone." Her immediate and stated purpose here is to defend Malachai, who has angered her grandfather by giving her access to space her grandfather considers dangerously sexualized and racialized. Her unstated purpose is to protect her access to that space.

This becomes apparent in the next episode, in which Estelle takes revenge on one of several boy cousins who precipitated this second episode: "They tore down my tree-house and scattered my precious dolls all over the ground. They even sat the biggest ones in the servants' privy like the dolls were real people." And this is the point. Estelle's tree house was her refuge from those boring children who respect the confines of Southern Ladyhood. Until her cousins' invasion, it had been a private place where, with her dolls as characters, she could invent her own world, one where blackness and sexuality do not signify shame. In this sense, then, Estelle is right. Her dolls *are* real people. Her cousins know this perfectly well, which is why they attempt to shame or humiliate her by sitting them in the "black" outhouse.

Yet, when Estelle's grandfather finds out, he is furious, not at his grandsons' violation and destruction of her property and house, not at the hurt to his granddaughter's feelings, but at Malachai, because he has exposed Estelle to an "unseemly" sight. "'Damn old Mal,' he spluttered, 'I had no idea that he'd overlook the proprieties—so—so indelicately.'"[35]

Here, in gently mocking her culture's obsession with her purity, Oldham also caricatures the myth of Southern Womanhood, which insists that "a white lady is prohibited from speaking a vernacular of bodily functions from sex to birth from menstruation to defecation because she is constructed to be 'innocent' of such things, chaste, orifices closed, a silent endorsement of the patriarchal representation of her as the designated work of art of Southern culture."[36] Her grandfather's refusal to acknowledge Estelle's feelings in this section repeats Nolia's refusal to acknowledge her feelings in the prior episode. Their teaching is designed to empty Estelle of curiosity and desire so that she can be transformed into a Lady, like her Aunt Carrie, whom she describes as an "unreal" but perfect Ice Maiden.

This tree house episode could be read merely as conventional scatological humor, but the specificity of its racializing and gendering, the firmness with which Oldham has woven the episode into her narrative, and the way in which Estelle swerves the conventional narrative so that her grandfather, rather than she, becomes an object of ridicule, all argue against such a reading.

The strongest evidence for the originality of the narrative and its content is the deep imprint this image made on Faulkner's imagination: that image is of a literally and figuratively soiled, rebellious little girl up in a tree, being looked at as, *and* looking at, something forbidden. In 1933 he will claim that an image uncannily like this was the inspiration and starting point for *The Sound and the Fury*. Oldham knew the power of the image because she understood its politics and was consciously exploiting them to serve her distinctly unladylike rhetorical design. That was what her fictional "I" was attempting. Her Estelle is soiled by her interest in sexuality and difference and her identification with Malachai's powerlessness—by her desire to see and know. Perhaps, most of all, she is soiled by her desire to continue to love Nolia, her black mother, and to tell her story about a little girl who refuses to fit in. It's the energy and originality and the lived reality of this subversion that Faulkner would later embrace and appropriate.

While in *The Sound and the Fury* and elsewhere, Faulkner will write a tragedy out of such material, Oldham writes comedy. Thus, unlike Faulkner's Caddy in similar circumstances, Oldham's Estelle has both agency and an ally in "blackness." Caring, as Caddy Compson will, for those who can't speak for themselves, Estelle moves to protect Malachai. Rather than confronting her grandfather directly, she diverts him by reciting that unsavory family history she "read in a book."[37] Telling the scandal of her *Mayflower* ancestor in the presence of Dr. Wohlenski has the desired effect of embarrassing and distracting her genteel grandfather. On the night of the old doctor's death, Estelle assumes his storyteller's role to deflate her grandfather's authority and increase her own. In this episode, she uses her imagination to slip out of conforming to her family's or town's notions of how little white Southern girls should behave.

Narrative tension derives from Estelle's need to define and speak for herself—a self that her grandfather's culture wants to silence. Despite the scoldings and spankings she receives from her elders, and her male cousins' teasing and physical assaults, she never portrays herself as a victim. Quite the contrary. Her energy, humor—often self-mocking—and curiosity are never daunted. Her voice grows increasingly compelling as, in her third and final tangle, she further aligns herself with blackness by mounting an inspired defense for the integrity of the stories she has heard in the kitchen. Here her cousin Pelham challenges her by daring her to prove the existence of Dr. Wohlenski's ghost, a ghost only black people claim they've seen. Baiting her, Pelham asks how she could possibly still love the dead Dr. Wohlenski when "he's only a pack of bones." She responds: "'It's his soul I love, which is the real man,' I parroted. 'Naturally I know that flesh rots.'" Pelham then tries to insult her by saying she's as irrational and superstitious as blacks: "Well, Miss Smarty, do you believe in ghosts like Isaiah?"

Estelle's retort, a subtle put-down, cements her alignment with and linking of black knowledge to her creativity: "How could I not when I hear truthful colored people swear they've seen them?"[38] Pelham continues to goad her: "You're a girl and maybe a witch, can't you conjure up a ghost for me?" But, when she does, it's Pelham's voice, not hers that sounds like a girl's—"high-pitched and a little hysterical." And although he calls her "crazy" as well, he's the one who becomes so frantic that he drops their lantern when she says she sees Dr. Wohlenski's ghost smiling at them and carrying the New Orleans doll he gave her, the one Pelham (a true Southern gentleman) had abused. In this way and in a kind of mock-Gothic moment, Estelle takes revenge on the male cousin who has been her chief tormentor. Their parents spank both children, but Estelle is so caught up in her fantasy that "I hardly felt it because I was so anxious to get to my dolls and count them."[39]

Although her New Orleans doll hasn't vanished, Estelle believes in her vision. For confirmation she seeks out one of her visiting uncles who, she says, is "jolly and full of life and a grand story teller" and who knows all about the "queer things most grown people don't believe in."[40] In other words, she thinks he'll listen to her story instead of trying to silence and shame her like her cousin: "I knew he wouldn't laugh at me." Unfortunately, her uncle has been reading some "new" psychology. Claiming that "it's all very natural," and sounding like popular interpretations of what the English-language newspapers that Estelle read in Honolulu and Shanghai referred to as the "new Freudian psychology," he attempts to dispel her belief: "Your unconscious mind stored that picture away and for a moment you actually saw him again with the doll. . . . Now, run along and play and forget all this."[41] Despite her white family's efforts to keep her ignorant, Dr. Wohlenski intervenes, literally from the grave, to give Estelle proof that the woman her doll represents actually exists and was his mistress, a far more appealing role than the chilly and silent image of white Southern Womanhood her family and Nolia would have her emulate. Dr. Wohlenski's will divides his estate between "his woman in New Orleans" and his black servant, Isaiah. So, in death, Estelle's ally, who in life was her grandfather's good friend, threatens to topple the pedestal on which Southern Womanhood stands by publicly acknowledging his violation of one of its greatest taboos—his long-time alliance with a woman of color and the black man who worked for him. But only when he's dead does he state his commitment to them and his debt; in his will he claims them as his only family. Oldham demonstrates here an acute grasp of Southern racial-sexual politics. Eighteen years later, when Callie Barr died, Faulkner duplicated his wife's fictional hero's act in reifying his black mammy once she was safely dead.

Here Oldham uses both Dr. Wohlenski and Estelle to exact revenge on her cousins' and grandfather's attempts to confine her to (white) ladylike spaces and realms of knowledge, to "make her forget all that." The feminine and feminized imagination, the irrational, sexualized, racially mixed, and spirit-charged world that Estelle has learned about from blacks' talk and Dr. Wohlenski, is pitted against Nolia's and her white family's narrative of a Jim Crow world that excludes her dissenting, mischievous, and curious voice.

Estelle's verbal sparring with white authority in all three episodes masks the child's unacknowledged emotional loss of her black mother, in two ways. First, it veils her anger about having to sacrifice to Southern Womanhood her identification with, idealization of, and love for Nolia, the only woman in this story who ever mothers her. Second, it masks her wish to be held again in Nolia's arms. This is poignantly illustrated in the final episode, where Estelle "conjures" Nolia's double, her other lost love—the ghost of Dr. Wohlenski. This ghost carries in his arms the New Orleans doll he gave her and then retrieved from shame—imaged by the most primal image of blackness Oldham can permit herself to summon.[42]

Faulkner's readers will recognize this theme, for it permeates his fiction too. It is the narrative of the white child's fall into racial difference; its most potent symbol is the lost black maternal. I suggest that when he read Oldham's stories in 1924 and 1925—for this loss and her attempts at reparation lie at the heart of all her work—he saw for the first time how he might begin to articulate the meaning of the relationship whose denial is responsible for the "paralyzed and numb" state of his poetry's pierrotiste persona. Oldham's story shows how Estelle's psychologically brutal education into white womanhood will wither every aspect of her sentient being as it walls her into white spaces. For example, although the child is still sharing meals in the kitchen with her family's black servants, Nolia is also educating her into racism by teaching her that "ladies" eat only in the dining room. For Faulkner, as for any sensitive white Southerner reading this story, such scenes touched a nerve. His imaginative response, as we have seen in earlier chapters, creates some of the most moving and painful reading of the ravages of racial prejudice in American literature. Think of Roth Edmonds's defining moment, the boy's crashing entrance into self-hating whiteness in the instant that he realizes he will eat alone at Molly's kitchen table (*GDM*, 113–14), or Joe Christmas's into self-hating blackness when he realizes he can enter only through Joanna Burden's kitchen door and sees his food "*Set out for the nigger. For the nigger*" (*LIA*, 237–38). Faulkner's fiction will clarify what Oldham's story obscures, that in repudiating that table, the white child must also deny the woman *and* the community responsible for her earliest and perhaps her only feelings of passionate physical and emotional attachment, and of tenderness, warmth, and comfort. This is the price of Southern Manhood and Womanhood and the cost of maintaining the Jim Crow culture that shaped Estelle Oldham's and William Faulkner's imaginations and lives, their marriage, and their treatment of their only child.

Although the damage to the child's affective life seeps through her narrative, Oldham herself does not appear to be conscious of it. She seems not to recognize that there is something odd about her descriptions of Estelle's responses to Nolia's anger and her cousins' cruelty, and even to Dr. Wohlenski's death: that they are devoid of negative affect. Equally emptied of feeling is the only moment of physical closeness Estelle experiences in "Dr. Wohlenski." In each of these episodes it appears that Estelle is immune to anger or grief. But if she really is, why do these emotionally muted moments always occur when she's resisting authority?

"Dr. Wohlenski" raises two other, related questions, both of which bear directly on Faulkner's and Oldham's relationship, on his fiction, and on both subjects as representatives of the larger culture that Faulkner, in his fiction, named Yoknapatawpha. The first concerns the omnipresence of alcohol in this and all of Estelle's extant stories. Why do whiskey fumes obsessively waft through (and at one point threaten to engulf) "Dr. Wohlenski"? Second, is there a relation between the ubiquity of alcohol, the acceptance of physical and psychological violence as normal, and the absence of any physical or emotional moments of love or affection in Estelle's world? "Dr. Wohlenski" marks the beginning of her education into the anesthetizing process of becoming the emotionally and intellectually stunted person who represents the best of Southern Womanhood. I use the word *anesthetizing* deliberately. The drug is alcohol, a dominant presence in *both* Faulkners' fiction, lives, and culture. It becomes as much a character in William Faulkner's fiction as the modern city is in Dreiser's. And, like racism, as I have shown in earlier chapters, it shapes Faulkner's poetics.

At an early and defining moment in Estelle's narrative, before she launches its three episodes, she identifies her story's two central and related conflicts. In doing so, she places these fumes at the center of her continuing attempts to sort out her identity in the context of what it means to be a man and what it means to be a woman within her family. For her, both whiskey and tobacco are firmly gendered male and therefore pivotal to her evolving understanding of Southern Manhood and Womanhood. The time is dusk of the evening her father tells her he is moving the family to Oxford in 1903. Her parents and grandparents have gathered for their cocktail hour in Papa Niles's library. Estelle, following her Mammy's instructions to "sit still and straight," to "put on a big smile," and to be "ladylike," is trying "hard not to fidget" during the "interminable time it took my elders to have their evening drink and conversation."[43]

While her grandfather and the other men in her family have spent their afternoon telling stories and drinking in her grandfather's office, her mother and grandmother have been doing one of the things women in Kosciusko in 1902 did—playing whist at Estelle's Great-aunt Carrie's.

"'How is my beautiful aunt?' Papa asked over the rim of his whiskey goblet." The ensuing adult conversation reveals that besides looking beautiful, Carrie is also "charming as always," serves "a delicious tea," and is "a delightful hostess."[44] Here Oldham sketches a succinct portrait of the ideal Southern Lady, which Estelle then subjects to a silent and withering critique. Ironically, but not unsurprisingly, these same adjectives and attributes appear constantly in the social columns of the Kosciusko newspapers, where the social life of Oldham's mother and grandmothers is recorded during these years. These adjectives followed the Oldhams to Oxford and followed Estelle Franklin, when she married Cornell, to Honolulu and Shanghai. She could not escape her culture except in her fiction. But her stories suggest that she once thought she could escape. And to some extent she finally did, by marrying Faulkner.

To Estelle, attempting to sort out the "tangle" of Southern Manhood and Womanhood, her model aunt, "a story book" character, is "without substance," like the "fragrance of a flower"; she has no body no sexuality. In contrast, the men in her family are "human—warm and comforting— smelling of horses and whiskey and tobacco." The ideal Lady lacks physicality. She is not a sexual or sensual being. Unlike men, she neither feels nor provides warmth and comfort; that is, love. In short, she is not human. Furthermore, although her aunt is in a book, it's men who write those books. Oldham's difficult task in her quest for an adult *feminine* identity was to wrest that power for herself.

Besides warmth and comfort, these mingled "human" scents have another association that may help to explain the role alcohol and tobacco played in Oldham's adolescence and in the Faulkners' life and art. Estelle identifies them here with intellectual communion. Her portrait of that communion, like that of humanness, is gendered masculine: "Papa Niles said one time that 'Josef and Fred and I are intellectually compatible.' I loved the sound of big words and memorized that." Even though Estelle associates the smells of alcohol and tobacco with men who are "human— warm and comforting," with "intellectual compatibility," and with language itself—the only thing she ever says she loves (besides Dr. Wohlenski's soul)—theirs is a warmth and community that excludes her. Although this girl child may memorize their words, she cannot join their party or share in their power, as her grandfather makes clear. Theirs is a world of men talking to men that is saturated with the mingled smells of whiskey, tobacco, and horses. Estelle associates whiskey and tobacco with being male and with her brief experience of being included in that male camaraderie in her grandfather's office and her rude ejection from it.

I have traced Billy Falkner's developing relationship with alcohol in earlier chapters. In the following chapters on Oldham's and Faulkner's shared adolescence, I suggest that this moment in "Dr. Wohlenski" replicates a painful exclusion that the seventeen-year-old Oldham endured when, in the summer of 1914, Phil Stone took what had hitherto been her place in Billy's intellectual and emotional life. Enamored of "little Billy's" genius (as Stone wrote of him to his mother), he and the young poet began an intensely charged friendship that flourished throughout Faulkner's long poetic apprenticeship. This close association began to disintegrate in late 1924, when Oldham returned home and Faulkner shifted to prose and to other mentoring relationships, with Sherwood Anderson, a much older but also much more intellectually and emotionally adventurous man, and with Estelle.

Biographers of both Faulkner and Phil Stone describe the early stages of their friendship as bonded by Stone's huge fund of knowledge about literature, his openly hostile attitude toward women, and his and Faulkner's mutual addiction to "white lightning." What the adolescent Estelle Oldham realized that summer of 1914, and it was a view her culture endorsed, was that alcohol and intellectual compatibility were linked and both were gendered male. This meant she was excluded. To drink, then, was to rebel against her gender. She resurrects the site of her exclusion and explains its source in this self-consciously autobiographical story. Because it's her story instead of her life, she invents a male writer who privileges her speech, inviting her to write with him. Wohlenski, therefore, offers a stark contrast to her grandfather, who explains with his "definite" dismissal of her from his office that "she's an impressionable girl," not a man, and who says that "we three old men forget the seeds of discontent we might be planting in an immature mind."[45] Estelle's grandfather has it all wrong. The seeds of discontent he fears manifest themselves in her *resistance* to the "rose tinted memories" that invented Southern Womanhood, in her pursuit of forbidden knowledge, and in her wish to invent and speak or write her own narrative, one that includes the dissonant voice of Dr. Wohlenski, who aids her in her confrontations with her grandfather and her young cousin (but not with Nolia). Psychologically this makes sense, because the permissive Dr. Wohlenski is a composite figure—among other things, a displacement of her wish to have her black mother restored to her and of her adolescent desire for the emotionally unavailable and socially unacceptable Faulkner.

In "Dr. Wohlenski" Estelle experiences another related exclusion that is dictated by the racial prohibitions that shape the construction of Southern Womanhood. There is no physical affection in Estelle's relationships—while her mother may "kiss" her baby sister goodnight, her parents "say" goodnight to her. She is never hugged or kissed, even though she is only six years old; grown-ups never hold her in their laps. In this story she has no relationship at all with her parents. Although she talks to many adults, other than a "good night" not a word passes between Estelle and her mother or father. Nolia is the only person whose body touches hers and who constantly cares for her, plays with her, and instructs her. Yet when Nolia says, "Come on now, let me get you dressed for supper" and then helps her to change, brushes her hair, and ties her sash—all the while constantly touching her—Estelle shifts into the passive and impersonal voice, as if to disembody and so deny the emotional closeness and the physicality and sensuality of the black woman's and white child's relationship: "Soon I was made presentable—hair smoothed and sash ironed and retied."[46] The rhetorical strategy of the passive voice robs Nolia of agency and substance. It denies the powers of touch. Estelle's language also transforms Nolia into a thing. Yet her denial and repression of her love for Nolia erupt in the thinly masked racially transgressive desires embodied in the secrets revealed to Estelle by Dr. Wohlenski's erotic life and Malachai's transgressively situated tree house.

I cannot emphasize enough how important it is that Estelle has no relationship with either of her parents—despite their biological ties and physical proximity in several key scenes. They never touch or talk. Their nonrelationship stands in stark contrast to her active relationship with Nolia and Dr. Wohlenski. From a developmental perspective, it is also important that the Oldhams' impending move to Oxford occurred at precisely the moment when, as part of her indoctrination into Southern Womanhood, she is being taught to deny her love for Nolia and others in the black family that raised her; this transpired, as it does in her story, when the real Estelle was six. Six is a vulnerable age, because gender-identity issues are especially active and intense at that time. In this culture, gender and racial identity are inseparable. Oldham replicates these conflicts in her story, using her imagination to make reparation for giving up the black maternal. By inventing the character of Dr. Wohlenski, she restores both the love of her black mother and its substitute, her adolescent love for Billy Falkner, which she lost when he deserted her for Phil Stone in 1914.[47] The identity she establishes for herself here is also a reparation. This irreverent, articulate six-year-old who can conjure idealizes a white man she figures as black and who supports her unladylike behavior. He encourages her to write, to learn about her sexuality, to entertain unconventional thoughts that mix up masculine and feminine, black and white—in short, to explore the possibility of a fluid sexual and racial selfhood. Yet in the story itself, Oldham does not make Estelle the narrator until after Dr. Wohlenski's death. Perhaps this, too, was prophetic.

Part of "Dr. Wohlenski's" value is what it tells about its author, what she was thinking during the seven years that preceded the Faulkners' marriage in 1929. For it is the bearing of Estelle Oldham's intellect and imagination on her relationship with William Faulkner that is of interest. That Estelle even wrote such stories throws into question all prior biographical portrayals. She wrote against the grain at a historic moment when, as Roberts and others have pointed out, the Jim Crow South was wrestling with the effects of "the hardening of racial attitudes and the enforcement and institutionalization of segregation in the 1920s and 1930s."[48] She was writing explicitly about sexuality and female subjectivity in addition to raising questions about race and gender as a means of exploring her characters' questions about their origins and identity—all subjects that will be central to Faulkner's fiction. As this story and her other fiction demonstrate, she seemed to understand that "what it means to be a white woman in the United States, particularly in the South, is still largely predicated on what it means to be black."[49] Furthermore, her experiences during her first marriage as a colonial wife enlarged her understanding of the power of the label of blackness; she came to see that white Westerners used it to include all those people or ideas or behaviors they felt threatened by and therefore wanted to silence or destroy.

15

Billy Falkner and Estelle Oldham, Oxford, 1903–1914

We were always sweethearts.
—Estelle Faulkner

E STELLE'S ICONIC love-at-first-sight account to a Richmond reporter, which she repeated a month later for her dead husband's
authorized biographer, Joseph Blotner, provides the romance narrative that appears in all biographies to date.[1] The fateful viewing takes place
sometime in winter 1904, shortly after the Oldhams moved to Oxford. In it
the seven-year-old girl stands beside a parlor window, where, to keep her
still while she cuts her straight dark hair, her nursemaid, Magnolia (Nolia)
Cottrell has told her to watch the passing street scene. It is early winter but
still warm enough for the Falkner boys to be out riding the ponies their
grandfather had given them. Since late fall 1903 the Oldhams have been
settled in a house near J. W. T. Falkner's on South Street, which Lem has
rented from a Mrs. Mary Bordeaux.[2] In this version of the story, Estelle's
wish to marry Billy Falkner was instantaneous. She sees him ride by and
claims him as her true love. Like a fairy-tale princess, or Scarlett O'Hara,
she announces to her faithful mammy that she will marry "that boy." Blotner interviewed Estelle at least four times. This is one of the rare instances
where he permits her direct speech: "'Nolia,' she said, 'see that little boy?
I'm going to marry him when I grow up.' Nolia kept on twirling the soft
hair around the broom handle. 'Hush yo mouf, chile,' she said. 'Folks what
say they goin' to get married while they little is sho to grow up to be ol'
maids.'"[3] Estelle's account to the Richmond reporter is somewhat fuller
and informed by subtle self-parody. After saying "We were always sweethearts," Estelle narrates:

> It was winter and I was sitting in the window of our house, and the maid
> was curling my hair. I had such awfully straight hair.

15.1. Studio portrait of Estelle Oldham, summer 1913.
(Courtesy of Victoria Fielden Johnson)

> Bill came riding down the street alone, and the two little boys [Jack and John] were behind him with their Negro grooms. I told my maid, "See that boy there?" Pointing out Bill. "I'm going to marry him when I'm grown." She told me to "shut your mouth, child," but I'd made up my mind. And poor Bill didn't know anything about it.[4]

Present here and missing from Blotner's version is a nice distinction: Estelle may shut her mouth but, like her fictional six-year-old namesake, she'll follow her own mind. Such agency and certitude align this image with the self-possessed and defiantly unsocial Estelle who appears in "Dr. Wohlenski." But Blotner's flat, narcissistic Southern Belle, not this little girl, only seven and already plotting a marriage that "poor Bill" knows nothing about, is the official Estelle.

Estelle also left another, even earlier account. In 1951, shortly after Faulkner had been awarded the French Legion of Honor, she supplied a New Orleans reporter with a more prosaic version in which she distinguished clearly between her childhood impressions of "Billy" and the sixteen-year-old who later fell in love with him.[5] She also portrays a less varnished version of Faulkner's parents' financial situation:

> Mrs. Faulkner says that she has known "Billy" since they were both children. "I fell in love with him when I was 16," she says.
>
> "The first impression I remember is seeing him with his two brothers, John and Jack, riding their ponies. They would ride by the house on their ponies with an old groom riding behind on an old nag to take care of them."[6]

Was Estelle just having some fun with the Richmond reporter and her husband's biographer, which is what her daughter suspects? Was she giving the public an image she had learned it wanted? Was she throwing up a protective smoke screen? She was sixteen years old in 1913. That September her parents sent her off to boarding school in Virginia, and she and Billy were separated for the first time in their sentient lives. The following summer, Billy left her for Phil Stone. This 1951 account may be the more accurate, recording as it does, in the flush of adolescence, the coincidence of her love for Billy Falkner with separation and then loss. It is also more self-revealing.

But just as Faulkner in his late years created himself as a caricature of the Southern Gentleman he immortalized in those final majestic photographic portraits of himself in full hunt regalia, Estelle, too, invented for the public and posterity a complimentary caricature of the Southern Belle. She had finally learned to appear to "behave" herself.

In all three of these stories, the *visual* image Estelle creates is that of a proper, quiet little girl. Yet, according to her fictionalized childhood memoir and the memories of others, as children, she and her sister, Tochie, led a physically active life. Until at least 1908 Estelle and Tochie spent much more time, in Billy Falkner's words, "running" over their neighborhood's "streets" and yards than they spent gazing demurely out of parlor windows.[7] Perhaps because its larger size and transient student population made Oxford a somewhat less homogeneous community than Kosciusko, the two sisters experienced there more freedom from social and familial strictures.

In that first decade of the twentieth century, a group of children including Estelle and Tochie, Billy and his brothers, and Ed Beanland, Rose Rowland, Katherine Andrews, and Sallie Murry may have played together in the sandy bottom that ran behind the Falkner and Oldham houses and hunted for the tiny pieces of sand-worn glass and pebbles they used to pave the walks and streets of the model towns they built with Lelia in the Falkners' yard.[8] In the late spring the children might have waged water fights in the stream, returning home just as wet and muddy as Quentin and Caddy Compson.[9]

When the children did play inside, they generally congregated at the Oldhams' or at J. W. T. Falkner's house. Katherine Andrews remembers great games of hide-and-seek at the Oldhams' and J. W. T.'s, where Sallie Murry's mother, Auntee, was in charge. Sallie Murry describes a wonderful indoor playground in loving detail: "It was white clapboard and stood in the middle of a big yard on South Lamar that included the whole block. It had a cellar and a full attic, two storeys of living space. . . . There was a porch across the back of the house and a servants' dining room and a big kitchen. Our meals were brought from the kitchen in covered dishes and served by a manservant. There was a tack hall downstairs also which got a great deal of use."[10]

In winter the children spent hours curled up reading books in the large upholstered wing chairs on either side of the Falkner grandparents' library fireplace or stretched out on the carpet, their faces turning pink from the heat of the embers, reading their own or their grandmother's books. Sometimes Estelle or Tochie had books they'd borrowed from their grandfather Niles. It was he who introduced Estelle to Dickens and Thackeray when she was a still a child and who suggested Voltaire when she was about twelve. The kids also shared new issues of their favorite magazines, such as *St. Nicholas,* to which Sallie Murry subscribed, *Boys' Life,* which belonged to the Falkner boys, and of course the *Confederate Journal,* which, like *The Clans-*

man, indoctrinated them into the myths and social codes of their fiercely Jim Crow world. It was also here that Billy Falkner and his brother first read those sentimental mammy testimonials whose rhetoric they absorbed and learned to substitute as "love" for their "second mother." In summer they spent many steamy rainy days poring over the stacks of old volumes of *St. Nicholas,* which included some of the best fiction published for children, as well as articles on science, history, and current events. The magazine was also an education in itself and connected them to the world beyond Oxford and the South.

When they grew bored with reading, they played dolls, including two social outcasts, Billy's Patrick O'Leary and, perhaps (if she existed in actuality), Estelle's New Orleans doll. Or they could troop up to J. W. T.'s attic for wilder games, like roller-skating. Although its walls and ceiling had been left unfinished, the Colonel had installed a wide-planked pine floor. On rainy days and during piercingly cold and damp winter afternoons, the children spent hours roller-skating in this large, open space. Their wheels made a tremendous noise—so loud that they could be heard across the street. One day an irate neighbor phoned to complain to Billy's Auntee: "I declare, I don't know how you stand the noise. It's driving me crazy all the way over here at my house." Auntee responded in a perfectly level voice, "Well, when they are skating up there I just take a big drink of gin and then run the sewing machine just as fast and as loud as I can."[11]

Estelle's description of her Niles grandparents' house in Kosciusko, one of the town's "big clapboard horrors" that "were beautiful to me, though," and of her indoor activities there on holidays when her cousins visited is very similar. They, too, rode bicycles down the long upstairs hall of an elegant Victorian. They played hide-and-seek in cavernous closets and spent hours reading by the fire in their grandfather's library or playing Parcheesi and "watching the flames from the burning wood make pictures" or painting and drawing in their grandmother's "studio."[12]

The Oldhams spent the hottest summer weeks of 1904 with Lem's mother, Mellie Mabry, at her cottage in the (relatively) cool hill country resort town of Monteagle, Tennessee, and did not return until after Labor Day.[13] Then Estelle entered first grade, Lem left to serve the court in Aberdeen in early October, and Lida entertained the Oxford Card Club. The Oldhams seemed to be settling into life in their new town.

In September 1905, shortly after Billy's eighth birthday, he and Tochie entered first grade. That year they and Estelle, who was now in the second grade, made honor roll. That Billy and Tochie were among just three honor students in their class indicates that to make the Oxford elementary school honor roll was really an honor. Recall that it was Billy's and Tochie's first-grade teacher who gave him *The Clansman*. Because Tochie also made the honor roll, it's likely that she, too, was awarded a copy. Its racist depictions of black male bestiality and brutality destroying the purity of Southern Womanhood were among these eight-year-olds' "history" lessons.

By the fall of 1906, Estelle and Billy were both in third grade because he had skipped second grade.[14] A classmate who was a good friend of Sallie Murry's remembers Estelle saying during a discussion of *The Life of Samuel Jackson* that "God could not let us win the war because slavery was wrong. But, he gave us the best generals."[15] Apparently *The Clansman* had not convinced Estelle. Her third-grade classmate remembers her dissenting voice and her attempt to cushion her critique.

That Christmas, the Oldhams set out as usual over the now muddy and sometimes snowy and slippery dirt roads that led due eastward through the hill country to the trace and then dropped down along it until it reached the short turn-off to Kosciusko. Both Lem and Lida's families were there, and the Oldhams wanted to spend the holidays and New Year's with Estelle's maternal grandmother, Miss Vic, and her grandfather Niles. Lida's sister, Etta, her husband, Fred Mills, and their three children were also going to visit, just as they do during the fictional Christmas of "Dr. Wohlenski."[16]

While the notices in the *Oxford Eagle*'s social columns document the Oldhams' comings and goings, Estelle's fictional memoir suggests something of the emotional texture of their lives. For example, she writes that "Christmas Eve was a wonderful day—almost better than the day itself, because expectancy heightens reality to a delightful pitch—and maybe because of the mystery that lies in all the gaily decorated boxes under the tree." In contrast, the day after was dreary and "a terrible let-down." Despite all the presents "brought to make us happy—somehow we weren't"; grown-ups "were to be avoided" as they were "maybe fighting hang-overs and indigestion."[17] A similar pall reigns on the day after Thanksgiving.

It is likely that similar conditions prevailed in the Falkner household. As we know, during the next seven years the Murry Falkners' finances continued to spiral downward, while the Oldhams' continued to appear more and more secure. During these years, as we've seen in Chapter 9, Estelle and Billy's relationship grew closer and closer.

I will return to that period, but for the moment I skip ahead to the critical summer of 1914 and Estelle's return to Mississippi after her year at boarding school.

In September 1913, when Estelle was sixteen, her parents sent their oldest daughter to Virginia to be "finished." At Mary Baldwin Seminary, she would be trained in an atmosphere reminiscent of the best "Christian Virginia homes." Yet Estelle enrolled in the school's demanding college program, suggesting that Lem and Lida (or perhaps Estelle herself) wanted their daughter to learn more than comportment and piano. She was among the seven Mississippians attending Mary Baldwin that year.

Located in the lush green foothills of the Shenandoah Valley, the school's classic Gothic buildings looked more like a Southern plantation than an educational institution. Although Mary Baldwin had been operating since 1842, it established its reputation after the Civil War, when it was taken over by "two consecrated women," Miss Mary Julia Baldwin and Miss Agnes McClung. Under their supervision it became a school "for the training of true womanhood." The Academic building housed classrooms, thirty-six practice rooms, science laboratories, and a wonderful library that contained over forty-five hundred books the year that Estelle attended.

Yet, as its 1913–14 catalogue explained, Mary Baldwin was at once "retired" and "accessible." Both the Chesapeake and Ohio and the Baltimore and Ohio railroads passed through Staunton, so it was easy to get to and from large cities like Washington, New York, and Boston. Students were permitted to take chaperoned excursions into Washington or nearby Charlottesville. Staunton, a city of twelve thousand people, had a public transport system of electric trolleys and "many of the advantages of a large city."

School rules were strict. Students could go home only at the holiday recesses and could receive visitors only on Saturday afternoons. "Young gentlemen" were admitted to visit a student only if the principal had received her parents' written permission and even then only at the discretion of the principal. Students could not leave the school grounds without permission, and all mail and telephone calls had to pass through the principal's office.[18]

Yet Estelle and her friends found loopholes in the system. One of their best was a Pernod-loving French teacher. Girls were permitted to attend weekend fraternity parties at the University of Virginia if they went in couples and were chaperoned by a Mary Baldwin teacher. According to Estelle, "We would always bring our French teacher who was definitely an alcoholic." The girls and their chaperone would settle in at Charlottesville's Queen Charlotte Hotel and "get our loves back then to buy her a big bottle of Pernod—her favorite drink—and we would leave for the weekend." Some of this is obviously tongue-in-cheek and meant to shock: Estelle also said she was only fourteen at the time (rather than sixteen) but that "girls were much more mature then, especially in the South."[19]

Coming from a home in which churchgoing was irregular at best and considered a social rather than a religious event, Estelle found this school somewhat oppressive. And understandably so, in that its stated objective was to be "as nearly as possible, in all its details, a Christian home, with all the purity and refinement that characterize a model Virginia home, the very atmosphere of which is an incentive to higher things and an inspiration to lofty ideals."[20] It wasn't all bad though—on Sundays they were not permitted to study.[21] Estelle was boarding at a school that did not even allow visitors on the Sabbath and whose aim was "to promote the highest intellectual development" of its pupils, "to give them good religious instruction, and surrounding them with all the influences of a refined home circle, to fit them for the duties of life" by appealing to their "pride of womanhood, and innate love of the Good, the True, and the Beautiful."[22]

The beautiful did not include clothes. At Mary Baldwin, dresses were confined to two colors—black or white. Low-necked dresses and short-sleeved dresses were not allowed. Necklines had to be "square or dutch" and sleeves could be "no shorter than elbow length." The school's catalogue stated firmly that "extravagance in dress is neither encouraged or desired" and made it clear that there was "no occasion when expensive dressing is necessary or suitable."[23] Nonetheless, the yearbook photograph of Estelle shows that a dutch neckline could reveal a good deal and that this dress code didn't interfere with the appearance of a pretty girl (see fig. 15.2).

Mary Baldwin's academic standards were as strict as its dress codes, as evidenced by the fact that students who completed its four-year college preparatory course could enter Goucher, Mount Holyoke, or Wellesley colleges without examination.[24] In 1914 Goucher College was rated as one of the most curricularly advanced institutions of higher education for women in the South. The College Board rated all three as Class A colleges.[25] Estelle's transcript for 1913–14, which gives her age as sixteen, shows that she did enroll in the college program. Her excellent high school grades allowed her to skip the entire freshman program and all but French in the sophomore program. Her courses included first-year French, third-year English, plane geometry, chemistry (both listed as fourth-year courses), and piano. Her final grades for the year were chemistry, 90; English, 91; French, 85; geometry, 89; and piano, 97, giving her a 90.4 average for her year's work. Had she returned for a second and final year, she would have been accepted for admission at three of the best women's colleges in the country. A comparison of her grades at Mary Baldwin with her mediocre performance during her freshman and sophomore years at the University of Mis-

15.2. Yearbook photo of Estelle and fellow members of the Bluestocking Club, from Mary Baldwin Seminary Yearbook, 1914.
(Courtesy of Mary Baldwin College Library, Staunton, Va.)

sissippi (1914–16) suggests that at Mary Baldwin she was not yet inhibited or distracted by the men in her life, the overwhelming presence of men in her classes, and the social pressure to get married. In 1914 only ten of the sixty-eight Ole Miss freshmen were women, and in 1915, only eleven of the fifty sophomores. At Mary Baldwin, where, despite the weekend charms of Charlottesville, Estelle did not participate in a constant round of social activities, she performed at the same high level she had maintained in the Oxford public school.[26] Although there is not necessarily a connection, Estelle began doing poorly in school after the summer Bill became immersed in his friendship with Phil Stone, and Estelle began accepting the attentions of Phil's law school classmate, Cornell Franklin. According to his descendants and relatives, Cornell had no liking for intellectually challenging women.

At Mary Baldwin, Estelle did well in all her courses, but she made the steadiest improvement in English and consistently excelled in music, where her lowest quarter grade in the fall term was 93, two points higher than her final English grade. One reason the Oldhams had chosen Mary Baldwin was its music program; the school owned forty pianos and two organs and employed four music teachers, two men and two women. As part of their training, students were required to "memorize an extensive repertoire of good compositions," something Estelle could have done with ease, since, according to her granddaughter, she had what might be called a photographic ear. Estelle's daughter amplifies: "She had what amounted to almost total musical recall."[27] In addition to practicing technique, phrasing, and the principles of composition, students were taught to understand and analyze the structure of the music they were learning to play. By their final year, Estelle's class was playing Chopin, Henselt, Rubenstein, Bach's larger works, and Mozart's and Beethoven's sonatas. They also learned at least one concerto by either Mozart or Beethoven.

By any standards, this was a rigorous curriculum which required that the student read music fluently and be much more than an average pianist. It is not known when Estelle stopped playing seriously. Jill remembers coming home from school one afternoon to find all the strings ripped out of her mother's piano. "Pappy had done it," she says. "He really took a hatchet and did a number on some of the wires and everything." By the late 1930s and early 1940s, Estelle seldom played classical music. "Occasionally she'd play light classical—Ravel nocturnes or Debussy. But mostly she played her own music and popular things. She seemed to be able to play anything she'd ever heard."[28] Her granddaughter, Victoria, didn't think she could even read music and considered her grandmother's lack of interest in formal techniques or serious music her way of rebelling against Lida Oldham's most cherished values.[29] But in 1913–14, Estelle was playing a great deal of classical music, and playing it well.

When, at various times, Jill or Victoria asked her to tell stories of her year at boarding school, Estelle described the forbidden caches of food she and her roommate stored on their dorm windowsill. She told of hanging out their window, even in bitter weather, to furtively smoke cigarettes. Jill did not think that Estelle had enjoyed the school very much.[30] Victoria's impression is different. Of her grandmother's year at Mary Baldwin she says, "I gather that she enjoyed it thoroughly. And enjoyed being away from Oxford. And didn't seem to miss anybody. She described it as a ball, you know. Having a great time." Estelle and the theatrical diva Tallulah Bankhead's younger sister, Eugenia, were classmates, and the stories Estelle told Victoria mostly concerned the two girls' "escapades and almost constant scrapes." Her granddaughter concludes, "It's amazing that they lasted at Mary Baldwin. What I suspect is that Eugenia got into most of them. I think Grandmama's stories about Mary Baldwin were like her stories about smoking opium in Shanghai. I think Eugenia did it and Grandmama watched, probably."[31] This was another character trait that she and Billy Falkner shared.

Given her good grades, one wonders why her parents didn't send her back for her senior year. Perhaps they thought success might be a liability to making a good marriage. Or maybe one year's tuition—almost five hundred dollars—was enough to spend on Estelle's education, particularly since they also sent Tochie to Immaculata, a Catholic boarding school in Washington, D.C., that year.

In any case, if she hadn't known it before her year at boarding school, Estelle returned to Oxford aware that, besides being pretty, she was also smart. But she had more than just intelligence. Her daughter says that in addition Estelle had "an amazingly accurate and highly visual memory for anything that had happened. There was no point in arguing with her about an incident for invariably, she would prove to be right."[32]

"I Fell in Love with Him When I Was Sixteen"

In May 1914 Estelle returned home from her first and only year at Mary Baldwin Seminary, in Staunton, Virginia. "It was a small Southern school for about 150 girls. We used to have a grand time at the fraternity parties in Charlottesville," Estelle Faulkner said in a 1972 interview with the University of Virginia newspaper.[33] She had left Oxford a pretty child; nine months later she arrived back in Oxford, a stunningly beautiful young woman (figs. 15.1, 2, and 17.3). Robert Farley, then an "ardent admirer" of

15.3. Snapshots of Estelle Oldham, Katrina Carter, and an unidentified
friend, taken near Oxford and at the Carters' home in town. On the porch
swing with Katrina and Estelle is Katrina's mother.
(Courtesy of Vinton C. and Jim Kyle Hudson, Jr.)

Estelle's best friend, Katrina Carter, gives some sense of the two girls' effect on Oxford's young men that summer. Both Katrina and Estelle had "rather deep-set eyes," and Estelle's, accentuated by her dark eyebrows, changed from gray to blue depending on the color of her dress. Their distinctive and engaging laughs "came from the throat, not a man's laugh, but deep and full instead of a girlish giggle." Katrina's short, wavy hair was brown and flecked with red highlights.[34] Estelle wore her dark red hair long or piled high on her head and held in place by combs and a ribbon. When she really dressed, as in her photograph for the 1913–14 Mary Baldwin yearbook, *The Bluestocking*, her intricate coif was reminiscent of Princess Eugenie. Both girls were slim and graceful. From the Carters' porch or on the tennis court, Billy Falkner could watch the girls at play and see the sunlight dappling through their organdy blouses and pale-colored lawn or dotted swiss tennis skirts. Estelle's slight, willowy figure made her seem taller than the five feet four inches registered on her 1921 passport.[35] Snapshots of the two friends swinging with Katrina's mother on the Carters' porch, leaning against one of their beaus' parked cars, perched on a fence with a group of picnickers, or laughing with their arms locked about each other as they try to pull another picnicker to his feet show two lively and pretty young women (fig. 15.3).[36]

Billy's withdrawal from Estelle, and their official break, accomplished by her marriage to Cornell in April 1918, had begun the fall of 1913, when she left for boarding school. Billy was about to turn sixteen, and she was sixteen and a half. But Estelle's absence only preceded an event whose causes had very little to do with her.

From Billy's perspective, marriage as practiced by his immediate relatives was nothing to embrace. Furthermore, it was clear that desire played no part in marriage. Men in his family divided procreation from sex. They had children with their white wives but sex with black women. The color of white Southern men's desire was black. Sexual pleasure, at least for his grandfathers, was sought with black women. Given his experiential knowledge of married life, it makes sense to suggest that he was disturbed and frightened by the increasing but highly ambivalent desire he felt for Estelle as she grew from a pretty little girl to an attractive and self-possessed young woman. Meta Carpenter Wilde, with whom Faulkner had an affair in the 1930s, described Faulkner's continuing ambivalence about sex and sexuality. Although he was a great "sensualist," he was also "obsessed with keeping from me the grossness of his physical self, running the water in the bathroom to cover evidence of his animality, bathing each time we made love."[37]

His ambivalence was so strong and so upsetting that traces of it resurfaced years later in his relationships with his daughter and step-granddaughter during their adolescence. Jill and Victoria's accounts of the cruelty to which Faulkner's anxiety drove him are heartrending.[38] But they serve as a valuable testament, if not to how he behaved toward Estelle between 1914 and 1918, at least to how he felt.

Estelle's desertion was to become a woman. As is apparent from the gender distinctions she makes in "Dr. Wohlenski," she knew this and may have tried to effect a remedy by imitating Billy. She began to drink and smoke. Like her fictional Estelle, she wanted to be part of the "warmth" and "humanness," the intermingled smells of whiskey and tobacco she associated with the "intellectual compatibility" men shared.

It's also possible that, ironically, her academic achievements, instead of impressing Billy, made him withdraw further. Unlike Phil Stone, who was four years his senior, and later Stark Young, who was fifteen years older, Estelle, besides being a girl, was his peer. Now, by all external measures, she had just completed a remarkably successful and final year of high school at Mary Baldwin. In contrast Billy had essentially stopped performing in school in the sixth grade. Although he continued to read voluminously, to draw, and to write reams of poetry, he simply refused to participate and succeed in a formal educational setting.

In some ways Estelle's and Bill's behavior mirrors the contrasting economic condition and emotional atmosphere in the Falkner and Oldham households. Although Lem Oldham's finances and social standing had improved visibly since his arrival in Oxford in 1903, Murry Falkner continued in the downward spiral set off in 1902 when his father sold his railroad interests.

After moving to Oxford, Murry Falkner made successive failures of the various businesses his father continued to assign him. The Falkners' shrinking income was reflected in their living conditions. By March of 1912 both Murry Falkner and Lem Oldham had offices on the square. But whereas Lem was still clerk of the U.S. District Courts for the Northern District of Mississippi (1903–19) and vice-president of the Bank of Oxford, Murry was merely a storekeeper. When he walked around the square, he could see the disparity between himself and Oldham, which was even more marked by the fact that Murry's father was president of Oxford's First National Bank.

The disparity was equally apparent when Murry wended his way home past the house the Oldhams had bought and lived in since 1905.[39] Since the Falkners' arrival in Oxford in 1902, they had moved to increasingly modest houses, whereas Lem Oldham and his wife had spent the years improving the lovely house they had bought in 1905. Murry's father—not Murry— and the Oldhams were two of the first three families in Oxford to own a car.[40] Along their semicircular drive fronting their house, Lem had directed the planting of symmetrically arranged flowerbeds filled with annuals and perennials. Cutting gardens were planted along either side of the house, and in the back lay another flower garden and a vegetable patch. In 1911 the Oldhams' latest auto was described in the *Oxford Eagle* as "one of the prettiest automobiles seen on the streets." It could be seen parked in their front drive waiting to take Lida to a tea or club meeting.[41]

There were other signs of success. Lem was reaping more benefits from his long-time commitment to the state Republican Party. In 1912 he was "appointed a member of Governor Brewer's staff with the rank of Major." He delighted in his orders, which were "to appear in full regimentals at all state occasions to assist in lending dignity to the governor of the state." His pride and pleasure are reflected in the handsome portrait of him taken shortly after his appointment (see fig. 15.4).[42]

In 1911, Lem was rich enough to make an investment that would ultimately be a factor in his financial collapse and ruin in the summer of 1926, the same year Estelle's marriage ended. He bought and began remodeling the old Coleman Hotel, which he sold at a loss in 1920.[43]

Even the Oldhams' children seemed more successful than the Falkners'. In the fall of 1913, when James Stone's boy, Phil, went off to Yale and Lem Oldham sent his two daughters to their respective boarding schools (and all three excelled), Murry Falkner's sons continued their mediocre performances in the Oxford public schools, where Billy distinguished himself primarily by his constant absences. No doubt Billy and Estelle were as aware of these disparities as their parents. Meanwhile Tochie and Estelle were in Washington, D.C., and Virginia, where among other advantages, their parents anticipated they would meet the daughters of families from the wealthier Southern states and perhaps marry their brothers. Describing their expectations for their daughters and importance of social connections to Lem and Lida, Jill Summers says that to her grandparents "the only thing that was acceptable for a well-brought up young lady to do at that time was get married. You simply didn't do anything else. Both my grandparents, but particularly Granddaddy was extremely—not ambitious—but he was determined that Mama was going to marry well. That is, into a good family which meant that it could trace every ancestor back a long, long time. In Mississippi family is important. I think down south it is. And probably when Mama was twelve or thirteen, Granddaddy and Nanny started scouting the eligible young men and decided in which direction they intended Mama to go. Her marrying Cornell Franklin was strictly an arrangement between Granddaddy and Mr. [Cornell] Franklin."[44]

Lem's and Lida's ancestors had migrated to Mississippi from Vermont,

15.4. Estelle's father, Major
Lemuel Earle Oldham, c. 1912.
(Courtesy of Cornell Franklin, Jr.)

Tennessee, North Carolina, and Virginia in the early 1800s. Jill Summers remarked that "North Carolina, South Carolina and Virginia are the places from which you want your ancestors to come if you live in Mississippi or Alabama. If they came from some place else, it was really not quite the thing. There was just this definite cachet about those three states. If you lived in the states that, so far as the South is concerned, are not quite respectable, that is Mississippi, Alabama, the lower end of Arkansas, the lower end of Tennessee,—[you were considered] the white trash of the South."[45]

This was the state of affairs in the Oldham and Falkner households the summer Phil Stone entered Estelle's and Billy's lives. Although his own drinking and her knowledge of his grandfather's and father's public drunkenness probably created tensions between Bill and Estelle (just as they increased the friction between Murry and Maud), it only drew Bill and Phil closer together. By the summer of 1913 Phil was already having blackouts. As an undergrad at Ole Miss, he had been drinking a quart of bourbon a day. Their culture sanctioned and facilitated their abuse of alcohol. In Oxford, manliness, drinking, and hunting, and to a slightly lesser extent drinking and talking, were synonymous. It was a firmly gendered way of life. So by becoming more and more involved in alcohol, Bill distanced himself from Estelle in a specific way. He threw himself into a social activity from which she was barred by virtue of her sex and social class. Besides pointing out that drinking is a sanctioned, almost hallowed masculine activity, a retired law professor at the University of Mississippi comments that "drinking takes the place of religion for those living out the mythological dimensions of southern manhood. You go to it for solace; you go to it to celebrate. You are taught from childhood that it's a part of manhood. In Oxford, probably because of the presence of the university and its fraternities embodying those never actually realized mythical ideals of the 'Old South,' it's worse. Listen to them talk. Willie Morris, for example, will talk for hours about alcohol—it's part of the drinking—to talk about it."[46] Alcohol—too much of it—symbolized entry into the adult male world. Paradoxically, besides being an essential feature of communal male activity, its effect was to relieve men of adult responsibility. Particularly it excused them for abusing their women, their children, and all black people. Southern fiction, from Mark Twain's to Faulkner's to Ferrol Sams's and Ellen Douglas's, is filled with terrifying and cruel scenes of such abuse. We cannot begin to understand the nature of human relationships in Billy's and Estelle's Oxford if we don't acknowledge the fact, meaning, and long-range effects of alcoholic addiction and the place of alcohol in their culture. It is equally important to understand the complicated relations between gender and economics in the Faulkner, Stone, and Oldham households, relations reflected in the town at large. By virtue of his education Stone had entrée and the ability to travel to a literary world and marketplace beyond Oxford. By virtue of his family's money he could and did help finance Bill's career up through the publication of *The Marble Faun,* in 1924, and beyond. Besides intellectual and emotional compatibility and support, he could offer material support, everything from stenographic services at his father's law office to actual capital. In contrast, while the Oldhams had money, Estelle did not have access to it. But even if she had, she could not have given, and Faulkner could not have taken from her, what he could accept from Phil simply because he was a man.

PART 4

First Loves, First "Marriages," 1914–1926

The other morning, Phil came in to wake me, and I said—Go away and let me alone, Mother.
— FAULKNER

16

Shifting Alliances, 1914–1918
From Estelle to Phil

> [You] ought to know this little Falkner boy who writes.
> —Katrina Carter

ATRINA CARTER, who was two years younger than Phil and two years older than Bill and Estelle, had, along with Maud and Estelle, been one of the earliest readers of Faulkner's poetry. That summer, when Phil Stone returned from his senior year at Yale, she had shown some of Billy's poems to him. Seeing that Phil was bursting with ideas about art and aesthetics and deeply interested in current experiments in poetry and prose Katrina suggested that he "ought to know this little Falkner boy who writes; he's always telling stories."[1] As she may have suspected, Phil was eager to mentor and mother a genius. In later years he often referred to himself as Faulkner's "wet nurse." One lazy summer afternoon he unfolded his thin, lanky body from the swing on Katrina's side porch and rose to shake hands with the slight teenager whose sharp brown (some said black) eyes seemed to bore right through him. Little did Stone suspect that he had just met the person who would become one of this century's greatest novelists. Nor, as Stone's biographer, Susan Snell, observes, did he dream that for the next seventeen years—if not for the rest of his life—William Faulkner would become the center of his reality.[2] Here is Phil's account of that summer and the two years that followed, during which, at his father's insistence, he took his (first) law degree at Ole Miss rather than returning to Yale: "[Bill] was painting some then, and was faintly interested in writing verse. I gave him books to read—Swinburne, Keats, and a number of the moderns, such as Conrad Aiken and the Imagists in verse and Sherwood Anderson in prose." Echoing Willard Huntington Wright, the aesthetician he most admired, and T. S. Eliot, Phil told Bill that "Swinburne had carried the oral resources of the language to their limits" and that "poets thereafter 'had to break the mold and start over again.'"[3]

Phil would return to Yale, this time for a second law degree, in the fall of 1916. Meanwhile, although enrolled in law school at Ole Miss and averaging As or high Bs throughout his tenure, Stone pursued his true avocations—poker, booze, and his mentoring of "little Billy Falkner."[4]

Faulkner's account of his poetic apprenticeship makes no mention of Stone. Rather, he portrays his learning as solitary. As he wrote retrospectively in April 1925, when he was in the midst of finishing his first novel, in 1914 "at the age of sixteen I discovered Swinburne. Or rather, Swinburne discovered me, springing from some tortured undergrowth of my adolescence, like a highwayman, making me his slave. . . . True, I dipped into Shelley and Keats—who doesn't at that age?—but they did not move me."[5] According to Faulkner, it was the sexually ambiguous Swinburne in whom he first found "a flexible vessel into which I might put my own vague emotional shapes without breaking them" and "who completely satisfied me and filled my inner life." Faulkner's description here of enslavement and mutual penetration places him in a suggestively subservient and homoerotic relation to the older poet.

Yet in January 1920 he dedicated *The Lilacs*, which appears to be the earliest of his handmade poem sequences, to Phil. As far as is known, it is the only one of his handmade booklets that he ever gave to another man. In it are adaptations and imitations of some of the most important poems by poets Phil had introduced him to. Bound in red velvet, it is a gaudy tour de force whose central thematic was Woman—especially Woman as the Decadents' perverse and fatal temptress. Poets imitated, adapted, and "translated" include Villon, Mallarmé, Aiken, Eliot, and, of course, Swinburne. As I've written elsewhere, this sequence is important on many levels. Stylistically eclectic, it displays an array of poetic techniques and voices from across the centuries. But its primary interest here is the light it sheds on the question of why, beginning in 1914, Bill Falkner began shifting his attention from Estelle to Phil. In this context, one poem in particular stands out: his intentional glossing and reworking of Swinburne's great lyric from *Poems and Ballads*.[6] Faulkner's adaptation becomes a means for extending his ideas about the relation of homoerotic love to creativity that he had begun in his first published poem, a reworking of Mallarmé's "L'Après-midi d'un faune." He included that poem, too, in *The Lilacs*. With both adaptations, he chooses to tell only part of the story. He recalls the Swinburne in order to offer a radical reinterpretation of the meaning of Sappho's life and songs. Most strangely, he omits the strophes that describe the stunning effect of Sappho's "visible song" of lamentation on the gods and on mortals. This change, coupled with another, casts an oddly judgmental light on the figure Swinburne uses to symbolize Sappho's new kind of poetry and poetics: lesbian love. In Swinburne's "Sapphics" lesbian lovers are a trope for the new life and speech that Sappho invents out of her grief at being betrayed by her lover, Anactoria.

> Clothed about with flame and with tears, and singing
> Songs that move the heart of the shaken heaven,
> Songs that break the heart of the earth with pity,
>   Hearing, to hear them.[7]

Faulkner's poem denies Sappho and her sisters such powers *because* they practice same-sex love. One can observe the difference in attitude toward lesbian desire between Swinburne's and Faulkner's personas by comparing the two poems.[8] It is curious that Faulkner, who was translating, imitating, and adapting the poems of older poets as a means of finding his own path to "visible song," should pass over the strophes that explicitly celebrated Sappho's great poetic achievement. His revision implies that Sappho's same-sex desire excluded her from Aphrodite's favor so that rather than singing songs "Made of perfect sound and exceeding passion," songs that "break the heart of the earth with pity," she and her sisters were condemned to "barrenness, cryings, and lamentations." Swinburne's women reject the fruits of heterosexual coupling so that they may bear a different kind of fruit—their new songs. In Faulkner's poem the Sapphic women are barren and songless because they have succumbed to the lures of homoerotic love. Theirs are merely "the cryings and lamentations / Of barren women." Possibly he missed the import of Swinburne's "Sapphics." But the accuracy with which he has condensed its opening strophes into the first three verses of his own version indicates that he made a careful study of the language and meter of Swinburne's lyric.

Faulkner's treatment of sexual love in his translation of "L'Après-midi d'un faune," which, with Phil's guidance and help he had published in the *New Republic* the prior summer, is also relevant to understanding why his version of "Sapphics" is diametrically opposed to Swinburne's. Faulkner excluded from his version of Mallarmé's poem the scene that is the specific source of his faun's erotic arousal. Mallarmé's faun creates music and initiates a fantasy in which he displaces his own homoerotic desire onto two intertwined and sleeping nymphs whom he surprises and then attempts to rape. This poem, although in a different way than "Sapphics" and in search of a different effect on its audience, is also about same-sex desire as a touchstone of creativity. The faun's music making triggers a homoerotic fantasy, which he then tells. The final product of his fantasy is a unique work of art, a poem that gives his fantasy coherence and form, making it available to others. The faun's (poet's) act is equivalent to what Sappho does with her grief in Swinburne's "Sapphics." She memorializes it in a new kind of poem. In both of these poems, written before the self-censorship resulting from the Wilde trials, Mallarmé and Swinburne are celebrating the myriad forms of sexuality—homosexual acts and fantasies in particular—from which they, as mature poets, derive imaginative inspiration. In contrast, Faulkner appears threatened by the underlying emotional currents in these poems. Although these and other homoerotic poems attract and fascinate him, he seems compelled to purify them. While claiming them as his, he also censors them as he adapts them to his conscious needs. One of these at this particular time in his life is to be defended against his increasingly close relationship and identification with Phil Stone, a man whose constantly voiced fear of women and self-characterizations as a "male Cassandra" and Billy Falkner's wet nurse indicate his irresolute sexual identity.

Both "Sapphics" and "L'Après-midi" interested Faulkner in part because they speak in new ways about the connection between creativity and sexuality. Although "L'Après-midi" may not be a poem about poets, it concerns the making of poetry, and Faulkner responded to it because it fired his imagination. In adapting these two poems, however, he either excludes or condemns homoerotic elements and ignores the connections Swinburne and Mallarmé make between homoerotic fantasies and the creative imagination. His censorship also forces him to omit their other common subject, the origins of new forms of poetry.

Clearly the resonances and dissonances Swinburne provoked have sent Faulkner's imagination into turmoil. His conscious morality makes him reject Swinburne's solution even as he is emotionally drawn to it. Not until late 1924, when Estelle returns precipitously from China and he begins to distance himself from Phil Stone, will he deal directly with this issue.[9] This is not to argue that Bill and Phil were lovers but rather to suggest that Faulkner's fears that he might desire a man rather than or as well as a woman express themselves in these poems, which he collected into this first known poetic sequence and which he gave to the man who replaced Estelle as his mentor and muse beginning in the summer of 1914 and on intermittently through 1924. It is also to suggest another reason why Phil supplanted Estelle beginning in that summer of 1914.

There are no letters or journals that record Bill and Phil's deepening relationship, although Susan Snell provides the most complete account of it, particularly of the years 1914–16, when Phil was earning his Ole Miss law degree. One of her most revealing primary sources is a sixteen-page autobiographical narrative Phil wrote in 1963, when, in his final, severely paranoid delusional state, he was committed to Whitfield, the state mental institution in Jackson.[10] However, after Snell's biography had already gone to press, Faulkner's letters that do document parts of their relationship were made public.[11] They form the basis of my account that follows.

Phil and Bill in New Haven, April–June 1918

Not surprisingly, one of their closest periods began shortly before Estelle's marriage to Cornell Franklin, Phil's fraternity brother and Ole Miss class-mate. In early April 1918, Bill, then twenty, left the South for the first time in his life and went to New Haven to stay with twenty-five-year-old Phil in his rooms at 122 York Street.[12] On the evening of Thursday, 4 April 1918, thirteen days before Estelle's and Cornell's marriage, Billy Falkner arrived in New Haven for a ten-week visit with Phil that ended with Billy's enlist-ment in the Royal Canadian Air Force (RCAF) and move to boot camp in Toronto. Phil, who was finishing his last year of Yale Law School, had taken the train to New York that morning to meet Billy's train at Penn Sta-tion. Before boarding another train to New Haven later that day, the two took a brief walk along Manhattan's most famous avenue. Billy describes the scene to his mother in a letter written the day after his arrival in New Haven: "I walked down Fifth Avenue to 66th St. and saw the convalescent French and British officers. The lobbies and Mezzanine floors of the hotels are full of them, with their service stripes and wings and game legs and sticks" (*TOH*, 45, 46).

His first impression in April 1918, his first real contact with what he saw as the drama and glory of the Great War, proved prescient. Here, in a few words—the service stripes, the game leg, and the stick—he sketches the wounded war-hero persona he will invent several months later on his dis-charge from the RCAF and will carry back to Oxford in December. In various guises this persona will haunt the poetry to which he dedicates him-self during the next six years, the first novel he writes with almost miracu-lous speed between March and May of 1925, and all the great novels that followed.

His first descriptions of New Haven are of local dress and drinking habits, which is not surprising for a young man who is preoccupied with both. In contrast to Oxford, "tight clothes and pink and yellow shirts are as rare here as negroes," but somehow, although people drink as much if not more than in Oxford, the liquor seems to have lost its punch. From his win-dows he can see "three or four Yale men going down the street with a tin bucket to get beer at the Taft or the Bishop [hotels]. And it's funny, they all drink, even the faculty members drink with them. But," he adds, "no body ever gets drunk." That he'd already checked out the Taft bar for himself that morning, his blanket assertions of universal sobriety, and his absurd claim to have already familiarized himself with local drinking customs after only a day in New Haven must have signaled his mother like so many red flags (*TOH*, 45, 46).

Three nights later, in Phil's boarding-house room, which they are sharing, Stone writes to his mother, Rosamond, about Billy. In his usual condescending manner, Phil expresses his belief in his protégé's talents: "He's a fine intelligent little fellow and I think he is going to amount to a lot some day." He adds that he doesn't think Billy will be "homesick" as "I've introduced him around to all of my friends and acquaintances, some of them rather brilliant people, and they seem to like him very much."[13]

Expecting him to stay awhile and knowing he will need money to support himself while continuing to write poems and possibly short stories, Phil has already arranged an office job for him through one of his drinking companions, Joe Biglin, "a blue-collar worker from Denver" who "had come east to make money in the war industries."[14] Billy will have a few days to settle in before starting work the following Wednesday, 10 April.

Phil's letter makes clear that contrary to prior accounts, Faulkner's exit from Oxford was no precipitous and emotionally charged departure. Advance planning, dating back at least to January, had preceded Billy's visit. He will even find a job waiting for him. The letter also records Phil's explicit and implicit explanations for his friend's presence in New Haven. Phil writes of the good the visit will do Billy and alludes to the good Billy's visit will do Phil; his remarks tell something about Phil's perception of his relationship with "little Billy" in 1918, a perception confirmed by Billy's letters home to his parents that same spring. Remarkably, considering the supposed circumstances of Faulkner's flight from Oxford and Phil's well-known dislike of Estelle, Phil never mentions her forthcoming marriage as the event precipitating his young friend's trip to New Haven.[15] Instead he gives very different reasons for getting him out of Oxford. He writes his mother, "Miss Rosie," that Bill's salary will be "only" twenty dollars a week—enough to cover his room, board, and laundry and still leave "a few dollars spending money left over each week." However, he thinks it a good thing that Billy will be on a tight budget: "He'll get along all the better without much money for awhile." Phil's next remarks, read in the context of Billy's comments on alcohol consumption at Yale, of Phil's ongoing battle with alcoholism, and of Faulkner's retrospective account of his own drinking habits during the three months he worked at his grandfather's bank prior to leaving Oxford are significant. They suggest that Faulkner's growing dependence on whiskey, his boredom, his professional frustration, and his irritation with his parents for not letting him volunteer in World

War I were the cause of whatever difficulties he was having in Oxford. *Not* Estelle.[16]

Susan Snell's description of the flowering of Phil and Bill's friendship, in which heavy drinking, gambling, riding around in roadsters, and consorting with various low-life characters were as important as any reading or literary talk, also suggests that his friendship with Phil and the company they kept, rather than Faulkner's love for Estelle, was more likely the source of what Phil calls Bill's "going to seed." Phil's patronizing, avuncular tone as he explains to his mother the need to get Bill out of Oxford seems designed to cover his own yearning for nurturance and home: *"I certainly am glad that I got him away from Oxford for he was going to seed there. Phone Miss Maud that he is alright and is behaving himself like a good boy and that I am going to take good care of him."*[17] Phil was an extremely intelligent and articulate young man. His assertion that Bill was going to seed provides a weak basis for concluding that Faulkner was pining away because the woman he loved was about to marry his rival.

Equally, if not more important from Phil's viewpoint, is the pleasure and comfort Billy's company will give *him*. After telling his mother that he doesn't "think Bill will be homesick," he then describes his own deep longing "to be at home so bad. It must be lovely in the country there now. I'd like to take you for a nice long ride in your little ford." As he speaks of his hunger for home-cooked food, fresh milk, butter, and eggs, his need becomes almost palpable. When he nears the end of his letter, his desire for mothering breaks through again: "It is certainly going to be a comfort to have Bill here this spring to keep me from getting restless and lonely."[18] Such acute homesickness for his mother and his mother's care from a twenty-six-year-old man, read in the light of Phil's constant complaints that his mother never loved him, perhaps explains why Phil needed Bill so badly and why he mothered Bill. When Bill began separating himself from Phil in 1924 (when he met Sherwood Anderson and when Estelle first arrived home from Shanghai) and (in Phil's eyes) completed the break by marrying Estelle five years later, Phil took out his grief and anger through hostility toward Estelle (and, to a lesser extent, Faulkner), which he sustained until his death. He said at the time and continued to believe that Estelle "was not worth a damn to anybody and never would be, but that she had always lived off the fat of the land and always would."[19]

One might expect Faulkner's first letters to his parents from New Haven to indicate some unhappiness or level of depression about Estelle's impending marriage, but his high-spirited and lively account of his train trip north through the Shenandoahs and Blue Ridge Mountains in Virginia, "the loveliest country I have ever seen," does not bring to mind a distraught, rejected suitor. He writes, for example, of blossoming fruit trees that look as though "myriads of white and coral butterflies were resting upon them and the dog wood like bits of silk upon green velvet"; of the soldiers he sees on the New York City streets and in hotel lobbies; and, later, of his first impressions of New Haven. The writerly eye he turns on everyone and everything, his humor and excitement, and his sheer exuberance portray a young man bubbling with ideas and impressions he is eager to share with his parents.[20] It's unlikely that a severely depressed twenty-year-old would be this open to new experiences and impressions and would write about them with such joy and enthusiasm (even if he were presenting a happy face to his parents).[21] To Maud he writes: "I have so much to tell you that I dont know where to begin" (6 April 1918). He describes the ocean, which he has just seen for the first time, as "a pale blue strip of paint on a sheet of glass." He's thrilled with his first Chinese restaurant—"paper flowers and butterflies and tea in tiny cups without handles" (7 April 1918). He reports that everyone "is nice to me," that "I'm having a great time" (9 April 1918), that "New Haven is a wonderful old place" (14 April 1918). When he goes to his first lacrosse game with Phil, about which he gives a hilarious account, he writes, "I never had as much fun in my life" (2 April 1918).[22]

Although he is shocked by the bitter dampness of that cold New England spring and writes frankly to both Maud and Murry about his homesickness (first to Maud: "I'm terribly lonesome"; and later to his father: "I am terribly homesick and I hope to hear from you by tomorrow"), his tone in both of his first long letters and those that follow is exhilarated, not sad or flat.[23] One might fairly argue that Faulkner, the master masker, simply withheld that part of himself from his parents' view. It is true that at least one of Phil Stone's retrospective accounts of the reasons for Faulkner's visit insists that Billy was the rejected suitor and that Phil's invitation saved his life. But Stone's 1918 letter tells a more complex tale and describes a very different emotional involvement—his own with young Billy. His tale is borne out by Billy's account of his relationship with Phil in letters home that spring and summer of 1918.

The letters also reveal other factors motivating Faulkner's exodus—the difficulty of finding a decent-paying job in Oxford in 1918, his wish to become a writer, not a husband, and to join the RCAF so he could both see the world and secure what he describes as a steady, reliable, and basically undemanding job in the military. In early May, when his parents express their reluctance to let Faulkner's brother Jack enlist, Billy responds, "I say let Jack go by all means. He is doing nothing there [in Oxford], and will continue to if you keep him there." As it always has, the army offered educational and employment opportunities for economically depressed parts of the population. Billy points out that if Jack "goes in the Q.M. Corps he can make something of him self, when as it is now, he'll keep on until they catch him playing cards or some similar kind of assinity [*sic*]. He can get things there now that he'll not be able to later."[24]

In June, arguing his own case, he is even more explicit: "I have got a chance to join up with the British and get a commission as a second lieutenant . . . in about three months after I'm sent to training camp. It's a wonderful chance as there's nothing to be had in the U.S. Army now, except a good job stopping boche bullets as a private." Pleading, he expands, "It's the chance I've been waiting for. Everything will be my way, I can almost have my pick of anything. I'll be in at the wind-up of the show. The chances of advancement in the English army are very good; I'll perhaps be a major at the end of a year's service. I've thought about it constantly." Pointing out how relatively safe he'll be in the British army, "where the elimination of risk is taught above everything," he closes by warning his parents of missed opportunities and a wasted life: "At the rate I'm living now, I'll never be able to make anything of myself, but with this business I will be fixed up after the war is over."[25] He seems to imply here either that he'll make a career out of the army or that his status as an ex-military officer will help provide him with a comfortable income for the rest of his life.

Phil's letter to his mother allows us to hear his feelings about "little Billy." But Billy's letters catch the essence of his feelings about Phil and his perceptions about the nature of their relationship in the weeks leading up to and months following Estelle's marriage to Cornell Franklin. The emotional intensity and tenderness of Phil's care that has been prefigured in Phil's earlier letter to his mother is instanced most dramatically in a dream Billy reports to Maud: "The other morning, Phil came in to wake me, and I said—Go away and let me alone, Mother, dont you know this is a heatless day?"[26] At this point in their relationship Faulkner seemed eager to play the child to Phil's "mother." Other letters announce that "Phil is going to mail this for me now" or that "I have broken into poetry again. Phil has sent it to a magazine and I am sending you a copy."[27]

Besides providing him with new friends, a home, secretarial services, and a job, Phil also opened up a whole new world to Bill. Bill wrote his parents repeatedly that "I never had as much fun in my life." He tells of playing bridge "nearly every night," of going to parties at Phil's law club, where service men and law students mix, and of camaraderie with his drinking buddies: "I took four quart milk bottles and went over to the Bishop hotel and got some beer. Then we sat around and smoked pipes and talked and the Boche [an ex–German soldier he has explained earlier] sang us some German drinking songs."[28]

On weekends he and Phil took streetcars to the shore and roamed the beaches, where they gazed at girls and sunned themselves. Describing one such excursion, Faulkner serves up an unsteady mix of interior monologue and conflicted images of the feminine imaginary from his early poetry that will reach fruition in Quentin Compson's wild figurations merging blackness and the feminine as he conflates and juxtaposes past and present forbidden, erotic images of "dirty" Natalie, the "little dirty" Italian girl he calls "sister," and his lost "virgin" sister, Caddy. Here the whiteness sails above, clean and chaste: "tiny white sails on the water and tiny white clouds, like their reflections in the sky, ambling along as gravely and demurely as very clean little girls on Sunday mornings." Meanwhile the blackness is sandwiched in between: "And canoes—one with the o sub aquatic propensiter of a U-boat—and Irish girls and teeth and chewing gum and the filthy, sturdy, unkillable infants of the very poor—verily, they shall inherit the earth—and the rustling of the sea like a ballroom full of ladies in silken dresses. We [Phil and he] lay on the sand and my hair is becoming sunburned on top again and didn't think and had a wonderful [*sic*]." On other Saturday afternoons and Sundays they go off to local sporting events like Yale-Harvard baseball games, boat races, and lacrosse matches, where the goalie is costumed "like . . . a deep-sea diver" and a player comes "tearing down the field with the ball in his 'Crosse' like a rock in a butterfly net."[29]

These and the rest of Falkner's 170 extant letters home, which he wrote during his five extended absences from Oxford (a total of almost twenty-two months), between April 1918 and December 1925, continually document his parents' economic and emotional support, despite the family's modest means. Most parents of a young man Faulkner's age would have eyed his way of life with trepidation, if not despair. Yet on the surface, it appears that between the ages of twenty and twenty-seven, Billy was on a perpetual paid vacation. Nonetheless he did hold jobs—in 1918 in New Haven and later that year in Canada, where he served for twenty-two weeks as a cadet-in-training for the CRAF, and in 1921 for a few weeks in New York clerking for Elizabeth Prall (later Anderson) at "Lord and Taylor's bookshop."[30] On all his sojourns, Maud and Murry Falkner made sure the oldest of their four sons received a constant flow of mail, goods, services, and money. "I got" the candy, the money, or various pieces of clothing is a constant refrain in these letters, which Faulkner wrote on the average of once every five days. Chocolate cakes whose icing is "good and bitter and rich," cookies, cheese, boxes of fudge, books and magazines, jams and jellies, and cans of tobacco pour in.[31] Shirts and coat-sleeve linings are made to Billy's explicit (and sometimes illustrated) specifications. Sheets and blankets are sent off. Overcoats and raincoats arrive when requested. As Faulkner himself remarks, "I think every time I write home, it is to say— Such and such a thing arrived safely, but I believe I do get something every day, so there is nothing for me to need."[32]

As these letters reveal, Maud and Murry were wiser and far more tolerant, generous, and loving in these years than any published biography has indicated. This is not to say that they were paragons or that they could not also be withdrawn, distant, or downright mean and cruel. Faulkner learned his legendary meanness and cruelty, as well as his remarkable generosity, from his earliest teachers. This is also not to say they were unconcerned. Although we don't have their portion of this correspondence, we can hear their anxiety echoed in their son's reassuring responses. On another trip East in 1921, first from New Haven and then from New York, he writes, "Now, Mother don't you be down hearted as I intend having the time of my life here," and "For heaven's sake, dont think I feel neglected. I take yours and my love for granted so much that I never worry about it at all. Cheer up! That's the first trace of exasperation I ever saw in your letters." From New Orleans in 1925, where he has gone to catch a freighter bound for Europe, he writes Maud: "I was so glad to hear from you; I was worried a little, your face looked so white and despairing. I'm so *darned* glad you and pop are willing for me to make the trip [to Europe] even though you think it foolish."[33]

Faulkner's letters to his parents dispel the notion that he went to New Haven as a despondent and rejected lover and document the extent to which Phil cared for Billy. In addition, they explain, perhaps, the primary source of his immense self-confidence and drive: Maud's *and*, it appears, Murry's trust and faith in his genius, a faith that frees him to tell them when he's homesick or having trouble writing, or to reveal his imagination at work in passages of lyric flights, tall tales, and thumbnail profiles. One week he writes, "[I] have an idea for a thing, but I'm enjoying myself too much, sitting in the sun watching the ocean, to write it yet." Then a week later, "have recovered my dog again and have written several things; I have one that is worth money at anytime, same as a commercial paper or a banker's note."[34] He simply knows that one day he will be famous. And in pursuit of this fame he has his parents' moral support and as much financial help as they can afford. He also has the pragmatic advantages of the friendships that Phil Stone and later Stark Young, William Spratling, and Sherwood and Elizabeth Prall Anderson offered.

The Beginning of a Friendship, 1914

Phil Stone and Bill Faulkner's friendship and Stone's mentoring of Faulkner's early work had begun in the summer of 1914. Phil was twenty-one and Billy five years younger in that halcyon summer that is memorialized in all the poetry and fiction of "The Great War." There is a double irony in the genesis of Bill and Phil's friendship. Katrina Carter, who first introduced them, was Estelle's best friend and according to Phil, his girl-friend. The flowering of Bill and Phil's relationship signaled the end of the young men's romantic interests (if, indeed, they had any at that time) in Estelle and Katrina, respectively.[35] Stone's biographer puts it succinctly. In April 1918 "William Faulkner left Oxford for New Haven and Phil Stone. And over an interval of almost 12 years [until Estelle's and Faulkner's marriage in 1929], literature was the only serious 'mistress' either man would have."[36] Phil had invited Bill to New Haven and arranged ahead of time an undemanding clerical job that paid twenty dollars a week, allow-ing the young writer plenty of time to read, write, and simply soak in the experience of living in a world so different from the one he had known for the first twenty years of his life. This was an opportunity that none of Faulkner's other local supporters could offer and one that he would ironi-cally memorialize in 1936 in Miss Rosa Coldfield's opening monologue: "'Because you are going away to attend the college at Harvard they tell me,' Miss Coldfield said. 'So I dont imagine you will ever come back here and settle down as a country lawyer in a little town like Jefferson, since Northern people have already seen to it that there is little left in the South for a young man. So maybe you will enter the literary profession.'" (*AA, 9*)

He also offered Billy an escape from an emotional relationship he was ill equipped to handle, as reflected in his early poetry, fiction, and behavior. At twenty-one, he did not need or want a wife. And once away from home, he found he could still receive his parents' care, especially his mother's, while keeping both at an emotionally more comfortable distance. But best of all, he had discovered another source of nurturance that fulfilled his wish to be mothered (as so many of his fictional boys are) by older, less tal-ented men.

What initially attracted the high school dropout who didn't even read French, much less Latin or Greek, and the patrician, fair-haired, and slightly balding young intellectual with two bachelor degrees and (later) two law degrees?[37] Stone claimed it was their mutual passion for literature that shortly had them "talking day and night of writing and the summer was very pleasant."[38] This is certainly true. In those early imitative poems that Billy showed his new friend, probably his variations on Swinburne's

"Sapphics" and Tennyson's "Atalanta in Calydon" and *The Princess,* Stone thought he recognized Faulkner's gift and began working indefatigably to shape and, later, promote it. Estelle could tell Billy about Hawaii and China, but it was Phil who provided him his first passport to places other than Oxford, Mississippi, and the opportunity to make connections that led to publication. Through Yale and his vast knowledge of Western literature, modern and ancient, Phil was connected to and conversant with an intellectual and collegial world beyond Faulkner's Mississippi. As Faulkner's letters from his 1918 and 1921 sojourns in New Haven reveal, this connection proved invaluable. Stone further expanded Faulkner's horizons by introducing him to another slightly senior Oxfordian, the novelist and New York drama critic Stark Young, who also provided him with the emotional, intellectual, and physical space to explore material he later reworked into the essential fabric of his greatest fiction.

But it was more, much more than that. By virtue of his gender, age, money, and the fact that he was not related to Faulkner, Stone gave Faulkner, whose most supportive readers until this point had been Oxford women, a very different and potentially more powerful audience. Both smart and educated, Stone seemed to have boundless energy and, as we shall see, considerable economic resources that he was willing to place at the service of Faulkner's art. Furthermore, as his April 1918 letter to Miss Rosie describing the care he will shower on his "fine intelligent little fellow" and his subsequent actions over the next seventeen years attest, he was eager to cater to the most infantile needs of the young would-be writer, a task neither Maud nor Estelle (for different reasons) could or would assume. Faulkner knew this. And so, throughout his life he made and discarded friendships with a series of men who served just this function. Stone was the first, and Faulkner's 1918 letters to his parents amply document the services he performed. He would be followed by Stark Young, Sherwood Anderson, William Spratling, the photographer Odiorne, Ben Wasson, and A. I. Bezzerides, among others. Most were silent about Faulkner's abuse and betrayal of their love. But those who did speak out—Stone, Wasson, and Bezzerides—sound like rejected yet uncomprehending suitors.

When asked to comment on the sacrifices genius exacts, Faulkner often said, rather dramatically, that an artist will both rob and destroy anyone in service of his art. Borrowing directly from Dostoyevsky's *Crime and Punishment,* Faulkner claimed: "If a writer has to rob his mother, he will not hesitate; the 'Ode on a Grecian Urn' is worth any number of little old ladies."[39] Clearly, Faulkner's ladies came in more than one gender. His friendship with Stone taught him that certain men could offer him a kind of mothering no woman could supply. When Faulkner no longer needed

Stone, he dropped him. Faulkner's friendship with Anderson, in its broadest outlines, followed a similar pattern. But because Anderson was a thoroughly established and famous writer and because he was threatening in other ways, Faulkner destroyed their friendship and tried to destroy Anderson. His treatment of both Stone and Anderson should have served as a warning to Estelle. But perhaps she didn't want to be warned. As she said, "I have lived a difficult life, but I have never been bored."

17

The Oldham-Franklin Wedding, April 1918

Yes, she was weeping again now; it did, indeed, rain on that marriage.
—Mr. Compson

THE BRIDE'S TEARS also fell at the Oldham-Franklin wedding, but Billy Falkner was not there to see them shed. For Cornell, his marriage that 18 April marked the climax of a sporadic four-year, long-distance courtship begun in June 1914, when the newly minted but empty-pocketed lawyer left Mississippi to seek his fortune in what was then called the Hawaiian Territory. Three years later, when Cornell officially proposed, his success appeared assured. On 1 June 1917, he had resigned from the Honolulu law firm in which he had practiced since his arrival in the summer of 1914 to accept a political appointment he'd been aiming for: deputy attorney general of the American Territory of Hawaii. He was one of the youngest lawyers ever awarded this post. The twenty-five-year-old Mississippian was jubilant; he had garnered an appointment that was considered a plum by Honolulu's American colonials. He would continue to rise. A little less than two years later, on 1 April 1919, President Woodrow Wilson appointed him First Judge of the First Judicial Circuit in the Territory, making him Wilson's youngest judicial appointment.[1] Franklin, who earlier had rejected the offer of an appointment as assistant U.S. district attorney because it paid too poorly, was also pleased with his salary increase.[2] At last he was in a financial position to ask Estelle Oldham's parents if he could marry their eldest daughter.

When he had left Oxford and Columbus in the summer of 1914, he believed he had secured Estelle's word that she would marry him. Estelle herself was mute on this subject. If she was engaged, the record of her social life in the Oxford papers from 1914 to 1917, when Cornell was away, gives no indication of such. During his five years (1909–14) at Ole Miss, during which he earned both his B.A. and LL.B., Cornell had cut quite a swath. He and Estelle had socialized since at least 1912, when, as only high school sophomores, she and Katrina were invited to join The Outlaws social club. Like Phil Stone, Cornell was an older man. As president of his class, he was popular with men and women. The combination may have made it hard not to be somewhat flattered by his interest. When Cornell pressed her before he left Mississippi for Honolulu, it was easier just to say yes than to argue with him. Perhaps in the light of Bill Falkner's increasing preference for Phil's company over hers that summer of 1914, Cornell's apparent infatuation offered some comfort. Besides, she knew he would be gone for some time. Furthermore Cornell, who had had to work while in college and law school to help pay his tuition, had no money to marry on. Finally, he was a formidable figure, accustomed to having his way. Like Thomas Sutpen, whom he resembled somewhat, he had a grand and rigid design in which form often triumphed over substance. For him, his four-year engagement to the Belle of Oxford may well have been such a form. Among his papers, along with the 1913 letters of introduction to Honolulu's legal community, he also kept a letter from a young woman in New Orleans, whom he met sometime between 1914 and 1916 when she was either living in or visiting Hawaii. It indicates he was not totally devoted to Estelle.[3]

Certainly the first months of their marriage were more form than substance. Instead of beginning their life together in a home of their own, Estelle would spend her first four months alone in Honolulu as a houseguest of the Watsons, the family of her husband's former boss. Cornell and she would not move into their own home until they'd been married for almost two years. Yet as early as 1914, Cornell began acquiring the equipment his wife-to-be would need to perform as a proper hostess. On his way to Honolulu he had stopped in Oakland, California, to visit his mother's sister, Jessie, and her two young daughters. There he had bought paintings (her copies of Old Masters) and the silver pieces he needed to complete his antique coffee and tea set.[4] Now, three years later, he was ready to support a wife.

Like Thomas Sutpen, however, Cornell assumed that Estelle's lovely and well-mannered surface mirrored an equally pliant interior. He did not know that she might enjoy manly pleasures like drinking, smoking, and gambling or that, as she makes clear in "Dr. Wohlenski," she was not a ladies' woman or a joiner. In return, most women cared no more for her than she claimed to care for them. "She was like a little partridge, a beautiful figure, lovely teeth and hair, and with charm too. She had everything," said Billy Falkner's cousin Sallie Murry. Then she added, "She was fast as a girl and in the Orient she played majong for high stakes."[5] Other contemporary accounts of Estelle are similar. "I remember Estelle getting drunk on

17.1. Estelle's first husband, Cornell Sidney Franklin, 1918.
(Courtesy of Victoria Fielden Johnson)

'cat' liquor. I never touched 'cat.' I only drank bonded. She was always doing something outrageous," recalled a Columbus contemporary.[6] Whether
these accounts were accurate is not so clear. Estelle did violate rules governing Southern Belles in conspicuous ways. Besides smoking and drinking,
she acknowledged her sexuality and her desirability. What she didn't seem
to understand was that despite all the men she attracted and the women
who felt threatened by her, she was still, at the most basic level, a piece of
valuable property. Until she married Cornell in 1918, her parents owned
her; until her divorce, she was owned by Cornell. This was one of the lessons she learned from her first marriage; it is a subject that she explores in
ever more complicated ways in the stories she began writing while married
to Cornell. And as the Caddys and the Judiths and the Clyties and the Ro-
sas of Faulkner's fiction show, it was a subject that became fascinating to
him as well.

By June 1917, when Cornell wrote his letter of proposal, almost three years had passed since he had made the seven-day, twenty-one-hundred-mile crossing by steamer from San Francisco and to Honolulu. Voted "Most Likely to Be a Millionaire" by his Ole Miss Law School class in 1914, Cornell appeared on his way to fulfilling that prediction.[7] With his quick mind, charm, and expertise at bridge and on the polo fields, he quickly carved out a place for himself in the island's legal and social circles. A network of Mississippi connections had smoothed his way into Honolulu's colonial power structure: he arrived bearing three glowing letters of reference to his fellow Columbian, Judge A. S. Humphries, from the Ole Miss chancellor and its law faculty;[8] in addition, his uncle, Malcolm A. Franklin, was then Collector of Customs for the Port of Honolulu. Nonetheless, Cornell's success was due largely to his drive, intelligence, and excellent ability to manage money and people. In December 1914, six months after his arrival, he had been admitted to the bar in Hawaii (California Court System, Ninth Circuit). From that December until his government appointment, he was in private practice with the law firm of Thompson, Milverton, and Cathcart.

Like Billy Falkner, Cornell was smart; unlike him, he demonstrated it in the usual ways. Besides maintaining an average that hovered between A and B plus, he was a campus leader.[9] Again unlike Billy, Cornell throve on athletic competition and lots of socializing, the staples of the American colonial communities of Honolulu as well as Shanghai, where he would spend most of his life. Besides belonging to three sports teams, he was a member of numerous campus social clubs including The Outlaws.

In 1913 Cornell had graduated as president of his undergraduate class. After one more year of study he earned his LL.B. degree and was admitted to the Mississippi Bar in May 1914, shortly before leaving to find work in the Hawaiian Territory. His quest for the wealth his father's early death had denied him began three months before the August assassination in Sarajevo that signaled the beginning of World War I.[10] It was hardly the best of times. Yet, considering his circumstances—that he began with little or no capital—he was remarkably successful.

Of all the places he could have chosen to settle, Hawaii, on the surface at least, presented an economic system of racial and class exploitation that Cornell found very familiar.[11] In many respects, the United States (aided in this process by European colonial powers) had transformed these islands, annexed in 1898, into what certain parts of the American South might have become had there been no Civil War. Contrary to the popular view of the islands as a "polyracial paradise" and the "showcase of American democracy," this colony was owned and controlled by a white Euro-American oligarchy consisting of a tiny minority of white plantation owners who

17.2. Cornell Franklin's "Southern Mansion" in Shanghai, c. 1935.
(Courtesy of Cornell Franklin, Jr.)

controlled the "so-called Oligarchy" of corporations known by 1915 as the Big Five.[12] In 1915 the islands' sixty sugar plantations made this Territory the fourth largest cane sugar producer in the world, exceeded only by what was then British India, Cuba, and Java. These plantations employed some fifty thousand laborers at a monthly wage of twenty to twenty-six dollars.

Like Thomas Sutpen, only a century later, Cornell Franklin went to the colonies to make his fortune. And like Sutpen, the first thing he did when, after divorcing Estelle, he began to make a good living in Shanghai, was build a white-washed brick Southern plantation mansion and stables that rivaled any Hollywood set in *Gone with the Wind* (see fig. 17.2).

But in 1917, rather than marry into a local family in the Hawaiian Territory and risking the possibility of mixed blood, he planned a more conservative and seemingly safer marriage into a family that, like his, could trace its American roots back into New England's Puritan soil. At some point during his last summer in Mississippi, at least as far as Cornell was concerned, he and Estelle Oldham, then seventeen, had reached an understanding, one he recalled in his letter to her mother, Lida, which he wrote in the flush of his first major legal and political appointment on the letterhead of the Office of the Attorney General, Territory of Hawaii. Full of the anticipatory pride of ownership and dated 22 June 1917, it reads:

My dear Mrs Oldham,

The last time I asked you for Estelle you ran into the house without giving me an answer. Now I am going to ask you again and this time I hope you will give her to me. I have loved her ever since the first time John Dinsmore took me to call and she met us at the door in a pink frock, with a rose at her waist, looking like a fresh rosebud herself. When I returned to the campus and Bill Bailey teased me about robbing the cradle my heart fluttered so that I knew then I was in love with your daughter. And I have known it ever since. If you give her to me I will do all in my power to make her happy. Her happiness and her well-being will be my chief aim in life and with me she will always come first.

It is no small matter to have Estelle leave you and especially when her home will be as far away as Hawaii. But I can assure you that she will be living in the most beautiful spot in the world and among some of the finest people I have ever known. And Honolulu does not seem as far away to those in Honolulu as it does to those at home.

Estelle has of course told you that she and I have been engaged since my last summer in Oxford [June 1914] so you see we are not "rushing in where angels fear to tread." After standing the test of three years separation I think we are safe. If I can possibly get away from my new official duties this fall we plan to be married then, otherwise next April. Everything is so unsettled now because of the war that it is impossible to make plans very far ahead.

My homecoming will be greatly saddened by the absence of little Ned [the Oldhams' fourth and youngest child, who died of rheumatic fever at age eight in December 1916]. I always associate you and he together. I often think and laugh over his telling you—"I heard Gouger tell Sister he loved her." You had my deepest sympathy when the bright little fellow was taken away.

I am sure Victoria [Tochie] is glad to be at home [from boarding school] once more. Ask her if she is going to the front as a nurse.

My love to all of you. May I sign myself

Your son,

Cornell[13]

In the photograph of Estelle that Cornell carried with him to Honolulu, she does indeed look like the girl-child of this letter (see fig. 17.3). She parts her pretty lips in a tentative smile revealing slight spaces between her tiny, perfectly aligned front teeth and adding fullness to her already round cheeks that have yet to lose their baby fat. A black woman, probably Missy

17.3. Estelle Oldham, c. 1913. In 1914, Cornell took this photo of Estelle with him when he went to settle in Honolulu. (Courtesy of Cornell Franklin, Jr.)

Robinson (by then Nolia Cottrell had become the Oldhams' cook), has carefully coifed and dressed Estelle's hair into a chignon fastened with feathers. But already a stray curl that was meant to frame her brow has escaped and sticks up rakishly, adding a wonderful ingenuousness and spontaneity to her expression in an otherwise highly formal portrait. The demure curve of her slightly scoop-necked taffeta gown scalloped with tiny rosebuds reveals the soft, childlike contours of her throat and shoulders. In it we see the image Cornell probably had before him on his desk as he wrote Estelle's mother his formal proposal.

What did it mean to a seventeen-year-old Southern girl from a "good" family in Oxford, Mississippi, in the summer of 1914 to be "engaged" to a young man five years her senior who took off for a foreign country thousands of miles away to make his fortune? Not very much, judging from her account and the local and university newspaper reports of Estelle's social activities at the time and over the next few years.[14] We have neither her mother's nor her own letters from this period, and the extant fragmentary evidence—as it is with most complicated people—is mixed. Cornell's letter sounds as if he is simply letting her mother know of two pledges, one made three years ago and one made perhaps as recently as within the last month, to which he and Estelle have agreed. However, the fact that her mother ran into their house without answering Cornell "the last time I asked you for Estelle" (June 1914) suggests that he had proposed unsuccessfully at least once and that the response, even from Estelle's parents, who are supposed to have been wildly in favor of this marriage, had not been promising. In one of Estelle's few surviving letters she writes retrospectively in 1929 of the "ghastly fear and abhorrence" she felt on leaving home after marrying him.[15] In the 1960s, trying to explain her first marriage to an interviewer, she said arranged marriages were not uncommon in her circle.[16] She also observed that although the Franklin and Oldham families knew each other well, and she "loved" Cornell's mother, Mamie Hairston, that Cornell had never paid any attention to her until he saw that "I would serve his purposes."[17] (Her repetition here of the phrase Mr. Compson uses when describing Sutpen's "design" may be either deliberate or uncanny. Unfortunately, her interviewer never asked her to elaborate.) Katrina Carter, who was one of her bridesmaids, said that just before Estelle walked down the aisle to be married, she turned to her and confessed, "I don't know whether I love Cornell, or if I want to marry him." Estelle told Joseph Blotner that she spent the night before her wedding in tears.[18] According to her, she was really in love with Bill Falkner and, but for Billy's insistence that they have both sets of parents' approval, would have eloped with him.[19]

Had she been interested primarily in a rich husband, she would not have chosen Cornell—even in 1917. She had plenty of reasonably well-off suitors in Oxford. In fact, because their money was family money, the economic risk in choosing them over Cornell was much less. Katherine Andrews, who grew up with Estelle and Faulkner and was a regular visitor at the Oldhams, commented, "The boys Mrs. Oldham would have liked for Estelle to marry were Henry Watson and Carl Smith. They were from prominent families, and rich too. I don't know why they didn't marry Estelle."[20] Why, then, did she choose to marry someone who, according to what she told her parents, an aunt, and Katrina Carter, she didn't love and who would take her to live in a country that in those days was at least a two-week journey from those who did love her and whom she loved in return?

Cornell's 1917 proposal letter gives some clues about external events (some related, some unrelated to Billy Falkner) that contributed to what I would call Estelle's increasing sense that she had little to offer beyond her looks and charm, even after her highly successful year at Mary Baldwin. To say she was merely a victim of her environment would be simplistic and inaccurate and provide as little understanding of her and her relationships with other people, particularly with her second husband, as earlier appraisals. She was both a product and, to some extent and under certain circumstances, a supporter of many of the values her parents and Oxford instilled. For her to deny and so lose her sense that her intellect was to be cultivated, used, and, most of all, prized, as she quickly did when she became a coed at Ole Miss in 1914, therefore placed her in a much more comfortable social position. People in Oxford made it clear that only girls like plain little Lucy Somerville, who excelled in their studies, might be among the two or three women in a class who went on to male bastions of professionalism like law or medical school.

For anyone, but particularly for adolescents in a small, essentially rural Southern town, it would have been almost imperative to have a companion in rebellion, or if not that, the support of one's parent(s). But Estelle's best friend, Katrina, left in the summer of 1917 to do YMCA volunteer work in Washington, an acceptable occupation for a marriageable Oxford woman too pretty to be permitted a profession. Her other companion in small mischiefs, her daredevil younger sister, Tochie, had also gone off to Washington in the fall of 1916 for her year of finishing school.[21] In the summer of 1917, Estelle had neither companions nor supporters.

Yet another contributing factor pushing Estelle into marriage, and perhaps more particularly motherhood, is also alluded to in Cornell's letter. On 1 December 1916, Ned, the Oldhams' youngest child and only son, died suddenly. He was the boy-child whom Lem and Lida saw as their immortality, the son who would fulfill their dreams. He was also a charming child whom Lem and Lida loved very much. In a note written to himself and found among his papers after his death, Lem recorded his grief: "During the last illness of my precious boy Ned, someone I believe Florrie Friedman, sent him some pink carnations. As I was leaving the sick room, just about three days before his death he said: 'Daddy, I want you to put one of my carnations in the lapel of your coat.' I did so and wore it until his death. The last gift from the 'Little Major' to Daddy." Born on Christmas Day in 1907, Estelle's little brother died twenty-four days before his ninth birthday.[22] Another reparation Estelle could make by marrying Cornell was to give her parents a son (in-law) who was a real major. It may be that chance was responsible for Estelle's becoming pregnant within weeks of her wedding, but the fact that she did not become pregnant again until 1923 suggests that either her wish to "replace" Ned or pressure from her parents or husband to produce a (male) heir played a role in the early pregnancy.

Thus, for Estelle, the years following her return from Mary Baldwin, while filled with a lively social life, were also marked more deeply by a series of losses. The devaluation of her intellect was implied by Billy's choice of Phil Stone and other men as his primary companions. Billy's already serious addiction to alcohol encoded his preferences in other ways. Several factors may have contributed to her apparent lack of further intellectual development and continued academic success: her experience as a coed at the university; her parents' failure to be interested in, and perhaps even their active discouragement of, her intellectual achievement; and the loss of her close and probably daily relationships with her sister and Katrina. Finally, her younger brother's death filled out the list of Estelle's personal losses. Although these losses differed in nature, their common effect seems to have been to push her toward conformity. Conformity for the Oldhams and for Oxford meant an appropriate marriage. For Estelle, marriage to Cornell was also, she may have thought, a means of coping with her losses.

But it is still not yet clear what happened between Estelle and Bill that convinced her it was hopeless to think she would ever marry him—and, perhaps, even that she should. The changing dynamics of Estelle's and Bill's outward circumstances and inner lives had a tremendous effect during these years, when both were trying so hard, as adolescents do, to find themselves in the welter of possible models imaged in the grown members of their families, their slightly older peers, and the culture at large. Bill's, his father's, and his grandfather's increasing dependence on alcohol between 1912 and 1918 and Murry's increasingly precarious financial state are well documented. There was already a high degree of tolerance and even encouragement of both early and heavy drinking (for white men) in Oxford, a situation exacerbated by Prohibition, but the real test of masculinity was being able to hold your liquor. Faulkner's grandfather, father, and Billy himself all failed it. In the summer of 1912 it seemed that father, son, and grandfather were vying for the title of town drunk. The summer of 1913 was the first one in which Billy worked as a bookkeeper in his grandfather's bank. In one of his somewhat mythical autobiographical reconstructions for the press (but one that he repeated privately and at a much later date) he dated the beginning of his daily drinking from that summer, during which he made the first of several failed attempts to hold a traditional kind of job: "Quit school after five years in seventh grade. Got job in Grandfather's bank and learned the medicinal value of his liquor. Grandfather thought the janitor did it. Hard on janitor."[23] Like so many of his fictional white boys, did Billy's father or grandfather force him to drink as part of his initiation into "manhood"? What was Billy self-medicating for? What did he want to obliterate? What did he not want to feel? Was he so sickened and humiliated by his father's failures that he resorted to this "medicine"? Did Estelle's imminent departure for Mary Baldwin mean that he was trying to cope with another anticipated loss of his own? In his story "Moonlight," which Faulkner claimed was the first he ever wrote, a sixteen-year-old boy, rebuffed by the girl he thinks loves him, drowns his sorrows and humiliation in his father's bootleg whiskey. It's a routine to which Faulknerian boys and men often resort. Such sots are often distanced with irony or humor, particularly in early fiction like "Moonlight" and in his first two novels. But as his work matures and Faulkner probes deeper levels of consciousness and motivation, he writes more and more about the tragic implications of such drinking. His characters drink to numb feelings of loss that are too intense to bear, or drink is used to brutalize helpless children like the young soldier in his first novel and, later, Temple Drake and Benjy Compson. Again and again, alcoholism, like racism, is taught from generation to generation. It has a similar effect: it paralyzes and dehumanizes.[24]

We do not have the Oldhams' reply to Cornell's letter of 1917, but the circumstances outlined above argue that his proposal came at a most opportune moment. Furthermore, by December 1917 he had added to his luster by joining the National Guard of Hawaii, where he was appointed to the office of judge advocate general, with the rank of major, the same rank his prospective father-in-law had held from 1912 to 1917 as a member of the Mississippi National Guard.[25] Needless to say, Lem Oldham retained his military title and took pride in it until his death.

Events may have intervened: in 1917 the United States entered World War I, and the United States government commandeered all passenger ships for the use of its troops and to save fuel. Or perhaps the Oldhams simply preferred an April wedding. In any case, this time they accepted Cornell's proposal, and by April 1918 the *Oxford Eagle* announced that he would arrive in Oxford on 12 April.

No time was allowed for Estelle and Cornell to become reacquainted. Throughout the six days preceding their marriage on Thursday, 18 April, they attended a nonstop series of bridge parties and dinners given in their honor. Wedding invitations, ordered from Tiffany & Co., announced that the marriage of Major and Mrs. Lemuel Earle Oldham's daughter Estelle would take place at the First Presbyterian Church at 7:30 in the evening.[26]

Tennessee Williams's grandfather, the Reverend W. E. Dakin, then a good friend of Cornell's mother, Mamie, performed an Episcopal ceremony. The Oldhams were not regular churchgoers, and their parents had been Baptists and Methodists, as had Estelle's prospective mother-in-law's. But both families were moving up socially; an important step in that process was joining the Episcopal Church. Mamie had known the Reverend Dakin when he was the rector of St. Paul's Episcopal Church in the staid old river town of Columbus. But recently he had been lured to Clarksdale, which the newly rich Delta planters had transformed into a boom town complete with gambling establishments and related entertainments.

Spring comes early in Northern Mississippi, so by April, roses, peonies, and lilies were in full bloom. On Estelle's wedding morning, Lida and her servants gathered flowers from her gardens and the gardens of all her friends. Servants carried them to the church, where she supervised the decorating. It was a magnificent, theatrical display. Standards of candles and tall potted palms formed the background for arrangements of countless lilies and roses. As guests found their seats and waited for the ceremony to begin, Estelle's Aunt Maude Mabry from Kosciusko and a group of her mother's friends performed a musical program. Mendelssohn's *Wedding March,* played by the church organist, signaled the entrance of the wedding party. Estelle's bridesmaids, Florrie Friedman, Nina Somerville, and Katrina Carter, and her maid of honor, Tochie, entered wearing long gowns of pink georgette crepe and carrying bouquets of Radiance roses. They were followed by the matron of honor, Cornell's mother, Mamie Hairston. Her ample frame was draped in a full-length gown of orchid satin and georgette crepe and she carried a bouquet of peonies and ferns. Estelle's little cousin from New Orleans, Blanche Mills, followed, scattering along the white pathway large, fragrant peony petals in shades of white, pale pink, and deep rose. Estelle, looking much thinner, her once thick eyebrows now plucked into a fashionably penciled line, entered on her father's arm. For the occasion he, like Cornell, was dressed in his major's uniform. Estelle's dress was made of white satin brocade trimmed in rose point lace, with a court train. She carried a shower of orchids and lilies of the valley. In her dark, shining hair was a coronet of orange blossoms from which hung her bridal veil. Cornell, resplendent in his white dress uniform, complete with masses of gold braid and a saber, met Estelle and her father at the altar. At the ceremony's completion the bride and groom exited together under an arch of glinting crossed sabers.

Afterward the Oldhams held a reception at their house on South Street. Decorated throughout "with a color scheme of pink, white, and green the house was ablaze with light and color." According to the Columbus paper, "gorgeous roses were used in every available place and the dining room was especially festive." There, the guests assembled for champagne and the cutting of the cake.[27] Their wedding cake contained Estelle's wedding ring and numerous prizes for the guests. Estelle and Cornell cut the first piece with Cornell's sword. In the library the couple's wedding gifts were on display. According to the *Eagle*, tables were "loaded with linens, silver, cut glass, and rare miscellaneous gifts."[28] In 1926, when Cornell demanded that she leave Shanghai, Estelle left most of these gifts behind.

The local papers reported effusively on the wedding ceremony, decor, dress, and food, all of which defined for the Oldhams perhaps the most important day in their public lives. Estelle's contemporaries, even in their nineties, still described it as the most memorable wedding they ever attended. There are no surviving photographs to document the event.

Estelle and Cornell left their reception after a little over an hour to catch the last train to Memphis. Arriving there shortly before midnight, they caught a taxi to the Peabody Hotel, where they spent their wedding night, before traveling on to Washington via Bristol and Lynchburg for five days of visiting with relatives there and in other nearby states.[29] They then returned to Cornell's mother's home in Columbus for two weeks of picnics, teas, luncheons, bridge parties, and dinner dances. Their honeymoon was not much of a private affair. They were constantly with family and friends, which is not surprising, given that this was Cornell's first trip home since the summer of 1914. To be always on display and on one's best behavior would have been a strain for anyone. Any ambivalence she felt about her choice had to be masked; besides, within a few weeks of her marriage, she had become pregnant.

By the first week in May the couple had returned to Oxford so that Estelle could serve as matron of honor in Tochie's much less lavish wedding to Pete Allen, on 6 May; on the 9th the Oldhams gave another party in the newlyweds' honor.[30] Afterward Cornell left again for Columbus, and Pete Allen, who was stationed in Atlanta, returned to his base. The two newly wed and already pregnant sisters were at home again with their parents until 21 May.[31] On that Tuesday, Estelle left to join her husband in Columbus, and Tochie took the train to Atlanta. A week later Estelle and Cornell returned to Oxford once more before boarding the train that took them to the West Coast, where they would catch a steamship to Honolulu. Their wedding announcement had said they would be "at home" in Honolulu on the first of June. But the war would change all that.

18

Marriage in the "Crossroads of the Pacific," June–September 1918

STELLE LEFT NO ACCOUNT of the first three years of her marriage and her life in Hawaii other than her statements to her daughter, Jill, and her granddaughter, Victoria Johnson, saying that she had loved living there. There are no surviving letters from friends or family and no record of contact with Bill Faulkner while there. (Recall that like Estelle, he, too, had changed his name the summer of 1918—when he enlisted in the Royal Canadian Air Force.) What follows is therefore a speculative reconstruction based on Cornell Franklin's business correspondence, official documents, archival sources like newspapers (especially the social pages), government records, and interviews with people who knew the Franklins in Honolulu. However, Estelle's fiction provides another rich source, as it did for her childhood, particularly her short story "A Crossing," which is valuable for two reasons. As a psychosocial commentary on the American colonial scene and as a psychological portrayal of a naïve American girl trapped in that world, it offers insight into Estelle's retrospective understanding of her place as the wife of an American colonial. When it is also read, as it should be, as Estelle's response to and revision of Faulkner's 1920 dream-play, *The Marionettes*, which he gave to her that summer, it provides evidence of a reopened literary dialogue and imaginative collaboration that was fed and flourished with Estelle's absence from Oxford and her marriage to Cornell.

"A Crossing" tells the story of an unworldly pretty girl's literal and metaphoric crossing: her seduction, betrayal, and ultimately forced marriage to a man she doesn't love. Edna Earl Tomlinson has always been the pawn of her elders. Raised by her mother to be a missionary and so "atone" for the sins of her father's family (their "bad blood"), she is ignorant of worldly pleasures and people. The story's setting was one Estelle knew well: a passenger steamer bound from San Francisco to Shanghai, with a layover in Honolulu. Her adventures begin when she sets sail unchaperoned for her missionary post in China. Her ship, the *S.S. President Adams,* is a den of various iniquities. It and Honolulu are the sites of Edna Earl's loss of innocence, her momentary rebellion, and then her very problematic shipboard marriage. Perhaps marking Edna Earl as part of her self, Estelle used her father's middle name and the first initial of her own. This and Chapters 20 and 21 read Estelle's first marriage and her renewed intellectual relationship with Bill Faulkner in these dual contexts.

Perhaps on their first voyage to the Hawaiian Territory Cornell abandoned his usual parsimony to sail first-class on a Matson Line steamer.[1] Despite his popularity, one of Cornell's campus nicknames was "Tightwad Corny." On future trips home during the time they lived in Honolulu, Estelle always took a troop transport ship, because the difference in fare was about $7 a day as opposed to about $160 one-way on the Matson Line.[2] There were only two classes: first class, for $65 and up (in 1915), and steerage, for $35.[3] Cornell's Aunt Bessie, who lived in Oakland, saw them off at the San Francisco docks. Like her fictional Edna Earl, Estelle had said good-bye to all her relatives when she left her small town in the middle of the continent. Like Billy's trip from Oxford to New York, Estelle's train trip across the continent also marked her first venture out of the South. Despite her physical discomfort and homesickness, she enjoyed the adventure of it all. Her early years of living with Faulkner and their infant daughter at Rowan Oak, which lacked central heating, running water, and electricity, make clear that she was not averse to roughing it. Like Billy two months earlier when he first arrived in New Haven, she, too, had never seen the sea before. Like him and like most people, she was struck by its colors, its vastness, and the eerie phosphorescence trailing through the ship's wake on dark nights. Almost four decades later, she re-created this experience in abstract ocean canvases she began painting after Faulkner's death.

Whether, like her lovely, leggy Edna Earl in "A Crossing," she was so alternately or simultaneously seasick and drunk that she had no memory of her first crossing is not known. Whether Cornell's shipboard behavior inspired the bisexual, seductive Madame Tingot, who plies Edna Earl with champagne cocktails and gorgeous gowns to bend her to her will, is a matter for conjecture. Whether Madame Tingot's estranged, "foreign," and feminized but equally seductive husband (originally an artist) also sprang from an autobiographical inspiration is unknown. It is a fact, however, that the boozy and sexually volatile climate Edna Earl enters when she boards the *S.S. President Adams* resembles the colonial world Estelle entered once the Franklins landed in Honolulu.

In 1918, steamers took at least half an hour to navigate around the live coral reef that protected the bay and pass the looming point cradling the 761-foot-high volcanic crater called Diamond Head before the city of Honolulu came into view. The water was crystal clear for hundreds of feet below the surface, and Estelle, as her series of abstract underwater seascapes shows, would have been fascinated by the reef's shoals, which in the 1920s were still pink and green and buff, depending on the nature of the sea floor and angle of the light.

Honolulu, which means "quiet haven," was already a noisy, busy, and crowded commercial port. Between 1910 and 1920, it was experiencing huge growth (its population rose from 52,183 to 83,327).[4] Although the island of Oahu is only forty-six miles long and twenty-five miles wide, its major city, compared to Oxford, Mississippi, was immense and cosmopolitan.

As they entered the harbor, immigration and customs officers boarded their ship. Among them was a familiar face—Cornell's uncle, Malcolm Franklin, the Collector of Customs, a position that under the wartime dry laws imposed in 1918 by Executive Order made him a great favorite with military officers. His blatant violations of the rules he had been hired to enforce, coupled with his alcoholism, would result in his forced resignation from his job in 1921 and his unhappy return to Columbus, Mississippi.[5] But when he welcomed his nephew's new bride to Hawaii in June 1918, he was, as Honolulu's society pages document, at the height of his career. Malcolm is important to Estelle's story for four reasons. First, as the friend of another Mississippian, the man who became brigadier general of Schofield Barracks, he helped further Cornell's military career. Second, when Malcolm lost his job and returned to Columbus, the letters he wrote to his nephew remain the only written evidence of how unhappy Estelle was, how essential booze was to the daily lives of the Franklin and Oldham men, and how precarious the Franklins' marriage and finances were. Third, Uncle Malcolm interested Estelle as a character and familiar type, in Oxford and abroad. In her Shanghai story, "Star Spangled Banner Stuff," she drew a brief but observant portrait of the behavior of an over-the-hill colonial alcoholic who passes his time in the bar at his club trying to pretend he can make it there each morning without a drink. Fourth, this fictional portrait, like her portrayal of Edna Earl's disoriented state in "A Crossing" and so much else in her stories written between 1922 and 1924, would have resonated with Bill Faulkner.

Also waiting to greet Estelle and Cornell were Judge Watson, Franklin's mentor, and his wife, Louise, who took the newlyweds to stay with them and their two daughters, Virginia Bradley (b. 1907) and Lillie Moore (b. 1912). The Watsons were a bit younger than Estelle's parents; Virginia, the eldest of their two daughters, had been born the same year as Estelle's youngest sister, Dorothy. From June until September 1918, when Cornell received his commission in the regular army and the Franklins were given officers' quarters at Schofield Barracks, Estelle remained the perpetual houseguest of the Watsons.[6] Yet Louise was too old and her daughters too young to have been friends for Estelle. A few times during this period, Estelle paid weekend visits to new friends she had made. Whether Estelle knew of this strained living arrangement prior to setting sail for Hawaii is not known. The Franklins' wedding announcement suggests not. If not, this was the first of several important decisions affecting their marriage that Cornell would make on his own.

The Watsons lived in a rambling one-story Victorian cottage set well back from the two bordering streets that formed a lushly planted peninsula-like lot at the intersection of Thurston Avenue and Green Street. Their heavily canopied garden was among the largest in this middle-class residential neighborhood, located just a few miles from the docks and the downtown area.[7]

Louise Watson was a piece of work. Although she could be charming in public and to visitors, within her own home she was often "domineering and bossy." Her children were terrified of her.[8] In the Watson household, according to a mutual friend of the Watsons and the Oldhams, "if you weren't already an alcoholic, you could easily become one. She [Estelle] was in the home of a lady who insisted on it the minute you came in the door—'Come on and have a drink.'"[9] Colonial memoirs and letters from and interviews with relatives of Americans in Cornell's and Malcolm Franklin's crowd in Honolulu, many of them also Mississippians, confirm that drinking a great deal was central to American colonial life in those years, particularly among the Bourbon Democrats, to whom Cornell owed his first job and his later government appointments.

Booze was so pervasive in their world that in 1937, when Estelle's daughter, Cho-Cho, then twenty years old, and her own baby daughter went to Shanghai to live with her father, Cornell made it clear to her that being able to hold her liquor was as essential to success in Shanghai's international settlement as good manners, expertise in bridge (and for men, polo as well), and a chic wardrobe. One of the first questions he asked her was "Do you smoke and drink?" When she answered no, he said, "Well you've got to learn to do both if you live in Shanghai."[10] As Franklin explained once, any "young American lawyer who was honest and could stay sober" and was proficient at polo "could make a fortune" in Shanghai.[11] However, feature stories in the English language papers of both Honolulu and Shanghai report on the many men and women who were not up to the task. Another North Mississippian, Dr. Anne Fearn, a well-liked Shanghai doctor, hostess, and activist, became both the obstetrician and a friend of Estelle's. In 1923 she delivered the Franklins' son, Malcolm. During the last decade of her long general practice she owned and ran a sanatorium that treated a large number of colonials addicted to alcohol, opium, or both. In her memoir she writes sympathetically and at length about this and other social and economic ills of colonization.[12]

A card enclosed with Cornell and Estelle's wedding invitation (and printed before the country's entry into the war) had announced that the couple would be "at home after the first of June at Honolulu, Hawaii" but gave no address. No one could have anticipated that immediately after the couple's arrival in Honolulu, Cornell, who was a major in the National Guard when war was declared, would have to report to Schofield Barracks for training. On Saturday, 1 June, three weeks before the Franklins' arrival in Honolulu, the Hawaiian National Guard had been mobilized. That night its thirty-three hundred men, including Cornell's First Hawaiian Infantry, reported for duty at Iolani Palace.

A newspaper article in the *Advertiser* of 2 July explains what Cornell did on his return to Honolulu and why he left Estelle to fend for herself within the first few days of landing in Hawaii. The headline reads: "Is Major One Day / Private the Next / Sergeant the Third: Cornell Franklin Resigns Commission to Enter Army as Draftee, Is Promptly Promoted to Non-Com, May Be Officer Again." It then explains why he resigned: "When the two National Guard Units were ordered to active duty a month ago Major Franklin was returning from Mississippi accompanied by his bride. As no one in the Judge Advocate's department was called to active duty, Major Franklin decided immediately upon arrival here, to accept the call of the draft board, resign his commission, and be just one of the 4992 drafted men from the Territory of Hawaii."[13]

This meant that Cornell spent June through August, the first three months of their marriage, in boot camp at Schofield Barracks, which was twenty-six miles from Honolulu. Some seven months later, when he applied to U.S. Attorney General T. W. Gregory for an appointment as First Judge of the First Judicial Circuit of the Territory of Hawaii, Cornell reiterated his reasons for resigning from the Guard: "When the National Guard was mobilized on June 1st, 1918, I was Judge Advocate General with the rank of Major. Due to the fact that none of the staff officers were called into Federal service, I resigned my commission and entered the ranks. After attending a regimental school for three months I was commissioned Second Lieutenant and have since been promoted to First Lieutenant."[14]

Perhaps he was driven by simple patriotism, but this letter and subsequent actions throughout his life suggest a more calculated motive. Had he remained an officer in the National Guard, he would have been shipped overseas with all the other reserve forces as soon as he returned from the States. By enlisting he avoided being sent to the European Front. Instead, after attending regimental school, he was quickly promoted to First Lieutenant on the basis of his prior service and served out the remainder of the war as aide-de-camp to Brigadier General John Heard, the commander of Schofield Barracks. His role became that of social secretary, and part of his duties included playing polo, the game that (in combination with his legal connections) was to open the way for the Franklins' move to Shanghai at the end of 1921. But none of this would happen until after he received his commission in early fall 1919.

Meanwhile, during her first months in Honolulu, while her husband was in boot camp, Estelle was essentially left to fend for herself.[15] Entries about her in the social columns indicate that she did a good deal of visiting during her first few weeks in the islands. Although Estelle is mentioned with some regularity, Cornell, other than in the article about his military status, is absent. They do not appear as a couple until late September, when the "Schofield Society" column announces that they have moved into one of the new bungalows recently completed for officers and their families at Schofield Barracks.[16]

Estelle's name first appears in the indexed notice of events that introduced the society pages for the last Sunday in June 1918. It had been a week of heavy socializing. In the course of four pages of announcements, she is mentioned several times. The featured event, a tea given on Thursday, 27 June, by Louise Watson, is billed as "An Afternoon for Mrs. Franklin." Mrs. Watson was an active organizer for the Hawaiian Red Cross relief, an organization as social as it was philanthropic. Among its officers were the wives of the richest and most influential men in the Territory. Mrs. Watson's good friend, the society editor, had seen to it that Estelle's arrival would be given proper attention. The tea was "in honor of Mrs. Cornell Franklin who has been Mrs. Watson's houseguest for the past week. About twenty of the younger set were present, and a very pleasant hour followed, the greater part of the time being devoted to knitting."[17] Knitting clothes for the troops and introducing Estelle to the right people were the purposes of Mrs. Watson's tea party. Among the guests were three young women in whose homes

Estelle would also be a houseguest during her first weeks in the islands.[18] These women took an immediate liking to Estelle. Her role as colonial wife had begun.

While Estelle's social life was confined to ladies' luncheons and teas, her uncle Malcolm's was more exotic. Had she been asked, she might have preferred being invited to what the papers described as a Japanese dinner party given by Colonel John Heard at the Japanese Club on Waikiki Beach. All the guests, which included Malcolm Franklin, were dressed in kimonos, sat on cushions "around the attractive Japanese table," and dined while geisha girls danced for their entertainment. After dinner Malcolm took the colonel, three captains, their wives, and a captain's daughter for a moonlight sail on the bay.

Colonel Heard would become both Cornell's boss and a fixture in the Franklins' social life. He too was a recent arrival to the Territory. He had come as the commander of the Fourth Cavalry, which moved from the mainland to Schofield Barracks in April 1917, when the United States had declared war on Germany. His credentials marked him as a member of the Southern network. Heard's dinner with Franklin was one of many, and the two men's friendship played importantly in Cornell's being appointed Heard's aide-de-camp when he was made Brigadier General at Schofield in October 1918.[19]

The marriage choice that Estelle's fictional Edna Earl Tomlinson is coerced into on her first ocean crossing determines her legally subordinate role as the wife of a missionary in the United States' colonial mission in China. Estelle was no missionary, but for nine long years she was a colonial wife. She draws on this world as well as her family background to create her story's narrative and its emotional texture. In Edna Earl, Estelle gently caricatures herself, just as Faulkner will poke fun at aspects of himself in his first three novels. Both women seem to have no good choices and realize that their chief value is their looks.

As Edna Earl's ship pulls away from its dock in San Francisco, she clings to the railing waving wildly to the only person she knows in San Francisco. Estelle seems to be molding Edna Earl's identity to strike a chord of recognition in the ears of the artist and writer whom she loves. Edna Earl's "exquisite profile" and "long slim legs" seem to be a mirror image of the drawings of Estelle that Faulkner had made for *The Marionettes*, where Estelle was clearly Faulkner's muse.

By the last week of June 1918, Red Cross work fell off as the club ladies of Honolulu moved out of the humid summer heat of the valley into their summer homes, hotels, or rental cottages on Oahu's windward side, or to mountain retreats in Tantalus for July and August. Mrs. Watson, however,

18.1. Estelle Oldham Franklin's United States Citizen's Identification
Card, issued in Honolulu on 9 July 1918.
(Courtesy of Cornell Franklin, Jr.)

was not among the deserters, and she pressed her houseguest to give more time to knitting, when Estelle would much rather have been serving the troops as a volunteer YWCA hostess at either Fort Armstrong or Schofield Barracks. But, as a recently married twenty-one-year-old, she could hardly be a chaperone.[20]

Some time in early July, Estelle went to the Immigration Department in downtown Honolulu, where she applied for her United States Citizen's Identification Card and had her official photograph taken.[21] She received her card on 9 July. Her identity card is the only surviving photograph of her taken during the first months of her marriage. Whereas she was slim in her engagement photograph (see fig. 11.3), her face is now so painfully thin that her delicate cheekbones seem about to break through her pale, pale skin. Her eyebrows are still plucked in an exaggeratedly fine line, but she has let her hair grow out of its fashionable bob. One is struck by the immense sadness in her eyes, by the slight downturn of her full yet unsmiling lips as she stares directly into the camera. Being left by her husband with total strangers in a strange land within days of arriving in Hawaii could not have been pleasant. That she was also pregnant and more than two thousand miles from home surely added to her anxiety and loneliness.

The purpose of identity cards was not so much to keep track of white United States citizens as to prevent the emigration to the mainland of Chinese, Japanese, and other foreign laborers whom American plantation owners had imported to provide cheap labor in the cane fields and on pineapple plantations. Such bias was not lost on Estelle. Although she might not have been aware of its implications in 1918, her stories, which draw on her experiences in the Pacific, the Far East, and the American South, comment explicitly on white America's exploitation of and bigotry toward the Chinese, Jews, and African Americans. They portray these attitudes as a logical extension of the prevailing Jim Crow mentality on the mainland.

Like its racial politics, Hawaiian sexual politics in 1918 also found their way into Estelle's fiction. In the islands, as in the States and in England, wartime conditions had resulted in increasing economic and social freedom for many women and a corresponding loosening of Victorian dress codes. In Honolulu that summer, what women could or could not wear on the beach became a major issue. On its surface this flap appears entirely frivolous, but because the site of the dispute is women's bodies, specifically *young* women's bodies, it is useful for giving depth and texture to the sexual politics of one of the colonial communities Estelle drew on for her stories.

In short, the Honolulu Women's Auxiliary claimed that the sight and presence of bared young female bodies on the city's beaches would cause nothing less than disease, pollution, and the destruction of the natural environment. Like unruly natives, sexualized white women threatened colonial order.[22] Was it because the market feared it might lose control of its most precious commodity, its daughters? Was it an unspoken fear of gender confusion and cross-dressing as the women invaded the men's departments of dry-goods shops to buy their bathing suits and then romped the beaches looking androgynous with their bobbed hair and men's suits that revealed their legs and arms but flattened their chests? Was it, as the 1918 headlines imply, the class and, possibly, racial barriers that were threatened when the young women were then fitted by "Men Tailors," many of whom were Asians?[23]

These questions raised by the bathing suit controversy relate to issues Estelle raises in her short stories. But her fictional flappers and their lovers cause even more trouble. As she writes it, Edna Earl is potentially much more transgressive than Honolulu's flapper bathing beauties. Sexually polymorphous, she passively entertains the desires of a woman who loves women as well as men; simultaneously she desires and is desired by the feminized, orientalized Jew, Sassoon. Drawn into a web of racialized gender border crossings, she is smitten by this "Levantine" with "oriental" eyes who is another incarnation of the "foreign," dark, sympathetic other who appeared first in "Dr. Wohlenski" and will be further developed in "Star Spangled Banner Stuff."

As the summer of 1918 wore on, and growing numbers of American men entered military service, more women began experiencing life on their own. The July social pages noted the increasing scarcity of men and wrote that the "debs are dancing with each other instead and commandeering the family car to go on a strictly feminine motor picnic."[24]

By 22 July 1918, the officers and families of the Second Hawaiian Infantry were moving into newly built quarters at Schofield Barracks, and by 4 August the papers reported that both the First and Second Hawaiian Infantry were now quartered at Schofield Barracks. According to the post office address on her identity card, however, Estelle was still living in Honolulu. And a report of her activities in the social columns indicates that she may have been behaving more like a flapper or, worse, a New Woman than a proper Southern Lady. She did make at least one trip on her own from Honolulu up the mountains to the barracks, a five-hour, twenty-seven-mile train ride on "The Pineapple Limited."[25] The papers note her presence, without her husband, at a hop given on Wednesday, 31 July, at the Twenty-fifth Infantry Clubhouse. She is listed as Mrs. Cornell Franklin of Honolulu.[26]

Even that summer, despite her inexperience and lack of alternative familial or societal role models, she was still not about to alter her behavior totally just to please her hosts and her husband's mentors. She was not willing to give up her privacy to advance her husband's business interests, something a more materially inclined or compliant young wife would have sacrificed. Unlike her six-year-old fictional Estelle in "Dr. Wohlenski" or her older, more disguised version, Edna Earl in "A Crossing," Estelle didn't actively rebel. She probably never said anything comparable to or as forthright as Edna Earl's desperate "I have to . . . make up my own words" or her furious "I hate it all. *All*, do you hear?"[27] Yet at twenty-one, she had already developed a remarkable reserve beneath her come-hither Southern charm, a reserve that could make even her elders feel uncomfortable and insecure.[28] To people she didn't like, she was polite but distant.

Increasingly, social life in Honolulu was revolving around Red Cross work. Although Red Cross activities dominate the society pages, Estelle apparently did not continue to pretend to share her hostess's enthusiasm for ladies' get-togethers. Her name is never mentioned. By mid-August the society editor noted that Red Cross meetings had replaced other forms of socializing.[29] By that time, Estelle's social life had come to a halt. During the rest of that summer, her name never appears in connection with any Red Cross work or other philanthropic women's club activities, which were, in effect, the unpaid occupations of all but a small minority of women of her class and color.[30]

The night of 25 August, the fantastic mile-long hedge of night-blooming cereus at Punahou school near the Watsons' house flowered, and many walked or drove over to see a full, golden moon shining on the unearthly sweet, milky white blossoms. Did anyone invite Estelle to see them, or did anyone offer to take her over to the big island to watch Mauna Loa erupting that August? We may never know. According to the social pages, after an initial flurry of invitations during her first weeks in Honolulu, Estelle's name seldom appears. After 8 August, she is not mentioned again until late September, when the "Schofield Society" section reports that the Franklins have moved into the new officers' quarters at the barracks. Clearly, she could not or would not capitalize on the introductions Louise Watson offered her through Red Cross work and her own social connections to the families who ran the Territory.[31] She was not invited again either to the home of the Williamsons or to that of the Lucases, where she had been a weekend houseguest earlier. When she and Cornell finally had their own house at Schofield Barracks, Eva Focke was the only one of her Honolulu hosts who visited her there.

At home in Oxford Estelle had never shared her mother's enthusiasm for socializing with other women in club activities; she had done the minimum required by Lida. Like her six-year-old heroine in "Dr. Wohlenski," she had always preferred her own company or the company of her few close female friends, like Katrina Carter, and of men. Now, newly married, pregnant, and on her own in a strange country, she was expected to behave in an entirely different way. Because she was married, her social life was limited to other women's company, women with whom she had little in common to begin with—and even less so as the war went on. Perhaps her greatest difficulty in this closely knit colonial society was that she was alone, whereas other women were often surrounded by generations of family and a common circle of friends and acquaintances. She could not enter into their family gossip; nor did she have children or servants, other popular topics of conversation. She had none of the housekeeping responsibilities associated with supervising the large staffs of Chinese and Japanese servants that the highly stratified society required "Haoles" to employ "in order to maintain the prestige and proper social distance from those less privileged."[32] Perhaps these months of intense emotional isolation, of observing instead of participating in a culture so like her own in Mississippi, was what first gave her the distance necessary to question its inherent racism and sexism in the fiction she had probably begun writing by that time.

On 9 September 1918, nine days after completing boot camp, Cornell, now a sergeant in the Machine Gun Company of the Second Hawaiian Infantry, was discharged to accept a commission as a second lieutenant in the First Infantry.[33] Now that her husband had finally received his commission, the Franklins would be eligible for housing in the officers' "bungalows" just being completed at Schofield. Estelle looked forward to being in her own home. At last she could set up her first household and live surrounded by a few familiar objects, including the Franklin silver and furniture given her by her mother-in-law and the pieces of Oldham furniture she had brought with her from Oxford. (All of this had been sitting in storage since the Franklins' arrival in June.) But most of all, she was relieved to escape the often disapproving voice and eye of Louise Watson, her bossy hostess.

At Schofield, where almost all the women would be newcomers and mainlanders like herself, she would fit in more easily and would again enjoy a semblance of the social life she had left behind in Oxford. She was not to be disappointed. In fact, the social whirl she was swept into exceeded her wildest dreams.

19

An Army Wife, Schofield Barracks, Hawaii, September 1918–May 1919

I N LATE SEPTEMBER 1918 the "Schofield Society" column in the *Advertiser* noted that "Lieutenant and Mrs. Cornelius [*sic*] Franklin have moved into one of the new bungalows recently completed between the 2nd Hawaiian Infantry and the 4th Cavalry Cantonment" at Schofield Barracks. This 29 September notice marks the paper's first mention of the Franklins as a couple since their June arrival. Five months after her wedding and more than four into her first pregnancy, Estelle finally began a married life something like what she had anticipated.

Mamie Hairston, acting as Cornell's mother and father, had taught her only child self-discipline, manners, and the value of education and social connections. Growing up as the poor relation had instilled in him a passionate desire for all the material wealth his father's early death had denied him. But this handsome, black-haired son had never learned to care, except superficially, about anyone besides himself. He was not a mean man, but he was immensely ambitious; he wanted professional fame and the best that money and position could buy, and he could be ruthless. As his college yearbook noted, he was a controlled and controlling person. Among some of his peers in Oxford and Columbus, but for very different reasons, he was no more popular than Bill Faulkner. People called him a "stuffed shirt," and "that shyster lawyer from Shanghai."[1] To get what he wanted, he restricted his personal and professional relationships to those that would build his fortune and reputation. This meant that in his relations with his wife, children, grandchildren, and even the younger lawyers he employed in Shanghai, Cornell came unabashedly first. Once he had paid for people, he considered them his property. Their primary purpose was to enhance his performance. When his children or grandchildren won praise and prizes at school for academic achievements, he appropriated them as his own. When they displeased him, they were shamed and banished. To his children he sometimes even seemed cruel. According to Jill Summers, neither Cho-Cho nor Malcolm was at all athletic. "When Cornell and Dallas [his second wife] returned from Shanghai in 1943 after their release from a Japanese POW camp and came to visit us in Oxford, I was out in the back riding my horse. Cho-Cho never let me forget that when he saw me riding, Cornell turned to our mother and said, '*That* is the child *we* should have had.'"[2] Similarly, Elizabeth Otey Watson recalls how he shamelessly exploited young lawyers like her husband who joined Franklin's firm in Shanghai.[3]

As Cornell grew rich (Standard Oil and Liggett & Myers were two of his accounts), he became almost a caricature of the mythical Southern patriarch of his earliest aspirations. According to Elizabeth Watson, the Southern plantation mansion replica that Cornell had built in 1926 on the outskirts of Shanghai and staffed with fifteen servants "looked like Mount Vernon" and was "ridiculous in that climate." Elizabeth Watson's mother-in-law remembers arriving at Cornell's mansion on a sweltering summer day—"it must have been 104 degrees"—and being served an "extraordinary Southern dinner, old Southern hospitality transported intact to Shanghai. There was fried chicken, corn pudding, everything!"[4]

Cornell's aspirations became less and less appealing to his Estelle as she realized her intended place in them. As the tensions that structure her fiction suggest, she came to understand that while her husband's demands and desires mirrored her culture's and her parents,' they were not hers.

She never lived in Cornell's Shanghai plantation house. Ironically, the government housing she and Cornell occupied at Schofield, or Castner, as it was called then, was to be the site of the happiest eight months of an eleven-year marriage whose disintegration can be measured, in part, by Estelle's ever more extended visits home to Oxford. Her first visit, in June 1919, lasted four months; her second, in March 1921, nine; and her third and final, in December 1924, eleven months, and ended then only because that fall Cornell returned to Mississippi and he and both families pled with her to return with him to Shanghai.[5]

What made life at Schofield appealing? Living conditions were pretty primitive. The red clay earth reminded her of home in Oxford, as did the mosquitoes, which were "large enough to fry" and so plentiful that everyone slept under heavy mosquito netting. Large red ants were ubiquitous; the only way to avoid them was to put the legs of all furniture in cans of kerosene and to mop the wooden floors daily with kerosene and water. Kerosene was also used for cooking and for lamps. Its fumes permeated indoor life. Just trying to stay clean and bug-free was a constant battle. One officer's wife remembered that "among our many battles, was a constant battle with those awful grass stickers and red and yellow dirt. Our dresses, skirts, hose, even shoes and trouser bottoms gathered those stickers by the thousands. So at the end of each day we scraped them off with knives, and picked by hand trying to get rid of them. All of our clothes had a reddish pink hue that hand washing could never remove."[6] Schofield itself was physically ugly, its grounds "a carpet of red and yellow dirt and devil grass" gridded by muddy roads (there were no paved streets or walks until after the war). The Franklins' and other officers' still un-landscaped and un-planted living quarters on the high plain above Honolulu, although new, were a far cry from Estelle's father's and other neighbors' carefully tended flower gardens and the wild and wooded hills and rolling fields of North Mississippi.[7] Its starkness, the wide, almost treeless vistas of this long plain, bordered with sweet-scented pineapple and wild guava fields abruptly broken by the high mountain ranges which bordered it on the north and south, made even the lush tropical gardens and parks of Honolulu seem more familiar. The Schofield Barracks society pages give no hint of these living conditions or of the difficulty of daily living, let alone entertaining and hosting houseguests.

Yet in Honolulu, Estelle had had no home and had been no one. She may even have felt a bit embarrassed over the awkward position in which Cornell had placed her. As a newcomer and young married woman with no family, profession, or independent income, she had neither status nor mobility. Without Cornell, Estelle was expected to restrict her social life to Red Cross work and to teas and luncheons with Louise Watson's contemporaries and the younger women her unofficial chaperone deemed suitable, the wives and daughters of the professionals and businessmen who ran Hawaii for its white, largely American plantocracy. But Estelle was not used to being so confined. In Honolulu, when she rebelled in the same ways she had in Oxford, she was punished. Louise Watson's journalist friends banished her from their society pages. Whether she also stopped receiving invitations is not known.[8] Schofield was an escape from the confinements of Honolulu.

As soon as she moved into Schofield Barracks, her situation changed dramatically. First of all, instead of being the only outsider, Estelle entered into a community where everyone was new. And she entered with status. At a base called the "Gibraltar of the Pacific," whose commander was a general from Mississippi, she came into her own as a Southern Belle whose reputation stretched from Jackson to Memphis and whose family tree included both Revolutionary and Civil War veterans. While in 1918 her father had still not advanced beyond the clerkship his influential father-in-law secured for him, her grandfather, Judge Niles, was known throughout the state. Now she was a wartime officer's wife. In its simplest and most superficial outlines, her social situation seemed like a magazine romance come true. In a society where women were defined by their husbands, Cornell's promotion and housing assignment had changed her situation from homelessness and a kind of unofficial widowhood to being a lieutenant's wife and the mistress of a brand-new home. Along with her house came another sign of her rise in status: her own staff of Japanese servants who lived in the row of quarters set, like Southern slave cabins, at the edge of the back gardens of all the officers' bungalows.

War news dominated the local headlines that fall, even after the armistice was declared in November. Yet for officers and their wives at Castner, socializing, if one includes sports like polo, appears to have taken up as much, if not more time than military maneuvers. The base boasted two of the finest polo fields in the territories, and matches were played every Wednesday and Sunday afternoon at 2:30.[9] Because Cornell was first player on the Schofield Rangers, Estelle spent at least two afternoons a week in the grandstands.

Besides polo, the Franklins' weekly calendar typically included an evening that began with a movie at one of the base's "various amusement halls," then a "Ladies Night" at the Fourth Cavalry Club, where they danced to music played by "a live military orchestra" and at ten o'clock were served "a very light Luncheon."[10] Almost every afternoon offered some form of planned entertainment such as swimming parties, picnics, or bridge parties. Nights were filled with dinner parties, more bridge, hops, and other dances.

Estelle had made one friend her own age in Honolulu, Eva Focke, a young woman whose ancestry on her mother's side placed her firmly in Honolulu's innermost social circle, but whose sense of humor, independent spirit, and love of adventure may have reminded Estelle of Tochie and Katrina Carter. On 3 October Estelle invited Eva to visit. Eva's maternal grandfather had served as attorney general to and played poker with Hawaii's last king. But Eva was famous on her own as well, in a way that suggests why she and Estelle had something in common. In the sixth grade, she had received a bouquet of roses from a not so young admirer. Concerned about what she considered her daughter's precocity, her mother immediately shipped her off to her sister, who lived in England. There Eva was enrolled in a German boarding school. When the war broke out, she returned to her aunt's in London and promptly volunteered as a nurse's aide in a British hospital for war amputees. Although Estelle was probably four or five months pregnant and so pushing limits by appearing in a bathing suit at all, she invited Eva to join her at the weekly swimming tea which was held at the pool near the 4th Cavalry cantonment. Eva did not disappoint. At Schofield there were no Honolulu matrons enforcing bathing dress codes or staring down young pregnant women.

That afternoon, after swimming and then changing into tea-gowns and dress uniforms, couples danced the newest dances to music furnished by the 4th Cavalry Band. That night the Franklins gave their first dinner party. Besides Eva, the only other woman, their guests included a Captain, a Lt. Colonel, and a Major. The following night the Franklins were dinner guests of Captain and Mrs. Owen Fowler, where Colonel John Heard, who later would make Cornell his aide-de-camp, was also a guest. After dinner, all the guests went on to another hop. Later, the weekend of 11–13 October, Eva Focke visited the Franklins again, this time as their houseguest.[11] (If a return invitation was issued, there is no record of it. Her name is never again yoked with Estelle's in the paper.)

Now that the Franklins were finally a couple, they were also invited to mixed social events in Honolulu. For example, one Saturday night they took the train down to the city to attend a dinner party with Myrtle and Merwin Carson's acquaintance from Honolulu.[12] The following week Cornell and Estelle had engagements every evening, including a small bridge party hosted by Colonel Heard and one at Captain and Mrs. Brighams'. Cornell was clearly a favorite of the senior officers, since he was always the most junior officer at their parties. That he had a desirable and amusing wife added to his appeal.

The second week in October, Colonel Heard was promoted to brigadier general. Besides a large party in his honor at Schofield, the general gave a luncheon for himself at the Alexander Young Hotel in Honolulu. Among the guests was Cornell's uncle Malcolm, who then "motored" up to Schofield with the general to spend the next two weeks as Cornell and Estelle's houseguest. According to the papers, Estelle welcomed her uncle-in-law with "a very attractive dinner party given at their beautiful new quarters at Castner on Friday evening before the 3rd Engineer hop at the 4th Cavalry Pavilion." Besides their uncle, the Franklins invited only three guests: General Heard and a Major and his wife. For her table centerpiece she filled the silver basket her mother-in-law had given her with pink and white roses brought from Honolulu. Dinner, prepared by her new Japanese cook and served by her Japanese maid dressed, as was the custom, "in her native garb," was reported to have been delicious.[13] Having Cornell's uncle as a long-term houseguest gave Estelle ample time to observe him. She would later draw on these observations in "Star Spangled Banner Stuff," where she describes the tissue of lies and evasions that compose the daily life of the pitiful old alcoholic club man. Strong resonances between Estelle's "old Fairman" and the Compson children's Uncle Maury in *The Sound and the Fury* suggest another aspect of the imaginative dialogue between Estelle and Bill Faulkner.

On 28 October Malcolm returned to the city "after a pleasant two weeks' visit" with his nephew and niece-in-law joining in their hectic social schedule, which had been packed throughout his visit. That schedule continued at the same pace during November and December. Cornell was now the Captain of the 1st Hawaiian Infantry polo team, which meant that polo practice continued even in the off-season.[14]

In mid-November, just as the Armistice was declared, Cornell received his first tangible reward for his wife's services as hostess, signaled by a notice in the papers that he had been made aide-de-camp to General Heard and promoted to first lieutenant.[15] Cornell's promotion may explain why Estelle's friendship with Eva Focke was apparently brief. Even if Eva had issued a return invitation to Estelle after her two visits to Schofield, Estelle could not have gone. At this point in her marriage, Estelle's presence as hostess was an asset to and requirement of her husband as well as his uncle.

Throughout December, although Estelle was now nearly eight months pregnant, they regularly made the arduous twenty-seven-mile trip over bad roads or twenty-five-mile trip by rail to Honolulu for dinner parties.[16] They also entertained at home with a series of parties culminating in a Christmas dinner for six that included the Brigadier General, Malcolm Franklin, and Captain Brigham and his wife.[17] Estelle was entertaining her husband's boss.

On New Year's Eve, many officers and their families motored down to Sanford Dole's legendary Haleiwa Hotel, the seaside resort where Hawaii's last queen, Liliuokalani, had vacationed but which, during the war, had been declared an officers' recreation site or liberty hotel. There they dined on the hotel's wide lanai, which overlooked magnificent Japanese gardens that spread down to the sea and danced beneath the twinkling lights of the delicately painted Japanese lanterns hung from the lanai rafters. Estelle continued to work hard at her job. On New Year's Day the Franklins arrived back in time for her to help serve refreshments at the brigadier general's afternoon reception.[18]

Perhaps partly in anticipation of the expenses of becoming a parent, and of being discharged from the army, Cornell chose the first week in January to write the Attorney General in Washington, the Honorable T. W. Gregory, to apply for the recently vacated position of First Judge of the

First Judicial Circuit of the Territory of Hawaii. Two years earlier, Gregory had offered to recommend him for the position of Assistant U.S. District Attorney, an offer Cornell refused, as he explained, "for financial reasons and because I did not feel that the experience gained would be of any value to me later." Apparently Gregory was not offended either by Cornell's earlier refusal or his obnoxious explanation, because on Cornell's 27th birthday, April 1st, President Woodrow Wilson gave him the position.[19]

The aftermath of the New Year's celebrations brought no halt to the usual round of socializing at the barracks, but Estelle seems to have stayed home and rested during the first ten days of the New Year. It's possible but not likely that as the birth of his first child grew more immediate, Cornell may have decided that Estelle, at least, should begin to obey the island-wide quarantine measures forbidding indoor public gatherings that had been in effect since the flu epidemic's outbreak on the mainland in the summer of 1918. Despite this quarantine, which extended through the spring of 1919, the flu had spread throughout Oahu.[20] But, by January 19th Estelle was back in the society pages, which reported a series of social engagements for the prior week in honor of her mother-in-law, Mamie Hairston, who arrived the weekend of 10 January.

Estelle was glad to see Mamie, whose company she vastly enjoyed, but she may have been surprised that her mother-in-law, not her mother, would come to be with her when her first child was born. She may have wondered if Lida was still mourning the death of Ned, the Oldhams' youngest child and only son, for she remembered that the summer of her engagement even Lida's pleasure in the prospect of gaining Cornell Franklin as her son-in-law had been muted by her grief. "She is so heartbroken," Estelle had written to her cousin, explaining why they could not come for a celebratory visit.[21] Now, once more, Estelle's mother was grieving, this time for her daughter Tochie and her unborn child who had both died that October in the flu epidemic. By withholding the news for so long, her parents had effectively made it impossible for Estelle to express her grief. Far away from anyone who had known Tochie, she could hardly observe a period of official mourning for her sister.

Estelle and Cornell seem to have kept Tochie's death to themselves. No announcement of it ever appeared in the Honolulu papers, and, judging from the entries in the Schofield social columns following Mamie's arrival, the Franklins continued their steady round of socializing. On 13 January the Brighams gave a huge tea party in Mamie's honor, and that evening there was a bridge party at which the Franklins and Cornell's mother were among the "favored" guests. Two days later Mamie was honored at another bridge party given by the wife of Colonel William Bibee, a polo teammate of Cornell's. Wednesdays and Sundays at 2:30, as Estelle had done since her arrival at Castner, mother and daughter-in-law went dutifully to the polo grounds to watch Cornell play.[22] There were at least three more teas or dinner parties in Mamie's honor before the end of January. Yet, with Mamie's arrival and perhaps with her support, Estelle had finally curtailed her social life. She accompanied her mother-in-law and husband to only one of these.

On 8 February at 2 P.M., less than three weeks after Mamie Hairston's arrival, Estelle bore the Franklins' first child, a daughter.[23] An army doctor officiated. Most likely sedating his patient with the drug of choice in 1919, "Twilight Sleep," as it was popularly called, he performed a forceps delivery.[24] A measure of her grief at her sister's and little brother's deaths and her desire to memorialize and undo is recorded in the names she chose for her first child: "Victoria" for her sister and "de Graffenreid," Ned's middle name. Victoria's Japanese nurse, or amah, nicknamed her "Cho-Cho san" ("little butterfly").

Estelle later told both her daughter Jill and her granddaughter Victoria Fielden Johnson that her first two pregnancies had been difficult and that both Cho-Cho and the Faulkners' first child, Alabama, were premature. One would never suspect this from the demanding social schedule she maintained until shortly before Cho-Cho's birth and then resumed a month after it. By 9 March, besides Mamie, the Franklins had two other houseguests in their tiny cottage, Malcolm Franklin again and a Colonel Hathaway. To all outward appearances, Estelle was proving a superb wife and hostess.

Besides Cho-Cho's birth, the greatest changes in the Franklins' lives were wrought by Cornell's discharge from the service on 8 April 1919, the day before he was sworn in as a judge. The Franklins maintained residence in Schofield and did not move to Honolulu until the late fall of 1919, some time after Estelle and Cho-Cho returned from a four-month visit to Mississippi.[25] Thus, from April until Estelle sailed for San Francisco on 19 May with her mother-in-law, her baby, and a Japanese amah, the Franklins saw each other only on weekends because Cornell's new job required his regular presence in court, a presence that is noted almost daily during his first months on the bench in a column called "Circuit Court Notes."[26] The Franklins' social activities are about equally split between Schofield and Honolulu. But as late as 6 May, the papers show that Estelle was still helping to serve tea at the weekly 17th Cavalry regimental band performance while her mother-in-law poured tea for General Heard at another performance. Clearly, they were very much members of the Schofield community, up until shortly before Estelle sailed for the mainland.[27]

The socializing Estelle and Mamie did in town those weeks was much more than Estelle was reported to have done when she first arrived in Honolulu the previous June. Many of the women's teas and luncheons Estelle and Mamie attended were given in Mamie's honor by the wives of prominent lawyers and businessmen, men who could prove helpful to Cornell.[28] Perhaps they went because Mamie, as a society page writer, was more experienced than her daughter-in-law and recognized the long-range importance of social networking in furthering her son's career.[29] Perhaps Estelle went along out of fondness for Mamie, in addition to a sense of social duty. Recall that when they married, Mamie had given her silver to her daughter-in-law, not to her son. Years later, when the Franklins divorced, Mamie took Estelle's side. Mamie never did acknowledge Cornell's second wife.

The week before Estelle and Mamie sailed for the States was filled with engagements both in Honolulu and at Schofield. Mamie's visit and their departure culminated in a dinner and dancing party for twenty guests that Cornell and Estelle gave for Mamie up at Schofield.[30] I mention this because the absence of any social activity at all prior to the Franklins' departure from Honolulu for Shanghai in December 1921 is such a contrast that it raises the question: what caused the Franklins' later fall from social favor?

On 19 May, draped in layers of leis and serenaded by the Royal Hawaiian Band's usual farewell melodies, they sailed at noon on the *USAT Sheridan*. Estelle and Cho-Cho would not return until the end of October. Cornell didn't join his family that summer. Instead he stayed in Hawaii, working and playing polo at least twice a week. When Estelle returned, she was the only married woman traveling alone on board the ship.[31]

By 5 June 1919, Estelle and Cho-Cho had been in Oxford several days. Yet, unlike her other trips home in the years that followed, there is no printed news about her activities that summer and fall. Other than announcements of her arrival and departure, Estelle's name is absent from Oxford's social columns during all of her four-month visit. She makes no known trips to visit relatives in Kosciusko, Aberdeen, or Columbus or even to shop in Memphis. Other than a note in the Columbus paper on 29 June saying that Mamie Hairston and Uncle Malcolm had left town earlier in the week to visit the Oldhams and that after their return from Oxford, Malcolm, who had been in the States since April, would sail for Honolulu "to resume his duties as collector of customs," there is no mention of her until October, when the *Oxford Eagle* noted that Estelle and Cho-Cho had left for Honolulu the previous Monday, 29 September.[32]

What was she doing in Oxford? In part, she was simply trying to pull her life together. In the past year she had married a virtual stranger, moved

19.1. Cornell's uncle, Malcolm Franklin (*left*), and other
Franklin relatives disembarking from the *USAT Sheridan*,
Honolulu harbor, c. 1920.
(Courtesy of Victoria Fielden Johnson)

with him to a foreign country, and spent the first four months with no home
or even a room of her own. She also had no real friends or family except
Cornell's bachelor uncle until Mamie arrived. Virtually ignorant about sex
and reproduction, she had survived her first pregnancy and the birth of her
first child. Months after the death of her favorite sister, she had to mourn
privately and in silence. Finally, since her arrival at Schofield, she had been
entertaining her husband's friends and family almost nonstop. She had
married Cornell to escape the unattainable Bill Faulkner and in hopes of
making a life for herself beyond the social and cultural confines of Oxford,
Mississippi. Like Edna Pontellier in Kate Chopin's satirical novel *The Awakening*, she had allowed herself the dangerous luxury of being taken in
by Cornell's romantic image, an image out of Southern history and myth:
the dashing army officer riding out of the West to claim his bride, the
Southern gentleman cavalier who, by virtue of his wits and education, escaped his Southern past only to re-create it on the new American frontier.
This is the myth that Southern writers like Chopin and, later, Ellen Glasgow so brilliantly expose by exploring the disastrous effects of such fantasies on the lives of their highly imaginative, potentially iconoclastic adolescent heroines.

Like Edna Pointellier or Glasgow's Dorinda Oakley, Estelle, too, had permitted herself to be gulled. Her first year of marriage to this fantasy brought to reality in the Hawaiian Territory had begun to educate her. The islands' colonial culture permeated Schofield and Honolulu, where most white women of her class and education had only one kind of public role—taking the forms of dancing partner, hostess, and chief housekeeper. The territorial economy and labor system enforced rigid and hierarchical separations between classes and races, and men and women. An array of servants was required to display social status and enforce the notion of wives as items of conspicuous consumption by making sure they had nothing to do but command their imported servants—all of this being an extreme form of the Jim Crow laws and Victorian conventions present in her life in Oxford. In Honolulu, transported white Southerners lived life in antebellum style. As her fiction indicates, she observed this and it made her aware of inequities which at home, in their familiar forms, she had never noticed. But she had no one with whom she could talk, so she stored her observations away, probably never thinking that a few years later she would transform these impressions into fictional critiques of colonialism at home and abroad.

In September 1918, when she had moved to Schofield Barracks, she at first had enjoyed the parties and the dances which came as a welcome respite after her stultifying four months at the Watsons'. But by December, she had become disenchanted. She was in the final weeks of her pregnancy; her back and legs ached from the extra weight her slight frame was carrying, and her ankles were sore and swollen. Yet Cornell insisted that she stand for hours pouring tea for the brigadier general's weekly dos and that they continue their almost nightly round of social engagements. Most difficult of all was her husband's seeming indifference to her needs or interests when they didn't coincide with his. Mamie's arrival in early January at least had given her a companion whom she loved as well as someone who easily assumed her duties. Mamie had protected her to some degree from Cornell's demands.

But now, in June 1919, she was home, surrounded by family and friends, and about to become involved again with Billy Faulkner, as she had been in 1913, before she had left for Mary Baldwin and Phil Stone had taken her place as Billy's most intimate player in his imaginative and actual worlds. The poetry and dream-play Faulkner wrote during the four months she and Cho-Cho were in Oxford that summer and fall of 1919, and during Estelle's second extended visit home from March to November 1921, and all three of Estelle's short stories, but especially "A Crossing," record their creative collaboration.

20

Stolen Interludes, 1919 and 1921
Estelle and Bill, A Continuing Dialogue

> MR. ESMOND: Say, they told me you were stupid. You don't sound stupid
> to me.
> LORELEI LEE: I can be smart when it's important. But (pause) most men
> don't like it.
> —Anita Loos, *Gentlemen Prefer Blondes*

T HE YEARS 1919 to 1921 mark the most innovative period of
Faulkner's long self-apprenticeship to poetry. His bursts of creativity coincide with Estelle's two extended visits home during the first
three years of her marriage to Cornell. Their renewed contact and ensuing dialogue—actual and literary—were crucial to Faulkner's becoming a
novelist.

The exchange above between Lorelei Lee and Mr. Esmond about
smart women is relevant to Faulkner and Estelle. Although Lorelei is speaking about her own problems with men, Estelle was dogged by similar problems in both her marriages. Her unwillingness to play dumb enough was
partly the reason for Faulkner's continuing ambivalence about the relationship he and Estelle resumed in the summer of 1919. To serve his emotional
needs, he wanted the women he loved to play dumb but be smart.[1]

The first part of this chapter discusses Faulkner's two most important
poem sequences, *The Marble Faun* (1919, 1924) and *Vision in Spring* (the latter
composed of love poems made for Estelle in 1921), and his dream-play, *The
Marionettes* (1920). The second part discusses Estelle's unpublished story "A
Crossing," as her imaginative response to the formal, psychological, and
personal issues shaping Faulkner's poetry, most explicitly in *The Marionettes*.
Estelle's populist Jazz Age take on his symbolist dream-play opened
Faulkner's imagination to the worlds he will explore in his first novels.

Summer 1919: *The Marble Faun* and *The Marionettes*

In December 1918, when Faulkner returned to Oxford from his brief stint in the RCAF, Estelle was still in Hawaii with Cornell. Manuscript evidence suggests that he worked on poems for his first commercially published book, *The Marble Faun*, during that winter and spring and continued to do so during and after Estelle's first visit home. His final dating of the sequence—"April, May, June 1919"—linked its completion with Estelle's arrival and their first time together since her marriage. In late May 1919, thirteen months after marrying Cornell, she and her three-and-a-half-month-old daughter, Cho-Cho, arrived in Oxford.[2] Manuscript evidence from poetry written during and after (namely *The Lilacs, The Marble Faun, The Marionettes*, and *Vision in Spring*), and inscriptions and poems Faulkner wrote in several books he lent or gave to Estelle, also suggests that he was deeply affected by this visit and her subsequent four-month visit in 1921.[3]

Lovers often give each other poetry they have shared, inscribing their love on a volume's flyleaf; Faulkner's gifts to Estelle also inscribed their imaginative dialogue. When she returned to Honolulu in late September 1919 with Cho-Cho and Lida, she took with her Faulkner's copy of Swinburne, which they had read together as teenagers and which had meant so much to him at sixteen, the year she said she fell in love with him.[4] To give it to her was a call to memory. It contained his fake RCAF title: "W. Faulkner / Royal Air Force / Cadet Wing / S of A / Borden." On the flyleaf he also wrote a passionate dedication, which she felt impelled to remove because of its incriminating tone. She possibly also carried with her Faulkner's similarly inscribed copy of Ralph Hodgson's *Poems*. Its equally imposturous inscription read: "W. Faulkner R.F.C./2 Squadron 43rd. Wing/Royal Flying Corps." Like the Swinburne, the Hodgson is missing its front endpaper. It also contains a poem fragment of Faulkner's whose content indicates that Pierrot of *The Marionettes* and his other early persona, the *Marble Faun*, once shared the same poem.[5] In giving her *Poems*, Faulkner confirmed her importance as sharer in his imaginative quest, for he placed in her care the only holograph copy of this poem, which is the earliest draft of the three extended writing projects he completed between 1919 and 1920.

The explicit sexuality of *The Lilacs* and *The Marionettes* and its explicit denial in *The Marble Faun* contrast sharply, suggesting the deep level of conflict Faulkner was experiencing in his relations with Phil and Estelle. Although Estelle would not return to Oxford again until March 1921, perhaps three months after Faulkner completed this play, *The Marionettes* is filled with her presence or, rather, the presence of her absence embodied in

Faulkner's text and illustrations—fragments of her clothing, a dancing slipper, a Chinese brocade stole (*TM*, 2, 3), and, most strikingly, the virgin Marietta drawn as Estelle. The likeness is eerie (see figs. 11.3 and 11.4). Inscribing Estelle's copy, Faulkner wrote, "TO 'CHO-CHO,' A TINY FLOWER OF THE FLAME, THE ETERNAL GESTURE CHRYSTALLIZED; THIS, A SHADOWY FUMBLING IN WINDY DARKNESS, IS MOST RESPECTFULLY TENDERED" (*TM*, 89).[6] The important figure here is not Cho-Cho, but the "flame," her mother. Faulkner celebrates not so much the child as the sex act itself, the "eternal gesture," of which Cho-Cho is the "flower." He juxtaposes Cho-Cho to his own creation, his play *The Marionettes*, which he describes in his dedication as a poor substitute. Faulkner persists in using the phrase "shadowy fumbling in windy darkness" in early criticism and other dedications in order to characterize love, his poetry, and, in his fictional self-parodies, bad art (see *Mosquitoes*). The flame also continues to figure in his poetry and prose as an indicator of his highly ambivalent and volatile feelings about feminine sexual power.[7] An example of how early and closely Faulkner linked it to Estelle appears in a poem about a failed marriage that he included in *Vision in Spring*, the sequence of love poems he wrote for her and gave to her to mark her visit home in 1921. It is a poem about estrangement and rebuffed desire.

In part, *The Marionettes* is Faulkner's thinly disguised attempt to come to terms with his feelings about Estelle's marriage and motherhood. In this strange play the author manipulates his characters rather than playing a character who is manipulated. Stage directions indicate that the characters are consciously patterned after puppets; their movements and costumes are highly stylized. But one has only to recall Faulkner's intricately choreographed seduction and rape scenes to recognize the incipient power of this early vision. Like their fictional offspring, Faulkner's first marionettes possess recognizably human forms whose actions Faulkner controls. The similarity of the settings in *The Marionettes* and *The Marble Faun*, as well as the similarity of Pierrot's physical state to the Faun's (both are immobilized and "dreaming"), suggests that the Faun's lamented "impotence," his inability to "sing," may also be sexual. Using language to connect Pierrot's malaise with the Faun's, Faulkner hints that he (as author) is not capable of fuller imaginative exploration until he has come to terms with his feelings about Estelle as a mother and someone else's wife. The objectives and results of leaving the protected pastoral garden in *The Marble Faun* and *The Marionettes* support such a hypothesis. However, Faulkner's ideas about the consequences of such a daring move changed during the months that lapsed between beginning *The Marble Faun* and writing *The Marionettes*. What do the walled-off gardens in both works represent; why are such virginal creatures, the Marble Faun and Marietta, tempted to leave; when they do escape, what role does choice play in their decisions; why are sexual desire and the wish to be active rather than passive always punished? These questions will recur in various forms throughout Faulkner's fiction. They are also the questions Estelle will take up and complicate in "A Crossing," which is among other things her most explicit response to Faulkner's *Marionettes*.

The Marble Faun has no real choice. He is a statue and therefore physically unable to escape from his sheltered garden. So he settles for dreaming and sleep; that is, for noninvolvement in the real world. In *The Marionettes* Pierrot abrogates choice by choosing to be drunk while the cloistered Marietta (Pierrot's dream creation), like the Faun, wants to leave her virginal garden in order to "know" and to be "free." Pierrot's ambivalence, figured visually in his black-and-white costume, is also revealed through his two dream characters. Thus, although he endows Marietta with volition, he has her claim that she lacks free will because she has been hypnotized by Pierrot's Shade. In retaining his subject but transferring his fictional voice from a persona-statue to these marionettelike characters, Faulkner permits himself an imaginative latitude denied in *The Marble Faun*. In *The Marionettes* the deeper implications of this subject matter begin to surface.

The Faun's inability to weep or be sad reflects Faulkner's inability in 1919 to write a successful poem in the poetic mode and form he chose for his first large-scale "test of invention." Because the epilogue recalls, in its form and language, the prologue, the cycle is technically completed or closed, but there is no thematic resolution to the Faun's dilemma. He is still constricted by Pan's suspect "gift of sleep" and dreams (*TMF,* 49). Failure itself, however, holds great interest because of the remarkable success that Faulkner later has with this kind of ending for the conclusions to his best novels.

Summer 1921: *Vision in Spring*

In late 1920, having pushed his infatuation with the 1890s to its limits in *The Marionettes,* Faulkner turned to contemporary poets. Concurrently, and in anticipation of Estelle's second return, he was working on his third poem sequence, *Vision in Spring. Vision,* in its form and content, presages by four years the shape and style of Faulkner's first novel, *Soldiers' Pay,* and other novels to come. Under Conrad Aiken's unknowing tutelage, Faulkner here took on the aesthetic and formal issues whose resolution led him into another genre entirely—and on to a new and enduring professional identity.

Vision in Spring is valuable for several reasons: among them are that it records his dawning realization, arrived at in part from imitating Aiken's extended narrative lyrics and symphonic poem sequences, that to become a great writer he must give up his dream of being a poet. Its further lasting value to Faulkner was its form. The poem sequence, built of a series of interior monologues and dialogues that are connected, in part, by the voice of a third-person narrator, showed Faulkner the limitations of his poetic voice—limitations in poetry that became the major strengths of his fiction. The answer to where Faulkner was going when he wrote his own musical sequence *Vision in Spring* lies partly in the formal structure of this "symphony," his secret tribute to the poet he so much admired. But only partly. Faulkner was still stuck with his poetic persona.

Vision marks Pierrot's final undisguised appearance in Faulkner's writing. The sequence suggests that there, he satirized Pierrot as a means of discrediting him. Faulkner permits him entrance again in 1925, when writing his first novel, and most notably, as we have seen, as Rider in "Pantaloon in Black" (see Chap. 6), but by then he no longer speaks as Pierrot the poet.

In *Vision*, Faulkner, as he imitated, learned the limits of imitation and of his poet self. Having learned these, he could then free himself of the pierrotique mask, that paralyzing presence that had dictated his poet's voice since he began *The Marble Faun*. In abandoning Pierrot, Faulkner begins to examine the emotional and professional limitations of idealizing himself as a poet.

Faulkner's reading of the Modernists and his growing facility with poetic technique cannot account completely for either the delicacy or the painful clarity of some of his insights in *Vision*. Faulkner made this booklet for Estelle and gave it to her when she and Cho-Cho returned to Oxford in March 1921 for what the Honolulu papers described as "an extended visit." This visit marked Estelle's second long stay in Oxford since her marriage. That Faulkner gave *Vision* to her is significant, because knowing that he chose to continue their relationship, despite or perhaps because of her marriage, is essential to understanding the preoccupations of *Vision in Spring*. Not only was she still married to another man and therefore safely unattainable; she was also mostly absent. Both facts made her an ideal recipient of and muse for the love poems Faulkner wrote in *Vision*.

Estelle had sailed from Honolulu on 17 February 1921. The Franklins' marriage had gone less smoothly once they moved from Schofield Barracks to Honolulu. Her departure for the States this time was unceremoniously abrupt, and she stayed in Oxford nearly nine months. Only Cornell's arrival in late September or early October 1921 and the combined pressure of both families made her agree to return to Hawaii with her husband, pack up there, and then move on with him to Shanghai. She and Bill would not see each other again for more than three years, during which time he wrote nothing that was new. By October 1921, with Estelle's capitulation and imminent departure, there was no longer any reason for Bill to postpone his second attempt to break into the New York publishing market, a trip he claimed he'd been anticipating ever since his 1918 return from Canada.[8] The first week of October, he headed for Stark Young's New York apartment. He was leaving Estelle, as he had in 1918, before she could leave him.

Estelle as Muse for *Vision in Spring*

For Faulkner, the months of Estelle's 1921 visit had proved very productive. As in the spring of 1919, when he marked her first return with his dating of *The Marble Faun,* so he would commemorate her second return with his third poem sequence, the love poems called *Vision in Spring.* Though he never published it, it would, as I have written elsewhere, be the pivotal work in his decade-long self-apprenticeship to poetry.[9] This cycle signals and describes his transformation from mediocre poet and dreamer to potentially brilliant novelist. Read in the context of his other poetry, his life, and both his early and best novels, this sequence of fourteen poems reveals fascinating information about how, during this apparently unrewarding period when he wrote poetry almost exclusively (c. 1916–24), the young Faulkner taught himself to write. It also suggests the myriad ways in which poetry in general and this sequence in particular informs the intention, the mode, and many of the thematic preoccupations of his great fiction. As might be expected, *Vision in Spring* is filled with images of illicit desire. A scene he observed the week Cornell arrived in Oxford may have inspired a late poem in the sequence. Faulkner gave it no name, but Estelle later penciled in the title "Marriage" (*VIS,* 67–75).

On a cool spring evening in "Marriage," a husband watches the firelight's reflection flickering along the ceiling and upon his wife "bathed in gold" as she plays piano music "of lustrous muted gold" (ll. 10, 9) She is engrossed in her playing and in her thoughts while he fantasizes about making love to her:

> His eyes like hurried fingers fumble and fly
> About the narrow bands with which her dress is caught
> And lightly trace the line of back and thigh. (ll. 35–37)

But something is wrong. He shuts his eyes:

As one concealed suppresses two loud cries
And on the troubled dark a vision sees. (ll. 43–44)

With great effort of will, her husband suppresses this dark vision and gives himself over to exploring his sexual fantasy. His wife, absorbed in her music and her own fantasies about her "concealed" because illicit lover and "a certain spring," then reveals the cause of her husband's anxiety: the "shattered spring that, softly playing,/She sought to build into a whole again" by conjuring the ghost of her lost love (ll. 77–78). "This she saw, and heard, and played" (l. 79). Meanwhile, her husband, more and more aroused, replays his fantasy of stripping and ravishing her. As he reaches its climax and "sees his brain disintegrate, spark by spark," she stops playing and "turns as if she heard two cries," the cries, we now know, of her secret love (ll. 91, 92). Abruptly, she exits toward the stairs. Her husband stands, watching her "subtle suppleness":

> This nervous strength that was ever his surprise;
> The lifted throat, the thin crisp swirl of dress
> Like a ripple of naked muscles before his eyes. (ll. 94–97)

He follows her to consummate his fantasy. But the poem is Faulkner's fantasy, and so the husband's desire will not be reciprocated. In the final couplet, his wife stops where the stairs turn, "and shivers there,/And hates him as he steadily mounts the stair" (ll. 101–2). *Vision in Spring* is the most successful work Faulkner had completed by the end of 1921, and this poem, much more skillfully than "The Lilacs" (in the sequence he made for Phil Stone in January 1920) simultaneously voices the antithetical emotions of its two speakers—a couple who, to all external appearances, seem in concert.

Though flawed, *Vision* is fascinating because it marks a turning point. As he wrote this sequence, and perhaps even more as he revised it (during those apparently fallow years of 1922 to 1924), he learned at last to separate himself from his dream of becoming a poet and so to begin to find his own voice. To be a poet was a dream he had tried to realize from the time (about 1916) he began to write in earnest, a dream expressed first in *The Marble Faun*, "for things I know yet cannot know." As stated by the Marble Faun, Faulkner's earliest pierrotique mask, to be a poet—to speak the unspeakable and sing like the god Pan—was not possible (*TMF*, sect. 17, ll. 5, 22, 39). Faulkner reiterates his wish to translate and transform his dreams and fantasies—things he knows but cannot know—throughout his apprenticeship. In *Vision in Spring* he begins this task. Here, Pierrot, his character enlarged, his voice range multiplied by Faulkner's reading of the Modernists, particularly Eliot and Aiken, and his conscious and sophisticated use of the sequence as a *narrative* poetic form, continues the quest he began in *The Marble Faun*. The more personal, colloquial voice Faulkner gives him in many of *Vision*'s poems permits him insights not granted his Marble Faun or the drink-numbed Pierrot of *The Marionettes*.

There are also personal reasons why this sequence is more emotionally accessible than his earlier works: *Vision in Spring* is his first extended love poem. Responding to a student's question in 1957, Faulkner said, "I don't know whether . . . any writer could say just how he identifies himself with his characters. Quite often the young man will write about himself simply because himself is what he knows best. That he is using himself as the standard of measure, and to simplify things, he writes about himself as—perhaps as he presumes himself to be, maybe he hopes himself to be, or maybe as he hates himself for being."[10] In the equivocal mode we associate him with, he here comments on the wide range of autobiographical motivation operating in young writers and more obviously visible in their early work.

As it will be in his fiction, the erotics of the forbidden is the subject of much of Faulkner's poetry. Like his earlier sequences, *Vision in Spring* provides a continuing record of the poet's thinly disguised attempts to come to terms with his sexual desires and identity, immensely complicated by their embeddedness in Jim Crow and by his deep and troubled identification with his black and white mothers, Callie and Maud, an identification in which Estelle, too, becomes implicated.

By 6 October 1921, although he had headed for New York, Bill was once again in New Haven, where he wrote Maud reassuringly, "Now, Mother, dont you be downhearted about me at all, as I intend having the time of my life here." Before he'd left Oxford, Stark Young had promised him a bookstore clerkship at Doubleday's in Manhattan.[11] But when he arrived, he found his patron out of town and so went on to New Haven, which was both more familiar and cheaper. There he first rented a dormitory room "with three other fellows" for two dollars a week, assuring Maud that "I can live on a dollar a day and another dollar a week for laundry." With the forty dollars he'd brought with him, he'd be fine until Young came back to New York and summoned him "to come down and go to work."[12] He stayed in the East only two months, returning home to accept the post office job his future father-in-law had secured for him.

No 1921 letters to or from Estelle survive, but the longest and most central paragraph in Faulkner's otherwise matter-of-fact letter to his mother seems almost to flood off the page in its effort to simultaneously mask and to express his feelings about Estelle's imminent ocean departure, to capture and contain his love with the only power at his command—language:

> There's only one sensation to be compared with seeing mountains, and that's seeing the ocean again. Coming up along the sound yesterday I was looking for it all the time; there's a strange feeling in the air: you pass through tight little New England villages built around plots of grass they call greens. The sky toward the sea is pale, about the color of salt, against which the inevitable white church spires are drawn clearer and whiter still. Every where the trees are turning—fall has already come here—ferns, and gum trees, all the underbrush is yellow and red, and over the whole thing is a queer feeling, an awareness of the slow magnificent ocean, like something you have heard or smelled, and forgotten. Then, suddenly, you see it, a blue hill going up and up, beyond the borders of the world, to the salt colored sky, and the white whirling necklaces of gulls, *and, if you look long enough, a great vague ship solemnly going somewhere. I cant express how it makes me feel to see it again, there is a feeling of the most utter relief, as if I could close my eyes, knowing that I had found again someone who loved me years and years ago.* (*TOH*, 145, italics mine)

That spring of 1921 he had indeed found Estelle again, yet soon and for an indefinite period the ocean, perhaps to his "utter relief," would separate them, leaving him secure in the knowledge of her love yet free to pursue his vocation (and his friendships with men like Phil Stone, Stark Young, and Ben Wasson). These friendships had their equally troubling erotic complications, which Faulkner muffled or anesthetized from consciousness with the large quantities of "moonshine" that served as their additional constant companion. Drinking could provide both the closet and the release of inhibitions for homoerotic fantasies and acts to flourish—homosocial bonding sanctioned and homoerotic content obscured.

"A Crossing": Estelle's Imaginative Response and Its Effects

Between early November 1921, when the Franklins left Oxford for Shanghai, and early December 1924, when Estelle made her precipitous return, Billy Faulkner wrote virtually nothing new. Three and a half years passed between the time he wrote *Vision in Spring* and the day he fired off a jubilant telegram to Phil Stone announcing he was well into his first novel.[13] These were the years he spent laboriously revising both his 1921 sequence and *The Marble Faun* in hopes that one or the other would be published. By summer 1921, although he did not know it, he had learned all he could from his long apprenticeship to poetry. Now through extensive reworking, he had to consolidate that knowledge in order to cut himself loose from his Pierrot mask.[14]

Faulkner's experiences with his male relations, friends, and mentors inform his first two novels, especially *Mosquitoes*. So also did Estelle Franklin's troubling, exciting, and almost continual presence in Oxford during all but three (possibly four) months of the five years preceding her marriage to Faulkner (December 1924–20 June 1929). Integral to this presence were her sexually and racially unsettling stories, which he first read in longhand and may even have begun typing for her in the weeks before he began writing his first novel.[15] Although Estelle wrote an earlier version of "A Crossing" in Shanghai, she did not have a typed draft until after she returned to Oxford in December 1924. On the first page of the earlier of two extant typescripts she has cancelled "Franklin" from the "E. Oldham-Franklin/Oxford, Mississippi," which appears at the left-hand corner. On the later draft and in the same place, her name appears simply as "E.O./Oxford Mississippi." This cancellation and change suggest that she and Faulkner worked on typed versions of this story perhaps as early as 1924, when she was still Estelle Franklin, and up until her separation and divorce in 1929.

Two of the three extant stories that Estelle wrote while living in Shanghai (January 1922–November 1924) were embedded in her colonial experiences there and in the Hawaiian Territory. These two, "A Crossing" and "Star Spangled Banner Stuff," are more surely crafted than the more discursive and overtly autobiographical "Dr. Wohlenski," but they share many of the same concerns with it and her later stateside stories that Faulkner chose to rework and make his own. All explore a female protagonist's difficulties with prevailing codes of conduct concerning how girls and women are defined and what they can say, think, feel, and do. Her stories are especially concerned with power relations between generations and races and are complicated by a resistance to the construction of human sexuality as strictly heterosexual and securely gendered masculine or feminine. Her interest in exploring homoerotic and bisexual desire and a black maternal imaginary may stem as much from personal experiences in Oxford and abroad as from fiction and the "new" psychology she was reading. In Oxford's tight community, as elsewhere, homosexuality and lesbianism, like that other taboo, miscegenation, were hardly unknowns. And as articles and book reviews in the Honolulu and Shanghai papers show, public fascination with Freud and Freudian theory was ubiquitous. From 1918 to 1924, Estelle was reading these papers. She even played a leading role in Susan Glaspell's then popular Freudian farce *Suppressed Desires*.

Estelle's shipboard romance, "A Crossing," is an excellent introduction to Faulkner's and her imaginative collaboration, which had recommenced that summer of 1919 or perhaps even earlier, once she had married Cornell. It is also very much part of the literary dialogue that Bill and Estelle had begun in childhood.

Edna Earl Tomlinson, her story's virginal heroine, hails from the modern Midwest rather than from a Beardsleyesque dreamscape, but her family background and the cloistered, puritanical upbringing against which her "wild blood" rebels recall that of Faulkner's virgin, Marietta, in *The Marionettes*. However, while Marietta's seduction is firmly heterosexual, Edna Earl's sexual initiation is both miscegenous and homoerotic, subjects Faulkner had not begun to touch in his poetry or dream-play. Drunkenness plays a significant role in both Faulkner's and Estelle's works, but here Faulkner's operates within the parameters of the genre he's imitating. In contrast, Estelle's more adventurous psychological approach anticipates addiction's complex thematic and tropic presence in the novels Faulkner will write once he embraces prose. Perhaps most important for Faulkner, Estelle's imagination expresses itself in a breezy and contemporary-sounding prose; she writes about a clearly identifiable now. Her response to Faulkner's Decadents-inspired *Marionettes* was to write the story of a 1920s American girl. Edna Earl's demise was very much Estelle's prose response and reimagining of the virgin with the "hot bed" that Faulkner had drawn to look exactly like his future wife. These and other factors make "A Crossing" much more than a thinly disguised account of Estelle's personal problems. Like her first marriage, which on its surface appeared to fulfill her parents', her community's, and even her own ideal of a perfect match, her story is not what it seems. Not surprisingly, considering the cultural context in which she wrote it, "A Crossing" initially appears to be a typical imperial or colonial romance.[16] She was familiar with this genre in that such romances were published regularly in the English-language Honolulu and Shanghai papers. Set in her own present, it's an adventure, an initiation or spiritual quest tale in which Edna Earl Tomlinson, a beautiful, innocent, golden-haired American missionary steams off on a ship bound from San Francisco to the mysterious, decadent, and "heathen" "orient."[17] As in the typical colonial romance, her first civilizing mission is to redeem "natives"— in her case, the Chinese.

Coding her Marietta-like character as a fictive self, she names her after the embattled heroine (herself a romance writer) in Augusta Evans's *St. Elmo* (1866), one of the most beloved novels of Estelle's and her parents' generation. Edna Earl's middle name was also Lem Oldham's. Her gray tear-filled eyes and long slim legs were Estelle's.[18] Through her characters, particularly her pure and impure mother and daughter figures, Estelle's authorial "I" explores feelings about race and sex, specifically the benefits and costs of asserting desire in a culture where sexually desiring women are always figured as "black."

On board Edna Earl meets the perfect mate of a colonial romance, a young minister who falls instantly in love with her. Although she cares nothing for him, he triumphs despite a series of interventions by exotic and sexually predatory surrogate parents. These are Mme. Tingot, an elegant dressmaker, and her estranged husband, Ahmed Sassoon, a pianist manqué who abandoned his music to pursue material riches. This olive-skinned gem merchant, referred to as "the Levantine," mesmerizes Edna Earl with his burning "oriental eyes."[19] He is not the only lure. Within the first seven pages we learn that Madame has a reputation for seducing young girls and that her still devoted ex-husband is as unmoored to any sexual binary as his ex-wife. Despite their different genders, Edna Earl is attracted to the femininity and the foreignness that characterize *both* ex-partners. Thus racialized, the Sassoons seem destined to be another of Estelle's always ambivalent fictional representations of the black maternal imaginary. They are, however, more explicitly racialized and sexualized than Dr. Wohlenski and therefore explicitly forbidden. Each has designs on Edna Earl—for sex and for use as a mannequin (marionette?) to display and market their wares on board ship.

Because it is, in part, a dialogue with Faulkner, Estelle's story abounds with more substantive evocations of *The Marionettes* in ways that foreshadow later Faulkner novels. The naive virgin is seduced as easily as Faulkner's Marietta and for some of the same reasons. Like Marietta, Edna Earl is genetically attracted to "darkness." She, too, has inherited "wild blood," only hers is from her loving, promiscuous, and beautiful paternal aunt Marcy rather than the loose-living mother in Faulkner's play. Like Caddy's illegitimate daughter Quentin, Edna Earl has minimal contact with her tabooed relative—the sexual woman. As the story reveals, Aunt Marcy, like Pierrot's Shade, is her niece's forbidden self; the self her mother attempted to erase by changing her name. When Mme. Tingot enters Edna Earl's life, she feels her aunt has been restored to her. She is Edna Earl's replacement "wild" woman, another blackened mother surrogate who offers all the physical pleasuring and material delights her mother denied her. Mme. Tingot and the feminized, orientalized Sassoon appeal to Edna Earl as "white" images of the black maternal. As Sassoon observes, they are outlaws who tempt Edna Earl to enjoy her body, to revel in her "bad blood," and to explore other taboo territory that her bigoted and hypocritical white culture has tried to repress.

Like Marietta's, Edna Earl's "proper" female relations have cloistered her all her life, stuffed her head with religion, and forbidden her to learn to dance. But in Estelle's story, as it does in Faulkner's poetry and play and will in his later fiction, dancing signals illicit and always racialized sexual foreplay. Edna Earl knows nothing about sex. Like Marietta, she is therefore ripe for ruin. The two "foreigners" waste no time in luring the simply dressed girl with their "caressing" bodies and voices and offering material goods including endless champagne, jewels, and Parisian gowns, all of it culminating in a screen test on their twelve-hour layover in Honolulu.[20] Here, too, Estelle's story responds to Faulkner's play where the virgin Marietta is drawn as a slim-hipped, small-breasted, long-legged, and plainly clad maiden. Once she's been seduced, Faulkner draws her as a bejeweled Wildean voluptuary sporting pendulous "breasts like ivory crusted jewels," rubies in her toes, jade-coated nails, and gold threads in her hair (*TM*, 45, and see fig. 11.2). Faulkner's is a stock image of the Decadents' femme fatale. In contrast, Estelle draws on pop and contemporary culture for her portrait of a virgin run amok. Like Pierrot, Edna Earl drinks herself into a stupor. Whereas Pierrot's drunkenness is willed, hers is coerced. Madame plies Estelle with booze without her knowledge of its effect. The "forgetting" it causes terrifies rather than soothes.

Estelle's treatment of liquor here as a drug given to gain control over and then exploit an ignorant young person suggests thematics that Faulkner will not attempt until he starts writing fiction. Consider, for example, the opening scene of *Soldiers' Pay*, in which an older soldier forces bootleg down a younger soldier's throat on a crowded troop train (*SP*, 10–11). As we've seen in earlier chapters, there are countless similar scenes in Faulkner's fiction. Edna Earl spends the five days it takes to reach Hawaii in an alcoholic haze. Despite all this, by the end of the voyage, her missionary zeal appears restored. Rather than going off with either Madame or Sassoon, in a sudden and unconvincing plot twist, she marries the prudish and preachy minister.[21]

The estranged Sassoons will remarry, and Madame will abandon her career as an international couturier. Thus, the heterosexual imperative and racial boundaries are restored. The unruly Sassoons resume their proper place in the colonial order, the new American Adam and his Eve continue on to China to conquer it for Christianity, and the popular missionary-colonial romance ends as it should.

Yet, Estelle has introduced so many subversive elements in her romance that her ending fails to convince. We are left with the sense that she has invoked the trappings of romance only to subvert them. In doing this, she exposes the difficulties the romance plot imposes on its characters, especially girls and women who insist on speaking their own words and who express a multiplicity of sexual desires. Still, the concluding scene of "A

Crossing" holds out about as much hope for its young heroine's marital bliss as Ellen Coldfield Sutpen's wedding ceremony in *Absalom, Absalom!*. Edna Earl allows marriage to silence her protesting voice and rob her of her economic independence.

Its trite ending aside, "A Crossing" is a modern-day story of multiple crossings, ones that Faulkner's fiction will engage as well: Edna Earl's from innocence to experience; the crossings implied in Mme. Tingot's homosexual and heterosexual liaisons and her husband's tolerance thereof; those implied in Edna Earl's attraction to both Sassoons' indeterminate gender and racial identities; the motivation for and consequences of her forced crossings into altered states of consciousness; the literal crossings of geographical boundaries; and Estelle's literary crossing into and revising of material in Faulkner's dream-play and other poetry.

From the opening paragraph, the battle between correct and unruly sex is foregrounded; the boundaries defining gender and sexual preference appear permeable and subject to reinterpretation. As her ship sets sail, Edna Earl's "exquisite profile" is the object of the predatory gazes of both the estranged couple and the very dull and proper young minister. The narrator observes that, as different as their interests appear, they share "a strange kinship," which gives their eyes the "same expression as they watched the girl." All three want to possess Edna Earl: "She was so young and fresh and beautiful, so unspoiled by contact with the world, that her simple, charming manner and the touch of sophistication that Mme. Tingot's costumes lent her made Edna Earl a rare combination indeed."[22] Such a plot, the explicit marketing of this rare combination, distinguishes this story from its contemporaneous romance counterparts. Of equal interest in the story is its focus on disturbing gender categories. Both themes are highly unconventional, and both will become a preoccupation of all three of the first novels Faulkner wrote, including the unpublished "Elmer."[23]

To contextualize "A Crossing" somewhat: the jeweler's surname, Sassoon, identifies him as related to one of the richest British Jewish families in Shanghai. Like many successful early American merchants, including Cornell Franklin's pre-Revolutionary New York City relatives, the British Sassoons had made their first fortunes in the "China Trade," a euphemism for opium trafficking.[24] The allusion contained in Sassoon's name would not have been lost on Estelle's assumed audience. It also has direct bearing on her story. In their attempts to subject or colonize Edna Earl, Mme. Tingot and Sassoon ply her with another addictive drug, one more pertinent to Estelle's, Cornell's, and Bill Faulkner's lives. Whether or not Estelle consciously intended this association, her portrayal of Edna Earl's initiation into colonial culture via drugs replicates Southern white boys' initiation into manhood. It also suggests that colonials poison themselves as well as their hosts with what they buy and sell.

By making religion one of the two issues of contention in Edna Earl's attempted rebellion against her upbringing, Estelle expands her economic critique to religion. Such a critique, had they read it, would also not have been lost on her contemporaries in Shanghai, who were well aware of and often chafed under the tremendous economic power American missionaries wielded there. "Next to London and New York," wrote the Presbyterian E. C. Lobenstine in the *China Mission Yearbook* of 1925, "Shanghai is the most important center of missions in the world." Nearly one-quarter of the two hundred mission operations in China were located in Shanghai, and missionaries and their families made up some four to five thousand of the ninety-eight hundred Americans living in China in the twenties. One China scholar writes that "informal estimates of American interests in China during the twenties suggest that, both in numbers of people and in economic investment, the Protestant missionaries were as important as the merchants and perhaps even outweighed them."[25] By making a missionary and two capitalists contend for ownership of her American Girl and pointing out the "strange kinship" among the three in her opening paragraphs, Estelle collapses any distinctions between spiritual and material colonizing. Considering that she wrote this story in the early 1920s, her narrative offers a fairly sophisticated cultural analysis and critique.

Besides being innocent, Edna Earl is very much a creation of her mother's psychosexual and social obsessions, her Mrs. Oldham–like concern with protecting the family's good name. Like Faulkner's Marietta, Edna Earl has been subjected to a joyless and repressive Calvinist upbringing and has lived by a set of rigidly defined religious, racial, social, and sexual laws and hierarchies. But the foreign Sassoons' allure and Madame's champagne change everything. Edna Earl's own unruly desires surface when she is drugged by drink and then tempted by the mystery and the exotic treasures of this sexually irresolute pair. At the same time, the proper young minister wants to marry her so she can help him help peddle Christianity to the Chinese.

Mme. Tingot (she has reclaimed her maiden name) awakens Edna Earl's sensuality, though any conscious sexual feeling toward another or even toward herself is absent. Edna Earl's wish to be touched manifests itself in three ways. The first is her physical pleasure in being cared for like a child. Madame unpacks her clothes and puts them away "in perfect order," and she relieves her mal de mer—"stay on your back so that the body becomes accustomed to the dance of the waves—I will give you something that will make you feel quite a seasoned voyager." Like a "mammy," she even dresses her: "Mme. Tingot knelt on the floor, gently pulling cobweb stockings over Edna Earl's slim legs." Edna Earl responds associatively by remembering another blackened woman, her "wild" aunt. Apparently, she is the only other grown-up who ever acknowledged the girl's body as something good and cared for her sensual needs. Simultaneously, to induce Edna Earl to model her gowns—"[Mme. Tingot] recalled how necessary to her was Edna Earl's appearance at dinner"—she constantly drugs her with champagne, which she claims is a remedy for seasickness.[26] This continues throughout the voyage. The cumulative effect of days of steady drinking on Edna Earl is a sort of psychological suspension and isolation, a state that first lulls and then terrifies her.[27]

Mme. Tingot's attentions also excite Edna Earl's pleasure in being looked at and desired by men and envied by women. Significantly, neither touch nor movement plays any part in this. Other than the dressing scenes, no one touches anybody. Even though a pointed exchange between Sassoon and the ship's purser makes clear that Mme. Tingot has a reputation for seducing young girls and suggests that she plans to seduce Edna Earl (7–8), nothing happens. Was Estelle being a narrative tease here, merely spicing up her tale by including a familiar New Woman stereotype, the rapacious phallic female who wants both men's jobs and their women? Or, in Edna Earl, was she creating a woman who could imagine desire but not permit herself to experience it?

Reading "A Crossing," Reading Herself: Biographical Implications

It is not much of a stretch to read "A Crossing" as, in part, Estelle's imaginative rendering of how she felt during her years in Shanghai as she tried to figure out what she wanted and what was best for her. During this time she was simultaneously caught between Bill's, Cornell's, and her parents' often competing agendas. The third-person impersonal narrator voices the internal and external pressures influencing the erotic and moral life of a young woman whose psychological core is, in some ways, similar to the author's. "A Crossing" therefore helps supplement the more traditional factual documentation concerning Estelle's first marriage, her continuing attraction to Faulkner, and his to her. It also provides insight concerning her perception of the societal pressures influencing her parents, who wished her to make a marriage that fulfilled their own, very conventional dreams. Finally, this story narrates Estelle's ambivalent critique and analysis of the roles played by young girls and women like herself in the neocolonial world of the Jim Crow South as well as the colonial cultures of the Hawaiian Territory and Shanghai's International Settlement. And, as a colonial anti-romance, it critiques the role romance fantasies play in Western imperialist endeavors.

While confirming its author's active and questioning mind and her ability to give pleasing formal shape to her fantasies, this story also suggests the nature and degree of her involvement with and collaboration in Bill Faulkner's imaginative life. When she wrote "A Crossing," she had been reading his apprenticeship work since at least 1914 and was therefore familiar with the fantasies and themes that governed it. Estelle was well aware of the role she played in those fantasies—or, rather, the stylized images of her that Bill drew, in both pictures and words. Most recently she had seen herself imagined as the virginal and then despoiled Marietta and, in *Vision*, as the faithless spouse and fatal dancer.

Responding to Faulkner's early work, "A Crossing" explores many of the same tensions but treats them differently. Bill's dream-play suggests his thinly disguised concerns about the nature of his desire and the relationship of his alcoholism to his sexuality and creativity. The play is also his imaginative response to his triangulated relationship with his mother and his abjured black mother, now concentrated in one woman and manifested in his illicit desire for the married Estelle, figuratively blackened for the purpose of returning his desire. In "A Crossing" Estelle addresses such miscegenous and sexually fluid desire through Edna Earl's relationship with the Sassoons.

Faulkner's dream-play is highly stylized and romantic. His maiden is seduced by Pierrot's Shade, is abandoned, and dies. Such is the alcohol-induced dream of the drunken Pierrot. Meanwhile, in her contemporary and realistic short story, Estelle revises Marietta (in part) to present her perspective on Marietta's seduction and perhaps to tell about a more personal betrayal. In Estelle's revision, Edna Earl makes the best of two bad choices: she agrees to marry the stuffy minister, a man who will please her family but with whom she will be unhappy, a familiar script. The apparent alternative, the Sassoons, live a life more like what Estelle might have imagined for herself had she married Faulkner in 1918. The multiple dimensions of the Sassoons' outsider status suggest her fears and wishes about her own and Bill's economic and creative potential. If she were to leave Cornell and marry Bill, could they survive and prosper, even though they chose to live an unconventional life? How would Oxford respond to their unorthodox union?

There is evidence that when Estelle and her children left Shanghai for good, early in 1926, after signing a separation agreement, she did try to support her family on her own. In a letter to her parents from Honolulu, she writes of her hope that Cornell will allow her to rent their old house from him beginning in June, when the current tenants' lease expires. He wants $100 per month for it—what the current tenants are paying—but she can only pay $75. And even then, she writes, "I'll be paying rent for my own furniture or, rather, Mother's [her mother-in-law, Mamie Hairston]." Her intention therefore was to try to make it on her own. After listing her monthly expenses—"My board here is $180 a month," the children's nurse $10 a week, and Victoria's school $25 a month—she writes that "I could run my house nicely and feel that I was nesting money here. . . . But unless I get my house my money will be just enough to get by on." She also tells her parents that she "had a wonderful letter from Mother and she said she would come out and spend several months with me." Mamie, who was herself a single working mother, had raised her son with little help from her richer relations. Perhaps hoping to emulate Mamie's independence, Estelle writes her parents, "If I ever get settled again I think I'll be reasonably happy."[28]

To supplement the three hundred dollars a month of child support plus school fees that Cornell had agreed to pay, she may have tried to market her writing and sewing skills. Through the Watsons, she would have known two of Honolulu's leading gossip columnists, in that they were Louise Watson's best friends and regular visitors at their home.[29] She also knew other local artists and writers through having acted in The Footlights, one of the better-known drama groups in Honolulu.[30] Unlike many of her contemporaries, Estelle continued into the early 1950s to make many of her own and her children's clothes. Letters Jill wrote her mother from college (1951–53) indicate that she was an accomplished dressmaker. She was inventive as well. Her daughter says that she seldom worked from a pattern, and if she did, it was her own design. Women in Oxford who served as her models or bought clothes from her remember several "fashion shows" she held in the Faulkners' house in the 1930s and 1940s. In the spring of 1926, however, Estelle's estranged husband was not as liberal with either his money or his affection as Mr. Sassoon. And perhaps Estelle, whose children were then seven and three, was not as enterprising as Mme. Tingot. Clearly, with two little children dependent on her, she was not as free. Estelle, Cho-Cho, and Malcolm remained at the Donna Hotel on Punaho Street until some time in late February or early March 1926, when she abandoned her brief dream of independence, packed up, said good-bye to the Watsons, and made the five-day crossing to San Francisco.[31]

Imaginative collaboration takes many forms, of which revision as part of a dialogue is only one. The language of "A Crossing" provides evidence of an even more intimate level of dialogue, "a marriage of speaking and hearing . . . in order to overpass to love," as Faulkner describes the story

Quentin and Shreve coauthor in *Absalom, Absalom!* Faulkner's voice is en-twined with Estelle's in this story. Self-consciously awkward grammatical inversions that occur in his early letters, and are prescient of phrasing in his earliest novels, occasional descriptions of Edna Earl, especially her looks or the ways her body registers her feelings, seem partly Faulknerian. As will be the case so often in Faulkner's novels, voyeurism, masking or illusion, erot-ics ungoverned by any binaries, and psychological mirroring and doubling are opening and sustaining themes in "A Crossing."

Estelle's belles in "A Crossing," in "Star Spangled Banner Stuff," and in the later "Selvage" and "A Letter to Grandmamma" suggest either that they were her inventions to begin with or that as he typed this story (and other stories) for her, her revisions of his Marietta—her wired little belles—stimulated Faulkner to, in turn, revise her narratives. When Faulkner first read Estelle's stories, in early December 1924, he would have found in her fictional heroines' troubles and escapades something that was lacking in his own lyric yet self-indulgent and often pathetically sentimental poetic ren-derings of adolescent angst. He responded, as he had to other writers he admired, by combining his voice with hers. In his earlier imitations and adaptations of Swinburne, Eliot, Aiken, and other poets, he had failed to transcend the bonds of imitation. Yet when he combined his voice with Estelle's, he created something bold and utterly new. Perhaps, in part, this was because Estelle wrote about the familiar—the funny, contemporary, and localized—in colloquial prose. Her girls and women were flappers, not Edwardian femme fatales. It was as if her fiction gave him permission to explore for the first time what he would later call his "postage-stamp of na-tive soil."[32] We cannot know for sure. What is clear, though, and most im-portant is the fact of their collaboration.

As we've seen in earlier chapters, the contemporary world figures only peripherally in Faulkner's poetry. Single lyrics and his three longer works, *The Marble Faun, The Lilacs,* and *The Marionettes* are all told from the perspec-tive of the classic adolescent pierrotiste, a solipsistic narrator (adapted from his careful readings of early Conrad Aiken and T. S. Eliot) who, before 1924, shows little interest in the interior lives of any fictional women, even in his few brief forays into prose fiction.

Like Faulkner's first poem sequences and his play, his earliest short story and prose sketch have a male adolescent voice as their central con-sciousness. The first, "Landing in Luck" (*Mississippian,* 26 November 1919), takes the form of a tall tale. His sketch "The Hill" (10 March 1922), like many of the short prose pieces he published in the *Double Dealer* and the *Times Picayune* in 1925, is a prose poem, an attempt to capture a lyric mo-ment rather than a story. Even Faulkner's early 1925 pieces for the *Double*

Dealer are sketches of single characters, primarily male loners, rather than fully developed multivocal narratives; many are unashamedly romantic. Because they are only tentatively about relationships, none are as formally sophisticated and psychologically complex as the short stories Estelle brought back with her from Shanghai.[33]

Assuming Faulkner did revise parts of her narratives, what it taught him as he mingled and merged his phrases with Estelle's was to see how to turn from the bookishly imitative and psychologically opaque figures in his poetry to the people and issues of his generation and world. The here-and-now physical and emotional geography of her stories suggested specific interior and exterior landscapes that were the antithesis of the undifferentiated dream spaces of his poetry. As he physically and emotionally immersed himself in her fiction, reading and then typing her sentences and paragraphs, he saw in her challenges to racial and sexual binaries how to move from fragmented lyric governed by the heterosexual imperative to Modernist narratives that often explored alternatives. The results of this collaboration are immediately evident in Faulkner's first two novels, where traces of "A Crossing" compose many of the scenes and emotionally charged crossings of adolescent girls and young women. All the young women in *Soldiers' Pay*—Emmy, Margaret Powers, and Cecily—begin in Estelle's Edna Earl. The same is true of *Mosquitoes*.

One example of the several moments in *Soldiers' Pay* that pay direct and unmediated homage to "A Crossing" occurs in another "dressing scene," wherein the world-weary, upper-class, bisexual Margaret lures the naive servant girl, Emmy, into a prolonged, prone embrace with promises of empathic listening, sensuous holding, and her beautiful cast-off clothes: "Suppose you come up with me and we'll try it on you. I can sew a little and we can make it fit you exactly. . . . I will lend you stockings to go with it, and a hat, too." Emmy's response asserts the heterosexual imperative: "'Where's your husband?' she asked irrelevantly" (*SP,* 122–23). Faulkner simultaneously screens and reveals Emmy's seduction, first with the irony of her highly relevant question, then with an ellipsis for the undressing and dressing scene that Estelle's story dwells on, and finally with the tale Emmy tells of being seduced and deserted by her employer's son. As Emmy told her tale, Margaret Powers, who "knew that lacking a bed any reclining intimacy was conducive to confidence," pulled the "unresisting" girl "down beside her in an ancient obese armchair" and "held her close" (*SP,* 124, 127). Faulkner's re-creation is sophisticated work in which a heated homoerotic scene plays out against Emmy's tearful recitation of a traditional heterosexual narrative of seduction and betrayal (*SP,* 122–29). But the psychological and narrative impulse began, I suggest, with his experience of writing himself into Estelle's stories.

Their family curse of wild blood causes the parents or parent surrogates in *The Marionettes* and "A Crossing" to wall off their adolescent virgins from the world. But these adolescents' inexperience cannot account for the awkward mix of voyeuristic eroticism and sexual anesthesia that suffuses *The Marionettes*, "A Crossing," Estelle's other stories, and Faulkner's first two novels. There may well be a connection between this anesthesia and the amount of alcohol their characters drink, particularly in Faulkner's play and "A Crossing." Both writers explore the effect of drinking on their characters' sense of responsibility for their choices, its use as a means of controlling the naïve and uninitiated, and its ability to distort perception and to deaden or mask severe emotional pain.

Perhaps because they believe they have more to hide, alcoholics do more masquerading than most people, so it is hard to say how much Estelle's and Bill's alcoholism exaggerated this aspect of their relationship. In her fiction Estelle focuses on the use of alcohol as a means of social control, whereas Faulkner veils his personal relation to the subject by explaining its presence in his text as part of the convention in which he was writing. Both writers make the causal relationships between alcoholism and masquerade, and between alcoholism and moral and emotional anesthesia and debauchery, central to their fictional worlds. Yet unlike Faulkner's emotionally evasive poetry, Estelle's fiction dealt with the pain and shame associated with intimate and forbidden subjects—namely, sex, race, and the always attendant alcoholism.

Alone in Shanghai in the early twenties, she had dared write about a space well known to him but silenced in his writing. Faulkner recognized in her responsive yet revisionist stories—her side of their dialogue—the vast imaginative potential of such tropes. She showed him how to move from convention to invention. In later novels, most extensively in *Sanctuary* and *The Sound and the Fury*, Faulkner will expand on the trope of alcohol to coerce, subjugate, and psychologically and sexually abuse children in families where it pervades almost every relationship white children have with their adult relatives or surrogate parents. As in the Faulkners' lives, this heritage became very much a part of their fictional dialogue and, later, Faulkner's mature artistic vision. It's no accident that Temple Drake calls Popeye "Daddy," that the Compson children's coercive father and maternal uncle are alcoholics, or that Benjy's older brothers torment him on the day he loses Caddy by further disorienting him with bootleg whiskey (*TSAF,* 13–15, 25–26).

In the early 1920s, when Estelle was writing "A Crossing," the fictional worlds of many American novelists reflected their country's cultural, social, and moral climates. The United States was locked in conflict over their most recent constitutional amendment (the Eighteenth) and the Volstead Act.[34] That Gatsby made his millions in bootlegging—his "drug stores"—is one of the finer ironies of Fitzgerald's 1925 bestseller. The perceptual and psychological effects of various degrees of inebriation permeate the pages of *The Sun Also Rises*, Faulkner's *Soldiers' Pay*, and dozens of other novels and short stories. But, almost without exception, this fiction, written by both men and women, valorizes and normalizes drinking. It is, without question, what real men (and the flapper "girls" who are their buddies) do. Booze floods their fictional worlds. In *Exiles Return*, Malcolm Cowley wrote about Hemingway heroes: "They drink early and late; they consume enough beer, wine, anis[e], grappa, and Fundador to put them all into alcoholic wards, if they were ordinary mortals; but drinking seems to have the effect on them of a magic potion."[35]

Faulkner, following Estelle, has a different agenda. What sets his work apart is that although many of his characters drink unremittingly, alcohol never acts upon them as a magic potion. Implicitly in his earliest work and explicitly in all of his finest novels, the narrative demonstrates understanding and fear of its destructive powers. Faulkner writes about the terrors, not the joys, of booze. He uses different aspects of alcoholic addiction as metaphors for total psychic dislocation. He also uses them to articulate compulsively self-destructive behavior whose root cause is a desire to repress unbearable and often unspeakably shameful racial and sexual pain, confusion, and desire. One thinks of Sutpen, of Quentin and Benjy, of Rider, of Temple Drake, and of Joe Christmas.

But Estelle Oldham explored these fears first, in "A Crossing" and the two other stories she brought to Oxford in 1924. In "A Crossing," alcohol becomes a metaphor for the essential rottenness of Edna Earl's colonial world. On the ship that is emblematic of this world, she is faced with a selection of bad choices. Whether she chooses to be the Sassoons' mannequin or a colonial missionary's wife, she will still be objectified, commodified, and silenced. She will never get to grow up. This colonial scene at this particular moment in American expansionism is the context in which Estelle sets Edna Earl's progress toward alcoholism, marriage, and silence. It describes her colonization and exploitation. Unlike the Faulkner of *The Marionettes* but very much anticipating the Faulkner of *Sanctuary*, here Estelle looks at this process through the mind of an adolescent girl. As is now clear, she was writing partly from self-observation. But her larger field of vision reached back to at least 1914 to include Bill's and Phil Stone's preoccupations with drinking, being drunk, and all the symbolic baggage alcohol carried in a Southern town. As is clear from her other two stories, Estelle was familiar with the importance of alcohol in homosocial bonding and its ritual role in exclusively male pursuits like hunting and sex. She was also knowledgeable about and interested in portraying a world in which grown-ups use the apparently antithetical opiates, alcohol and religion, on young people (as their ancestors had on their slaves) to deprive them of their wills and educate them into culturally prescribed roles. Alcohol's effects and Estelle's feelings about its effect on her are recorded in "A Crossing." Edna Earl's only intimate relationship is with or under the influence of booze.

Recall that the girl passes the five days it takes to reach Honolulu in a drug-induced haze. Emerging from it, "she felt a little frightened. Where had she been, what had she done, to have been blinded like this? Why, she'd scarcely been aware of being at sea at all. True, every day before tiffin she had come out on deck for a promenade, but she'd always had the feeling that she was a beautiful actress playing her part on the stage. Clothed in strange luxurious fabrics and furs and looked upon with mingled admiration and envy, she had gloated over her masquerade. And in the evenings, in smart, exquisitely beautiful dinner gowns, she had come out on this very deck to the dances."[36]Edna Earl's sense of disassociation, of watching herself as if that self were another person, articulates an alienation to which Faulkner's imagination was also attracted; it was a revisioning of Faulkner's splitting of his Pierrot character in his dream-play. Once the alcohol wears off, Edna Earl suffers the terrific pangs of her relentless Calvinist conscience: "You have not read your bible. . . . You have not written . . . your mother" and "every day you drink wine; wine is a mocker." This last charge proves too much. Hysterically she screeches, "But if I didn't drink a little, I'd be sea-sick." In response, an obliging steward orders more champagne, which she refuses as vehemently as, two pages later, she "scornfully" rejects the young minister's advances and his prayer-book method of salvation. Both threaten to destroy what remains of her fragile sense of self. When he insists that she read with him prayers for her soul, she resists: "That kind of praying doesn't help me. . . . I have to shut my eyes and make up my own words." As in her earlier story, Estelle's heroine claims that her personal salvation lies in her ability to speak for herself and to imagine her own narrative. The minister persists, calling on (this must be ironic) "the comfortable words of St Paul." Edna reacts appropriately: "'Don't!' [she] screamed and stuck her fingers in her ears. 'I hate it all. All, do you hear? My Tomlinson blood is cropping out, and I'm glad!' She rushed from the room."[37] Meanwhile Sassoon, lurking in a corner, is watching all this and silently urging her on.

The problem is that, like Temple Drake at Miss Reba's whorehouse, she has nowhere to go. Given her upbringing and lack of education and economic resources, her choices are either to do the missionary work for which she has been trained since childhood or become Madame's drugged sex slave and private mannequin. The latter appears as, by far, the more interesting choice.

As it does for Faulkner's Pierrot, drunkenness also seems to serve as a metaphor for her impotence. When the ship docks for its brief layover in Honolulu, Edna Earl is still drunk. She can't "remember the details of her day in port. . . . She couldn't recall things clearly. . . . She couldn't remember." Again, the Sassoons "take care of her." She reels off a list of material splendors they've arranged for her, the stuff of every soap opera heroine's dreams; gorgeous gowns, orchids, and even a screen test. Estelle really piles it on here for the same reason her minister quotes St. Paul—she wants to be sure her audience understands why Edna feels indebted to the Sassoons. She thinks she must do what they ask because they've "been so good to me."[38] Her authoritarian upbringing makes it impossible for her to realize that they have used her.

"A Crossing" further elucidates Estelle's side of their dialogue at the time she wrote this story and suggests how her revisions of and additions to Faulkner's political and sexual economies in *The Marionettes* and other apprenticeship works helped him move from poetry to prose. Estelle's narrative fiction, so personal and autobiographical in ways known only to Bill, gave him a different kind of formal and emotional model, a new way of seeing and experiencing the world he was to write out of for the rest of his life.[39]

Because "A Crossing" is, in part, a dialogue with Bill, it abounds with more substantive echoes of *The Marionettes*, which she revises in ways that foreshadow Faulkner's later novels. Like Marietta and like Caddy's illegitimate daughter, Quentin, Edna Earl has minimal contact with her tabooed relative—the sexual woman. She's only been allowed to see her twice. But all her associations to her aunt are both childlike and sensuous. As the story reveals, Aunt Marcy, like Pierrot's Shade, is a tabooed dark double. Mme. Tingot briefly revives that part of Edna Earl: "You remind me of Aunt Marcy. . . . She is beautiful like you and has lovely things too. Things that smell like a whole garden of flowers at night." Her aunt, "the most wonderful aunt in the world," also believes women can be smart. Edna Earl describes to Mme. Tingot how she cares for and rewards her niece's intellect *and* her femininity: "She has sent me clothes all my life and she came when I graduated from high school and again when I graduated from the

Female College in Martinsville."[40] Perhaps some wish fulfillment is at work here. Recall that although Estelle earned As and Bs in Mary Baldwin's rigorous college preparatory program, which included chemistry and geometry, her parents felt one year there was enough.

Aunt Marcy is the antithesis of Edna Earl's mother, who has had her "trained since I was a baby to be a missionary, to help in my humble way to compensate the world for the misery the Tomlinsons have caused in it." Yet, Edna Earl idealizes her racy, self-supporting, and unmarried aunt. Although Faulkner will transform the combined unruliness of all of Estelle's rebellious women into figures like Caddy—a tragic yet ultimately silenced image of the disruptive feminine—Estelle's original Bad Girl–Woman is an ideal and a success. Mme. Tingot's sensuality is, in part, what makes her so appealing to Edna Earl. She is her replacement "wild" woman, another blackened mother surrogate who offers Edna Earl all the sensual physical care and material delights her mother denied her. She and Sassoon, both replacements for Aunt Marcy, appeal to Edna Earl, being white images of the black maternal, outlaws who try to teach Edna Earl to pleasure her body, to revel in her "bad blood," and to explore other taboo territory that her white culture has denied her. With perhaps an intuitive grasp of the intimate tie between eros and creativity, Estelle highlights Madame's erotic relationship with her imaginative creations: "with an intense solicitude that was almost sensuous she lifted the beautiful expensive gowns and wraps from the dark recesses and laid them tenderly on the bed or hung them gently in the wardrobes and along the wall." As she arranges the collection she has designed, "her long white hands caressed over and over each single garment."[41] Yet the metaphor of sexual play and arousal that Estelle develops in these sentences never travels from the clothes to Edna Earl's body, and there is no expansion of the purser's assertion to Sassoon that Madame will seduce Edna Earl as she has another young woman. Estelle suggests but never develops an explicit lesbian seduction. She only permits Mme. Tingot to make love to the clothes in which she so lovingly dresses Edna Earl.

As in *The Sound and the Fury*, Estelle's and Bill's earlier narratives police and punish sexually active female adolescents. Dancing serves in both narratives as a prelude to and euphemism for sexual play. Both Bill's and Estelle's virgins have grown up in homes where they are forbidden to dance. When the virgins do "dance," they are punished. Both narratives close with the maiden's literal or spiritual death. *The Marionettes* and many of Faulkner's early poems repeat this formula. Estelle would have been familiar with Bill's poem "The Dancer," because he wrote it for that sequence of love poems he gave her in 1921. This dancer creates a

> flame that, like a music from your hair,
> Sheds through me as though I were but air;
> That strips me bare, my sudden life reveals.

She "haunts" and "tempts" her lover, knowing that she has "mazed your life against your will" ("The Dancer," *VIS*, 65). In "A Crossing," Estelle takes a fresh approach to Faulkner's trope of the fatal dancer as she draws on her own experience of being the dancing girl who is being looked at *and* looking. Forbidden to dance and consequently not knowing how to when given the opportunity, Edna Earl turns *not dancing* into a tool for seducing others. But her guilt at her ingenuity overwhelms her. Thus her sin of omission, her *not* dancing, is far "worse" (than had she joined the other dancers) because "you were aware of being more beautiful *still* than the other women were in motion, and so you told the truth and said you couldn't dance. Then you lay in a long chair, your beautiful body mocking all the other bodies of women. And they hated you, lying there so wholly enticing, declaring you couldn't dance."[42] By transforming the still figure's gender from the drunken and immobilized Pierrot to her own tipsy Edna Earl, Estelle fictionalizes a familiar scene from their shared adolescence, those dances in the university gym or at the Oldhams' home in Oxford. At those, she had been the dancer who gazed hopelessly upon the still, silent, beautiful, and probably inebriated Bill as he stood or sat motionless on the sidelines, refusing to dance. She said that although he'd never ask "to escort me because he didn't care for dancing and really couldn't," he "would be there, impeccably dressed," which she loved and which "attracted" her to him. She thought "he was the first boy in Oxford to own a set of tails," which his grandfather "probably had made for him in Memphis, as Mr. Murry would have none of that kind of nonsense." At these dances Billy "would stand on the sidelines. Occasionally he'd ask me to dance or cut in, pushing me around for a few minutes until someone else cut in," and occasionally she'd sit out a dance with him.[43] Here, Estelle, in a wishful role reversal, imagines herself as Bill. In this reversal—Edna Earl as watcher—she performs an imaginatively bold move as, for a moment, just for the length of a sentence, she puts her female heroine in charge of desire.

Back at sea, when Madame and her ex team up to dress Edna Earl in gowns and jewels they hope to sell to colonial matrons who will display them at venues like the Shanghai Race Meet, we see how completely they have transformed and framed her as an object of the colonial gaze, a spectacle of colonial desire. When one passenger decides "she must have that costume," Sassoon observes that Edna Earl is now "perfect" because she supplies "the proper background for his favorite gem." The Sassoons have made her into their personal icon of consumerist desire: "A hush came over the room. Against the deep blue of the slim little gown a single pear-shaped diamond glowed and sparkled as it swung on its almost invisible platinum chain."[44]

At the moment that Edna Earl stands framed as the background for the Sassoons' wares, the ship's doctor appears and commands her service. The young minister has caught scarlet fever and is mortally ill. The doctor claims that only her words can comfort him. By saying that the minister talks about nothing but her, the doctor implies that her indifference has made him sick. Edna Earl instantly reverts to the role for which she's been trained, the self-sacrificing, self-effacing woman. But as soon as she agrees to the doctor's demand, she suddenly feels "as if she herself were dying"— which, of course, she is.[45] From this point on, Edna Earl slides swiftly from missionary nurse into the role of docile, Bible-spouting spouse. In the con- clusion, she sits beside the minister's hospital bed intoning the Father's Word as she reads from her husband's previously rejected prayer book. She'll never again "make up [her] own words."

Edna Earl's dilemma resonates with her author's. Through the charac- ter of Mme. Tingot, Estelle has tried to write an alternative plot to mar- riage. But even Madame, talented and successful and sexually liberated, returns to her old marriage. The meaning of her return manifests itself in Sassoon's proprietary response: "My Jeanne and my ruby."[46] The author can't resolve the conflicts she's created for Edna Earl any more successfully than she can solve her own. Even Estelle's most rebellious woman, Mme. Tingot, returns to respectability. A sentimental, tacked-on ending that re- unites the Sassoons nullifies both women's bids for independence and iden- tities separate from their husbands.

Both "A Crossing" and *The Marionettes* raise questions relevant to the future of Estelle and Bill's relationship. Estelle's questions are, can a woman leave her marriage to pursue a career and still be thought normal? Does a daughter who has been rigorously trained to uphold the values of her par- ents and her culture have a chance of becoming a person in her own right, of speaking in a different voice, "my own words"? What are the costs of abandoning one's art for material gain? Can a man be an artist without be- ing feminized; can a woman be one without being masculinized? Or, will the culture marginalize all difference by charging it with sexual deviancy? And, most important, should it matter? What does a woman find erotic about racial and sexual taboos and about men who seem more feminine than masculine or about another woman's desire? What is racial-sexual difference and what is its appeal? What is the cost of allowing oneself to be silenced—either by alcohol or by cultural expectations and constraints for which alcohol serves as a metaphor? Like her earlier story about her childhood, "A Crossing" concerns a young girl who tries to speak for herself and to create and explore a culturally taboo maternal imaginary. The fictional child Estelle succeeded where Edna Earl, Mme. Tingot, and Mr. Sassoon ultimately fail. What about the real Estelle?

As with "Dr. Wohlenski," we will never know for sure the source of these imaginative germs in "A Crossing," which come to fruition in Faulkner novels. But that they are woven through all of Estelle's stories and brought together, reconstituted, and transformed in Faulkner's fiction argues for their origins in Estelle's modest and forgotten tales.

Estelle's second visit home, in 1921, had lasted twice as long as her first. During the nearly three and a half years the Franklins lived in Hawaii, Estelle had spent more than a year on the mainland. Of the remaining time, Estelle's and Cornell's mothers spent nine months between them visiting their children in Hawaii. During their first four months on the island, the newlyweds were separated when Cornell went off to boot camp, leaving Estelle alone in Honolulu. The intervals they did spend together were brief—until the nearly three years they lived in Shanghai, from late November 1921 to the end of November 1924.

In Shanghai their marriage fell apart.

21

The Marketing of Estelle and Her Rebellion
Honolulu, 1919–1921

I N THE TWENTY-FIRST CENTURY, the concept of men in modern
Western societies exchanging women to strengthen their social bonds,
maintain the status quo, and stimulate their capital is no longer new.
Like the slave economies that preceded them, plantation-based economies,
into which Estelle, Cornell, and Faulkner were born, were extremes of this
model. With rare exceptions, their political, social, and economic structures
were run by and for white men. The Oldham-Franklin marriage is a case
in point. By 1921 in Oxford, Mississippi, their union had produced precisely this effect, for it stimulated other "exchanges" among groups of men.
These began with Estelle's male in-laws and her father and resulted in financial gain for all—all, that is, except Estelle. Although she facilitated
these exchanges, she was excluded from participating in either the economy or the resulting homosocial bonding within that community of men.
The exchanges resulting directly and indirectly from Estelle's first marriage
are important, first, for understanding the shifting dynamics of Estelle's
and Bill Faulkner's relationship before their own marriage in 1929 and, second, because these exchanges benefited the young artist at a significant moment in his career. Third, these exchanges are relevant for the fictional capital that first Estelle and then Bill would make of them.

Exchanges of women in race-obsessed colonial and postcolonial communities drive the plots of Estelle's "A Crossing" and "Star Spangled Banner Stuff," as well as "Selvage" (published as "Elly") and "A Letter." They
will also define the Byzantine familial relationships in all of Faulkner's novels. As we've seen in *Absalom, Absalom!* and *Go Down, Moses,* for example,
black slaves, African Americans, and white women and children are constant objects of exchange. I suggest that although Faulkner's long involve-

ment with Estelle led to his acute awareness and understanding of the emotional climates in families ruled by such exchanges, the initial impulse to *write* about their sexual and economic politics, particularly their impact on the women involved, was Estelle's. As postcolonial critiques, her stories, set in a mutually shared culture, were Billy's most emotionally and experientially intimate models. It is no wonder that when he read them, he wanted to try to rewrite her two stories with Southern settings, "Selvage" and "A Letter."

Marketing Estelle Oldham

How did such exchanges work within the Oldham, Franklin, and Falkner families—in Estelle's and Billy's actual experience? In 1918, after capitalizing on his daughter's alliance with Cornell, Lem Oldham then widened the circle of exchange by using his newly acquired political powers to improve the financial condition of two young men in Oxford. Surprisingly, these were Faulkner and Phil Stone, the poet's financial backer and best friend at the time.[1] Part of Lem's motive for helping Phil was to strengthen the legal business partnership, or the financial marriage he had made previously with Phil's father, James Stone. Why he wished to help Billy Faulkner, whom he had rejected and would continue to reject as a son-in-law, probably had more to do with his liking for Billy than with any expectation of economic gain. One of the Oldhams' most telling objections to Billy had been his financial situation. This may explain why Estelle's father stepped in to get Billy a job only *after* she had married Cornell.

Estelle's first marriage, or marketing, set in motion a series of political appointments and economic alliances that resulted in jobs and incomes for all sorts of men, including her first husband and the man who would become her second husband.[2] Although she may not have realized this in the first years of her marriage, her fiction shows that by 1922 she understood it very well.

Because Estelle never found a means to become economically independent and therefore free of Franklin, she ended up making her body and mind, the only commodities she could control, the sites of her two forms of resistance. By becoming an alcoholic, she ultimately succeeded, wittingly or not, in transforming herself from Franklin's asset to his liability. And by using her imagination, at first to act in Honolulu's amateur drama groups and then to write fiction critiquing her culture's trafficking in women and its racism, she achieved some degree of intellectual and emotional independence. Most important, writing also extended and expanded her dialogue with Billy Faulkner. In "A Crossing" and "Star Spangled Banner

Stuff," the education, the codes of conduct, and the consumables of her culture that her first husband and parents meted out become the fictional nexus for her challenge to the marketing of women, imperialism, and racism.

Initial and Subsequent Exchanges: Lem Oldham and Cornell Franklin

By early 1922, shortly after the Franklins moved from Honolulu to Shang-hai, the initial exchange of Estelle between Cornell and Lem produced another tangible result. Cornell, now the "Judge," wrote his father-in-law to request that the "Major" use his political influence to "have me ap-pointed attorney for the Shipping Board in China."[3] The effects of Estelle's marketing continued long *after* her 1929 divorce from Franklin as financial exchanges between Cornell and Lem continued. The terms of the Frank-lins' divorce settlement graphically illustrate how their marriage had been, for all financial purposes, a union between two men—Estelle's father and her first husband. Although she got custody of their children, she received no alimony. Cornell did pay child support but sent his checks to Lem, not to his ex-wife. This economic arrangement continued during most of Es-telle's second marriage.[4] Explaining her understanding of Cornell's child support arrangement, Sallie Murry wrote that Cornell sent money to Lem "because he was Victoria's and Malcolm's guardian and he kept the money for his family [Lida, Dorothy, and himself] to live on."[5] While Cornell may in fact have sent child support checks to Lem, court papers state that Estelle was to receive the money.

Although in 1929 the Oldhams still opposed Estelle's marrying Faulkner, they again benefited financially from her marriage. With the loss of Lem's government job and subsequent demise of his business ventures, their new son-in-law also began contributing to their economic support.[6] Thus, after 1929, Lem would have *both* his daughter's husbands supporting him.

In early February 1919, Lem resigned from the government appoint-ment *his* Republican step-father-in-law had secured for him fifteen years earlier to enter a law partnership with Phil Stone's father, James. Stone was a member of the Delta plantocracy and one of the richest Democrats in Oxford.[7] The two were already financially allied. By 1910 Stone, president of the Bank of Oxford, had made Oldham his vice president. Further-more, both men held substantial shares in the ill-fated Lamb-Fish Lumber Co., whose general counsel was Stone's eldest son, Jack.[8]

In November 1919, nine months after Lem Oldham's resignation,

President Warren Harding, a Republican, won his landslide victory over Woodrow Wilson. Lem, who, like Lida and her family, had been a lifelong worker for the state's Republican Party, began lining up support in his bid for another government appointment—United States District Attorney for the Northern District of Mississippi, a considerably more lucrative post than his prior clerkship. Chief among his supporters was Thomas B. Franklin, a Democrat from Columbus, Mississippi, and the influential uncle of Lem's new son-in-law.

In mid-March 1920, Thomas Franklin wrote Cornell in Honolulu to report Lem's success: "Mr. Oldham has just returned from Washington where he landed the US District atty-ship—in place of my old friend Shed Hill who died about a month ago. . . . It afforded me *real* pleasure to help Mr. Oldham—John Wood and myself got the Columbus Bar to endorse Mr. Oldham."[9] Even though Oldham was a lifelong Republican, his new relative, a Democrat, wrote a letter on his behalf and arranged for the Columbus Bar Association to support his appointment. The position, which Lem held until 25 January 1926, paid an annual salary of thirty-five hundred dollars. Lem made up his lost income almost exactly when he started receiving Cornell's child support payments later that year.

In 1922, the Franklins' first year in Shanghai, Lem made his son-in-law a much needed loan of fifteen hundred dollars. In March 1925, from Shanghai, Cornell wrote to Lem: "You must think me very neglectful of my obligations not to have even mentioned for nearly three years the loan you were good enough to let me have." He assures Lem that repayment with interest will be forthcoming in June or July. In fact, Cornell would not repay the loan until 2 February 1926, shortly after he had determined that Estelle was no longer an asset to his quest for fame and fortune in Shanghai's International Settlement and so got rid of her. As her Shanghai lawyer (a good friend of Cornell's) wrote to her, "It is admitted that Cornell required that you go home."[10]

Given that the economic picture in Mississippi in 1921 was even worse than usual, Lem, Phil, and Bill were especially fortunate to get the jobs brought about by the Democratic and Republican party networks they made use of through Estelle's marriage. Meanwhile, the news from Honolulu was not happy. Harding's election emboldened a Republican investigation of Malcolm Franklin, Cornell's uncle, which resulted in his forced resignation as Customs Collector and his return to Mississippi in May 1921.[11]

Meanwhile, in Oxford, once Lem was back on the party payroll, he wasted no time in exercising his new political clout. In short order he recommended that his law partner's son, Phil, be made his assistant, at fifteen hundred dollars a year, a position Phil held until 1923.[12] Between 1918 and

1924 Phil, in turn, invested a lot of time and money in Bill Faulkner's bid to become a published poet. Ironically, Phil, who disliked Estelle and actively opposed her relationship with Bill, reaped a significant profit from her first marriage, for it helped to finance *his* economic and emotional alliance with "little Billy," a relationship Phil's biographer likens to "a marriage."

More Exchanges and Bonding: Lem Oldham and Billy Faulkner

Although Lem Oldham did not want Bill Faulkner to marry Estelle, during the early years of her marriage to Cornell, he evidenced great fondness for Bill. In May 1920, when Lida and Estelle's sister, Dorothy, went to visit the Franklins in Honolulu, Lem invited Bill to move in with him.[13] Oxford wags began referring to Faulkner as "Lem Oldham's yard boy."[14] The racial overtones and emotional reverberations of this epithet find expression throughout Faulkner's fiction. One of his most inventive reworkings and transformations is his subversive drama of another "marriage" between a would-be Southern gentleman, Thomas Sutpen, and his white-trash "yard boy," Wash Jones, a marriage sealed in drink and consummated with the "exchange" of Wash's fifteen-year-old granddaughter, Milly. When she fails to produce a male heir, Sutpen dismisses her, saying, "Well, Milly, too bad you're not a mare like Penelope. Then I could give you a decent stall in the stable" (*AA*, 151). His failure to honor the exchange he made with Milly's grandfather drives Wash to kill Sutpen. The white master is destroyed by his own design and by the one man he betrays who is most like his own white-trash father.

When and why Lem conceived his liking for Billy we will never know for sure. Like Oldham in the early years of his marriage, Faulkner was his town's ne'er-do-well; they both were visually breathtaking; they both loved to dress up; like the fictional couple Sutpen and Wash, during the long Mississippi summers Lem and Billy drank together and enjoyed each other's stories. Perhaps Lem saw his younger dream-filled and ambitious self in the poet–wounded warrior–town tramp–dandy personae Bill alternated among. The emotional flexibility and freedom Faulkner's impostures projected perhaps reminded Lem of the self who had existed before his business failures in Texas and Kosciusko had forced him, in the early years of his marriage, onto his step-father-in-law's dole. In 1903, he had moved off it, but only by means of the clerkship Judge Niles had procured for him in Oxford. Now, nearly twenty years later, another judge whose friendship Lem had gained by exchanging his daughter, Estelle, would provide another sinecure. Lem's financial solvency depended thoroughly on exchanges of his wife and daughter. Perhaps Lem also liked Faulkner because he saw in the young man, who by 1920 had already made one trip East in search of fame and fortune, a history of striving and a wanderlust with which he identified. In short, the qualities that Lem may have found most attractive in the young Faulkner were also what made him unacceptable as a son-in-law: the poet had nothing material to offer in exchange for Estelle.

So on her first trip home, Estelle must have been surprised to find a new closeness between them. Once again, another man seemed to have slipped into the role she longed for. But, just as Wash made his daughter's compliant body the "vessel" for his worshipful love for Sutpen, so Estelle may have perceived Lem's love for Bill as legitimating hers.

Estelle's marriage to Cornell helped Bill in more tangible ways as well. Faulkner had been on his second visit to New Haven just over three weeks when, on 1 November 1921, he wrote Maud that he had received "a wire from Major" saying that he should "answer immediately" if he wanted the job of university postmaster. Apparently the major's haste was unnecessary; Faulkner did not take up his offer until two weeks later (*TOH*, 155). Within a month of his daughter's reluctant departure for China, Lem had secured the post office sinecure for Bill, which paid fifteen hundred dollars a year, a post he held until September 1924, despite having scored lower on the postal examination than the other candidate.[15] To claim that Estelle's first marriage financed Bill Faulkner's apprenticeship years would be an overstatement, but it certainly helped. In the early 1920s, a yearly income of fifteen hundred dollars for a single man living at home in Oxford, Mississippi, was a generous income.

Ironically, while Estelle's marriage to Cornell improved her husband's and father's economic prospects almost immediately, and indirectly fostered Bill's financial and emotional independence, the benefits it brought to her parents and her husband only further constricted her. Monetary interests combined with social conventions to keep her in an emotionally and intellectually barren marriage in which she was totally financially dependent on her husband. Neither family wanted Estelle and Cornell to divorce; until the very end, both families and Cornell worked hard to keep the marriage intact, at least in the legal sense.

Estelle's Market Value: Its Rise and Fall, Honolulu, October 1919–November 1920

Estelle's ship from San Francisco reached Honolulu on 25 October 1919. Perhaps refreshed by her five-month visit home that summer and buoyed by the knowledge that her mother and sister planned a long visit the following spring, Estelle resumed the demanding social schedule required of the wife of a lawyer on the rise in the Hawaiian Territory. Franklin's cases were reported regularly in the *Pacific Commercial Advertiser*'s column on the circuit court; its social columns chart Estelle's attendance at luncheons and the couple's evening social engagements with stunning regularity.

During his wife's absence that first summer Cornell had bought a small, newly built bungalow for his family at 1670 Kewalo Street. It was a middle-class neighborhood of modest homes about ten blocks from the Watsons' house on Thurston, where Estelle had stayed upon arriving in Hawaii more than a year and a half earlier. There is no record of Estelle's feelings about resuming this life. She probably enjoyed much of it, just as she enjoyed the clothes her husband lavished on her. Louise Watson's daughter remembers going with her mother to visit Estelle and Cho-Cho. "Estelle came to the door dressed in a silk kimono trimmed all around with pale pink ostrich feathers. She looked so beautiful and so exotic, I remember thinking she must be a movie star. I couldn't believe she was just the wife of one of the young American lawyers my father had befriended."[16]

Two island visits by the Prince of Wales provided the high points of the spring and summer social season of 1920. On his first visit at a ball given in his honor, the playboy prince chose Estelle as "one of four dancing partners he alternated between" that night. "Sporting a double violet lei entwined with maidenhead ferns and a lei of white violets" along with his "engaging manner and democratic smile, he danced for almost two hours."[17] Estelle later told relatives in Columbus that "he danced and danced with her and then asked her for a date." She gleefully mimicked his surprise when she told him she had to go home to care for her baby daughter. In the envelope containing Estelle and Cornell's invitation to the ball, which Cornell saved, is a lock of blond hair.[18] Cornell and Cho-Cho were both dark-haired. Was the lock really the prince's, or was this simply an elaborate joke of Estelle's?

Before the ball the Franklins had also attended a traditional Hawaiian dinner for the prince. Tables were covered with mats of fern and sweet-smelling mountain vines and decorated with rare old polished calabashes brimming with tropical fruits. Servants brought the guests steaming bundles of food wrapped in palm leaves—roasted pig, lailau chicken, taro, poi, and other island delicacies. As the guests ate, Dude Miller's band played and Hawaiian girls danced the hula for them. For Estelle, moments like these still held the glamour and mystery of all events foreign and theatrical that made the staid little Mississippi town of Oxford seem a distant and provincial world, where Bill Faulkner's idea of dressing up was to don a new pair of tight black "stovepipes" from Halle's department store in Memphis. But by February 1921, the lure of such entertainment had palled for Estelle. Suggesting that her marriage, too, had palled, the newspaper announcing her second trip home reported that she would remain in the States for "an extended stay." But that April evening, as Cornell basked in Estelle's success, he may have felt that with such a wife by his side he could not fail to succeed in the "Eden of the Pacific."

Some time toward the end of May or beginning of June 1920, about five months after Estelle's return to Honolulu, her mother and her youngest and now only sister, thirteen-year-old Dorothy (known as Dot), arrived for nearly a four-month visit.[19] Thus, other than this five-month period alone with Cornell, Estelle was with her family either in Oxford or Honolulu during much of 1919 and 1920.[20]

After the ball for the Prince of Wales in April, Estelle almost disappears from the social columns. But with her mother's and sister's arrival in early June, the pace quickens. Estelle first gave a luncheon to introduce Dot to what the papers called the "Sub-Debutante" set. Next she hosted the largest affair she had ever supervised, a tea party for her mother attended by 120 guests. Estelle's huge Thursday afternoon party in mid-June honoring Lida was the featured event, and she was listed as one of the hostesses of the week in the society pages for Sunday, 20 June.[21]

Her social life remained exceedingly active throughout the summer. As the papers reported, the women's clubs had closed down for the summer, but "there will still be dancing and bridge, luncheons, dinners, teas. Honolulu would not be Honolulu if hospitality were to cease, even for a short time." And it didn't. As the papers predicted, "There will be moonlight dances at the Outrigger and Country Club, moonlight hikes to Nuuanu Pali, surfing and swimming parties, songfests and plenty of other jolly times."[22] Often the Franklins gave or attended dinner parties before going to dances at the Country, University, or Elks clubs. In addition, important members of the legal and business community entertained them regularly, as did the governor, whose box they had shared during the April festivities for the Prince of Wales.

The Oldhams' and Franklins' activities during these months make clear that by this time Estelle's social life was completely independent of her original sponsors, the Watsons. In fact, in early June, shortly after the Oldhams arrived, Louise Watson and her daughter, Virginia, left town to spend the summer and fall in California.[23] Thus all the events Estelle planned for her mother and to which they were invited were the result of her own efforts to succeed in the community her husband had chosen.[24] Estelle saw to it that her mother's and sister's first summer in Honolulu was a great deal more entertaining than her own had been. Her efforts on their behalf also strengthened Cornell's business relations.

Meanwhile in Chicago that June, where Lem was attending the Republican National Convention as a Mississippi delegate, the suffragists won the right to full equality in committee membership by a margin of one vote, the Equal Representation Principle carried on the third ballot after two defeats, and Harding and Coolidge headed the ticket in a tenth-ballot landslide.[25] Although the Honolulu paper carried articles at least once a week noting the numbers of women who had registered to vote for the first time—there were 10,000 eligible women voters in Oahu—it is not known whether Estelle was one of the 4,296 women who actually did register, even though Lida surely urged her to do so. Unlike her parents and Dot, she had no interest in Republican Party concerns, even though, or perhaps because, it had been the main source of her family's income for her entire life.

Summer passed quickly; Wednesdays and Saturdays were reserved for watching Cornell play polo, and the rest of the week was spent attending luncheons and beach parties. The week of Lida and Dot's departure, Lida attended both a luncheon and a bridge party given in her honor at Honolulu's most fashionable hotel, the Moana, in Waikiki.[26] On Sunday, 5 September, at almost midnight, Estelle and Cornell watched from the wharf as the Oldhams, their necks buried in multicolored, sweet-smelling leis from various well-wishers, waved from the deck of their Canadian-Australian steamer, *Niagara*, as it was towed away from its dock in Honolulu harbor. It was the month of good-byes.[27]

From this point until early November, the Oldhams' social life abruptly ceased because Cornell, whose circuit included other islands, was hearing cases throughout the Territory. Estelle accompanied him on these trips now that Cho-Cho was old enough to be left with her Japanese amah. In this time she visited all eight of the then inhabited islands except Molokai.[28]

By 4 November, the Franklins were home, and Cornell had returned to his courtroom.[29] On 6 November, Estelle once more took up her social responsibilities. For the next week she engaged in a constant round of entertaining and being entertained. A daily luncheon and dinner party were the norm.

But then, something happened. The Franklins would not move to Shanghai for another year. Nor would Estelle return to Oxford again until mid-February 1921. Yet an elaborate dinner party on Saturday, 13 November, was the last social event the Franklins ever hosted or were invited to in Hawaii. Even the Watsons and the Thompsons, the Franklins' original sponsors and employers, did not invite Estelle and Cornell to their houses again. Because heavy socializing was essential to Cornell's rise in Honolulu's economic and social hierarchy, the failure of this party and the consequences of that failure (as reflected in the social columns during the months that follow) bear scrutiny. Why did the party fail? Why were the Franklins suddenly social pariahs? A clue may lie in the Franklins' guest list, which consisted of Cornell's business and potential business associates, who, for the most part, were of the same generation as the Franklins' parents.

For Estelle, even with servants, the party was a complex undertaking. Just the mechanics of arranging the cooking and serving of an elegant six-course dinner for fourteen guests in their bungalow's small dining room presented a challenge. Then, the space had to be cleared and rearranged for card playing. Their house, as one of the Watson daughters observed, was "just a little cottage."[30] Other guests included Cornell's original mentors, the Billsons, the Watsons, and Frank Thompson, who was a good friend of Judge Watson as well as a polo player, an admirer of Cornell's legal skills, and a partner in the law firm Cornell had joined when he first arrived in Honolulu. The presence of two of Cornell's most influential sponsors and the new couples invited indicate the party's purpose. Both older men were Cornell's and Estelle's parents' ages; one was a stockbroker and vice president of the Honolulu Stock and Bond Exchange, the other a Harvard Law School graduate who had taught Admiralty Law there before going to Honolulu in 1905 and establishing a lucrative private practice with one of the reigning lawyers there.[31]

One can only speculate about what happened that night to bring the Franklins' social life to a halt. Probably it was a scene between Cornell and Estelle that even their hard-drinking guests found beyond the pale. By all accounts, particularly their children's and grandchildren's, those Bourbon Democrats lived up to their name. Watson and his colleagues, whose conservative economic and social politics placed them firmly in the pockets of the Dillinghams, Bishops, Castles, Cooks, and other wealthy families who made up the Hawaiian plantocracy in the early decades of the twentieth century, were hardly teetotalers. But even they thought Estelle Franklin overdid it.[32] Their censure fell on Estelle because of the double standard that prevailed and is still replicated and reiterated in all biographical accounts of Estelle's two marriages. Bill and Cornell drank; Estelle was a drunk. In fact, all three were alcoholics.

Both Estelle's and Faulkner's fiction depict addiction as endemic to the worlds represented in their writing: the post-Reconstruction South and American colonial culture in Hawaii and Shanghai. As one of Estelle's fictional ancestors in "Dr. Wohlenski" explains, "One tosses it down purely for the effect it gives—that of well-being, a lift from care."[33] All three of her extant stories make clear that she recognized both the dangers and pleasures of addiction. Yet in Honolulu in the fall and early winter of 1920–21, it may have seemed, for the moment, to make her life as Cornell's wife a lot easier. Years later Jill said that although she thought her mother drank "as an escape" and "to relieve tension," her ultimate goal was "oblivion—just to get away from things. She drank to get drunk, as a means for coping with her everyday life. Living as she did was more than she could face." She remembered as a child that when her mother was going to start drinking, "she began at daybreak. I don't remember a time when it was not a fact of life." She elaborates with telling insight: "My mother was not a happy person: she was a lot more sophisticated and intelligent than anyone gave her credit for and I think that's why she was unhappy."[34]

Intentionally or not, the unladylike behavior Estelle initially adopted in Oxford, perhaps in hopes of maintaining her old place in Billy's world, became a cause for her exclusion from Honolulu social circles. It's also possible that her ostracism was self-orchestrated. The manner in which she spent the next eleven months until her second departure for Oxford suggests that once relieved of the intense daily round of socializing, she began doing what she wanted, using her intellect and imagination for her education and enjoyment.[35] In Shanghai in 1922 Estelle will repeat this pattern, and produce, in the space she carved out by doing so, her novel (which she may have begun in Honolulu) and a series of short stories. The fall of 1920 in Honolulu marked her first known attempt to create and claim an identity and self that was independent of her marriage to Franklin and that also strengthened her long-distance dialogue with Faulkner. Like Billy that same fall, Estelle became involved in local amateur theater. After their disastrous November dinner party, Estelle disappeared from the luncheon, bridge, and dinner party circuit but turned up for the first time, and in quick succession, in two local theatrical performances. Although sponsored by the University Club and the Elks Lodge, two staid and prestigious men's clubs to which Cornell belonged, many of the members of these two drama groups hailed from Honolulu's avant-garde. When she joined The Footlights, a part of Estelle's life in Honolulu began to mirror Billy's back in Oxford. That fall the company produced two plays whose subject matter— the Pierrot character and Freud and his "new psychology—also figures prominently in the poetry Faulkner was reading and imitating and in the dream-play he was writing in 1920–21.

Going Her Own Way: Estelle's and Billy's Theatrical Forays, 1920–1921

By joining the island's leading amateur theater group, The Footlights, in fall 1920, Estelle added to her imposed roles of colonial wife and mother that of actor in a very different kind of public theater. This one was ruled by stage, not social, conventions. More important, she was exposed to and became immersed in the nuts and bolts of theatrical performance and contemporary dramatic narrative. She would use both when she began writing fiction. But just as Faulkner's theater experience on the University of Mississippi campus that same fall helped him distance himself from the roles he was playing in real life and so transform his fantasies and daydreams into art, so her theater experience gave her new perspectives on her life. At least one play in which she played a major role was, like the stories she later wrote, exceedingly modern and au courant. On many levels she experienced the possibility of playing something other than what her husband and her parents had scripted for her.

Estelle's awareness of the theater of everyday life, particularly those roles constructed for women and other minorities, is central to her fiction. Her portrayals of such theatricality, of characters who have a great capacity to disassociate and to watch themselves watching themselves will be of great interest to Faulkner. He will make use of her insights in early February 1925, when he begins writing his first novel.

The Footlights was founded in 1915 as a women's dramatic society.[36] It began admitting men when it became associated with the University Club, where many of its performances were held. The first play the Footlights produced that fall, a fifteenth-century French farce admired by Rabelais and Molière, *Maistre Pierre Patelin,* gave Estelle another specific connection with Faulkner's current project—his Pierrot play.[37] The hero of what the papers described as "this rough and tumble comedy" was that smooth-tongued, libidinous slickster Pierrot.[38] In this version, Pierrot appears as a devious and rascally lawyer whose wife aids and abets him in his schemes. This is the comic as opposed to the semitragic Pierrot of Faulkner's play. Yet both share the Pierrot figure's dominant characteristics—his egotism, his libidinousness, his deviousness, and his adolescent solipsism.

It may be only coincidental that Estelle's involvement with The Footlights and her stage appearances occurred during the same months in which Bill, back in Oxford, joined The Marionettes, played behind-the-scenes roles in their productions, and then wrote and illustrated his own play by that name about Pierrot and a heroine drawn as Estelle. It may also be only coincidental that Faulkner's subject—the relation of dreams to suppressed and repressed desires—though treated very differently, is also the subject of Susan Glaspell's Freudian farce, *Suppressed Desires,* in which Estelle played one of the leads. But by naming his initially naïve heroine Marietta, Faulkner appears to link his play's heroine both to Estelle and to Glaspell's similar foils, the Greenwich Village Freudian groupie, Henrietta

Brewster, and Mabel, her naïve country sister. As in *Suppressed Desires*, Marietta's opening lines directly invoke the title and subject of the comedy in which Estelle acted: female sexuality, the relation between conscious and unconscious desires, and the importance of dreams.

"I cannot sleep," Marietta wails. "My bed is heavy and hot with something that fills me with strange desires. Why," she asks, "am I filled with desire for vague, unnamed things because a singing voice disturbed my dreams?" Like many neurotics, including her Faulknerian predecessor, the Marble Faun, she wants to know yet fears the answer: "No, no, I do not want to know, I am afraid to know!" (*TM*, 10, 11). Specifically, in classical psychoanalytic terms, *The Marionettes'* plot issuing from dreams represents Pierrot's fantasies of his own and Marietta's desires, wishes, and fears. The summer of Estelle's second visit (1921), Faulkner would further interpret his drawings of Estelle-Marietta in a poem called "Pierrot, Sitting Beside the Body of Columbine, suddenly [*sic*] Sees Himself in a Mirror."[39] The subject here is not so much his lover's death as Pierrot's tenuous sense of a self that is separate from Columbine. Although he sits beside the dead girl, his thoughts are on his own extinction. He feels the darkness

> Coldly descending like water upon him, and saw his hands
> Dissolve from his knees . . .
> Pierrot saw his face in the mirror before him
> Slowly extinguished like a match. . . .
> Leaving the mirror empty. (ll. 2–7)

In the poem's final strophe Pierrot's mirrored image is "like a dead match" (l. 36), while dead Columbine

> Now lying crushed and lifeless and infinitely pitiful, seemed to him
> The symbol of his own life: a broken gesture in tinsel. (ll. 40–41)

The familiar mirroring, then merging, resulting in death, further clarifies Pierrot's deep identification with, desire for, and fear of the feminine.

The origins of *The Marionettes* stem, in part, from Faulkner's ambivalent response to Estelle's marriage, but equally important to its composition may have been discussions between Estelle and Bill about aesthetic and psychological issues that both were being exposed to and exploring in their reading and their local theater groups. Yet, other than this textual and contextual evidence, there is no record of what Estelle said or wrote to Bill when she read his ambivalent tribute to her imagination and her love, this first work in which she figures explicitly. As "A Crossing" demonstrates, however, her fictionalized response, primarily her revision of Marietta, is preserved in that short story and figures prominently in her ongoing literary dialogue and collaboration with Faulkner in the years preceding her marriage to him.

Although she may well have written Bill about *Pierre Patelin* giving rise to his fantasies of an Estelle-like figure playing opposite a Faulkneresque Pierrot, Estelle had no acting role in that play. But, as I have noted, she did play one of the three roles in a play whose subject, the public infatuation with popularized notions of psychoanalytic dream theory, was of even more interest. On 27 January 1921, she appeared as Henrietta or her sister, Mabel, in The Footlights production of Susan Glaspell's and George Cram Cook's 1915 spoof on radical new women, modern marriage, and psychoanalysis.[40]

In the 1920s and early 1930s Glaspell was considered one of the country's leading playwrights. In 1932 Ludwig Lewisohn wrote, "Susan Glaspell was followed by Eugene O'Neill. The rest was silence; the rest is silence still."[41] One of the reasons for this particular play's worldwide popularity was that throughout at least the first four decades of the twentieth century, psychoanalysis was a hot topic, even in Shanghai and Honolulu. Between April and July of 1920, John Barry, the culture and book review editor of the *Pacific Commercial Advertiser,* devoted at least two long columns to Freud. Both Barry's essays and Glaspell's *Suppressed Desires* articulate popularized conceptions of psychoanalysis to which Estelle was exposed at a time when she was beginning to make profound changes in her life. It appears that she may have applied what she learned to the fiction she later wrote.

Her exposure to Freud is even more important in terms of following her ongoing intellectual and imaginative dialogue with Bill. For, as she was absorbing Freud and critiques of his theories through Barry's columns and Glaspell's "naughtily Freudian" play, so, back in Oxford that same fall and winter, Bill was reading Conrad Aiken's Freudian-inspired poem sequences, his "symphonies in verse," which served as Bill's first psychoanalytic filter.[42] Partly through reading and then imitating Aiken's poems, he absorbed the formal techniques and themes that would inform his next major writing project, *Vision in Spring.* Popularized Freudian theory informs Faulkner's dream-play, his early unfinished novel about an unsuccessful artist, "Elmer," and his second published novel, *Mosquitoes.* All three are also concerned with the sexual preoccupations of unsuccessful artists. More sophisticated use and spoofing of Freud occurs throughout Faulkner's fiction.

Popularizing Freud in the *Pacific Commercial Advertiser*, April–November 1920

Freud delivered the first of his famous five lectures in America at Clark University in Worcester, Massachusetts, in the fall of 1909. In the following years, articles on the "new psychology" appeared regularly in such magazines as *McClure's*, *Vanity Fair*, *Cosmopolitan*, the *New Republic*, and the *Friday Literary Review* and in large circulation newspapers throughout the country.[43] By 1920 even Honolulu columnists were popularizing the new psychology. The intellectual buzz in Honolulu in 1920 was not far removed from the buzz in Glaspell's Greenwich Village when she wrote and produced her play (1915–16). Barry's first essay is an interview with an imaginary psychoanalyst who outlines some of Freud's most catchy theories and their applications.[44]

In July, when Barry wrote his next column on the subject, "Aspects of Psychoanalysis," he had read further on the subject. He defines transference and discusses its function in psychoanalytic treatment as the analyst's principal tool: "The business of the analyst is to develop this dependence [on himself] into independence by leading the patients to the self-control that enables them to draw on their own powers and to stand upon their own feet." He also notes the importance of interpreting the analysand's "resistance," which he characterizes as "the war between the conscious and the unconscious that is the cause of so many miseries in life." He notes that resistance hides from consciousness "painful memories and ideas." Effective use of transference and interpretation of resistance depends on the analyst's interpretive skills. Toward this end, he then asks, "What we do when we try to understand another person?" and "What makes a good psychoanalyst?" Enlarging on empathy, which he had noted in his earlier column, he includes an attentiveness to all kinds of unconscious behavior, which he characterizes as "what is going on in peoples' minds when they are off their guard." Barry underscores his belief in the similarity between good artists and good psychoanalysts, noting that "what is most essential is the analytical faculty as a natural gift." As in his prior essay, he reiterates that this gift is most often present in writers and other kinds of artists. Henry James and John Singer Sargent serve as his exemplars of psychologically astute artists.[45]

Reading Barry's columns, attending lectures at the University Club, and acting in *Suppressed Desires*—all of which perhaps stimulated Estelle to read some of Freud's work—gave her extensive exposure to such ideas as the power of the unconscious, the essential sexual nature of its contents, and its varied ways of expressing itself—in body language, slips of the tongue, jokes, and dreams. Like many Americans, she maintained a life-long and eclectic interest in religious, spiritual, and psychological self-help books.[46] For someone seeking better ways to understand herself and others, as Estelle was, Barry's columns explained and championed the liberating and socially valuable function of psychoanalytic theory. Acting in a play that made fun of people who treated such theories as the new Gospel would have encouraged her to think critically about this new "science" and "art" of the mind. The play's topicality, realism, and humor are all qualities that mark her later fiction. Its foregrounding of the "new sexual consciousness of the era" and "greater sexual openness," with lines like "the living Libido [is] in conflict with petrified moral codes," may have freed her to invent the wayward couples and coupling featured in stories like "A Crossing."[47] And the experience of day-to-day involvement with a dramatic production that was being hailed by New York City's avant-garde gave her a chance to be with people whose interests and values were much more like Faulkner's than her husband's.

Estelle and Honolulu's Bohemians

Suppressed Desires was performed as the feature at a dinner dance at the University Club on 27 January. The male lead, Don Blanding, who became instrumental in developing theater on the island, was then closely identified with Honolulu's bohemian set, as was another Footlighter, Sara Lucas's brother, Harry.[48] There are no accounts of the play's reception, perhaps because of the more unconventional nature of the avant-garde. There is, however, an extensive and detailed description of the Elks Club Valentine's celebrations of February 1921, in which Estelle also played a part. The latter event captures the essence of these functions and of the traditional public roles performed by women who were married to Americans on the make in the Territory and other colonial enclaves farther east.[49]

For its Valentine's celebration the Elks clubhouse at Waikiki mixed nationalism with cupids and hearts. According to the social column, the evening's hostesses, costumed in American Colonial gowns, greeted guests and danced in rooms and on lanais decked out in a "brilliant holiday red. Between dances various members performed cabaret numbers including a Valentine tableau—a Valentine who came to life." A fashion show of the "very latest modes" was also part of evening festivities; Estelle was "among the thirteen models who posed so gracefully for the exquisite gowns that they received rounds of applause." The scene evokes Estelle's fictional model, Edna Earl. There was also a series of dance solos, but Estelle, like

Edna Earl, did not dance that night. Although the Elks Club sponsored another dance for its four hundred members on Valentine's night and a huge carnival on 19 February on the theme of "Rome in the Days of Caesar"—complete with "strings of slaves and captives"—Estelle did not attend. With Cho-Cho and her amah, she was already crossing the Pacific again, headed for Oxford and Billy.

February 1921: Back to Oxford

The same day as the Valentine's Ball and fashion show, the following notice had appeared in the personals column of the *Pacific Commercial Advertiser:* "Mrs. Cornell Franklin, wife of Circuit Judge Franklin, expects to leave by the U.S. Army transport *Sheridan* next Tuesday [Feb. 15] for San Francisco, and is on her way to her former home in the South where she will make an extended visit to relatives and friends."[50] Thus, only five months after Estelle's mother and sister had returned to Oxford from Honolulu, she and Cho-Cho were making their second trip home. Although she didn't know it at the time, this departure marked the end of her residence in Hawaii. When she returned that November, it would only be to pack up and sail on to Shanghai, the family's final colonial outpost.

On this trip, Estelle was chaperoned. Cornell's younger step-brother, Billy Hairston, who had clerked for him since 1919, sailed with her.[51] The day she actually departed, the papers carried the headline "Nine Marriage Knots Slashed by Court." Although she may have wished that her marriage, too, had been "slashed," she would have been mortified to have been included under such a headline. When women of her class separated, as had the wife of Attorney General Ingrahm Stainback, the papers announced that they had gone to the mainland for "an extended stay." There they obtained discreet divorces.[52] Lida Oldham's departure from Honolulu in September 1920 had followed days of farewell parties, but no one gave a luncheon, tea, or dinner for Estelle. A second notice on 17 February announcing her rescheduled departure on the *Sheridan* at 4 P.M. that day was all that marked her leave-taking.

PART 5

The Emergence of a Mature Novelist

Faulkner and Estelle's Collaboration, 1924–1933

With her listening, Bill found he could talk.
—JOHN FAULKNER

22

Estelle's Shanghai Sojourn, 1922–1924
From Franklin to Oldham

Aᴌᴛʜᴏᴜɢʜ Cᴏʀɴᴇʟʟ ᴍᴀʏ ʜᴀᴠᴇ ᴍɪssᴇᴅ his wife and daughter, in many ways it was easier for him to lead the life he loved without them. In the 1940s, explaining his decision to move from Honolulu to Shanghai, he described that bachelor summer of 1921 to a news reporter. He was due a paid holiday for having served as a territorial judge since April 1919 and had always wanted to visit the Far East. So, rather than return to Mississippi, he sailed for Japan and from there to China. On shipboard he met another polo-playing lawyer who invited him to play polo in Shanghai. He played a week there, a week in Peking, and then returned to play a third week in Shanghai. This, he said, gave him entrée into the international colony in the city. His fellow polo enthusiasts told him that "a young American lawyer who was honest and could stay sober could make a fortune" in the former British Crown Colony. "Judge Franklin returned to Honolulu, resigned his Judgeship, boarded the T.K.K.S. Taiyo Maru and arrived back in the Chinese city on New Year's Eve, 1921."[1] Cornell omits both Estelle and Cho-Cho from this adventurer's scenario, even though they went with him when he returned to Shanghai.

Long before the reunited Franklin family reached Honolulu again in November 1921, Cornell had decided to move to China. It is not known whether he returned to Oxford to coax Estelle back to Hawaii because of her negative reaction to his most recent decision. Whatever the case, it was one of several times that, through the force of his personality and with the support of both sets of parents, he convinced her to return to their marriage. On 29 November, just days after their arrival in Hawaii, Cornell tendered his resignation as judge, "to take effect December 11, 1921." He was in high spirits. In his almost jaunty letter to the U.S. attorney general he

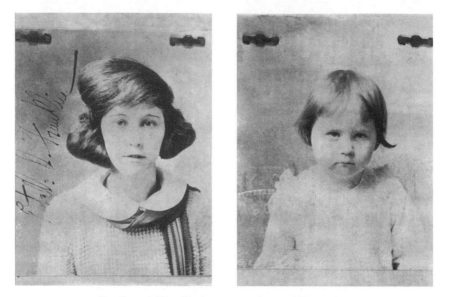

22.1. Estelle and Cho-Cho's passport photos, 8 December 1921.
(Courtesy of Cornell Franklin, Jr.)

noted that his term would be up 30 June 1923 and that "my position would naturally be filled by a Republican. In this policy I heartily agree for I am a believer in the time honored theory that 'to the victors belong the spoils.' Such being the case, however, I must of necessity, give some thought to the future and I have decided to retire from the bench at once and open offices in Shanghai for the general practice of law."[2] He received a telegram on 7 December accepting his resignation.

The next day Estelle and Cho-Cho were issued their joint passport, good for one year. According to this document, she and Cho-Cho planned only to travel in China, via Japan and Hong Kong.[3] Perhaps that was her private intention, or perhaps it was just her hope. In contrast with the photograph taken in Oxford the summer before, in her passport picture she looks even more waifish and childlike (fig.22.1). Dressed in what looks like a schoolgirl's uniform, her thick, dark red hair now much longer and held in place by barrettes, she lacks any trace of the stylish sophistication projected in either the summer photograph or photographs taken before her marriage, or even in her 1918 passport photograph. As in the latter, she is unsmiling and her slightly downcast green eyes seem almost haunted. She looks beaten, withdrawn, depressed. Cho-Cho, just two months shy of her third birthday, looks equally morose.

The day following, Judge Franklin resigned from his Elks Lodge and from the vice presidency of the Honolulu chapter of Phi Delta Theta. Two days later, on the balmy Sunday of 11 December, Estelle, Cornell, and Cho-Cho sailed out of Honolulu's harbor for the Far East. They were headed for the more open markets in the International Settlement of Shanghai, then China's largest treaty port.[4]

Three years would pass before Estelle's precipitous return to Oxford on 9 December 1924—just six days before the Four Seas Press published Bill Faulkner's first book, *The Marble Faun*. What happened to her during those years, what she accomplished intellectually, and the decisions she made about her marriage that changed the course of her life and that of William Faulkner is a story untold until now.

Estelle's Shanghai in Fact and Imagination, December 1921–November 1924

It was bitter cold, made colder by a biting north wind from Siberia, on New Year's Eve of 1921, when the Franklins' ocean liner steamed from the mouth of the Yangtze River up the partly frozen brown Huaangpu River toward Shanghai.[5] Boasting a population that had expanded from 1 million in 1910 to 2.5 million by 1920, Shanghai was China's most industrialized and cosmopolitan city.[6] Like so many other Westerners, Cornell had come to make his fortune in that expansion.

At the port of Wusong the Franklins debarked from the *Taiyo Maru* and boarded a steam-tender, which transported passengers eighteen miles farther up river to the landing jetty on Shanghai's famous Bund. A local guidebook notes that on this last leg of the voyage a visitor would "see little that suggests the Orient to him. The river is crowded with shipping, the waters dotted with large and small steamers, lighters, tugs, and sampans. The smokestacks of many factories stand out in a skyline which would look familiar in any port of Europe or America." Huge shipyards, warehouses, factories, and docks lined the river bank on both sides.[7] As they approached the city's waterfront, the Franklins could see the magnificent sweep of the skyline of the Bund—the business district and showpiece of Shanghai's International Settlement.[8] From a distance, the European architecture of its huge banks, office buildings, and hotels made it look like any of the great cityscapes of the Western world. But once the Franklins landed and were taken through Shanghai's crowded streets, they entered a different world, one of noise and confusion; of tramcars, rickshaws, sedan chairs, wheelbarrows, bicycles, and carriages drawn by Mongolian ponies; and of crowds speaking dozens of Chinese dialects, plus pidgin English. Dr. Anne Fearn, a long-time Shanghai resident who would become Estelle's obstetrician

22.2. Estelle and Cornell's house in Shanghai *(top)*; Estelle, Cho-Cho,
and her nurse in their garden, c. 1922–23.
(Courtesy Victoria Fielden Johnson)

and friend describes the scene: "Chinese men walk the streets dressed in
their traditional long silk gowns, blue cotton ones, or the latest western
style. Some Chinese women are beautifully dressed, with smart waved
heads, silk stockings and high-heeled shoes, and some cling to the divided
skirts and embroidered jackets of tradition. There are Japanese, Indians,

Anamites and Europeans, a conglomeration of every nationality under the sun."[9]

British friends of Cornell's met the Franklins at the Custom House and took them back to their home. British interests governed the economic and social hierarchy of Shanghai's International Settlement. Cornell intended to scale that hierarchy and these were friends who could help him. The Franklins "sojourned" with them for almost five months, as Cornell wrote his father-in-law.[10] Not until the end of May did they move into their own house, which, according to her husband, cured Estelle of a week-long "bilious attack." He added, "I wish you could see how delightfully situated we are. The house is most attractive but is really a little too small for us." He wrote Lem that Cho-Cho not only owned her own rickshaw but had acquired a British accent and "the habit of taking tea every afternoon" as a result of living with their British friends.[11]

In the words of a tourist guidebook, the Franklins had moved from the "Paradise of the Pacific" to, as Cornell wrote, the "Paris of the East."[12] He did not mention Westerners' more infamous sobriquet for Shanghai, the "Whore of the Orient." This bustling port was a shopper's heaven, in flesh and fashion. In 1922 its three Chinese luxury department stores (including one named Sassoon's) carried the latest Paris fashions, and individual Paris designers regularly advertised showings of their collections in the daily English-language newspapers. Shanghai's foreign population, which in the early twenties numbered about twenty-four thousand people, accounted for a disproportionate percentage of such sales. These foreigners' "*raison d'être* . . . was business."[13] During the years Estelle lived there, the city also had a lively intellectual and cultural scene, which included many famous Western visitors. One could view the latest Western films at any number of movie theaters as well as attend the theater, ballet, and opera. A sample month in 1923 offered the following events: the Grand Italian Opera from Milan performing eight operas; a Chopin recital; Einstein lecturing on Zionism and relativity; and popular films of the time such as *What Every Woman Learns*, *The Married Flapper*, *Her Husband's Wife*, and *The Branded Woman*, "a picture that goes to the heart of love and marriage" with a lead "whose burning struggle gives this girl a soul." A more highbrow version of marriage gone awry was portrayed in Henrik Ibsen's *A Doll's House*. At the American Club, Estelle could have heard Jane Addams speak about her work in the slums of Chicago and a noted sinologist lecture on the development of Chinese art.[14] In the *China Press*, the books of note reviewed in one week alone included Freud's *Group Psychology* and *Beyond the Pleasure Principle*, a Freud biography (all under the headline "Freud Is More Than Ever in Vogue"), and a review of Ring Lardner's *How to Write Short Stories*, all of which would have been of interest to Estelle.[15] The city earned its racy reputation from its gangsters, drug trafficking, nightclubs that never closed, and hotels that supplied opium with room service. Shanghai's criminal population also included "war-lords, spy-rings, international arms dealers, and the peculiar delights on offer at Chinese brothels."[16] In short, allowing for some variations (namely, the impressive lack of any economic oversight or regulation), Shanghai's virtues and vices were those of the largest Western metropolises, especially its ports. That was its great attraction.

Shanghai's unusual status as a treaty port made it, if one were bright and industrious like Cornell, a potential "Lawyer's Paradise."[17] As the steady stream of news reports on Cornell's clients shows, he threw himself into his work, pleading the case of almost any American who walked through his office door on the Bund. That winter and spring of 1922 he defended a sailor accused of "murderous assault," a drunken wife who "molested" her husband ("she threatened to throw glass in my eyes" and said she'd kill him), and two alleged extortionists and blackmailers. He also pled but lost a stay of execution of a judgment against the Hamburg Amerika Shipping Line in the Mixed Court.[18] The last case excepted, such clients made good stories but not much money, and so, through his personal and political connections, Cornell pursued other avenues. These included writing to ask his father-in-law to have him appointed "attorney for the Shipping Board in China," because "the prestige and advertisement will be worthwhile and you can work it from that end." He also asked Lem to arrange for a pay increase for the counsel-general, Edwin Cunningham, with whom Franklin was friends and hoped to further ingratiate himself.

At first Estelle was equally busy. While Cornell spent his days and nights politicking and drumming up business, she plunged into the social swing. Because they arrived in the winter, there were no obligatory polo matches to attend and no meets of the Shanghai Race Club. Yet her calendar was filled with an endless round of engagements designed to further her husband's career. Within three weeks of the Franklins' arrival, the *China Weekly Review*, the Settlement's leading English-language newspaper, listed "Mrs. C. S. Franklin" as one of the principal performers in the George Washington Birthday Ball pageant, a time-consuming commitment but a good introduction to Shanghai social life.[19] For Americans living there, the ball was the most important social event of the year. Held at the Town Hall, which, for the 1922 celebration, was transformed into a replica of George Washington's Mount Vernon home, it attracted a crowd of over sixteen hundred people, including the Settlement's most influential foreign set. This historical pageant consisted of a series of period dances (the polka, quadrille, gavotte, and minuet), each performed by four couples. Only five married women, among them Estelle, participated without their husbands. Nine other single women were among the thirty-two dancers. During the four weeks preceding the ball, Estelle, one of eight polka dancers, attended daily rehearsals at 6:30 P.M. at the Palace Hotel, directed by a Russian dance mistress, as well as dress rehearsals the weekend before. Estelle loved to dance, although her husband (like Billy Faulkner) was a poor partner. Perhaps this was why she chose to audition and participate in the pageant. Perhaps she just wanted to get out of the house and see what Shanghai had to offer.

In any case, this experience gave her the chance to meet the socially active members of Shanghai's young and older American set and observe its social life, whose essence she captures and satirizes in "Star Spangled Banner Stuff" and, to a lesser extent, in "A Crossing."[20] It was also through the ball that she may have first become friends with the legendary Shanghai Southerner, Dr. Anne Walter Fearn, whose professional achievements, triumph of will in her own unpleasant marriage, and encouragement may have inspired Estelle to be less passive about her lot. It was a cross-generational friendship sustained long after "Annie," as she was called, had retired to her family home in Mississippi. Jill remembers visits with her parents to Dr. Fearn throughout her childhood. Other than these two facts, there is no direct evidence of any significant relationship between Annie and Estelle. Yet incidents in Fearn's life appear in both of Estelle's anticolonial romances, and I suspect that Annie's marital and economic-professional self-reliance and assertiveness may have encouraged Estelle to write fiction—and perhaps even leave Cornell in November 1924. In her memoir, Fearn wrote that "it is one of the joys of my life to know that my warmest friendships had their beginnings in a physician-patient relationship, many of them starting at my hospital."[21] Ever the social diplomat, the doctor remained on good terms with Cornell, testifying in 1926 concerning the mental health of one of his more infamous clients.[22]

Annie Fearn was raised not far from Oxford, in Holly Springs, Mississippi. Her upbringing and, to some extent, her marriage were similar to Estelle's, yet she had carved out an independent and professionally fulfilling life. In her memoir she wrote that at sixteen she, too, was the belle of her town and that although she loved music and piano, "I was qualified for nothing but the life of a social butterfly."[23] There, Fearn's upbringing veers from Estelle's. Of Lida Oldham's generation, Annie had dared her mother's threat to disown her and, with her older brother's support, earned an M.D. in 1893.

After graduating from medical school, she sailed for China to fill in at a missionary hospital for one of her mentors. She loved her work and ended up staying forty-four years. Trained as "a surgeon who degenerated into obstetrics," she practiced medicine in various capacities, married a missionary doctor whose religious impositions she ultimately defied, and bore a daughter in 1897, the same year as Estelle's birth, who died of dysentery in 1902. She spent years working in public health and, through the American Women's Club, spearheaded social reforms to improve the health care of Shanghai's working class—orphans, the rickshaw pullers, itinerant sailors, and particularly prostitutes, many of whom were Westerners. She also treated other "foreigners" for alcoholism, opium addiction, and depression—which she claimed were the three most prevalent diseases among Shanghai's foreign residents. When she first went into private practice, "aside from a few rich Chinese," her patient population shifted to primarily foreigners "from all walks of life." In her new practice "the diseases of colonialism replaced those resulting from filth, superstition, and ignorance." She added, "I was now to fight the sickness of alcoholism, free and easy living, and the mental depression caused by financial and marital worries." Retrospectively, she would write, "I often felt I should have trained in psychiatry and opened a home for mental cases." In 1916 she did open her own small hospital and sanatorium whose patients and staff "were as cosmopolitan as Shanghai itself." Cases included everything from "confinements," appendectomies, dysentery, drug and alcohol addictions, "d.t. cases," and STDs to severe and long-term emotional disorders like shell shock and depression. On 3 December 1923, twenty-five months after the Franklins' arrival in Shanghai, Estelle delivered their second child, Malcolm Argylle Franklin, at the Fearn Sanatorium.[24] There are no surviving records to indicate whether Dr. Fearn was also treating her for alcohol abuse and depression, but Estelle's account of her Shanghai years confirms the former.

As her patient, Estelle may have heard Dr. Fearn describe her rebellion against her autocratic husband, John, who "was born to give orders as definitely as I was born not to take them." Fearn's story bears a striking resemblance to that of Estelle's fictional heroine, Edna Earl. John Fearn was obsessed with religious observance. He demanded that every morning at the hospital begin with at least an hour of prayer and Bible reading. Not even a medical emergency could interrupt: "All hospital work stopped during this time." One morning, in violation of his orders, his wife was summoned for an emergency C-section. When John insisted that they finish the reading, she revolted. "Springing up tempestuously I cried, 'I can't bear it! I wish I'd never seen the damn thing!' Flinging the Bible to the floor, I rushed . . . to the operating room."[25] They never resumed their Bible reading and he never forgave her, but neither sought divorce. Their thirty-year marriage ended only with John's death, in 1926. Even among educated professionals like Annie, the social opprobrium of divorce and the code of the double standard were as fixed in Shanghai as they were in Mississippi.

After Estelle's Washington Ball debut in February 1922, she disappeared from public view. Her name appeared only once more in the social columns of the Shanghai papers—in December 1923, when her son is born. By her own account she was desperately unhappy, in part for reasons made clear in her stories about women whose lives are dictated by the needs and desires of their parents, suitors, and husbands. She drank, as she explained in the 1950s, because it "seemed to me an ideal escape" from "unfortunate occurrences."[26] Summarizing her life in Shanghai, Estelle once told her daughter, "I don't think I took a sober breath for three years." Estelle's behavior was not atypical. A contemporary describes the Shanghai expat scene: "Boozing went on excessively and ceaselessly, pickmeups in the morning, heavy, boozy tiffins [lunches] and cocktail parties, teas, receptions and the late dinners, and the whole, long night of drinking, dancing, and carousing, stretching ahead of it. Few . . . could resist it. Few did."[27] As she later described her years there, "There was no escape from it. If you lived in China when I did, you drank. It started at about eleven in the morning and ended about three or four the next morning. There was nothing else to do—no housework, no anything, and in the American and British communities it was expected that the people in a certain position were expected to do a certain amount of entertaining. And you never declined an invitation so that it was literally non-stop."[28] Contemporaneous accounts in the English-language Shanghai papers confirm Estelle's description, as do Annie Fearn's and others' memoirs.[29]

In a letter Estelle wrote home in 1954, when she was visiting her daughter and son-in-law in Manila, she recaptures the quality of the need to escape she had felt in Shanghai in the twenties: "The artificially induced gaity of the Far East is very pronounced here—a feverish clutching at nothing that is little short of terrifying—As I sit here now, looking out on Manila Bay with its warships and carriers—every one of them ready for instant action—I feel an insecurity verging on panic." The scene she gazed on— an image of the United States on alert at the height of the Cold War— probably reminded her of instances between 1922 and 1926 when the ever-present British and American gunboats massed in Shanghai's harbor to protect their "nationals," first from rival Chinese warlords fighting for control of Shanghai's arsenal and economy, then from Chinese Nationalists, who began challenging its Western "guests'" constantly expanding imposition of foreign privilege in their Settlements, and later from the warring factions of Chinese revolutionaries.[30] For Estelle, these external wars could serve as a metaphor for the internal battles she fought at different times with both her first and second husbands, her family, and herself for the right to some kind of autonomy and selfhood. In Manila, she also resorted to her old ploy for dulling the panic and anger she felt at having no control of her life: "But, in a little while, I'll go out to tea, cock-tails, dinner and what-have-you, and join all the inconsequential chatter of the internationals."[31]

Memoirs of Estelle's contemporaries and newspaper accounts of cultural, political, and social activities in Shanghai's Western sectors demonstrate that there *were* other "things to do," and perhaps with Fearn's help or perhaps on her own, Estelle did find them. They changed her life.

Besides taking up painting and drawing, she started to write stories. It's possible that she even joined a group of amateur and professional writers called the Shanghai Short Story Club. Founded the summer of 1923 by a group of both published and unpublished writers who were living in Shanghai, their objective by 1926 as "realists" was to write fiction that depicted "truthfully local color, customs, and characteristics." They wanted "to help dispel the delusions and possibly some of the illusions held abroad about this land in which we live." The club held workshops in the art and craft of short story writing, which is where Estelle might have learned some of the narrative strategies evident in all her extant stories.[32] Or she may have simply learned on her own. In either case she read the stories that came out of this club, in that many were first published in the *North China Daily News*, the *China Press*, and the *China Weekly Review*.[33] The club also published two collections of stories—in 1924 and 1927.[34] Introducing their second collection, club members observed somewhat caustically that although truth may be stranger than fiction, "no truth can be stranger than Chinese fiction, or to put it more properly, Western fiction about China," most of which is "so fictitious as to be fantastic."[35] A survey of "Chinese" stories published by American and Shanghai English-language presses in the second decade of the twentieth century and through 1926 confirms that such a goal in 1926 was quite unusual.[36] "A Chinese Woman Speaks," Pearl Buck's first short story, also published in 1926, uses what her biographer, Peter Conn, calls a kind of reverse Orientalism, or "occidenticalism," to challenge and critique Western stereotypic portrayals of the Chinese. As he notes, to the Chinese woman who is the story's narrator, "it is the West that appears somewhat exotic," animalistic, crude, and primitive.[37]

But even more unusual is that sometime between 1922 and 1924, with or without the influence of the Short Story Club, Estelle attempted a similar reality in her own Shanghai story, in which she portrayed Westerners' drinking and mating habits from the multiple perspectives of an ironic impersonal narrator and a modern-day upper-class Chinese businessman and his Chinese servants. This was one of the narrative devices she coupled with the story's edgy and often wry tone to satirize that "feverish" world of Shanghai's international business community. In doing so, she exposed the hypocrisy of International Settlement businessmen and lawyers like her husband, whose exploitation of their host country and unabashed marketing of even their wives and daughters undercut their professed support of democratic ideals, their "Star Spangled Banner Stuff." Estelle, making an inside joke, cribbed her title from the "theme" of Shanghai's 1923 Washington Birthday Ball.[38] On a more private level, her tale provided further space to play with her racialized erotic fantasies.

What happened to Estelle during her three years in Shanghai is crucial to the role her unexpected return home and her writing played in Faulkner's sudden and dramatic shift from poet to novelist in February 1925, less than six weeks after her return from China in December 1924. The stories she wrote in Shanghai testify to her increasing awareness of racial prejudice, social injustice, and the centrality of gender and sexuality in all human relationships. Because no letters or journal notes she may have written survive, these stories are the only testament to her perspective at the time.

There is precedent for the critical perspective she developed with regard to gender and racial prejudices and social inequalities. The intellectual awakenings of at least two other Southern women of her generation who also lived in China in the 1920s offer insight. For the writers and activists Lillian Smith and Pearl Buck, both of whom worked in missionary settings in China, the daily presence of racism and sexual exploitation proved transformative. Retrospectively, Smith would call her China experience, specifically observing the dichotomy between what white missionaries preached and what they practiced, her "racial epiphany." Estelle's Shanghai story and "A Crossing" critique a similar and related dichotomy drawn from observing the behaviors of Shanghai-bound colonials and Shanghai's Anglo-American business community. Smith wrote that "I saw white supremacy over there . . . and the further away from home I was, the worse it looked. . . . I had taken it for granted in Jasper [Florida, where she grew up]. . . . I was stirred intellectually by what I saw in China. I was at a distance; I could analyze, criticize, look at, rebel."[39] Pearl Buck's Southern missionary father was a misogynist fundamentalist who, like Edna Earl's missionary suitor-husband in "A Crossing," cited St. Paul to justify subordinating his wife and daughters and who despised and constantly denigrated the Chinese he had come to "serve"; through him Pearl came to hate both organized religion and the racial and sexual domination and segregation that her father practiced.[40]

His unintended lessons were reenforced when, at boarding school, she volunteered to teach at the Door of Hope, a well-known Shanghai shelter for Chinese slave girls and prostitutes. According to Buck's biographer, "From the Ming dynasty through 1949, 'China had one of the largest and most comprehensive markets for the exchange of human beings in the world.'" In Shanghai this traffic in women's flesh was "accelerated by the presence of white men," namely, the Western colonials. These women and children had often been "tortured, starved, repeatedly raped" and beaten.[41] Dr. Fearn had also volunteered her medical services there: "I made daily visits . . . to give them treatments, for their venereal infections, bind up their broken bones, their suppurating sores, their mutilated bodies."[42] When Buck returned to the States in the early thirties, she, like her friends W. E. B. Du Bois and Paul and Eslanda Robeson, was already aware of the global reach and implications of American racism; in response, she became a civil rights activist, publishing regularly in *Opportunity* and *Crisis* as well as the white mainstream press. Conn notes that both her feminism and "her sensitivity to racial inequality and to white discrimination was rooted in the decades she had lived in Asia."[43] Estelle's mind, too, was changed by her cumulative experiences with American spiritual and secular imperialism abroad, first in Hawaii and then in Shanghai. Her political awakening was not so unusual. It was replicated in the lives of other sensitive Southern American women of much greater intelligence and talent. What is unusual is that she translated her insights into fiction, fiction that spoke to Billy Faulkner in a way that changed the course of his career.

Writing fiction that questioned the terms and values by which the Americans and the British governed Shanghai's International Settlement, Estelle redirected her reader's gaze to their self-serving nature. Specifically she focused attention on their linked politics of racism, misogyny, and economic privilege. The stories she wrote there all germinated in this boozy and avaricious colonial world. Her experiences as Cornell's wife inform both "A Crossing" and "Star Spangled Banner Stuff." The colonial reality the latter story depicts reveals the "Stuff" of her ambiguous title to be trash. That title stakes out the tropological space of her would-be empire builders, chiefly some of the young men who work in the Shanghai offices of Standard Oil and the tobacco company Liggett & Myers, companies that later became clients of Cornell Franklin.[44]

To exploit the democratic terms and so illuminate the true nature of "Star Spangled Banner Stuff," Estelle invents a drama whose narrative tension derives from the clash between the professed democratic ideals of the American Marc Montjoy (specifically, "All men are created equal") and his actual beliefs, which are sexist and racist. Montjoy is democratic at heart as long as he isn't threatened and panicked by "innocent little [white] girls" and "honorable Chinese gentlemen" engaging in interracial sex, an act he can conceive of only as rape. Although the story's overall tone is comedic, its critique is serious. In it a "blonde and beautiful" and "brainless" nineteen-year-old girl's seduction of an attractive Western-educated Chinese businessman, Needham Chang ("Needy" for short!), unveils Montjoy's racism.[45] In "Star Spangled Banner Stuff," Estelle revises the traditional narrative of interracial sexual transgression and colonial rape. She will return to this theme in her later and much darker story, "Selvage," set in the neocolonialist contemporary South.[46]

"Star Spangled Banner Stuff" casts Emma Jane Morrison, the only daughter of an unscrupulous American capitalist, as a parody of the Imperial Belle. At first she appears as little more than her parents' mechanical doll, whom her father, with his wife's cooperation, plans on marrying off to consolidate a business deal. She functions in this story like her male counterparts—as colonialism unmasked. Her constant and unself-conscious racist comments and acts draw attention to the more subtle racism and classism of her parents and her male admirers. Their more practiced bigotry shows itself fully only under duress and in a situation in which Emma Jane's desire is the catalyst. Estelle uses Emma Jane as a device for stripping her fictional American colonizers in Shanghai of their pretensions to democratic ideals. She shows their colonial machinations *in process*. By doing this, she makes a mockery of its professedly democratic practitioners. Writing fictional critique and becoming an alcoholic were Estelle's ways of coping with and exploiting her own marketing. "Star Spangled Banner Stuff" is most useful for exploring the actual and "fictional" reality of those years and their relevance to her continuing imaginative dialogue with Bill.

Unlike Edna Earl, the naïve and slightly loopy missionary of "A Crossing," Emma Jane has no redeeming graces. Like a baby doll, a precursor to Cecily in *Soldiers' Pay*, she is "all gold curls and blue eyes, her slim little arms and body and legs so quick and eager with the latest dance steps." Her materialism and narcissism demand steady infusions of the praises, gifts, and gazes of male admirers. No conflict complicates or cracks the mirrorlike surface of her psyche. What it mirrors is an image of an American grotesque. A puppetlike doll of a flapper daughter who has been programmed for consumption, Emma Jane is, as one of her would-be suitors notes prophetically, "a knock-out."[47] And that is the irony. Built for consumption, she becomes the site over which the very culture that built her almost consumes itself as all her would-be owners literally slug it out—supposedly to redeem her honor, but in fact to enforce white racial superiority. From the moment she enters, this baby doll is a "disturbance."

To Faulkner readers this will sound eerily familiar: *Soldiers' Pay* draws on this character for the ambience surrounding Cecily, most particularly her necking scenes on the porch swing and the jazzy country club dance sequence. In *Sanctuary* he transforms Estelle's flapper and the melee she causes into a horrifying depiction of Jim Crow sexual myths and mores. In Estelle's Shanghai narrative Emma Jane speaks-parrots the hysteria of a culture fixated on imperialist expansion and its attendant racism. But because she is a puppet out of control, she also (unwittingly) challenges it. Like everyone in "Star Spangled Banner Stuff," she's a caricature. That is the point of this smart and comic but serious fictional critique of Shanghai's colonial culture.

Three years would pass before Estelle returned to Oxford. During these years, Bill Faulkner continued struggling with his poetry. Constantly and obsessively he revised his poems and poem sequences, sometimes retaining as many as eleven almost indistinguishable drafts of a single poem. He could neither improve or escape his poet's voice. Then, on 17 November 1924, Estelle and her children suddenly left Shanghai.[48] When she arrived home in early December, she brought with her the products of her first marriage: two children and a sheaf of manuscript pages including her novel and stories like "Star Spangled Banner Stuff."

Faulkner was in Oxford when she arrived, having just returned from his first brief trip to New Orleans to meet Sherwood Anderson. Through Sherwood's new wife and his old friend Elizabeth Prall, Faulkner had struck up an instant friendship with the man who was then considered America's greatest writer of contemporary fiction. Although still a poet, he now had something more public to show for it. That October, for a fee of four hundred dollars the Four Seas Company had agreed to publish his first poem sequence, *The Marble Faun*. Its release date was 15 December. Earlier that year saw his first national exposure: one poem in the *New Republic* and several in the *Double Dealer*.

By 4 January 1925, Faulkner had returned to New Orleans, where he moved in with Elizabeth and Anderson's eighteen-year-old son. "She is so nice to me—mothers me, and looks after me, and gets things to eat which I like," Faulkner wrote Maud in mid-January.[49] Sherwood was away on a lecture tour and did not return until March. But in Oxford, between Faulkner's November and January trips to New Orleans, something miraculous had happened that gave him the freedom and self-confidence to access his genius: the poet became a novelist. His transformation first manifested on a smaller scale. In New Orleans in January, he began writing a series of short sketches that he published beginning in February in Mc-Clure's newspaper, the *Times Picayune,* and in the February issue of the *Dou-*

ble Dealer (*TOH*, 174, 175, 178–80). Then in mid-February, he wrote his mother that "right now I am 'thinking out' a novel" and that "as soon as I get it straight, I will begin work" (184). That happened in early March, right after another trip home to Oxford and Estelle (187, 208).

Perhaps letters he wrote Estelle from New Orleans that winter and spring more explicitly acknowledged his debt. However, the only existing record of his feelings during these months is in his mostly cocky and self-confident letters to Maud that winter and spring. By mid-January the "Mississippi Poet" wrote that "I am writing a series of short sketches [stories] which I am trying to sell to a newspaper. Took one to the editor of the *Times-Picayune* yesterday."[50] John McClure first told Faulkner to leave his work and call back in "a day or two; then he glanced at the title, read the first sentence, then the first page, then the whole thing with a half finished letter in his typewriter and three reporters waiting to speak to him. He was tickled to death with it and has put it before his board. I have finished another one which I shall take him tomorrow." In his next letter Faulkner wrote that the paper "took those things, and the editor wants all I can do like them" (*TOH*, 174–75). His first sketch, "Mirrors of Chartres Street," appeared on 8 February. Its radical shift in genre and voice signaled the modest beginning of a tremendous creative leap forward.

The next year, Faulkner bound ten of his New Orleans sketches, along with a new one entitled "Hong-Li," into another handmade book for Estelle. He dated it 29 October. Its chaste dedication read: "To Estelle, a/ Lady, with/Respectful Admiration:/This." Written expressly for her, "Hong Li" has been read as one of Faulkner's "epistolary persona(e)" whose "bitter misogyny constitutes a nasty corrective to the sequence of writing [for Helen Baird and Estelle], private and published that goes before it in this pattern."[51] Evidence of his continuing ambivalence about Estelle, "Hong-Li" also underscores the centrality of Faulkner's and Estelle's ongoing dialogue as, in this sketch, he invokes but recasts her Chinese protagonist's lament to his own fickle flapper love. For Faulkner, perhaps not consciously, their dialogues gave him permission to begin to explore and mine that ambivalence. Yet not until 1928, when Estelle is legally free of her first husband, would Faulkner realize the full imaginative potential of such collaborative moments.

This time Estelle stayed in Oxford for eleven months. In November 1925, under great pressure, she returned with Cornell to Shanghai. Yet sometime in early 1926, and for unknown but multirumored reasons, Cornell, who the prior fall had begged her to return, "required" that his wife leave Shanghai.[52] With no money of her own, and with the two Franklin children, Estelle headed for Honolulu, where, with Cornell's child support plus whatever she could earn, she hoped to become economically independent for the first time in her life. We do not know why this plan failed. We do know that its failure depressed her enough that she may have attempted suicide prior to returning to Oxford. That she and Bill Faulkner resumed a relationship that began in childhood and culminated in marriage is well known. The fiction she wrote in Shanghai shows that much of its substance was the stuff of an intellectual and literary dialogue that began when both were adolescents and continued through Estelle's first marriage. During the next five years (1925–29), Faulkner and Estelle worked together on her material; meanwhile her unsettling but exciting presence and her voice continued to feed his new-found genius.

While living with her parents in Oxford from the spring of 1926 until her marriage to Faulkner in June 1929, Estelle also revised her novel *White Beaches*. Faulkner then typed it for her and submitted it to Scribner's. The novel no longer exists. Both she and her sister told Joseph Blotner she had burned the rejected manuscript. She also completed "Selvage" and at least two more short stories, "Idyll in the Desert" and "A Letter to Grandmamma." She and Faulkner then worked together on at least one of these short stories; he later published two of them under his own name.[53] No biographer mentions Oldham's three extant stories that Faulkner did not try to revise and publish, although a catalogued version of "Star Spangled Banner Stuff" has been in the University of Virginia Faulkner Collection since the early sixties. Embedded in her imperial antiromances are her imaginative responses to and revisions of Faulkner's earliest poetic and dramatic portrayals of romantic and erotic desire. As such these stories form half of an imaginative dialogue whose written record begins as early as 1920.

After she married Faulkner, Estelle stopped writing but, as we know from Jill, her parents continued their imaginative collaboration. They transformed what was originally a written dialogue into the theater of their everyday life. The effects of Faulkner's and Estelle's continuing dialogue were far-reaching. They helped shape the psychodynamics of human relationships in all of Faulkner's major novels, most significantly perhaps in *The Sound and the Fury*.

During 1930–31 Faulkner submitted "Idyll in the Desert" to seven magazines (*USWF*, 701). Ultimately, Random House bought it for four hundred dollars and released it in December 1931 in a limited edition.[54] Both "Elly" ("Selvage") and "Idyll" appeared under Faulkner's byline. In February 1930, Faulkner also sent out his revised version of Estelle's "A Letter to Grandmamma," now retitled "A Dangerous Man."[55] A surviving typescript of Estelle's version with her name and P.O. box typed on the title page suggests that, as with "A Crossing," "Selvage," and her other short stories, her original intent was publication.[56]

Estelle never did publish any of her fiction, although after Faulkner's death, she made further revisions to "Dr. Wohlenski" and "Star Spangled Banner Stuff." Also, after Faulkner's death, she resumed the painting she had started in Shanghai and continued until 1929.

Estelle's art and music, which I have discussed elsewhere, offer evidence of her creativity and the pleasure she took in it, particularly during the two brief periods when she was not living with either of her husbands. Her fiction, however, tells the most about the person she was, her imaginative dialogue and collaboration with Faulkner, and her understanding and criticism of the different cultures in which she lived during the years leading up to their marriage.

23

Collaborating with Estelle, Oxford, 1924–1925
"Star Spangled Banner Stuff," Her Shanghai "Romance"

E STELLE'S ORIGINAL manuscript of "Star Spangled Banner Stuff" is missing. The earliest of its three extant typescripts, however, provides evidence of Faulkner's and Estelle's collaboration. The latest, an unmarked original and its revised carbon copy, typed for Estelle by Jill in 1964, is marked with Estelle's additional revisions.[1] These further emphasize her flapper's lack of any real agency and her own critique of Shanghai's colonial culture. They also provide continuing evidence of her still very active intellect, but because she made these revisions in the 1960s, they are not part of this story.

Faulkner's and Estelle's Marks: The Paper Trail

"SSS" #1, a sixty-three-page typescript dating from 1924, has been available to scholars since the mid-1960s. According to an accompanying note by the donor, this story "by Mrs. William Faulkner, then the wife of Judge [Cornell] Franklin, [was] written ca. 1924 in Shanghai. William Faulkner subsequently read the story in Oxford, Miss., and, according to Mrs. Faulkner, offered suggestions regarding its construction—The story was never published." The mixture of carbons and original typescript pages indicates that "SSS" #1 is a revision of an earlier (now missing) typescript. The majority of the pages are carbons. Original typescript pages are preceded or followed by large page breaks, where portions of the manuscript were significantly rewritten. One revised page is typed on the reverse side of letterhead from Estelle's father's office, dating from the mid-1920s.[2] Both Faulkner and Estelle have made ink holograph corrections throughout this typescript, providing a rare handwritten example of their collaborative work. Both have also made minor substantive revisions. Estelle has also inserted many of the apostrophes that Faulkner removed in typing, and she has capitalized both "Chinese" and "Chinaman," which he had consistently lowercased. In 1964, when Estelle asked Jill to type a clean copy of "Star Spangled Banner Stuff" from the 1924 typescript, she included both parents' holograph revisions ("SSS" #2). Estelle then made further substantive revisions on the carbon copy ("SSS" #3). Because our interest here is Estelle's and Faulkner's collaboration and its effects on Faulkner's dramatic transformation from poet to novelist in February 1925, all references (unless otherwise noted) are to "SSS" #1, which was published in a scholarly journal in 1997.[3]

"Star Spangled Banner Stuff" is of a piece with Estelle's "A Crossing" and "Selvage." Again her subject is a "white" girl simultaneously fascinated and repulsed by her attraction to the "dark," artistic outsider. As in Estelle's other tales, her flapper is indifferent to the proper white man she ends up marrying. Alcohol is a prevalent thematic, along with a main character's remorse for choices made when he or she was drunk; and there are allusions to and revisions of Faulkner's poetry. As in "A Crossing," stylistic turns and some diction and phrasing anticipate the language of *Soldiers' Pay* and the novels that follow. Its brazen nineteen-year-old is a Cecily Saunders or Pat Robyns in embryo. At two crucial points in "Star Spangled Banner Stuff," in a move reminiscent of instances in *Soldiers' Pay* and *Mosquitoes*, where Faulkner writes fragments of his own poems into his fictional characters' speeches, his pierrotiste poet's laments are voiced by this story's "foreigner," its racialized "ivory-skinned" Chinese businessman, Needy Chang.

In late 1924, Faulkner had not yet written any modern fiction. To date, his only known works of prose fiction were "Landing in Luck," a twenty-five-hundred-word comic war story, and "The Hill," an eight-hundred-word prose poem or sketch, which were published in the *Mississippian* in November 1919 and March 1922, respectively. Neither gives any hint of the novels to come. In contrast, Estelle's story does. Marked by racialized gender confusion and its dismantling of iconic figures like the Southern Belle and the New Woman, it anticipates Faulkner's *Soldiers' Pay*, which he began writing within less than two months of Estelle's return, and *Mosquitoes* (begun in 1925). In "Star Spangled Banner Stuff," aspects of Faulkner's pierrotiste persona appear in the heroine's unacceptable male lover, the feminized dark male "other" who inhabits all her stories. Not until much later would Faulkner tackle directly the kinds of questions Estelle explores in her stories. But as he typed "Star Spangled Banner Stuff" and entered her imagination through its prose narrative, he enriched his own. He emerged from that feminine space, which he often referred to as his "empty vessel," reborn as a novelist. Had he left the Pierrot of his poetry in Estelle's story, where, speaking through her character, he had begun its transformation? Or had Estelle's prose incarnation and critique of that character given him a perspective he needed to free himself from its hold on his voice? In any case, her revised Pierrots taught him something: further remnants of her Pierrots form a dominant trope in his first novel, where he uses them to piece together and critique all of the novel's "soldiers."

Estelle was not an influence in any conventional sense; rather, because of their intense personal relationship, composed of intricate layers of feelings expressed over time and in both spoken and written language, her impact on Faulkner's creativity was unique. Of course, and as many have observed, there were important other influences. But Estelle's fiction spoke from an inner space of herself and the Southern history and culture she and Faulkner shared. In that culture in 1924, as a disgraced and banished wife, she now figured in her community as black. It was the act of placing himself inside of her figuratively blackened mind, another permutation of the black maternal, which taught him how to write a world that to date had been unspeakable.

Reading "Star Spangled Banner Stuff"

Estelle sets her fast-paced and jazzy Shanghai tale about race, seduction, and power in famous and, to her, familiar spaces: in the gaming rooms and bar of the American Club; in the public and private rooms of the opulent Astor House, with its parquet dance floor, palm garden, and great French chef; and at the famous Carleton Café—"Everyone who goes about in Shanghai reaches the Carleton sometime between eight P.M. and 4 A.M. on Saturday night. There's usually a fair show and always good music." A gambling scene and a beating mark her story's beginning and end. The gamblers and beaters are four Americans. But Needy Chang, a major player in this story's "game," is absent from the table. Club membership is closed to Chinese. Even so, the most openly prejudiced of the Americans, Freddy Bowen, is not adverse to playing with Chang's money or using him. Chang's prize for winning is supposed to be an introduction to the "nifty Round-the-worlder," a visiting American flapper named Emma Jane Tomlinson.[4]

As in Estelle's other stories, the relation between a young girl's commodification and her limited emotional range is an important theme, one that Faulkner will seize upon to explore in greater depth. Like her Faulknerian offspring, Emma Jane has been bred to be desired by men and then married off to the highest bidder. She herself may not express desire. Interestingly, though, Emma Jane ends up with somewhat more agency than Faulkner's more nuanced "silver-frocked," long-legged, "virginal" Cecily or his "fallen" Caddy Compson.

Needy Chang is also forbidden to express desire, and his imperialist confrères objectify him with a similar gendered, racist, and racializing gaze. So do two women who are in and out of the story: the unnamed narrator and Emma Jane. This is why Emma Jane spells trouble. Chang Wong Pao Needham (Needy Chang "to his intimates") has one English name but is not biracial. Rather his Western-educated father, "a grand old man" who holds a British knighthood and is full of "wisdom and tolerance," either "through acknowledgement thereof or a fine sense of humor, had tacked a good old English name" onto his beloved son. For some months, Needy, a wealthy Yale- and Cambridge-educated businessman from Shantung province, has been a fixture at the Astor House, where his "ivory skin," Western education, impeccable manners, sumptuous rooms, and endless liquor supply have gained him the appearance of a friendship with this group of American would-be tycoons. Three are young Southerners who work for the Shanghai offices of Standard Oil or Liggett & Myers Tobacco. However, to make this a thoroughly American tale, its most obvious villain is the unapologetic racist, Freddy Bowen, a New York bond trader. His opening pronouncements at the mah-jongg table that "I couldn't come right out and tell [Chang] that I couldn't introduce a nice white girl to a Chinaman, even if he is Croesus," and that he couldn't say, "You yellow chink, I can't introduce you to a white girl," set up the terms of engagement for the battle between East and West played out in this story. Freddy is quickly seconded by one of the Southerners who adds, "It's different for a man to be seen going about with a Chinaman, but for a white girl, and American—hell, no."[5]

Shanghai's Anglo-American business community provides a rich setting for Estelle to foreground her fascination with the marketing of women and her interest in and figuring of the black maternal in her portrayal of yet another dark-skinned foreign gentleman, the "smitten" Needy (pun intended?) Chang. The attractions of his difference are apparent in the unnamed narrator's first highly erotic but feminized portrait of him. While the Americans are gambling at their club, Chang passes the afternoon in his rooms at Astor House reading Keats, smoking his pipe, and drinking tea: "His light, embroidered silk dressing-gown was open, and it revealed his deep smooth ivory skin from his throat to the pale yellow cummerbund binding the white silk trousers about his slender waist. It was July, and he was hot despite the breeze from the Whang Poo below that billowed the fine draperies. . . . His slender ivory fingers held the open dressing-gown at either side and his head lay back against the chair . . . [as he] lost himself in daydream." He is tended by servants, a "coolie who stood behind his chair and fanned his master unceasingly and from time to time another servant poured pale scalding tea into a shallow cup on the little table, and Chang read and sipped and mused."[6]

When Chang muses "in Chinese" about his infatuation with the American flapper, he sounds a bit like Faulkner's Marble Faun: "Ah, woe is me that at last among foreign surroundings have mine eyes beheld the woman that I have dreamed after all my life; a woman as far beyond my reach as the evening star, and as shining. The whiteness of her dims my dream." But despite his Faulknerian lament, this revised Marble Faun still has more in common with Edna Earl's orientalized Ahmed Sassoon, even quoting him at one point. The Americans Chang has to bribe with booze, whom he refers to as "worms," already drink like fish, so this is hardly necessary.[7]

Reading with a twenty-first-century sensibility, it is hard to know whether Estelle intended aspects of her portrayal of Chang to be slightly campy: Chang's heightened aggrandized language was given to all Chinese in Anglo-American stories being published when Estelle was writing. But it's also the language of Billy Faulkner's poet persona, to whom Chang is related, with his Keats, his pipe, his delicate, feminine frame, and his sighs and dreams about the "Shining One." Meanwhile the "Shining One's" hypersexualized and stylized movements and her (c)rudeness anticipate Faulkner's first full-blown flirts, like Cecily Saunders or Pat Robyns.[8]

In fact, though, Emma Jane is no shining one. She's a royal pain in the neck. This is evident to readers and Chang's Chinese servants but not to all the young men who pursue her. This makes the chaos she creates for the American businessmen, her parents, and the love-struck Chang ultimately more amusing than tragic and sorrowful.

Emma Jane's brattiness has a purpose: her initial and ultimate resistance to her father's plan to use her charms to lure Chang to invest in his business gives Estelle an opportunity to further showcase American racism and materialism. At the same time, Emma Jane's attraction-repulsion to Chang affords a splendid opportunity to explore Estelle's making of blackness (in this case, Chinese-ness), a subject central to her two other stories.

In "Star Spangled Banner Stuff" Estelle extends her experiments (begun in "Dr. Wohlenski") with multiple and constantly shifting points of view and with more complex plotting. Chang has bought into the sexual values of the Western imperialists. Against his better judgment, he becomes smitten with Emma Jane: "'She is like white jade,' he said to himself . . . 'Pure and untouched.'" Like Jay Gatsby, another outsider who loved a flapper dream, though slightly more self-aware, and like the orientalized Sassoon in "A Crossing," Chang recognizes that he must consort with "worm[s]," her parent-owners and the American businessmen who have access to them, merely for the privilege of shaking hands: "I . . . must first make drunk a worm, bribe him, then beg of him the favor of merely being allowed to touch her fingers in greeting."[9] As we've seen, Estelle understood both the use of alcohol in temporarily suspending racial boundaries and the paradox of the taboo of touch in a racist culture. Such moments occur in all her stories. A decade later, when Faulkner writes the scene of Clytie Sutpen and Rosa Coldfield's first confrontation in *Absalom, Absalom!* he explains the meaning of Clytie's "touch," but only from the white Southern Lady's perspective. Here, writing alone in a house filled with Chinese servants in Shanghai's American sector in the early 1920s, Estelle is already attempting to let her counterparts to Clytie tell about that touch from *their* perspectives.

Emma Jane is dancing at the Astor House with Freddy Bowen when she first sees Chang sitting at a nearby table. Instantly her "round blue eyes were held in staring fascination by the long narrow black ones of the stranger." She begins flirting from afar. But when Bowen tells her that Chang's a "Chink," she's horrified: "In her heart was a growing horror of what she had done—flirted with a Chinaman and enjoyed it." She then looks "with relief" at Freddy and even the disgusting Fairman: "'They are white,' she said to herself over and over, yet despite herself and with a sort of horror her blue eyes sought those still black ones again."[10]

The racism and hypocrisy of American "foreigners" in this Chinese treaty port setting are critiqued by their Chinese "hosts." Chang, the upright (politically correct?) Chinese counterpart of Marc Montjoy, notes the hypocrisy of the sexual politics governing American ideals. After bribing Freddy Bowen, the slimiest of the young Americans, to introduce him to the "nifty looker," Chang gives Freddy his word that "I'll never ask you again to do anything that evidently seems improper to your American sense of decency."[11]

The story's plot charts Chang's seduction by Emma Jane and its predictable result. At the end, Chang, sadder but wiser, leaves Shanghai, that evil foreign enclave, to return to Shantung province.[12] In the soliloquy that precedes his departure, he lapses again into a polyglot of an infatuated but otherwise sensible young man and Faulkner's pierrotiste persona, as he pictures himself walled away in solipsistic despair, writing blazons to an imagined life and love: "Chang stretched himself on a couch and turned on the fan. He touched the [hotel room] wall lightly with his fingertips. She lay sleeping somewhere, perhaps just beyond this wall. Dangerous fires! He would go to old Li tomorrow. A final stone laid on the wall of his life, walling him away into gardens of old and grave content. She is like a white jade vase that holy hands had placed among lighted candles."[13]

Like Faulkner's Faun and Pierrots, Chang too will find peace in his retreat to his walled garden.[14] But for quite different reasons. Unlike Faulkner's emotionally frozen and paralyzed pierrotistes, Chang follows Estelle's more realistic and pragmatic script. He recovers, marries the right mate (that is, a Chinese woman from his own class), has "three beautiful, strong sons," and names one of them after the only American who recognizes and makes a stab at apologizing for his own and his friends' racist treatment of Chang.[15] Because the story attempts to represent a complex discursive space, neither its colonials nor its Chinese speak with the same voice. Rather, Estelle's story, like Faulkner's later, much more gifted novels, reaches toward polyphony.

It also depicts and critiques hierarchies within, and external to, the ruling structure of Shanghai's International Settlement. Geography plays an essential role in defining both the strengths and weaknesses of that colonial structure. Although Estelle's American men hatch their plots within the walls of their all-white male clubs, to execute them they must venture into the more democratic and volatile space of Shanghai's prestigious Astor House. Whoever can afford the hotel is welcome there, and so rich Chinese and foreigners mingle in its opulent rooms, in the palm courtyard, and on its parquet dance floor. But because Astor House allows women and Chinese to enter and take rooms, it is a site where disruption can and does occur.

The setting of Estelle's story attests to the breadth and depth of her knowledge of this sector of Shanghai society. Opening and closing scenes occur, appropriately, at the gaming tables in Shanghai's American Club, a famous bastion of white male privilege and symbol of the American presence in China.[16] Its president, ironically named Fairman, is probably a composite satire inspired by Estelle's husband, her husband's uncle Malcolm from Honolulu, and Stirling Fessenden, an important figure in International Settlement politics in the 1920s. Fessenden, an American lawyer and, like Fairman, an ardent Anglophile, was elected chair of the British-controlled Shanghai Municipal Council in 1923.[17] Many Americans considered Fessenden "more British than the British themselves" and saw him as "a pawn occupying a position of eminence to give a veneer of internationalism to what was otherwise an almost entirely British show."[18] Estelle would have known him personally and had ample time to observe him, since he was also the law partner of Cornell's good friend, Major Chauncy

P. Holcomb. Holcomb will represent Estelle in the divorce proceedings her husband instituted in Shanghai in 1928.

In all International Settlement social clubs, race and gender discrimination was rigidly enforced. Prior to 1925, the period during which her story occurs, neither the Shanghai Club (British) nor the American Club admitted Chinese except to serve or entertain their members. The rules were essentially the same for women. At the American Club, white women, along with their children, were admitted as guests on patriotic holidays (whose social events the wives organized) like the Fourth of July and the Washington Birthday Ball.[19] Club hierarchies replicated the economic and social hierarchies within Shanghai's Anglo-American community. Fairman, who runs the American Club, also belongs to the Shanghai Club, "a sign," as one Chinese cultural historian notes, "of arrival in Shanghai [white] society, which is not to say all members were equals. Junior members of the leading British firms . . . remember the strict . . . lineup at the [club's world-famous] Long Bar, its polished mahogany shining under dark Jacobean paneling—the taipans at one end and the griffins, or newcomers, at the other."[20] Estelle's narrator notes that the American Club "was a haven for the young man just out from home but just another place to drop in for the older men, who for the most part preferred the Shanghai Club, supposedly cosmopolitan but essentially English."[21]

Estelle drew on her knowledge of the American Club's function and club members' habits to portray the violent world in which all men drink constantly but only the biggest creeps like Freddy and Fairman are said to be drunks. Surveillance in this clubby community is essential for maintaining social hierarchies. Fairman, who habitually "started his afternoon going with a visit to the Shanghai Club bar," ends his afternoon many drinks later with a patrol of the American Club, "by which hour he was in a state of prowling, slightly pop-eyes officiousness."[22] Foregrounding the weakness and fluidity of this colonial power structure, Estelle makes its chief of surveillance a lush. Fairman is the man charged with keeping the myth of the white man's natural supremacy in place. She pokes more fun at Fairman in a later scene, where his "boy" silently "watched with interest" as his "master" sneaked a morning "pick-me-up." Estelle is attentive to class distinctions. While earlier the aristocrat, Chang, had mocked the Americans, here Estelle writes an amusing scene viewed from a Chinese servant's unflattering perspective. In it Fairman, dressed as a pillar of Western imperialism in his "morning coat, top hat, and gleaming boots," gulps his gin before breakfast and then swinishly wipes "his lips on the cloth that covered the buffet." As is often the case in Estelle's tale, American colonials are the true grotesques. The servant's critical mind observes his colonial employer enslaved to the bottle: "the boy stood quietly and watched" Fairman's "unsteady hand," his "initial shudder," and "the steady pulsing of the master's swallowing throat." His servant's distanced, ethnographic eye, focusing on the alcoholic's compulsive behavior and his gross physicality, anatomizes another taboo narrative pervading Western colonial outposts. As with Edna Earl in "A Crossing," Estelle's critique of alcoholism becomes explicit when Chang, filled with "remorse," blames his fatal moment of bad judgment on his being drunk.[23]

This colonial society, as Estelle portrays it, seems more preoccupied than most cultures with exclusion. The hatreds and desires such preoccupations can unleash are central to Estelle's characterizations. Fairman, for example, is barely tolerated by his peers at both clubs; at the American the members laugh at him behind his back but have elected him their president so as to "eliminate a nuisance from the card-room." Yet he clearly enjoys pushing the junior men around: "the younger members hated him and feared him a little, for . . . he held suspension over them like a sword." Fairman's power to exclude his junior associates turns out to be of far greater concern than Montjoy's professed wish that his fellow Americans treat Chang decently.[24] Despite resenting Fairman's power, they nonetheless aggressively enforce this pecking order of exclusion, and claim, in the vocabulary replicating exclusion arguments in Shanghai's English-language newspapers, that their behavior is "natural."

The club setting for Estelle's story is fitting, as sexism, racism, white male privilege, and alcohol are activities around which club life revolves. In fact, all the anxieties of her story's representative Americans are registered in these tropes. Imperialism's economic and erotic desires further propel its action. The club, after all, is the place where deals are made, and the deal on the gaming table involves a white American girl whom all the men want to own.

Estelle's plot, where the economic exchange of a human commodity is effected by men playing a game of chance, is only slightly less complex than some of Faulkner's. In order to break into Shanghai's import-export market, Fairman, "a stickler for rules—for other people," and his friend Morrison, a visiting American businessman, need to borrow money from Chang, a rich young Chinese businessman whom they don't know. Morrison proposes, and his wife concurs with, a plan to use their daughter, Emma Jane, as bait. She is the goods that will be proffered to facilitate the expansion of Morrison's business in Shanghai. In order to accomplish their scheme, their daughter must be silenced and deprived of agency; one way to accomplish this is to infantilize her. Thus Mrs. Morrison instructs Emma

Jane that "as long as we are in China, my baby mustn't speak disrespect-fully of the Chinese," adding, "so you see, my little daughter, should we meet Mr. Chang . . . we will have to be nice to him." But, as her mother's qualifying phrase ("as long as we are in China") suggests, Emma Jane has been well schooled in racial hatred. She exposes her mother's hypocrisy by responding that she's "not going to run after yellow Chinamen" to help her father clinch a business deal and that "I hate Chinks!" whom she calls "Old, creepy, long-clawed thing[s]." To Freddy Bowen, Emma Jane says "hysterically" that she'd "scream if she had to touch a Chinaman's hand."[25]

Later that night at the Carleton Café, when she threatens to leave the table "if a Chink sits down" with them, her mother says fatuously "you simply cannot go to foreign countrys [sic] and avoid meeting the natives oc-casionally." It's a wonderful moment. Then Mrs. Morrison explains apolo-getically that this notion of what the Chinese are has been taught to Emma Jane by her old "nurse."[26] Another outsider (here, a black American ser-vant) is always available for blame and excuse.

In a comic scene between mother and daughter, Emma Jane questions her exploitation in a dialogue that explains (implicitly) why Mrs. Morrison cooperates in marketing her daughter. Asking why she's needed, she asserts that "Papa's got enough cash for me" and "enough business . . . without making us run after yellow Chinamen." In response, Mrs. Morrison tells her daughter to leave business decisions "to papa, as I've always done, and profit by it."[27] Mrs. Morrison has learned how to take advantage of her commodification, and she is trying to pass on her knowledge. But Emma Jane refuses to cooperate. She has other plans.

The Morrison seniors, Fairman, and their would-be successors—the young Americans who serve as the link between Chang and Fairman—ex-pect Chang and Emma Jane to adhere to their sexist and racist assump-tions and are shocked when she doesn't—sort of. When she actually sees Chang and learns that he doesn't look like the racist caricatures of Chinese "creeps" in her nursery books, she becomes fascinated by his "difference" and determines to add him to her "collection" of young men. Here, for the second time, Estelle calls attention to the fact that racism, like sexism, is taught and that both are based on myths and culturally constructed. Chang, like all the Westerners except the narrator, also objectifies and ide-alizes Western women; his upper crust Anglo-American education has in-doctrinated him into Western standards of feminine beauty as well as busi-ness. Worldly-wise in all matters but love, Chang has already become infatuated with this "looker."[28] All he sees are her golden curls, slim legs, the "full radiance of her shining hair and the silver shimmer of her frock." Like the Americans, and despite all evidence to the contrary, he insists she is "pure and untouched." Unlike his more observant servants, he doesn't notice her shallowness or hear her "harsh" and "petulant voice." Nor does he observe that "there was something of the pea-fowl in Emma Jane" or note her "shrill little mind." Acquisitive himself, neither he nor the young Americans notice that swinging Emma Jane, as she herself puts it, "always had one eye out for young men; a girl needed so many nowadays." Neither he nor her American suitors see that this material girl makes no distinction between acquiring them and picking up other bargains in rugs, silks, and curios. All are collectibles. As she says to her mirrored reflection "You are beautiful, old thing. [She's nineteen!] If you work it right, Needy will give you something grand to show around at home. Gee, I wish they could have seen you making a mandarin go cuckoo last night."[29]

Estelle's American men are racists, but they and Chang are united in thinking of women as booty they can exchange at the gaming tables. They see nothing wrong with the right to be introduced to a woman as the prize for winning at mah-jongg, although Chang, like Sassoon in "A Crossing," chafes at being beholden to a white man he considers inferior. Gender unites all Estelle's men in agreement that women are property, whereas race—which determines who has the rights to which women—divides them.[30]

A conventional resolution would follow if Estelle's story fit the formulaic plots of the popular colonial romances about contemporary China reviewed in the Honolulu and Shanghai English-language newspapers of the time. Using his compliant daughter as a lure, the Westerner would get a piece of the Chinese market, and the Chinese businessman "who loves the hero[ine] would be disposed of heroically but finally in order to obtain *the correct resolution for the story's other principals.*"[31] But Estelle is not writing typical colonial romance. Her spoof on this genre underscores the misogyny and racism masking as democratic idealism—"star spangled banner stuff"— and explores the inherent paradox of insisting that all white women are quintessentially innocent and pure while educating them to be racists, "material girls," and sexual teases. With Emma Jane, Estelle also revises the interracial rape fantasy to show the grotesque results of forcing women to negotiate for power within the cultural norms for marriageable young girls in this society.[32]

Swerving from that fantasy, she casts Emma Jane as an aggressive seductress rather than the more typical, unwitting victim. Although her suitors' idealized view of her dominates, the reader first sees her through the eyes of a Chinese servant whose vision has not been tainted by a Western education. Watching the "foreign woman" from his employer's hotel hallway, Pang appraises the "light leave-taking of the Shining One" and a young (white) man: "A kiss. What did a chink servant matter? A quick embrace, and the Shining One pushed the young man away and left him staring at the gold lettering on her door." Although "he had never been out of Shantung province [before] and he knew little of the ways of foreigners . . . the radiance of the Shining One was dimmed." He's disgusted by sexual behavior that is devoid of pleasure: "the strange way she had put her mouth on the mouth of the man," and then pushed him away.[33] His stripped-down sentence makes the reader feel his disgust.

Estelle later confirms the accuracy of Pang's view. Like her Edna Earl, Emma Jane experiences her body as something separate from herself—a machine designed, tuned, and then constantly retuned to create desire in any man who watches her. And all do. Prefiguring Faulknerian female adolescents and young women, she spends a great deal of time before her mirror speaking to and tending this "body" that precipitates desire in others yet feels no desire. She seems more automaton than human. Emma Jane has been taught to *look* and *act* but not to *feel* erotic. Her job is to direct her energy into creating concrete proofs of her market value. Like her mother, she is bent on wresting material treasure ("profit") from her victim, the evidence that she has seduced a "Chinese lord." She is the American girl as consummate violator and consumer, an imperialist visitor collecting human feelings (hearts?) and other "oriental" trophies to take back to civilization in Toledo.

Estelle also suggests that by idealizing its women and placing them on pedestals, colonial culture, like the Jim Crow South, invests them with the power to destroy men of color. Emma Jane doesn't have to protect her reputation by claiming rape, because, to "protect their property," white men will make the claim for her. Her behavior is outrageous and campy. Saturated with images from Hollywood romances, she waltzes into Chang's rooms in her mother's chiffon and lace negligée. "Emma Jane walked—as she had seen cinema queens walk—into Chang's arms." Even though the Americans find her in Chang's bed, her "honor" is secure because of her white suitors' need to believe in her "innocence" (read lack of desire or agency). They think they are fighting for her *honor*, whereas she, who finds their violence "thrilling," understands very well that they are fighting for *possession*.[34]

Estelle appears to treat Chang, the alleged rapist, more conventionally. His role is often replicated in contemporaneous popular fiction as well as in late imperial romances—white men accuse him of raping a white woman and beat him. But the intent of Estelle's story is different. As in her more serious story "Selvage" / "Elly," she wants to challenge racism and misogyny, not justify them. The reader knows that Chang is innocent and that the Americans' accusations against him are racially motivated: "You yellow cur, to bring that innocent little girl to your rooms!"[35] To return to the language of the *Honolulu Star Bulletin*'s book review column, Estelle's narrative purpose is to disrupt the "correct resolution" sought by popular fiction, not confirm it. The accusation and beating scene in which Montjoy's racism is unmasked and his "Star Spangled Banner Stuff" proved empty rhetoric accomplishes this.

Estelle uses Emma Jane's and Chang's transgressive behavior to reveal the inherent racism, sexism, and denial that define and control female and "native" sexuality in colonial cultures. Ultimately, though, Chang plays the role that colonialism has scripted for him, since he is brutally beaten for allegedly stealing and "dragging off" white female property, thereby destroying its value. In contrast, not only does Montjoy deny Emma Jane's participation; he also insists on interpreting Chang's alleged rape as further proof of her natural innocence. Yet, by "aveng[ing]" her, that is, by nearly killing the innocent Chang, the white men undermine order rather than restore it. Chang then creates an appearance of order by first retreating to the Chinese sector of the city and then to Shantung, where he marries a Chinese woman chosen by his parents. In the brief flash-forward concluding the story, Chang describes her as a good wife because she's a good breeder, having borne him three sons, a resolution that is silent on his wife's feelings.

Chang's attitude toward and treatment of Emma Jane and his wife is as sexist as any white man's. By idealizing Emma Jane, he reinforces the Western image of the golden girl.[36] In this sense, then, Estelle doesn't idealize Chang either. Rather, her story shows that neither white nor Chinese men allow women agency. Both respond only to Emma Jane's physical appearance—her whiteness, her golden ringlets, deep blue eyes, and "pomegranate lips." They ignore her acts and words.

Perhaps the end Estelle invents for Montjoy and Chang is their payoff for believing and investing in a Gatsby-like dream of femininity. They have confined Emma Jane to this dream-image, and her negotiations for power within its confines compose the story's plot, which unfolds as it does because her captors can't see through the golden nimbus in which they've enfolded her. "Shining One" says it all. Their idealization is also Emma Jane's immunization to any taint of racial (which is always sexualized) pollution. Considering her confines, she does pretty well. She marries the gullible Montjoy, who is her choice, not her parents'; and her marriage removes her both from the market economy of her parents and from a life as a colonial wife. Four years later and, according to one of Montjoy's Shanghai associates, still "blond and beautiful," she and her husband "step high" in New York City.[37] Unlike her Chinese counterpart or her mother, she's also apparently unencumbered by children. Emma Jane is clearly no "mother-woman." Here, as in "A Crossing," New York becomes the home of the woman who has flouted social conventions and a marketing intended to keep her in her place. But this time it's the girl herself who has this agency, not her loose-living black sheep of an aunt.

Of the four young men in "Star Spangled Banner Stuff," Marc Montjoy stands out initially because he constantly criticizes his companions for their racist behavior toward Chang. Montjoy's problem with Chang is similar to Emma Jane's. That is, Chang's racialization is far from simple. Like the Creole, Paul de Montigny, in "Selvage" / "Elly," he doesn't segregate easily from the social classification of "whiteness." As we know from the other Americans, a "Chinese" is a certain thing. However, Chang constantly confuses their categories of Chinese and white; that is, by merely changing his clothes, he can pass as either Chinese or Western. Yet, he's a man who is coded feminine and even "queer" by both the narrator and Emma Jane. For example, as Emma Jane gloats over the jewel Chang places "reverently around her neck" (shades of Sassoon), she thinks "it was cold—cold and queer like the man who gave it to her."[38] Here Estelle continues probing the coding of the "stranger's" racialized sexuality, as she does in two of her other miscegenation stories, "A Crossing" and "Selvage." Chang, too, resists easy signification.

The true blue Montjoy bases his criticism of his compatriots' racism on his own American sense of decency, his belief in American ideals of fair play, and his market values—that Chang's money and education make him the equal of whites—or "Star Spangled Banner Stuff," as his friends call it. What Marc Montjoy defends here is Chang's "whiteness," a whiteness that turns yellow the moment Montjoy imagines him guilty of raping a white girl. Ironically, it is he, not his unabashedly racist friends, who, fired by a fantasy of interracial rape, nearly kills Chang because he thinks he has dragged Emma Jane ("the poor innocent girl") to his rooms and raped her. In the face of overwhelming evidence to the contrary, Montjoy insists on Emma Jane's essential innocence and a Chinese man's essential guilt. In fact, Emma Jane's portrayal as a sexual tease clarifies the limits of Montjoy's democratic ideals, which are predicated on his initial belief that Chang is "honorable" and "a gentleman." According to Montjoy, a Chinese gentleman will admire but not covet Western women. Although he sees and even acknowledges that Emma Jane has "flirted with Chang and that Chang had," as she predicted, "fallen in love with her," Montjoy insists that Chang will "go home now," leaving Emma Jane for white men.[39]

Yet to preserve his value system Montjoy continues to insist on her innocence—"What a thoroughbred Emma Jane was."[40] His metaphor, however, reveals his motive and his values. For Montjoy and his friends, as for Estelle's first husband Cornell (the passionate polo player), a good woman was as valuable as a thoroughbred horse. The metaphor also invokes racially inscribed gender categories. Only a "thoroughbred" *can* be a good woman-girl. Montjoy has to insist on seeing Chang, not Emma Jane, as the aggressor; to reverse the roles would upset his beliefs about race, masculinity, and femininity.

Estelle captures the moment of confrontation that marks Montjoy's unveiling: "In the eyes of the two Americans was concentrated all the racial antipathy of yellow and white. 'Chang,' Montjoy said in his dry toneless voice, 'Taylor and I came here last night, believing you were our friend and a white man under your damn yellow skin. . . . You yellow cur, to bring that innocent little girl to your rooms!' and he sprang at Chang again."[41] Estelle's critique of the bigoted underpinnings of Shanghai's American business community in "Star Spangled Banner Stuff" expresses itself in the hypocrisy, violence, and acquisitiveness of all the Americans involved.

In their basic outlines, the players and the plot climax in Estelle's tale bear a marked similarity to E. M. Forster's late imperial romance *Passage to India* (1924), which was published during her third year in Shanghai. That is, the political and economic desires of her colonialists are all played out in the sexual arena. She recasts the story of alleged interracial rape to reveal the contradictions or fissures in her Americans' colonial discourse of legitimation, the "Star Spangled Banner Stuff." But in regard to gender, she tells a very different story. Unlike Forster, she never allows her reader to entertain the "repulsive possibility" that Chang attempted to rape a nineteen-year-old white American girl.[42] Nor does she permit her reader to "play into the hands of racist Anglo-India," which in Estelle's case would be racist Anglo-American Shanghai. And although she often romanticizes and orientalizes her Chinese characters, particularly her Chinese servants, she does not, as one critic observes of Forster, indulge in "Oriental indeterminacy." Her intentions are antithetical to Forster's in that she is not concerned about preventing the reader "from finding him [the alleged Oriental rapist], or anyone else, guilty of the book's offenses against women in general." Rather, her intent is to portray the various forms of exclusion and cruelty sanctioned by a society that encourages and abets racism and sexism. For Estelle is equally interested in exploring the relationship between her colonialists' demonization of "the Oriental" and their idealization of white Womanhood. This is why her plot turns on the alleged crime of interracial rape. She also chose this plot because she knew her intended audience was obsessed with the subject and that, like most white Mississippians (and other white Americans), much of the foreign population in Shanghai viewed this crime as a serious threat to its authority. Dr. Fearn, who treated many female prostitutes, noted that before the arrival of White Russian refugees in 1919 "the residents of Shanghai's bordellos were, for the most part, American and British women."[43]

According to John Pal, an Australian journalist working in Shanghai in the twenties, by 1925 the influx of Russian women fleeing the Revolution "had so lowered the moral tone of our city that the then League of Nations became alarmed, and formed a special committee to investigate the effects . . . of female Russian penetration." Following this remarkable metaphor, Pal quotes the 1925 League of Nations report: "Owing to the growth of the number of Russian girls and women engaged in prostitution, and competition between them and the numerous prostitutes of Oriental nationality, the Russian women and girls . . . are driven to offer themselves to Chinese. . . . That this extensive prostitution of Russian girls and women and the breach by them of the natural racial barrier which has . . . existed between white women and natives in China, cannot but have a demoralizing effect . . . [because] the appearance of a white woman . . . among natives . . . affects very deeply the prestige of the Western nations in the Orient."[44]

The greater threat to colonial authority here is not prostitution per se but interracial sex, as the bodies of the Russian "women and girls" become the body—the prestige, the moral superiority—of "Western nations in the Orient." Estelle's story engages these same arguments to examine the sources and meanings of this fear. Hence, for Marc Montjoy, Emma Jane's body becomes emblematic of the (white) community. In this respect, "Star Spangled Banner Stuff" is Estelle's exploration of one of white America's most deeply ingrained fantasies. Originally, when Montjoy claims Chang as his equal, he unconsciously deconstructs the binary oppositions on which racial privilege depends. When he feels threatened and scrambles to reconstruct them, he reveals just how *unnatural* and self-serving these socially constructed categories of difference are. For example, when he thinks Chang has taken the economic and sexual property American imperialism defines as his, Montjoy instantly names Chang a "yellow cur." Estelle elaborates on this theme in her much darker story, "Selvage" / "Elly," where Elly insists that her lover can't really be a "negro" because he's wealthy and he attended the University of Virginia and Harvard. "Elly" transforms the somewhat campy social satire of "Star Spangled Banner Stuff" into Gothic, psychological drama. Because there are no existing drafts of this story (neither Estelle's nor Estelle's and Faulkner's), we cannot know, but I rather suspect this shift was Faulkner's contribution. What came first, however, were Estelle's short stories; her fictional narratives that posed these problems; her recognition of their centrality to the marriage plot; her creation of various unruly female sensibilities; and the family and racial dynamics through which to filter them.

In the short stories she brought home from Shanghai in 1924 and in the stories she continued to write before her marriage to Faulkner, Estelle had transformed her experience and the experiences of girls and women like her into ironic and often funny critiques of these romantic and restrictive conventions so destructive to women's autonomy and individualism. Transforming her own reality was a more difficult task.

24

Faulkner's Other Collaboration, New Orleans, 1924 and 1925

ETWEEN NOVEMBER 1924 AND MAY 1925, when Faulkner finished *Soldiers' Pay*, Sherwood and Elizabeth Anderson and Estelle were instrumental in providing him with the actual and imaginative environment he needed to begin to transform himself from poet to novelist. The prior chapters narrate Estelle's and Faulkner's relationship up to her unexpected return from Shanghai in early December 1924 and Faulkner's initial reading of the fiction she had written during their three-year separation. As they are temporally and psychologically intertwined, I turn now to Faulkner and Anderson's concurrent brief friendship, literary dialogue, and collaboration. It's a well-known story that fits snugly into the Bloomian paradigm of anxiety of influence. Yet when the dynamics of their friendship and falling out are seen as part of the larger picture — those interactions among the structures, processes, and people who claim a continuing dominant place in Faulkner's interior life—this paradigm proves inadequate.

Speaking to an undergraduate writing class of young men at the University of Virginia in the 1950s, Faulkner described the weeks he and Anderson spent together in New Orleans in the fall of 1924 and the following spring. Watching, walking with, listening to, and drinking with Anderson convinced him that "if that was the life of a writer, that was the life for me" (*FIU*, 21–22). The bohemian, alcohol-filtered scene Faulkner paints is one of master and acolyte, the speaker and the listener. Here, paraphrasing his own 1953 elegiacal and reparative essay "A Note on Anderson," the great novelist feeds his words to the ever receptive and always listening apprentice.[1] Faulkner's repeated image of his silent drinking in of Anderson's language, along with the contents of shared bottles of bootleg—"we'd walk and he'd talk and I'd listen . . . and we'd sit around till one or two o'clock drinking, and still me listening to him talking"—creates the sense of a continuous present of creative excess: "Then in the evening we would meet again, with a bottle now, and now he would really talk; the world in miniscule would be there in whatever shadowy courtyard where glass and bottle clinked and the palms hissed like dry sand in whatever moving air" ("A Note," 9).

Like an infant at the breast, he was being fed and filled with Anderson's words, the world in miniscule, the essential food he needed, the "secrets," as he wrote his mother, of what the master did every morning when he "was in seclusion working" (*TOH*, 195). The actual fluid that they share here in the socially sanctioned act of men drinking through the night together both facilitates and masks this memory's relation to his always racialized maternal imaginary and its homoerotics; alcohol fuels what will become their mutual imaginings and washes away (obliterates) that conjunction. It also apparently obliterated Faulkner's memory of his ultimately vicious attack on Anderson. Twice in this account, he insists on how much they liked each other and how well they got along. This is what he remembers.

What is washed away tells a richer history that bears directly on Faulkner's and Estelle's much longer collaboration. It is the story that began this account of the origins, growth, and fruition of Faulkner's creativity in a racialized maternal imaginary. He invented, pieced, quilted this imaginary from the remnants of his passionate attachment to and violent, shameful disavowal of his black "mother," Caroline Barr, the "Mammy" his culture had forced him to simultaneously denigrate and sentimentalize. In differing but complementary ways both Estelle's and Sherwood's collaborations with Faulkner gave him permission to write directly out of that maternal imaginary. And, for reasons that will soon become clear, "loving and hating," he punished them accordingly.[2]

The Background

On 5 November 1924 Faulkner included Estelle's Shanghai address on the list he sent his publisher of people who were to receive copies of *The Marble Faun*. He had no idea that by early December, she and her two children would be his neighbors again or that he would put off his imminent European tour until the following July. On 10 November Four Seas wrote that his publication date had been delayed until 1 December, the day he had planned to board a freighter in New Orleans and sail to Europe. When *The Marble Faun* arrived some ten days later, Phil Stone hosted a book-signing party for his protégé, at which Faulkner gave Estelle's parents an inscribed copy.[3]

At some point that fall, either in late October or early November, Faulkner had made a quick trip to New Orleans to meet the already famous Pulitzer Prize–winning author whom he then believed had written the best short story in America.[4] In early January 1925, Faulkner returned to New Orleans, again intending to set off for Europe. As he wrote his mother on 6 January, "I am so darned glad you and pop are willing for me to make the trip, even though you think it foolish" (*TOH,* 169). Yet he changed his mind. Sherwood was on a lecture tour, but Elizabeth Anderson invited him to stay temporarily in their apartment. Faulkner became one of the group of artists and writers who lived in the Vieux Carré. At this time, his public persona was still a poet; in January 1925, the New Orleans *Times Picayune* even ran a photograph of him captioned "Southern Poet in New Orleans" (*TOH,* 179).

Although their months together in New Orleans appear in every biographical account of either author, its most significant element for Faulkner's imaginative growth has been missed: the insight he gleaned from Anderson for imagining race and alternative sexualities as aspects of style. Estelle's stories had domesticated these themes for him and so led him from poetry to prose. With Phil Stone he had read the High Modernists and their predecessors. Anderson introduced him to the "refused" of High Modernism, probably by lending him and certainly by discussing with him the experimental novels of Gertrude Stein (*Three Lives,* 1909) and Jean Toomer (*Cane,* 1923), both of which, through style, foregrounded an American English of racialized sexuality.

When asked if he recalled Anderson discussing "her [Stein's] work and its influence upon himself," Faulkner answered simply "Yes" (*FIU,* 230). In the 1950s no one asked him about Toomer. If they had, his response would have been the same. During the time Anderson and Faulkner were together, both novels were much on Anderson's mind as he worked on *Dark Laughter,* the awkward, tone-deaf novel they inspired.[5] In October 1924, in the midst of writing it, Anderson had written Stein praising *Three Lives,* especially her stripped-down sentences and her portrait of the "graceful, pale yellow, intelligent, attractive negress," Melanctha Herbert: "Why ["Melanctha"] hasn't been included in some of the lists of great short stories I don't know."[6] Recommending *Cane* to Stein earlier that same year, he said that it had "real color and splash—no fake negro this time, I'm sure. Do look it up."[7] He admired *Cane* for two reasons: for its portrayals of African American life and its highly experimental style, which he praised as having "consciously the artist's impulse." After reading *Cane* he wrote Toomer from

New Orleans that "you I am sure belong to us, nervous distraught ones, us moderns." And then, condescendingly, that "it is quite wonderful to think you belong also to the men I saw working on the docks, the black men."[8] Anderson was one of many who admired Toomer's *Cane* for its stunning experiments with subject matter, form, and language. His insistence that African Americans had no interiority, however, precluded any real understanding of this novel, which, through its highly experimental form, was exploring modernity through the consciousness of varieties of black masculine subjectivity. Being party to his mentor's writing process and watching Anderson's failure with his "jazz" novel, *Dark Laughter*, gave Faulkner valuable lessons in how NOT to write such a novel. Estelle's stories had shown him his subject and genre; Anderson, and through him Toomer and Stein, helped Faulkner to begin writing a racialized aesthetic that is the conflicted and passionate heart of his fiction.

In January 1925, however, Faulkner had a ways to go. Shortly after moving into the Andersons' apartment he began publishing short prose pieces in the *Times-Picayune* and the *Double Dealer*.[9] These stilted, stylized, and highly imitative sketches show that he could still sustain only a lyric moment; he did not quite know how to tell a story. As in his poetry, the tone of these early sketches is often masked and muted by ornate layerings of baroque imagery—I refer particularly to his nymphs and fauns—a Southern version of the Georgians and the pierrotiste personas of the early Modernists. Unlike the narrators of Estelle's short stories, which he probably read prior to his second trip to New Orleans in January, the voice of these poems and early prose sketches speaks from a void that is out of space and out of time. To see the contrast, one need only compare the character in his 1925 monologue titled "Wealthy Jew" with the Jewish jeweler and one-time concert pianist in Estelle's story, "A Crossing," or the lamenting Chinese lover of his 1925 sketch "Hong Li" to Estelle's Needy Chang. Faulkner's Jew and Chinese are merely Pierrot with another name. Their solipsistic yearnings severely limit both range and depth. The poet was indeed, as he writes in one of his Pierrot poems, trapped "in a cage of moonlight" (*VIS*, 10). His subject, like that of so many early male Modernist poets, is still only a limited and oddly distanced view of the psychic struggles of his adolescent self.

That Faulkner, at some level, had long been aware of his inability to articulate a richer range and depth of feeling in his writing is reflected in his book reviews of others' work. He might have been writing about himself. And, judging by his 1924 poems, he was still far from a solution.[10] Yet within the next two months the new directions initiated by four significant events of that fall ended Faulkner's artistic stasis. These were the mutual electricity generated by Anderson's and Faulkner's meeting in November, the culmination of his self-apprenticeship to poetry with the publication of *The Marble Faun*, Estelle's unexpected return to Oxford and to him, and reading Estelle's realistic short stories, which were, in part, her response to and critique of that poetic apprenticeship.

Faulkner's brief collaboration with Anderson, like his lifelong collaboration with Estelle, was both immensely productive and deeply disturbing. Anderson was away when Faulkner returned to New Orleans in January, but by March he'd returned. A month later, Faulkner published two pieces that are keys to understanding his strong ambivalence about their friendship and collaboration. The first was a short prose sketch called "Out of Nazareth," which Anderson judged "rotten." The second was his retrospective review of Anderson's work in the *Dallas Morning News*. Overall, the review was a wicked piece; even Faulkner's praise was double-edged. Although he lauded the high Modernist style of *Winesburg, Ohio*, particularly its authorial erasure, he also suggested that Anderson was incapable of writing a real novel: "The only indication of the writer's individuality which I find . . . is his sympathy for [the characters], a sympathy which, had the book been done as a full-length novel, would have become mawkish." Among his sharpest jabs were that Anderson's fiction demonstrated "a fundamental lack of humor" and that at almost fifty, he had still not matured as a writer.[11]

Anderson's Talk: His Gifts of Stein and Toomer

The issue is not whether Faulkner was right but why he chose to attack, particularly at this moment. During Faulkner's first meeting with Anderson and that same spring of 1925, as they walked and talked and drank, Anderson gave Faulkner the schooling that helped him unmoor from the Europeans on both sides of the Atlantic and begin experiments with form and language that created his distinct voice. Anderson's own experiments and his advocacy of Toomer's and Stein's helped Faulkner realize that the elements capable of giving his voice a unique subject, tone, and style lay in his native North Mississippi. Perhaps most surprisingly, Stein's *Three Lives* gave him, as it had for Anderson, both the license and the beginnings of a language for exploring the linked American geographies of race and sexuality, particularly irresolute sexuality.

Anderson's enthusiasm for Jean Toomer's *Cane* would further illuminate Faulkner's realization of the imaginative potential of his own racist and racialized world. Faulkner responded to *Cane*'s consciously racialized aesthetic, its daring interweaving of varieties of literary genres with black musical forms, particularly folk spirituals and jazz, to create a montage of black American lives, both urban and rural, Northern and Southern, in a novel that took Modernism to new levels.

Some of the best writing in Faulkner's *Soldiers' Pay* was inspired by *Cane*: its highly elliptical form; its syncopated opening scene of American soldiers on a train heading home to Georgia; the country club dance where flappers and "boys of both sexes swayed arm in arm, taking sliding tripping steps" to the jazz rhythms and phrases from the blues of black musicians (*SP*, 190); the singing from a black church that performs a choral role in the novel's final section; and throughout, scenes where dialogue is set as in a play, blurring and blending American genres and cultures. Faulkner's version of Georgia, was, as Waldo Frank wrote of Toomer's, the "South" freed at last "from the mists of muteness."[12] Perhaps Faulkner set *Soldiers' Pay* in Georgia to acknowledge *Cane*'s value to him.

After his fall 1924 trip to New Orleans, Faulkner returned to Oxford, where he and Phil fumed about his book's delayed publication date and Phil worked on circulating advanced publicity to various newspapers and little magazines. Estelle's arrival on 9 December changed Faulkner's plan to catch a freighter to Europe as soon as he had copies of *The Marble Faun*. It also changed his life. As we have seen, Estelle's returns during the years 1918–26, when she lived abroad with her first husband, always coincided with significant advances in Faulkner's creative development.[13]

Even though Faulkner did not spend most of his time in Oxford the spring of 1925, he knew Estelle was there, he saw her when he wanted to, he wrote poems dated to commemorate her arrival, he read and typed the stories she had brought with her from Shanghai, and he knew her marriage was over. In short, as his first novel shows, she and Anderson created a strongly felt presence in his imagination throughout that winter and spring.

Becoming a Novelist: Oxford and New Orleans, Spring 1925

Stylistically, *Soldiers' Pay* signals Faulkner's break into a Modernism grounded in what he had absorbed from Anderson, Stein, and Toomer. As Anderson tells it, the literary sources compelling his own figuring of blackness as the "backdrop" that counterpointed and contained the foregrounded white love story in his Jazz Age, postwar novel *Dark Laughter* were Stein's "Melanctha," in *Three Lives,* and Toomer's *Cane*. But unlike theirs, Anderson's figuring of race was filled with clichés and emptied of psychological complexity; it conformed to his stereotyped notions of what the African American was.[14] Anderson saw race as an unproblematic identity—

an unchanging essence intimately tied to a manhood that was assumed to be white. *Dark Laughter* and stories like "Out of Nowhere" articulate this viewpoint and its connections to eugenicist notions of racial dominance. In these works, Anderson encodes many of Southern patriarchy's simultaneously most feared and cherished fantasies concerning black men and white masculinity. His construction of blackness as animalistic, primitive, physical, exotic, and, most important, emptied of all intellectual complexity stands in marked contrast to its characterizations in *Three Lives* and *Cane*. The black community he invented in *Dark Laughter* bore no relation to that portrayed in Stein's Bridgepoint or Toomer's Washington, D.C., or Georgia. His racist construction of black life wasn't new or unusual. It's the essence of American minstrelsy present in many Modernist texts. His fiction, at moments so wonderfully fluid and insightful in articulating a continuum of (white) homosocial and homoerotic desire, revealed his racial politics as pure Jim Crow. In *Vanity Fair*, a year after publishing *Dark Laughter*, he wrote, "In regard to the Negro I am Southern. I have no illusions about making him my brother. Liking Negroes wanting them about—not wanting them too close. In me the Southern contradiction so puzzling to the North."[15]

As Anderson had misread Toomer's *Cane*, so he misread Stein's *Three Lives*. Like most white Modernist poetry and fiction, her very early experimental novel appears to reflect contemporary racist beliefs; often she does appropriate and exoticize. Stein's treatment of race, however, is ultimately as irreverent and challenging as her treatment of conventional beliefs about class, marriage, and the primacy of the heterosexual imperative.[16] Although her portrait of race is not free of racism, she uses race as a mask beneath which she challenges homophobia and denaturalized heterosexism. Faulkner will follow her here, particularly in novels like *Light in August* and *Absalom, Absalom!* In contrast, Anderson's "negroes" were simply stereotypes, perhaps one reason for the great commercial success of *Dark Laughter*. As one of his biographers writes, despite good sales figures, it was "an astonishingly bad book."[17]

"Out of Nazareth"

In April 1925, although Faulkner was then following Anderson's advice as he wrote the strongest and most experimental sections of *Soldiers' Pay*, he publicly mocked his teacher. He mounted his attack on two fronts, which, but for Anderson's generosity, could have easily backfired. His brief but intense connection to Anderson, the *only* such relation he was ever to have with a famous living writer, excited a complex reaction between his psychic needs and fears and the racialized aesthetic he was then beginning to develop. As Faulkner's writing about Anderson that April shows, such excitement and stimulation was both exhilarating and threatening. His simultaneous imaginative engagement with Anderson and Estelle during these months gave him what he needed to find his own voice. Despite vast differences between Estelle and Anderson, Faulkner engaged both in a similar pattern. He collaborated with and then betrayed each in similar ways. This similarity, together with the pattern's fictional manifestations in Faulkner's art, provides the context that will reveal another facet of Faulkner's literary collaboration with Estelle.

Only one of Faulkner's extant letters of 1925 indicates that he was brewing trouble with Anderson that spring. In a brief paragraph in a letter postmarked 7 April, he tells Maud that his friend Bill Spratling had done a sketch for one of his stories that they were "sending off tomorrow."[18] Faulkner then adds, "Sherwood says it is a rotten story. But then he may be right. I think it is pretty good, myself. Maybe he doesn't like it because (not for publication) I left the worm out" (*TOH*, 197). One reason Sherwood may have thought it rotten was that it parodied his portraits of Faulkner and himself in Anderson's earlier story, "A Meeting South." More threatening perhaps, it portrayed Anderson as unabashedly homosexual.

"Out of Nazareth" was Faulkner's first direct venture into same-sex eroticism; parody served as his protective mask. Although his poet persona, David, is the object of both Spratling's and Anderson's desire, David is oblivious. Faulkner thereby succeeds in simultaneously avowing and disavowing the queer spaces he's created. Ten years later, with *Absalom, Absalom!* Faulkner will invoke the same iconic tale of David and Jonathan, this time without disavowal.

A few days after "Out of Nazareth" was published, Faulkner wrote Maud that he was "in a writing slump now—cant seem to do anything. have it all in my head but cant put it on paper for some reason. Stale, I guess" (*TOH*, 200). Or feeling guilty about what he had done and what he was going to do next.

Faulkner's review of Anderson appeared in the *Dallas Morning News* of 26 April 1925, a few days after he had written his mother that "I have got a dog-gone good novel. Elizabeth and Sherwood both say so. Sherwood says he wishes he had thought of it first. They have taken me in charge, wont even let me read anything until I finish it." After summarizing the plot of *Soldiers' Pay*, he adds that "I hope to have it finished by the end of June. And Sherwood is going to try to make his publisher take it and give me an advance on it, the book to appear next fall."[19] Faulkner's letter makes his review all the more shocking. By the first of June he had finished *Soldiers' Pay*, and both Andersons had read it (*TOH*, 209, 210). Ten days later Faulkner wrote Maud from Pascagoula that "Sherwood Anderson is all blowed up over the novel. He has written Liveright two letters about it and Liveright has written asking me to send it on to him. Sherwood thinks it is going to be a sensation. I hope so. The coast is certainly grand now. I wish you and pop and the captain [his youngest brother, Dean] would come down. I have about persuaded Sherwood and Elizabeth to spend the weekend at Pascagoula" (210–11). There is no record that the Andersons ever went.

Various causes are given to explain why Anderson wrote his publisher on 19 April 1926 that Faulkner had been so "personally nasty" to him that they were no longer on speaking terms. Biographers cite Faulkner's 1925 review. In an essay written in 1930, Anderson wrote that the cause was "a silly drunken quarrel." Faulkner claimed it was the parody he and Spratling published six months later in December 1926, when Faulkner and Spratling, after their joint trip to Italy and France, were again living together in New Orleans. Spratling remembered that when Faulkner and he gave their book to Anderson, hot off the press, "he turned it over, looked inside, scowled and said, 'I don't think it's very funny.'"[20]

In Faulkner's fiction, collaboration always serves as a metaphor for dangerous and generally illicit forms of love or desire. As "Out of Nazareth" suggests, Faulkner's friendship with Anderson, which included the merging of their imaginations, incited homoerotic fantasies about Anderson that, because of Faulkner's racism, were always racialized. He responded by lashing out. By the early 1930s, in *Absalom, Absalom!* Faulkner could write a passionate, nonjudgmental, and deeply felt story of same-sex, interracial, and incestuous desire and its progeny, a marvelous imaginative collaboration that results in that novel. Perhaps he could now explore this tabooed terrain because marriage and children, plus at least one affair, secured his White Manhood in his own mind. But in spring 1925, his description of his and Anderson's collaborative process in another letter home suggests the underlying feelings their collaboration may have stirred up in Faulkner that shortly provoked his hostile response. Another letter to Maud speaks to his inner confusion and resulting anxiety: Is he the author or the fictions in this friendship? What is "documentary—that is, a true incident" and what is "me as I really am, not as a fictitious character"? But most troubling, *where does he end and Anderson begin?* Anderson is "now writing a book about childhood, his own childhood [*Tar: A Midwestern Childhood* (1926)]; and I have told him several things about my own which he is putting in as having happened to him" (*TOH*, 195). Asserting his claim and contribution to two of Anderson's stories, the first of which was probably "A Meeting South," he writes, "Yes, the story of Mr. Anderson's was started by me. It is not documentary—that is, a true incident. I just kind of cranked him up. What really happens, you know, never makes a good yarn. You have got to get an impulse from somewhere and then embroider it. And that is what Sherwood did in this case. He has done another about me as I really am, not as a fictitious character" (194–95). Faulkner's boundary confusion suggests that what homoerotic issues were present in the Faulkner-Anderson narrative have been subsumed by the more polymorphous and infantile erotic and narcissistic needs of Faulkner's maternal imaginary. By the spring of 1925, as he literally moved back and forth between Estelle and Anderson, they were commanding considerable space in his psyche. Having divulged these "secrets of our profession" he notes that Anderson has a seven-thousand-dollar contract for his book—the "childhood thing"—and then reveals another secret that helps explain his conflicting desires. He wants both to merge with and destroy the famous writer. "Someday, I'll be that good. In secret, remember. He and I are getting our book along, and I am writing one of my own, a novel."[21]

As Faulkner was writing *Soldiers' Pay*, the Andersons read his manuscript, praising and encouraging him. In January and February Elizabeth Anderson had given him free room and board when they could ill afford it, and, by Faulkner's account, Sherwood initiated, and he responded to, a constant flow of spoken and written dialogue. He also critiqued Faulkner's work in a joint writing project he originated. The "Al Jackson" letters, a continuous tall tale that they wrote to each other that spring, were writing exercises. Sherwood was a "stern" but "generous" teacher. He also taught him to approach and treat his "craft with his own humility and respect" ("A Note," 7, 8, 9).

Years later, explaining the "pull" New Orleans exerted on him and other artists in 1924, Faulkner said it allowed him "to be with people that have the same problems and the same interests as him, that won't laugh at what he's trying to do, won't laugh at what he says no matter how foolish it might sound" (*FIU*, 231). In this same exchange, as he thinks associatively, he observes that one reason Anderson liked Gertrude Stein personally was that he could "trust" her: "that she would never do anything to hurt him." Elaborating, he repeats "hurt" four times (230, 232). In light of this statement, Faulkner's hurtful public laughter at Anderson's expense seems especially gratuitous. But it is of a piece with Faulkner's wedding-night desertion of Estelle and the series of staged events he arranged in the course of their marriage to "hurt" her and expose her to public ridicule.[22] In this same uncharacteristically personal analysis of Anderson, Faulkner foregrounds gender by sexing his own laughter when he explains why Anderson trusted Stein: "he knew that she was—well you might say a lady, and wasn't—was never going to hurt him." Following this line of thought, he also sexes genius, saying that Anderson (unlike himself) lacked "the ruthlessness to, well, rob from any and every source he wanted" and that "a writer must be interested in people the same way the surgeon is interested in cadavers—he don't have to like people at all, he can loathe people, but he's got to be interested in them, and Anderson . . . was afraid of people" (*FIU*, 232). Here Faulkner seems to speaking as much about himself as Anderson. His self-portrait as the ruthless robber and the misogynist surgeon, loathing people but dedicated to understanding their inner workings, is, as well, the portrait of a man who was afraid of people. Particularly, as he says here, of their laughing at him. Faulkner was afraid. Once asked why he drank, he replied, "Fear." Like Quentin and his shadow or Roth and his black family or Clytie and Judith, when he talks about Anderson, he cannot separate himself from him or distinguish between where his own body begins and Anderson's ends—even in 1958.

Faulkner's ridicule and plundering of Anderson took different forms. It was not just his April 1925 review, in which he used Anderson's own words about himself and his work to skewer him and implied that whatever genius he possessed was similar to that of an idiot savant's. Nor was it just "Out of Nazareth," his April 1925 sketch mocking Anderson's story about meeting him. Faulkner took the highly experimental central structuring concept as well as the general plot outline of *Dark Laughter*, the novel Anderson was rewriting that fall and spring, for his own much more sophisticated and effective first novel. As one reviewer wrote of *Soldiers' Pay*, it was much too rich a "compound of imagination, observation, and experience" to make it "one for facile categories."[23]

Not content with skewering Anderson in his *Dallas Morning News* review and in "Out of Nazareth," Faulkner and Bill Spratling next published *Sherwood Anderson and Other Famous Creoles*, a series of pictorial and written sketches with a foreword by Faulkner that satirized Anderson and parodied everything from his dress and mannerisms to his literary style.[24] Their intended audience included Spratling's, Anderson's, and Faulkner's mutual friends in New Orleans. Faulkner's 1953 explanation of what he had done states his intentions: "We had made his style look ridiculous; and by that time, after *Dark Laughter*, when he had reached the point where he should have stopped writing . . . he too must have known . . . that there was nothing else left" ("A Note" 10, 6). Faulkner wanted to destroy Anderson's sense of self by ridiculing his art. Not until 1953, twelve years after Anderson's death and at a time in his life when Faulkner felt *he* had nothing else left, did he begin to acknowledge the hurt he had inflicted and his debt. Yet, as in its companion piece, "Mississippi," and for some of the same reasons, he laced his elegiac and reparative essay with demeaning statements. Even as

24.1. William Spratling's drawing of Faulkner and himself in New Orleans, 1926. From *Sherwood Anderson and Other Famous Creoles*. (Courtesy of Jill Faulkner Summers)

he called Anderson the "father of us all," and praised his generosity toward the writers of Faulkner's generation, he told readers that Anderson was only "a one- or two-book man" and that, in "fumbling for exactitude," he had made such "a fetish of simplicity" that his writing "finally became just style" (6, 5).

In its hyperbole, even the tone and language of some of Faulkner's praise of Anderson is similar to that he bestowed on Callie Barr in "Mississippi." Of course Faulkner was lauding Callie's character, her self-sacrificing and endless ministrations, and her devotion and fidelity to his family, whereas with Anderson, his exemplary devotion to his art and younger artists reveals his "generous" character. Yet Faulkner describes Anderson's devotion to his writing and toward Faulkner as very much like Callie's devotion to the Falkners: "he worked so hard and so laboriously and so self-sacrificingly" ("A Note," 9). Like Callie, Anderson was "sound and strong and valuable, but without recorded pedigree" (4); yet he "never failed to approach writing except with humility and an almost religious, almost abject faith and patience" (6–7). Like Callie Barr, Anderson taught Faulkner "to believe in the value of purity, and to believe more. To believe not in just the value, but the necessity for fidelity and integrity" and to practice his craft "with humility and respect" (9).[25] Anderson's singular contribution to Faulkner's genius, specifically to his racialized aesthetic, has a liminal presence here in Faulkner's elegiacal language and his rhetoric. Both link him in Faulkner's unconscious with Callie Barr, the founding source of his maternal imaginary. Faulkner's final sentence in this essay exquisitely compresses his dreadful need to destroy what he craves. After the "unhappy caricature affair," Anderson "declined to see" him. Years later, Faulkner glimpses him across a crowded room in New York "and I knew that I had seen, was looking at, a giant in an earth populated to a great—too great—extent by pygmies, *even if he did make but two or perhaps three gestures commensurate with gianthood*" ("A Note" 10, my italics). The cruelty of Faulkner's cut here—elegizing and degrading in the same sentence—is much more than a typical demonstration of Bloomian anxiety of influence. It speaks the terrible legacy of slavery on his soul.

While Faulkner includes Spratling in his account of his meanness to Anderson, as far as Anderson was concerned, Faulkner alone was responsible. On 19 April 1926, nearly a year after Faulkner's review had been published, Anderson wrote Horace Liveright about Faulkner's talent and marketability: "He is a man who will write the kind of novels that will sell. He is modern enough but not too modern; also he is smart." He told their joint publisher that he could pass on his compliments to the younger writer if he felt Faulkner needed encouragement but that "I do not like the man personally very much. He was so nasty to me . . . that I don't want to write him myself." He would, however, "be glad if you were to do it in this indirect way."[26]

Although Faulkner dedicated his third novel, *Sartoris,* to Anderson, "through whose kindness I was first published," and in June 1953 published his somewhat more honest acknowledgment of his debt to him in the *Atlantic,* he continued to lie, both in public and privately to Estelle, about Anderson's early and vital contribution and support. He claimed that, rather than praising it, Anderson had *disparaged* his first novel and that Anderson had told Elizabeth that "he would do anything for him [Faulkner] so long as I don't have to read his damned manuscript."[27] Estelle said her husband never forgot those words. Yet Faulkner's 1925 letters home reveal that he didn't forget them because he had invented them.

There is no rational explanation for his behavior toward Anderson. However, Faulkner's earlier intensely maternal fantasies about Phil Stone coupled with his childlike descriptions of Elizabeth Anderson's attentions suggest a further internal logic. In Elizabeth, whose husband was then absent, he had found another nurturing maternal ideal, so nurturing that Faulkner had begun "thinking out" his first novel while living at the absent Anderson's house.[28] In the guise of another "son," he had usurped both Anderson's place and that of Anderson's son, Bob. Besides mothering him and cooking dinner "for me every night," Elizabeth even sees that he and Bob, who was then eighteen years old, "have enough cover, and takes care of our money for us" (*TOH*, 173, 180).[29] When Anderson returned, Faulkner was forced to find new quarters and to give up being babied by Elizabeth. He later wrote and spoke about the artist robbing his mother with impunity in service of his art. His actions in New Orleans in 1925 and 1926 suggest rather that he was robbing first the mother and then the father who mothered him. The spoils were his first and second novels. But before he could claim the adult status such achievement conferred, he had to denigrate and disavow this generous, nurturing maternal ideal who so bounteously fed his physical and emotional needs. In short, Anderson's generosity opened an old wound; Faulkner reacted accordingly.

I suspect that the emotional abuse Bill Faulkner dealt Estelle on their wedding night and during their honeymoon in Pascagoula in 1929 was, in some ways, similar in origin and intent to that he had dealt Sherwood Anderson in 1925 and 1926. He had been nurtured and he had borrowed—he would say robbed—extensively from both Anderson's and Estelle's fiction; he had merged his erotic and creative life with theirs in mutual collaborations. It didn't matter that Anderson was an older man and a famous writer, or that Estelle was Faulkner's contemporary, an unknown who had never published. At critical stages between 1924 and 1929, Faulkner collaborated with both and also took their fiction to refashion and publish as his own— which it was. That Anderson and Estelle were so generous with their imaginations and art confirmed in Faulkner's unconscious the similarity of their relation to his imaginative processes. He had rifled their imaginations to feed his own. Accepting their gifts and incorporating them meant he had acknowledged his need for their love. Incapable of experiencing love and its complement—his art—as, in part, the result of a mutually shared experience, he had to destroy the givers. That was the repetition, a recurrent theme in Faulkner's life and art. Those he perceived as helping him to become a writer in any significant way, those who loved him and with whom he made an intellectual and emotional commitment, paid a price. I observe this not to criticize but to try to understand the complex (and probably completely unconscious) motivation that led him again and again to denigrate and try to destroy the people he loved, people whose love he judged essential to his creativity.

For Faulkner, nurturing love and generosity recalled his first "holding me," as he visualizes that warmth and comfort in his three-year-old's screen memory. It opened his imagination's richest lode. Yet that lode was also the site of his original narcissistic wounding: his forced betrayal of his "second mother," Callie Barr, his self-loathing and anger for his vulnerability to that wounding and for his still unrepressible desire for her trashed love and nurturance. Although he wrote ever more moving and eloquent fiction about white children, mostly boys, caught in these bleak Jim Crow rituals, he could no more control his personal need to repeat them than he could control his need to drink. They figured painfully in every intense love relationship he entered and in every intense love relationship represented in his greatest fiction. I use this analogy deliberately, because so often in Faulkner's fiction, rejection of love is enacted by physical and verbal violence followed by gorging and then vomiting of proffered food and alcohol. (Joe Christmas, Roth Edmunds, and Rider are just three of numerous examples.) There are instances earlier than Anderson and later than Estelle of similar attempted destructions, the most important being Callie Barr.

Because Faulkner's ridicule of Anderson is so close in time to his cruelty toward Estelle in Pascagoula, because it is so well documented, and composed of many similar elements, it increases our understanding of Faulkner and Estelle's relationship. Perhaps Faulkner was drawing on more than commonplaces or poetic convention when he spoke and wrote in praise of artists eliminating either their mothers or old women in service of their art and filled his early poetry with images of "moon mad" mothers and more old women whose "presence like shed scent,/ Holding him body and life within its snare" all keep the poet from singing.[30] It was not mothers or children; it was Faulkner's Jim Crow world that was mad. Yet out of this world, and at great cost, he wrested his magnificent art.

Anderson's and Estelle's imaginative responses to Faulkner's fantasies, their alternative yet complimentary perspectives, fed him with the love and approval he needed to push further off on his own. But their devotion, attention, and generosity also appear to have made him very angry. That Anderson and Estelle gave willingly of themselves only exacerbated his rage.[31] Faulkner used his facility with language to attempt to destroy Anderson and Estelle. Yet the footprints of these creative collaborations haunt Faulkner's fiction. Faulkner's recognition of his debt to and conflicted love for his imaginative collaborators suffuses his work. It expresses itself covertly in those twinned autobiographical essays he wrote in 1953 and in *Go Down, Moses* and *Absalom, Absalom!*. With Estelle, as we shall see in the next two chapters, that reparation will not be completely revealed until long after both Faulkner and Estelle were dead.

25

The Sound and the Fury and
Its Aftermath, 1925–1933
Faulkner and Estelle

> It began with the picture of the little girl's muddy drawers.
> —Faulkner

I N THE EARLY SPRING OF 1928, Faulkner entered the most creative and productive period of his life. Within the next four years, publishing a novel a year, he would write four of the twentieth century's most remarkable works of fiction: *The Sound and the Fury, Sanctuary* (the first and final versions), *As I Lay Dying,* and *Light in August.*[1] In between and while working on these novels, he also wrote at least twenty-seven short stories. These two final chapters draw together Estelle, Callie Barr, and Maud Falkner and bring to a climax the story of Estelle and Faulkner's literary collaboration, which culminates in the June 1933 introduction to his most beloved novel, *The Sound and the Fury.* The novel and its introduction, like *Go Down, Moses* and "Mississippi," are the evidence Faulkner left of his debt to Callie Barr, Maud Falkner, and Estelle. Read in concert and context, these texts confirm Callie's, Maud's, and Estelle's lifelong roles in shaping, sustaining, and constantly renewing his creative imagination.

The years 1925–33 are a period of Faulkner and Estelle's intensifying collaboration, the importance of which Faulkner acknowledged in his 1933 introduction, which he never allowed to be printed. It is the most detailed description Faulkner left of his creative process. From it we learn that he used Estelle and her fiction as his transformative "vase" or "vessel"—his terms—for his intertwined imaginaries of his two mothers, Callie Barr and Maud Falkner. As a vessel or holding place, Estelle served as his mask or, perhaps, closet. Through and with her, he could perform a kind of creative miscegenation. Inhabiting her past and present, her mind (imagination?), her spoken and written patterns of speech, and her body, he could at last integrate and merge those hitherto segregated feminine imaginaries represented by his black and white mothers. In short, he could perform the unspeakable. According to his 1933 introduction, the first "explosion" from this "vase" was his reimagining of the six-year-old heroine, Estelle, of Estelle's "Dr. Wohlenski," as the initiating and dominant image of *The Sound and the Fury.*

From childhood, he had absorbed the stories Callie Barr and other members of Oxford's black community had told him and the stories he'd heard from his white parents and grandparents. From an early age, his visual imagination had been engaged, stimulated, and taught by his white mother and maternal grandmother. Only Estelle actually wrote stories, which gave Faulkner the means to translate himself from the stuck poet to the great novelist. When he allowed his imagination to dwell in and explore the tone and rich content of her fiction, he found his genius.

The events and creations of the years beginning shortly after Estelle's unexpected arrival home in December 1924, namely, Faulkner's first three novels and then in 1928, and most spectacularly, *The Sound and the Fury* and his three following novels; the complicated progress of Estelle's separation and divorce; Estelle and Faulkner's intellectual and emotional collaboration during these years formalized in their marriage in June 1929; the births of two daughters and the death of the first; and the short stories Faulkner submitted during those years that had begun as Estelle's, and his 1933 introduction to *The Sound and the Fury*—these are the puzzle pieces of this miraculously productive period of Faulkner's life.

Faulkner did not dedicate *The Sound and the Fury* to anyone. He did not need to, as the coded signs of his long collaboration with Estelle are all over it. Three other documents provide external evidence. The first is that introduction. In 1933, within days of his second daughter's birth, Faulkner began drafting the essay that memorialized Estelle's greatest gift to him: his "mental picture" of the "beautiful and tragic little girl" with the muddy bottom who, in the moment when she stooped to comfort her mute, retarded brother and he heard and felt "her fierce hotbreathing," "the entire story . . . seemed to explode on the paper before me." The mythic origins of this beloved, "mudstained," "soiled," and "shamed" white female body, "the naked backside of that doomed little girl," lay deep in Faulkner's and Estelle's shared history and memory, but Estelle had first translated it to words and images that he could hear and feel and see (*TSAF,* 230, 231). Through her authorial "I," particularly her story of the attempted shaming of Estelle's feisty six-year-old fictionalized self in "Dr. Wohlenski," she made conscious, speakable, and palpable that little girl's "courage," her "fierce hotbreathing," and her "doom" (*AL*, 280). Estelle's own unraveling drama, her history, her now constant presence, and the ensuing dialogue between Estelle and Faulkner lent it immediacy and materiality.

The second piece of evidence is a series of five thirty-five-millimeter photographs Faulkner took of his two- or three-year-old daughter Jill playing in the branch in Rowan Oak's woods with her twelve-year-old half brother, Malcolm Franklin, probably in 1935. They could serve easily as illustrations for the crucial opening scenes of *The Sound and the Fury*. This was not the first time Faulkner would write his art on the bodies of his family, but in this instance his writing was private.[2] (Later I will say more about how these photographs, read with Faulkner's suppressed introduction, provide a unique view of his creative process and Estelle's role in it. For the moment just note that both were valuable documents that he made only for himself.) Although he kept the photographic proof sheets, he never enlarged or framed them. Similarly, even though he killed publication of his introduction, and was so anxious to suppress it that in 1946 he offered to buy it back from his publisher, he nonetheless kept at least ten drafts of it. Together, these drafts and final version show the process by which he worked and reworked his account of the powerful imaginative force of the novel's initiating image.

In "Dr. Wohlenski," the fictional Estelle's boy cousins, like Caddy Compson's brothers, attempt to punish and humiliate her for not acting "like a lady": they tear down her tree house and stuff her dolls in the black people's outhouse. In doing so, the cousins figuratively blacken her by smearing her dolls with black people's excrement. In both, Estelle's and Caddy's "mammies" literally or figuratively try to scrub them clean—or make them act white.[3] Faulkner's image of Caddy's outspokenness, her defiance of the codes of Southern Womanhood—the (always racialized) stain of that same outhouse (what he calls her "shame" and "doom")—is smeared across her muddied drawers. In 1935 he once again memorialized Estelle's blackened little white girl in his photographs of their daughter. His marking of Jill also identified Estelle as the creator (maker?) of this image. I suggest that his introduction and his later photographs of Jill as the "doomed" but also "fierce" and "courageous" little Caddy Compson were all expressions of his gratitude to Estelle for her collaborative role in his life and art.[4]

The third piece of evidence is Estelle's and Faulkner's short story "Selvage," which was published as Faulkner's "Elly" in 1931. "Selvage/Elly" was originally Estelle's. During the same months he was writing *The Sound and the Fury*, Faulkner and she revised it together. He then submitted "Selvage" to *Scribner's* under their joint byline in December 1928, shortly after returning from New York, where he had gone to read galleys for his third novel, now titled *Sartoris*, and make final revisions on *The Sound and the Fury*.

Fall 1925–August 1933: An Overview

Through the fall of 1926, Faulkner continued spending either weeks or months at a time away from Oxford. This was a pattern he'd begun in April 1918 when, some weeks before the Oldham-Franklin wedding, he left Oxford to visit Phil Stone in New Haven. Estelle's clear break with Cornell announced by her unexpected arrival in early December 1924 did not alter Faulkner's habits, although he may have increased the frequency of his trips home. Beginning in January 1927, however, this pattern changed: for the most part he stayed in Oxford, where, in the space of four years, he wrote four of his best novels and many of his greatest short stories. Among the latter were "A Rose for Emily," "That Evening Sun," "Dry September," and "Spotted Horses." Then there were his lesser novels, *Mosquitoes* and *Flags in the Dust/ Sartoris* and two collections of short stories. In addition Faulkner wrote and illustrated several more unique booklets. Among these last, all dated 1926, were *Vision in Spring* (dated 1921 but rebound for Estelle on 26 January); *Mayday* (for Helen Baird, dated 27 January); *Helen: A Courtship* (for Helen, dated June); and *Royal Street* (for Estelle, dated 29 October). Also in 1926 there appeared *Sherwood Anderson and Other Famous Creoles*, Faulkner and Bill Spratling's satire (December), and his second novel, *Mosquitoes*, which he dedicated "To Helen" (11 January 1927, *SL*, 34).

Faulkner proposed marriage to Helen Baird in 1925 and in the next two years dedicated three books to her. For these reasons biographers have considered her a significant player and another indication that when he married Estelle in 1929, it was because he felt obligated, not because he needed and loved her. So before turning to Faulkner and Estelle's relationship from 1925 to 1933, we need to understand Faulkner's love affair with Helen. The actual time they spent together between 1925 and 1927 was negligible. A Memphis debutante and doll maker, she often visited New Orleans to sell her work and be with other artists. He first met her there in the spring of 1925. Although in letters home from New Orleans that spring, he mentions other young women he has met, he says nothing about Helen. None of the people who hung out with Faulkner in New Orleans mention her either. Helen's family owned a summer house in Pascagoula, where she stayed in the summer of 1925. That summer Faulkner made two trips to Pascagoula, spending about fifteen days and staying at the Stones' summer house there. Faulkner was living in New Orleans at the time but prefaced each trip to Pascagoula with a trip to Oxford and Estelle, where he spent a total of about thirteen days—a similar amount of time. On his second Pascagoula visit, he was finishing revisions on the typescript of *Soldiers' Pay*.[5] According to both Faulkner and Helen, he proposed marriage to her shortly before she left to spend the rest of that summer in Europe. She refused. Although he claimed to Helen's aunt that he was smitten with her, his filthy and disheveled appearance and the company he kept in Pascagoula seemed designed to discourage anyone's romantic interest. Long-haired, barefoot, and ragged, his once white duck trousers held up by a rope, Faulkner had as his main companion an equally ragged beachcomber and "local character" similar to the old town drunk he had befriended in Oxford.[6] Faulkner also spent some of the next summer in Pascagoula, but Helen was in Europe. As he had in 1925, Faulkner stayed at the Stones' house, where he typed and revised *Mosquitoes*, the novel he dedicated to Helen in late January 1927 (*SL*, 33–34). A week later, again as if to neutralize this dedication to Helen, he wrote a birthday fable for Cho-Cho, his "dear friend on her eighth birthday." It was about another little girl who, like Cho-Cho, was sick on her birthday. Like Estelle, her mother was "beautiful, so slim and tall with her grave unhappy eyes changeable as seawater and her slender hands that came so softly about you when you were sick" (*Wishing Tree*, 81). By that March, Helen Baird had married someone else.[7]

In the fairly bad but interesting sonnet sequence he gave Helen, his opening portrayal of her in "To Helen, Swimming" is reminiscent of the girl-boys in his earlier poems to Estelle and in his first novel. He describes her with "her boy's breast and the plain flanks of a boy"; as she swims

> Hands of water hush with green regret
> The brown and simple music of her knees. (*Helen*, 1)

In a later sonnet the poet claims it doesn't matter that she's refused his bed, because all that is really important is what he can do in his imagination, where, "I've lain lonely nights and nights with you" (*Helen*, 10). That was the extent of Faulkner and Helen's one-sided affair. Like many other tales of disappointed love that he had told Elizabeth Anderson, Helen's aunt in Pascagoula, and anyone else who would listen, it was his fantasy. Helen found him amusing but had no romantic interest in him. Once she told a friend that he looked like a furry little animal and that he smelled. On 30 April 1927, when *Mosquitoes* was published with its dedication to Helen, she was already married to Guy Lyman. *Mayday*, Faulkner's first book for her, is an imitative and ironic fable of a young knight's failed quest for perfect love. Its dedication

> To thee
> O wise and lovely
> this:
> a fumbling in darkness

combined a phrase he'd used in the 1920 copy of *The Marionettes* that he'd given to Estelle—"a shadowy fumbling in windy darkness" with one he'd use again four months later in dedicating *Royal Street* to Estelle.

So, why Helen and why then? Between 1924 and 1927, while Estelle and Cornell were negotiating the end of their marriage, Faulkner seems to have needed to enforce periods of physical and emotional distance between Estelle and himself, as he did throughout their lives. His infatuation with Helen Baird helped serve this need, as did, in part, his summer visits to Pascagoula. Besides Estelle, he subjected others who were close to his emotional and creative life to similar distancing. On his trips to New Orleans, where he lived with Bill Spratling in the spring of 1925 and again during the fall of 1926, he worked on divorcing himself from Sherwood Anderson, another emotionally threatening relationship. Spratling and Faulkner's various sophomoric and often homoerotic joint ventures in New Orleans were all aimed at embarrassing the famous writer, who had done so much to help both younger men. Faulkner's "devastating yet oblique parody" of Phil Stone, which he sent from Paris to H. L Mencken at the *Dial* (with a copy to Phil), was another instance of this kind of behavior, a sign that Faulkner chafed under what he owed Stone.[8] By the fall of 1928, besides serving as his unpaid secretary, publicist, and agent, Phil had lent Bill more than seven hundred dollars.[9]

During Faulkner's stretches of time in Oxford in 1925 and 1926, he immersed himself in writing. He also read Estelle's short stories and her novel, *White Beaches,* typing the latter probably in late 1926 or early 1927. In 1928 and 1929 they collaborated to revise several short stories that were originally hers. Faulkner sent out at least one under their joint byline in December 1928. So Faulkner's relationships with Helen Baird and Estelle couldn't have been more different: though he dedicated works to both, and may have proposed marriage to both, only his love for Estelle was reciprocated. He collaborated only with her.

Faulkner and the Franklin Divorce

What active role, if any, did Faulkner play during the five years that Estelle and Cornell were negotiating their long-distance divorce? Ignoring facts to the contrary, the prevailing narrative of Faulkner and Estelle holds that he married reluctantly and out of a sense of honor and obligation to a woman no one else would have. However, between Estelle's arrival home in 1924 and the legal end of the Franklin marriage in February 1929, Faulkner was not a passive bystander. As he explained, "It's a situation which I engendered and permitted to ripen which has become unbearable, and I am tired of running from the devilment I bring about." He wanted Estelle to leave Cornell and supported her efforts to do so.

Aside from the somewhat ambiguous evidence of the books he made for her, the first clear indication of Faulkner's activism occurred in fall 1925. Three months after leaving with Spratling for his first and only Grand Tour, he was ready to come home. On 17 October 1925 he wrote his father a nostalgic letter: "I have been away from our blue hills and sage fields and things long enough. So I am making arrangements to come home." He had "plenty of notes and data to last me a long time: all I need now is to settle down at home comfortable again and bang on my typewriter" (*TOH*, 218). He was waiting for Boni and Liveright to send him his contract and two hundred–dollar advance for *Soldiers' Pay* and was "reasonably certain" that he'd be sailing home from France by 1 November (219).

He was also eager to be home and homesick for another, more intimate reason to which his parents were probably not privy. An ocean crossing in 1925 took ten days, which meant that had he left as planned he would have been back in Oxford *before* Estelle was due to return to Shanghai and would have been there when the Franklins and Oldhams were pressuring her to go back with Cornell. However, because he could not cash Liveright's check when it arrived—almost two weeks later, on October 26th—he did not sail from Cherbourg to New York until 2 December on the *S.S. Republic*, eleven days after Cornell and Estelle had sailed from San Francisco bound for Shanghai on the *S.S. President Wilson*. Meanwhile in Paris, he spent much of November trying desperately to cash his advance and berating his publisher. As he missed ship after ship, his letters home brimmed with increasing homesickness, irritation, and vitriolic remarks about the idiocy of Liveright sending him a personal check that no one would honor—"Damn that Jew" (*TOH*, 229).

Although there are no extant letters between Faulkner and Estelle to document the dual sources of his anxiety to return home, there are several from the Franklins that speak to Estelle's disenchantment with her marriage and her desire not to return to Shanghai. By early March 1925, although she'd been in the States almost four months, Cornell had heard little from his wife. Writing to his father-in-law to assure him that he'd soon pay back the fifteen hundred–dollar loan Lem had made him when he and Estelle had first arrived in Shanghai on New Year's Eve 1921, he asked for news: "You know Estelle's letters well enough to know what meager news I get from her so please write me what you think of the Franklins and how they look and what they are doing. Would also appreciate a Kodak picture or two."[10] By June 1925, Cornell had appointed his secretary to write Estelle. She closed her account of her boss's doings in court and on the polo field by writing that he was "counting a great deal on his visit home" at the summer's end and adding wistfully that "I'd like to see him fetch you back" to Shanghai.[11]

Shortly after Estelle's return to Oxford in December 1924, her mother-in-law and Cornell's uncle Malcolm, who had spent much time with Estelle and Cornell in Honolulu, arrived from Columbus to visit the Oldhams. Writing to Cornell about their visit and responding to an anxious letter from his nephew written four days before Estelle had returned to Oxford, Malcolm heaped both praise and blame upon her. She "was so greatly improved and her clothes about a mile and a half *ahead* of "Vogue"—Her gowns are *stunning*—I am eager for her to get to Columbus—She will make the Columbus women look like an oyster cook on a hand cart." Estelle looked the part of the proper lady, but that wasn't enough; Malcolm complained at length that she'd been remiss in her bootlegging duties. Although they had had a fine visit with the Oldhams, "it was *dry*—just as *dry* as summer *dust*—Estelle *failed* to have things fixed in Honolulu and the Major was out of corn—but some of his friends came to his rescue—we had a few drinks of corn, but nothing like enough." Sounding like one of Estelle's relatives in her fictionalized memoir, he continued to dwell on her failure to fulfill his craving, saying that he was "damned tired of *corn*—it is a *horrible* drink, I haven't had a drink of real whiskey since I left Honolulu—*nearly four years ago*—I am so anxious to get to Shanghai." There he'd have unlimited supplies of booze and could drink himself into a genteel stupor on a daily basis, like the man who ran the American Club in Estelle's Shanghai story.[12] In choosing to take a dry, rather than a wet, ship home in November 1924 and in refusing to bring back an illegal supply of whiskey from Honolulu, Estelle may have been fighting her own addiction. She was also refusing to perform as scripted by her male relations—her husband, father, and uncle.

That fall of 1925, while Faulkner's frustration over being stuck in Paris mounted, Estelle caused more trouble as she tried unsuccessfully to remain at her parents' home in Oxford rather than return with Cornell, who had, indeed, come to "fetch" her back to Shanghai. Perhaps she was encouraged by the same news Faulkner had sent his parents at the end of October. About his contract offer from Boni and Liveright for *Soldiers' Pay* and the next two novels he had written, "my future looks alright financially—only you and Pop will have to furnish the parched corn for a while longer, until the loot starts coming in." Besides a $200 advance on his first novel, Liveright had offered him a "$400 advance on each" of his next two novels, "he and I to divide the movie rights" (*TOH*, 223, 30 October 1925).

Malcolm's letters to his nephew written before the Franklins sailed that December of 1925 also indicate that the Franklin marriage was in poor shape. Malcolm writes that he hopes that by March of the coming year "your financial condition will be, of course, better—your home life running smoothly." His last good-bye letter makes clear that Estelle held out until the very end. With great relief he writes, "Your leaving with your family has filled me and your mother with joy unspeakable" and "pray[s] that every cloud which o'er your household lowered, will be buried in the bottom of the deep sea."[13]

Malcolm and the Oldhams were to be disappointed. In less than four months, Estelle and the children were back in Oxford. It is not known whether Faulkner's success with *Soldiers' Pay* and promise of advances for twice as much on his next two novels also fueled Estelle's resolve to behave so badly that Cornell was able to legally "require" that she leave their Shanghai home, probably in late January or early February 1926. She sailed first to Honolulu where she tried, briefly, to set up her own household. As a measure of her unhappiness, despite having no realistic prospect of economic self-sufficiency, she nonetheless wrote her parents, "I have an awful horror of divorce but at least I believe I would be happier if everything was over."[14] By 17 March 1926 the *Oxford Eagle* had announced that Estelle and her children had "returned Sunday evening from Honolulu for a visit." Estelle's "visit" lasted the rest of her life.[15] The Sassoons' separation in her story "A Crossing" is at one level a fictionalized portrayal of one aspect of the state of her marriage on the Franklins' second and last trip to Shanghai together. Through Edna Earl (the innocent Estelle of her first voyage in 1918); the dark "Levantine" Sassoon and his estranged fashion designer wife, Mme. Tingot; and the St. Paul–quoting Christian missionary suitor, Estelle's authorial "I" tries to work out an equitable resolution for a relationship that the law then defined as unequal.

Faulkner did not return to Oxford until New Year's Eve 1925, having stopped first in New York to see his publisher and read page proofs of *Soldiers' Pay*. Although Estelle had gone, she left in his care her well-worn handmade booklet *Vision in Spring*, the sequence of love poems he had given her in 1921, just before the Franklins moved to Shanghai. Near the end of January 1926, possibly after hearing that Cornell had kicked her out and that she was going to try to make it on her own in Honolulu, Faulkner made new covers for it of a "brownish-green mottled paper" and hand-lettered its title on a small square of white linen paper that he pasted on the cover. Opposite the sequence's last page he printed in black ink "REBOUND 26 JANUARY 1926. OXFORD. MISSISSIPPI." The next day, as if to erase the personal significance of either gift, he dated Helen's *Mayday* 17 January 1926. By the end of February 1926 Faulkner was back in New Orleans, living again with Spratling and supported by money borrowed from Phil Stone. He returned home shortly, however, in that he needed to borrow more from Stone. He was there when Estelle arrived on 14 March and did not leave again until July, when Estelle and her children also left to spend the hottest months in Monteagle, Tennessee. That summer, Stone stepped in once more to help Faulkner, suggesting that he spend a few weeks at his family's Pascagoula summer house and writing Liveright (under Faulkner's signature) to ask for an advance of fifty dollars.[16] Beside his time with the Stones, and with Spratling in February and again in December, his trips away from Oxford became less frequent once Estelle arrived for good. On 29 October, probably just before leaving for New Orleans, he made another booklet for her: *Royal Street* included the sketches he had published in the New Orleans *Double Dealer* in 1925, plus one new one. "Hong Li," the spurned and distraught Chinese lover, like Estelle's in her Shanghai story, comforts himself with the metaphor of his "bereaved" soul as a diseased garden. To restore it to health he knows he must "root out and destroy the tares which her dead and delicate feet sowed across my heart." Though, like Estelle's Needy Chang, he realizes this, he remains obsessed: "Ehee, Ehee, her little little feet."[17] Meanwhile, in Shanghai by that December, Cornell Franklin and his future wife were being seen and photographed in public as a couple.[18]

As of January 1927, Faulkner began staying mostly in Oxford because Estelle was there. This change coincides with the beginning of the most creative period of his entire career. The year began inauspiciously. Liveright returned the galleys of *Mosquitoes* with four passages deleted. These all depicted what we would now call very explicit instances of "gender trouble" or highly eroticized same-sex desire. Faulkner was angry at first but then acceded, performing some gender trouble of his own in the process. Referring to himself as "practically a vestal in the field of professional lit," he wrote that "I understood why the deletions were made, and I was merely pointing out one result of it that, after all, is not very important." He believed in the "truth" of the deleted material. Thus while he gave in one sentence, he took in the other, portraying himself as both a woman AND a virgin. He then thanked Liveright for "the enclosed memoranda showing why [the cuts]" (*SL*, 34). Liveright's deletions from his second novel taught Faulkner what the mass market would and would not tolerate. He took the lesson to heart. As Minrose Gwin notes, "In the process of writing and publishing the book, he very likely discovered not only what he might be capable of writing but also what he would not be able to write about openly." In short, "to be published in a mass market, he would need, at least in part, to muffle and veil explicit same-sex eroticism, i.e., gender trouble" in his future treatment of homoerotic and homosexual themes.[19]

The deleted material in *Mosquitoes* also had direct bearing on his literary collaboration with Estelle. Stories like "A Crossing," with its suggestive title, its sexually irresolute characters, and its shipboard cabin scenes of the "married" bisexual Mme. Tingot seducing the cross-named virgin, Edna Earl, inspired similar seduction and fantasied seduction scenes between Emmy and Margaret Powers, first, and then Cecily and Margaret in Faulkner's first novel and also in their more explicit elaborations in *Mosquitoes* (*SP*, 124–29, 263–68). Besides Estelle's treatment of race and racism, her challenges to marriage as an institution and to gender assignments as natural and fixed in all her fiction had opened Faulkner in a very personal way to the imaginative possibilities and social implications raised by characters who question and subvert the concept of race and "notions of sexuality as either 'natural' or fixed."[20]

Faulkner's activism is also evidenced by his encouraging Estelle to publish her own fiction. By mid-February 1927, he had almost finished typing her novel for her as he thought it good enough to be published. At the same time, he had begun writing *Flags in the Dust*, which he then thought was his breakthrough novel (published as *Sartoris* in February 1929). He was immersing himself in her authorial voices and simultaneously finding new registers for his own. On 18 February Faulkner wrote his publisher that he planned to send him Estelle's novel as soon as Liveright returned from Europe. Describing it, Faulkner wrote, "I have dug up something else for you." Simultaneously deprecating but protective—he did not name the author's gender—he added that it was "a mss. by one who has no literary yearnings whatever and who did this just to pass the time." He then added, "I have persuaded the author to give you first shot at it. I think it is pretty fair. I'll get it on for you to see when you return from Europe" (*SL*, 34–35). He was doing for Estelle what Sherwood Anderson had done for him two years earlier. Although it is unclear whether Faulkner ultimately sent Estelle's novel to Liveright or to Scribner's, it was rejected. Faulkner remained deeply invested in it: when he heard that Estelle had then burned it, he was furious. Nothing of it survives.[21]

Throughout spring and summer of 1927, Faulkner remained in Oxford working steadily on his third novel. When he hit "a dry spot," he wrote stories. Meanwhile Estelle and her children spent June in Columbus with

Mamie. There Bill and she could visit with impunity as Estelle's mother-in-law was fond of him and much less concerned with propriety than the Old-hams. In July he wrote Liveright, "The new novel is coming fine. It is much better than that other stuff. I believe that at last I have learned to control the stuff and fix it on something like rational truth" (*SL*, 37).

That September Estelle went to Kosciusko for the weekend. She created a splash in her hometown when she arrived for the wedding of the season.[22] No one there had any idea she was in the middle of a divorce. With her ermine cape in the oppressive Mississippi summer heat, her designer dresses from the "Orient," and the sheer force of her personality, she made an indelible impression. Lilly Reynolds Brown, six years younger than Estelle, and her cousin, Zaida Woodward, remembered their exotic cousin's visit with awe, pleasure, and a tinge of envy.

Lilly's daughter, Polly, and her cousin, Zaida, explain another source of the women's awe. Recalling what her mother told her about Estelle, Zaida says, "She was just a darling, a most attractive person. She just drew people to her. Evidently the men liked her a lot, too." Their cousin, Charlene, elaborates, again only by speaking indirectly. Another relative, Marilyn Jackson, too, was "kind of that kind of person": Marilyn was "a wild vivacious, didn't-care girl. She shocked me the way she'd come to visit at Grandmother's. She'd undress before anybody and that, to me, was absolutely shocking. Her male cousins would come over there and Marilyn would come by in her bra or something. She was loud talking, very vivacious and she would wear bright red and she kind of reminded me of some type of loose woman."[23]

Estelle was no ice maiden. She broke age-old codes of conduct for Southern "ladies." Speaking of her later conduct, Zaida puts it succinctly: "I stood a little bit in awe of her. She was one of the first in the family to get a divorce. It was an *event* in the family history." Even more appalling, she then married a man who was disreputable to begin with, but worse, wrote *Sanctuary.* "I was always a little bit embarrassed that Estelle would marry anybody who would write about things like that. We just didn't talk about those things."[24] At the same time, and again indirectly as they explain what marriage was like for women of Estelle's and their mothers' generation, they defend her for daring to leave a bad marriage at a time and in a place when most women like her stayed married at all costs. Charlene explains: "Fortunately mother married a sweet person. But she used to tell me that there were a lot of women in Kosciusko that married men who were mean and they were treated just terribly. She'd give me vivid examples and then say 'but they had no place to go.' Their husbands could treat them any way they wanted to and the men evidently knew that and played it for what it was worth, if they didn't understand the meaning of love, which so few people do."[25]

As the two generations talk, a portrait emerges, one very like the domestic worlds portrayed in Faulkner's fiction and in historical accounts of the era. One thinks of those desperate wives trapped in loveless and violent marriages—Mrs. Hightower, Ellen Coldfield, or the lynch-mob leader's wife in "Dry September." Then there are their equally desperate daughters—Judith Sutpen, Temple Drake, Caddy Compson, or the daughters in Estelle's stories, all marketed like so many cattle. Her cousins' placing of Estelle's narrative in its historical and familial context provides a better understanding of what it meant to their community for Estelle and Faulkner to marry. Estelle had refused to be marketed and refused to silence her sexuality. Like the Texan's spotted horses in her husband's story by that name, she brought an aura of excitement and color to her Kosciusko relatives' staid, sleepy town and, for its women, the vision of another kind of life unshackled by laws and conventions that constrained them, a life sparkling with glamour and the shimmer of imagination.

Faulkner, too, was breathing in her ether. When he sent off the typescript of *Flags* that October his cover letter was filled with joy: "I have written THE book, of which those other things were but foals. I believe it is the damndest book you'll look at this year, and any other publisher" (*SL*, 38). To his shock and disappointment Liveright rejected it. On 30 November Faulkner wrote back, "Its too bad you don't like *Flags in the Dust*." He asked his publisher's permission to submit it elsewhere, as "I still believe it is the book which will make my name for me as a writer" (39). Eventually, after many submissions and extensive cutting and editing by Ben Wasson, *Flags*, now called *Sartoris*, was published in 1929. But by then Faulkner really had transformed into the gifted artist. Between March and September of 1928 he wrote *The Sound and the Fury*. Had he written nothing else, this novel would have assured his fame. Another liberation occurred simultaneously, which would make possible the next stage of Estelle Franklin's and Bill Faulkner's relationship. During those same months, Estelle's final negotiations with Cornell began and were completed.

The Franklin Divorce: 1926–1929

As they had since Estelle's marriage began, Faulkner's creative surges seemed to spike with each new phase of its disintegration. Only bits and shards of the Oldham-Franklin divorce narrative survive. But they are telling. In early February 1926, a month before Estelle's arrival home, Cornell finally paid off the large loan her father had made him in 1922.[26] Rather

than his usual fulsome letter, Lem sent only a terse statement acknowledging receipt of Cornell's check. By at least that December, Cornell and Dallas Lee Chesterton Meclewski were openly carrying on their affair. A de-
scendant of Robert E. Lee, her family was from Richmond, Virginia, a cut
above Oxford, Mississippi. They had first met when Dallas consulted Cornell about divorcing her abusive first husband, a naval officer then stationed
in Shanghai.[27] Sometime after Cornell began this affair, probably in 1926
or 1927, he wrote Estelle in Oxford once more, urging her agreement to a
divorce. "Too much water has run under the bridge for us ever to start over
or try again—it just couldn't be done. Won't you be reasonable?" By then
he was so eager to be free to marry Dallas that he offered to let her file:
"You can bring an action on the ground of desertion or cruelty and have a
good case." (He would withdraw this offer by the following spring, as Estelle's Shanghai lawyer and Cornell's friend Chauncy Holcomb's letters to
her show.) He then adds, almost pleadingly, "We could still be just as
friendly as we are now and regardless of what happens for my part I will
always have a great deal of affection for you. Let me know what you intend
to do, give me a definite and final answer."[28]

When Estelle's divorce proceedings moved into high gear in 1928, so
did Faulkner's pace and creativity. As he later described that February and
March in his suppressed introduction to *The Sound and the Fury*, something
remarkable occurred: "One day I seemed to shut a door between me and
all publishers. . . . I said to myself, Now I can write. Now I can make myself
a vase. . . . And so I . . . made myself a beautiful tragic little girl."[29] For the
first time in his writing life he was aware of himself as completely free of
any judging voices, real or imagined. In early March he wrote optimisti-
cally to Liveright: "I have got going on a novel, which, if I continue as I am
going now, I will finish within 8 weeks" (*SL*, 40). A few blocks away that
same early March, Estelle, having agreed to go forward under the terms
offered by Cornell in his pleading letter, had received her first letter from
Holcomb. He offered to represent her and then outlined Cornell's new and
very different terms. Meanwhile, as Faulkner worked on through that
spring and summer, he experienced a creative ecstasy, a "quality" of mind
previously "absent" from his writing process. Four years later (also in that
same introduction) he described it as "that emotion definite and physical
and yet nebulous to describe: that ecstasy, that eager and joyous faith and
anticipation of surprise which the yet unmarred sheets under my hand held
inviolate and unfailing."[30] This metaphor, like others in that introduction,
speaks to the erotic and personal sources of his creative ecstasy. He came
into possession of his vision, his "vase," once he knew Estelle would be free.
That knowledge seems to have freed him to transform her fictional image

of her childhood self into *The Sound and the Fury:* "She was my heart's darling. That's what I wrote the book about, . . . to try to draw the picture of Caddy" (*FIU,* 6; *TSAF,* 236). He would continue redrawing her in the many drafts of his 1933 introduction to the novel and in the 1934–35 photographs he took of Jill as another progeny of his and Estelle's collaboration.

During those same months, Estelle's divorce negotiations with Cornell, begun in February, when Faulkner began his new novel, were completed. That June she replied to Holcomb, questioning his motives in representing her in light of his closeness to Cornell and, more particularly, in maintaining he could see no legal way for her to file for divorce, even though Cornell had already told her she could file, because she'd have to prove two years' residence prior to filing, "which would be rather hard to prove." She was no dummy. If he were indeed her advocate, he would be looking for alternatives—for ways for her to prove residency in Shanghai so that she could file. With no real advocate and no practical way to obtain one, she ultimately gave in to her husband's humiliating terms. These were, as Holcomb wrote in March and then reiterated in August 1928, that not she but Cornell "applies for divorce here on the grounds of desertion," because "I know of no other cause for a divorce except desertion." This despite the fact that "it is admitted that Cornell required that you go home." She would get three hundred dollars a month in child support, in that "Cornell says it is impossible for him to pay more than $300.00 monthly."[31] That was it. Later, all she would tell her childhood friends Christine Drake and Katherine Andrews was that Cornell had "hurt my feelings," nothing more.

In Shanghai, on 13 November 1928, Cornell took the first official step, filing an Interlocutory Order for Divorce in the U.S. Court for China. He would have to wait ninety days until filing the final divorce order. On 15 February 1929 it was filed, Cornell having waited exactly ninety days. Ten days later the Franklin marriage was legally over.[32] A copy of the Franklins' final divorce decree would not be filed in the Oxford Courthouse until 6 June 1929, two weeks before William Faulkner and Estelle Oldham married.[33] However, Estelle's typescript and carbon of a later typescript of "A Crossing" indicate that she had reclaimed her maiden name by the fall of 1928. Just "E.O." was typed on the carbon version.[34] On the earlier typescript version Faulkner had typed her byline as "E. Oldham-Franklin,/Oxford, Mississippi." Then at some point, either she or he had crossed out "Franklin" with black ink. Also during that spring and summer of 1928 when Faulkner was writing *The Sound and the Fury,* he and Estelle began revising her story "Selvage." In December, shortly after he returned from New York, where he had gone to finish up both *Sartoris* and *The Sound and the Fury,* Faulkner sent "Selvage" to *Scribner's* magazine under their joint byline, "E. Oldham and W. Faulkner." On 23 February 1929, eight days after Cornell filed the final divorce decree, Faulkner sent *Scribner's* the carbon copy of "Selvage." Not hearing back from them, he thought the magazine had lost the original. *Scribner's* letter rejecting this now missing typescript and carbon of "Selvage" is the only known public record of Estelle and Faulkner's long and fruitful literary collaboration.

In his letter accompanying the carbon, he announced that he had "got involved in another novel." This was his only best-seller, his infamous and devastating critique of a southern community and larger world where there was no *Sanctuary*. It is, however, the ignored and demeaned "Selvage," another gift of Estelle to Faulkner, that is now most relevant to the story of the couple's extended and extensive imaginative merger. Without Estelle's original version of the story or any of its jointly written versions, the process by which it became their mutual creation is lost. Yet Faulkner's excision of Estelle from the story's byline in the extant drafts of "Selvage" and his resubmission of it in 1931 to *Story* magazine as "Elly" does not erase her authorial voice.[35] His excision also anticipates his later and much larger erasure of her transformative imaginative presence—his pulling from public view and then supposed destruction of his 1933 introduction to *The Sound and the Fury*.

"Selvage/Elly," 1928: A Bad, Bad Southern Belle

When Estelle read *Sanctuary* in manuscript or typescript, "she was furious and said it was horrible. 'It's meant to be,' he said. 'It will sell.'"[36] And it did. Although it echoes that of her Kosciusko relatives, Estelle's appalled response rings somewhat false in the context of the contemporaneous "Selvage," which she and Faulkner first submitted for publication in the fall of 1928. Set in 1920s Mississippi, it is probably one of her later stories and certainly her raciest. In it, the crazy restrictions governing Southern Belledom drive the seventeen-year-old virgin Elly to plunge into promiscuous and interracial sex and then commit a double murder to preserve her reputation. This raging and hysterical adolescent girl registers the societal sickness produced by the laws and customs governing Southern Womanhood, most particularly those requiring its women's racial and sexual purity. Elly is thus part of Estelle's larger project that we have seen unfolding in her earlier stories. Yet here no irony and humor mute her critique. Desperately, Elly seeks alternatives to life in a rigidly hierarchical and racist society where she is forbidden to feel desire and can do nothing with her life but destroy it or marry the man her family approves of. Her desperate alternative to victimhood is murder.

Faulkner and Estelle's collaboration on this story, coming when it does, shows Estelle's fiction very much in dialogue with Faulkner's, particularly about an adolescent girl clearly related to Faulkner's novels that bracket it, *The Sound and the Fury* and *Sanctuary*. Elly is even the same age as Caddy when the latter marries. Their joint revisions on "Selvage" were made during the same months that Faulkner was writing *The Sound and the Fury*. I suggest that reworking with Estelle the three-pronged relationship among Elly, her patriarchal grandmother, and Elly's lover, biracial Paul, gave Faulkner the raw material and the collaborator he needed to create in Elly a more crude rendering of the various, much more nuanced psychosexual and psychosocial tensions informing the novel he was writing and the one that he would shortly write. The collaborative experience of "Selvage/Elly" coupled with his reading and typing of her other stories and her novel provided him with a kind of staging area or creative playing ground. He would take the images, themes, and emotions he found there, those that touched him most, to refine and re-create as his own.

"Selvage" is only one of several known stories that began as Estelle's and that Faulkner then submitted under their joint byline. By 1930 he had sent out several other stories that were originally hers. Among these is "Idyll in the Desert," which, Blotner writes, "had begun with an idea Estelle had explored and abandoned. Her husband had become interested in it and reworked it in a 4-page manuscript."[37] Blotner obviously saw a version with Estelle's byline on it. However, it, too, is now missing. It is not known how many other manuscripts of Estelle's are also missing. Yet even this sparse evidence confirms that between at least 1928, when he began writing *The Sound and the Fury*, and 1931, Faulkner and Estelle were collaborating on quite a few stories that had begun as Estelle's. Faulkner submitted "Idyll" to at least seven magazines beginning in early January. Like "Selvage," it was published in 1931. By 1979, when Blotner included it in Faulkner's *Uncollected Stories*, his notes no longer mention Estelle's coauthorship. There is also another story, a complete six-page typescript, called "A Letter to Grandmamma," with Estelle's byline given as "E. Oldham/Oxford Mississippi/Box 170." Faulkner's two revised versions bearing his byline are retitled "A Letter."[38]

Extant drafts of "Selvage/Elly" are all apparently Faulkner's.[39] Since we don't have Estelle's original versions of "Selvage" or any versions with their joint byline, we can't know what of this story was originally Estelle's. Nor can we even know whether Faulkner's version of "Selvage" is closer to Estelle's original than "Elly." Length is not necessarily a useful indicator of his revision process here in that her version or their jointly authored version may have been longer before he began crafting a version on his own from their collaborative work. Regardless, surviving drafts indicate that the basic material was Estelle's. Elly is one of her series of contemporary girls (whose first names all begin with E) who are trying to find ways to act independently, speak their minds, and express their sexuality in communities and cultures whose intent is to make them into ice maidens.

Past critical response to Estelle's coauthorship of "Selvage/Elly" has been either to erase its collaborative aspects or to blame her for the story's initial rejection. We are therefore told that when *Scribner's* wrote Faulkner rejecting the version "'done by you and Estelle Oldham.' . . . The editor found the piece to be 'too febrile,' an interesting judgment about Estelle's mental condition at this time."[40] As is generally the case, anything positive about Estelle's relationship with Faulkner provokes wild analysis.

"Selvage/Elly": The Narrative

Elly is a killer. In one murderous lunge at a steering wheel, she eliminates both her racist deaf grandmother, from "whose sight nothing escaped" (*CS*, 223), and the Harvard-educated New Orleanian Paul de Montigny, who is rumored to have "negro blood" and with whom Elly has had consensual sex just three weeks before her arranged marriage to a proper "white" Southerner ("Selvage," TS, 2–3). She's the only survivor of this car crash. There are no witnesses. She will pay neither for her capital crime nor her crime of breeching the color line and despoiling her family's "honor." As a character type, Elly breaks the mold. Although bad Southern Belles were a staple of white Southern fiction, they always paid for their misdeeds, generally with their lives. In contrast Elly, like her less excessive Shanghai counterpart, just goes on.

In this story Estelle continues probing the instability and unreliability of so-called racial markers: Elly's badness is as complex as her racial identity. Her grandmother is also from New Orleans, suggesting that she, too, is passing. Consequently, Elly's family may be just as "negro" as Paul's. Further emphasizing the paradoxes of Jim Crow, Elly's grandmother speaks for Southern patriarchy—its virulent racism, its negation of white women's sexual desire, and its attendant hypersexualizing of "negroes." Ironically, in her attempts to escape, Elly acts out all of her grandmother's prejudices. There is a kind of sexual blankness to Elly. She feels only numbness and despair when engaging in the promiscuous sex she constantly seeks. Night after night she necks on her front porch "with a different man," always keeping her virginity intact, always dismissing beaux peremptorily at 11 P.M. These bouts leave her deeply depressed: "weary and dulled with kissing with a feeling of the pointlessness and emptiness of life more profound than the rage or the sense of persecution" caused by her hated grand-mother, the "old bitch." Alone in her room she asks herself, "Why do I do it? What is the matter with me? I don't want any man, anything" (*CS*, 209, 211). At her grandmother, she shouts her rage and frustration: "What else can I do, in this little dead hopeless town? I'll work. I don't want to be idle. Just find me a job—anything, anywhere, so that it's so far away that I'll never have to hear the word Jefferson again" (212). Marriage "to a sober young man of impeccable character" is her only choice (213). Such moments are familiar in Estelle's fiction. In "A Crossing," for example, Edna Earl, responding to her shame and fear that "my Tomlinson blood is cropping out," succumbs to marrying the minister—but not before her "choice" makes her feel as if she is dying.[41] Elly's transgressions are much worse, and she puts up more of a fight.

Although she doesn't love Paul, like every one of Estelle's women, she is fascinated by his "blackness," rumors of which she claims not to believe because, like another of Estelle's interracial couples, Emma Jane and the Cambridge-educated Needy Chang, her New Orleans Creole, doesn't perform "negro": Elly insists, "He is not a negro he went to Virginia and Harvard and everywhere" ("Elly," *CS*, 218). Simultaneously, she wants to have sex with him because she thinks that this violation of racial-sexual taboos will free her from her grandmother's surveillance. It doesn't, because her grandmother is only an external sign of her entrapment in Southern Womanhood. Elly has so internalized her grandmother's values that when Paul balks at killing the "old bitch," she decides to kill *him* too. As their car ploughs through the symbolic "white railing" beside the precipice, "it flung her free," while "Paul's face, her grandmother, the car, had disappeared as though by magic." Elly's a survivor—her only wound, a cut hand ("Elly," 123, 124). In its published form, as in Faulkner's extant drafts, the plot is incredible, but as a dream of Elly's nightmare life, it makes sense. Most important, like Estelle's "Doctor Wohlenski" and her other stories, it links her fiction to the imaginative worlds that opened up to Faulkner once Estelle's freedom from her own "proper" marriage began to take solid form.

Besides this and other short stories, Faulkner spent the spring and summer months of 1928 working steadily and ecstatically on his new novel. "He showed Estelle parts of it when he had nearly all of it written. In 1965 she still considered it "his best novel and thought that he [too] was satisfied with it."[42] In his 1933 introduction, Faulkner described the process of writing it: "It was like I had taken a pill or like when a chemist puts a precipitant into an inextricable and indistinguishable mass of matter." In "a series of delayed repercussions like summer thunder" the words, sentences, and paragraphs formed effortlessly on the page, so different, he said, from his poetry and even his first three novels (MS C, *AL*, 273). That June he got more good news. His new publisher, Harcourt Brace, had accepted *Sartoris*, with the manuscript to be delivered 7 October and the book to be published 31 January 1929. The repercussions continued. Within the next fourteen months Faulkner wrote and submitted *The Sound and the Fury* (March–October 1928), *As I Lay Dying* (fall 1929), his first version of *Sanctuary* (January–May 1929), and some short stories. Additionally, there were Estelle's short stories that they were then working on together. Besides "Selvage," there may well have been other joint submissions, now lost.

It is clear, then, that Faulkner's marriage in June 1929 only increased his creativity and productivity. By the end of October 1929 he had also begun *As I Lay Dying* (published in October 1930), which he finished in forty-seven days (MS B, *AL*, 252). That fall and winter, when they were living in a rented apartment in the house of Estelle's relative, Elma Meek, Faulkner worked the night shift at the university powerhouse, where he wrote *As I Lay Dying.* "In the mornings he brought Estelle what he had written during the night."[43] Although her interviewer Carvel Collins must have asked what happened next, Estelle's answer does not appear in his notes. Presumably her husband wanted her to read and respond to his novel as he wrote it. She was the audience inside his head. In these same interviews Estelle describes Faulkner's writing process once they had moved into Rowan Oak in June 1930. "He'd get up in the middle of the night which was why they had separate bedrooms. She liked to stay up and read by kerosene lamp [when they moved in, the house had no central heating, electricity or plumbing] but often he'd retire at ten and wake at about one and go down to his office to work. Estelle said she'd smell toast, which was how she'd know he was up, and that 'he'd leave the kitchen in a hell of a mess.' In the day he'd go into the office, sometimes only to read mail. Often in the car or the paddock he'd take a letter out of his pocket or a scrap of paper and write a few lines. Even when he was not writing, he was working. There were hours of silence on car trips." She went on to describe her husband at work: "He kept library paste on his desk and would cut off a sentence or paragraph and stick it in. Then he'd do a typed version from the cut and paste." She also told Collins that "when he wrote, he wrote hard. He skipped meals. No one dared interrupt him—except the negroes who worked at the farm. They wouldn't interrupt him at a nap but they would at the typewriter."

Estelle also served as his common reader. He'd bring her work in progress, saying, "If you can understand it, anyone can." When editors returned manuscripts with queries, "he'd bring me passages people said were unclear and ask me if I got them." Faulkner's unsurpassed creativity continued unabated through 1935, with *Light in August* (October 1932), *Pylon,*

(March 1935), and *Absalom, Absalom!* (October 1936), a steady stream of short stories, including more collaborations with Estelle, and several short story collections.

Estelle and William Faulkner: 1929–1933

The first four years of the Faulkner marriage played out against professional triumph and a terrible personal loss. By the fall of 1931, *The Sound and the Fury, As I Lay Dying,* and *Sanctuary* had all been published to critical acclaim. *Sanctuary,* which had been released that February, was also, as Faulkner had predicted to Estelle, selling well. His first short story collection, *These 13,* released in late September, had gone into a third printing less than a month later. He was being published in London and Paris and sought out and lionized by New York publishers and Hollywood producers. Yet he still could not keep up his mortgage payments or make very basic improvements on his recently purchased house. In June 1930, when they had been married a little more than a year, Estelle, her two children, and Faulkner had moved into the old Shegog place, which they had bought for six thousand dollars at 6 percent interest, with no down payment and an agreement to pay the seller seventy-five dollars a month.[44] They renamed it Rowan Oak. They installed electricity and basic plumbing that summer, with Faulkner doing a good deal of the work. They did not add central heating until 1933 (*SL,* 73–74).

That spring and summer of 1930 Faulkner continued writing and submitting short stories—eight in February, eight more in March, and three in May. Simultaneously he worked on his novel. By July, Estelle was pregnant with their first child. Faulkner was ecstatic. Echoing and confirming Estelle's 1929 elopement letter to her parents, he wrote Ben: "I am content and I am happy. Right now all the bells in the world seem to be ringing for me."[45] On 11 January 1931, the infant was born two months prematurely, in a hospital without an incubator. Alabama, named for Faulkner's favorite aunt, died nine days later. Estelle's recovery was prolonged. By October 1931 she was still anemic and often very tired. Some of her behavior in New York that fall suggests that her grief was further complicated by postpartum depression. Faulkner, too, appeared emotionally unhinged. Shortly after Alabama's death, he floated a bizarre tale of shooting their obstetrician. That summer he claimed to have "deliberately" run his car into a telephone pole where "I laid my skull bare in a wreck" (*SL,* 50–51).

That fall of 1931, on business trips to Virginia and New York, he was drinking heavily.[46] Even in New York, where everyone in Faulkner's crowd drank a lot, he far exceeded their norm. He continued to binge and began disappearing for days at a time. This behavior peaked near the end of November, when, after an extensive search, Faulkner's publisher Hal Smith found him holed up in the Algonquin Hotel, drunk, "agitated, and emotionally upset" and adamant that "he did not want to be left alone." Smith asked Ben Wasson to wire Estelle to come to New York and care for him.[47] She arrived on 30 November. There is no account from either Faulkner on what happened next, but plenty from Bennett Cerf, Dorothy Parker, and Marc Connelly, members of the group of writers and publishers who were wooing, wining, and dining Faulkner, as opposed to those like Smith and Louise Bonino, who were trying to protect him from himself. Cerf recalled a party at his Central Park South apartment where Estelle's response to the cityscape view was, "When I see all this beauty, I feel just like throwing myself out the window." Parker told of taking her shopping only to have Estelle hysterically tear her dress and threaten to jump out another window. Placed in the context of the high drama that, according to their daughter and others, occupied a good part of their lives together, Estelle's behavior, like Faulkner's under stress, takes on a familiar cast.

Both Faulkners, in their own ways, were distraught and out of control. Yet all accounts of their equally flamboyant, hysterical, and self-destructive behavior make Estelle out as the sole nutcase, who is also somehow to blame. Here, for example, is Connelly's oft-repeated tale: "To Marc Connelly she seemed 'a very nervous girl who occasionally had some kind of slips of mental processes, of thinking, and so on.' He would remember one particular night. 'I don't know what she did, but it was something with which Bill was obviously familiar. And quite objectively, without a bit of reproachment in it, he looked at his wife and reached out and slapped her face very hard. . . . She went right back to completely normal conduct, and Bill, without any apologies or anything else, continued whatever he had been talking about.'"[48]

A shocking scene. However, Connelly's account of it and Blotner's comment—"What was the cause of *her* hysteria?"—are more shocking. Not only does Connelly not know what Estelle did to cause Faulkner to slap her, but he (and apparently Faulkner's biographer) see Faulkner's assault as normal, justified, and acceptable behavior. And even though Connelly can't tell us what Estelle said or did that was at all *abnormal*, he claims that Faulkner's slap instantly returns her "to completely normal conduct."[49]

As troubling as the double standard being applied and the use of self-contradictory evidence is the lack of clarification or retrospective commentary from Estelle. All we are told is that she was disturbed by the increasingly manic tone of Faulkner's letters home to her during the five weeks they were separated and that "it sounded as though he was headed for another collapse."[50] What was the state of Estelle and Faulkner's marriage that fall? The only surviving evidence is Faulkner's few existing letters from those months published in his *Selected Letters*. No letters at all from Estelle survive. In editing Faulkner's for publication, all his loving remarks to Estelle were deleted. I include them here because they enrich our understanding of the Faulkners' passionate, playful, complex, and often tense relationship.

Faulkner left for the Southern Writers' Conference just nine months after Alabama's birth and death. From the Monticello Hotel on the day of his arrival in Charlottesville, Faulkner closes his brief letter with, "I don't think that I will need to tell you to give my love to the children, any more than to tell you that you already have about 1,000,000 tons of it yourself. But I do, nevertheless. Oh well, just darling, darling, darling. [signed] Billy." Included in his letter are a snapshot of himself in his RCAF uniform and a silly poem, ostensibly for Cho-Cho and Malcolm. Its nonsensical language, however, had a private meaning for Estelle. Another deleted passage in a later letter makes clear that this nonsense, "Tinkie," in particular, is also part of the vocabulary of their sexual intimacy.[51]

> Merry Xmas morning,
> Merry Xmas tree;
> Tinkie Poochie Peachie,
> Such a happy girl was she
> That when the star was lighted
> And silver shine was made,
> Tinkie Peachie Poochie
> Put the shining in the shade.[52]

The snapshot of himself in his RCAF uniform, his first imposture as the soldier with the metal plate in his head who often drank himself into oblivion to dull his war wounds, gave a hint about his state of mind. David Minter puts it well: "The chief accomplishment of the conference in Charlottesville was to establish Faulkner's public reputation as a drinker."[53] Sherwood Anderson had also been invited. Writing to friends, he described the scene: "Bill Faulkner had arrived and got drunk. From time to time he appeared, got drunk again immediately, and disappeared. He kept asking everyone for drinks. If they didn't give him any, he drank his own."[54]

In New York Faulkner cemented this reputation, which did nothing to deter various publishers like Bennett Cerf and Alfred Knopf from pursuing him. Hollywood agents were also wooing Faulkner. Nor, according to his letters to Estelle, did his binging slow down his writing. And it would not for another ten years. On 4 November he wrote her that one agent had assured him that he could earn $500 to $750 a week writing film scripts in Hollywood and asking whether she'd like to go: "I think the trip would do you a lot of good. We could live like counts at least on that, and you could dance, and go about." He added that he had already made $300 since arriving in New York and wanted to stay another month because "I believe I can make 1000.00 more." He enclosed a large check for her to deposit and draw on and said he was "mailing checks for all the old bills" so that she "could just tear up the ones you received on the 1st addressed to me." He also suggested that Estelle "have Cho Cho's teeth fixed now and closed with "write me about the California trip, and I love you, darling." Four days later he wrote again, saying, "I think of you all the time" (*SL*, 53). He was "writing a movie for Tallulah Bankhead" for $10,000, plus working on his novel, a theatrical production of *Sanctuary*, for which rehearsals were starting the following week, in addition to writing a short story commissioned by *Cosmopolitan* for $1500. He had "created quite a sensation." Besides luncheons "in my honor" and constant "evening parties" he "had learned with astonishment that I am now the most important figure in American letters. That is, I have the best future." He added that he was "glad I'm level-headed, not very vain. But I dont think it has gone to my head" (53–54).

Less than two weeks later, Estelle received the telegram from New York confirming her judgment about Faulkner's increasingly manic condition. On 30 November she took the train from Memphis to New York. After two more apparently horrendous weeks in New York, Estelle and Faulkner finally left for home. On the way, they spent a night in Baltimore, where they dined with Mencken. Then Estelle went to bed while Faulkner and he spent a night of "hard drinking" together.[55]

Once home, there is no more mention of either film scripts for famous actresses or a Broadway play of *Sanctuary*. *Light in August* was going well, and Faulkner seemed content and happy. To Ben at the end of January 1932 he wrote, "I cant send you LIA because none of it is typed yet. I had not intended typing at all until I finished it. It is going too well to break the thread and cast back, unless absolutely necessary. But I may strike a stale spell. Then I will type some." Although Ben had written with an offer from Metro-Goldwyn-Mayer, Faulkner demurred: "I will be better off here until this novel is finished. Maybe I can try the movies later on" (*SL*, 59). By mid-March he had sent the typed manuscript to Ben, saying that he wanted five thousand dollars for it "and no editing." Cape and Smith had met his price, but fifteen months later, Faulkner had only realized one thousand dollars of it, for his publisher had gone into receivership and then liquidation (64). Needing money, he signed a six-week contract with MGM for five hundred dollars a week, to begin work on 7 May.

By 2 June, Faulkner was writing Estelle from the MGM studio lot in Hollywood and sending her household money: "Sweetheart—Here is $100.00. . . . Write me if you need more. Otherwise I will go ahead applying it [the rest of his salary] on debts." In the omitted paragraphs he writes of his love for her: "I have just found your letter on my desk. I came in so steamed up to write you that I never noticed it until this minute, right in the middle, your letter. Isn't that coincidence? Perhaps I knew . . . when I left my room that your letter would be here." He closes with "I love you and am homesick as the devil. I think it is because I want to sleep with you, in our bed and our room. That must be it. [signed] Billy."[56]

Faulkner stayed until the first week in August, when his father died of a heart attack; he returned to Oxford to take on responsibilities for his immediate and extended family. To Ben he wrote bluntly, probably in late September, that his father had left Maud "solvent" for about a year. "Then its me." At home he read and returned the galleys for his seventh novel, *Light in August*. Despite the fall interruption, he had completed one of the century's best novels in less than eight months. In this same letter, his satisfaction with it and at being home again is evident: "I was too busy and too mad all the time I was in Hollywood to write to you. Now I am home again, eating watermelon on the back porch and watching it rain. I just finished reading the galley of LIGHT IN AUGUST. I don't see anything wrong with it. I want it to stand as it is."[57] On 6 October it was published and Faulkner returned briefly to Hollywood to fulfill his contract with MGM and in high hopes that Paramount would buy the film rights to *Sanctuary*, the book that Murry, in one of his last rebukes to his oldest son, had tried to have banned in Oxford. Once he had signed with Paramount for six thousand dollars, he headed back to Oxford. Estelle was pregnant again and he was anxious to be home.

26

Faulkner's Suppressed Tributes to Estelle, 1933–1935

> It was not the talking alone which did it, . . . but the happy marriage of speaking and hearing.
> —*Absalom, Absalom!*

THIS TIME Estelle carried their child to term. Jill was born on 24 June 1933. Her father was immensely happy and gratified. These feelings would be the immediate impetus in what for him was an extraordinarily self-revealing piece of work, his introduction to *The Sound and the Fury*.[1] Within three days of Jill's birth he wrote Ben Wasson, "Well, bud, we've got us a gal baby named Jill. Born Saturday and both well" (*SL*, 71). He was ready "to start right away" on the introduction for a commissioned special edition of *The Sound and the Fury* in which he would use different color inks to signal various time shifts.[2] By mid-August he sent Ben the introduction that he would denounce thirteen years later and beg his publisher to return. Why?

Estelle as Mask for the Black Maternal: *The Sound and the Fury*, Its Introduction, and "Dr. Wohlenski"

"When I was little there was a picture in one of our books, a dark place into which a single weak ray of light came slanting upon two faces lifted out of the shadow. *You know what I'd do if I were King?* she never was a queen or a fairy she was always a king or a giant or a general *I'd break that place open and drag them out and I'd whip them good* It was torn out, jagged out. I was glad" (*TSAF*, 109). Caddy Compson, the passionate center of his first great novel, never speaks to us directly. We are not allowed inside her head. The only way we ever hear her speak is through the minds of her three brothers. For each, her speech, her smell, her feel, her taste, the sight of her slight, lovely, literally and figuratively blackened body, almost constantly in motion, is the erotic core of their being. Fantasies of her dominate their waking lives. Her image rules their dreams. Her fierce courage, her constant violations of authority, her humor and compassion, her sheer sexual energy simultaneously excites and repulses them.

Here, Quentin's memory and fantasy—Caddy's Kingship, her punishing of those whom he imagines as the Compson children's terrible parents—make him glad. This is an aberration. Only in his secret world of make-believe can he revel in her courage. In real life he condemns it. Seven pages into his monologue Quentin observes that to call someone black is a behavioral definition: "that a nigger is not a person so much as a form of behavior" (*TSAF,* 55). From childhood, the Compson children have been taught by their black and white caretakers alike that because Caddy refuses their authority, because she refuses to be shamed by her body, because she is curious and honest, she is "doomed." Her behavior makes her family and culture try to define and confine Caddy as black and therefore powerless. Yet, her voice, always resisting, even in defeat, and her actions, always in opposition, drive them crazy. It speaks its fantasies (claiming Kingship and its attendant powers) or insists on the realities that everyone else in her family is intent on hiding—her grandmother's death, her uncle's dalliances, her mother's cruelty and hypocrisy, her youngest brother's idiocy, her own desire.

Most outrageous are her violations of Southern patriarchy: she will not act like a lady; she will not act white. She will wet her dress playing in the branch water; she will break white taboos of touch, ordering the black child Versh "to unbutton" it so she can take it off to dry; she will not be fazed by Quentin's slaps that knock her in the branch, leaving her "all wet and muddy behind" (12); she will get Versh to push her by her muddied bottom up into the forbidden pear tree. As she says when her brother threatens her, "Let him tell. I don't give a cuss" (13). And, like her literary forbearer, Elly, she will have sex out of wedlock. Unlike her, she will enjoy it (104). Try as they may, the Compson brothers cannot contain her. Quentin has absorbed his mother's values: *"Why wont you bring him to the house, Caddy? Why must you do like nigger women do in the pasture the ditches the dark woods."* But in the midst of recollecting his mother's voice, his desire takes over, concluding and cutting off his thought: *"hot hidden furious in the dark woods"* (59). She is simultaneously their reason for living and their reason for self-destruction. In essence, she is their creative force. But because each brother seeks to suppress and repress her, rather than open himself to the imaginative possibilities she offers, to "drag out" their dreadful parents and "whip them good," he is doomed.

This is *The Sound and the Fury*, a story Faulkner could tell once he realized that he had to get "outside" of Benjy, Quentin, and Jason: white boys whose fear, shame, and hatred of their desire to embrace Caddy's blackness causes their demise. His realization that he must write from both "inside" and "outside" freed him to complete this novel in 1928 and to marry Estelle Oldham in 1929 (MSS E, F, *AL*, 278). *Go Down, Moses* and "Mississippi" were Faulkner's elegies and love letters to Callie Barr; *The Sound and the Fury* and its suppressed introduction are his memorial and love letter to Estelle. Family secrets are buried in all four texts. To know Caroline Barr's influence and inspiration in Faulkner's imaginary illuminates our reading of his fiction and his other intimate lifelong relationships, particularly with his wife. By the force of her personality, her actions, and her authorial self-invention in her writing, Estelle became in Faulkner's imaginary an alternative transformation and figuration of the black maternal—a woman who looked "white" but acted and thought and imagined "black." Like Estelle's Estelle in "Dr. Wohlenski," Caddy wants no part of Southern Ladyhood. Unlike that Estelle's Aunt Carrie, Caddy is no "fairy out of a story book," no properly pedestaled, disembodied Southern Lady "without substance." Instead she would be "King," or "a giant or a general." Like Estelle, she identifies "human" with embodiment, with sexuality, and with caring and speaking for those who cannot speak for themselves.[3] Faulkner called her "my heart's darling."

The Suppressed Introduction to *The Sound and the Fury*, 1933

In mid-August 1933, when the Faulkners had been married for a little over four years and their daughter Jill was nearly two months old, Faulkner elaborated on and revealed the depth of his imaginative identification with Caddy Compson's ferocity, courage, and creativity in what was to be an eight- to ten-page introduction to a limited edition of *The Sound and the Fury*. The last version, which he sent to Ben Wasson, had gone through at least ten drafts.[4] Faulkner's evident satisfaction with this essay and his life at this moment are apparent in his cover letter: "The enclosed explains itself. I have worked on it a good deal, like on a poem almost, and I think it is all right now. We are fine. Jill is getting fatter and fatter. Estelle has never been so well" (*SL*, 74).

The edition was never published and his introduction lay in the Random House files until mid-May of 1946 when, contemplating a Modern Library edition containing both *The Sound and the Fury* and *As I Lay Dying*, Robert Linscott returned his essay with a request that he revise it to introduce this new project. Faulkner wrote back: "Bless you for finding the introduction and sending it back to me. Random House paid me for it and I remembered writing one, but *I had forgotten what smug false sentimental windy shit it was. I will return the money for it, I would be willing to return double the amount for the chance of getting it out of danger and destroyed"* (*SL*, 235, my italics).

Why did Faulkner suppress this essay, one in which he originally took pride? Why was his concern so great that he even offered to buy it back? What "danger" did it pose? And finally, if it was so dangerous, why, once it *was* returned to him, did he carefully keep it with its nine other drafts instead of destroying it? It has been argued that Faulkner withdrew the essay because it reveals that for him Caddy "fills the role of substitute mother for the three brothers" and that "their responses toward her may, in fact, represent three aspects of Faulkner's complex feelings for the mother or mother figure." The essay was thus "an extraordinary confession of Faulkner's own obsession with the woman whose body was once connected to his." This reading also assumes that Faulkner's mother or mother figure is only his biological mother, Maud. Furthermore, this explanation seems dubious because similar material appears in his most psychologically transparent writing, the early poetry (see, e.g., *The Marionettes*, 1920) and throughout his fiction, including *The Sound and the Fury*. This suggests that, on the contrary, Faulkner felt no need to censor this aspect of his material.[5] What we now know about the history and dynamics of Faulkner's lifelong relationships with both his white and black mothers, and with Estelle, especially their centrality to Faulkner's emotional and imaginative life, suggests a somewhat different interpretation.

What *was* in the introduction and its drafts were other, much more private feelings. It's likely that he suppressed but did not destroy this essay and its drafts because he realized, perhaps not when he wrote it but certainly on rereading it from the distance of thirteen years, that in explaining the genesis of *The Sound and the Fury*, he had revealed too much about his collaborative relationship with Estelle. In revealing the personal meaning (as he does in the various drafts of this essay) of the novel's core or organizing fantasy, he acknowledged her imagination's role in giving him access to the long-buried memories and emotions from which he created not only *Soldiers' Pay* but, most important, *The Sound and the Fury*—her role in giving him himself.

Faulkner's intense need to publicly denigrate and suppress this introduction and his fear of it—he characterizes its circulation as "dangerous" and calls it "shit"—yet his failure to destroy either the returned manuscript or its earlier drafts suggests that the material was dangerous precisely *because* Faulkner valued it. Faulkner confirms this in his original covering letter to his editor, where he gave it the understated praise he characteristically reserved for his own and other writers' best work. Its value lay in its private meaning, which he feared he had revealed.

Faulkner's introduction to *The Sound and the Fury* has two subjects; first, how he learned to be an artist by subjecting the initiating image for this novel, what he calls "the dream," to a fierce and courageous scrutiny and, second, how that dream of Caddy inscribes what he most loved, hated, and feared about Estelle, that is, the conflicting desires at work in his relationship with her. He claims he discovered this vein of creativity as he began to let himself imagine Caddy and her world—to literally see her—as in a dream or vision.[6]

It is the origins of Faulkner's initial dream image for his breakthrough novel that I want to speculate about here. The image is familiar to all Faulkner readers, since he always claimed in interviews that it was *The Sound and the Fury*'s imaginative beginning: "the only thing in literature that will ever move me very much: Caddy climbing the pear tree to look in the window at the grandmother's funeral while Quentin and Jason and Benjy [look up at the muddy seat of her drawers] and the niger [*sic*] children looking up at the muddy seat of her drawers."[7] Like his book, this is a portrait of tense ambivalence: a dirty little girl performing multiple forbidden acts yet caught in a male gaze whose intent is to expose, humiliate, and punish her. Where did this, his most precious "dream," ever come from?

Following Faulkner's lead here we might think about this image that spilled out of his unconscious as a fantasy or daydream. Having "closed the door" on his critical voices and "with no plan at all in mind," he began writing the novel that became *The Sound and the Fury*.[8] At first he wrote about a brother and sister playing in a stream or branch, not an anecdote but "a picture" that was so explicit it could be "caught without dialogue by a camera," something he would actually do two years later.[9] Faulkner makes clear here that the only language is visual. Like a startling dream image, drawing, or photograph, it is vivid and jolting, yet wordless. Initially, then, we are in the realm of the presymbolic.

Like the day residues present in a dream, the origins of this highly condensed, silent image lay in a series of real feelings, images, and events. Among these was Faulkner's lifelong relationship with Estelle, whom many in Oxford and Kosciusko thought of as akin to Caddy. But also there was an explicit visual and speaking image, Estelle's imaginative rendering of her childhood self in "Dr. Wohlenski," her fictional representation of herself as the outspoken six-year-old. Perched in an old crab apple, her tree house on the color line separating her white and black families, she, too, gains access to forbidden knowledge. She, too, expresses desire, defying gender and color lines. For her disobedience, specifically for challenging the fixity of gender and color, she, too, is physically attacked and humiliated by her male peers.

As Faulkner describes his creative process in the various drafts of his introduction, it becomes clear that he has first appropriated and then transformed Estelle's imaginary self into a little girl and her brothers and the black people who acted as their mothers in order to mirror his own wishes, fears, and desires. His story's origins are alluded to and acknowledged in two analogies he makes between sexual desire and his creative process. They appear in the draft that follows his first mention of the content of that wordless, camera-quality image from his creative unconscious that gave him *The Sound and the Fury.*

Faulkner's next immediate associations lead him to acknowledge the image's most intimate source (see MSS C, D, *AL,* 274–75). "I wrote this book and learned to read. I had learned a little about writing from Soldiers Pay [*sic*]—how to approach language words: . . . with a kind of alert respect, as you approach dynamite; even with joy, as you approach [unpredictable] women; perhaps even with the same secretly unscrupulous intention."[10] What Faulkner may have felt as his secretly unscrupulous intention here was the joy he took in Estelle's dynamite, the gifts she proffered of her imagination (her stories) and now, at last, her sexual self. The latter is made explicit later on in the same paragraph. Here he equates his anticipation of making love to his actual writing of *The Sound and the Fury.* While writing he felt "that emotion definite and physical and yet nebulous to describe: that ecstasy, that eager and joyous faith and anticipation of surprise which the yet unmarred sheets under my hand held inviolate and unfailing." Although he deleted his first association in all later drafts, he retained the second in the version he sent his publisher in August 1933.

In later typescript drafts, including the version he sent to his publisher, Faulkner further asserts the essay's and the novel's autobiographical components, claiming that art is "a very personal thing" because for the artist "it is himself that he is writing about." Identifying with Caddy, he characterizes his creative process with the same language he has used to describe Caddy as she tries to assert her selfhood: "the single furious breathing (or writing) span." He adds that "we more than other men unconsciously write ourselves into ever [*sic*] line and phrase." He writes with "rage" and his writing is "a savage indictment" (TS H, *AL,* 279; *TSAF,* 229). He then illustrates by describing the process of writing himself into and out of *The Sound and the Fury.* Part of that process was writing himself into and out of Estelle's imagination. "Now I can make myself a vase. . . . And so I made myself a beautiful and tragic little girl."[11]

Until he wrote the novel's fourth section, "I was inside the book: I was

Quentin and Jason and Benjy and Dilsey and T.P., learning each day what I could do, doing each day things that I had not imagined even, with joy and peaceful eagerness and surprise" (MSS E and F, *AL*, 278). But most of all, like Caddy's brothers, he was inside Caddy (Estelle). In his next draft, Faulkner further clarifies his identification with and reasons for analyzing and thus separating or distancing himself from his initial fantasies: "So I wrote Quentin's and Jason's sections, trying to clarify Benjy's. But even then I knew I was merely compromising, temporizing; that I was still being each of them in turn; hence the story was not clear yet. (I was thinking now in terms of print, readers) I saw that I should have to get completely out of the book. I realized that there would be compensations, that in a sense I could give a final turn to the screw and extract some ultimate distillation. Yet it took me better than a month to decide to take pen and write *The day dawned bleak and chill* before I did so. I am not sorry now" (TS H, *AL*, 282). Being inside the vase, inside all his characters, but especially being inside the fierce little girl he first fantasized in that germinal dream image (MS E, *AL*, 277), one that, like many vivid dream images, had no language, gave him access to the material that transformed this initial silent image, his private fantasy, into a work of art that spoke to others.

In shifting from his initial fantasy of being inside his vase, that is, identifying and often merging with his characters, learning from being inside to begin to speak the meaning of that fantasy, to a more distanced identification of being on the outside, "giving myself a fourth section in which to talk some myself," Faulkner speaks of the "compensation." It costs a great deal to give up the oceanic bliss of total identification, of being held inside the vase or vessel that was Estelle. But unless he separates, he cannot complete his novel. Here again, to emphasize the importance of making this move, he invokes James—"the final turn of the screw"—a literary father. Metaphorically, in describing his own creative process, he moves fluidly between feminine and masculine sites of erotic pleasure and (re)production. Nonetheless, he writes, it took him more than a month to make this decision, to leave his vase: Here the pleasures of remaining inside are further clarified by a simultaneous reading of the holograph and typescript versions of this section:

> I suppose I knew at the time that I could not live forever inside [th] my [Rom] [Gre] Tyrrhenian vase, that perhaps to have it so I could lie in bed and look at it and touch it now and then would be better. . . . Much better the muddy bottom of a little doomed girl climbing a tree in April, to look in a window at the funeral. (MS F, *AL*, 278; see also MSS B, C, D, E, *AL*, 272–78)

In the later draft Faulkner writes,

> Well, I had made my vase, but I suppose I knew all the time that I could not live forever inside of it; that perhaps to have it so that I too could lie in bed and look at it would be better. (TS H, *AL*, 282)

Why "better" remains the same and equally ambiguous in both versions:

> Its fine to think you will leave something behind you when you die, but it's [much] better to have made something you can die with. Much better the muddy bottom of a little doomed girl climbing a blooming pear tree in April to look in the window at the funeral. (282)

The difference, as I read it, is the difference between a private fantasy—being Caddy-Estelle inside the vase—and creating a work of art.

Radiating from his introduction as it does from the novel itself and from every public comment he ever made about *The Sound and the Fury* is this image: "the only thing in literature that would ever move me very much: Caddy climbing the pear tree to look in the window at her grandmother's funeral while Quentin and Jason and Benjy and the negroes looked up at the muddy seat of her drawers."[12] The image is explicitly oppositional; in it Caddy is not an ice queen or a fairy. Rather she is a King. She is also a six- or seven-year-old Southern girl defying gender categories and sexual and racial taboos. Like Estelle's fictional self in "Dr. Wohlenski," Faulkner's Caddy will look at and embody what has been forbidden and reveal what is supposed to be concealed. As such, her initial actions in his novel lay down the first of many challenges to her brothers, her parents, and the black people who work for the Compsons about what she can see (know), do, and show. Also present in this introduction, yet absent from his much later public statements about the novel, is Faulkner's identification with and internalization of Caddy. Read along with Estelle's story of herself as a child, it suggests the cornucopia of autobiographical secrets Caddy held for Faulkner. He identifies Caddy's fierceness, her courage, her violence with the emotions he felt as he invented her. Faulkner's Jamesian "impression" of Caddy is endowed with the same emotions he associates with being an artist. His cameralike "picture," as he carefully called it and which he will later photograph, resonates uncannily with Estelle's fictional image of her six-year-old self in "Dr. Wohlenski." At bottom Caddy is Estelle.

Freud explains that the artist "possesses the mysterious ability to mold his particular material until it expresses the ideas of his fantasy faithfully; and then he knows how to attach to this reflection of his fantasy-life *so strong a stream of pleasure that, for a time at least, the repressions are outbalanced and dispelled by it*."[13] This is how Faulkner describes his state of mind when writing *The*

Sound and the Fury. Identifying Caddy as the driving force of his creative energy, he writes that "when she quit the water fight and stooped in her wet garments above him [Benjy], the entire story, which is all told by that same little brother in the first section, seemed to explode on the paper before me." He explains that for Quentin and for the "idiot" brother Benjy, "all knowing must begin and end with that fierce, panting, paused and stooping wet figure which smelled like trees." Writing *The Sound and the Fury* "taught me both how to write and how to read, and even more: It taught me what I had already read, because on completing it I discovered, in *a series of repercussions like summer thunder,* the Flauberts and Conrads and Turgenievs which as much as ten years before I had consumed whole and without assimilating at all, as a moth or a goat might" (*TSAF,* TS J, 230, 231, my italics).

In another draft Faulkner puts it even more forcefully. Claiming that Benjy

> knew that she would stop what she was doing to comfort him, that she was *courageous* enough to quit the water fight to do so, and sure enough she did. When she did so, the entire story, which is all told by Benjy in the first section, seemed to *explode* all about me. I saw in a *flash and a glare* what they both knew: that she would always quit water fights to comfort him; only I saw more than they knew, than Caddy could know then and that Benjy would ever know since to him all knowing must begin and end with that *fierce, hotbreathing, paused and stooping* ["wet" is typed above] *figure* that smelled like trees. (TS H, *AL,* 280, my italics)

Conveying the tremendous erotic force of the explosion triggered by his initial image of Caddy, he continues:

> That was all clear yet momentary, like something seen in a lightning flash; there was no time to assimilate it and understand it clearly; it was going to [*sic*] fast then; I was [driving a runaway team] riding a horse which had bolted beneath me. They had been sent to the pasture to play to get them away from the house during the grandmother's funeral in order that the three brothers and the nigger children could look up at the muddy seat of Caddy's drawers (again hers was the courage, the courage which could face with honor the shame which she was later to engender, which Quentin and Jason could not face . . .) as she climbed the tree to look in the window at the funeral. And I had gone beyond that scene before I realized the symbology of the soiled drawers. I had already gone on to night and the bedroom and Dilsey—. . . already trying to cleanse with the sorry byblow of its soiling that body, flesh, whose shame they prophesied   —with the mudstained [*sic*] drawers scrubbing the naked behind of that doomed

and courageous and tragic little girl. The story was complete, finished. (TS H, *AL*, 281)

Note that in this scene Dilsey's role is similar to the one Nolia plays in "Dr. Wohlenski." Here Faulkner seems to be saying that when he accepted Caddy-Estelle both for herself and as part of himself, he became an artist. The experience Faulkner describes here is the point at which he finally acknowledged and accepted that his need and desire for Estelle was grounded in just those qualities he gives to Caddy—her courage, her compassion, her deeply disturbing sexuality, and her sense of honor, which give her the strength to ignore hypocritical conventions. That is, he loves her not in spite of what he figures as her blackness but *because* of it. She is indeed his vase, his vessel, and his closet. Only in and through her can he safely and secretly embrace the black maternal. Although he publicly disavows his introduction as "a piece of shit," privately he clings to it. Even though it's "dangerous," he cannot throw it away. His essay tacitly acknowledges that their emotional and intellectual relationship, difficult as it might be, is essential to his creativity. That also was why it was so dangerous.

However, the story Faulkner writes is about what happens to three brothers who fail to acknowledge this, who fail to listen to Caddy, who try to shut her up. As he explains in his introduction, Caddy's "was the courage which was to face later with honor the shame which she was to engender, which Quentin and Jason could not face: the one taking refuge in suicide, the other in vindictive rage." Like his brothers, but for different reasons, Benjy also remains inside the vase of his fantasies. He is not capable of understanding or judgment. His mind can "never grow up to where the grief of bereavement could be leavened with understanding and hence the alleviation of rage as in the case of Jason, and of oblivion as in the case of Quentin." In this sense Benjy's understanding of Caddy's meaning for him comes closest to Faulkner's initial dream image. For Benjy lives in a perpetual dream state, "in time yet not of it save that he could nightly carry with him that fierce, courageous being who was to him but a touch and a sound that may be heard on any golf links and a smell like trees, into the slow bright shapes of sleep."[14]

In February 1927 Faulkner had begun writing in a white heat that would continue for the next nine years. I suggest that part of what freed him to invent the imaginary world of Yoknapatawpha was his decision to marry Estelle.[15] Thus when, in his suppressed introduction, he describes the "ecstasy" of writing *The Sound and the Fury*, he's alluding as well to an equally fulfilling personal and relational ecstasy he was experiencing.[16] As long as he could make his remarks about creating *The Sound and the Fury* sound like a love letter to Caddy—which he did in all public statements about the novel—the material remained innocuous. The "danger" of the written versions was that they revealed the real subject of his love letter. It was a debt and a love he never publicly acknowledged. Still, he could not let it rest.

In the summer of 1934 or 1935, he would reinscribe his debt in that visual medium whose tricky language he had first learned from his artist grandmother. Armed with the Leica he had bought recently through the studio for the bargain price of seventy-five dollars, he made a stunningly uncanny and beautiful series of photographs of "Jill baby" as little Caddy Compson. Along with his early screen memory, Caddy had now become and remained the image at the heart of his maternal imaginary. As such she also symbolized the inspiration—the explosion, the flash, and the glare that continued to emanate from his and Estelle's long collaboration. What better way to celebrate and rededicate it than to "write" it on the innocent baby body of their only child?

Faulkner's Photographic Homage to the Women Behind His Maternal Imaginary, 1934–1935

The series of five photographs Faulkner took of Jill in 1934 or 1935, when she was about two, records his continuing fascination with his initial dream of Caddy. He never enlarged or framed these photographs, but he kept them—as contact prints for his private use (viewing?). As with his dangerous essay on *The Sound and the Fury*, their privateness is what makes them important. So besides the obvious parallel with Caddy and Quentin, he must have seen something more in them. I suggest that what he saw was her nascent and always racialized sexuality, so crucial to his creative process and so emblematic of his relationship with Estelle (fig. 26.1).[17] His camera images of Caddy held in and on her body the quintessence of Faulkner's maternal imaginary. Playing in the woods with his daughter and stepson on a summer's day, perhaps shortly after his return from Hollywood with his new camera, Faulkner began to photograph.[18] What he caught on film was a liminal, primal world of Jill's and Malcolm's watery, muddy encounter in the branch that ran through the woods surrounding Rowan Oak. Although Malcolm is ten years older and twice as tall, Jill dominates each photograph; her half brother seems to serve as Faulkner's second pair of eyes. What strikes one as immediately odd about the sequence is that in all the frames Jill's face is obscured or partially obscured, leaving the camera's eye free to gaze only on her body: she is symbol, specifically and as Faulkner wrote in his 1933 suppressed introduction to the novel, "the symbology of

26.1. Faulkner's proof sheet of his sequence of five 35-mm images of his daughter, Jill, as Caddy Compson, c. 1935. "Then I looked back at *The Sound and the Fury* and discovered for the first time . . . that the action, the desires of the people all came to one single head . . . in a picture [so explicable] that it could be acted by lay figures and caught without dialogue by a camera" (MS B, *AL*, 273).
(Courtesy of Jill Faulkner Summers)

the soiled drawers." His daughter's reality-actuality, her identity as his and Estelle's joint creation is equally crucial, but not herself, not Jill. Here she also symbolizes Estelle and Faulkner's other collaboration and its offspring: the novelist's fictional voice.

In these beautifully composed photographs of a feisty baby girl with a soiled behind Faulkner reimagines and portrays a visual rendering of that collaboration, which led to the birthing of *The Sound and the Fury*. Rewriting the private and secret narrative of his collaborative creative process on these half siblings' bodies, he photographs the moment of his novel's conception; that instant when he saw Caddy stooping above her brother and *The Sound and the Fury* "seemed to explode on the paper" before him. The liminal space and fluidity of this moment; the running branch water—the oozy mud, the contrast of light and dark and shadow—and the camera eye's constant probing of what is not seen or meant to be seen, creates an atmosphere as magical and potent as his 1953 word portrait of Callie Barr teaching the seven-year-old Jill how to piece a quilt that disappears when Callie dies. Here Faulkner composes a world or field of dreams and secret confessions, a primal moment where the photographer's unconscious drives are enacted through and on the bodies of the two children. As his camera moves in closer and closer, he creates a cinematic unfolding through a montage of temporally connected shots. But the ruptures breaking those filmed moments, like similar scenes in *The Sound and the Fury*, also brim with what cannot (should not?) be spoken or seen.

Jill's face being either obscured or in shadow suggests both her symbolic status and the primal dreamlike quality of the unconscious drives being enacted by the camera eye. In contrast, Malcolm's face or expression, in constant dialogue with and mirroring the fantasies and desires of that eye, is registered in three of the four frames in which he appears.

In the first frame, an older crouching boy looks at a small, just-walking girl whose very facelessness transforms her from individual to symbol (fig. 26.2). This frame also sets up the power structure of the visual field: the gaze belongs to the boy and the camera eye. In this dream field, only the boy-brother is doing the looking. His face in profile, revealing just his cheek, suggests that he is grinning at something about the little girl that is directly in his line of vision: not her face but the mystery of what lies below. Her pale-colored diaphanous sunsuit clings to her body suggesting that she has just emerged from the shadow-dappled water. Like a wood nymph— "Caddy smelled of trees"—she picks her way, prancing delicately along the dark woodsy bank as her half brother, kneeling in the muddy stream, watches. Her head is bent, her eyes cast down. A lock of hair further obscures her already shadowed face. Her very facelessness emphasizes her

26.2. First frame: "So I . . . set out to make for myself a beautiful and
tragic little girl" (TS H, *AL*, 280).
(Courtesy of Jill Faulkner Summers)

dreamlike aura and the liminal quality of this wet, wild space. Jill's skimpy
sunsuit tugs at her crotch, making a series of creases that catch the light
and shadow, highlighting and seeming to enlarge her pubic area. Creating
in this visual and wordless medium, Faulkner much more explicitly eroti-
cizes the little girl. The boy's gaze and the camera's are trained on her
highlighted, wet, shadow-stained baby-sex. As in *The Sound and the Fury* and
its antecedent, Estelle's "Dr. Wohlenski," what is seen is not meant to be
seen: the soiled baby girl as erotic object of the male gaze. What more perfect symbol of Caddy's ultimate silencing and Faulkner and Estelle's silenced collaboration than these photographs of the Faulkners' not-yet-talk-
ing daughter?

As in the novel, there are also narrative ambiguities. Jill, like the fictional Caddy, seems oblivious to her half brother's mocking gaze or to the
shame and ridicule it confers. Furthermore, her barefoot stride on sturdy
little legs, like her stance in the second, third, and fourth frames, is assertive, almost Amazonian. If she could talk, one can imagine her saying, like
Caddy to her brother: "Let them tell: I don't give a cuss" (*TSAF*, 13).

Faulkner's narrative of male collusion continues in the second frame.
Here Malcolm, still kneeling and therefore still below Jill, grins directly at
the camera, while she is caught with her back to it, her muddied bottom in
full view (fig. 26.3). Foregrounded but still faceless, she's the object of her

26.3. Second frame: "We watched the muddy bottom of her drawers" (*TSAF*, 25). (Courtesy of Jill Faulkner Summers)

half brother's knowing grin. In the rupture between the first and second frame, the dark sash around her waist that we first saw in frontal view appears to be a harness that is knotted at the small of her back and then tied between her legs. Perhaps the sash was there for safety, its purpose being to be able to quickly lift Jill from the water if she fell. But in this photograph, where it looks like a harness, it seems ominous (almost pornographic?): the harness trusses and cuts her little behind in two and further draws attention to its soiling—a dark mud-stain smeared across her left buttock. Meanwhile, Malcolm and the man behind the camera eye are there and still sharing a joke that excludes Jill. The boy grins somewhat tentatively at his stepfather, at something taking place behind Jill's back. Like Caddy's brothers, he has been "look[ing] up at the muddy seat of her drawers" (TS J, *TSAF*, 230). With his camera, Faulkner is reimagining the moment when Caddy's brothers (all of whom Faulkner's introduction claimed were originally him) fasten their eyes on Caddy's blackened bottom, the symbol of her "dishonor and shame." Rewritten on Jill here is Faulkner's "symbology of the soiled drawers" (230). How did she get muddy? In that rupture between the first and second frame, did she slip and fall? Had she fallen before her father began filming? Surely her half brother didn't push her, as Quentin pushed Caddy into the muddy branch. Did Faulkner, as orchestrator of this optic field, arrange her muddied bottom or was it just chance?

26.4. Third frame: "My boy cousins tore down my tree-house and scattered my precious dolls all over the ground. They even sat the biggest ones in the servants' privy like the dolls were real people" ("Dr. Wohlenski," 23). (Courtesy of Jill Faulkner Summers)

The third frame partially reveals Jill's face for the first and only time (fig. 26.4). She stands ramrod straight and ankle-deep in the running water of the branch. Her shadowed gaze is downcast, as she looks intently at something that Malcolm, still kneeling and almost out of the frame, is holding or playing with between his legs. Her navel is visible through the now soaking-wet cloth of her sunsuit. Ambiguity floods the frame. At this camera angle, her sash looks quite jaunty. One tip of it sticks out behind her like a small holster gun or a phallus. Here she's at once a little swashbuckler and a speechless baby girl who is confined by the gaze of her father and brother. Because most of Malcolm is cut off by the frame, we, unlike Jill, cannot see what Jill sees. Again, in this shot its subject gazes on something hidden. Again there's ambiguity for the subject and object of the gaze have been reversed. Now Jill, standing and looking, looms over the much larger boy. Her attention is drawn to something the camera occludes from our sight. Like Caddy in her pear tree or "Estelle" in her crab apple, her vantage point gives her access to forbidden knowledge. Is it, in a photographic

26.5. Fourth frame: "Caddy was all wet and muddy behind. . . . Caddy smelled like trees in the rain" (*TSAF,* 12). (Courtesy of Jill Faulkner Summers)

slip, an unconscious reversal of the first frame, what *she* imagines might be between his legs? Another teasing shot of a little girl looking at something not meant to be seen. As if to recall the consequences of such looking and also to link it with Caddy's imaginative beginnings, on the ground behind Jill and to the left lies a muddied, naked baby doll. Perhaps it reminded Faulkner of Estelle's contributions to his imaginative breakthrough, those other muddied dolls in her story that lay behind his mind's "picture" that inspired Caddy. Sunlight also highlights Jill's doll in the final frame of Faulkner's sequence.

We are familiar with Faulkner's syntactic acrobatics. His stylistics of repetition with a difference is essential to his narrative strategies, which mime the logic of dream and the unconscious. The fourth frame captures such a moment, reversing the first to suggest that throughout the sequence the camera eye is tracking Jill as she walks back and forth in Malcolm's gaze (fig. 26.5). Such repetition calls attention to the boy as an auxiliary eye and an extension of the father and the patriarchal codes of gender carried by that eye. Yet the fluid, labile quality of those gender codes in this liminal, primal dream space is also very much a part of each frame's composition. In the first shot we saw a frontal view of Jill prancing toward Malcolm. Now that composition is repeated in reverse as a foregrounded rear-view shot of Jill. This time she nearly fills the frame, suddenly appearing much larger than her brother. The camera eye catches her as she moves toward him. Looking at her and the camera, Malcolm kneels in the water, buried up to his wrists in the muddy ooze of the bank where he has been digging. In this fourth frame his lower face is in shadow, obscuring his mouth, but the baleful expression in his eyes suggests a kind of wariness; he is no longer smiling. Another rupture. What has angered or upset him? Attentive readers may be reminded of the adolescent Quentin "plunging" in the mud that substitutes for his wish to "plunge" into a hyperracialized and eroticized dark, wet, oozy feminine, that image that Faulkner wrote as Caddy and now photographs on his baby daughter. In the barn scene of *The Sound and the Fury*, where he "dances" with "dirty Natalie" and then, furious and ashamed by his desire, jumps "hard as I could into the hogwallow the mud . . . up to my waist stinking I kept on plunging until I fell down and rolled over in it." He then tells Caddy, "I was hugging her that's what I was doing. She turned her back I went around in front of her. I was hugging her I tell you." Caddy's assertive and indifferent response—"I don't give a damn what you were doing"—further infuriates Quentin. He grabs her and, as he had when she asserted her will at seven, smears mud on her "wet hard turning body" as she tries to fight him off (*TSAF*, 86, 87).

This frame catches Jill mid-stride, still the little swashbuckler or baby Amazon, her arms gracefully outstretched for balance, her firm little legs straddling the watery branch below. Sunlight beams on her gold hair; sun highlights her plump, capable little shoulders and the tips of her bare feet and toes. Her sash looks even more like a small sword or pistol. Dangling at her backside, it could be a weapon that is concealed from Malcolm but revealed to us by the camera eye. Yet below Jill's insignias of power and undercutting them lies the ocular proof of her "dishonor" and "shame," her now completely mud-smeared bottom. Thus Faulkner captures in this shot his beloved novel's ambiguity and ambivalence—"The story is all there." On the one hand his baby daughter's stance asserts that her body has a right to that space: like the child, Caddy, she is the courageous one. On the other, the camera and Malcolm still own the gaze, simultaneously eroticizing and shaming as they train it on the baby girl's wet pubic area and the "muddy seat of [her] drawers" (TS J, *TSAF*, 231, 230). Faulkner maintains this visual triangle in his sequence's first, second, and fourth shots. His montage uncannily re-creates the racialized, gendered power relationships

26.6. Fifth frame: "All
knowing must begin and end
with that fierce hotbreathing,
paused and stooping wet
figure that smelled like trees"
(TS H, *AL*, 280).
(Courtesy of Jill Faulkner
Summers)

he initially imagined and played out in the spring of 1928 while writing the
first section of *The Sound and the Fury*. In this later photographic rewriting,
while Jill is caught between the gazes of the camera and the boy, her foregrounding, her aggressive, assertive, centered, self-contained, and utterly
unself-conscious stance in front of her self-conscious half brother is manifest. The viewer perceives both the mark of Caddy's "dishonor" and the
ambivalence and ambiguity pervading the power play between Caddy, her
brothers, and other authority figures in the scene that Faulkner, in his suppressed introduction and in all subsequent remarks, claimed was his initiating "dream" or "mental picture" for *The Sound and the Fury*.

The fifth and final frame reprises the third one, performing another
repetition with a difference in the sequence. Jill has moved back toward her
half brother and to the same pool where Faulkner filmed both children
playing in the third shot. She now stands closer to Malcolm, their bent
backs and their gazes aligned and in concert as they study the same task or
object in the muddy water by the bank (fig. 26.6). Now her foregrounded

figure nearly covers her brother's. She stands in partial profile, facing away from the camera and stooping slightly to pick up or examine something in the glinting water. Light falls on the back of her head, her back, and the upper curve of her buttocks. Her damp sunsuit clings to her bottom, revealing the beginning indent between its two curving cheeks and once more drawing attention to her mud-stained little butt. Just below, shadow extends to cover her legs, blackening her further. The skin of her lower body contrasts sharply to the paleness of Malcolm's back, which is about all we see of him in this frame. In this last shot, like Caddy, Faulkner's baby daughter stands unveiled, stooping in what his camera eye has created as an anarchic pool of desire and taboo, a world where dreams like Caddy form, as the artist dreamer gives his unconscious drives free rein.

Filmed here and expanding upon his suppressed 1933 introduction is this lovely and loving wordless narrative of his creative process. Loving because, like his introduction and like his much later essay "Mississippi," it acknowledges the collaborative nature of that process and its roots in a feminine imaginary that is a composite of Callie Barr, Maud Falkner, and Estelle Oldham.

By 1933 Faulkner had reached the height of his imaginative powers, and my story of the roles played by his relationships with these three successive generations of Mississippi women in the origins and development of his creativity is complete. With *The Sound and the Fury* his greatness had emerged and was acknowledged. His introduction to it had confirmed Estelle's primacy and her collaborative role in the growth of his artistry. With increasing difficulty, as his alcoholism took its toll, Faulkner would continue to reap the rewards of those three relationships as he probed ever more deeply and painfully into his vision with *Absalom, Absalom!* in 1936 and *Go Down, Moses* in 1942, both of which we now know are entwined with and fueled by the maternal imaginary he created out of the history, myth, memory, and reality that composed his lifelong attachments to these women.

My narrative of Faulkner, Callie, Maud, and Estelle ends here, even though he continued to write, would go on to win the Nobel Prize in 1949, and lived until 1962. But this is the story of Faulkner and three crucial relationships. It is an account of how his imagination was forged, from infancy and early childhood, in the bodies and minds and imaginations of the most important women in his life—Callie Barr, Maud Falkner, and Estelle. Faulkner's relations with these three Mississippi women within the claustrophobic, defining, and deforming prison of slavery and Jim Crow plays out in the erotics and aesthetics of his art to create the most moving, profound, and painfully sad chronicle of a legacy that still haunts this nation.

Abbreviations

FREQUENTLY CITED INDIVIDUALS

JFS   Jill Faulkner Summers
MBF   Maud Butler Falkner
SB   Sallie Falkner Burns
WF   William Faulkner

BOOKS AND COLLECTIONS OF WORK BY FAULKNER

AA   *Absalom, Absalom!* (1936). New York: Vintage, 1990.
CS   *Collected Stories of William Faulkner* (1950). New York: Vintage, 1977.
EPP   *Early Prose and Poetry.* Edited by Carvel Collins. London: Jonathan Cape, 1963.
ESPL   *Essays, Speeches, and Public Letters.* Edited by James B. Meriwether. New York: Random House, 1966.
FITD   *Flags in the Dust.* New York: Vintage, 1973.
FIU   *Faulkner in the University: Class Conferences at the University of Virginia, 1957–1958.* Edited by Frederick L. Gwynn and Joseph L. Blotner. New York: Vintage, 1965.
GDM   *Go Down, Moses* (1942). New York: Vintage International Edition, 1990.
Helen   *Helen: A Courtship* and *Mississippi Poems.* Introductory essays by Carvel Collins and Joseph Blotner. Oxford: Yoknapatawpha Press and Tulane University, 1981.
IITD   *Intruder in the Dust.* New York: Vintage, 1948.
LDB   *Faulkner: A Comprehensive Guide to the Brodsky Collection.* Vol. 2, *The Letters.* Edited by Louis Daniel Brodsky and Robert W. Hamblin. Jackson: University Press of Mississippi, 1984.
LIA   *Light in August* (1932). New York: Vintage International Edition, 1990.
LIG   *Lion in the Garden: Interviews with William Faulkner, 1926–1962.* Edited by James B. Meriwether and Michael Millgate. New York: Random House, 1968.

MOS	*Mosquitoes.* New York: Liveright, 1951.
"A Note"	"A Note on Sherwood Anderson." 1953. See *ESPL*, above.
S	*Sanctuary* (1931). New York: Vintage, 1993.
SL	*Selected Letters of William Faulkner.* Edited by Joseph Blotner. New York: Random House, 1977.
SP	*Soldiers' Pay.* New York: Boni and Liveright, 1926. Reprint, New York: Liveright, 1954.
TM	*The Marionettes: A Play in One Act.* Edited and with an introduction by Noel Polk. Charlottesville: University of Virginia Press, for the Bibliographical Society of the University of Virginia, 1978.
TMF	*The Marble Faun.* Boston: Four Seas, 1924.
TOH	*Thinking of Home: William Faulkner's Letters to His Mother and Father, 1918–1925.* Edited by James G. Watson. New York: Norton, 1992.
TSAF	*The Sound and the Fury* (1929). New York: W. W. Norton, 2d ed., 1994.
USWF	*Uncollected Stories of William Faulkner.* Edited by Joseph Blotner. New York: Random House, 1979.
VIS	*Vision in Spring* (1921). Edited by Judith L. Sensibar. Austin: University of Texas Press, 1984.
Wishing Tree	*The Wishing Tree.* New York: Random House, 1964.

OTHER FREQUENTLY CITED SOURCES

AC	Estelle Oldham Faulkner, "A Crossing." Unpublished short story.
AH	*Kosciusko-Attala History.* Kosciusko Attala Historical Society. N.p.: Walsworth Publishing, 1976–77.
AL	Philip Cohen and Doreen Fowler, "Faulkner's Introduction to *The Sound and the Fury*," *American Literature* 62:2 (June 1990): 262–83 (8 drafts designated as MS A-F or TS H-I).
ASTS	Sherwood Anderson, *A Story Teller's Story: Memoirs of Youth and Middle Age.* With a preface by Walter Rideout. New York: Penguin, 1969.
Bitterweeds	Malcolm Franklin, *Bitterweeds: Life at Rowan Oak with William Faulkner.* Irving, Tex.: Society for the Study of Traditional Culture, 1977.
Faulkner (1974)	Joseph Blotner. *Faulkner: A Biography.* Vol. 1: pp. 1–909; vol. 2: pp. 912–1846. New York: Random House, 1974.
Faulkner (1984)	Joseph Blotner. *Faulkner: A Biography.* New York: Random House, 1984.
FOM	Murry C. Falkner. *The Falkners of Mississippi.* Baton Rouge: Louisiana State University Press, 1967.
Goodspeed	*Biographical and Historical Memoirs: Southern Arkansas.* Chicago: Goodspeed Publishing, 1890.
MBB	John Faulkner. *My Brother Bill.* New York: Trident Press, 1963.
Moak	Franklin E. Moak. "The Mystery of William Faulkner's Grandfather Butler." Unpublished Manuscript.
My Days	Anne Walter Fearn, M.D. *My Days of Strength: An American Woman Doctor's Forty Years in China.* New York: Harper and Bros., 1939.
SA/GS	Ray Lewis White, ed. *Sherwood Anderson/Gertrude Stein: Correspondence and Personal Essays.* Chapel Hill: University of North Carolina Press, 1972.
SE	Sigmund Freud, *The Standard Edition of the Complete Psychological Works*

	of Sigmund Freud. 24 vols. Edited and translated by J. Strachey et al. London: Hogarth, 1953–74.
"SSS"	Estelle Oldham. "Star Spangled Banner Stuff." Edited by Judith L. Sensibar. *Prospects: An Annual of Cultural Studies* 60 (December 1997): 379–418.
WFO	James W. Webb and A. Wigfall Green, eds. *William Faulkner of Oxford.* Baton Rouge: Louisiana State University Press, 1965.
Williamson	Joel Williamson. *William Faulkner and Southern History.* New York: Oxford University Press, 1993.

REPOSITORIES

CSFA	Cornell Swinton Franklin Private Archive.
FCUM	Faulkner Collection, John Davis Williams Library, University of Mississippi, Oxford, Miss.
FCVA	William Faulkner Foundation Collection, Alderman Library, University of Virginia, Charlottesville, Va.
HRC	Harry Ransom Humanities Research Center, University of Texas at Austin.
JFSA	Jill Faulkner Summers Private Archive.
JFSA/UVA	Jill Faulkner Summers Archive, Alderman Library, University of Virginia, Charlottesville, Va.
SEMS	Blotner papers, Southeast Missouri State University, Cape Girardeau, Mo.
VJA	Victoria Johnson Private Archive.

NEWSPAPERS AND JOURNALS

Church Minutes	Minutes of the Oxford Baptist Church, 1858–80.
Democrat	*Attala Democrat.*
FJ	*The Faulkner Journal.*
Heritage	*Lafayette County Heritage.*
HSB	*Honolulu Star Bulletin.*
Ledger	*Attala Ledger.*
NCH	*The North China Herald.*
OXE	*The Oxford Eagle.*
PCA	*Pacific Commercial Advertiser.*

Notes

Book epigraph, p. vi: WF, speaking at the University of Virginia, 11 March 1957, in *FIU,* 45.

PREFACE

    1. JFS, interview with author, 18 September 1987.

    2. See Brodie, *Thomas Jefferson;* Gordon-Reed, *Thomas Jefferson;* and Smith, "Tests Link Jefferson, Slave's son."

    3. See Ellis, *The American Sphinx;* Ellis and Lander, "Founding Father"; and Gordon-Reed, "Why Jefferson Scholars Are the Last to Know."

    4. Bessie Sumners, interview with author, 19 May 1988.

GENERAL INTRODUCTION

    1. *Bitterweeds,* 109–14; JFS, interview with author, 20 August 1980.

    2. Hines, *William Faulkner,* 146.

    3. Louise Meadow, interviews with author, 25 May, 5 June, and 26 June 1986.

    4. "Seems like yesterday, Ed, Vic, and Stelle and Sallie and us, running over the streets"; (WF to MBF, 21 October 1918, *TOH,* 117–18). See also Katherine Andrews, interview with author, 10 August 1987.

    5. "Dr. Wohlenski," an unpublished short story fragment by Estelle Oldham, with holograph revisions and corrections; thirty-three typed, legal-size pages. See JFSA/UVA. For more on this story, see Chaps. 14 and 26, this vol.

    6. JFS, interview with author, 9 July 1986.

    7. Ibid.

    8. Her unpublished short story, "A Crossing," set partly in Honolulu, features a bisexual woman who has left her husband to become an internationally successful fashion designer (JFSA/UVA).

    9. JFS, interview with author, 2 November 1995.

10. WF to Alabama McLean, September 1925, in *SL*, 20.

11. For examples, see Faulkner's early short story "Moonlight" (which may have begun as one of Estelle's), *Soldiers' Pay, The Sound and the Fury,* and most important, *Sanctuary.* This theme is central to Estelle's "A Crossing," which is discussed in Chap. 20, this vol.

12. That Estelle divorced Cornell is another myth (see Chap. 25, this vol.). Regarding the Oldham-Franklin divorce, all biographies cite Joseph Blotner, who wrote that Estelle divorced Cornell (*Faulkner* [1974], 1:613). Cornell insisted on filing for divorce in both Oxford and Shanghai. See Oxford Court House Court Case Index, book 5, p. 353, no. 6144, and Shanghai Archives, where on 15 February Cornell filed the final divorce decree, which was granted on 25 February 1929 (author's photocopy of document). See also letters to Estelle cited in Chap. 25, this vol.

13. Quoted in *Faulkner* (1984), 240.

14. Oates, *William Faulkner,* 83, 84. For similar assessments, see Karl, *William Faulkner,* 354, 356–57, 376, 377, 378; Williamson writes that "Estelle—seemingly wrist-cutting, self-drowning, window-jumping Estelle, already with two children when he married her and a body threatening death if she attempted a third—was such a fragment of life itself." And, "As a Belle at Ole Miss Estelle had had her fling . . . but fell hard and fractured badly. It seemed that she could never be put together again" (250, 251–52).

15. JFS, interview with author, 2 November 1995.

16. Oates, *William Faulkner,* 84.

17. Ibid., 87.

18. For example, see WF to Robert Haas, 3 May 1940, *SL,* 122–24.

19. Meta Carpenter Wilde, interview with author, 4 March 1982; Joan Williams, interview with author, 20 June 1983.

20. Westoff, "A Faulkner Flirtation," 69–78. In *Soldiers' Pay,* Faulkner, like his fictional character Jones, quotes and paraphrases from Faulkner's own love poems "Atthis," "Eros," and "Leaving Her" (poems 17 and 25 of *A Green Bough* and poem 12 of *Helen: A Courtship,* respectively). For more on Jones as a self-parody, see Sensibar, *Origins,* especially 155–57.

21. For Faulkner's Pierrot persona, see Sensibar, *Origins;* for the Cyrano persona, see *Origins,* 250n27, 268n25.

22. JFS, interview with author, 26 February 1986.

23. Ibid., 9 July 1986.

24. Ibid., 7 November 1995.

25. Ibid., 21 February 1986.

26. Ibid., 9 July 1986.

27. *Faulkner* (1974), 1:604.

28. JFS, interview with author, 2 November 1995.

29. Ibid., 23 February 1987.

30. Ibid.

31. Estelle Faulkner, interview, *Charlottesville Daily Progress,* 26 January 1969.

32. JFS, interview with author, 23 February 1987.

33. Ibid.

34. Ibid.

35. Ironically, of the two, Estelle is the only one who ever filed for divorce. In August 1936, she and Jill had driven with Faulkner to Hollywood. Evidence suggests that when she found out that he was having an affair with Meta Wilde—the dinner party at their house where Faulkner arranged for Meta to come as Ben Wasson's "date"—she filed for divorce in Los Angeles (October). She withdrew her claim in December 1936. See legal papers in Estelle Faulkner folder, Carvel Collins files, HRC; *Faulkner* (1974), 2:1941–47; Wilde and Borsten, *A Loving Gentleman,* and Wasson, *Count No 'Count.*

36. JFS, interview with author, 23 February 1987.

PART 1: WILLIAM FAULKNER AND CAROLINE "CALLIE" BARR

Epigraph: WF's inscription on Caroline Barr's gravestone. (See Chaps. 5 and 6 for a discussion of Faulkner's naming and appropriation here.)

INTRODUCTION TO PART 1

Epigraph: WF to his nephew James M. ("Jimmy") Faulkner (May or June 1961), *SL,* 454.

1. James Rudd, interview with Pat Tingle, 12 May 1998. Rudd said that he had heard that the family came originally from Nottoway County, Virginia. But according to Faulkner's daughter, Callie Barr told her she'd come from South Carolina. Because she was freed in South Carolina, she may have considered that state as the site of her spiritual and political rebirth. Although the African slave trade was abolished in 1807, domestic slave trade continued and expanded from then until the Civil War. See McPherson, *Battle Cry of Freedom,* 38.

2. In his memoir, Faulkner's brother John repeats a ghost story Callie Barr told about the Ku Klux Klan terrorizing her family. See *MBB,* 50.

3. Jones, *Labor of Love,* 81, 80–84.

4. Sensibar, *Origins,* 52, 237n34.

5. Faulkner's family and friends called him Willie until about 1912, when he became Billy or Bill. In 1918 Faulkner changed the spelling of his last name from Falkner to Faulkner.

6. *MBB,* 49.

7. Morrison, "Faulkner and Women," 296, 297.

CHAPTER 1: CAROLINE BARR IN BLACK AND WHITE VOICES

1. Besides legalizing separate and unequal, this ruling also effectively denied "the existences of mixed race people" and naturalized the notion of race. See Hale, *Making Whiteness,* 23.

2. In 2002 James Rudd owned eighty acres of land between Batesville and Sardis; James Rudd, interview with author, 13 March 2002.

3. Notices in the social columns of the *Oxford Eagle* for 1902 make clear that Lelia had gone to New Albany and then Ripley to assist with the births of her daughter's first two children, in 1897 and 1899, and made a permanent move to Ripley in June

1901 (*Faulkner* [1984], 7–8). Maud's third pregnancy in four years was difficult, which is why Lelia arrived well before John's birth, on 24 September 1901.

4. JFS, interview with author, 28 February 1989.

5. Ibid., 16 May 1983.

6. WF to the Reverend Robert Elijah Jones, 15 March 1940, Robert Elijah Jones papers, Amistad Research Center Library, Tulane University, New Orleans, La.

7. Rachel McGee and Mildred Quarles, interviews with Pat Tingle, 20 March 1989.

8. WF to the Reverend Robert Elijah Jones, 15 March 1940, Robert Elijah Jones papers, Amistad Research Center Library, Tulane University, New Orleans, La.

9. See the Swift-Butler genealogy (fig. 7.3). In late 1887, during Charles Butler's second term as Oxford's town marshal he absconded with city funds, deserting his wife and daughter.

10. James Rudd, interview with Pat Tingle, 29 November 1989. We will never know their names or how many there were because slaves are listed only by numbers in the surviving slave records from Georgetown and Williamsburg, the counties where her slave owner's plantation probably was.

11. *MBB*, 70.

12. Tucker, *Telling Memories Among Southern Women*, 32.

13. See both Blotner biographies throughout for accounts of Faulkner's father's, grandfather's, and great-grandfather's alcoholism and violent behavior.

14. Besides the one move prior to Willie's second birthday (from New Albany to Ripley) and the family's second move (from Ripley to Oxford on 22 September 1903), the Falkners moved no fewer than five times as Murry's father shifted him from one job to another between 1903 and 1918, when J. W. T. finally had his errant son appointed assistant secretary for the university and the family moved into a house on campus, where they stayed until several years before Murry's death, in 1932.

15. These volumes were in the Faulkners' library at Rowan Oak (JFSA/UVA).

16. Williamson, 131, 133.

17. "'Mammys' . . . who, with everlasting devotion and loyalty, became second mothers to white children" (*FOM*, 13).

18. JFS, interviews with author, 15 and 16 October 1987.

19. Ibid., 20 August 1980. Blotner says that when Maud had to take her husband to Byhalia to be dried out, she brought the children along too, as an object lesson. It failed. All the brothers (except, possibly, Jack) became alcoholics. See Blotner throughout.

20. Ellison, "Change the Joke and Slip the Yoke," in *Shadow and Act*, 45–59.

21. His brother John writes that "I think . . . he would play drunk simply to get waited on. For the time being, he had got tired of waiting on himself" (*MMB*, 148). Malcolm Franklin provides a detailed description of the way Wallace Lyles, a black man whom Franklin describes as "one of the most loyal friends Faulkner ever had," would be called in to nurse his stepfather "during heavy drinking periods," which occurred "perhaps two or three times a year, lasting from three to six weeks" (*Bitterweeds*, 117, 118).

22. Mildred Quarles, interview with Pat Tingle, 20 March 1989.

23. Faulkner, Woolf, and Watkins, *Talking About William Faulkner*, 11–12.

CHAPTER 2. CAROLINE BARR'S ORIGINS

Epigraph: Rhyme recited by Callie Barr to JFS.

1. JFS, interviews with author, 23 February 1987, 2 May 1989, and 7 November 1995. Charles Joyner, a historian specializing in South Carolina slave communities, says that the terms in this rhyme are common to Gullah culture (Joyner, telephone interview with author, 2 May 1989). You might ask why, if Callie spoke Gullah, none of Faulkner's black characters share this distinction. Simply because it would have distracted from the story he wanted to tell—he wasn't prepared to individualize his black characters in this way. He wrote what he knew, which was Southern white male subjectivity. His black characters have rare moments of individuality—of speech—just as his white women do. Those moments perhaps come from his experiences with Callie Barr, her family, and community. But he didn't want to particularize or historicize in any way that detracted from his central novelistic preoccupation. Gullah would have done that; it also would have required him to introduce another story-history into his fiction, one that required him to articulate a black consciousness and subjectivity. This was something he could not have done in any sustained way.

2. *Bitterweeds*, 109. "She was born in South Carolina." JFS, interview with author, 1 November 1995.

3. *MBB*, 48, 50.

4. James Rudd, interview with Pat Tingle, 12 May 1989, and interview with author, 13 March 2002.

5. *Bitterweeds*, 109.

6. Joyner, *Down by the Riverside*, chaps. 1, 3, pp. 9–89.

7. John Faulkner writes that when Oxford was invaded, a Colonel Barr who "owned nearly all of the land from Oxford to Burgess (12 miles west of Oxford)," moved his slaves to Pontotoc—which was where he freed Callie. She then continued working for him as a paid servant (*MBB*, 48, 50). This seems unlikely, however, as the Lafayette County census has no listing for a Colonel Barr. John also says that Callie didn't begin working for his parents until 1907, when Willie was ten. Since John and Jack report Callie's prolonged absences of anywhere from three to five times during their childhoods, one of those absences may have occurred sometime between John's third and sixth birthday. Thus what he recounts here is *his* first memory of Callie's being part of his life (*MBB*, 51, and *FOM*, 12–15).

8. Jones, *Labor of Love*, 52.

9. *Bitterweeds*, 109, 110.

10. *MBB*, 50.

11. Ibid., 48.

12. James Rudd, interview with Pat Tingle, 12 May 1989.

13. JFS, interviews with author, 18 July 1988, 21 and 28 March 1989.

14. *Bitterweeds*, 109, and JFS, interview with author, 21 March 1989.

15. McFadden, "Meteors Put on a Show."

16. Davis, "The Game of Courts," 130, and Sensibar, "Who Wears the Mask."

17. Charles Joyner, interview with author, 2 May 1989.

18. Ibid., 17 May 1989; see also Joyner, *Down by the Riverside*.

19. A George Barr is listed as one of the county's original settlers, and both black

and white Barrs appear on county records from the beginning of the eighteenth century until the 1920s. See Boddie, *History of Williamsburg*, 469, 526.

20. Ibid., 250.

21. In Williamsburg's 1870 census James Barr, the only Barr listed, owns three slaves. The largest slaveholder in the county owned eighty-three slaves, twice as many as the next largest owner. Although many families owned no slaves, an equal number held one to nine (Boddie, *History of Williamsburg*, 154–55).

22. Jones, *Labor of Love*, 15 and 16, quoting a slave owner.

23. Ibid., 17, 15.

24. Genovese, *Roll, Jordon, Roll*, 328.

25. Jones, *Labor of Love*, 24.

26. *MBB*, 49.

27. *Bitterweeds*, 109.

28. Jones, *Labor of Love*, 52.

29. 1870 and 1880 census records for Phillips County, Arkansas, show a large influx of both black and white South Carolinians, but not Caroline Barr.

30. James Rudd, interview with author, 13 May 2002.

31. There are only two or three photographs of Callie Barr, all taken by white cameramen or women. Rachel McGee had a scrapbook that included photographs, but she says she lent it to the only other black person who came to interview her. He then sold it to "a white man from Greenville." Rachel McGee and Mildred Quarles, interviews with Pat Tingle, 16 February, 20 March 1989; Pat Tingle, interview with author, 16 February 1989.

32. Rachel McGee and Mildred Quarles, interviews with Pat Tingle, 16 February 1989.

33. Mildred Quarles, interview with Pat Tingle, 20 March 1989.

34. Evelyn Wortham Golliday, interview with Pat Tingle, 8 March 1989.

35. Earl Wortham, "So I Could Ride Along with Him," in Webb and Green, *William Faulkner*, 167, 168.

36. Evelyn Wortham Golliday, interview with Pat Tingle, 8 March 1989.

37. Ibid.

38. JFS, phone interview with author, 21 March 1989. See also *Bitterweeds*, 110.

39. Rachel McGee, interview with Pat Tingle, 16 February 1989.

40. Ibid. Fred Booker (b. 1909), confirmed in interview with Pat Tingle, 15 February 1989.

41. Rachel McGee and Mildred Quarles, interviews with Pat Tingle, 16 February, 20 March 1989.

42. Jill and her mother returned in late May 1937, and Faulkner followed in late August. JFS, interview with author, 21 March 1989.

43. Mildred Quarles, interview with Pat Tingle, 20 March 1989.

44. JFS, interview with author, 21 March 1989.

45. *Faulkner* (1974), 2:1776, and Floyd Watkins, interview with Jim Faulkner, *Talking About William Faulkner*, 63–64.

46. Wilson and Ferris, *Encyclopedia of Southern Culture*, 493.

47. James Rudd, interview with Pat Tingle, 12 May 1989.

48. Rachel McGee, interview with Pat Tingle, 2 February 1989.

49. See Sorensen, "The Life of Slave Women," 6.

50. At least one black person in Ripley thought that Callie had a husband (perhaps another brother, nephew, or a son?) named Joseph Barr who was either a trustee or a deacon at one of the churches in town. But neither her Sardis nor Oxford relatives know anything about a Joseph Barr. People in Ripley say that a Joseph Barr belonged to St. Paul United Methodist Church; Jill Summers remembers that it was the Ebenezer Baptist Church. Wilda Bayliss, interview with Pat Tingle, February 1989, and JFS, interview with author, 21 March 1989.

51. Rachel McGee, interview with Pat Tingle, 16 February 1989.

52. James Rudd, interview with Pat Tingle, 12 May 1989.

53. Ibid.

54. Rachel McGee and her daughter, Mildred Quarles, interview with Pat Tingle, 16 February 1989. Rachel was seventy-six years old at the time of this interview. After Pat turned off the tape, Rachel explained to her how important it is to know all your brothers and sisters even if you don't know who the fathers are so as not to intermarry.

55. *Bitterweeds*, 109. Faulkner's biographers have virtually ignored Malcolm's memoir. Malcolm (b. 1923) was six when his mother and Faulkner married. He spent his childhood and adolescence living either with his mother and stepfather or with Estelle's parents, Lem and Lida Oldham. His perspective on the Faulkners' household is the only published extant insider view.

56. James Rudd, interview with Pat Tingle, 12 May 1989.

57. James Rudd, interview with author, 13 March 2002.

58. James Rudd, interview with Pat Tingle, 12 May 1989.

59. Ibid., and James Rudd, interview with author, 13 March 2002.

60. James Rudd, interview with Pat Tingle, 12 May 1989.

61. Ibid.

62. Rachel McGee and Mildred Quarles, interviews with Pat Tingle, 16 February 1989 and 20 March 1989.

63. Williamson, 157.

64. Mildred Quarles, interview with Pat Tingle, 20 March 1989.

65. Williamson, 156, 157.

66. Ibid., 161.

67. Ibid., 162.

68. Bessie Sumners, interview with author, 21 May 1988.

CHAPTER 3: NEGOTIATING THE "MAMMY" TRADITION

1. Smith, *Killers of the Dream*, 19.

2. *MBB*, 48–49.

3. *FOM*, 15, 14.

4. John Faulkner writes that she had a brother, Wes Barr, who lived over in the Hollow and children and grandchildren still living in Oxford (1963). He also writes that Molly Barr was one of Callie's children (*MBB*, 48, 51). This is wrong. According to Rachel McGee, Molly Barr's daughter, both Wes and Molly were the children of Callie's brother, Ed Barr. Rachel McGee and Mildred Quarles, interview with Pat Tingle, 20 March 1989.

5. *Faulkner* (1974), 1:76, and *Faulkner* (1984), 219.

6. Snead, *Figures of Division*, 36, 37, 39.

7. Freedman Town is "a section comprising about seven blocks, adjoining the railroad tracks northwest of the center of town" (*Faulkner* [1974], 1:75). According to Rachel McGee, Callie Barr's great-niece, Freedman Town was "over by North 7th street," which is now Martin Luther King Drive. In the 1920s and 1930s Rachel, Mildred, and her family lived in what was then country: "back up there from Freedman Town where all them row of houses, that use to be a field and woods. We didn't have nothing around us, you know." Rachel McGee and Mildred Quarles, interviews with Pat Tingle, 20 March 1989.

8. James Rudd, Rachel McGee, and Mildred Quarles, interviews with Pat Tingle, 12 May and 20 March 1989; Taylor, *Faulkner's Oxford*, 122.

9. Herbert Wiley and Mildred Quarles, interviews with author, 17 March 2002; and James Rudd, interview with author, 13 March 2002.

10. The "Faulkner Farms" ledgers, 1938–42, JFSA/UVA (placed there in summer 1998), and Federal Reserve Bank of New York, "Prime Rate as It Changed, 1929 to Present"; *ftp://ftp.ny.frb.org/prime/Prime.txt*.

11. Hunter, *To Joy My Freedom*, 168.

12. Hurston, "Characteristics of Negro Expression," in *"Sweat!,"* 67.

13. A useful sociological study of origins and development of black lower- and working-class "social dance arenas" like jooks is Katrina Hazzard-Gordon's *Jookin'*. Hazzard-Gordon argues that the jook "was the first secular cultural institution to emerge after emancipation" (77).

14. Hunter, *To Joy My Freedom*, 179–80.

15. Hurston, "Characteristics of Negro Expression," 68, 69.

16. This information about Molly Barr comes from her daughter and granddaughter and from Evelyn Golliday, Susie Marshall, and James Rudd. The women spoke only off the record about Molly Barr's jook-joint business, thinking it reflected badly on the Barr family and so blemished the image of Callie Barr as a responsible caretaker of the Falkner children. But to cut Molly Barr out of Callie's life just perpetuates the uncomplicated mammy mask worn by Callie Barr in all previous biographical portrayals and does a disservice to her and to Faulkner. If we see only the mask, we cannot understand why Faulkner's education into racial narratives, in part through his relationships with the Barr family, became central to his imaginative vision.

17. See Davis, *Faulkner's "Negro,"* especially her discussions of *Soldiers' Pay* (chap. 2) and *Go Down, Moses*, and her essay "From Jazz Syncopation to Blues Elegy."

18. For the larger personal and aesthetic dimensions and context of Faulkner's complicated and important feelings about "black" and "white" music, see Sensibar, *Origins*, 206–21.

19. Explaining why he had named Nancy's husband Jesus, Faulkner told a University of Virginia undergraduate writing class that he had wanted to "emphasize the point that I was making, which was that this negro woman [Nancy] who had given devotion to the white family knew that when the crisis of her need came, the white family wouldn't be there" (*FIU*, 21).

20. Although Joseph Blotner says she had another daughter, MayBell Clark, her Sardis and Oxford relatives had never heard of her. Faulkner did write a letter to a

woman he addresses as "May Bell," telling her about Callie's death, but there is no indication in the letter that she is Callie's daughter. Though the gravestone Faulkner had made for Callie Barr is engraved "Callie Barr Clark," none of her relatives know who Clark was. For letter, see FCVA, accession no. 6271AB.

21. *FOM*, 13.

22. *MBB*, 51.

23. *FOM*, 191. Faulkner's brother John is equally vehement (*MBB*, 268). Because the brothers' memoirs serve as Faulkner's biographers' primary source for Caroline Barr, their accounts reflect and perpetuate this bias.

24. The Falkners were the norm. All over the Jim Crow South, white middle- and working-class children were raised similarly. See Smith, *Killers of the Dream*, for a personal account, and Hale, *Making Whiteness*, for a historical account. Susan Tucker's interviews with African American women and the white women they cared for as children are an invaluable source; see Tucker, *Telling Memories*.

25. WF to Maud Falkner, 31 March 1925, in *TOH*, 194–95.

26. *FOM*, 13.

27. *MBB*, 53.

CHAPTER 4: CALLIE BARR AND MAUD FALKNER

1. The *Confederate Veteran*, published from 1893 to 1932, was the official monthly magazine of the Daughters of the Confederacy, the Confederate Veterans, and other Southern memorial associations. Its masthead states that it is published "in the interest of Confederate Veterans and Kindred topics." The 1906 masthead also provides its ideology and backers, stating that "Though men deserve, they may not win success;/ The brave will honor the brave, vanquished none the less." It also declares that "the *civil* war was too long ago to be called the *late* war." The term they will use is the "War between the States." Furthermore, it states that the "terms 'New South' and 'lost cause' are objectionable to the *Veteran*" (*Confederate Veteran* 14:3 [March 1906]: masthead). By 1906, the journal cost a dollar a year; it was probably a fixture in both the Falkner and Oldham households. Its sole purpose was to memorialize the war and mythologize the pre–Civil War South.

2. Wickham, "My Children's Mammy." *The Confederate Veteran* 34 (1926): 413.

3. See James Dahl's interview with Maud Falkner, "A Faulkner Reminiscence," 1027, 1028. Dean Wells elaborated by giving this example: Her grandmother "loved the songs, 'Oh It's Only a Paper Moon' and 'Mona Lisa' which she had on a 78 rpm record and used to play over and over. Then one day she found out Nat King Cole was black and she broke them and never listened to either song again" (Dean Wells, interview with author, 18 May 1989, 38). At the same time, and with no apparent sense of contradiction, members from all the generations of Falkners/Faulkners claim that everyone in the family obeyed Callie Barr unquestioningly. Rachel McGee and her daughter concur. When asked how Callie got along with Estelle, Mildred said, "Just fine." Her mother followed with, "See, she was the boss of that house. Aunt Callie— whatever Aunt Callie said, they wouldn't buck it." Rachel then compares Faulkner's relationship with Callie to her own relationship with the white child she reared: "Now,

I got a place and I been there fifty-five years and I'm the boss there. They [the children] are all grown. The boy is in Atlanta and he calls me and I tells him what to do. He is a man. The white children I raised" (Rachel McGee, interview with Pat Tingle, 20 March 1989).

4. For legal battles fought as late as the 1940s concerning racial classifications, see Victoria E. Bynum's "'White Negroes' in Segregated Mississippi."

5. *Oxford Globe*, 2 July 1981.

6. Dahl, "A Faulkner Reminiscence," 1027.

7. Ibid.

8. For examples, see photographs in Cofield, *William Faulkner*, 94, 103, 106, 112.

9. JFS, interview with James B. Meriwether (JBM), September 1982. See photo of Maud's self-portrait and descriptive note that JBM sent JFS, 30 September 1982. JFSA.

10. Dean Falkner Wells, interview with author, 18 May 1989.

11. *FOM*, 189.

12. Ibid., 12–16, 188.

13. Ibid., 199.

14. Dahl, "Faulkner Reminiscence," 1027, 1028. Dahl interviewed Maud in 1953, when he was a twenty-year-old college student at the University of Minnesota.

15. Bessie Sumners, interview with author, 12 May 1989.

16. JFS, interview with author, 23 February 1987.

17. Ibid. 21 March 1989.

18. Hunter, *To Joy My Freedom*, 129.

19. JFS, interviews with author, 21 March 1989 and 23 February 1987.

20. Ibid. 23 February 1987. Shifting the enforcer's gender and item of clothing, Estelle told a similar but more risqué story to Joseph Blotner. She was gardening in shorts and was seen by the old black servant, Ned Barnett, who had also worked for William's grandfather. He told the cook to "please tell mistress I can't come up to the house while she's in her underwear." She went in, changed, "and never appeared in shorts again" (*Faulkner* [1974], 2:998, citing his interview from 1967).

21. Lula Brown Law, interview with author, 10 May 1989. Law met Cho-Cho in fall 1933 at the boarding school in Holly Springs, Miss., that they both attended.

22. This is often a theme in postbellum fictional constructions of the Mammy figure. See Roberts, *The Myth of Aunt Jemima* and *Faulkner and Southern Womanhood*, and Hale, *Making Whiteness*. Both point out that the mammy figure was not a reality but "an ideological tool, a creation of white culture to aggrandize and perpetuate itself" (Roberts, *Faulkner*, 42), and see Hale, 113, 114.

23. JFS, interview with author, 21 March 1989.

24. Davis, "Faulkner in the Future," 19. Davis elaborates: "With more insight, clarity, and artistry than any other writer of his generation . . . Faulkner represented issues of race, racialization, racial construction, and racial division" (16).

25. Davis notes that George Kent was the first to make this point in his *Blackness and the Adventure of Western Culture* (Chicago: Third World Press, 1972) 18.

26. Davis, "Faulkner in the Future," 17.

27. *FOM*, 148.

28. JFS, interviews with author, 21 February 1987, 22, 24, and 16 October 1987.

29. Jack Falkner contradicts William: "To her, Father was 'Mist' Murry and Mother was Mis' Maud" (*FOM*, 16).

30. In "Mississippi," which he first published in *Holiday* magazine in 1954, Faulkner writes about his fictional and "real" families. He refers to himself first as the "child" and later as the "middleaged." Central to Faulkner's characterization of "Caroline" is her means of using naming to attempt to level the racial playing field: "Caroline, never calling the child's [WF's] father nor the father's brother and sister by anything but their Christian names even when they themselves became grandparents" and "calling the middleaged 'Memmy' still, from the fifty-odd years ago when that was as close as his brothers could come to 'William.'" "Mississippi" is reprinted in *ESPL*, 17, 41.

31. *MBB*, 51.

32. As Diane Roberts and others have noted, "Aunt Jemima flourished in the minstrel shows before she became a corporate brand name: the archetypal 'mammy,' her shiny, scrubbed black face beaming, her crimson head-rag tied smartly in a square knot. The mammy typifies the mythic Old South of benign slavery, grace and abundance; she rules the kitchen or she instructs the young ladies in decorum or she buries the family silver in the orchard so the Yankees won't steal it" (Roberts, *Aunt Jemima*, 1). Roberts notes that "Hortense Spillers says these names (and other raced terms whites have invented for blacks) 'are markers so loaded with mythic prepossession that there is no easy way for the agents buried beneath them to come clean' ("Mama's Baby," 65)" (Roberts, *Aunt Jemima*, 1). See also Spillers, "Mama's Baby."

33. JFS, interview with author, 20 August 1980.

34. Ibid., 16 October 1987.

35. Ibid., 26 February 1986.

36. Ibid., 18 July 1988.

37. Ibid., 16 October 1987.

38. Ibid., 26 February 1986.

39. Ibid., 2 November 1995.

40. Ibid., 23 February 1987.

41. *MBB*, 49.

42. *FOM*, 200, 27, 13.

43. *MBB*, 50.

44. *Bitterweeds*, 109–10.

45. JFS, interview with author, 18 July 1988.

46. Eulogy, 4 February 1940. See *SL*, 118–19.

47. JFS, interview with author, 23 February 1987.

48. Ibid., 26 February 1986 and 3 February 1987.

49. Ibid., 22 February 1986.

CHAPTER 5: CAROLINE BARR AND FAULKNER'S POETICS

1. See, e.g., Bleikasten, *The Most Splendid Failure* and *The Ink of Melancholy;* John Mathews, *The Play of Faulkner's Language;* Richard C. Moreland, *Faulkner and Modernism;* Gail Mortimer, *Faulkner's Rhetoric of Loss.*

2. Faulkner's interview with Jean Stein vanden Heuvel (1956) and his unpublished 1933 introduction to *TSAF*. Both reprinted in *TSAF*, Norton Critical Edition, 233, 227.

3. By *racialization* I mean the mechanisms by which race is made visible, mobilized, and experienced.

4. See, e.g., Tyson and Tyson, *Psychoanalytic Theories of Development*, 1.

5. Faulkner makes numerous statements like this throughout his life. In 1944 he wrote his editor, "I am telling the same story over and over, which is myself and the world" (Cowley, *The Faulkner-Cowley File*, 14).

6. Besides many fictional accounts by white Southern writers, see Lillian Smith, *Killer of the Dream*, Tucker, *Telling Memories*, and Hale, *Making Whiteness*. The latter gives as one of her examples U. B. Phillips, a historian trained at Columbia University who was a Georgian by birth; Phillips wrote that "white children hardly [knew] their mother from their mammies or their uncles by blood from their 'uncles' by courtesy. Negroes equaled home" (Hale, *Making Whiteness*, 63).

7. Hale notes "the common theme of the twinned/integrated childhood" in whites' stories about their childhoods (*Making Whiteness*, 103).

8. Smith, *Killers of the Dream*, 17. In "Mississippi" Faulkner claims that perhaps by age four he was consciously asserting the privileges of being white when he played with his black "twin brother" (17).

9. Michael Millgate was among the first and remains the most reasoned and articulate proponent of this view. See his *The Achievement of William Faulkner*, 201.

10. Smith, *Killers of the Dream*, 18.

11. Ibid., 19.

12. See Hale, *Making Whiteness*, in which she examines white Southerners' fictional and actual portrayals of the mammy figure as an invention and tool for the "making of whiteness." She argues that it's another stereotype that whites designed to construct and perpetuate their whiteness (118). Mammy stories were "circulated widely in magazines, memoirs, and autobiographies between 1890 and 1940" (98). See also Fred Hobson's *But Now I See*, which claims that memoirs constructed around this theme, beginning with *Killers of the Dream*, are so prevalent that it's really a subgenre with roots in the Puritan Conversion Narrative.

13. Morrison, "Faulkner and Women," 296.

14. Even in 1925 Faulkner recognized this screen memory as both highly charged emotionally and in need of censorship. The following day he sent a self-censored version of it to Vannye at her Paris hotel: "The last time that I saw you that I remember, I was 3 years old and crying: you and Natalie had brought me home from Aunt Willie's in Ripley, where I had gone to spend the night, and I lost my nerve. You held a kerosene lamp, and your hair looked like honey" (WF to Vance ["Vannye"] Carter Witt [probably 11 September 1925], *LDB*, 3–4).

15. JFS, interviews with author, 23 February and 16 October 1987.

16. Freud suggests that the discrepancy exists between the vividness of the memory and its apparently banal content because "the relevant scene may perhaps have been incompletely retained in memory, and that may be why it seems so unenlightening." What is remembered "is not the relevant experience itself" but "*another psychical element closely associated with the objectionable one*" (my italics). For example,

Faulkner's screen memory concludes in what should be a moment of relief—his aunts rescuing him and carrying him home. But as he tells it, we can see that it's not a moment of relief at all. In fact, as soon as one begins to translate a screen memory into language—to interpret it, to communicate it to someone else, as Faulkner did in this letter—the so-called indifference falls away, revealing the essential instability of the construction. Freud makes an analogy that is useful here: "there is a common saying . . . about shams, that they are not made of gold themselves, but have lain beside something that *is* made of gold. The same simile might well be applied to some of the experiences of childhood which have been retained in the memory." He further notes that sometimes "screen memories will . . . be formed from residues of memories relating to later life." These "owe their importance to a connection with experiences in early youth which have remained suppressed." Finally he suggests that "it may indeed be questioned whether we have any memories at all *from* our childhood: memories *relating to* our childhood may be all that we possess. Our childhood memories show us our earliest years not as they were but as they appeared at later periods when these [early] memories were [again] aroused. In these periods of arousal, the childhood memories did not, as people are accustomed to say, emerge; they were formed at that time. And a number of motives, with no concern for historical accuracy, had a part in forming them, as well as in the selection of the memories themselves" (Freud, "Screen Memories," *SE*, 3: 306–7, 320, 322). See also "Introductory Lectures on Psychoanalysis," *SE*, 15, 200–201. It is impossible to date a screen memory with any accuracy.

17. The codes of Southern life required that (other than in infancy and very early childhood) white subjects have no place where they could express or acknowledge any positive emotional relationship (be it love, kinship, relation, or even kindness) with blackness; no positive relationship that they could express in public or private spaces and have it be embraced or accepted by anyone. Faulkner's screen memory perhaps relives this complex system of being required to shut down all public and eventually all private positive emotional relationships with black or figuratively blackened people (except when he was drunk).

18. Those ubiquitous scenes of "touch"—always placed in private spaces (a bedroom, a kitchen, a bathroom, a deserted barn or stairwell, a cabin), exploding with passion and violence, and always summarily shut down or cut off—originate in this core or screen memory and are Faulkner's powerful imaginative reconstructions of this memory.

19. That Faulkner had two early object-choices, both of whom were women, may have further complicated the oedipal anxieties of a young boy who experienced his alcoholic and emotionally distant father primarily as "lack." (Many of these points were clarified for me in conversation with Harvey Strauss, M.D., President Emeritus, Chicago Institute for Psychoanalysis.)

20. Faulkner renders the extremes of this degradation in what may be his first fictional translation of this memory. In *Soldiers' Pay* a small white boy "wanting his mother" finds "himself running suddenly through the hall toward a voice raised in comforting, crooning song." This nameless voice is his "Mammy," "a friend mountainous in blue calico" with "undulating elephantine thighs." She asks what's wrong, "but he did not know. He only clung to her" weeping "in uncontrollable sorrow." As she picks him up and rocks him, "holding him against her balloon-like breast," he's

comforted. Faulkner can only allow the boy (a fictional self?) to be comforted if he renders the black mother of his desire a repulsive grotesque (*SP,* 298–99).

21. In Faulkner's fiction such figuring of blackness is not gender specific. For example, Temple Drake, Horace Benbow, and even Tommy the "feeb" experience Popeye, the white bootlegger and gangster "whose face had a queer bloodless color . . . a dead dark pallor," as black: "He smells black," Horace thinks, "like that black stuff that ran out of Bovary's mouth." Thus blackness translates as poison, suicide, and blood—the result of illicit desire. Identifying him with Emma Bovary, Horace feminizes and racializes Popeye—a typical rhetorical strategy for constructing the other. He also frames him with an iconic literary moment in a vain attempt to fictionalize and thus contain this man who mirrors him as he acts out Horace's own deepest fears and desires (*S,* 7; see also *S,* 4, 5, 19, 42, 49, 67, 109, 121, 219).

22. Quentin, Mrs. Compson, and Jason all make this connection explicit in their derogatory racist responses to either Caddy's or young Quentin's sexual behavior.

23. Jenkins observed that characters like Henry often serve as a "reminder of the [white character's] dream of violated fraternity." Thus Faulkner writes Roth's "shame" and "grief" at his cruelty to Henry while Henry "is never shown as having been capable of anticipating the event, of having been hurt or offended by it. . . . He [like other black characters] is simply rendered as already having assumed . . . the mask of submission." As such, he appears "not as a human but as a nonhuman, a thing, without rights or feelings, an object . . . to whom things are done." Jenkins then wonders "if this is what Faulkner is referring to when he declares that 'the white man has forced the Negro to be always a Negro rather than another human being'" *(Faulkner and Black-White Relations,* 21, 22).

24. "'Mammys' . . . became second mothers" (*FOM,* 13).

25. WF to Robert K. Haas, 5 February 1940, *SL,* 117.

26. By public and private discourse I mean to differentiate between what he is reported to have said or what he wrote in essays, speeches, and letters or other "non-fictional" texts and what he wrote in his poetry, short stories, and novels.

27. *Faulkner* (1974), 2:1038; WF to Robert Haas (7 February 1940), *SL,* 118.

28. *Faulkner* (1974), 2:1034–36; WF to Robert Haas (7 February 1940), *SL,* 118–19.

29. Critics have written eloquently and contentiously about Faulkner's fictional representations of these paradoxes and contradictions. The most thought-provoking readings are from Davis, especially *Games of Property;* Donaldson, "Cracked Lens"; Gwin, *The Feminine and Faulkner;* Roberts, *Aunt Jemima* and *Faulkner;* and Sundquist, *Faulkner* and *To Wake.* See also Davis, "The Game of Courts," 129–54, 101–28.

30. Linda Wagner-Martin's request that I write an essay for *New Essays on Faulkner's* Go Down, Moses led me to realize that Faulkner's earliest and most enduring narrative consciousness, Pierrot in all his permutations, was perhaps the site from which to begin to study the contradictions in the racial consciousness tearing at the seams of *Go Down, Moses* by trying to answer the question I'd been ignoring for years: Why is Pantaloon/Pierrot here and why is he black?

31. When I first raised these issues at a Faulkner conference in Oxford, Mississippi, in August 1987, I drew many deeply felt and thoughtful responses. I include here one of those because it is representative as well as being among the most articulate and sensitive, and, all unconsciously, it makes precisely the same point: "As regards the

question you raised about how Callie Barr's attitudes about and experiences with men might have influenced Faulkner's. I suspect that you will find that they were minimal, given the whole Southern social system. Let me share my experience, which is probably characteristically Southern. My mother died a few days after my birth and my brother and I were raised by a Black mammy for four years, until my father remarried. Afterwards, she continued to work for the family for the next 25 years until her retirement. After that I continued to take care of her, to regard her emotionally as a mother surrogate, and when she died I overruled my family's resistance and buried her in my cemetery plot. But in spite of that lifetime of emotional closeness, I never regarded her attitudes about men and marriage or religion as anything other than particular and peculiar to her own culture. I suppose some equivalent for a Northern family would be, say, a Lutheran family with a Catholic nanny. In spite of their closeness on a personal level, they would regard her attitudes about church, sexuality, sin, politics, or marriage as exotic. So I doubt you will find Callie Barr's perceptions ultimately threw much weight with Faulkner" (Thorton F. Jordan, Columbus, Georgia, in a letter to the author, 9 August 1987). Since then Susan Tucker's invaluable *Telling Memories* has appeared. Oral histories of black domestic workers and their white employers, "a collective memory of these women of the South," is the author's attempt to record "the stories as well as the silence . . . about two groups of Southern women" (1). Many of the interviews confirm the emotional climate and unspoken codes of conduct that Patricia Tingle and I recorded in our interviews with the Barr and Faulkner families.

32. Limon, "The Integration of Faulkner's *Go Down, Moses*," 423.

33. I remind readers here, as Faulkner reminds readers in his essay "Mississippi," that throughout his life Caroline Barr called him "Memmy," a twinning Faulkner encodes in this story about an imagined black self (*GDM*, 131). *The Jazz Singer*, Al Jolson's movie in which Jolson, in minstrel mask, sings his famous rendition of "Mammy," was first released in 1927. Michael North notes the "prevalence of blackface routines in film, onstage, and even on radio." For example, 1927 also saw the release of *Uncle Tom's Cabin*, D. W. Griffith's comic version of Stowe's novel, and blackface films starring Eddie Cantor and W. C. Fields. See North, *The Dialect of Modernism*, 4–8, 197–98 nn6, 7.

34. Ellison, "Change the Joke and Slip the Yoke," in *Shadow and Act*, 49, 53.

35. Two others were "The Old People," which Faulkner had sent to his agent Harold Ober on 3 October 1939, and "The Fire and the Hearth," which he had sent along with "Pantaloon" (WF to Robert K. Haas, Wednesday [22 May 1940], *SL*, 124).

36. WF to Robert Haas (28 April 1940), *SL*, 122, italics mine.

37. In an attempt to get his publisher to raise his fees, he also began negotiations with a new publisher, which left him only the time and energy, he wrote, to write "trash" (*SL*, 121). By the end of July, the negotiations had fallen through and Faulkner again wrote Random House about *Go Down, Moses* saying that he needed to write one more story, "a novella, actually," to complete the book but that he'd have to write a book he could sell fast first (more "trash"), as he didn't want the novella published separately (*SL*, 135).

38. *Faulkner* (1984), 424; Dardis, *The Thirsty Muse*, 70. Dardis's chapter documents Faulkner's addiction as being well beyond his control by January 1936 (26).

39. See, e.g., Davis's reading of the bear as Faulkner's symbolic representation of "Negro" in her conclusion to *Faulkner's "Negro"* (242–47). Other blacks that white men subject to ritual killings in *Go Down, Moses* are Rider, in the novel's third section, and Butch Beauchamp, in its concluding chapter. Blacks subjected to symbolic killings by white men are Eunice, who drowns herself after learning that her daughter, Tomasina ("Tomey"), has been raped and is bearing a child by her white master and father, Carothers McCaslin; Molly, Lucas, and Henry Beauchamp, Roth's black family that he must kill to become a white man; and Roth's distant cousin and lover, the unnamed woman (who can pass for white but chooses not to) and their son. But as the latter (and her inventor) point out, Roth is "not a man yet" (*GDM*, 343). He will never be one. Only acknowledging his love for her and the rest of his black family will make him a man. There are at least six other scenes in which alcohol is reified in *GDM*.

40. WF to Robert Haas (1 May 1941), *SL*, 139–41.

41. These constrictions are, as well, the dungeon that Quentin Compson describes so eloquently as that "dark place into which a single weak ray of light came slanting upon two faces lifted out of the shadow. . . . The dungeon was Mother herself she and Father upward into weak light holding hands and us lost somewhere below even them without even a ray of light" (*TSAF*, 109–110).

42. WF in letter to Robert Haas (7 February 1940), *SL*, 118–19.

43. Rachel McGee and Mildred Quarles, interview with Pat Tingle, 16 February 1989.

44. Pat Tingle, interview with author, 6 March 1989.

45. Mildred Quarles, interview with Pat Tingle, 29 March 1989.

46. *MBB*, 216.

47. Ibid., 217. In fact the Faulkner family treated Maud's funeral as an intensely private affair—the antithesis of Callie Barr's. At the funeral only the family carried Maud's casket; "no outsider touched it until the undertaker's men took charge of it as it left the porch of the house" to be taken to St. Peter's Cemetery. In *William Faulkner*, Frederick Karl writes that "if Faulkner grieved, he did so without too much display" (1012). For a different opinion, see *Faulkner* (1974), 2:1764–65.

48. North, *The Dialect of Modernism*, 5–8.

49. Lott, *Love and Theft*, 188, 189.

50. Juxtaposing Faulkner's early Pierrot persona with Rider allows crucial insight to the writer's creative process. The imagery of Rider's psychic world derives from Pierrot of *The Marble Faun* and *Vision in Spring*. In his waning years, Faulkner kept Estelle's copy of *Vision in Spring* on his bedside table. The stuff of dreams, it had been a touchstone for his genius.

51. Here, too, as in many other American novels besides Faulkner's, miscegenation is also figured as incest, thereby racializing the oedipal conflict.

52. Interview with Faulkner's nephew, Jimmy Faulkner, in Faulkner, Wolff, and Watkins, *Talking About William Faulkner*, 77. Jimmy spells it "Memi," but his father, John, spelled it "Memmie" (*MBB*, 51). Faulkner's own spelling is "Memmy."

53. The resonance here between Rider and Joe Christmas, perhaps Faulkner's most racially and sexually irresolute protagonist, is conscious and deliberate. Faulkner's readers are meant to hear and explore its aesthetic, personal, and political meanings.

54. After Roth becomes a racist, Molly feeds him but refuses to let him eat with

her family. The emptiness—the lovelessness he feels—is imaged in that section, as it is in "Pantaloon," as food made by the black mother/lover but no longer shared with her. Put simply, the breast denied. Edmonds speaks with his body, as does Rider.

55. Rider's act also prefigures and prepares the way for Roth Edmonds's lover's answer to Ike McCaslin when he tells her to go North and "marry a man in your own race" so that she'll forget about Roth. She retorts, "Old man . . . have you lived so long and forgotten so much that you don't remember anything you knew or felt or even heard about love?" (*GDM*, 346).

CHAPTER 6: FAMILY SECRETS

1. Faulkner gave "Mississippi" to his agent Harold Ober on 25 March 1953 (*Faulkner* [1984], 570). After appearing in *Holiday* (April 1954), it was reprinted in *ESPL*, 11–43. All subsequent references are to this reprint. *Brown v. Board of Education* reversed the "separate but equal" doctrine of *Plessy v. Ferguson*, the legal basis for de jure segregation and the rule of Jim Crow.

2. Blotner, who gives no source for this letter and does not include it in *Selected Letters*, writes that it is dated "August 20th" and that Faulkner could have written it "at any time during the previous fifteen years," i.e., August 1952 to August 1937 (*Faulkner* [1974], 2:1452).

3. Yeats, "Among School Children," *Norton Anthology*, 445. I'm taking poetic license here, in that Faulkner was only fifty-six years old.

4. For detailed, firsthand descriptions of Faulkner's severe deterioration, see Saxe Commins's letters to his wife and to Robert Haas and Bennett Cerf at Random House, written when Estelle had begged Commins to come to Oxford to try to keep Faulkner from drinking himself to death. These are published in *LDB*. See also Williamson, 285–96; Wasson, *Count No 'Count*, 180–89; and Blotner (1974) and (1984).

5. *Faulkner* (1984), 574.

6. Saxe Commins to Robert Haas and Bennett Cerf, 8 October 1952, in *LDB*, vol. 2, 90–91. See also Commins's letter to his wife: Saxe Commins to Dorothy Commins, Oxford, Miss., 8 October 1952, *LDB*, vol. 2, 89.

7. *Faulkner* (1984), 560–61.

8. *Faulkner* (1974), 2:1442.

9. Ibid., 1454; Bernard Wortis, interview with Joseph Blotner, 17 August 1965; and *Faulkner* (1984), 568.

10. Williamson, 287, quoting from Joseph Blotner's interview notes.

11. On 24 February 1953 Faulkner gave his Anderson essay to Harold Ober, who sold it for three hundred dollars to *The Atlantic*, which published it that June. See *Faulkner* (1974), 2:1451, and *Faulkner* (1984), 569.

12. See Patricia Yaeger's revisionist reading of "Southern literature" and of its relation to other American literatures (*Dirt and Desire*, 99, 97). My reconstruction of the Faulkner family's, most particularly Faulkner's and his mother's relationships with Caroline Barr and her family, and my readings of how Faulkner translated the casual and systemic and psychically violent discrimination into a poetics of unmournable loss suggest a different conclusion.

13. "He touched now and then on the concerns that had brought him into controversies in Letters to the Editor columns, . . . but this was no predominant note" (*Faulkner* [1974], 2:1456).

14. In Faulkner's first Yoknapatawpha novel (written in 1927), its tortured homicidal-suicidal and sadistic white hero, a twin who feels responsible for his brother's death and so spends the rest of his short life running and drinking, seeks shelter one cold night with a nameless black family. They lend him a quilt "ragged and filthy to the touch, and impregnated with that unmistakable odor of negroes." Bayard "rolled himself into the quilt, filth and odor and all." In the morning he "dragged" himself from "his odorous bed" (*FITD*, 389, 390). Similar scenes cast in similar language appear as well in two works from the 1940s (see *GDM,* 195–96, and *IITD,* 9–12). Always, the white man's or boy's desire to seek comfort from and envelop himself in the bed and body of the dark other has to be masked (quilted?) with disgust.

15. *FIU,* 31.

16. Ibid., 26, 74.

17. Faulkner, interview with Jean Stein vanden Heuvel, 1956; reprinted in *TSAF,* 232, 233.

18. *FIU,* 31.

19. Ibid., 1, 17, 31.

20. In a letter to his editor about a week later, Faulkner wrote that she didn't suffer. She "lost consciousness within 30 minutes and never regained it." Caroline Barr died the following Wednesday "while my wife was sitting by her bed. She couldn't have gone better, more happily" (WF to Robert K. Haas, 5 February 1940, in *SL,* 117).

21. Williamson, 64.

22. James Rudd, interview with Pat Tingle, 12 May 1989.

PART 2: FAULKNER'S MOTHER, MAUD BUTLER FALKNER

INTRODUCTION TO PART 2

Epigraph: To "Dear Miss Lady" from "Yure erfexxionnate sun/Billie"; WF to MBF, 16 August 1912, *TOH,* 39–40.

1. Christine Drake, interview with author, 6 February 1989; Carvel Collins's impression, 2 April 1950, in MBF file, Collins papers, HRC; Dean Wells, interview with author, 14 May 1989; *Memphis Press Scimitar,* 14 September 1954.

2. Gray, *William Faulkner,* 76.

3. In two of the most terrifying instances—between Joanna Burden and Joe Christmas in *Light in August* and between Roth's father and Lucas Beauchamp in *Go Down, Moses*—Faulkner's characters perform a kind of ritualized death dance.

4. None of Maud's writing from this period is extant.

5. Only one painting for this period, a still life dated 1903, survives. It is owned by Jill Summers.

6. Katharine Andrews, interview with author, 10 August 1989.

7. JFS, interview with author, 16 May 1983.

8. Louise Meadow, interview with author, 3 July 1986.

9. *Faulkner* (1984), 679.

10. Ella Somerville, interview with Joseph Blotner, 18 August 1964. Blotner papers, SEMS.

11. MBF to SB, 4 March (1950?), Collins papers, HRC.

12. Dean Wells, phone call to Ann J. Abadie, Associate Director of the Center for the Study of Southern Culture, Oxford, Miss., 15 March 2002; repeated to author by Ann Abadie.

13. His precise words were, "I have some of her nigger pictures somewhere," which he repeated several times during his interview (Chooky Faulkner, interview with author, 18 March 2002). His house is decorated with many other paintings by his grandmother and his father, John (Maud's third son). Considering Chooky's attitude toward his grandmother's cabin scenes, it seemed odd that his father's cabin scenes were prominently displayed on Chooky's living room wall. Whatever the reason, the result is a censoring of Maud's art.

14. Louise Meadow, interview with author, 5 June 1986.

15. MBF, interview in *OXE*, 14 October 1954.

16. MBF, interview with Margaret T. Silver, 1956. "*McCall's* Visits 'Miss Maud,'" typescript for *McCall's* article; held at the University of Mississippi Library.

17. Obituary, *Memphis Commercial Appeal* (AP release), 17 October 1960.

18. Lelia's advertisement for such services reads as follows: "New Porcelain Painting / This new art of painting, or coloring photographs, is taught for $3. / Can be learned by ANY ONE in a single lesson. / Pictures colored to order. / Mrs. L. D. Butler"; *Oxford Globe*, 2 July 1891. Franklin Moak, letter to author, 29 March 1990.

CHAPTER 7: MAUD'S MYSTERIOUS ANCESTRY

Epigraph: Williamson, 87–88.

1. *Marriage Bonds Book 2, 164*, Lafayette County Courthouse, Lafayette, Miss.

2. Her gravestone in St. Peter's Cemetery, section 4, gives her dates as "3.5.49 to 6.1.07," as do the *Lafayette County, Miss., Cemetery Records*, vol. 2, 45–46.

3. The *1880 U.S. Census for Lafayette County, Miss.* lists Lelia as age thirty, her birthplace as Mississippi, and her parents' birthplace as Tennessee.

4. In Maud's idealized final revision, a plump, pretty, and plainly but well-dressed woman is seated in a tufted red velvet Victorian armchair. A young girl of about eight or nine, Lelia, stands at her side but slightly behind her. The girl's right wrist and hand, like her mother's elbow, rest on the chair's arm. The acute angles made by the mother's and daughter's arms, and the similarity in the poses of the mother's and daughter's right hands, form a compositional relationship that emphasizes their familial relationship, which also asserts itself more obviously in their similarly bland facial features. The painting's iconography identifies it as a mourning portrait. Lelia's mother is dressed in black; her only jewelry is the enamel mourning brooch clasping the white lace collar of her dress. Although Mahalah's now unlined face and bared neck look very young, her hair, which was black in the original painting (see fig. 4.3), is now prematurely gray. Centering the painting are her brooch and the Bible she is holding. It is probable that besides transforming both subjects' faces and necks, Maud also repainted her grandmother's hands. Perhaps this is the family Bible

from which Lelia read when she taught Sunday school at Oxford's First Baptist Church. This painting, especially its detail, its attention to fabric colors and textures, and the intricacy of Lelia's mother's lace collar and bonnet trimming, are reminiscent of the attention to detail in some of Maud's portraits, suggesting either more retouching or the possibility that Lelia herself might have been the artist.

5. Lelia was baptized in the Oxford Baptist Church "on the third Sabbath in June 1873, five years after her marriage" (Church Minutes, 28). Robbie Eades, "A Love of Drawing," and Rose Rowland, "William and His Grandmother," in Webb and Green, *William Faulkner of Oxford*, 22–27.

6. A stark, undated still life signed "Lelia Dean Butler" hangs in the living room of one of her great-great granddaughters. Three ears of dried Indian corn bound by their pale and shriveled husks are mounted against a weathered, soft, dark gray-green, wooden background, probably a farmhouse door; the kernels of the two foregrounded ears are a dull reddish-brown, the color of the North Mississippi clay her father's slaves farmed; the kernels on the third are a pale yellow white, slightly darker than the husks. Lelia's painting evokes the sere end of autumn. A practiced piece, it is the product of an experienced and disciplined hand. This is all that is left of a lifetime of work.

7. Williamson, 144.

8. Cowley, ed., *Faulkner-Cowley File*, 114.

9. *MBB*, 123–24.

10. Louise Meadow and Dean Wells, interviews with author, 18 May 1989.

11. *FOM*, 9.

12. Ibid., 8.

13. Rose Rowland, "William and His Grandmother," in Webb and Green, *William Faulkner of Oxford*, 24–25.

14. One of the few socially acceptable ways to earn income for a middle-class white Southern woman of Maud's and Lelia's eras was to take in female boarders. Elly Spence, interview with Carvel Collins. Also see Carvel Collins papers, MBF file, HRC, for the Mrs. Calvin Brown interview, 22 March 1962. Marjorie Lewis, phone interview with author, 2 February 1990.

15. *Faulkner* (1974), vol. 1.

16. See Williamson, chaps. 3 and 4, 77–141, for the story of the Butlers, the family of Maud Falkner's father, especially Charlie Butler's years as the county's marshal-sheriff, and his disappearance. As for Lelia Dean Swift's family, Williamson writes, "Exhaustive searches in the censuses of 1850, 1860, and 1870 for Mississippi, Arkansas, and Tennessee have not found Lelia" (87).

17. John R. Swift is listed as the editor in the 10 August 1888 issue of the *Cleveland County Democrat*, published in Kingsland. Stan Sadler, editor and publisher of the *Cleveland County Herald*, Rison, Ark., telephone interview with author, August 1990. Sadler was reading from a county centennial publication. There are no extant copies of either of these papers from the 1880s or 1890s.

18. "History of Arkansas, Cleveland County," in *Biographical and Historical Memoirs: Southern Arkansas*, 630. This was essentially a vanity press where you paid your money and got your biographical entry. These were generally written by their subjects.

19. In a land deed recorded 3 August 1850, "John Tate Swift and Mahalah A. Swift" sold Levi Nope 250 acres of land in Lafayette County, "namely the west part of

Section 25 Township 7 Range 4 West of the Meridian," for $600. All parties were then citizens of Lafayette County. This is the *only* place where John's whole name is given and Mahalah's is correctly spelled. All other documents give Lelia's father's name simply as John T. Swift. See *Lafayette County Deed Record Book F,* 56, County Courthouse, Oxford, Miss.

20. The North Carolina, Georgia, Mississippi, and Arkansas tax and land records, agricultural schedules, Lafayette County Police Board minutes, Baptist Church minutes and other documents give a further dimension and a sense of pathos.

21. Sobotka, *A History of Lafayette County,* 24, and the *1850 Census for Lafayette County.*

22. As household #22 in the *1850 Lafayette County Federal Census: Population Schedule,* the Swift farm would have been very close to the town.

23. *1843 Lafayette County Combination Tax Roll.*

24. Any tract over 100 acres qualifies as a plantation in this period.

25. John R. writes that in 1861 he joined Company I, First Arkansas Infantry, which fought that year in Virginia. He was in the first battle of Bull Run. In the latter part of the war he fought at Shiloh and was in Raleigh, N.C., when Lee surrendered. See Goodspeed, 630, and "Mississippi," 17.

26. Hathorn, *Early Settlers,* 42.

27. Williamson, 83; Haynes, *Heritage,* 29.

28. John Swift's slaveholdings are taken from the *Lafayette County, Miss., Personal Tax Rolls* of those years. For the move to Drew County, see the *Lafayette County, Miss., Personal Tax Rolls.* The Swift family, minus Lelia, appears in the *1860 Drew County, Ark., Census,* as do George (the Oxford school teacher) and Sarah Prouse, with whom two of the Swift children were boarding in Oxford in 1850. See household of George and Sarah Prouse (there spelled Prosise), *1850 Lafayette County Census.*

29. Dougan, *Confederate Arkansas.*

30. Creativity among the Swifts was not limited to Lelia. In 1886, William Tate Swift, another brother, was the editor of the *Kingsland Sauce.* Both brothers owned their newspapers in Arkansas. Stan Sadler, interview with author, August 1990.

31. Charles G. and Berlina Butler were among the wealthier and more influential families in Oxford. In the first county election (2 May 1836), Charles was elected sheriff of Lafayette County, and in July of that year he was employed to survey and lay off into lots for the town of Oxford the fifty acres that three men had donated to the county board. In 1837 Charles is listed as one of the men superintending the sale of stock for a proposed railroad to be built from Oxford to Pontotoc (a pipe dream). By 1850, besides their inn, which was established in 1837, the Butlers owned 230 acres of farmland valued at $1,000 (Hathorn, *Early Settlers,* 18, 29, 44, 60, 87, 90, 96). The 1850 census lists the Butler family as follows: Charles G., 45, Innkeeper, Tenn.; Berlina W., 40, N.C.; William R. or K., 20, student, Tenn.; Emily C., 18, Tenn.; Henry S[herwood], 16, student, Miss.; Mary A., 12, Miss.; Martha J., 10, Miss.; Charles E., 2, Miss. (*1850 U.S. Federal Census, Lafayette County, Miss.,* no. 1335, 136).

32. Williamson, 82.

33. *1860 U.S. Federal Census, Lafayette County, Miss.*

34. Moak, "Mystery of Grandfather Butler"; Williamson, 85. For this and much subsequent information relating to the Butlers, I am indebted to Professor Franklin E.

Moak's carefully researched, unpublished essay, "The Mystery of William Faulkner's Grandfather Butler."

35. *Marriage Bonds Book 2*, Lafayette County Courthouse.

36. Bessie Sumners, interview with author, 11 February 1989.

37. Freeman, *The Wedding Complex*, 75.

38. Williamson, 120.

39. Ibid., 89.

40. The *1880 Lafayette County Census*, the first in which Charles and Lelia appear as a family, lists their children's birthplace as Mississippi.

41. On 3 September 1871, Charlie Butler was selected "as a delegate to the meeting of the [Baptist] association which was to convene at Clear Creek Church in October" (Church Minutes, September 1871).

42. Williamson, 86.

43. Tax Rolls, Lafayette County, 1874.

44. Williamson, 89.

45. *Marriage Bonds Book 2, Lafayette County, Miss.,* 164.

46. For the first mention of Charlie's affair and escape with "a beautiful octoroon woman," see *Faulkner (*1974), 1:57, and, for greater detail, see Williamson, 124–32.

47. Bessie Sumners, interview with author, 11 February 1989; Marjorie (Mrs. Will) Lewis, interview with author, 16 February 1989; Maud (Mrs. Calvin) Brown, interview with Carvel Collins, 23 September 1962, MBF file, Collins papers, HRC.

48. *Deed Book EE*, 653–54, Lafayette County Courthouse, Oxford, Miss.

49. *OXE,* 5 April and 12 April 1888.

50. *Lafayette County Heritage*, 35. Although the town eventually settled for $874.83, Williamson argues convincingly that the actual amount was somewhere between $3,000 and $5,000 (116–19).

51. See, e.g., *OXE,* 11 October 1888.

52. Williamson, 93.

53. *Deed Book EE,* 114.

54. Williamson, 92.

55. Butler killed Thompson on 8 May 1883 (*Oxford Eagle,* 17 May 1883).

56. The editor's story, though interesting, is not part of this narrative except as an example of the interest Oxford took in policing its citizens' sexual behavior, particularly when race was involved.

57. Williamson, 110.

58. Moak, "Mystery." See *Deed Book 1,* Lafayette County, Miss.

59. Church Minutes, 1858–80, 28; Moak.

60. Ibid.

61. Church Roll information; Moak.

62. Church Minutes, 1880–91, 67–68.

63. Murry C. Falkner to Franklin E. Moak, letter, 7 March 1973, courtesy of Franklin Moak.

64. The school's "mission" as stated in its 1889–90 catalog, where Maud is registered for the business course. College records indicate she also attended in 1891–92, although the catalog for that year is missing. Maud appears again in the

1894–95 catalog, where she is registered for drawing as a Special Student in the Industrial Arts.

65. *Oxford Globe*, 2 July 1891, and other issues of the Oxford papers.

66. During the first five years of Maud's marriage, when she and Murry lived in New Albany and Ripley, Lelia addressed her letters to "Miss M. Butler, care of Mr. Murry Falkner." Murry begged his wife "to get your mother to stop this," but she continued until she moved in with them in Oxford in 1902. Interview with Mrs. J. W. T. Falkner, Jr. (Sue Harkins, Holland's and Murry's sister-in-law), 31 December 1974, in Wells, *Dean Swift Falkner*, 5.

67. *Faulkner* (1984), 6.

68. *AH*, 1.

CHAPTER 8: WILLIE FALKNER'S CHILDHOOD WORLD, 1896–1907

1. Nell Irvin Painter argues that we must attend to "sex and the psychological aspects of white supremacy and Southern identity" because it was not merely an ideology. Rather it was a belief system, deeply "rooted in sex and personal gendered identity." See "Three Southern Women and Freud: A Non-Exceptionalist Approach to Race, Class and Gender in the Slave South," in her *Southern History*, 220n7.

2. Jimmy Falkner, interview with Joseph Blotner, 12 April 1977.

3. Sallie Murry Williams, interview with Joseph Blotner, 26 November 1965.

4. SB, interview with Carvel Collins, 4 August 1963, Collins papers, HRC.

5. Women's Book Club Minutes, vol. 2, n.p.; courtesy of Mary Hartwell Howorth. Sallie Murry's good works extended beyond her own congregation and family. On Thanksgiving she took baskets to the county poor farm. But "she did it quietly, without fanfare and not for fame," said her niece Sallie Burns. She also "sensed the deprivation of the non-fraternity boys" at the university, "their exclusion from all social and extra-curricular affairs. They were not even included in the college Annual or Yearbook unless they were athletes. In defiance of the general snobbishness she always invited them over and many sang in her church choir" (SB, interviews with Carvel Collins, 4 and 6 August 1963, Collins papers, HRC). "She was elegant and although she had never been to college, was a great reader" (Bessie Sumners, interview with author, 21 May 1988). Sallie Murry Falkner was "outspoken, utterly frank, scorning all pretense, and making very plain her likes and dislikes"; she was loved and respected as "a very sweet and kindly and generous old lady with her bark far worse than her bite" *Faulkner* (1974), 1:78.

6. SB, interview, 7 August 1963, Collins papers, file 2, Burns, HRC.

7. *MBB*, 236.

8. *FOM*, 9–10.

9. MBF, interview with Carvel Collins, 13 April 1950, Collins papers, HRC.

10. SB, interview with Carvel Collins, 4 August 1963, Collins papers, HRC.

11. Dean Wells, interview with Joseph Blotner, 11 June 1980, SEMS.

12. Christine Drake, interview with author, 6 and 9 February 1989. Drake (from Aberdeen) boarded with Maud from 1951–1953 when she was teaching adult education at the University of Mississippi. A Thompson, her family connections to Oxford date from its founding. Dean Wells writes that Maud was a great saver, especially of things

belonging to her children: "baby teeth, locks of hair, letters and postcards. . . . She kept a cigar box for each child." See Wells, "Dean Faulkner, Dean Swift Faulkner [*sic*]: A Biographical Study," master's thesis, University of Mississippi, 1975. The whereabouts of Maud's cigar boxes and their contents is not known.

13. As early as 1912 Faulkner owned a camera, probably the only camera in the family, since he lent it to his mother when she went on a trip. See "Dear Miss Lady," WF to MBF, 16 August 1912, in *Thinking of Home*, 39.

14. *Faulkner* (1974), 1:112–13.

15. See, for example, Hightower being caught by news photographers as he exits his church in disgrace, a moment told from two narrative perspectives—once to introduce Hightower's story and once near its conclusion so that this photographic image itself frames Faulkner's telling of Hightower's tale (LIA 68 and 489).

16. WF, quoted in Cohen and Fowler, "Faulkner's Introduction," 280, 273.

17. SB, 1963.

18. Upon returning from military service, Faulkner's actions mirror those of his great-grandfather in 1847. On his homecoming, the Colonel wrote his first book, a long, melodramatic narrative poem with little literary merit, *The Siege of Monterey* (1851). He also claimed to have a war wound, a claim not supported by his discharge papers. Much of the rest of this chapter is drawn from *Origins*, chap. 4, and my "William Faulkner, Poet to Novelist."

19. See Greenacre, "The Relation of the Imposter to the Artist," 526.

20. Williamson, 44, 45.

21. Helene Deutsch quotes her patient: "Jimmy, while firmly pretending that he *was* what he pretended to be, asked me again and again, sometimes in despair: 'Who am I? Can you tell me that?'" (497). Many of Faulkner's poetic personae, as well as his fictional characters, ask this same question.

22. Whenever Faulkner places himself in a new situation or strange surroundings, he either elaborates on his current imposture or assumes a new one. Additions occur when he enrolls at the University of Mississippi, where he alternates among the wounded hero, the impeccably dressed aesthete, and the ragged poet, and in New Orleans, where he adopted a new mentor, Sherwood Anderson and further exaggerated his limp and head wound. During these stages of his imposture he was already drinking fairly heavily (*Faulkner*, 1974).

23. *Pontotoc True Democrat*, May 1886.

24. *Faulkner* (1974), 1:14–19, and Sensibar, *Origins*, chap. 4.

25. Ibid., 1:37.

26. Ibid., 1:68.

27. Murry was promoted to general passenger agent on 28 September 1896 and to his next position on 7 November 1898.

28. MBF to SB, undated letter (1950s), Collins papers, MBF file, HRC.

29. WF to the Reverend Robert Elijah Jones, 15 March 1940; published in the *Georgia Review* 55:3 (Fall 2001): 536–42.

30. Ibid.

31. "She [Maud] wasn't snobbish at all but she was very much aware of everybody's status. One afternoon we were sitting on her porch and I told her that Vasser Bishop and her father and mother had invited me to come and have a sandwich

Sunday night. 'You couldn't have chosen a better family than the Bishops and the Somervilles, especially the Somervilles' she said." Christine Drake, interview with author, 6 February 1989.

32. WF to the Reverend Robert Elijah Jones, 15 March 1940.

33. JFS, interview with author, 28 October 1998.

34. *OXE*, 27 March 1902.

35. *Faulkner* (1974), 1:80. In *Elmer*, the unfinished novel Faulkner wrote sporadically between 1925 and 1929, he returns to this family argument. In his fictional representation Elmer's mother, not his shiftless father, is the parent who insists on moving to Texas. There she is punished for her rash and willful actions: she loses her house to fire and her daughter to the streets, and dies an early death. Worst of all, her son Elmer, unlike the real Faulkner, fails to become an artist.

36. *OXE*, 2 October 1902.

37. Typescript of "Oxford Women's Book Club History to 1929," courtesy of Mary Hartwell Howorth.

38. Women's Book Club Minutes, vol. 2, n.p.

39. Ibid.

40. Ibid., vol. 3, n.p.

41. See Sensibar, *Origins*, 14–18, and Chap. 5, this vol.

42. Maud's obituary said that she had painted "as a young woman" and that "after her marriage, she painted a little, mostly pictures of her children. But bringing up four boys, she gave up painting" until 1941. *Memphis Press Scimitar*, 17 October 1960.

43. *FOM*, 48.

44. Negatives from the front endpapers of the Falkner family Bible, JFSA; now at Rowan Oak.

45. *FOM*, 83, 89, 9, 150.

46. *Faulkner* (1974), 1:81.

47. *OXE*, 10 August 1905.

48. Ibid., 16 July 1908.

49. *Faulkner* (1974), 1:18.

50. *OXE*, 15 September 1904.

51. Sallie Murry Williams interview, 19 August 1964, Blotner papers, SEMS.

52. Dixon, *The Clansman*, 3.

53. Ibid., 267, 374, 179; see also 304–5.

54. Ibid., 291, 290, 291.

55. Ibid., 292–93.

56. JFS, interview with author, 23 October 1980.

57. Ibid., 16 October 1987.

58. *FOM*, 45.

59. As Tom Dardis and others who write about the history and culture of American addiction note, the main ingredient in over-the-counter pain medications was and is alcohol or another addictive ingredient, especially opiates and opiate derivatives. See Dardis, "50 to 80 Proof," in *Thirsty Muse*, 33.

60. More questionable was Keeley's drug therapy. He and his successors treated all chemical addictions as well as neurasthenia over a four-week period by injecting

patients four times daily with double chloride of gold, composed of gold, alcohol, and strychnine.

61. Keeley, *Non-Heredity of Inebriety.*

CHAPTER 9: FROM HONOR ROLL TO TRUANCY, 1907–1914

1. *MBB,* 70.

2. Estelle Faulkner, interviews with Blotner; Blotner papers, Estelle Faulkner file, *SEMS.*

3. Bessie Sumners, interview with author, 19 May 1988.

4. *OXE,* 16 July 1908.

5. Dixon, *The Clansman,* 321, 244.

6. *MBB,* 210. "She was particularly fond of Joseph Conrad, a man's writer, and we came to know him through her. A collection of Conrad was always on Bill's bookshelf. *The Virginian* was a favorite of hers and ours too, as well as Shaw and Samuel Butler" (*MBB,* 236). His comments regarding his dislike of school are from an unpublished portion of the class conference at the University of Virginia, 5 June 1957.

7. Bessie Sumners, interview with author, 19 May 1988, and Ralph Muckenfuss, Faulkner's desk mate that year (*Faulkner* [1984], 33).

8. *Faulkner* (1974), 1:123.

9. In the 1950s he told Robert Linscott, an editor at Random House who spent time with him, that "his grandfather used to give him heeltaps [the last drops in the glass]." Inge, *Conversations with William Faulkner,* 96.

10. *Faulkner* (1974), 1:125.

11. Ibid., 1:120.

12. Ibid., 1:155.

13. *MBB,* 122.

14. *Faulkner* (1974), 1:180.

15. Ibid., 1:157, 175.

16. Estelle Faulkner, interviews with Blotner, n.d., Blotner papers, Estelle Faulkner file, SEMS.

17. Sallie Murry Williams, interview with Blotner, 19 August 1964, Blotner papers, SMW file, SEMS.

18. Mrs. Calvin Brown, interview with Carvel Collins, 22 March 1963, Collins papers, Mrs. C. Brown, Sr., file, HRC; and Bessie Sumners, interview with author, 19 May 1988.

19. *FOM,* 47–48.

20. Markette, "Railroad Days," *WFO,* 29.

21. *Faulkner* (1974), 1:142.

22. *MBB,* 122.

23. *Faulkner* (1974), 1:143, 148–49.

24. *FOM,* 11.

25. *MBB,* 127; *Faulkner* (1974), 1:151.

26. Bessie Sumners, interview with author, 21 May 1988.

27. "There was a ferocity in Nanny" and a "Spartan" quality. "She painted all the

panels of her safe with moss roses. But in general, her house was as Spartan as she. I don't remember ever seeing fresh flowers. She wasn't interested in gardening or in anything that had to be cultivated, including grass. She didn't like to cook but we'd always have a big breakfast—scrambled eggs, waffles, fresh whipped cream. She liked her toast charred on both sides. She'd cut it very carefully in three strips with a minimum of butter and then she'd just crunch that toast" (Dean Wells, interview with author, 14 May 1989).

28. Christine Drake, interview with author, 9 February 1989.

29. Marjorie Lewis, interview with author, February 1989.

30. See Billie to Maud, 16 August 1912, *TOH*, 39–40.

31. Robert Farley, interview cited in Wells, "Dean Swift Falkner," 34.

32. Jimmy Falkner, interview with Carvel Collins, 17 March 1965, Collins papers, HRC.

33. Wells, "Dean Swift Falkner," 34, 38.

34. *Faulkner* (1974), 1:151.

35. Louise Meadow, interview with author, 22 June 1989.

36. *Faulkner* (1974), 1:160.

37. Estelle Oldham, interview, 1951, FCUM.

38. Jimmy Falkner, interview, 21 March 1965, Blotner papers, SEMS.

39. Meriwether, *Literary Career of William Faulkner*, 87. This early version no longer exists. The two surviving versions were written after Faulkner had finished *Soldiers' Pay* (*USWF*, 495–503). Facsimiles are printed in the Garland Edition, vol. 25. Typescripts of the two extant versions are in FCVA.

40. This Bible, owned by Jill Summers, is at Rowan Oak. It is not clear to whom it belonged, since "Maud Falkner" is written beneath "William Falkner" on its inside front cover. Maud wrote this note on the book's free endpaper in the back.

41. MBF, interview with Carvel Collins, 13 April 1950, Collins papers, HRC. Other than the few phrases in quotations, Collins simply paraphrases what Maud said. Again, her voice is occluded.

42. *Faulkner* (1974), 1:192.

43. Sallie Murry Williams, letter to Blotner, 5 September 1967, Blotner papers, SEMS.

44. *Faulkner* (1974), 1:233.

45. Martha Ida Wiseman, Murry Falkner's secretary, interview with author, 11 May 1989.

46. Ibid.

47. *Faulkner* (1984), 73–74, 308.

48. Quoted in ibid., 308.

CHAPTER 10: CHOOSING ROLES AND ROLE MODELS

1. For the story of this apprenticeship, see Sensibar, *Origins,* and for a complete listing of Faulkner's poetry, see Sensibar, *Faulkner's Poetry.*

2. See Sensibar, *Origins,* xv–19.

3. Millgate, *The Achievement of William Faulkner,* 1. Faulkner jealously guarded his "new" name. In the early 1940s his brother John decided he, too, could write for a

living and altered the spelling of his last name to ride on his older brother's coattails. Faulkner was "infuriated. A few weeks later Pappy, then famous, philosophically commented, 'If putting a "u" in his name would get a leech off my back, I am happy'" (*Bitterweeds*, 99).

4. This and the official photographs Faulkner poses for throughout his career are interesting for what they reveal about the character he wished to project upon the public. In them he always looks tall, cocky, and authoritative. Actually he was only five feet five inches tall, whereas his brother Jack, his father, and his grandfather were all six-footers.

5. Phyllis Greenacre mentions Goethe, Fritz Kreisler, and Thomas Chatterton ("The Impostor," 525).

6. Bate, *John Keats*, 137–40.

7. "Sustained imposture . . . is the living out of an oedipal conflict through revival of the earliest definite image of the father. In so far as *the imposture* is accomplished, *it is the killing of the father through the complete displacement of him. It further serves to give a temporary feeling of completion of identity* [sense of self]" (Greenacre, "The Impostor," 370–71; emphasis added). Finkelstein gives the most succinct and authoritative definition of a pathological impostor. "The impostor is a person who assumes a false name or identity for the purpose of deceiving others; he is a type of pathological liar who hopes to gain some advantage from his deception. Unlike the show-off or poseur who fails to deceive people and leaves them chiefly impressed with his pretentiousness, the impostor succeeds at least for awhile in charming his audience into believing his deceptions. His role playing differs from more normal forms of pretending and acting a part, which are forms of mastery or play, because it involves driven, repetitious behavior that stems from unresolved pathological inner conflicts" (Finkelstein, "The Impostor," 85).

8. What psychoanalysts call "defective superego functioning" or what we would call lack of conscience or amorality directs the behavior of all impostors described in medical literature. See Finkelstein, "The Impostor," 91–92.

9. See Abraham, "History of an Impostor"; Deutsch, "The Imposter"; Finkelstein, "The Impostor"; Greenacre, "The Impostor"; and Rank, *The Myth of the Birth*.

10. Faulkner, in a letter to his publisher Horace Liveright (16 October 1927), *SL*, 38.

11. WF to Horace Liveright (late July 1927), *SL*, 37.

12. See Sensibar, *Origins*, 19–28.

13. WF, interview with Jean Stein, in Meriwether and Millgate, *Lion in the Garden*, 255.

14. WF, quoted in Blotner, "William Faulkner's Essay," 125.

CHAPTER 11: LEARNING TO SPEAK WITH HIS EYES

1. See Jones, *Tomorrow*, 41–46.

2. WF to Malcolm Cowley, c. January 1946, *SL*, 216.

3. Louis D. Rubin, Jr., quoting from a Virginia newspaper editor's welcoming speech to Charles Dickens, 1842, in *Writer in the South*, 12.

4. See Rubin, quoting from George W. Cable's 1883 commencement speech, in *Writer in the South*, 10. Rubin notes that, until Faulkner, the only accomplished writers

who seriously challenged the status quo—Samuel Clemens and Edgar Allan Poe—left the South. Faulkner's male friends who wished to be artists and writers—Ben Wasson, Lyle Saxon, William Spratling, and Stark Young—followed their example. Obviously, Faulkner was not the only writer working in the South in the 1920s. The Nashville Agrarians represent, as Rubin notes, an "essential stage in the history of Southern literature" (82). Besides Allan Tate, Robert Penn Warren, and the others, Thomas Wolfe published *Look Homeward, Angel* in 1929, and first novels by Erskine Caldwell and Hamilton Basso appeared the same year. Ellen Glasgow, James Cabell, and other novelists had been publishing steadily throughout the early 1920s. Faulkner's challenge and achievement seem even more exceptional and unique when he is read in their context.

5. Jones, *Tomorrow*, 44, 34, 44. Paradoxically, however, the questioning of these values began in the South's historical endorsement of women writers, beginning in the 1840s and 1850s (45). See also Susan V. Donaldson, "Cracked Lens," 51–81.

6. WF to MBF, *TOH*, 95n1.

7. See Sensibar, *Origins*, chap. 12, for discussion of Southern women artists Faulkner chose as friends and lovers.

8. Jones shows how certain Southern women writers used similar tactics. Faulkner's fictional Southern "authoress," Rosa Coldfield, demonstrates his intimate understanding of such women.

9. Berger, "The Primitive," 64. In 1941, Maud Butler had her only "formal" lessons, with the exception of a college Industrial Arts class. "The instructor insisted her technique was all wrong, that she should sketch the whole portrait before painting. But Miss Maud said she was left to her own devices" (Silver, "*McCall's* Visits 'Miss Maud,'" 2).

10. Berger, "The Primitive," 64.

11. "The primitive begins alone; she inherits no practice. . . . She does not use the pictorial grammar of the tradition—hence she is ungrammatical" (Berger, "The Primitive," 68); I have changed "he" to "she."

12. Berger, "The Primitive," 68.

13. MBF to SB, 4 March and 24 November 1958 and 22 July 1960. Collins papers, HRC. There are eighteen letters in the two Sallie Faulkner Burns folders. Originally there were thirty. No one at the HRC seemed to know where the others were.

14. MBF, interview, summer 1953; quoted in Dahl, "A Faulkner Reminiscence," 1028.

15. MBF to SB, 26 December 1954, Collins papers, MBF file, HRC.

16. All quotes are from MBF's letters to her niece SB, dated as follows: 10 October 1956; 14 August 1955; 26 March 1956; 14 August 1955; Collins papers, HRC.

17. Silver, "*McCall's* Visits Miss Maud," typescript, 2, JFSA. Subsequently published in *McCall's*, October 1956, 22–23, 25.

18. Barthes, "The Photographic Message," in *Barthes Reader*, 206–7.

19. Barthes, *Camera Lucida*, 85; Sontag, *On Photography*, 57.

20. See Brody's *Impossible Purities*, 8, for an elegant historical tracing and discussion of the impossibility of purity and the inevitability of hybridity from British Victorian to modern American representations of ethnicity, sexuality, gender, and race.

21. Fictional photographs also permit Faulkner's characters to release otherwise

silenced emotions. For more on these works, see Sensibar, "Faulkner's Fictional Photographs."

22. Tydeman and Price, *Wilde: Salome*, 177, 179, 115.

23. Dahl, "A Faulkner Reminiscence," 1028.

24. In her catalogue to a photographic exhibition, "Rrose is a Rrose is a Rrose: Gender Performance in Photography," Jennifer Blessing notes that "the medium of photography yields the perfect arena for the play of gender and sexuality." Like the nineteenth- and twentieth-century artists and ordinary people whose photographs are featured in this catalogue, Faulkner's self-portraits in various masquerades show he recognized that "photography's strong aura of realism and objectivity promotes a fantasy of total gender transformation, or, conversely, allows the articulation of incongruity between the posing body and its assumed costume" (8).

25. *Faulkner* (1974) and (1984); Goffman, *Presentation of Self*; Grimwood, *Heart in Conflict;* Sensibar, *Origins* and "'Drowsing Maidenhead'"; and Strauss, "A Discussion of Judith L. Sensibar's 'William Faulkner, Poet to Novelist.'"

26. Dahl, "A Faulkner Reminiscence," 1027.

27. *SL;* Cowley, *Faulkner-Cowley File.*

28. Watson, *William Faulkner,* 50.

CHAPTER 12: READING FAULKNER'S "MOTHERS"

1. For some of the most interesting treatments of Rosa Coldfield and Clytie and Judith Sutpen, see the following works by Gwin: *Black and White Women of the Old South and The Feminine and Faulkner,* and "The Silencing of Rosa Coldfield," in Hobson, *Absalom, Absalom!,* 151–88. See also Davis, "The Signifying Abstraction," 69–107, in Hobson, *Absalom, Absalom!;* Boone, *Libidinal Currents,* 289–322.

2. Gwin was first to question the judgment of the male gaze in *Absalom, Absalom!* and brilliantly argued that Rosa "is both artist and participant. It is she who insists not only that the story be told, but that it be understood." See her *Black and White Women,* 116, and *The Feminine and Faulkner,* 75.

3. Jones, *Tomorrow,* 42.

4. Berger, *Ways of Seeing,* 64, 54–55.

5. Describing the Southern writer's audience, Faulkner said, "I think that most Southerners know that his home folks ain't going to like what he writes anyway. That he's not really writing to them, and that they simply do not read books. . . . The non-writing Southerner, the non-reading Southerner, he wants the sort of brochure that the Chamber of Commerce gets out. There are things in his country that he's not too proud of himself, but to him it's bad manners to show that in public." William Faulkner, interview, 13 May 1957, *FIU,* 136–37.

6. I say series because Faulkner was using his Leica camera. He probably enlarged the two best shots, one of Callie with Jill sitting beside her on a log out in back of Rowan Oak and one of Callie Barr sitting alone and smoking what looks like a cigarette. On one copy of the former photograph, Faulkner has written "Camera— Leica / Lenz—1.3, 5 F-50mm / L is at 4.5 / shutter 1 / 60 / Eastman Panchromatic Film/Overcast 5:00 PM / May '39" (Collins papers, HRC). See James Watson's transcription in *William Faulkner,* 35.

PARTS 3, 4, AND 5: WILLIAM FAULKNER AND ESTELLE OLDHAM

Epigraph: WF to Tom Kell, Pascagoula, Miss., July 1929; quoted in *Faulkner* (1984), 243.

INTRODUCTION TO PARTS 3, 4, AND 5

1. *Faulkner* (1974), 1:142.

2. Besides my prior work, see Moser, "Faulkner's Muse."

3. WF to Estelle Oldham Faulkner (20 July 1934), *SL*, 82–83.

4. *SL*. See FCVA for the uncensored versions of these letters.

5. *SL*, 235–36.

6. Some of the more recent assessments of the Faulkners' marriage are as follows: "That early relationship . . . helped create their doomed marriage—doomed before they married" (Karl, *William Faulkner*, 257); "During their honeymoon when she fearlessly and absentmindedly entered the tragic and mundane daily life that was to be hers, his wife attempted suicide" (Glissant, *Faulkner, Mississippi*, 36); and "[Faulkner] must have seen he was stepping into a doomed relationship, one based on a fantasy of home and hearth, but he could not stop himself" (Parini, *One Matchless Time*, 130).

7. Louise Meadow and Maggie Brown, interviews with author, 26 June 1989 and 26 May 1986, respectively; Jill Faulkner Summers and marriage and birth announcements in *OXE*.

8. There, I discuss "Dr. Wohlenski" in the context of the Franklins' divorce, the Faulkners' marriage, and the 1933 introduction Faulkner wrote for *The Sound and the Fury* and then withdrew from publication. In "Mississippi," Faulkner's fictional memoir, he spoke of his debt to Callie Barr from behind a safe veil or masquerade. In this earlier essay, Faulkner acknowledges less obliquely his debt to Estelle.

9. "Star Spangled Banner Stuff" was published in 1997. See Sensibar, "Writing for Faulkner, Writing for Herself," and Oldham, "Star Spangled Banner Stuff."

10. Franklin earned some of his tuition and board working in the university post office (CSF, Oath of P.O. Employee, University of Mississippi, 23 August 1910 and 30 October 1912, CSFA). Interviews with Franklin friends and relatives reveal that, in direct contradiction of all published accounts, Cornell Franklin was not at all wealthy when he and Estelle married (interviews with author: Merrill Thomas, 28 August 1989; Lilla Pratt Rosamond, 28 August 1989; and Katherine Searcy, 24 May 1988). Mamie worked for Searcy's father, who was the owner and editor of the *Columbus Dispatch*.

11. Undated (c. 20 June 1929), handwritten, hand-delivered letter addressed to "Mama and Daddy." Courtesy of Estelle's granddaughter from her first marriage, Victoria Fielden Johnson.

12. Katherine Andrews, interview with author, 10 August 1987.

13. Jim Godfrey, interview with author, 17 May 1993.

14. Faulkner's first publisher was Boni and Liveright. See WF to Horace Liveright, 18 February 1927, in *SL*, 34–35. According to Blotner, Estelle's novel was ultimately sent to Scribner's, not Boni and Liveright (*Faulkner* [1984], 197).

15. Davis first observed Anderson's contribution to what I call Faulkner's racialized aesthetic in *Faulkner's "Negro,"* 32–64. Building on Davis I suggest that Faulkner's immersion in Anderson and, through him, in Stein and Toomer

taught Faulkner much about a racialized stylistics that makes its first appearance in *Soldiers' Pay.*

16. *TOH,* 219, 228–29.

17. JFS to author. The complete sentence is "Some of the good people of Oxford declined to let their children play with me." Years later, Jill elaborated: "People weren't wild about their children playing with Pappy's offspring. I had a solitary life. They thought Pappy was a no-good drunkard" (JFS, interviews with author, 31 July 1980 and 7 November 1995).

18. Katherine Andrews, interview with author, 10 August 1987.

19. Maggie Brown, interview with author, 26 May 1986.

20. Leo Falk, M.D., interview with author, 21 April 1993.

21. JFS, interview with author, 24 March 1993.

22. "Hong-Li" was first published in Noel Polk's "'Hong-Li' and *Royal Street:* The New Orleans Sketches in Manuscript," in *Mississippi Quarterly.* It was reprinted in Meriwether, *A Faulkner Miscellany,* 143–44, and in Polk, "William Faulkner's 'Hong Li' and *Royal Street,*" *Library Chronicle of the University of Texas at Austin,* n.s. 13 (1980): 27–30.

23. JFS, interview with author, 28 February 1993.

CHAPTER 13: ESTELLE OLDHAM'S MISSISSIPPI FRONTIER FAMILY

1. Interview with Estelle Faulkner, *Richmond News Leader,* 3 November 1964.

2. "Estelle" to "Mama and Daddy," holograph envelope and undated two-page ink holograph, on letterhead stationery from "Rice-Stix Manufacturing Wholesalers, St. Louis" (letter courtesy of Victoria Fielden Johnson). This is one of Estelle's five known extant letters or letter fragments dating from 1917–29.

3. Elizabeth Otey Watson, interview with author, 8 February 1994.

4. In November 1924, Mamie abruptly canceled her trip to the Franklins' Shanghai house when she learned of Estelle's imminent and unexpected arrival in Mississippi. See letter from Cornell's secretary to Mamie Hairston, CFSA.

5. The Faulkners left Columbus on 1 July and arrived in Pascagoula two days later, when Faulkner wired Mamie that they had arrived safely. On 4 July Mamie replied with a four-page letter: "My precious Children/ Bill's wire yesterday made us all happy—The first question Pops [her husband] asked when he came last night was—'Have you heard from Estelle and Bill?' We thought of you all day Monday and Tuesday—wondering where you spent Monday night etc. I failed to put in the oranges and tomatoes ordered especially for your lunch—The University called Bill Monday night—I told *Central* that he and family left Monday morning for Pascagoula." She goes on to give some family news and say she has forwarded mail to her new son-in-law, paid some bills "with the check Estelle left," and hopes that their "four trunks reached Pascagoula promptly." She closes with "I wish I could tell you how painfully I miss every one of you. I think of this home as yours too . . . Love and Kisses for all of you—Devotedly, Mother—" (Hairston to WF, 4 July 1929, accession no. 10817, box w/10443, 4 July 1929, FCVA).

6. Carolyn Neault, Historian and Librarian, Columbus, Miss., Public Library, interview with author, February 1989. Neault had heard this story from Rufus Ward, a contemporary of the Faulkners'.

7. *Faulkner* (1984), 245.

8. JFS, phone interview with author, 8 February 1994.

9. Glissant, *Faulkner, Mississippi*, 36.

10. At the same time that Faulkner left Harcourt, Brace, in early 1928, Hal Smith, his editor there, also left to start a new publishing house with Jonathan Cape (Cape and Smith). Smith took the manuscript of *The Sound and the Fury* with him and contracted to publish it on 18 February 1929. This was Faulkner's fourth publisher in just over four years (*Faulkner* [1974], 1:603).

11. The legal chronology of Estelle's and Cornell's divorce is as follows: on 13 November 1928, Cornell files an Interlocutory Order for divorce in the United States Court for China. A ninety-day wait is required before he can file the final divorce decree, which he does on 15 February 1929. Another ninety days must elapse before that becomes final, about 15 May 1929. Faulkner and Estelle marry on 20 June 1929. See *Minutes of Chancery Court*, book 8, Oxford, Miss., and official transcript from the records of the United States Court for China, 25 February 1929 (CSFA).

12. Undated letter to his publisher, Harrison ("Hal") Smith, of Smith and Haas, Berg Collection, New York Public Library, and quoted in *Faulkner* (1984), 239.

13. "Mama was a rather venomous woman when it came to other women. . . . She didn't like Estelle, Jill, or me." Victoria added that "[after Blotner's biography came out] we were both riled up over the errors in it, about us. . . . I think she may have decided that no other person, scholar, researcher, academician, journalist, whatever, was going to paw over personal correspondence with her mother. I doubt she thought Estelle might be researched as a writer in her own right" (Victoria Johnson, letter to author, 9 October 1999). Jill says that "Vicky told me that just before Victoria [Cho-Cho] died, she burned all Mama's paper and letters. Cho-Cho told Vicky that she had burned everything because she hated my mother so. She just wanted to get rid of every evidence of her" (JFS, interview with author, 23 February 1987).

14. See *SL*, 42–43, 41.

15. WF to Robert Haas, Random House (7 June 1940), *SL*, 129.

16. Lem Oldham's great-great grandfather was Jesse Oldham, from Prince William County, Va. (c. 1733–1814), who with Daniel Boone founded Boonesboro. He stayed there two years before going to North Carolina, where he served under his brother, Captain John Oldham, in the Revolutionary War. Lem's grandfather Baylis Earle (1809–90), described in a local history as a pioneer settler in Attala County, was one of the founders of Kosciusko, and an uncle, Sylvanus Thaddeus (1834–1902), was a graduate of Cumberland Law School and a major in the Confederate Army. By the time the eighth child was born to Lem's father, Emmett C. Baylis (1845–73), the family's wealth—enough to send the first three children to college and law school— had dwindled. Sylvanus's family, along with a sister and her husband, had emigrated to Dublin, Texas. In 1873, Lem's father, who was deeply embroiled in local politics, was "shot and instantly killed in the court house by Burrell Johnston. The latter was tried and acquitted and now [1893] lives in the county." "A Short Account of White Men and Women That Have Been Killed Within the Bounds of the County Since Its Organization [1833]—Items of Much Interest" (see *Kosciusko Star*, 1893); "Attala County: Murders," Sanders File, Kosciusko Library. See also Oldham Death Notice file, Rowan Oak. Emmett's oldest son, Lem, was three. Lem's mother, Melvina

Murphy Doty (Mellie), was a direct descendent of the infamous Edward Doty, who instigated the *Mayflower* mutiny and whose name is carved on Plymouth Rock (Joyce W. Sanders, letter to author, 6 July 1987, and Rowland's profile of Lemuel Earle Oldham [1870–1945] in *History of Mississippi*, 189–90). (In "Dr. Wohlenski," Estelle embarrasses her grandfather by telling the story of this relative.) Mellie did not remarry until 1883. See Doty family Bible, Rowan Oak, Miss., and Kosciusko *Star Ledger*. Meanwhile the Oldhams' economic situation was precarious.

17. Judge Henry Clay Niles, like his father, Jason, was United States district judge for Mississippi. In 1889, at the age of forty Henry Niles was appointed a federal judge for Mississippi. He served in that position in the Oxford area for twenty-eight years. Lem Oldham probably read law under him. Both the Niles and Oldham families were Republicans (Joyce W. Sanders, letter to author, 22 July 1987, and Rowland, *History*, 189).

18. Alumnae records of the Mississippi University for Women, Columbus, Miss., and of the New England Conservatory of Music, Boston, Mass.

19. George A. Leighton, letter to Mrs. L. E. Oldham, 26 June 1921; courtesy of Victoria Fielden Johnson.

20. *Kosciusko Star*, 5 July 1895.

21. *Ledger*, 9 July 1897. Niles's grandfather was an Episcopal bishop in Vermont, but his son Jason (Henry's father) had no interest in entering the church. Leaving the East, he settled in Kosciusko in 1848, practiced law, and became involved in state politics, always as a Republican. In 1868 he participated in the Mississippi Constitutional Convention and sat in the legislature after that. He was circuit judge of the Northern District until 1891. Jason was well liked, considered a good judge, and owned one of the largest private libraries in the state, which his son, Henry, inherited (Mrs. E. C. Fenwick, interview with author, 9 August 1987).

22. *Mississippi Farmer*, 9 September 1897.

23. *Ledger*, 31 December 1897.

24. *Democrat*, 31 January 1899.

25. Ibid.,2 October 1900.

26. *Kosciusko Herald*, 28 November 1902.

27. "Hon. Lemuel Earle Oldham," in Rowland, *History*, 189–90.

28. Founded in 1859 by the highly successful businessman, self-promoter, and one-time mayor of Poughkeepsie, Harvey G. Eastman, it was a forerunner by decades of today's business schools. Lem Oldham probably learned of Eastman from a newspaper advertisement (Myra Morales, Local History Librarian, Adriance Library, Poughkeepsie, N.Y., interview with author, 1987; see also Eastman's obituary in the *New York Times*, 14 July 1878).

29. Mrs. E. C. Fenwick, interview with author, 7 July 1987. Register of the Department of Justice, Federal Documents Depository, Old Gym, University of Mississippi, Oxford, Miss.

30. JFS, interview with author, 18 July 1988.

31. Besides teaching piano, Lida was (like both Cornell and Faulkner) the university postmistress.

32. Joyce Sanders, letters to author, 18 and 27 August 1987.

33. Katherine Andrews (Mrs. L. C.), interview with author, 10 August 1987, and

letter to author, 22 August 1987. Mrs. Andrews had relatives in Kosciusko, but her family was from Oxford and related to the Shegogs, the family that built Rowan Oak, which she said was built in 1848, not 1840 as is written. Katherine was born in Oxford in 1893 and lived on the same block as the Falkners and Oldhams, whom she played with and had known since childhood.

34. See Allen-Oldham family correspondence: Cornelia Benton to Victoria Allen, 15 January 1875, and Cornelia Benton to Victoria Allen, 22 November 1875, VJA.

35. Walter Davis, interview with author, 7 August 1987. Jason and Swanson were Miss Vic and Judge Niles's twin sons. They appear in Estelle's fictional memoir.

36. Interviews with author: Walter Davis, 7 August 1987; Mrs. E. C. Fenwick, 7 July 1987; and Katherine Andrews, 10 August 1987.

37. Etta graduated in June 1887.

38. Registration card for Lida Allen, Kosciusko, Miss., Alumni Office, New England Conservatory of Music. For more information about Lida's experience, see the *Prospectus of the New England Conservatory of Music, 1892–93*.

39. *OXE*, 12 January 1888.

40. Joseph Blotner, interview with Mrs. J. Hudson (Katrina Carter), *Faulkner* (1974), 1:204.

CHAPTER 14: KOSCIUSKO CHILDHOOD, SOUTHERN BELLEDOM, AND ESTELLE'S FICTIONAL MEMOIR, 1897–1903

Epigraph: WF, *The Town* (New York: Random House, 1957), 6.

1. Estelle's birth date recorded by her father in the Oldham-Doty family Bible in Estelle's desk at Rowan Oak (JFSA). According to all previous biographers, and in keeping with their image of Estelle as the older woman, she is supposed to be "a year and a half older than he" (*Faulkner* [1984], 40). In fact, she's eight months older.

2. *The D. M. Anderson Business Directory and Handy Guide of Bonham, Fannin County, Texas, 1894* (Dallas: D. M. Anderson Directory Co., 1894), 28, and interview with Tom Scott, Fannin County Museum of History, 4 August 1998. His granddaughter remembers Lem as always changing into another "snowy white dress shirt" when he returned home for luncheon from "Oldham Enterprises," his second-floor office overlooking Oxford Square, where Square Books is now located.

3. *Ledger*, 5 March 1887.

4. There are extant photocopies of three of Estelle's short stories. One of these, "Dr. Wohlenski," is a thirty-three-page typescript (on legal-size paper), eleven thousand words in length, of what appears to be the first two parts of a story. Typed upper left on the first page is "Dr. Wohlenski/Part I." Part I is canceled in ink holograph and then "Dr. Wohlenski" is repeated in ink holograph at the top center of the page. Page eleven of the typescript is followed by a one-page ink holograph insert written on lined legal-pad paper and labeled "11–2" in the upper left-hand corner. On page fifteen the story is divided with a centered title, "II 1904." In fact, this would have been 1902, in that the Oldhams moved to Oxford in the fall of 1903. To avoid confusion, I use the correct dating in my text. The last ten lines of the last extant page have been canceled in the same ink as that used on the insert page. Prior to these revisions, the page had ended in mid-sentence. All three stories are now included in the FCVA.

5. According to the narrator, her sister, Victoria, is called Tochie because "there were so many Victorias in the family . . . [that] one of them had to have a nickname" and the baby, "not being able to help herself, was called Tochie. They blamed it on me, but I didn't quite believe them—for I knew that I could have made up something better" ("Dr. Wohlenski," 19). Throughout her story, the remarks and observations Oldham gives to Estelle reinforce the reader's sense of her independence, self-confidence, sense of humor, and imaginative powers.

6. Like the slaves from whom they were descended, these African Americans are identified only by their first names in Joseph Blotner's biography.

7. The title of the second half of her story is "Part II 1904." However, this must be Oldham's error, in that one of the events around which it revolves is her parents' imminent move to Oxford, which occurred in late fall 1903. See *OXE*, 22 October 1903. On 28 March 1903 Lemuel Oldham was appointed Clerk of the Circuit Court for the Northern District, fifth circuit, a post he held until 1912, when the office was phased out. The family moved to Oxford because the court met there most often. *Register of the Department of Justice*, Federal Documents Depository, Old Gym, University of Mississippi, J1.7, 1.5.

8. Oldham, "Dr. Wohlenski," 19.

9. The huge library of Jason Niles, Estelle Oldham's step-great grandfather, was inherited by his son and Estelle's step-grandfather, Henry Niles.

10. In *Haunted Bodies*, Susan Donaldson and Anne Jones write that "in the South gender and race haunt one another as they haunt the region's bodies" and that Southern literature is obsessed with "the region's preoccupation with manhood, womanhood, and their 'proper' boundaries" (16, 17).

11. Oldham, "Dr. Wohlenski," 2–11.

12. In *Killers of the Dream,* one of the earliest nonfictional analyses of the psychic cost of racial segregation to white Southerners of the Faulkners' generation, Lillian Smith begins by saying what Estelle Oldham's story confirms: "Even its children know that the South is in trouble. No one has to tell them; no words said aloud. To them it is a vague thing weaving in and out of their play, like a ghost haunting an old graveyard or whispers after the household sleeps—fleeting mystery, vague menace, to which each responds in his own way. Some learn to screen out. . . . Others deny even as they see plainly, and hear. . . . This haunted childhood belongs to every Southerner. . . . The white man's burden is his own childhood. Every Southerner knows this" (15, 17).

13. "Deriving from and similar to the nineteenth century cult of Victorian Domesticity, the cult of True Womanhood was built on the four cardinal virtues—piety, purity, submissiveness, and domesticity" (Welter, "Cult of True Womanhood," 152).

14. Oldham, "Dr. Wohlenski," 2, 21.

15. Ibid., 21, 24.

16. Families worked their own small farms and more prosperous farmers owned and used some slave labor as well. The 1850 census lists Attala County's total (white and slave) population at 10,999, with 1,431 dwellings (an average of 7.6 persons per household) and 1,336 farms under cultivation. The 1850 slave roll for the county shows only 15 families owning more than 20 slaves and the vast majority owning fewer than 10 (*AH*, 32). By 1860, of the 692 slave owners in the county, almost half owned fewer

than 3 slaves and many farmers owned no slaves at all. The county's largest slaveholder owned 96 slaves. No Jacksons are listed as large slaveholders. By 1870 the population of 14,776 people was 60 percent white and 40 percent black (*AH*, 47).

17. Oldham, "Dr. Wohlenski," 20, italics mine.

18. Ibid., 20–21.

19. Ibid., 15–16.

20. Morrison, *Playing in the Dark*, 20.

21. Oldham, "Dr. Wohlenski," 17, 18, 21.

22. Ibid., 20.

23. Ibid., 17.

24. See Long, *Great Southern Babylon*.

25. Roberts, *Aunt Jemima*, 10, 19.

26. Oldham, "Dr. Wohlenski," 17.

27. Roberts, *Aunt Jemima*, 2.

28. *Faulkner* (1984), 229.

29. Blanche Mills Harding, interview with author, 21 September 1992. This is Etta and Pelham Mills's younger daughter and Estelle's cousin.

30. JFS, interview with author, 23 February 1987.

31. Oldham, "Dr. Wohlenski," 23.

32. Ibid., 21, 22.

33. Ibid., 22.

34. Roberts notes that "personifications are limited and contained; persons are troubling and volatile" (*Faulkner and Southern Womanhood*, xii). In one of Oldham's later stories about a young white American missionary whose blood is "cursed" by her wayward father and his sister, the battle reaches a much higher pitch. Its resolution marks its heroine's full surrender to the Law of the Father and the end of her brief and almost hysterical bid for independence and selfhood.

35. Oldham, "Dr. Wohlenski," 23. Roberts uses Bahktin's idea of *classical* and *grotesque* bodies as her model for reading the "different representations of women in Southern culture and in Faulkner's interrogation of it," and I am struck by how suited this paradigm is to analyzing this episode in Estelle's story and to understanding the meaning of Faulkner's transformation of it in *The Sound and the Fury* (Roberts, *Aunt Jemima*, 3).

36. Roberts, *Faulkner and Southern Womanhood*, xiv.

37. Oldham, "Dr. Wohlenski," 23. This book would have been the profile of the Oldham family from Rowland's *History of Mississippi*, 189–90.

38. Oldham, "Dr. Wohlenski," 32.

39. Ibid., 33.

40. Ibid., 26.

41. Ibid., 33.

42. Developmentally, the image is exquisitely age-appropriate.

43. Oldham, "Dr. Wohlenski," 19.

44. Ibid.

45. Ibid., 19, 18, 16.

46. Ibid., 17.

47. In an important respect this loss was also a repetition. While it is true that

Faulkner left Estelle for Phil Stone, it is also true that Estelle's parents considered Faulkner a totally inappropriate husband. In this sense, he too becomes figured as black and identified, at an unconscious level, as Oldham's invention of Dr. Wohlenski and the other dark lovers in her stories shows, with her first passionate love—her black mother.

48. Roberts, *Aunt Jemima*, 158. Roberts notes that "legal definitions of 'black' actually tightened between 1910 and 1930" and that "paralleling this narrowing of racial boundaries was the institutionalization of segregation in the 1920s and 1930s and the shocking number of lynchings between 1880 and 1950" (154); she adds that 1892–1907 was the period of the greatest number of lynchings in the South (172). According to Lillian Smith, most of the Jim Crow laws were passed between 1890 and 1910: "White and Colored signs went up over doors and stayed there. Railroad stations, rest rooms, drinking fountains were labeled. A South mushroomed in strange duality; sin and its shadow crept over the land. White church—colored church; white school—colored school; white toilet—colored toilet . . ." (*Killers of the Dream*, 203).

49. Roberts, *Aunt Jemima*, 9.

CHAPTER 15: BILLY FALKNER AND ESTELLE OLDHAM, OXFORD, 1903-1914

Epigraph: Estelle Faulkner, speaking to a Richmond, Va., reporter; quoted in Churn, "William Faulkner's Widow Is Mood Painter."

1. *Faulkner* (1974), 1:85, and (1984), 15; Blotner's interviews with Estelle Faulkner, 9 December 1964, and Dorothy Oldham, 20 November 1966. Blotner interviewed Estelle Faulkner after Faulkner's death. Dorothy could not have corroborated this story because she wasn't born until 1905.

2. *Faulkner* (1984), 15, 9, 29; *OXE*, 22 October 1903.

3. *Faulkner* (1974), 1:85.

4. Churn, "William Faulkner's Widow Is Mood Painter," 11.

5. *Faulkner* (1984), 548.

6. Holder, "Wife Finds Life 'Nice,'" *New Orleans Item* clipping, 1951, Mississippi Room Collection, University of Mississippi Library.

7. WF to MBF, 21 October 1915, *TOH*, 117–18.

8. Rowland, "William and His Grandmother," in *WFO*, 24–28; Sallie Murry Williams, interview, 26 November 1963, Collins Collection, HRC.

9. Earl Wortham, interview, Collins Collection, HRC. Estelle and Tochie didn't own ponies, but they often begged rides on the wagon of the local blacksmith, Earl Wortham, when he drove his oxen into their drive to deliver stove wood. The girls ignored their mother's scoldings not to do so; she finally gave up objecting when Wortham assured her the girls would be perfectly safe.

10. Sallie Murry Williams, letter to Joseph Blotner, 10 August 1967, Blotner papers, SEMS.

11. Estelle Faulkner, interview, 16 August 1963, in *Faulkner* (1974), 1:87; Sallie Murry (Mrs. R. X.) Williams, interview, 26 November 1963, Collins collection, HRC.

12. Oldham, "Dr. Wohlenski," 20, 31, 18, 27.

13. *OXE*, 8 September 1904. This house, willed to Estelle by her maternal

grandmother, was the one to which she would return and take up her painting again for part of the summer after she and Cornell separated. However, because she could not pay the taxes, she lost it (see Estelle to Cornell, undated letter fragment, probably summer 1926, CSFA).

14. *Faulkner* (1974), 1:103.

15. Bessie Sumners, interview with author, 19 May 1988.

16. *Kosciusko Star Ledger,* 30 December 1904.

17. Oldham, "Dr. Wohlenski," 30, 31.

18. *Mary Baldwin Seminary Catalogue,* 1913–14, 18.

19. Hand, "Faulkner's Widow Recounts Memories," 1, 4.

20. *Mary Baldwin Seminary Catalogue,* 1913–14, 9.

21. Ibid., 9.

22. Ibid., 17, 13.

23. Ibid., 16.

24. Ibid., 23.

25. Solomon, *In the Company of Educated Women,* 80.

26. Her grades at Ole Miss for the two years were as follows: German, B and C; French, A and B; English, C and C; Psychology, D; Mathematics, D. In her sophomore year she also took Spanish (C), History (D), and Domestic Science, for which she took an incomplete. Estelle Oldham, Student's Record Transcript, University of Mississippi, 1914–16. Admissions and Records, University of Mississippi.

27. Victoria Johnson, interview with author, 22 February 1990; JFS, interview with author, 17 October 1989.

28. JFS, interviews with author, 15 October 1987 and 17 October 1989. "Pappy hated for Mama to play the piano. . . . I get a definite feeling that when Mama played the piano she was removed and Pappy was jealous." See also Sensibar, *Origins,* 206–18.

29. Victoria Johnson, interview with author, 22 February 1990.

30. "I don't think she particularly enjoyed a girls' school"; JFS, interview with author, 9 July 1986.

31. Victoria Johnson, interview with author, 16 August 1989.

32. JFS, interview with author, 17 October 1989.

33. Hand, "Faulkner's Widow Recounts Memories," 1, 4.

34. Snell quoting and paraphrasing from her interview with Robert Farley, February 1976, in *Phil Stone of Oxford,* 76.

35. Passport issued in Honolulu on 8 December 1921 to Estelle and Victoria Franklin for travel to China, CSFA.

36. Photocopies of snapshots belonging to Katrina's son, Jim Kyle Hudson, Jr.; letter to author, March 1991. Hudson's wife, Vinton, sent me the original snapshots on 10 May 2008.

37. Wilde, *A Loving Gentleman,* 279. For more on this, see *Origins,* 155–57.

38. The most famous incident is Jill's account of her father's response to her sixteenth birthday: "It was just before my birthday and I knew that Pappy was getting ready to start on one of these bouts. I went to him—the only time I ever did—and said, 'Please don't start drinking.' And he was already well on his way, and he turned to me and said, 'You know, no one remembers Shakespeare's child.' I never asked him again" (JFS television interview; transcript in Abadie, *William Faulkner,* 92).

39. His financial collapse in July 1926 occurred the summer of the final collapse of the Franklin's marriage.

40. The other two were Lee Russell and J. W. T. Falkner.

41. *OXE*, 9 November 1911.

42. Ibid., 22 February 1912.

43. Oldham papers, Rowan Oak. These papers are now in the Faulkner collection at UVA.

44. JFS, interview with author, 9 July 1986.

45. Ibid. Estelle's granddaughter Victoria Johnson concurs (interview with author, 11 September 1989).

46. Aaron Condon, interview with author, 16 May 1989.

PART 4: FIRST LOVES, FIRST "MARRIAGES," 1914–1926

Epigraph to Part 4: WF to MBF (19 May 1918), *TOH*, 57.

CHAPTER 16: SHIFTING ALLIANCES, 1914–1918

Epigraph: Katrina Carter to Phil Stone, 1914, in Snell, *Phil Stone of Oxford*, 76.

1. Snell, *Phil Stone of Oxford*, 76.

2. Ibid., 2–3.

3. Quoted in ibid., 78.

4. See Snell's account of those years in *Phil Stone of Oxford*, 77–89.

5. "Verse Old and Nascent," *EPP*, 114.

6. A. C. Swinburne, *Poems of Algernon Charles Swinburne*, ed. Ernest Rhys (New York: Random House, 1919). According to his daughter, Faulkner kept this edition on his bedside table throughout his lifetime and taught her much of Swinburne's poetry.

7. "Sapphics," in Swinburne, *Poems*, 139.

8. See my discussion of Faulkner's immersion in Swinburne and of these two poems in *Origins*, 77–90.

9. Snell thinks the initiation of Estelle's divorce proceedings, which she dates as January 1927, signaled the end of the intense period of Phil and Bill's friendship: "Phil Stone and William Faulkner would go on as before, but psychologically they began to live apart" (*Phil Stone of Oxford*, 204).

10. Snell, *Phil Stone of Oxford*, 342–43n2. Stone was committed in January 1963. The final diagnosis was "Chronic Brain Syndrome associated with Cerebral Arteriosclerosis with Psychotic Reaction." But Stone had been suffering from chronic depression and paranoid delusions for years. As Snell notes, "Even the cacophonous medical jargon does no justice to Stone's thirty-three years of anguish" (328).

11. These letters are printed in *TOH*.

12. Snell, *Phil Stone of Oxford*, 67.

13. Phil Stone to Rosamond Stone, Monday (8 April 1918, New Haven), William Faulkner letters, box 1, HRC.

14. *TOH*, 54; Snell, *Phil Stone of Oxford*, 100–101; and Phil Stone to Rosamond Stone, 8 April 1918, HRC.

15. Stone was never shy about voicing his dislike and fear of women in general

and of Estelle in particular. As he aged, he became increasingly hostile. Yet even years later, describing the reason for Faulkner's visit to him at Yale, Stone wrote that when he "came home Christmas 1917 he told Bill about this [scheme to enlist in the RCAF] and they schemed to ship Bill to the Canadian Air Force. In the spring of 1918 they manipulated for Bill to come up to New Haven early in April and Phil got him a job." Phil Stone, unpublished memoir, quoted in Snell, *Phil Stone of Oxford*, 102.

16. Stone was familiar with Faulkner's drinking problem. During the fall of 1913, his first term as a Yale undergraduate, he claims to have finally been able to quit— "there was no more failing"—and he abstained for the next twelve years, "until he knew he could taste whiskey without trouble" (Snell, 64, quoting from Stone's sixteen-page 1963 autobiographical fragment).

17. Phil Stone to Rosamond Stone, 8 April 1918, HRC (italics mine).

18. Ibid.

19. Snell, *Phil Stone of Oxford*, 101.

20. WF to MBF, 5 April 1918, HRC.

21. Ibid.

22. WF to MBF, HRC.

23. WF to Murry Falkner, 6 April 1918, HRC.

24. WF to "Dear Mother" (5 May 1918), *TOH*, 55.

25. Ibid. (7 June 1918), *TOH*, 63–64.

26. WF to MBF, 19 May 1918, *TOH*, 57.

27. WF to MBF, 24, 28 April 1918. Even as late as 1925, he wires Phil to send him clothes in New Orleans—"what I want is my Brown Two pants tweed suit, my knickers and my heavy gray socks and sweater" (WF to Phil Stone, 22 June 1925, *TOH*, 211).

28. WF to Maud and Murry Falkner, 24 and 21 April 1918, *TOH*, 52–53, 51–52).

29. WF to MBF, 19 May and 21 April 1918, *TOH*, 56–57, 51–52.

30. Even while he was in training, his parents sent him "nearly three-quarters of the amount he was paid at the cadet-pilot rate of $1.10 a day" *(TOH*, 23).

31. 1 May 1925, *TOH*, 204–6.

32. WF to MBF, Long Branch, 15 September 1918, HRC.

33. WF to Maud and Murry Falkner, 6 October and 23 November 1921, and 6 January 1925, HRC.

34. WF to Maud and Murry Falkner, 13 and 20 October 1921, HRC.

35. Susan Snell suggests that one reason Faulkner and Stone came together was "because women gave them trouble. Oxford assumed that Katrina Carter was destined for Phil Stone, while Bill Faulkner believed he had an understanding with her friend Estelle Oldham. When, for different reasons, neither courtship readily progressed to the altar, Phil and Bill found consolation in the security of masculine companionship." Yet her account of the progress of that friendship reveals a different sequence of events in which their mutual friendship displaces their earlier romantic and intellectual friendships with Katrina and Estelle, respectively. See Snell, *Phil Stone of Oxford*, 102.

36. Ibid., 9.

37. Faulkner dropped out of the eleventh and, then, the final grade of Oxford High School in December 1914. Although in the fall of 1915 he returned to play football, he withdrew permanently later that fall. *Faulkner* (1984), 748.

38. Snell, *Phil Stone of Oxford,* 75.

39. WF, interview with Jean Stein, *Writers at Work,* 124.

CHAPTER 17. THE OLDHAM-FRANKLIN WEDDING, APRIL 1918

Epigraph: *Absalom, Absalom!,* 45.

1. Cornell Sidney Franklin to the Honorable T. W. Gregory, 8 January 1919, CSFA.

2. Editorial on Cornell Franklin, *Shanghai Evening Post and Mercury,* 18 November 1948, and CSF to Gregory, 8 January 1919, CSFA.

3. "Miss Nancy" to Cornell Franklin, 1 July 1916, CSFA. She writes from New Orleans, "Have you forgotten me? . . . I've often wondered because I really think you were sorrier to see the boat pull out that morning than anyone else, . . . You were the last one to turn away. I saw that in spite of the fact that my heart was breaking in two. . . . The last thing you said as you took my hands was, 'I'll see you in New Orleans this time next year.' Does that still hold good?"

4. "Aunt Jessie" to Cornell S. Franklin, c/o Messrs. Thompson and Milverton/12 Campbell Block/Honolulu, 10 November 1915, CSFA.

5. Sallie Murry Williams, interview with Joseph Blotner, 14 November 1966, 1918 file, SEMS. Sallie Murry confirmed that Estelle and William were born the same year. In contrast, Ben Wasson told Blotner that Estelle "was at least two years older." He also elaborated on the meaning of "fast" by saying that Estelle, Ella Somerville, and Katrina Carter all smoked in college and were therefore considered fast. Ben Wasson, interview with Joseph Blotner, 28 March 1965, SEMS.

6. Katherine Searcy, interview with author, 13 February 1989.

7. His undergraduate peers had a similar assessment. Two comments appearing under his photograph in different yearbooks—"I want to grow as beautiful as God meant me to be" and, in his senior year, "the glass of fashion and the mold of form" (*Annual,* 1912, 1913)—speak to one of his attractions. In his senior *Annual* his classmates wrote that he was "an all round man whose record is clean and bright alike in the classroom, on the athletic field, as post-master, as social light and in closer associations of friendship. He will make a splendid lawyer and besides, expects to be the first governor of Texalette." This was an insider joke referring to Mississippians' proclivity for leaving their perennially economically depressed state and heading to Texas in search of a better living. It was also a comment on Cornell's potential as politician and capitalist. Another joking remark cites him as the author of a "how-to" book titled "Smiles and Success" (Ole Miss *Annual,* 1913, University of Mississippi Library, Special Collections).

8. The letters of introduction Cornell carried with him to Honolulu that summer of 1914 offered enthusiastic testimony to his intelligence, his high moral character, and his excellent family background. The dean of the Ole Miss Law School, L. J. Farley, whose son Robert was part of the "gang" who clustered around Katrina Carter and Estelle and who in 1929 filed Estelle's and Cornell's Shanghai divorce papers in the Oxford courthouse, wrote that Cornell was a "studious, painstaking student" and a young man "of more than ordinary ability, well equipped naturally and

by application for his chosen profession, the Law." He predicted that Franklin would be "a brilliant success." Professor Kimbrough claimed Cornell had "the legal mind preeminently" and wrote that "in his Moot Court work he has shown independent and logical thought, and has developed a clear and concise power of presentation." He also praised Cornell's writing and speaking talents and noted that "his command of the English language is unusual." Although all three wrote of his high moral character and good manners, the chancellor, Andrew Kincannon, waxed eloquent in his praise of Franklin's family background and upbringing, writing that he possessed "those splendid traits of head and heart characteristic of his paternal ancestry, which render manhood both admirable and lovable" and that his mother, Mamie Wyckoff Taylor [Mamie Franklin Hairston], who "comes of a prominent Mobile family and is a woman of unusual intellectuality and charming personality," had "reared her son with great pains, and she has every reason to be proud of her handiwork" (L. J. Farley to the Honorable A. S. Humphries [ASH], 25 April 1914; D. M. Kimbrough to ASH, 25 April 1914; and Andrew A. Kincannon to ASH, 25 April 1914, CSFA).

9. Ken Wooten, registrar, University of Mississippi, interview with author, 9 February 1989.

10. Mamie Hairston worked to support herself and her son: "Cornell's mother wrote the society page for my father, the Editor of the Columbus paper, and rented out rooms in her house for income." Katherine Searcy, interview with author, 13 February 1989.

11. See Weinman, *Hawaii*, 3; quoted in Lind, *Hawaii*, 3. In 1911 an American journalist wrote that "Hawaii furnishes a vivid illustration of the way in which private business organization in its final stages of development permeates, influences, and controls the life of a country. Sugar is King in Hawaii to a far greater extent than cotton was in the Old South" (Baker, "Wonderful Hawaii," 28; quoted in Lind, *Hawaii*, 6). In 1934 an even more critical assessment claimed and prophesied that "there are three main reasons why American imperialists paint a roseate view of Hawaii. First, it screens the slavery in the sugar and pineapple plantations. Second, it conceals military preparations for the next Pacific war. Third, tourists, readers, and movie fans pay millions for illusions of paradise." As revealed in Estelle's "Star Spangled Banner Stuff," her only extant short story dealing explicitly with American colonial exploitation, none of this was lost on her.

12. Vander Zanden, *American Minority Relations*, 326; quoted in Lind, *Hawaii*, 2. See also Lind, *Hawaii*, 20.

13. Cornell Franklin to Lida Oldham, 22 June 1917, CSFA.

14. See Faulkner (1974), 1:191–94. His notes of the three interviews he conducted read, in part, "She thought Cornell began courting her when she returned from Mary Baldwin. When he proposed, she accepted just as she had accepted other boys' fraternity pins with no thought that he had taken it any more seriously than she. She found out how he had taken her acceptance when a ring arrived for her" (1918 file, SEMS).

15. Estelle Oldham Faulkner to her parents, undated letter (June 1929), VJA.

16. Estelle Oldham Faulkner, interview with Joseph Blotner, 29 April 1968, SEMS.

17. Ibid., 22 August 1964.

18. *Faulkner* (1974), 1:204, and note in which he cites his source as "Interview with Mrs. James Hudson [Katrina Carter], 21 November 1965."

19. *Faulkner* (1974), 1:194; *Faulkner* (1984), 54 (no source given in the latter edition). Blotner's interview notes on this say that Billy told her if they married "he'd support them by working at the bank even though he hated it." She also added that he, who was "always a great one for points of honor," insisted on telling both their fathers, who "blew up." In conclusion she said "it was probably all for the best. He'd never could have [sic] been a writer if they married then." Estelle Oldham Faulkner, interview with JB, 9 December 1964, SEMS.

20. Katherine Andrews, letter to the author, 22 August 1987.

21. *OXE*, 28 September 1916.

22. Lem Oldham to himself on letterhead of U.S. Clerk for Northern District of Mississippi, Carvel Collins papers, HRC.

23. WF, interview with Marshall Smith, *Memphis Press Scimitar,* 10 July 1931; reprinted in *LIG,* 7.

24. In 1953, when Faulkner thought he was losing his mind, a psychiatrist he consulted asked him why he drank. "Fear," he answered. In novels like *The Sound and the Fury, Sanctuary, Go Down, Moses,* and *Absalom, Absalom!* Faulkner invents a new poetics to convey such complete disorientation and a numbness that is never quite effective (see Chap. 6).

25. Rowland, *History of Mississippi,* 4:190.

26. Tiffany wedding invitation, CSFA.

27. *Columbus Commercial,* 21 April 1918.

28. *OXE,* 25 April 1918.

29. *Mississippian,* 24 April 1918.

30. Ibid., 17 and 24 April 1918; *OXE,* 9 May 1918.

31. We know from Cho-Cho's birth date that Estelle was pregnant.

CHAPTER 18: MARRIAGE IN THE "CROSSROADS OF THE PACIFIC," JUNE–SEPTEMBER 1918

1. Worden, *Cargoes.*

2. Virginia O'Connor Vilmaire, interview with author, 19 January 1994. By 1923, first-class one-way fares cost a minimum of $110 (*Aloha Guide Supplement,* 1923, 3).

3. *Aloha Guide Supplement,* 1923, 9.

4. *Hawaiian Annual,* 1920 and 1922, census figures, p. 17 in both volumes.

5. Letters of complaint and resignation, CSFA.

6. In 1918 and 1919 Cornell gives their address as the University Club (*Polk's City Directory,* 1918, 1919). However, this was not a residential club, so Estelle could not have stayed there. When the Franklins moved to Shanghai in January 1922, they followed a similar pattern, staying with friends of Cornell's for the first three months.

7. Watson from Holly Springs, Miss., was one of many Bourbon Democrats President Wilson appointed to administrate territorial affairs. According to his daughter, Lillie Moore Nelson, they were brought out to keep the traditionally Republican plantation owners in line. In fact, as representatives of the conservative wing of the Democratic Party (as was Wilson) and as descendants or would-be

descendants of mainland plantation aristocracy, their political interests were often similar. *Famous Men of Hawaii* (1921), 409, and (1925), 847–48. Minerva Tuttle Hairston, interview with author, 24 May 1988.

8. Christianne O'Connor, interview with author, 19 January 1994.

9. Walter Davis, interview with author, 26 May 1988. By the early 1940s when Davis met her, Judge Watson had died and Mrs. Watson was an alcoholic. She lived with her recently divorced eldest daughter, Virginia O'Connor (later Vilmaire), who also became an alcoholic. Christianne O'Connor, interview with author, 19 January 1994, Dennis O'Connor (Virginia's son), Honolulu, 18 January 1994, and Mrs. William T. Nelson (Lillian "Tootles" O'Connor, Virginia's sister), 1 February 1994.

10. Lula ("Tootsie") Law, interview with author, 25 July 1989. Law, who had known Cho-Cho since they were in boarding school together and remained friends with her until her death (14 February 1975), said she was an alcoholic and traced its source to her colonial experience. Law says, and Corny Franklin (Cornell and Dallas Franklin's son) confirms, that both his father and his mother were "heavy drinkers."

11. *Charlottesville Daily Progress*, 2 August 1956.

12. Fearn, *My Days*.

13. *PCA*, 2 July 1918.

14. CSF to the Honorable T. W. Gregory, 8 January 1919, CSFA.

15. *Polk's City Directory* would not list a home address for Cornell until 1920, a year after the birth of the Franklin's first child, Victoria.

16. *PCA*, 29 September 1918.

17. Ibid., 30 June 1918.

18. They were Eva Focke, Sara Lucas, and the recently married Ada Tree (Mrs. William Williamson).

19. Brigadier General John Heard file, Tropic Lightning Museum Archives, Schofield Barracks, Hawaii.

20. *PCA*, 1 and 6 July 1918.

21. Estelle's identity card, issued on 9 July 1918, a little over a month after her arrival in Hawaii, gives her vital statistics as follows: "Age: 21; Occupation: Housewife; Complexion: Fair; Hair: Brown; Height: 5'5"; Eyes: Grey; Marks: None." Estelle Oldham Franklin, United States Citizen's Identity Card, Honolulu, CSFA. Jill remembers her mother's hair as "dark, dark red," the color reported in a 1931 interview with Estelle (*Memphis Commercial Appeal*, 1931).

22. By mid-July the *Pacific Commercial Advertiser* first playfully equated scantily suited women with disease when it reported that one lady, "apparently a stranger to Honolulu," discarded her blouse and stockings and cavorted in the ocean in "a tight fitting silken suit of brilliant yellow, something the color of a quarantine flag" (*PCA*, 9 July 1918).

23. A front-page headline reads, "Men Tailors Fitting Bathing Suits on Women, Is Report: Outrigger Auxiliary Directors in Formal Statement Outline Things They Object to and What They Want to Accomplish" (*PCA*, 3 July 1918).

24. *PCA*, 22 July 1918.

25. *Schofield Barracks Historic Guide.* A newspaper ad that appeared regularly until well after the war's end claims that if you miss the last train to the barracks, you can

leave by taxi from Honolulu as late as 3:30 A.M. and arrive at Schofield in time for reveille.

26. *PCA*, 4 August 1918.

27. AC, 17.

28. Leo Falk, M.D., interview with author, 21 April 1993.

29. *PCA*, 18 August 1918, and *Hawaiian Annual*, 1919, 149.

30. Castle, *Hawaii Past and Present*, 244–45 and n48.

31. See *Hawaiian Annual*, 1919, 141 and *Centennial Memoirs of the Pacific Club*, 65.

32. The term *Haole* means "white skinned person" in Hawaiian and is used by all races and classes. Lind notes that "because of the very profound impact of the plantation upon the entire life of the Territory, many of the peculiar characteristics of master-servant relations on the Hawaiian plantations have been extended to the urban setting as well. For example, the widespread impression that all Haoles must employ servants in order to maintain their proper social position is clearly borrowed from the plantations" ("The Changing Position," 76, 78). In well-entrenched colonial cultures this form of stratification and definition still prevails, since it strengthens the colonial social and political structure. For example, in 1990 an American woman who had just received her degree from Brown University and accepted a teaching job at the American School in Jakarta was assigned a servant whose job was to wait on her in the joint living quarters provided by the school. The living arrangement also included a cook, housekeeper, and gardener. I had a similar experience in 1964–66, when I lived in Kingston, Jamaica. When I told my employers I did not need a cook, a gardener, and a woman to do the cleaning and laundry, they made clear to me that I was behaving very oddly. When I did attend the obligatory women's lunches and pool parties, the main topic of conversation was servants.

33. Cornell Franklin, Honorable Discharge Certificate, and Cornell Franklin to T. W. Gregory, U.S. attorney general, letter of application for judgeship, 8 January 1919, CSFA.

CHAPTER 19: AN ARMY WIFE, SCHOFIELD BARRACKS, HAWAII, SEPTEMBER 1918–MAY 1919

1. *College Yearbook*, 1913; Robert (Bob) Hardy, interview with author, 14 February 1989, Columbus, Miss., and Will Lewis, interview with author, Oxford, Miss., 23 May 1988.

2. JFS, interview with author, 24 March 1993.

3. Elizabeth Otey Watson, interview with author, 8 February 1994. Her husband, Cornell's nephew, worked for Franklin in Shanghai.

4. Ibid.

5. See letters from Uncle Malcolm to Cornell; A. E. (Cornell's secretary) to Estelle Franklin, 4 June 1925; and Malcolm Franklin to Cornell Franklin, 23 November 1925, CSFA and VJA.

6. Bessie S. Edwards, widow of Dr. Thomas H. Edwards, Major, VC U.S. Army, to commanding officer, Schofield Barracks, 26 August 1959, Schofield Archives, Castner, Hawaii.

7. Patricia Alvarez, interview with author, 17 January 1994. See also her *A History of Schofield Barracks Military Reservation*. Prepared for the Department of the Army, U.S. Army Engineer Division, Fort Shafter, Contract DACA84–81-Q-0274, March 1982. According to Alvarez, there was no money allocated for planting and landscaping until after World War I. A rash of suicides among civilian dependents was the impetus for the planting.

8. *PCA*, 4 August 1918.

9. Ibid., 25 January 1919.

10. Ibid., 29 September 1919.

11. Ibid., 6 October 1918. That Estelle would choose such a friend seems natural. It is ironic that she should visit the weekend that Tochie Oldham Allen died in the 1918 flu epidemic, while living on another American army base. Yet there is no newspaper announcement of Tochie's death among the other mourning notices. Perhaps fearing the news would jeopardize Estelle's health and not wanting to risk losing a third child or another unborn grandchild, the Oldhams decided to write nothing. Estelle would not hear that Tochie had died until Mamie Hairston arrived the following January.

12. *PCA*, 29 September and 6 October 1918; *Men of Hawaii*, 1921, 77.

13. *PCA*, 20 October 1918.

14. Dated and captioned photograph of Cornell and his team, CSFA.

15. *PCA*, 17 November 1918.

16. *Aloha Guide*, 1915, 156.

17. *PCA*, 29 December 1918.

18. Ibid., 5 January 1919.

19. Boyce Loving, interview with Cornell Franklin, *Charlottesville Daily Progress*, 2 August 1956. Cornell Franklin to the Honorable T. W. Gregory, U.S. attorney general, 8 January 1919, CSFA.

20. *PCA*, 17, 23, 24 January 1919, and *Hawaiian Annual*, 1920, 144.

21. When they learned of Estelle's engagement, the Mills, the family of her mother's sister Etta, wrote to congratulate Estelle and begged her and her mother to come for a visit so they could celebrate together. Estelle wrote back, thanking them for their good wishes: "Your very dear father surprised and delighted me so and I'm terribly glad you think so much of me! Yes, I think I'm very fortunate for Corny is a love positively." She had begun sewing her trousseau: "I have embroidered some awfully pretty linens and," she added naughtily, "before long will start on my 'undies.'" But she didn't think she was going to visit the Mills soon: "I want to see you all and am trying to persuade Mama to go down but I doubt . . . that she'll leave home. Oh, she is so heartbroken." Estelle [Oldham] to Mary Vic[toria Mills], undated, but probably summer or fall 1917. Catalogue item 296a, box 5, folder 3, William B. Wisdom collection, Howard Tilton Memorial Library, Tulane University.

22. *PCA*, 25 January 1919.

23. Victoria De Graffenried Franklin, certificate of birth #2879, Hawaii Dept. of Health, Honolulu.

24. Victoria Johnson, interview with author, 26 March 1993.

25. *PCA*, 9 April 1919. Franklin does not begin paying taxes on their Honolulu house until 1920.

26. *PCA*, April–December 1919.

27. Ibid., 29 April and 11 May 1919.

28. E.g., in mid-April Estelle attended a bridge party given by Mrs. S. H. Kemp, a woman her mother's age, whose husband had just been appointed associate justice of the Supreme Court of Hawaii (*PCA*, 7 March 1918). Prior to that he had held Cornell's new position, first judge of the First Circuit (1917–18) and asst. U.S. attorney (1916–17) (*PAC*, 20 April 1919, and *Men of Hawaii*, 1921, 231). Even more significant was the luncheon Mrs. A. G. M. Robertson gave in Mamie's honor. Besides being native-born and a friend of Louise Watson's, this well-known local singer was the wife of the president of the Bar Association, a prominent Republican politically associated with Dole and the Chief Justice of the Supreme Court from 1911 to 1917 (*PCA*, 27 April 1919, and *Men of Hawaii*, 1921, 340–41).

29. Katharine Searcy, interview with author, 24 May 1988.

30. *PCA*, 18 May 1919.

31. Ibid., 28 October 1919; "Circuit Court Notes" columns and sports pages, May–October 1919; passenger list for the *Sherman*, *PCA*, 26 October 1919.

32. *PCA*, 18 April 1919; *OXE*, 5 June 1919; *Columbus Commercial*, 29 June 1919; *OXE*, 2 October 1919.

CHAPTER 20: STOLEN INTERLUDES, 1919 AND 1921

Epigraph: From the screenplay of Anita Loos's *Gentlemen Prefer Blondes*.

1. Marilyn Monroe in the 1953 film version of Anita Loos's *Gentlemen Prefer Blondes* (1925), directed by Howard Hawks, with screenplay by Charles Lederer; based on the musical comedy by Joseph Field and Anita Loos and the novel by Loos, *Gentlemen Prefer Blondes* (New York: Boni and Liveright). By February 1926, Faulkner had read this recently published "diary" of Lorelei Lee. Much impressed with it, he wrote Anita Loos to offer "my envious congratulations" for her best-seller, *Gentlemen Prefer Blondes*. He was especially taken with Loos's narrative technique, in particular her choice of voice: "the way you did [Dorothy] through the intelligence of that elegant moron of a cornflower. . . . My God, it's charming. . . . The Andersons even mentioned Ring Lardner in talking to me about it" (WF to Anita Loos, "Something Febry 1926," *SL*, 32).

2. *OXE*, 5 June 1919. Their four-month stay ended 29 September 1919. *OXE*, 2 October 1919.

3. Sensibar, *Origins*, 24–28.

4. "At the age of sixteen . . . Swinburne discovered me . . . making me his slave." Faulkner, "Verse Old and Nascent" (April 1925), in *EPP*, 114, and Sensibar, *Origins*, 77–104.

5. Sensibar, *Origins*, 24.

6. This dedication appears in the second Texas copy of *TM*, verso of title page, HRC. This page is reprinted in the published version of *The Marionettes*, as cited parenthetically.

7. Sensibar, *Origins*, 25.

8. In early November Faulkner wrote to Maud about whether to take Lem's offer

of a job as university postmaster: "I hate to think of leaving the east after taking three years to get here" (1 November 1921, *TOH*, 155). Yet before Christmas he had returned to Oxford and accepted the position.

9. See introduction to *Vision in Spring*, ix–xxviii, and *Origins*, 59–77.

10. WF, 25 February 1957, in *FIU*, 25.

11. Young, a novelist and critic, was a fellow Oxfordian some ten years older than Faulkner. Like several of the men who cared for Faulkner, particularly between 1916 and 1926, Young, too, was gay.

12. WF to MBF, 6 October 1921, in *TOH*, 144.

13. *Faulkner* (1974), 1:397.

14. What is known of these years suggests that the strain of being so apparently unproductive was considerable. Faulkner maintained and embroidered up on his various impostures at home, during his brief New York sojourn, and on frequent short trips to Memphis and New Orleans. He also drank more and more heavily, a factor that contributed to his eventually being fired from his detested post office job and his volunteer position as Boy Scout master.

15. The byline on the earlier typescript reads "E. Oldham-Franklin,/Oxford Mississippi." "Franklin" has been x'd out with ink. The byline on the later version reads "E. O./Oxford, Mississippi." All page references are to the later version. See the two extant typescript versions of "A Crossing," JFSA and JFSA/UVA, Special Collections.

16. There is confusion over the terms for identifying this genre or these "narratives of empire" or "colonialism," as Suleri calls them interchangeably, in arguing that "the conventions of romance control the literatures of Anglo-Indian colonization" (*Rhetoric of English India*, 7, 11). Sharpe and McClure prefer the term "imperial romance" (McClure, *Late Imperial Romance*, and Sharpe, *Allegories of Empire*).

17. AC, 2.

18. Ibid., 2, 11. Edna Earl, its autobiographical heroine, gives up her successful career as a romance writer for marriage. In *The Wishing Tree*, a fairy tale about another birthday girl, which Faulkner wrote and hand-bound into a book that he inscribed to Cho-Cho on 5 February 1927, her eighth birthday, he will more accurately describe Dulcie, the fictional birthday girl's mother as "beautiful, so slim and tall, with her grave unhappy eyes changeable as seawater and her slender hands that came so softly about you when you were sick" (81).

19. AC, 18.

20. Ibid., 4, 5, 13, 20.

21. Ibid., 27.

22. Ibid., 1, 2, 13.

23. It was the principal subject of Faulkner's unfinished novel about a failed painter named Elmer. For a discussion of "Elmer's" role in Faulkner's growth as an artist, see, *Origins*, 206–21.

24. Clifford, *Spoilt Children*, 48–49.

25. In the 1920s American mission land and property holdings made up anywhere from "$43 to $80 million of a total of $150 million in American investments in China and the missions spent roughly $10 to $15 million a year in the country" (Clifford, *Spoilt Children*, 52).

26. "AC," 10–11, 11.

27. Humorously rhapsodizing on alcohol as a curative for "mal de mer" a Honolulu newspaper columnist explained, "Champagne, of course, has long been regarded as a very good remedy and in severe cases it is generally used." Its "secret" is "that it lifts one out of ordinary mental processes" and "one's soul suddenly becomes more important than the body and the cares of the world are forgotten in a glorious contemplation of things far more remote than mal de mer." Claiming seasickness as cause for an ocean binge was apparently common enough among regular travelers to the East to be a source of popular humor. *Honolulu Advertiser,* 2 November 1927, 13.

28. Undated ink holograph letter fragment, 3, signed "Devotedly, Estelle, Victoria, *Malcolm,*" Collins papers, HRC. Estelle told Blotner that she returned a final time for three weeks after Christmas in 1926 to take care of legal matters, but I find no documentation for this.

29. Virginia O'Connor Vilmaire, interview with author, 19 January 1994; Mrs. William T. Nelson, interviews with author, 1 February and 6 March 1994.

30. *PCA,* 16 January 1921: "A Play at University Club, *Suppressed Desires,* a Comedy by Susan Glaspell. The cast of three persons includes Mrs. Cornell Franklin."

31. Virginia Vilmaire, interview with author, 25 January 1994; Mrs. William T. Nelson, interview with author, 1 February 1994.

32. Stein, "William Faulkner," 141.

33. Faulkner's "Moonlight" is the only exception (see Chap. 17, p. 333). If he wrote this very short story in 1920–21, then it was an aberration; its genre, content, and tone are nothing like his other writing from those years. More likely, he wrote "Moonlight" in 1924, shortly after he began reading Estelle's stories.

34. The Eighteenth Amendment was approved in 1919. To enforce it, Congress passed the Volstead Act that same year.

35. Dan Wakefield's essay-review, which includes this sentence from Cowley, describes some of the reasons why writers of Faulkner's and succeeding generations have exalted alcohol's properties and the rationales they have used to explain their drinking ("Through a Glass Darkly," 166–69).

36. AC, 14.

37. Ibid., 17.

38. Ibid., 20–21.

39. Janet Malcolm notes that among writers "narrative theft is a common phenomenon," especially when that narrative is compelling. Certainly this was the case with Faulkner, who found Estelle's fictional narratives personally compelling (*Two Lives,* 170).

40. AC, 12.

41. Ibid., 10–11.

42. Ibid., 14–15, my italics.

43. Estelle Faulkner, interview with Joseph Blotner, 9 December 1964, SEMS.

44. AC, 22.

45. Ibid., 23.

46. Ibid., 27.

CHAPTER 21: THE MARKETING OF ESTELLE AND HER REBELLION

1. Beginning in November 1920, after Bill officially withdrew from the University of Mississippi (where he had been enrolled as a "special student" since the previous fall), Snell writes, "Faulkner used his [own] father's house as a base and Stone as a bank" (Snell, *Phil Stone of Oxford*, 132, and *Faulkner* [1974], 1:287). The alliance of Phil's father, James Stone, Murry Falkner, and Lem Oldham originated at Ole Miss, where all three were fraternity brothers. Unlike their male counterparts, white women in Mississippi had no comparable organizations. Although Oldham and Falkner women were founding members of their respective towns' Federated Women's Clubs, they did not serve the same purpose as fraternities because their members were not financially independent. Like Estelle's fictional young women and like Faulkner's, they were "on the market." Their brothers, husbands, and fathers were their traders.

2. Estelle's marriage also linked Oxford to the national and global economies. In a town in the poorest Southern state where, even among the white middle class, barter was still a major form of economic exchange, the outside money Estelle's marriage generated for the town—her father's, Phil Stone's, and Bill Faulkner's salaries were all paid from Washington and, later, Cornell's child-support payments were sent from Shanghai—was a nice addition to the town's money economy.

3. Cornell Franklin to Lem Oldham, 29 January 1922, Rowan Oak, Oldham file.

4. Sallie Murry Williams to Joseph Blotner, 2 March 1971, *LDB* collection, SEMS.

5. Ibid.

6. Financially, Faulkner's relationship with Estelle was no more enlightened or less patriarchal than Cornell's. Throughout most of their marriage, his letters to her and to others show that his practice was to dole out money to her in arbitrary quantities along with detailed instructions as to how she was to spend it. This was especially onerous when he worked in Hollywood for months at a time, while Estelle stayed in Oxford caring for the Franklin and Faulkner children, managing their finances, and running their household as well as their farm. It was not until the mid-1950s, with their grown daughter's intervention on her mother's behalf, that Faulkner was finally prevailed upon to at least settle a monthly allowance on his wife. See letters from WF to Estelle Oldham Faulkner in the 1930s and 1940s and from JFS to WF in the 1950s, Blotner materials, LDB collection, SEMS; *SL;* letters from WF to EOF, UVA; and JFS letters to her mother from Pine Manor in the 1950s, JFSA. In a well-known incident, Estelle rebelled against this system by overcharging on all the Faulkners' Oxford accounts; in response, her husband subjected her to public humiliation by running a notice in the Oxford paper claiming he was not responsible for any debts his wife incurred.

7. *OXE*, 13 February 1919, and Snell, *Phil Stone of Oxford*, 132.

8. *Faulkner* (1974), 1:133, 115.

9. Thomas B. Franklin (Columbus, Miss.) to Cornell Franklin (Honolulu, Hawaii), 13 March 1921, CSFA.

10. Letters from Cornell Franklin to Lemuel Oldham, 9 March 1925, Oldham

File, Rowan Oak; interest note signed received by Lemuel Oldham, 2 February 1926, CSFA; Chauncey P. Holcomb, Esq., to Mrs. Cornell Franklin, 2 August 1928, VJA.

11. Malcolm's demise was one of the casualties of American expansionism. Having lived as a colonial for most of his adult life, he was ruined for life back at home in the small Southern town of Columbus. In the larger context, Malcolm is an exemplar of colonialism's destruction of its own best servants—a point well made in Estelle's portrayal of a similar figure in "Star Spangled Banner Stuff." Letters containing the charges against him—that he was aiding and abetting the illegal importation of alcohol into the Territory and that he himself was habitually drunk when serving in his capacity as Collector of the Port—make clear that his conduct had gone unremarked for years. They also make clear that many local Bourbon Democrats were beneficiaries of Franklin's "aiding and abetting."

12. Snell, *Phil Stone of Oxford,* 132.

13. *Faulkner* (1974), 1:274.

14. *Faulkner* (1984), 239.

15. WF to MBF, 16 November 1921, *TOH,* 160–61. The letter firing Faulkner was postmarked 2 September 1924 (*Faulkner* [1974], 1:362). Faulkner's other November 1921 letters to his parents give further details of Lem Oldham's lobbying on his behalf (*TOH,* 154–55, 160–61).

16. Virginia Watson Vilmaire, interview with author, 21 January 1994.

17. The Prince of Wales visited Honolulu from 13 to 15 April and again from 30 August to 3 September 1920. Besides Estelle, his two other partners at the first ball were the governor's daughter, Miss Anne Parker, and Estelle's friend Margaret Frances (Mrs. Reynold) McGrew (*PCA,* 12, 13, 14, 18 April 1920).

18. Merrill Thomas, interview with author, 28 August 1989.

19. Lida and Dorothy left Oxford on 14 May and returned by 23 September. *OXE,* 13 May and 23 September 1920; *PCA,* 6 September 1920.

20. In both 1919 and 1920, Estelle spent Christmas in Honolulu. Thomas B. Franklin to Cornell Franklin, Columbus, Miss., 9 March 1921, CSFA.

21. *PCA,* 6 and 20 June 1920.

22. Ibid., 20 June 1920.

23. Ibid., 24 October 1920.

24. Ibid., 10 August 1920.

25. Ibid., 10 and 13 June 1920.

26. Ibid., 6 September 1920.

27. A week later, Estelle's friend Sara Lucas also left the island to spend the winter in New York, where Nils Larsen, the Norwegian pathologist whom she would marry in 1921, was finishing his residency (*PCA,* 12 September 1920).

28. Estelle Oldham Faulkner, interview with Joseph Blotner, 9 September 1965, SEMS. From 5 September to 6 November, the Franklins were absent from the *Advertiser*'s and the *Star Bulletin*'s social columns. Also absent were notices about the cases being heard in Cornell's court, which had appeared regularly in the *Advertiser*'s "Around the City" columns during his mother-in-law's visit. They began appearing again in December 1920. See *PCA,* 11, 13, 16–24, and 27–30 December 1920. For social columns, see the *Honolulu Star Bulletin,* 6 and 13 November 1920.

29. *Honolulu Star Bulletin,* 4 November 1920.

30. Virginia Watson Vilmaier, interview with author, 21 January 1994. The Franklin's lot at 1670 Kewalo Street was a fairly ample 8,400 square feet. On it were "1–1 story residence; garage and quarters" worth $3,595 in 1926. *Field Assessment Books,* book 5C, folio 56, for the city and county of Honolulu for 1926–30. The Assessment Books for 1900–25 were not available.

31. *Men of Hawaii,* 1921, 301.

32. Corroboration comes from the following interviews with author: Barbara Thompson, 21 January 1994; Dennis O'Connor, 18 January 1994; "Lil" Watson Nelson, 1 February 1994; and interviews with JFS and CSF, Jr.

33. Oldham, "Dr. Wohlenski," 10.

34. JFS, interview with author, 27 February 1987.

35. The poignant parallels here between Estelle and Kate Chopin's fictional Mme. Pontellier tell something about the universality of this experience. As Mary Poovey, Carol Smith-Rosenberg, and many feminist biographers have documented, historically many women have used illness as a means to establish intellectual independence. Emily Dickinson, Louisa May Alcott, Edith Wharton, and Charlotte Perkins Gilman are only a few examples.

36. Wright, *Honolulu Community Theater.*

37. *PCA,* 31 October 1920.

38. Like the Modernist avant-garde in Paris, London, and New York, the avant-garde in Oxford, Miss., and in Honolulu were also intrigued with Pierrot at that moment.

39. For poem, see Sensibar, *Origins,* 231 n. 8.

40. *PCA,* 16 January 1921. In 1915 as one of the first four plays presented by the famous Provincetown Playhouse, *Suppressed Desires* quickly became, according to Glaspell's bibliographer, "one of the most popular one-acts to come out of the little theater movement." Glaspell herself wrote that "it has been given by every little theater, and almost every Methodist church; golf clubs in Honolulu, colleges in Constantinople; in Paris and China and every rural route in America" (Papke, *Susan Glaspell,* 17).

41. Lewisohn, *Expression,* 398, quoted in Gainor, *Susan Glaspell in Context,* 1.

42. The drama critic Joseph Wood Krutch, quoted in Gainor, *Susan Glaspell in Context,* 28. For Faulkner and Freud, see Sensibar, *Origins,* 60, 101, and chap. 7, "Aiken and Freud: New Shapes for Faulkner's Inner Voices," 104–37. For the imaginative roles Eliot and Aiken play in Faulkner's apprenticeship, see *Origins,* chaps. 7 and 12.

43. See Gainor's chapter on *Suppressed Desires,* in *Susan Glaspell in Context,* 20–36.

44. John D. Barry, "Psychoanalysis," in his "Ways of the World" column, *PCA,* 11 April 1920.

45. John D. Barry, "Ways of the World" columns, *PCA,* 10 July and 4 November 1920.

46. At Rowan Oak, Estelle's bedroom bookshelves included William James's *The Varieties of Religious Experience* (1929), Joseph Smith's *The Book of Mormon* (1950 ed.), Paramhansa Yognanda's *Autobiography of a Yoga* (1956), Emmet Fox's *The Power of Constructive Thinking,* Ralph S. Harlow's *A Life After Death,* Bishop Fulton Sheen's *Way to Happy Living* (1963), George H. Hull's *Salvation: Parts 1–3,* Ambrose and Olga Worrall's

The Miracle Healers (1965), and Marcus Bach's *Had You Been Born in Another Faith* (1963), among others works.

47. Gainor, *Susan Glaspell in Context*, 31.

48. Although he plays a heterosexual husband in *Suppressed Desires,* Blanding was gay, which scotches speculations about any sexual improprieties with a fellow actor being the source of Estelle's removal from the social scene. Virginia Watson Vilmaire, interview with author, 21 January 1994; Mary Judd, interview with author, 21 January 1994.

49. The following February (1922) in Shanghai's Treaty Port sector, Estelle made her first public appearance at a similar though more sedate Washington Birthday Ball.

50. *PCA*, 12 February 1921.

51. Ibid., 11 December 1921.

52. Dennis O'Connor, interview with author, 18 January 1994.

PART 5: THE EMERGENCE OF A MATURE NOVELIST

Epigraph to Part 5: John Faulkner, *MBB*, 122.

CHAPTER 22: ESTELLE'S SHANGHAI SOJOURN, 1922–1924

1. *North China Daily Herald*, 7 January 1922; *C'ville Daily Progress*, 2 August 1956. Estelle and Cho-Cho had been in Oxford since March 1921 and would remain for 15 months. For the importance of sport, especially polo, to members of Shanghai's foreign legal community see Allman, *Shanghai Lawyer*, 116, 129, 149, 151, 152 (a reference to Cornell).

2. CSF to the Honorable H. M. Daugherty, attorney general of the United States, 29 November 1921.

3. CSF to the Honorable H. M. Daugherty, attorney general of the U.S., 29 November 1921; telegram from Daugherty to CSF, 7 December 1921: "Resignation effective December tenth," and passport for Estelle Olden [*sic*]. Franklin and her daughter, Victoria Franklin, CSFA.

4. Parts of this chapter appeared originally in "Writing for Faulkner, Writing for Herself: Estelle Oldham's Anti-Colonial Romance." It and Estelle's story "Star Spangled Banner Stuff" were published in *Prospects: An Annual of American Cultural Studies* 60 (December 1997): 357–417.

5. *North China Herald*, 7 January 1922. *NCH* reported a temperature of 27.1 degrees F for the day they arrived (31 December 1921).

6. Bergère, "'The Other China,'" 4–5, in Howe, ed., *Shanghai.*

7. Crow, *Traveler's Handbook for China*, 83, 86.

8. This is an Anglo-Indian word meaning "quay." The British foreigners, the first and most powerful in Shanghai, were quick to colonize with language.

9. *My Days*, 141.

10. CSF to Lemuel Oldham, 29 May 1922. Rowan Oak, Oldham file.

11. CSF to LEO, Glenline Building, Shanghai, 29 May and 29 January 1922, CSFA.

12. CSF to LEO, 29 January 1922, CSFA.

13. Bergère, "The Other China," 7.

14. Jane Addams spoke at the American Club in 1923, one of several years in which Fearn was president (Fearn, *My Days*, 212); "Albert Einstein Lectures to Jewish Community on Relativity and Zionism," headline in social pages of the *China Press*, 6 January 1923. Announcement for Ibsen's *A Doll's House* and *The Prisoner of Zenda NCH*, 2 February 1923.

15. *China Press*, January 1923, passim; for book reviews, see *China Press*, 16 November 1924.

16. Sargent, *Shanghai*, 3.

17. Allman, *Shanghai Lawyer*, 115–16.

18. *NCH*, 11 March 1922:708; *NCH*, 22 April 1922: 266, 267; *NCH*, 27 May 1922: 635.

19. *China Weekly Review*, 21 January 1922: 350–351, 11 February 1922: 480–481, and *NCH*, 25 February 1922: 525.

20. By 1926 Cornell Franklin had been elevated to organizing the ball; his future wife served on the refreshments committee. Knowing the degree to which this actually figured in all three peoples' lives further sharpens the irony of Oldham's reference to the ball at the conclusion of "Star Spangled Banner Stuff."

21. Fearn, *My Days*, 296.

22. Willie Fondell, an African American sailor who was a fixture on Shanghai's waterfront bar scene. Cornell successfully defended him against charges of habitual vagrancy, drunkenness, and insanity, calling on Annie Fearn to give a medical opinion concerning his state of mind. *North China Daily News*, 21 April 1926.

23. Fearn, *My Days*, 4, 6.

24. Ibid., 182, 183, 220, 230, 221–24. Birth notices in the *Shanghai Press*, 3 December 1923, and the *China Press*, 14 December 1923.

25. Fearn, *My Days*, 95, 96.

26. Estelle Oldham Faulkner to Saxe Commins, 5 November 1956, *LDB*, 2:199.

27. Milly Bennet, an American journalist who was job hunting in Shanghai in 1927; quoted in Clifford, *Spoilt Children*, 75.

28. JFS, interview with author, 28 February 1993. For a sketch of the Shanghai foreign scene in 1924, see *Vogue* essay quoted in Clifford (*Spoilt Children*, 74–75) and elaborated on by Candlin, who concludes that for foreigners such as the Franklins and herself "it was a world of total service" (*The Wall*, 55). For a less exaggerated account, see Clifford, 77.

29. In 1922, *The North China Herald* ran a series of articles and letters to the editor arguing about the American Women's Club and British Women's Association proposals to force the Chinese domestic workers to "register" with the Municipal Police and carry papers attesting to their good character. The letters, more con than pro, provide a good picture of the average colonial's treatment and expectations of their household help. See *NCH*, 25 February 1922, 530, and also Fearn, *My Days*, 183.

30. See Clifford for a good account of the political situation in Shanghai in the twenties. Describing the effect of political instability on daily life, another American woman wrote, "The ordinary person just hung on. If he were a foreigner, generally he lived in that superficial comfort many good servants assure, but all too often the very ground seemed to quiver, even when he rang bells for the boy, the cook, the gardener,

the coolie, the amah, the chauffeur" (Candlin, *The Wall*, 38). For summer 1924, and a description of the political situation in Shanghai in the months preceding Estelle's first trip home that December, see Clifford, 85.

31. Estelle Oldham Faulkner to Dorothy and Saxe Commins, 13 December 1954, *LDB*, 2:175.

32. In 1926 the club planned to spend the first half of the year taking a writing class. Their textbook was *A Handbook on Short Story Writing*, by Blanche Colton Williams, regarded as a standard work on the subject.

33. *Short Stories Written in Shanghai by Members of the Short Story Club*, foreword, 2, 250, 252–53, 256.

34. *North China Daily News*, 6 October 1926, "Shanghai Short Story Club," 12.

35. *Shanghai Stories*, Introduction.

36. Some examples are Louise Jordan Miln's *The Flutes of Shanghai* (London: Hodder & Stoughton, 1928); L.S. Palen, *White Devil of the Black Sea* (New York: Blach & Co, 1924); Upton Close, *In the Land of the Laughing Buddha: The Adventures of an American Barbarian in China* (New York: Putnam's, 1924); James W. Bennett and Soon Kwen-ling, *Plum Blossoms and Blue Incense and Other Stories of the East* (Shanghai: Commercial Press, 1926). Similar stories were published in British and American magazines like *Scribner's* and *The Freeman* and in Shanghai's English-language newspapers.

37. Conn, *Pearl S. Buck*, 84.

38. "The theme, carried out in decorations—the flags of all the states—is 'Star Spangled Banner Stuff'" (*The China Press*, 11 February 1923).

39. Smith elaborates: "Everywhere one found white arrogance, white colonialism in all its manifestations. . . . Always, always, we British and Americans segregated the Chinese—even the Christian Chinese from our 'fun'"; quoted in Hale, *Making Whiteness*, 256, 273–74.

40. Conn, *Pearl S. Buck*, 20.

41. Ibid., 389, 42–44.

42. *My Days*, 144.

43. Conn, *Pearl S. Buck*, 250 and passim.

44. Cornell S. Franklin, Jr., interview with author, 5 April 1990.

45. "SSS," 12, 16–17, 28.

46. In December 1928, Faulkner submitted a co-authored version of "Selvage" to his editor at Scribner's, which they rejected in February 1929. A further revised version called "Elly" was published in *Story* magazine in 1934, in a collection of his own stories, *Dr. Martino and Other Stories* later that same year, and in 1950 in *CS*.

47. "SSS," 6.

48. Passenger List for the *T. K. K. Shinyo Maru*, China Press, 22 November 1924.

49. WF to MBF (probably 12 January 1925), *TOH*, 173. Stark Young introduced WF to Elizabeth Prall when Faulkner came to New York in fall 1921. Faulkner worked for her at Doubleday's bookstore on Fifth Ave. and Forty-third St.

50. *TOH*, 168. Stone had placed an announcement in the New Orleans *Times-Picayune* before Christmas 1924 announcing the publication of Faulkner's book and the imminent arrival of the "Mississippi Poet" in New Orleans.

51. Watson, *William Faulkner*, 50, 55.

52. Chauncy P. Holcomb to Estelle Oldham Franklin, 2 August 1928, VFJ.

53. Scribner's rejection letter to WF states "the story 'salvage' [*sic*] done by you and E. Oldham" (Alfred Dashiell to WF, 23 February 1929, Princeton University Library). Faulkner had mailed the manuscript to Dashiell in December, 1928 (WF to Alfred Dashiell, n.d., Princeton University Library). It seems unlikely that Faulkner would have been cavalier about coauthorship. Estelle's version of "Selvage" is, apparently, lost and there is no extant coauthored version, or at least no version that acknowledges Faulkner and Oldham as coauthors. Joseph Blotner indicates that he saw Estelle's version of "Selvage," but his account doesn't clarify matters. Drawing on his 1968 interview with her, he writes that "Estelle had thought of an idea for a story and written it up only to find it thin and unsatisfactory. When she showed it to Bill he suggested that they rewrite it together. She decided she didn't want to, but she'd be happy for him to try it if he liked. In the six manuscript pages that he composed, the plot line remained much the same, but the texture thickened and darkened" (Blotner, *Faulkner* [1974], 1:604). The available typescripts and holographs of both "Selvage" and of "Elly," the title of the version Faulkner finally published, are reproduced in McHaney, *William Faulkner Manuscripts.*

54. *Faulkner* (1984), 294.

55. Ibid. As far as I can tell, the one surviving typescript of "A Dangerous Man" bears no relation to any of the surviving typescripts or holograph versions of either "A Letter to Grandmamma" or "A Letter." *Faulkner* (1974), 1:646; Blotner repeats this claim in *Faulkner* (1984), 256.

56. Rowan Oak papers, University of Mississippi Library, now at UVA.

CHAPTER 23: COLLABORATING WITH ESTELLE, OXFORD, 1924–1925

1. All citations are from the 1997 published version of the earliest draft (#1) of "Star Spangled Banner Stuff," hereafter, "SSS." See note 2, below. All typescripts of this story are now located in the Faulkner collection, UVA. On "Selvage," see below.

2. Lem's letterhead reads "U.S. District Attorney for the Northern District of Mississippi, 1921–25/ The Oldham Building, Oxford Mississippi." "SSS," 51.

3. For the published version of "SSS" #1, see Estelle Oldham, "Star Spangled Banner Stuff" *Prospects* 22 (1997): 379–418. "SSS" #3, the carbon of "SSS" #2 (typed by Jill Summers), has slight revisions throughout in Estelle's hand. She has also reworked the conclusion, which somewhat tightens the narrative and, at the end, heightens the colonial critique.

4. "SSS," 2.

5. Ibid., 2, 3, 7.

6. Ibid., 4.

7. Ibid., 4–5.

8. Ibid., 22. One of the town boys describes Cecily's entrance at a dance: "Then as they turned the angle of the porch he saw Cecily clothed delicately in a silver frock, fragile as spun glass. She carried a green feather fan and her slim, animated turned body, her nervous prettiness, filled him with speculation. The light falling diffidently on her, felt her arm, her short body, suavely indicated her long, virginal legs" (*SP,* 192–193).

9. "SSS," 5, 10.

10. Ibid., 10.

11. Ibid., 4.

12. Estelle uses historical accuracy here to make her point. Shantung or Shandong, a coastal province, was the home of the war-lord who came to power in Shanghai in January-February 1925. Clifford, *Spoilt Children*, 88.

13. "SSS," 21.

14. Ibid., 21.

15. Ibid., 29.

16. Norwood F. Allman, one of the few Chinese-speaking American lawyers practicing in Shanghai in the 1920s and, with Franklin, a member of the American Troop polo team, describes the role clubs played for foreign businessmen: "In no other place in the world was a man's club more important to him than in Shanghai. The American Club, [a] five-story male sanctuary with luxurious fittings and some fifty rooms for members, was the center of social life for Americans" (*Shanghai Lawyer*, 156).

17. Chauncy P. Holcomb to Estelle Oldham Faulkner, March and August 1928. VJA. Holcomb and his law partners were among the "handful of Americans . . . who had reached the highest levels of what was otherwise a very British Shanghai establishment" (Clifford, *Spoilt Children*, 22).

18. Clifford, *Spoilt Children*, 22; see also 35, 36, 262.

19. Chinese were not admitted to either the British or the American Club. The American Club began admitting Chinese in 1929. Clifford, *Spoilt Children*, 36, 71.

20. Ibid., 71.

21. "SSS," 1.

22. Ibid., 1.

23. Ibid., 1, 18.

24. Ibid., 1–2.

25. Ibid., 1, 6, 7.

26. Ibid., 13.

27. Ibid., 26, 27.

28. Chang's degrees are similar to those of other Western educated Chinese businessmen whose names appear in the "Men and Events" columns of the *China Weekly Review* (11 February 1922). For example, a Doctor H. L. Huang, the assistant manager of the China Banking Corporation, was Phi Beta Kappa at Princeton, where he received his A.M., Ph.D., and Litt. B. degrees.

29. "SSS," 10, 21.

30. Ibid., 4, 8, 9, 14, 15.

31. From a review of *The Yellow Corsair* by James W. Bennett in a review essay, "A Sheaf of Fall Fiction Based on Various Themes of China and Chinese Life," *Honolulu Star Bulletin*, 5 November 1927, 12, italics mine. Reviews like these appeared periodically in Shanghai and Honolulu throughout the years in which Oldham lived in these cities. John McClure outlines three other formulas for popular imperial romance: "the romance of a life of adventure on the imperial front lines, the romance of heroic sacrifice in the name of civilization," and "the familiar liberal humanist story of the heroic individual who stands alone against the mob and preserves civilization from its

own pathologies" (*Late Imperial Romance,* 124). Oldham's story "A Crossing" exposes the first, and "Star Spangled Banner Stuff" mocks the third.

32. Oldham pursues the potential tragic implications of this theme in her later story "Selvage," in which she explores the erotic lives of homegrown colonized subjects.

33. Ibid., 5, 6, 24.

34. Ibid., 25, 26, 24, 22.

35. Ibid., 23.

36. Ibid., 10.

37. Ibid., 28.

38. Ibid., 23.

39. Ibid., 4, 9, 16.

40. When Montjoy's more honorable sidekick wants to apologize to Chang, the "whitefaced" Montjoy says, "You can't go back, now," repeating to himself, "that innocent girl" ("SSS," 26).

41. "SSS," 23.

42. See Restuccia, "'A Cave of My Own,'" which argues that misogyny is given free rein through this trope in *Passage to India.*

43. Fearn, *My Days,* 264.

44. Quoted in Pal, *Shanghai Saga,* 87. No citation given for the report.

CHAPTER 24: FAULKNER'S OTHER COLLABORATION,
NEW ORLEANS, 1924 AND 1925

1. See "A Note on Sherwood Anderson," reprinted in *ESPL,* 3–10. Anderson's story was "I'm a Fool."

2. As many have noted, Faulkner gives this sentiment about the South to Quentin Compson in *AA* and to himself as the narrator of "Mississippi."

3. Snell, *Phil Stone of Oxford,* 161–63.

4. Ben Wasson, interview with Blotner, in *Faulkner* (1984), 120.

5. Townsend, *Sherwood Anderson,* 223.

6. Stein, *Three Lives,* 86.

7. Sherwood Anderson to Gertrude Stein (New Orleans, October 1924; Reno, March 1924), in *SA/GS,* 39, 37.

8. Sherwood Anderson to Jean Toomer (New Orleans, Christmas 1923), in *Sherwood Anderson: Selected Letters,* 53.

9. WF to MBF (January 1925), *TOH,* 174–75, 178.

10. Sensibar, *Origins,* 104–221.

11. "Sherwood Anderson," *Dallas Morning News,* book page, 26 April 1925. Reprinted in *William Faulkner: New Orleans Sketches,* 132–39.

12. Quoted in Littell's review of Toomer's *Cane.*

13. See Moser, "Faulkner's Muse."

14. In 1923, responding negatively to Toomer's idea for starting a black magazine, Anderson asked, "Where, in God's name, are you going to get material . . . when you

are the only negro [*sic*] I've seen who seems really to have consciously the artist's impulse" (quoted in Turner, "An Intersection of Paths," 105).

15. Quoted in Helbling, "Sherwood Anderson and Jean Toomer," 116.

16. The two German immigrant serving "girls" whose lives bracket "Melanctha"—the "good Anna's" and the "gentle Lena's"—reveal the social coerciveness of that imperative for both men and women, particularly those inclined to same-sex desire. Mrs. Lehntman is "the only romance Anna ever knew" and "a woman other women loved" (Stein, *Three Lives*, 52). The gentle Lena's husband-to-be, Herman, is defiantly not. Terrified of marriage, he runs away for "He liked to be with men and he hated to have women with them" (251). The African American, Melanctha, quests for "world wisdom" (103). Her wish "to understand what everybody wanted and what one did with power when one had it" is a deeply imagined analysis of the power plays inherent in multiplicitous varieties of friendship and of sexual desire (106). And this was the problem—Toomer's and Stein's black characters often resisted racist stereotyping.

17. Townsend, *Sherwood Anderson*, 223.

18. "Out of Nazareth" was published 12 April 1925, *TOH*, 197 n. 1.

19. WF to MBF (postmarked 23 April 1925), *TOH*, 203–4. Faulkner's review is reprinted in the *Princeton University Library Chronicle* 18 (Spring 1957): 89–94.

20. Spratling, *File on Spratling*, 29.

21. WF to MBF (postmarked 31 March 1925), *TOH*, 194–95.

22. The most well known are the advertisement Faulkner took out in the *Oxford Eagle* stating he was no longer responsible for Estelle's debts; the time he invited his lover, Meta Carpenter, to come to dinner as Ben Wasson's "date" (Estelle knew that Wasson, no great fan of hers, was gay); and the time he invited Jean Stein to visit the Faulkners' home in Rowan Oak, again as Wasson's "date."

23. Kronenberger, *Literary Digest International Book Review* 4 (July 1926): 522, in Inge, *Contemporary Reviews*, 15.

24. In December 1926 the authors "paid the Pelican Press to print 400 copies and sold them all in a week at a dollar and a half each" (*Faulkner* [1984], 195). See also Faulkner and Spratling, *Sherwood Anderson and Other Famous Creoles*.

25. "[Callie Barr] who had been, as he had been from infancy, within the scope and range of that fidelity and that devotion and that rectitude" (Faulkner, "Mississippi," 42).

26. Sherwood Anderson to Horace Liveright, 19 April 1926, New Orleans in Anderson, *Letters of Sherwood Anderson*, 155.

27. Quoted in Blotner, *Faulkner* (1974), 1:431, and *Faulkner* (1984), 146. Faulkner includes a less nasty variation on this incident in "A Note," 10.

28. "Right now I am 'thinking out' a novel. As soon as I get it all straight, I will begin work. I expect to come home this week. I will wire you as soon as I can just when to expect me" ("Billy" to MBF, 16 February 1925, *TOH*, 184).

29. Billy to Maud (12 January, mid-January, and early February 1925), *TOH*, 173, 174, 180.

30. From Faulkner's *The Marionettes* (1920) and "After Fifty Years" (December 1919).

31. At one point Phil Stone wrote the Four Seas Co. (publishers of *The Marble*

Faun) that Faulkner had delayed his trip to Europe because "Sherwood Anderson has been kind enough to write a novel in collaboration with him" (*Faulkner* [1984], 135). Blotner notes instances of Faulkner "stealing" from Anderson, in *Faulkner* (1984), 139, 140, 145.

CHAPTER 25: *THE SOUND AND THE FURY* AND ITS AFTERMATH, 1925–1933

Epigraph: Faulkner responding to a student's question as to why there was no "section giving [Caddy's] views or impressions of what went on" (*FIU*, 1).

1. Manuscript versions of these novels were completed as follows: *The Sound and the Fury* (March–October 1928); *Sanctuary* (January–May 1929, which he then tore down in galleys and completely rewrote during November–December 1930); *As I Lay Dying* (October–December 1929); and *Light in August* (August 1931–February 1932).

2. When his youngest brother, Dean, was killed, Faulkner had engraved the epitaph for his fictional pilot, John Sartoris, on Dean's headstone. Maud was appalled.

3. See Oldham, "Dr. Wohlenski," 10; *TSAF*, 47–48; and Faulkner's suppressed introduction, reprinted in *TSAF*, 231.

4. TS H, Faulkner's suppressed introduction, reprinted in Cohen and Fowler, "*Faulkner's Introduction*," 281. All quotations from Faulkner's introduction are taken from its ten extant drafts. Two of these have been included in *The Sound and the Fury*, Norton Critical Edition, 225–32 (hereafter *TSAF*). These are designated TSS G and J in Fowler and Cohen (see below) but are not reprinted there, as both were already available in the Norton. The other eight drafts and draft fragments (MS A-F and TS H-I) were published in a bibliographical essay by Cohen and Fowler, "Faulkner's Introduction" (hereafter cited as MS or TS, *AL*).

5. Faulkner's letter to Maud says that he left New Orleans for Pascagoula 6 June and returned to New Orleans on 11 June (WF to MBF, 11 June 1925, *TOH*, 210–11). He made a second visit to the Stones 22 June and stayed until the end of the month (*TOH*, 211–12). He then went home to Oxford before going to New Orleans and sailing with Spratling to Genoa on 7 July (WF to MF, 22 and 25 June, 1925, ibid.,). See Collins's accounting of Faulkner's travels from 1925 to 1927 in his introduction to *Helen, A Courtship*, 17–24, passim.

6. *Helen*, 24. By the time he was eighteen, Charlie Crouch, "the town drunk," and Faulkner were steady companions (*Faulkner* [1974], 1:180).

7. *Helen*, 12 and 88. He says 4 March on one page and 4 May on the other.

8. Snell, *Phil Stone of Oxford*, 185. I'm indebted to Susan Snell for pointing out this parallel between Faulkner's treatment of his two very different male mentors; see especially 185–87.

9. Ibid., 185, 186, 204.

10. Cornell S. Franklin to Lemuel Oldham, 9 March 1925, Oldham file, Rowan Oak papers.

11. Cornell's secretary to Estelle Franklin, June 1925, Oldham file, Rowan Oak papers.

12. Malcolm A. Franklin to Cornell S. Franklin, 7 January 1925, CSFA.

13. Ibid., 16 November 1925; ibid., c/o the *S.S. President Wilson*, San Francisco, 28 November 1925, CSFA.

14. Undated letter fragment, Estelle Franklin to Lem and Lida Oldham, Estelle Faulkner file, Collins papers, HRC.

15. Estelle is supposed to have returned to Shanghai in September 1926 and then returned to Oxford for the last time in January 1927 (*Faulkner* [1974], 1:524, 1:539, and *Faulkner* [1984], 189–90). Estelle's name appears on the passenger lists published in either the Honolulu or Shanghai newspapers of all the other voyages she made back and forth between Honolulu or Shanghai from 1918 to 1925. Her arrivals and departures are also noted in *OXE*. I cannot find her on any lists published through 1927. Nor can I find any announcements of a later trip in the Oxford paper. However, there is no mention of her at all in the *OXE* social columns from 7 July 1926, when she leaves for a visit to Monteagle, to 19 January 1927, when she entertained at her mother's home in Oxford. Arguments against the possibility that she returned are Holcomb's 1928 letters to her, her own stated wishes to divorce in her letter to her parents from Honolulu (January or February 1926?), and the huge expense of such a trip at a time when her father's finances were a shambles. In July 1926 Lem's ice plant, insured for $7500, burned in a fire that caused $75,000 in damages. He never rebuilt, and the fire signaled the beginning of the Oldhams' financial collapse (*OXE*, 16 and 20 July 1926).

16. Snell, *Phil Stone of Oxford*, 187, 188.

17. Faulkner also writes on it, "single mss. impression—Oxford, Mississippi—29 October 1926." See Noel Polk, "'Hong Li' and *Royal Street*"; reprinted in Meriwether, *A Faulkner Miscellany*, 143–44.

18. 27 December 1926, Paper Chase photo, CSFA.

19. Gwin, "Did Ernest," 122.

20. Ibid., 138.

21. *Faulkner* (1984), 197. Estelle did compose and write lyrics for a song she called "White Beaches." Her granddaughter, Victoria Johnson, owned a recording of Estelle performing it.

22. This was the Jackson-Filler wedding. Estelle was related to the Jacksons. See her "Dr. Wohlenski" and Lilly Reynolds Brown, interview with author, May 1988.

23. Zaida Woodward, Polly Brown, Charlene Woodward, interviews with author, 15 February 1989.

24. Zaida Woodward, interview with author, 15 February 1989.

25. Charlene Woodward, interview with author, 9 August 1987.

26. Note from Lem to Cornell dated 2 February 1926, acknowledging receipt of $1,960 "in settlement of a loan made to said Franklin in 1922 in the sum of $1500.00 with added interest" (CSFA).

27. Peter Meclewski, interview with author, 21 May 1990 (Peter was Dallas's son from her first marriage); Lilla Pratt Rosamond, interviews with author, 24 May 1988 and 28 August 1989; and Dallas Lee Chesterman (Meclewski) Franklin's 1930 photograph album, which includes photos dating from 1926 (CSFA). The first photograph of Cornell Franklin shows him with a group of men, women, and children at the 1926 American Consulate Fourth of July celebration. I assume Dallas took the snapshot,

which is why it is included as probably another private reminder of the beginning of their affair. The first photo of Cornell and Dallas strolling together is captioned "First Paper Chase, December 27th 1926." It is the only picture, other than those taken on national holidays such as the Fourth, that is precisely dated. After her rancorous divorce, Dallas and Cornell were married in Shanghai, on 2 September 1929, a little more than three months after Faulkner and Estelle's marriage.

28. Cornell Franklin to Estelle Franklin, undated fragment, Faulkner/Estelle file, Collins papers, HRC.

29. MS E: box 2, folder 39, Rowan Oak papers, Faulkner collection, University of Mississippi. Reprinted in Cohen and Fowler, "Faulkner's Introduction," 277. All subsequent references are to those drafts of Faulkner's introduction printed in *AL*, unless otherwise noted.

30. Faulkner, MS D, *AL*, 275.

31. Chauncey P. Holcomb to Mrs. Cornell Franklin, 15 March and 2 August 1928, VJA.

32. Interlocutory Order for Divorce filed in U.S. Court for China (Cause no. 3119, Civil no.1335). See documents, CSFA.

33. Chancery Court Cases, Docket 5, Case 6144, Minutes of the Chancery Court Book 8, Oxford, Miss., Courthouse.

34. See two typescript versions of Estelle Franklin's and Estelle Oldham's "A Crossing," JFSA/UVA.

35. "Elly," originally "Selvage," was published in *Story* 4 (February 1934). In the spring of 1930 he submitted it to *Forum* and *Liberty*, both of which also rejected it.

36. Carvel Collins's notes from interviews with Estelle Oldham Faulkner, 18 and 23 February 1965, Collins papers, HRC.

37. *Faulkner* (1974), 1:643.

38. "A letter to Grandmamma," six-page complete TMS by E. Oldham; "A Letter," seven-page TMS fragment by William Faulkner; "A Letter," thirteen-page carbon fragment by William Faulkner (Rowan Oak papers, no. 9817, now in FCVA). Blotner claims that "A Dangerous Man" (sent to *American Mercury* on 6 February 1930) is yet another version of this story. The only thing the two stories have in common is a character who is a train agent (see Blotner [1974], 1:646).

39. They consist of one six-page holograph draft; one fourteen-page typescript titled "Selvage," with Faulkner's holograph corrections; an eleven-page holograph copy titled "Elly"; and the published version of "Elly" that appeared in *Story* magazine and was included in his collection *Dr. Martino and Other Stories*. See McHaney, *William Faulkner Manuscripts II*.

40. Ibid., x. This strangely reasoned judgment has been repeated in most subsequent Faulkner biographies. For bias and misogyny it ranks with the other constant assertion in the face of biological impossibility that Malcolm Franklin was Faulkner's son. See, most recently, Parini, *One Matchless Time*, 97, 257n.

41. AC, 17, 23.

42. Notes from interviews with Estelle Oldham Faulkner, 18 and 23 February 1965, Collins papers, HRC.

43. Ibid.

44. *Faulkner* (1984), 259.

45. Wasson, *Count No 'Count*, 98.

46. Blotner adds that on the second morning of the conference Faulkner had drunk so much that he became "violently ill" at a public event at the local country club (*Faulkner* [1974], 1:714).

47. *Faulkner* (1984), 274, 295–96. All information about the Faulkners' trip to New York can be found in Blotner's authorized biography.

48. Ibid., 295–96.

49. Ibid.

50. Blotner uses his own words here rather than quoting Estelle directly. The effect is to essentially silence her. See *Faulkner* (1974), 1:737, interview with Estelle Oldham Faulkner, 9 July 1968.

51. From Hollywood, 12 July 1934, Faulkner writes, "I had both your letters at one time yesterday. They were the nicest ones I ever had from you because they sounded hopeful and like you had a good grip on yourself and are at peace. *Maybe Tinkie is responsible.* I love you and miss you damn bad. God bless you and Cho and Mac and little bit, Jill. [signed] Billy" (my italics). For rest of letter, see *SL*, 82.

52. WF to Estelle, 22 October 1931. For rest of letter see *SL*, 52.

53. Minter, *William Faulkner*, 133.

54. Anderson, *Letters of Sherwood Anderson*, 252.

55. *Faulkner* (1984), 296.

56. The uncensored letters are located in FCVA.

57. Faulkner to Ben Wasson (probably late September 1932), *SL*, 66.

CHAPTER 26: FAULKNER'S SUPPRESSED TRIBUTES TO ESTELLE, 1933-1935

Epigraph: Narrator, *Absalom, Absalom!*, 253.

1. All quotations from Faulkner's introduction are taken from its ten extant drafts. Two have been included in *The Sound and the Fury* (Norton Critical Edition). These are TS G and TS J. The other eight drafts and draft fragments (MS A-F and TS H-I) were published in a bibliographical essay by Cohen and Fowler, "Faulkner's Introduction" (hereafter cited as MS or TS, *AL*).

2. According to Blotner, "Faulkner marked the Benjy section of his own copy of the novel with three colors to indicate time shifts and sent the book to Cerf, who sent it on to Grabhorn Press. The project fell through, and Faulkner's book was never returned to him" (*SL*, 71 n. 2).

3. Oldham, "Dr. Wohlenski," 20.

4. Linscott asked for an introduction of eight to ten pages. We do not know which of the extant typescripts Faulkner sent to Random House, but, because he was writing on demand, it seems reasonable to assume that the ten-page draft (TS J, *TSAF*, 228–32) was sent to and later returned by Faulkner's publisher. It is also the only version Faulkner dated—"Oxford/19 August 1933"—and typed his name on. My reading is based on this assumption.

5. He felt no need to censor this material because it was the part of his fantasy or daydream that corresponded to the manifest content of a dream which his dream-work had made unreadable. As Freud observed, although everyone has day-dreams and

fantasies, only a "true artist . . . understands how to elaborate his day-dreams, so that they lose that personal note (which grates upon strange ears) and become enjoyable to others; *he knows how to modify them sufficiently so that their origin in prohibited sources is not easily detected"* (my parentheses and italics). Freud, lecture 23, "The Paths of Symptom Formation," *General Introduction*, 384–85.

6. "It seemed to me that the book approached nearer the dream if the ground-work of it was laid by the idiot who was incapable of relevancy." Asked in 1957 whether he wrote the novel's sections as they appear, Faulkner said yes and that in telling the story from four different perspectives and then even twenty years later when he wrote the appendix he was "still trying to make that book what [*sic*]—match the dream" (*FIU*, 63–64, 84).

7. MS E, *AL*, 276.

8. MS C, *AL*, 273.

9. MS B, *AL*, 273.

10. MS D, *AL*, 274.

11. MS E, *AL*, 277.

12. This is from the five-page typescript where the image appears twice. It appears as well in the longer typescript but it is an earlier image of Caddy "when she quit the water fight and stooped in her wet garments above him" (Benjy who was crying for her) that causes "the entire story, which is all told by that same little brother in the first section, seemed to explode on the paper before me" (from the five- and ten-page typescript versions of Faulkner's suppressed introduction for *The Sound and the Fury*, reprinted in *TSAF*, 218–24. For transcriptions of other manuscript and typescript drafts, see Cohen and Fowler, *AL*, 262–83).

13. Freud, *General Introduction*, 385, my italics.

14. TS J, *TSAF*, 231, 230, 231.

15. WF to Horace Liveright, 16 October 1927 and early March 1928, *SL*, 38, 40. Blotner thinks the manuscript Faulkner writes about in the latter letter was *The Sound and the Fury*.

16. MS D, *AL*, 275; TS H, *AL*, 282; TS G and J, reprinted in *TSAF*, 226, 231.

17. Racialization refers to the mechanisms by which race is made visible, is mobilized, and is experienced.

18. To Estelle from Hollywood, Faulkner wrote, "By the way, I'm hoping to wangle via the studio, the camera I have wanted, the little one with the German lens that takes pictures indoors and out both. The good ones cost $200, but I hope to be able to get one for about $75. If I can do so, I may buy it. Then we can keep a regular diary of the children and Rowanoak [*sic*]" (WF to Estelle, 21 July 1934. For published portion of letter, see *SL*, 82–83).

Select Bibliography

WILLIAM FAULKNER: FICTION, PROSE, POETRY, LETTERS, AND COLLECTIONS

Absalom, Absalom! New York: Random House, 1936. Reprint, New York: Vintage, 1990.

As I Lay Dying. 1930. Vintage, 1990.

The Collected Stories of William Faulkner. New York: Random House, 1950. Reprint, New York: Vintage, 1977.

Early Prose and Poetry. Edited by Carvel Collins. London: Jonathan Cape, 1963.

Faulkner: A Comprehensive Guide to the Brodsky Collection. Vol. 2, *The Letters.* Edited by Louis Daniel Brodsky and Robert W. Hamblin. Jackson: University Press of Mississippi, 1984.

Faulkner in the University: Class Conferences at the University of Virginia, 1957–1958. Edited by Frederick L. Gwynn and Joseph L. Blotner. New York: Vintage, 1965.

Flags in the Dust. 1926. Edited and with an introduction by Douglas Day. New York: Vintage, 1974.

Go Down, Moses. 1942. New York: Vintage, 1990.

The Hamlet. 1940. New York: Vintage, 1956.

Helen: A Courtship and Mississippi Poems. Introductions by Carvel Collins and Joseph Blotner. Oxford, Miss.: Yoknapatawpha Press; New Orleans: Tulane University Press, 1981.

Intruder in the Dust. 1948. New York: Vintage, 1972.

Light in August. 1932. New York: Vintage, 1990.

Lion in the Garden: Interviews with William Faulkner, 1926–1962. Edited by James B. Meriwether and Michael Millgate. New York: Random House, 1968.

The Marble Faun and *A Green Bough.* 1924 and 1933. Reissued in one volume. New York: Random House, 1965.

The Marionettes: A Play in One Act. Edited and with an introduction by Noel Polk. Charlottesville: University of Virginia Press, 1978.

"Mississippi." 1954. In *Essays, Speeches, and Public Letters by William Faulkner.* Edited by
James B. Meriwether. New York: Random House, 1966.

Mosquitoes. 1927. Introduction by Frederick Karl. New York: Liveright, 1997.

Sanctuary. 1931. New York: Vintage, 1993.

Selected Letters of William Faulkner. Edited by Joseph Blotner. New York: Random House,
1977.

"Selvage," "Elly," and "Selvage/Elly." See Thomas L. McHaney, ed. *William Faulkner
Manuscripts II: Dr. Martino and Other Stories.* Holograph manuscripts and typescripts.
New York: Garland, 1987.

Sherwood Anderson and Other Famous Creoles. In collaboration with William Spratling.
Austin: University of Texas Press, 1966. Reprint.

Soldiers' Pay. 1926. New York: Liveright, 1954.

The Sound and the Fury. Edited by David Minter. Norton Critical Edition. 1929. New
York: Norton, 1994, 2d ed.

The Sound and the Fury. Suppressed introduction and drafts. In "Faulkner's Introduction
to *The Sound and the Fury.*" Edited and with an introduction by Philip Cohen and
Doreen Fowler. *American Literature* 62:2 (June 1990): 262–83.

Thinking of Home: William Faulkner's Letters to His Mother and Father, 1918–1925. Edited by
James G. Watson. New York: Norton, 1992.

Uncollected Short Stories of William Faulkner. Edited by Joseph Blotner. New York: Random
House, 1979.

Vision in Spring. Edited by Judith L. Sensibar. Austin: University of Texas Press, 1984.

William Faulkner: New Orleans Sketches. 1925. Edited and with an introduction by Carvel
Collins. New Brunswick: Rutgers University Press, 1958.

The Wishing Tree. 1927. New York: Random House, 1964.

OTHER SOURCES

Abadie, Ann J., ed. *William Faulkner: A Life on Paper.* Jackson: University Press of
Mississippi, 1980.

Abadie, Ann J., and Doreen Fowler, eds. *Faulkner and Popular Culture.* Jackson: University
Press of Mississippi, 1990.

Abadie, Ann J., and Donald M. Kartiganer, eds. *Faulkner and the Artist, Faulkner and
Yoknapatawpha, 1993.* Jackson: University Press of Mississippi, 1996.

Abraham, Karl. "The History of an Impostor in the Light of Psychoanalytical
Knowledge." *Psychoanalytic Quarterly* 4 (1935): 570–87.

Allen, Neil Walsh, and Joel Snyder. "Photography, Vision, and Representation." *Critical
Inquiry* 2 (Autumn 1975): 143–69.

Allman, Norwood F. *Shanghai Lawyer.* New York: McGraw Hill, 1943.

Anderson, Elizabeth, and Gerald R. Kelly. *Miss Elizabeth: A Memoir.* Boston: Little
Brown, 1969.

Anderson, Sherwood. *Letters of Sherwood Anderson.* Edited by Howard Mumford Jones
and Walter B. Rideout. Boston: Little Brown, 1953.

———. *Sherwood Anderson: Selected Letters.* Edited by Charles E. Modlin. Knoxville:
University of Tennessee Press, 1984.

Arnheim, Richard. "On the Nature of Photography." *Critical Inquiry* 1 (September 1974): 149–61.

Baker, Ray Stannard. "Wonderful Hawaii: A World Experiment Station." *American Magazine* 11, November 1911.

Barthes, Roland. *Barthes Reader.* Edited by Susan Sontag. New York: Hill and Wang, 1982.

———. *Camera Lucida.* Translated by Richard Howard. New York: Hill and Wang, 1981.

Bate, Walter Jackson. *John Keats.* London: Chatto and Windus, 1979.

Berger, John. "The Primitive and the Professional" in *About Looking.* New York: Pantheon, 1980, 64–68.

———. *Ways of Seeing.* Middlesex: Penguin, 1972.

Bleikasten, André. *The Most Splendid Failure: Faulkner's* The Sound and the Fury. Bloomington: Indiana University Press, 1976.

———. *The Ink of Melancholy: Faulkner's Novels from* The Sound and the Fury *to* Light in August. Bloomington: Indiana University Press, 1990.

———. *William Faulkner: Une vie en romans, biographie.* Paris: Alden, 2007.

Blessing, Jennifer. *Rrose Is a Rrose Is a Rrose: Gender Performance in Photography.* New York: Guggenheim Publications, 1997.

Blotner, Joseph. *Faulkner: A Biography.* Vol. 1. New York: Random House, 1974.

———. *Faulkner: A Biography.* Vol. 2. New York: Random House, 1974.

———. *Faulkner: A Biography.* New York: Random House, 1984.

———. "William Faulkner's Essay on the Composition of *Sartoris.*" *Yale University Library Gazette* 47:3 (January 1973): 121–25.

Boddie, William Willis. *History of Williamsburg* (1924). Spartansburg, S.C. Reprint Co. Publishers, 1980.

Boone, Joseph. *Libidinal Currents: Sexuality and the Shaping of Modernism.* Chicago: University of Chicago Press, 1998.

Brodie, Fawn McKay. *Thomas Jefferson: An Intimate History.* New York: Norton, 1974.

Brodsky, Louis Daniel. "The Faulkners, the Franklins, and the Fieldens: A Conversation with Victoria Fielden Johnson." *Southern Review* 25:1 (Winter 1989): 95–131.

Brodsky, Louis Daniel, and Robert W. Hamblin, eds. *Faulkner: A Comprehensive Guide to the Brodsky Collection, The Letters,* vol. 2. Jackson: University Press of Mississippi, 1984.

Brody, Jennifer DeVere. *Impossible Purities: Blackness, Femininity, and Victorian Culture.* Durham: Duke University Press, 1998.

Bynum, Victoria E. "'White Negroes' in Segregated Mississippi: Miscegenation, Racial Identity, and the Law." *Journal of Southern History* 64:2 (May 1998): 247–76.

Candlin, Enid Saunders. *The Wall: A Memoir of Old China.* New York: Paragon House, 1973.

Castle, William R. *Hawaii Past and Present.* New York: Dodd, Meade, 1926.

Centennial Memoirs of the Pacific Club, 1851–1951. Privately printed, 1951.

Churn, Virginia. "William Faulkner's Widow Is Mood Painter." *Richmond News Leader,* 3 November 1964, 11.

Claridge, Laura, and Elizabeth Langland, eds. *Out of Bounds: Male Writers and Feminist Inquiry.* Amherst: University of Massachusetts Press, 1990.

Clifford, Nicholas R. *Spoilt Children of Empire: Westerners in Shanghai and the Chinese Revolution of the 1920s.* Hanover: Middlebury College Press, 1991.

Cofield, Jack. *William Faulkner: The Cofield Collection*. Oxford, Miss. Yoknapatawpha Press, 1978.

Cohen, Philip, and Doreen Fowler. "Faulkner's Introduction to *The Sound and the Fury*." *American Literature* 62:2 (June 1990): 262–83.

Conn, Peter. *Pearl S. Buck: A Cultural Biography*. Cambridge: Cambridge University Press, 1996.

Cowley, Malcolm, ed. *The Faulkner-Cowley File: Letters and Memories, 1944–1962*. New York: Viking, 1957.

Crow, Carl. *The Traveler's Handbook for China*. 2d ed. Shanghai: Kelly and Walsh, [1920?].

D. M. Anderson Business Directory and Handy Guide of Bonham, Fannin County, Texas, 1894. Dallas: D. M. Anderson Directory Co., 1894.

Dahl, James. "A Faulkner Reminiscence: Conversations with Mrs. Maud Falkner." *Journal of Modern Literature* 3 (April 1974): 1026–30.

Dardis, Tom. *The Thirsty Muse: Alcohol and the American Writer*. New York: Ticknor and Fields, 1989.

Davis, Thadious. "Faulkner in the Future." In *The Achievement of William Faulkner: A Centennial Tribute. Proceedings of the C. William Gibson Symposium*. Ashland, Va. Randolph-Macon College, 1997, 15–19.

———. *Faulkner's "Negro": Art and the Southern Context*. Baton Rouge: Louisiana State University Press, 1983.

———. "From Jazz Syncopation to Blues Elegy: Faulkner's Development of Black Characterization." In *Falkner and Race, Faulkner and Yoknapatawpha*. Edited by Doreen Fowler and Ann J. Abadie. Jackson: University Press of Mississippi, 1987, 70–92.

———. "The Game of Courts: *Go Down, Moses*, Arbitrary Legalities, and Compensatory Boundaries." In *New Essays on* Go Down, Moses. Edited by Linda Wagner-Martin. London: Cambridge University Press, 1996, 129–54.

———. *Games of Property: Law, Race, Gender, and Faulkner's* Go Down, Moses. Durham: Duke University Press, 2003.

Deutsch, Helene. "The Impostor. Contribution to Ego of Psychology a Type of Psychopath." *Psychoanalytic Quarterly* 24 (1955): 483–505.

Dixon, Thomas, Jr. *The Clansman: An Historical Romance of the Ku Klux Klan*. New York: Doubleday, Page, 1905. Reprint, Lexington: University of Kentucky, 1970.

Donaldson, Susan. "Cracked Lens: Faulkner, Gender, and Art in the South." In *Faulkner and the Artist, Faulkner and Yoknapatawpha, 1993*. Edited by Ann J. Abadie and Donald M. Kartiganer. Jackson: University Press of Mississippi, 1996, 51–81.

Douglas, Ann. *The Feminization of American Culture*. New York: Knopf, 1977.

Ellis, Joseph. *The American Sphinx: The Character of Thomas Jefferson*. New York: Vintage, 1998.

Ellis, Joseph, and Eric S. Lander. "Founding Father." *Nature* 396 (5 November 1998): 13–14.

Ellison, Ralph. *Shadow and Act*. New York: Vintage, 1995.

Evans, Augusta Jane. *St. Elmo*. New York: Dillingham, 1866.

Falkner, Murry C. *The Falkners of Mississippi: A Memoir*. Baton Rouge: Louisiana State University Press, 1967.

Faulkner, Jim, Sally Woolf, and Floyd C. Watkins. *Talking About William Faulkner:*

Interviews with Jimmy Faulkner and Others. Baton Rouge: Louisiana State University Press, 1996.

Faulkner, John. *My Brother Bill*. Athens: Hill Street Press, 1998.

Fearn, Ann Walter, M.D. *My Days of Strength: An American Woman Doctor's Forty Years in China*. New York: Harper and Bros., 1939.

Finkelstein, Lionel. "The Impostor: Aspects of His Development." *Psychoanalytic Quarterly* 43 (1974): 85–155.

Fowler, Doreen, and Ann J. Abadie, eds. *Faulkner and Race, Faulkner and Yoknapatawpha, 1986*. Jackson: University Press of Mississippi, 1987.

———. *Faulkner and the Craft of Fiction*. Jackson: University Press of Mississippi, 1989.

———. *Faulkner and Women: Faulkner and Yoknapatawpha, 1985*. Jackson: University Press of Mississippi, 1986.

Franklin, Malcolm A. *Bitterweeds: Life with William Faulkner at Rowan Oak*. Irving, Tex. Society for the Study of Traditional Culture, 1977.

Freeman, Elizabeth. *The Wedding Complex: Forms of Belonging in Modern American Culture*. Durham, N.C.: Duke University Press, 2002.

Freud, Sigmund. *A General Introduction to Psychoanalysis*. New York: Perma Books, 1958.

———. *Introductory Lectures on Psychoanalysis* (1915–17). Vol. 15 of *The Standard Edition of the Complete Psychological Works of Sigmund Freud*. Translated and edited by James Strachey et al. London: Hogarth Press, 1953–74.

———. "Screen Memories" (1899). In *Early Psycho-Analytic Publications*. Vol. 3 of *The Standard Edition of the Complete Psychological Works of Sigmund Freud*. Translated and edited by James Strachey et al. London: Hogarth Press, 1953–74.

Gainor, J. Ellen. *Susan Glaspell in Context: American Theater, Culture, and Politics, 1915–1948*. Ann Arbor: University of Michigan Press, 2001.

Genovese, Eugene. *Roll, Jordon, Roll: The World the Slaves Made*. New York: Vintage, 1975.

———. *The World the Slave Holders Made: Two Essays in Interpretation*. New York: Pantheon, 1969.

Glissant, Edouard. *Faulkner, Mississippi*. Chicago: University of Chicago Press, 2000.

Goffman, Erving. *The Presentation of Self in Everyday Life*. New York: Anchor, 1959.

Gordon-Reed, Annette. *Thomas Jefferson and Sally Hemings: An American Controversy*. Charlottesville: University of Virginia Press, 1997.

———. "Why Jefferson Scholars Are the Last to Know." *New York Times*, Op Ed essay, 4 November 1998.

Gray, Richard. *The Life of William Faulkner: A Critical Biography*. Cambridge, Mass. Blackwell, 1994.

Greenacre, Phyllis. "The Impostor." *Psychoanalytic Quarterly* 27 (1958): 359–82.

———. "The Relation of the Impostor to the Artist." *Psychoanalytic Study of the Child* 13 (1958): 521–40.

Grimwood, Michael. *Heart in Conflict: Faulkner's Struggles with Vocation*. Athens: University of Georgia Press, 1987.

Gwin, Minrose. *Black and White Women of the Old South: The Peculiar Sisterhood in American Literature*. Knoxville: University of Tennessee Press, 1985.

———. "Did Ernest Like Gordon? Faulkner's *Mosquitoes* and the Bite of 'Gender Trouble.'" In *Faulkner and Gender Trouble: Faulkner and Yoknapatawpha, 1994*. Edited by

Donald M. Kartiganer and Ann J. Abadie. Jackson: University Press of Mississippi, 1996.

———. *The Feminine and Faulkner: Reading Beyond Difference.* Knoxville: University of Tennessee Press, 1990.

Gwynn, Frederick L., and Joseph Blotner, eds. *Faulkner in the University: Class Conferences at the University of Virginia, 1957–1958.* New York: Random House, 1965.

Hale, Grace Elizabeth. *Making Whiteness: The Culture of Segregation in the South, 1890–1940.* New York: Pantheon, 1998.

Hand, Barbara. "Faulkner's Widow Recounts Memories of College Weekends in Charlottesville." *The Cavalier Daily,* 20 April 1972, 1, 4.

Hathorn, John Cooper. *Early Settlers of Lafayette County, Mississippi, 1836–1860.* Oxford, Miss. Skipwith Historical Society, 1980.

Hawaiian Annual. Honolulu: Honolulu Star-Bulletin, 1919, 1920, 1922.

Haynes, Jane Isbell. *William Faulkner His Lafayette County Heritage Lands Houses and Businesses.* Ripley, MS: Tippah County Historical and Genealogical Society, 1992.

Hazzard-Gordon, Katrina. *Jookin': The Rise of Social Dance Formations in African-American Culture.* Philadelphia: Temple University Press, 1990.

Helbing, Mark. "Sherwood Anderson and Jean Toomer." In *Jean Toomer: Critical Evaluations.* Edited by Therman B. O'Daniel. Washington, D.C. Howard University Press, 1988, 111–20.

Hines, Thomas S. *William Faulkner and the Tangible Past: The Architecture of Yoknapatawpha.* Berkeley: University of California Press, 1996.

"History of Arkansas, Cleveland County," *Biographical and Historical Memoirs, Southern Arkansas.* Chicago: Goodspeed Publishing, 1890.

Hobson, Fred. *But Now I See: The White Southern Racial Conversion Narrative.* Baton Rouge: Louisiana State University Press, 1999.

———, ed. *William Faulkner's Absalom, Absalom! A Casebook.* London: Oxford University Press, 2003.

Hodes, Martha, ed. *Sex, Love, Race: Crossing Boundaries in North American History.* New York: New York University Press, 1999.

Howe, Christopher, ed. *Shanghai: Revolution and Development in an Asian Metropolis.* Cambridge: Cambridge University Press, 1981.

Hunter, Jefferson. *Image and Word: The Interaction of Twentieth-Century Photographs and Texts* Cambridge, Mass. Harvard University Press, 1987.

Hunter, Tera W. *To 'Joy My Freedom: Southern Black Women's Lives and Labors After the Civil War.* Cambridge: Harvard University Press, 1997.

Hurston, Zora Neale. *"Sweat."* Edited and with an introduction by Cheryl A. Wall. New Brunswick: Rutgers University Press, 1997.

Inge, M. Thomas, ed. *Conversations with William Faulkner.* Jackson: University Press of Mississippi, 1999.

———. *William Faulkner, The Contemporary Reviews.* New York: Cambridge University Press, 1995.

Jacobs, Karen. *The Eye's Mind: Literary Modernism and Visual Culture.* Ithaca: Cornell University Press, 2001.

Jenkins, Lee. *Faulkner and Black-White Relations: A Psychoanalytic Approach.* New York: Columbia University Press, 1981.

Jones, Anne Goodwyn. *Tomorrow Is Another Day: The Woman Writer in the South.* Baton Rouge: Louisiana State University Press, 1981.

Jones, Anne Goodwyn, and Susan V. Donaldson, eds. *Haunted Bodies: Gender and Southern Texts.* Charlottesville: University of Virginia Press, 1997.

Jones, Jacqueline. *Labor of Love, Labor of Sorrow: Black Women, Work, and the Family from Slavery to the Present.* New York: Basic, 1985.

Jones, Norman W. "Coming Out Through History's Hidden Love Letters in *Absalom, Absalom!*" *American Literature* 76:2 (June 2004): 339–66.

Joyner, Charles. *Down by the Riverside: A South Carolina Slave Community.* Chicago: University of Illinois Press, 1984.

Karl, Frederick R. *William Faulkner: American Writer.* New York: Weidenfeld and Nicholson, 1989.

Kartiganer, Donald M., and Ann J. Abadie, eds. *Faulkner and Gender: Faulkner and Yoknapatawpha, 1994.* Jackson: University Press of Mississippi, 1996.

Keeley, Leslie E., M.D. *The Non-Heredity of Inebriety.* Chicago: S. C. Griggs, 1896.

Kent, George. *Blackness and the Adventure of Western Culture.* Chicago: Third World Press, 1972.

Lewis, Will. *The Story of Banks and Banking Activity in Oxford Through the Years: A Contribution to the Celebration of Oxford's Sesquicentennial, 1987.* Oxford, Miss. Privately printed by Will Lewis, 1986.

Limon, John. "The Integration of Faulkner's *Go Down, Moses.*" *Critical Inquiry* 12 (Winter 1986): 422–38.

Lind, Andrew W. *Hawaii: The Last of the Magic Isles.* London: Oxford University Press, 1969.

———. "The Changing Position of Domestic Service in Hawaii." *Social Process in Hawaii* 15 (1951): 71–87.

Littell, Robert. Review of *Cane.* *New Republic* 37 (26 December 1923): 126.

Long, Alecia. *The Great Southern Babylon: Sex, Race, and Respectability in New Orleans, 1865–1920.* Baton Rouge: Louisiana State University Press, 2004.

Loos, Anita. *Gentlemen Prefer Blondes.* New York: Boni and Liveright, 1925.

Lott, Eric. *Love and Theft: Blackface Minstrelsy and the American Working Class.* New York: Oxford University Press, 1993.

Mathews, John. *The Play of Faulkner's Language.* Ithaca: Cornell University Press, 1982.

McCabe, Susan. *Cinematic Modernism: Modernist Poetry and Film.* Cambridge: Cambridge University Press, 2005.

McClure, John. *Late Imperial Romance.* London: Verso, 1994.

McDowell, Deborah E. "'Must Have Been Some Kind of Love': Sexualities' Attachments in Faulkner." In *Faulkner's Sexualities.* Edited by Annette Trafzer and Ann J. Abadie. Jackson: University Press of Mississippi (forthcoming).

McFadden, Robert. "Meteors Put on a Show, and Comet Swings By," *New York Times,* 17 November 1998, A29.

McHaney, Thomas L., ed. *William Faulkner Manuscripts II: Dr. Martino and Other Stories.* Holograph manuscripts and typescripts. New York: Garland, 1987.

McPherson, James M. *Battle Cry of Freedom: The Civil War Era.* London. Oxford University Press, 1998.

Meriwether, James B. *A Faulkner Miscellany.* Jackson: University Press of Mississippi, 1974.

―――. "William Faulkner's 'Hong Li' and *Royal Street.*" *Library Chronicle of the University of Texas at Austin,* n.s. 13 (1980): 27–30.

―――, ed. *The Literary Career of William Faulkner: A Bibliographical Study.* Columbia: University of South Carolina Press, 1971.

Meriwether, James B., and Michael Millgate, eds. *Lion in the Garden: Interviews with William Faulkner, 1926–1962.* Lincoln: University of Nebraska Press, 1980.

Millgate, Michael. *The Achievement of William Faulkner.* Lincoln: University of Nebraska Press, 1963.

Minnick, Cheryl, "Faulkner and Gender: An Annotated Select Bibliography (1982–1994)." *Mississippi Quarterly* 48 (Summer 1995): 523–53.

Minter, David. *William Faulkner: His Life and Work.* Baltimore: Johns Hopkins University Press, 1980.

Mitchell, W. J. T. *Iconology: Image, Text, Ideology.* Chicago: University of Chicago Press, 1986.

Moak, Franklin E. "The Mystery of William Faulkner's Grandfather Butler." Unpublished, unpaginated essay.

Moraitis, George, and George H. Pollack, eds. *Psychoanalytic Studies of Biography,* Emotions and Behavior Monograph Series of the Chicago Institute for Psychoanalysis, no. 4. Madison, Conn.: International Universities Press, 1987.

Moreland, Richard C. *Faulkner and Modernism: Rereading and Rewriting.* Madison: University of Wisconsin Press, 1990.

Morrison, Toni. *Beloved.* New York: Alfred A. Knopf, 1987.

―――. "Faulkner and Women." In *Faulkner and Women: Faulkner and Yoknapatawpha.* Edited by Doreen Fowler and Ann J. Abadie. Jackson: University Press of Mississippi, 1986, 295–302.

―――. *Playing in the Dark: Whiteness and the American Literary Imagination.* Cambridge: Harvard University Press, 1992.

Mortimer, Gail L. *Faulkner's Rhetoric of Loss: A Study in Perception and Meaning.* Austin: University of Texas Press, 1983.

Moser, Thomas C. "Faulkner's Muse: Speculations on the Genesis of *The Sound and the Fury.*" In *Critical Reconstructions: The Relationship of Fiction and Life.* Edited by Robert M. Polhemus and Roger B. Henkle. Palo Alto: Stanford University Press, 1994: 187–211.

North, Michael. *The Dialect of Modernism: Race, Language and Twentieth-Century Literature.* New York: Oxford University Press, 1994.

Oates, Stephen B. *William Faulkner: The Man and the Artist.* New York: Harper and Row, 1987.

O'Daniel, Therman B., ed. *Jean Toomer: A Critical Evaluation.* Washington, D.C.: Howard University Press, 1988.

Oldham, Estelle. "Star Spangled Banner Stuff." Edited by Judith L. Sensibar. *Prospects: An Annual of American Cultural Studies* 60 (December 1997): 379–418.

Painter, Nell Irvin. *Southern History Across the Color Line.* Chapel Hill: University of North Carolina Press, 2002.

Pal, John. *Shanghai Saga.* London: Jarrolds, 1963.

Papke, Mary E. *Susan Glaspell: A Research and Production Sourcebook*. Westport, Conn.: Greenwood Press, 1993.

Parini, Jay. *One Matchless Time: A Life of William Faulkner*. New York: Harper Collins, 2004.

Polhemus, Robert M., and Roger B. Henkle, eds. *Critical Reconstructions: The Relationship of Fiction and Life*. Stanford: Stanford University Press, 1994.

Polk, Noel. "'Hong Li' and *Royal Street:* The New Orleans Sketches in Manuscript." *Mississippi Quarterly* 26:3 (Summer 1973): 394–95.

Powdermaker, Hortense. *After Freedom: A Cultural Study in the Deep South*. New York: Viking, 1939.

Rank, Otto. *The Myth of the Birth of the Hero: A Psychological Interpretation of Mythology*. New York: Nervous Disease Press, 1909.

Restuccia, Frances. "'A Cave of My Own': E. M. Forster and Sexual Politics." *Raritan* 9 (Fall 1989): 110–28.

Roberts, Diane. *Faulkner and Southern Womanhood*. Athens: University of Georgia Press, 1994.

———. *The Myth of Aunt Jemima: Representations of Race and Region*. New York: Routledge, 1994.

Rowland, Dunbar. *History of Mississippi, The Heart of the South*, vol. 4. Chicago: S. J. Clarke, 1925.

Rubin, Louis D., Jr. *The Writer in the South*. Athens: University of Georgia Press, 1972.

Sargent, Harriet. *Shanghai: Collision Point of Cultures, 1918–1939*. New York: Crown, 1990.

Schnack, Ferdinand J. H. *The Aloha Guide: The Standard Handbook (for) Honolulu and the Hawaiian Islands*. Honolulu: Honolulu Star Bulletin, 1915. Supplement, 1923.

Scott, Anne Firor. *The Southern Lady: From Pedestal to Politics, 1830–1930*. Charlottesville: University of Virginia Press, 1995.

Sensibar, Judith L. "'Drowsing Maidenhead Symbol's Self': Faulkner and the Fictions of Love." In *Faulkner and the Craft of Fiction: Faulkner and Yoknapatawpha, 1987*. Edited by Doreen Fowler and Ann J. Abadie. Jackson: University Press of Mississippi, 1989, 124–47.

———. "Faulkner and Love: The Question of Collaboration." In *Faulkner at 100: Retrospect and Prospect. Faulkner Centennial Essays*. Edited by Donald Kartiganer and Anne J. Abadie. Jackson: University Press of Mississippi, 2000, 188–195.

———. "Faulkner's Fictional Photographs: Beyond Patriarchy?" In *Out of Bounds: Male Writers and Feminist Inquiry*. Edited by Laura Claridge and Elizabeth Langland. Amherst: University of Massachusetts Press, 1990, 290–315.

———. *Faulkner's Poetry: A Bibliographical Guide to Texts and Criticism*. Ann Arbor: UMI Research Press, 1988.

———. "Faulkner's Racialized Aesthetics: Modernist Loss and Initiation Rites in Faulkner and in Literary Studies." *The Faulkner Journal of Japan* 9 (April 2007): 103–14. English version available at www.faulkner-in-Japan.net.

———. "A New Beginning: 'The Thunder and the Music of the Prose.'" In *William Faulkner: Modern Critical Views*. Edited and with an introduction by Harold Bloom. New Haven: Chelsea House, 1986, 269–79.

———. *The Origins of Faulkner's Art*. Austin: University of Texas Press, 1984.

———. "Pop Culture Invades Jefferson: Faulkner's Real and Imaginary Photos of

Desire." In *Faulkner and Popular Culture.* Edited by Ann J. Abadie and Doreen Fowler. Jackson: University Press of Mississippi, 1990, 110–41.

———. "Who Wears the Mask? Memory, Desire, and Race in *Go Down, Moses,*" In *New Essays on* Go Down, Moses. Edited by Linda Wagner-Martin. London: Cambridge University Press, 1996, 101–28.

———. "William Faulkner: Poet to Novelist: An Impostor Becomes an Artist." In *Psychoanalytic Studies of Biography: Emotions and Behavior Monograph Series of the Chicago Institute for Psychoanalysis, Monograph 4.* Edited by George Moraitis, M.D., and George H. Pollock, M.D., Ph.D. Madison, Conn.: International Universities Press, 1987, 303–32.

———. "Writing for Faulkner, Writing for Herself: Estelle Oldham's Anti-Colonial Romance." *Prospects: An Annual of American Cultural Studies* 60 (December 1997): 357–78.

———. "Writing Loss in a Racialized Culture: William Faulkner's Jim Crow Childhood." *Journal of Aesthetic Education* 33:1 (Spring 1999): 55–61.

Shanghai Stories, by Members of the Short Story Club. Shanghai: Kelly and Walsh, 1927.

Sharpe, Jenny. *Allegories of Empire: The Figure of the Woman in the Colonial Text.* Minneapolis: University of Minnesota Press, 1993.

Short Stories Written in Shanghai by Members of the Short Story Club. Shanghai: The Oriental Press, 1924.

Smith, Leef. "Tests Link Jefferson, Slave's Son: DNA Study Suggests a Monticello Liaison." *Washington Post,* 1 November 1998, A1.

Smith, Lillian. *Killers of the Dream.* New York: Norton, 1949.

Snead, James A. *Figures of Division: William Faulkner's Major Novels.* New York: Methuen, 1986.

Snell, Susan. *Phil Stone of Oxford: A Vicarious Life.* Athens: University of Georgia Press, 1992.

Sobotka, John C., Jr. *A History of Lafayette County, Mississippi.* Oxford, Miss.: Rebel Press, n.d.

Solomon, Barbara. *In the Company of Educated Women.* New Haven: Yale University Press, 1985.

Sontag, Susan. *On Photography.* New York: Farrar, Straus, and Giroux, 1977.

Sorensen, Leni. "The Life of Slave Women on Middling Virginia Farms, ca., 1775–1800." *Dispatch, A Quarterly Newsletter of the Jamestown-Yorktown Foundation* (Fall 1998).

Spiegel, Alan. *Fiction and the Camera Eye: Visual Consciousness in Film and the Modern Novel.* Charlottesville: University of Virginia Press, 1976.

Spillers, Hortense. "Mama's Baby, Papa's Maybe: An American Grammar Book." *Diacritics* 17:2 (Summer 1987): 65–81.

Spratling, William. *File on Spratling: An Autobiography.* Boston: Little Brown, 1932.

Stein, Gertrude. *Three Lives.* New York: Vintage, 1909.

Stein, Jean. "William Faulkner." In *Writers at Work: The Paris Review Interviews.* Edited by Malcolm Cowley. New York: Viking, 1959, 119–43.

Steiner, Wendy. *Pictures of Romance.* Chicago: University of Chicago Press, 1988.

Storey, Robert. *Pierrots on the Stage of Desire: Nineteenth-Century French Literary Artists and the Comic Pantomime.* Princeton: Princeton University Press, 1985.

————. *Pierrot: A Critical History of a Mask*. Princeton: Princeton University Press, 1978.

Strauss, Harvey, M.D. "A Discussion of Judith L. Sensibar's 'William Faulkner, Poet to Novelist: An Imposter Becomes an Artist.'" *Psychoanalytic Studies of Biography*. Edited by George Moraitis, M.D., and George H. Pollock, Ph.D., M.D., *Emotions and Behavior Monograph Series of the Chicago Institute for Psychoanalysis*, no. 4. Madison, Conn.: International Universities Press, 1987.

Suleri, Sara. *The Rhetoric of English India*. Chicago: University of Chicago Press, 1992.

Sundquist, Eric J. *Faulkner: The House Divided*. Baltimore: Johns Hopkins University Press, 1983.

————. *To Wake the Nations: Race in the Making of American Literature*. Cambridge: Harvard University Press, 1993.

Szarkowski, John. *Looking at Photographs: One Hundred Pictures from the Collection of the Museum of Modern Art*. New York: Museum of Modern Art, 1973.

————. *The Photographer's Eye*. New York: Museum of Modern Art, 1966.

Taylor, Herman E. *Faulkner's Oxford: Recollections and Reflections*. Nashville: Rutlege Hill Press, 1990.

Townsend, Kim. *Sherwood Anderson: A Biography*. Boston: Houghton Mifflin, 1987.

Trachtenberg, Alan, ed. *Classic Essays on Photography*. New Haven: Leete's Island Books, 1980.

Tucker, Susan. *Telling Memories Among Southern Women: Domestic Workers and the Employers in the Segregated South*. Baton Rouge: Louisiana State University Press, 1988.

Turner, Darwin. "An Intersection of Paths: Correspondence Between Sherwood Anderson and Jean Toomer." In *Jean Toomer: Critical Evaluations*. Edited by Therman B. O'Daniel. Washington, D.C.: Howard University Press, 1988, 99–110.

Tydeman, William, and Steven Price, eds. *Wilde: Salome*. London: Cambridge University Press, 1996.

Tyson, Phillis, Ph.D., and Robert L. Tyson, M.D. *Psychoanalytic Theories of Development: An Integration*. New Haven: Yale University Press.

Urgo, Joseph R., and Ann J. Abadie, eds. *Faulkner's Inheritance: Faulkner and Yoknapatawpha 2005*. Jackson: University Press of Mississippi, 2007.

Vander Zanden, James W. *American Minority Relations*. New York: Ronald Press, 1966.

von Tempski, Armine. *Born in Paradise*. New York: Literary Guild of America, 1940.

Wagner-Martin, Linda, ed. *New Essays on* Go Down, Moses. New York: Cambridge University Press, 1996.

Wakefield, Dan. "Through a Glass Darkly." Review of *A Drinking Life: A Memoir*, by Pete Hamill. *The Nation* 7 (February 1994): 166–69.

Wasson, Ben. *Count No 'Count: Flashbacks to Faulkner*. Jackson: University Press of Mississippi, 1983.

Watson, James G. *William Faulkner: Self-Presentation and Performance*. Austin: University of Texas Press, 2000.

Webb, James W., and A. Wigfall Green, eds. *William Faulkner of Oxford*. Baton Rouge: Louisiana State University Press, 1965.

Weinman, Samuel. *Hawaii: A Story of Imperialist Plunder*. New York: International Pamphlets, 1934.

Wells, Dean. "Dean Swift Falkner: A Biographical Study." Master's thesis, University of Mississippi, 1975.

Welter, Barbara. "The Cult of True Womanhood: 1820–1860." *American Quarterly* 18 (Summer 1966): 151–74.

Westoff, Leslie Aldridge. "A Faulkner Flirtation." *New York Times Magazine,* 10 May 1987, 69–78.

White, Ray Lewis, ed. *Sherwood Anderson / Gertrude Stein: Correspondence and Personal Essays.* Chapel Hill: University of North Carolina Press, 1972.

Wickham, Julia Porcher. "My Children's Mammy—An Appreciation." *Confederate Veteran* 34 (1926): 413–15.

Wilde, Meta Carpenter, and Orin Borsten. *A Loving Gentleman: The Love Story of William Faulkner and Meta Carpenter.* New York: Simon and Schuster, 1976.

Wilde, Oscar. *Salome.* Illustrations by Aubrey Beardsley. London: Elkin Matthews & John Lane, 1894. Citations from Dover reprint, New York: Dover Publications, Inc., 1967.

Williamson, Joel. *William Faulkner and Southern History.* London: Oxford University Press, 1993.

Wilson, Charles Reagan, and William Ferris, eds. *The Encyclopedia of Southern Culture.* Chapel Hill: University of North Carolina Press, 1989.

Woodson, Carter Godwin. *A Century of Black Migration.* Washington D.C.: Association for the Study of Negro Life and History, 1918.

Worden, William L. *Cargoes: Matson's First Century in the Pacific.* Honolulu: University Press of Hawaii, 1981.

Wright, Norman J. *Honolulu Community Theater (formerly known as The Footlights): A Brief History: 1915–75.* Honolulu: privately printed, 1975.

Yaeger, Patricia. *Dirt and Desire: Reconstructing Southern Women's Writing, 1930–1990.* Chicago: University of Chicago Press, 2000.

Yeats, William Butler. "Among School Children." In *The Norton Anthology of Poetry,* rev. ed. New York: Norton, 1975, 445.

Index

Absalom, Absalom! (Faulkner). *See* chapter 12; 6, 22, 32–33, 77, 82–83, 119, 129, 198, 203, 211–12, 221–33, 238, 276, 320, 377, 391, 429, 476; alcoholism in, 32; film and photographs as tropes in, 22, 211–12, 221–23, 228–29, 230; filmic scenes in, 221, 224–25; homoeroticism in, 448, 449; initiation rites in, 224–25; love and desire in, 225–26, 228–31; maternal imaginary in, 210, 227–28, 233, 500; role-playing in, 221–22; Rosa as poet, 223–24; triadic relationship of Judith, Clytie, and Charles Etienne in, 226–28; triadic relationship of Rosa, Clytie, and Judith in, 212, 225–26

addiction, 7, 184–85, 528n60; among expatriates, 339–40, 414 *(see also* Watson, Louise; Franklin, Malcolm; Fearn, M.D., Anne); in Estelle Faulkner's fiction, 284–86, 372–73. *See also* alcohol; alcoholism

"After Fifty Years" (Faulkner), 231

Aiken, Conrad, 198, 309, 310; and Faulkner's poetry, 362, 363, 377, 400

alcohol: as aspect of Southern Manhood, 7, 31, 284–86, 304–5; as part of life in Hawaii, 339–40; and same-sex desire, 367, 375, 383; as theme in Estelle Faulkner's fiction, 284, 286, 338, 371, 379–82, 396, 432; as trope in Faulkner's fiction, 3, 7, 16, 31, 32–33, 104, 333, 379–82

alcoholism: and emotional anesthesia, 116, 183, 333, 379; of Estelle Faulkner, 237, 379, 414; Faulkner family history of, 161, 180, 195, 237, 332, 507n19; of Murry Falkner, 29–30, 158, 176, 179, 180, 184–85, 332; in Southern fiction, 305; treatment for, 176, 184–85, 528–29n61; of William Faulkner, 30–31, 114–17, 237, 304–5, 314–15, 332–33, 476–77, 478

Alcott, Louisa May, 177

Allen, Etta, 261, 262, 264, 550n21

Allen, John Wilbourn, M.D., 261

Allen, Pete, 335

Allen, Victoria Swanson. *See* Niles, Victoria Swanson Allen

Anderson, Elizabeth Prall, 319, 420, 441, 443, 450, 453–54

Anderson, Sherwood, 309, 315, 319, 321, 420, 478, 534–35n15; Faulkner's ambivalence toward, 445, 447–55, 461; Faulkner's collaboration with, 449–501; Faulkner's review of, 445, 448; racial stereotypes in work of, 446–47; and relationship with, 117, 244, 286, 322, 441–42, 443–46, 450

Andrews, Katherine, 133, 242, 245, 292, 330, 470, 537–38n33

art: gendered notions of, 205–6, 231–33; as subversive force, 66, 181. *See also* Butler, Leila Dean Swift; Falkner, Maud Butler; Faulkner, William

As I Lay Dying (Faulkner), 456, 475, 476, 483
"Atalanta in Calydon" (Tennyson), 321
Awakening, The (Chopin), 357–58

Baird, Helen, 11, 252; Faulkner's love affair
    with, 459–61
Bankhead, Tallulah, 299
Barr, Alex, 35
Barr, Caroline ("Callie"), 1, 15; age of,
    37–38, 45–46; Barr family's recollections
    of, 30,31, 50–53; childhood of, 19, 26, 35,
    37–40, 539–40n16; children of, 28, 35, 50;
    contradictory images of, 21–22, 46,
    123–24; death of, 101, 106–8, 123, 124–25,
    511–12n20, 521n20; as disciplinarian, 46;
    early years of, 19–20; Maud Falkner's
    painting of, 71, 72–75, 208; Maud
    Falkner's relationship with, 28–29, 72–76,
    80, 81, 83–84, 129, 134, 140, 174–75, 186;
    and the Falkner women, 25–30, 512–13n3;
    family of, 2, 19, 20, 25, 48–51; Murry
    Falkner, 29–30; family origins of, 34–35,
    41, 506n1; and Estelle Faulkner, 79–80,
    512n3; Faulkner children's recollections
    of, 43–48, 63; Faulkner family's sense of
    ownership of, 107–8, 119, 133; Faulkner's
    epitaph for, 133; and eulogy for, 86–87,
    101, 106, 108–9, 282; and Freedman
    Town, 2, 57, 61, 81 (*see also* Molly Barr);
    genealogy of, 26–27; funeral of, 107–8; *Go
    Down, Moses* as elegy for, 89, 90, 101–2,
    105, 108–10, 483; gravestone of, 18, 19,
    100, 105, 512n20; as influence on
    Faulkner's imaginative vision, 20–21, 38,
    55, 61–62, 64–65, 100, 124, 442, 483, 500;
    intelligence of, 22, 46; journey to
    Mississippi, 42–43; and Mammy myths,
    174; many names of, 63; masks of, 21, 62,
    63, 81, 84, 100, 203; "Mississippi" as elegy
    for, 21, 89, 91, 111, 117, 118–19, 125, 233,
    452, 483, 563n23; as moral arbiter, 86–88,
    174–75; as "mother" and "Mammy" to
    Fa(u)lkner males, 2, 20, 21–22, 25, 30–31,
    57, 63, 64–65, 76, 78, 81–82, 85, 93, 174,
    514n29; mythologizing Callie as Dilsey,
    46, 57, 72; and naming of Falkner family
    members, 82, 514n29, 518n33; photo-
    graphs of, 36, 44, 72, 122, 232, 509n31;

quilts and quilting of, 2, 35, 47, 76, 121,
    123; as racialized maternal imaginary, 111,
    453, 500; and racial violence, 53–55; racist
    stereotypes of, 21, 56–57, 64–65, 80, 90,
    123, 174: James Rudd's recollections of,
    50–53; as sharecropper, 48–49; as slave,
    34, 35, 37, 38–40, 50, 506n1; snobbery of,
    84–85, 175; as storyteller, 21, 22, 29–30,
    34, 85–86, 457; teaching methods of, 20,
    29–30, 53, 82, 108, 121, 493; temperament
    of, 50–51, 52–53; on the truth, 87–88;
    work life of, 40, 45, 46
Barr, Ed, 25, 28, 49, 50, 510n4
Barr, Joseph, 510n50
Barr, Molly (Callie Barr's niece), 25, 44, 47,
    49, 80, 510n4, 511n16; as businesswoman,
    25, 59; jook joint of, 57–61, 511n16; as
    midwife, 59, mother, 25; reputation of, 61,
    85
Barr, Samuel, 28
Barr, Wes, 49, 510n4
"Bear, The" (Faulkner). See *Go Down, Moses*
Beardsley, Aubrey, 213, 214
Berger, John, 208, 229–30
Bezzerides, A. I., 321
Biglin, Joe, 314
Bishop, Vasser, 527–28n32
black community in Oxford: Maud
    Falkner's paintings of, 67, 71–76, 208. *See
    also* Caroline Barr and Molly Barr
Blanding, Don, 402, 557n48
Blotner, Joseph, 57, 112, 135, 171, 173, 189,
    289, 291, 330, 422, 472
Boni and Liveright, 462, 463–64
Brown, Mrs. Calvin, 190
Brown, Lilly Reynolds, 467
Brown v. Board of Education, 520n1
Buck, Pearl S., 416, 417–18
Burns, Elizabeth (Lizzie) Murry, 164
Burns, Sallie Falkner, 132, 134, 136, 164–65,
    167, 526n6; Maud Falkner's correspon-
    dence with, 208, 209
Butler Hotel, 150, 151
Butler, Berlina House, 141, 145, 150, 151–52,
    153, 524n31
Butler, Charles G. (father of Charlie Butler),
    141, 145, 150, 151, 524n31
Butler, Charlie (father of Maud Falkner),

133, 140, 144, 152–53, 154–57, 523n16; family history of, 151–52; felony of, 132; and miscegenation, 132, 179

Butler, Lelia Dean Swift (mother of Maud Falkner), 25, 28, 29, 66–67, 68, 70, 130, 194; as artist and rebel, 140, 142–43, 150, 180–81, 207, 523n6; death of, 144, 178; emotional limitations of, 179–80; family history of, 140, 143, 144–51; genealogy of, 146–47; as influence on Faulkner's visual imagination, 134, 137, 141–42, 143, 144, 150, 206; marital difficulties of, 132, 152–53, 154–57, 179; marriage to Charlie Butler, 140, 141, 144, 152; and opposition to Maud's marriage, 29, 158; painting of, 68, 70, 71, 138, 141, 522n4; as support to Maud Falkner, 174, 175, 176, 178, 506–7n3

Butler, Maud. *See* Falkner, Maud Butler

Butler, Sherwood Tate, 132, 145, 153–54

Butler, William R., 151, 152

cabin genre paintings, 67, 68. *See also* Falkner, Maud Butler

Cane (Toomer), 443–44, 445–46, 447

Cape, Jonathan, 536n10

Carpenter, Meta. *See* Wilde, Meta Carpenter

Carson, Merwin, 352

Carson, Myrtle, 352

Carter, Katrina, 262, 300, 301, 309, 320, 330, 334

Cerf, Bennett, 115, 245, 477, 478

Chopin, Kate, 357, 556n35

Clansman, The (Dixon), 182–83, 186, 188, 292–93, 294

Clark, Callie Barr. *See* Barr, Caroline ("Callie")

collaborative fantasy: and cultural mythologies, 8

Commins, Saxe, 115–16

Confederate Journal, 64, 292

Confederate Veteran, 66, 106, 512n1

Connelly, Marc, 477

Cottrell, Magnolia (Nolia), 289, 329. *See also* "Doctor Wohlenski"

Cowley, Malcolm, 205, 218, 380

creative process: in Callie Barr (*see* Barr, Callie, teaching methods of); Maud

Falkner; 67–75, 134, 136–37; in Estelle's fiction, 268, 271, 272, 281, 342, 383, 423; in Faulkner, 1, 6, 7–9, 91, 95, 100, 109, 111, 120, 205–6, 217–18, 238, 246, 359, 442, 454, 458, 486, 491, 519n50

Crime and Punishment (Dostoyevsky), 321

"Crossing, A" (Estelle Oldham [Faulkner]), 31, 194, 241, 358, 388–89, 402, 417, 425, 429, 444, 464, 474; alcohol as weapon in, 373–74, 380–82, 387; as anti-romance, 371–72; desire in, 344, 370, 371–72, 385–86, 429, 466; colonial critique in, 336–38, 374, 380, 384–85, 417; dance as trope in, 384; female agency in, 380, 381, 382, 383, 385, 386; as imaginative dialogue with Faulkner, 358, 368–74, 376–77, 378, 382; Faulkner's homage to, 378, 379, 380, 386, 466; as inspired by Estelle's colonial life in Hawaii and Shanghai, 336–38, 342, 344, 345, 374–75; marketing of women in, 373, 385, 388–89; marriage as theme in, 337, 342, 371, 374, 380, 385, 417, 464, 474; maternal imaginary in, 370, 377, 382–83, 386; the other in, 344, 370, 371, 373, 428, 464; racialized gender crossings in, 344, 370, 371–72, 385–86, 429, 466; as response to Faulkner's *Marionettes*, 336, 359, 362, 368–71, 382, 385–86, 399–400; seduction in, 371, 373; transgressive erotic desire in, 337, 344 378, 383, 385–86, 466

Crouch, Buster, 193–94

Cunningham, Edwin, 412

dance: in Faulkner's fiction, 8; and poetry, 383; in Estelle's fiction, 383–84. See also *The Marionettes; "A Crossing"*; and Fatal Dancer

"Dancer, The" (Faulkner), 231, 384

Dark Laughter (Anderson), 443, 444, 446–47, 451

Davis, Thadious, 38, 61, 81, 534–35n15

Dixon, Thomas, Jr., 182

"Doctor Wohlenski" (Estelle Franklin [Faulkner]), 14, 80, 241, 291, 324, 344, 368, 386, 423, 428, 474, 508n4; alcohol in, 284, 285, 302, 396; desire in, 276; as dialogue with Faulkner, 286–87;

"Doctor Wohlenski" *(continued)*
education into Southern Womanhood,
271–72, 275–76, 278, 280, 282, 283, 284,
285, 286, 458; female agency in, 269, 272,
274, 275, 281; figuring race in, 273,
276–77, 280, 281, 287, 458, 496, 497;
"Mammy" in, 80, 268, 274–75, 278–79,
287; maternal imaginary in, 268–69, 271,
283, 287; as fictionalized memoir, 267–88;
narrative voice of, 273–74, 287; New
Orleans doll as trope in, 275, 282; plot of,
270–71; racialized loss and mourning in,
268, 271, 276, 283; sexual knowledge in,
268, 270–73, 274–77, 279, 281, 282,
286–88; and *The Sound and the Fury,* 245,
269, 281, 457, 458, 483, 485, 488, 490,
494, 496; Southern Manhood in, 276,
280; Southern myths as aspect of, 272–73;
structure of, 269–70
Dole, Sanford, 353
dolls, 181, 275, 276, 280 282, 293, 496, 497
Donaldson, Susan V., 532n5, 539n10, 571n29
Dostoyevsky, Fyodor, 321
Douglas, Ann, 108–9
Douglas, Ellen, 305
Drake, Christine, 133, 192, 470, 526n13,
527–28n32
"Dry September" (Faulkner), 459, 468
DuBois, W. E. B., 418
"Dulcie," 71–72, 76. *See also* Falkner, Maud
Butler: paintings by

Eastman College, 260, 537n28
Einstein, Albert, 411
Eliot, T. S., 198, 309, 310, 377
Ellison, Ralph, 30, 103
"Elmer" (Faulkner), 400, 528n36
"Estelle Oldham," 80, 267–68, 271, 283. *See
also* "Doctor Wohlenski"; *The Sound and
the Fury:* suppressed Introduction to
Evans, Augusta Jane, 177, 369. *See also* "A
Crossing"

Fable, The (Faulkner), 212
Falkner, Colonel William Clark, 1, 69, 114,
130, 167, 170–73; genealogy of, 146–147;
shadow family of, 114, 125, 131, 146–47,
170, 183; *See also* Falkner, Emeline Lacy

Falkner, Dean Swift (William's brother), 28,
43–45, 186
Falkner, Emeline Lacy, 125, 146–47
Falkner, Henry, 172
Falkner, Jack (Murry Charles, William's
brother), 157, 164, 167, 316–17; and Callie
Barr, 56, 57, 81, 85; and Lelia Butler, 143;
childhood recollections of, 179–80, 184;
and his two mothers, 63, 76
Falkner, John Wesley Thompson, "J. W. T.,"
(William's paternal grandfather), 29, 69,
141, 158, 167, 171, 172, 187; black mistress
of, 152; and Murry Falkner, 172–73,
175–76, 180, 190, 195, 507n14
Falkner, Mary Holland ("Auntee"). *See*
Wilkins, Mary Holland Falkner
Falkner, Maud Butler, 1, 2–3, 20, 25–26, 32,
144, 159, 187, 240, 480, 512n3, 526–27n13,
529–30n27; appearance of, 129–30; as
artist, 3, 66–76, 133, 135–37, 164, 178, 196,
206–10, 522n13, 522–23n4; and Callie
Barr, 3, 28–29, 65–68, 72–76, 80–81,
83–84, 129, 174–75, 178, 186, 456, 500,
512; biographical sources for, 135–37;
birth of, 154; childhood of, 28, 154–55,
156, 157; children born to, 173, 175; death
of, 108; education of, 157; epitaph of,
133–34; family history of, 132, 141–42,
154–57, 524n31; Faulkner's relationship
with, 129, 130, 134, 137, 183, 194–95,
318–19; friendships of, 133, 161–62,
163–64, 176–77; genealogy of, 146–47;
gravestone of, 133–34; as influence on
Faulkner's imagination, 72–73, 129, 130,
131–32, 134–35, 206–10, 500; insecurities
of, 158–59; intellectual life of, 132, 177–78;
marriage to Murry Falkner, 152, 158, 172,
173, 184–85; her mother as support to,
174, 175, 176, 178; and Murry's alcoholism, 184–85, 190, 201; paintings of,
66–88; parents of, 140; on race relations,
76–77; reading habits of, 3, 132, 164;
religion as viewed by, 156, 179; teaching
methods of, 164, 178, 183; and Jill
Faulkner Summers, 81–82, 133; and
Auntee Wilkins, 132, 158, 161–62, 163
Falkner, Murry Cuthbert (William's father),
3, 45, 69, 131, 133, 134, 187, 240, 480;

alcoholism of, 29–30, 158, 176, 179, 180, 184–85, 190, 196, 507n19; and Callie Barr, 29–30, 56, 57; death of, 196, 480; family history of, 140; father's treatment of, 172–73, 190; financial difficulties of, 177, 180, 191–92, 195, 302; marriage to Maud Butler, 152, 158, 172, 173; and his mother-in-law, 29; temper of, 158, 179, 193

Falkner, Sallie. *See* Burns, Sallie Falkner

Falkner, Sallie McAlpine Murry (Maud's mother-in-law), 161, 163–64, 174–179, 324

family secrets: 28, 111–25, 483. *See also* dolls; "Doctor Wohlenski"; "Mississippi"; *The Sound and the Fury:* Faulkner's suppressed Introduction to

Farley, Robert, 299–301, 545n8

Fatal Dancer: Estelle Faulkner as, 7–8, 375, 384; in Estelle Faulkner's fiction, 384; and bedroom battles, 130–31

Faulkner, Alabama, death of, 476

Faulkner, Estelle Oldham Franklin, 1, 16, 20, 22, 115, 181, 192, 199, 513n20; as actress, 245, 368, 397–400; alcoholism of, 237, 286, 324–25, 388, 396–97; as artist, 4; and Callie Barr, 22, 79–80, 123; birth of, 264, 266; childhood of, 266, 292–94; colonial experiences of, 263, 344 *(see also* fiction of); conflicting views of, 9–11; as creative force for *The Sound and the Fury,* 245, 269, 353, 422, 457, 469–70, 471, 484–91; death of, 240; education of, 7, 268, 273, 275, 294, 298; efforts to support herself, 375–76, 421–22; on falling in love with Faulkner, 289–91; family history of, 4–5, 140–41, 239–41, 303–4, 536–37n16; as Fatal Dancer, 7–8, 375; Faulkner's letters to, 10, 237–38, 478, 480, 567n51; figured as black maternal imaginary, 426, 481, 483, 490; genealogy of, 256–57; grief following death of Alabama, 476–78; independence of, 14, 245, 291, 345, 397, 468; intelligence of, 91, 288; letter announcing her marriage to Faulkner, 249–50, 252–54, 255; literary tastes of, 292–93, 556–57n46; losses suffered by, 331–32; marketing of, 387–92, 554nn1–2; on marriage to Faulkner, 242, 244; at

Mary Baldwin, 294–99, 383; mother-daughter relationships in family of, 261, 266; as musician, 298–99; myths about, 5, 9, 10, 14, 238, 254, 291, 505n12, 566n40; parents of, 255–63; photographs of, 8, 215, 236, 264–65, 267, 290, 297, 300, 328–29, 408, 410; relationship with former mother-in-law, 250; relationship with parents, 250, 253–254, 261; return to Oxford in December 1924, 244; self-image of, 245, 330–31, 397; in Shanghai, 243, 245, 263, 397, 407–23; as Southern Lady, 10, 244–45, 255, 270, 291–92; theatricality of, 8–9; Phil Stone's hostility toward, 315; suicide attempt by, 251–52, 505n14; as unconventional woman, 159, 255, 385–86, 397, 467–68. *See also* Faulkner, William; Faulkner, Estelle Oldham

—fiction of, 5, 13–14, 31, 238, 245, 254, 325, 538n4; addiction as theme in, 7, 372–73; alcohol as theme in, 284, 285, 286, 302, 338, 371, 379–82, 396, 432; black maternal imaginary in, 283, 383, 427; as imaginative collaboration with William, 241, 336, 353, 358, 368–74, 376–86, 388, 422–23, 424–25, 439, 454, 455, 456–59, 466, 470–71, 472–73; dolls as trope in (see "Doctor Wohlenski"); experiences in Shanghai, 245, 397, 416–20, 422, 425–39; Jim Crow South as depicted in, 3–4, 268, 270, 288; parental figures in, 254–55; racialized gender issues as theme in, 80–81, 241, 418–20, 473–74; religion as subject in, 373; sexuality in, 383, 466; as source of insight into Estelle's life, 336–38, 342, 344, 345, 374–75, 423; Southern Manhood as represented in, 8, 21, 201–202, 213, 224, 230; Southern Womanhood as represented in, 239, 241, 271–72, 275–76, 280, 284, 285, 286, 471. See also "A Crossing"; "Doctor Wohlenski"; "Selvage"/"Elly"; "Star Spangled Banner Stuff"

—and Cornell Franklin: divorce of, 243, 375–76, 389, 390, 461–62, 464, 468–71, 505n12, 564n15; early relationship with, 298, 323–24, 329–30; Estelle's

Faulkner, Estelle Oldham Franklin
(*continued*)
—and Cornell Franklin
ambivalence about relationship, 329–30;
external events leading to marriage of,
330–32; Faulkner's feelings about
marriage of, 361; marriage of, 5, 6–7, 8,
195, 242–43, 245, 253, 255, 261, 262, 301,
303, 323, 333–35, 357–58, 363–64, 388,
554n2; proposal of marriage, 326,
327–28, 333, 546n14; wedding ceremony
of, 333–35
—in Hawaii, 242, 245, 336–47; birth of first
child in, 355; dress codes as issue for, 344;
pregnancy in, 348; role in *Suppressed
Desires*, 245, 368, 401, 402; at Schofield
Barracks, 348–58, 548–49n25; social life
of, 341–43, 345–46, 347, 350–52, 354–56,
358, 392–96, 551n28; U.S. Identification
Card of, 343–44; visits home to Oxford,
349, 356–58, 360, 403; at the Watsons',
339, 341–42
Faulkner, Jill. *See* Summers, Jill Faulkner
Faulkner, Jimmy (William's nephew), 46, 48;
alcohol as initiation rite for, 31–32
Faulkner, John (William's brother), 143, 173,
187, 191; alcoholism of, 31–32; recollections of Callie Barr, 22, 28, 37–38, 40, 56,
61, 64, 82, 83, 85, 107–8, 508n7;
recollections of Maud Falkner, 164;
recollections of Estelle Faulkner, 191, 237;
recollections of William Faulkner, 166,
191, 237
Faulkner, Murry Cuthbert ("Chooky,"
William's nephew), 46, 135, 522n13
Faulkner, William: alcoholism of, 30–31,
114–17, 237, 304–5, 314–15, 332–33,
380–81, 441–42, 477, 478, 507n21, 544n16,
547n24, 553n35; and Sherwood Anderson, 117, 244, 286, 322, 420, 441–55, 461,
534–35n15; artistic pursuits of, versus
Southern codes of masculinity, 7, 8, 167,
188–89, 201, 205–6; aunts as remembered
by, 93–95; and Helen Baird, 459–61;
Callie Barr as moral influence on, 86–87;
Callie Barr as "mother" to, 2, 20, 21–22,
25, 33, 78, 81–82, 93, 174, 220, 233, 455;
creative process of, 1, 134, 189, 454, 456,
458, 469, 486, 487, 491, 493, 500, 519n50;
creativity and sexuality, 301, 312, 375, 377
(see also *The Sound and the Fury*); as dandy,
199, 219; disapproval of, 85; dolls, playing
with, 181, 293; early drinking of, 3, 188,
193–94, 197; education into race, 2, 21, 81,
95, 182–83, 511n16; emotional damage of,
183–84; Estelle as childhood friend of,
186–87, 189; extramarital affairs of, 252;
and Maud Falkner, 129, 130, 137, 183,
188, 194–95, 220; family history of,
140–41; fashion-consciousness of, 188–89;
father-son relations in family of, 170–73,
201; genealogy of, 146–47, 168–69; grief
of following death of Alabama, 476; in
Hollywood, 480; Hollywood agents in
pursuit of, 478–79; imitating Estelle, 189,
190, 198–202, 203–4, 218–19, 221, 313,
478, 527n23, 531n7, 552n14; letters to
Estelle Faulkner, 10, 237–38, 478, 480,
567n51; and love, xiv, 20, 21, 33, 91,
96–98, 360, 442; marriage as viewed by,
301–2; marriage of, 9–10, 11, 249–50,
252–54, 476–80, 506n35, 534n6, 554n6;
maternal imaginary of, 450, 500; mental
and physical health of, 114–17; military
posing of, 198, 199, 200, 218, 313, 478;
modernist poetics of, 22, 32, 89, 90, 112,
113, 137, 206, 211, 366, 443, 444, 447; as
myth, xii-xiii, 5, 16; in New Haven,
313–19, 392; in New Orleans, 441, 443;
and Lem Oldham, 391–92; painting of,
69; photographs by, 122, 232, 491–500,
568n18; photographs of, 160, 198, 218–20,
531n4; photography as interest of, 137,
165–66, 218; poetry of, 191, 197–98, 199,
202, 310–12, 320–21, 359, 360, 361–66,
377, 420; and psychology of impostors,
199–201, 531n7; as public man, 113;
racialized worldview of, 81, 181–83;
reading habits of, 188; role-playing of,
198–202, 203–4, 218–19, 221, 313, 478,
527n23, 531n7, 552n14; romantic
relationships of, 11–12; screen memory of,
6, 93–97, 181, 455, 515n14; self-portraits
by, 206–7, 218; sexuality as viewed by,
301–2; spelling change in last name of,
167, 170, 198, 336; and Phil Stone, 179,

193, 195, 242, 244, 286, 291, 298, 304–5, 309–22, 332, 367, 391, 442–43, 446, 453, 459, 461, 465, 544n35; as student, 186–91, 293–94, 302, 303, 544n37; Swinburne as inspiration to, 310–12, 321, 360, 543n6; truancy of, 188, 190–91; two mothers of, 6, 21, 23, 30, 66, 78, 94, 137, 212; as viewed by his parents-in-law, 255; visual aesthetic of, 67, 131, 137, 165–67, 206–8, 231, 233; on writing and writing process, 64, 90, 123–24, 474–75

—and Estelle Oldham Faulkner, 385–86; alcohol as factor in relationship, 7, 239, 251, 252, 280–81; childhood friendship of, 186–87, 189, 193, 241; conflicting views of relationship, 5, 9–11, 15–16; early relationship of, 241–42, 244, 289–91, 302; and Estelle's divorce from Cornell Franklin, 461–62, 468–71; Faulkner's ambivalence toward, 21, 245, 251, 252, 484–91, 315, 367, 485; and Faulkner's creative development, 237, 238–39, 246, 254, 283, 288, 359, 360–62, 364–66, 420, 425–26, 446, 469–70, 475–76, 484–91, 500; imaginative collaborations of, 241, 254, 336, 353, 358, 368–74, 376–86, 388, 422–23, 424–25, 439, 454, 455, 456–59, 466, 470–73, 484, 493, 494, 497, 500; marriage of, 9–10, 11, 249–50, 252–54, 476–80, 506n35, 534n6, 554n6; as racialized maternal imaginary, 490, 491; role-playing and theatricality in relationship, 12–13, 78, 88, 124, 203, 219, 246, 251, 253; self-representation of, 8; violence towards, 298, 477; wedding night of, 250–51, 454

—fiction of: alcohol as trope in, 3, 7, 16, 31, 32–33, 104, 333, 379–82; Sherwood Anderson as influence on, 244, 445–46, 453–55; Callie Barr as influence on, 20–21, 38, 55, 61–62, 64–65, 100, 124, 212, 456, 483, 500; black maternal imaginary in, 283, 481–83, 516–17n20; blackness figured in, 110, 111, 166, 318, 360, 483, 517n21; Lelia Butler as influence on, 134, 137, 140, 141–42, 143, 144, 150, 207, 217; collaboration as metaphor in, 449; constructing race and gender in, 2, 3, 6,

7, 21, 23, 54–55, 62–63, 81, 82–83, 86, 95–97, 131, 139–40, 182, 206, 211–12, 444, 466, 513n24; in context of other Southern writers, 532n4; dance as trope in, 8, 383–84; dolls as trope in, 181, 496–97; early successes, 420–21; Maud Falkner as influence on, 131–32, 134–35, 206–10, 212, 217, 456, 500; family myths as influence on, 167, 170; flâneuse in, 139–40; and Freudian theory, 399, 400; homoeroticism in, 448, 449, 465–66; imposture in, 201–3; male family members as influence on, 167, 170–71; marriage as subject in, 1; and the maternal imaginary, 206, 212, 244, 442, 450, 456, 491, 500; parent-child relationships in, 254–55; photography as trope in, 210–12, 222, 223, 228–29, 230, 233; Pierrot mask in, 202; quilts as trope for forbidden and disavowed love in, 76, 102, 123–24, 183, 442, 493, 521n14; racialized visual aesthetic in, 166–67, 206, 207–10, 231–33; religion in, 156; role-playing and theatricality in, 8–9, 11–13, 77–78, 203–4, 398; Gertrude Stein as influence on, 443–44, 445; Jean Toomer as influence on, 443–44, 445–46; tropes of racialized loss in, 2, 3, 22, 33, 89, 90–91; White Supremacy as represented in, 161, 182–83; women as influence on, 1–2, 21–22, 93–95, 130, 140, 456, 500. *See also titles of works by Faulkner*

Fearn, Anne, M.D., 340, 409–11, 413–15, 416, 439

Fearn, John, M.D., 414–15

Fessenden, Stirling, 430

Finkelstein, Lionel, 531n7

"Fire and the Hearth, The" (Faulkner). See *Go Down, Moses*

Flags in the Dust (Faulkner), 124, 201–3, 211, 459. See also *Sartoris*

Focke, Eva, 346, 351, 353

Footlights, The, 376, 397, 398, 400

Forster, E. M., 438

Frank, Waldo, 446

Franklin, Cornell, 252, 534n10, 545n7, 545–46n8, 558n20; ambitions of, 255, 349; army enlistment of, 340–41, 347–48; divorce from Estelle Oldham, 243,

Franklin, Cornell (continued)
   375–76, 389, 390, 461–62, 464, 468–71,
   505n12; education of, 326; in Hawaii, 242,
   245, 336–47, 393–97; intelligence of, 255;
   marriage to Estelle Oldham, 5, 6–7, 8,
   195, 242–43, 245, 253, 255, 261–62, 301,
   303, 323, 333–35, 357–58, 363–64; and
   Dallas Meclewski, 469, 565–66n27; in the
   National Guard, 340–41; and Lem
   Oldham, 389–90; photograph of, 325;
   proposal to Estelle Oldham, 327–28, 333;
   at Schofield Barracks, 340–41, 345, 347;
   selfishness of, 348–49; in Shanghai, 242,
   327, 407–9; social connections of, 326;
   Southern mansion of, 327; Jill Faulkner
   Summers's view of, 15, 349
Franklin, Estelle Oldham. See Faulkner,
   Estelle Oldham Franklin
Franklin, Malcolm (Cornell and Estelle's
   son), 20, 84, 250, 252, 458, 507n21,
   510n55; birth of, 340, 414; myth about
   parentage, 566n40; photographs of, 216,
   493–498, 500; recollections of Callie
   Barr, 34, 37, 38–39, 40, 42, 46, 48–50,
   86
Franklin, Malcolm A. (Cornell's uncle), 326,
   338, 342, 352–53, 356, 357, 390, 430, 463,
   464, 555n11
Franklin, Mamie (Cornell's mother). See
   Hairston, Mamie Franklin
Franklin, Thomas B., 290
Franklin, Victoria ("Cho-Cho," Cornell's
   and Estelle's daughter), 49, 79–80, 84,
   236, 249, 250, 254, 349, 360, 403, 460,
   536n13, 548n10, 552n18; birth of, 355;
   photographs of, 408, 410; in Shanghai,
   408–10
Freedman Town, 57, 58, 61, 63, 511n7
Freud, Sigmund, 368; on the artist and his
   fantasies, 488, 567n5; Estelle Franklin's
   exposure to ideas of, 400, 401–2, 411. See
   also screen memory; Suppressed Desires

Genovese, Eugene, 39
Gentlemen Prefer Blondes, 359, 551n1
Georgetown District, South Carolina, 37,
   40, 41
Glasgow, Ellen, 357–58

Godfrey, Jim, 243
Go Down, Moses (Faulkner), 6, 38, 88, 89–110,
   120, 139, 211, 226, 500, 518n37; "The
   Bear," 104; constructing race in, 77,
   82–83, 86, 90, 91–93, 97–100, 108–10,
   283; creativity figured in, 110; as elegy for
   Callie Barr, 89, 90, 101–2, 105, 108–10,
   483; erotic desire in, 100; "The Fire and
   the Hearth," 91, 108; loss and mourning
   in, 90, 109; "Pantaloon in Black," 21, 91,
   100, 101–3, 110, 117, 363; racial unconscious as manifested in, 118, 517n30;
   racialized maternal loss in, 90, 91–93,
   97–100, 108–10, 283; racist fears as
   manifested in, 77, 96, 131, 519n39
Golliday, Evelyn, 45, 46
Graffenried, baron de, 141
Gullah language, 35, 84, 508n1. See also
   Caroline Barr: family origins of
Gwin, Minrose, 466, 533n2

Haas, Robert, 101, 103–4, 105, 111–12, 115
Hairston, Billy, 403
Hairston, Mamie Franklin (Cornell
   Franklin's mother), 242, 250, 330, 333–34,
   348, 535n5, 546n8; Estelle's relationship
   with, 354–56, 358, 467
Hale, Grace Elizabeth, 515n12
Hamlet, The (Faulkner), 11, 101
Harcourt Brace, 475
Hawaiian folklore: in Estelle Faulkner's
   stories, 13
Hawaiian Territory, The, 546n11; as
   American colony, 326; Cornell Franklin's
   arrival in, 323, 326; race and class issues
   in, 326–27, 546n11, 549n32. See also
   Faulkner, Estelle Oldham Franklin: in
   Hawaii
Hawks, Howard, 237–38
Heard, John, 341, 342, 352, 353
Helen: A Courtship (Faulkner), 197, 459
Helena, Arkansas: Barr family in, 41, 42;
   freed slaves in, 42
"Hill, The" (Faulkner), 377
Hodgson, Ralph, 360
Holcomb, Chauncy P., 430–31, 469, 470,
   561n17
Holiday magazine. See "Mississippi"

Hollywood, California: Faulkner in, 480

Holman, Millie (Callie Barr's daughter), 35, 43, 48, 50–51, 63

homoeroticism: and alcohol, 367; Faulkner's fears regarding, 312, 367, 449–50; in Estelle Faulkner's fiction, 368, 372; in William Faulkner's fiction, 448, 449, 465–66; in "Sapphics," 311

"Hong Li" (Faulkner), 246, 421, 444. See also Royal Street

House, Sherwood, 145

Humphries, H. A., 326

Hurston, Zora Neale, 53–54, 60–61, 85

Ibsen, Henrik, 411

"Idyll in the Desert" (Estelle Oldham and William Faulkner), 241, 422, 472

impostors. See Faulkner, William: military posing of; role-playing

Ivory, Fanny (Callie Barr's daughter), 35, 43, 48, 49, 50–52, 63

Jackson, Marilyn, 467

James, Henry, 90, 203, 401, 487

Jezebel, Falkner myth of Callie Barr as, 57, 64

Jim Crow South: in Estelle Faulkner's fiction, 3–4, 268, 270, 288; as influence on William Faulkner's worldview, 7, 16, 124; mentality of, as manifested in Hawaii and Shanghai, 344, 374–75, 435; race relations in, 22–23, 78–79, 80–81, 83, 500, 521n1, 541n48. See also race; White Supremacy

Johnson, Else, 252

Johnson, Victoria Fielden (Estelle's granddaughter), 254, 298, 336, 536n13

Jolson, Al, 108, 518n33

Jones, Anne Goodwyn, 205, 206, 270, 532n8, 533n3, 539n10

Jones, Fanny Ivory (Callie Barr's daughter). See Ivory, Fanny

Jones, Jacqueline, 39–40

jook joint, 22, 57–61. See also Molly Barr

Joyner, Charles, 39, 508n1

Keeley, Leslie E., 184–85, 191, 528–29n61

Keeley Institute, 184–85

Kells, Tom, 251

Killers of the Dream. See Smith, Lillian

Knopf, Alfred, 478

Ku Klux Klan, 19, 37, 182–83

"Landing in Luck" (Faulkner), 377

"L'Après-midi d'un faune" (Mallarmé and Faulkner), 310, 311–12

Larsen, Nella, 139

Law, Lula, 79–80, 548n10

"Leg, The" (Faulkner), 198, 211

"Letter to Grandmamma, A" (Estelle Faulkner), 241, 377, 387, 388, 422, 472

Lewis, Dora, 20

Lewis, Marjorie, 192

"Liggens, Preacher Green" (Maud Falkner's painting, 71–72, 76, 208

Light in August (Faulkner), 139, 156, 203, 456, 475, 479, 480; autobiographical traces in, 114, 156; constructing race in, 62, 165, 166, 211, 283, 447; desire and loss in, 6, 11, 123; photographic tropes in, 166, 246 maternal imaginary in, 6, 11, 97

Lilacs, The (Faulkner), 197, 310; erotics of, 360

Limon, John, 103

Linscott, Robert, 483, 529n9, 567n4

Liveright, Horace, 453, 462, 465–66, 467, 468

Loos, Anita, 551n1. See also Gentlemen Prefer Blondes

loss: as trope in Faulkner's fiction, 2, 3, 22, 33, 89, 90–91, 111 210, 227–28, 233, 453, 500. See also racialized loss

Lott, Eric, 102, 103, 108, 109

love and desire: in Faulkner's life and art, 1–2, 6, 11, 16, 20, 21, 23, 33, 56, 62, 82, 91, 95, 98, 111, 114, 116, 117, 118, 119, 123, 180, 183, 293, 366–67, 449, 454–64, 483, 485–6, 490–91

Lucas, Harry, 402

Lucas, Sara, 402

lynchings, 54, 110, 187. See also The Clansman; Ku Klux Klan

Mabry, Groves, 258

Mabry, Maude, 334

Mabry, Mellie, 293

Malcolm, Janet, 553n39

Mallarmé, Stéphane, 310

"Mammy," 514n31; white Southerners' memorials to, 64, 66, 106, 293; as "second mothers," 57, 66. *See also* Barr, Caroline ("Callie"); Cottrell, Nolia; Faulkner, Estelle and Faulkner, William: fiction of

Marble Faun, The (Faulkner), 197, 201, 242, 305, 359, 360, 361–62, 364, 365, 367, 428, 519n50; publication of, 442–43, 445, 446

Marionettes, The (Faulkner), 6, 8, 31, 95, 131, 197, 201, 245, 336, 342, 359, 379, 484; and Estelle's "A Crossing" 359, 362, 368–71, 382, 385–86, 399–400; Faulkner's drawings as subversive countertext for, 131, 213–17 , 206, 212–18; inspiration for, 212–13; as masked autobiography, 213–18, 360–62; Pierrot character in, 213–14, 215, 217, 360, 362, 398–99; relation to Estelle, 213, 220, 361; to Maud, 213; sexual desire in, 360–61

Mary Baldwin Seminary: Estelle as student at, 294–99, 383

masculinity: Southern codes of, 7, 167, 188–89, 201, 205–6, 230. *See also* Southern Manhood

masking: as legacy of slavery, 81, 84; in Faulkner's fiction, 8, 100, 105, 203. *See also* role-playing; theatricality

Mayday (Faulkner), 197, 465

McClean, Aunt Bama, 93

McClure, John, 421, 561–62n31

McGee, Rachel (Callie Barr's niece), 20, 27–28, 44, 46, 47, 49, 61, 63, 509n31, 510n4, 511n7, 512–13n3; and Callie Barr's death, 106–7

Meadow, Louise, 3, 133, 134, 155

Meclewski, Dallas Lee Chesterton, 469, 565–66n27

"Meeting South, A" (Anderson), 449–50

Melville, Herman, 203

memoirs, fictional. *See* "Doctor Wohlenski"; "Mississippi"

Mencken, H. L., 461, 479

Mills, Blanche, 334

Minter, David, 478

"Mirrors of Chartres Street" (Faulkner), 421

miscegenation, 114, 519n51; of Charlie Butler, 132; in Faulkner's fiction, 276–77;

of Faulkner's paternal great-grandfather and grandfather, 152, 153, 179, 181–83

"Mississippi" (Faulkner), 38, 62, 78, 82, 140, 500, 514n29, 515n8; Callie Barr's death in, 123–25; desire and love in, 123; as elegy for Callie Barr, 21, 89, 91, 111, 117, 118–19, 125, 233, 452, 483, 563n23; family secrets in, 114, 117, 125; legacies of slavery in, 120–21, 131; magic in, 124; masks and myths inherent in, 113–14, 119; narrative structure of, 111–14; quilt as trope in, 122–24; racialized loss in, 111, 117–18, 121, 124

Mississippi Industrial Institute and College, 157, 262

Mississippi State College for Women, 157

Modernism: 89, 137, 139, 446

"Moonlight" (Faulkner), 194, 333, 553n33

Morrison, Emma Jane, 272, 419, 428. *See also* "Star Spangled Banner Stuff"

Morrison, Toni, 23, 93, 274

Mosquitoes (Faulkner), 63–64, 111, 202, 361, 368, 378, 400, 425, 459, 460, 465

New Haven, Connecticut: Faulkner and Phil Stone in, 313–19, 392

New Orleans Woman: in "Doctor Wohlenski," 276–79, 282; Estelle as, 276

Niles, Henry C., 4, 241, 258, 259, 261, 292, 391, 537n17, 537n21

Niles, Jason, 537n21

Niles, Victoria Swanson Allen ("Miss Vic"), 240–41, 259, 261–62, 266, 351

"Note on Anderson, A" (Faulkner), 441–42

Ober, Harold, 103, 114

Odiorne, William, 244, 321

Oldham, Carrie Estelle, 262, 264

Oldham, Dorothy (Estelle's sister), 4, 240, 391, 394

Oldham, Estelle. *See* Faulkner, Estelle Oldham Franklin

Oldham, Lemuel (Estelle's father), 3, 4, 5, 187, 192, 240, 241, 258–63, 289, 293, 304, 412, 462; as businessman, 259–61, 266; family history of, 536–37n16; fashion-consciousness of, 265–66; and William Faulkner, 391–92; marriage of, 255, 259;

social standing of, 302–3; and son's death, 331; and Phil Stone, 388, 389, 390–91, 554n1

Oldham, Lida Allen, 4–5, 159, 192, 240–41, 258–59, 262–63, 264, 266, 293, 303, 354, 391, 394, 403; education of, 240, 259, 262; family background of, 261–62; marriage of, 255, 259

Oldham, Melvina Victoria ("Tochie") (Estelle's sister), 186, 192, 240, 266, 292, 299, 303, 334, 539n5; death of, 354; as student, 293–94; wedding of, 335

Oldham, Ned, 328, 331, 332

"Out of Nazareth" (Faulkner), 448, 449, 451

Page, Thomas Nelson, 270

Painter, Nell Irvin, 526n1

"Pantaloon in Black" (Faulkner). See Go Down, Moses

Parker, Dorothy, 477

Passage to India (Forster), 438

Patton, Nelse, 54, 187. See also lynchings

photography: see Faulkner, William: childhood of, fiction of, and visual aesthetic of; Butler, Lelia; Falkner, Maud

Pierrot: as Faulkner's poetic persona, 198–99, 201, 363, 368, 519n50. See also Go Down, Moses; The Marble Faun; The Marionettes; Vision in Spring

Plessy v. Ferguson, 25, 520n1

Powdermaker, Hortense, 48

Pullen, George, 145

Pylon (Faulkner), 475–76

Quarles, Mildred, 20, 45, 47, 49–50, 53, 63, 107, 511n7

quilts and quilting, 2, 35, 47, 102. See also Faulkner, William: fiction of, as trope for forbidden love in

race: as performative, 62, 77–78; social constructions of, 274. See also miscegenation; racialized loss

racialization, 568n17

racialized loss, poetics of: see Barr, Caroline; Estelle: fiction of; Falkner, Maud; and Faulkner, William: fiction of

racial segregation, 539n12; as constitutional, 25, 520n1. See also Jim Crow South

racial violence, 53–54, 182–83. See also lynchings, The Clansman, Ku Klux Klan

racist stereotypes, 21–22, 56, 57, 64–65, 446–47, 563n16. See also Barr, Caroline; Faulkner, Estelle

Ramey, Myrtle, 252

Reconstruction, aftermath of, 53–54, 131

religion: in Faulkner's fiction, 156; as satirized in Estelle Faulkner's fiction (see "A Crossing"; "Doctor Wohlenski")

Roberts, Diane, 276, 514n31, 540nn34–35, 541n48

Robeson, Eslanda, 418

Robeson, Paul, 418

Robinson, Taylor, 28, 49, 50

role-playing, 12–13, 78, 88, 124, 198–202, 203–4, 218–19, 221, 246, 251, 253, 313, 478, 527n23, 531n7, 552n14

"Rose for Emily, A" (Faulkner), 123, 154, 459

Rowan Oak, 476

Rowland, Rose, 143, 144, 292

Royal Canadian Air Force (RCAF), 198, 313, 316, 318, 336

Royal Street (Faulkner), 246, 459, 461

Rudd, James (Callie Barr's great-great grandson), 20, 35, 37, 38, 43, 49, 63, 125, 506n35

Salome (Wilde), 213, 214

Sams, Ferrol, 305

Sanctuary (Faulkner), 31, 211, 212, 379, 380, 420, 456, 467, 471, 476, 479, 480

"Sapphics" (Faulkner and Swinburne), 310–12, 321

Sargent, John Singer, 401

Sartoris, 203, 211, 453, 459, 468, 475. See also Flags in the Dust

Scott, Anne Firor, 6, 141

screen memory, Freud's theories of, 93, 95, 515–16n16; of William Faulkner, 6, 93–97, 181, 455, 515n14, 516nn16–17

"Selvage"/"Elly" (Estelle Oldham [Faulkner] and William Faulkner), 13 387, 388, 425, 435, 470–74; critique of Southern patriarchy in, 473, 474;

"Selvage"/"Elly" *(continued)*
destabilizing racial contructions in, 471–74; Elly as Bad Southern Belle, 473, 482; female agency in, 471, 473, 474; as imaginative collaboration with William, 241, 377, 422, 439, 458–59, 470–73, 475; marriage in, 470; the other in, 474; plot of, 471, 473–74, 560n53; and *Sanctuary,* 470–71; and *The Sound and the Fury,* 472, 482; transgressive sex in, 471, 473, 474

Shanghai, 558–59n30, 561n16; as American imperialiast enclave (*see* "Star Spangled Banner Stuff"); American missionaries in, 373; birth of Estelle and Cornell's son in, 414; cultural and intellectual life in 1920s, 411–12, 416–18; discrimination and segregation in, 416–18; Estelle in, 243, 245; Estelle's departure from, 243, 263, 421–22; Estelle's unhappiness in, 415–16; Cornell Franklin in, 242, 327, 407–9, 412; the Franklins' arrival in, 407–9; the Franklins' social life in, 412–13. *See also* "Star Spangled Banner Stuff"; Fearn, Anne, M.D.

Sherwood Anderson and Other Famous Creoles (Faulkner), 459

Short Story Club (Shanghai), 416–18

slave narratives, 32–33

slavery: in *Absalom, Absalom!,* 32; aftermath of, 19–20; legacies of, 7, 16, 21, 88, 135, 181–82, 211, 453

Smith, Hal, 9, 10, 252, 253–54, 536n10

Smith, Lillian, 56, 91, 92, 271, 417, 539n12, 541n48

Smith-Rosenberg, Carol, 556n35

Snead, James, 57

Snell, Susan, 242, 309, 312–13, 315, 543nn10–11, 544n35

Soldiers' Pay (Faulkner), 8, 31, 117, 139, 197, 198, 202, 244, 254, 362, 419–20, 441, 447, 460, 462, 464; Sherwood Anderson's enthusiasm for, 448–49, 450; black maternal in, 516–17n20; as imaginative collaboration with Estelle Faulkner, 378–79, 425; Jean Toomer and Gertrude Stein as influences on, 445–47

Somerville, Ella, 134

Somerville, Lucy, 331

Somerville, Nina, 334

Sound and the Fury, The (Faulkner), 6, 10, 31, 57, 61, 62, 72, 203, 250, 371, 456, 468, 476, 536n10; agency in, 458, 481–82; alcohol as weapon in, 379–80; 277, 281, 383, 469, 472, 484; Caddy Compson as desiring woman, 77, 382, 482; conception of the novel; 90, 166, 470, 481; as "dream," 487; as imaginative collaboration with Estelle, 241; inspiration for, 90, 123–24, 166; and Faulkner's private photographs, 458, 485 491–500; Estelle Faulkner's role in, 245, 269, 353, 422, 457, 469–70, 471, 483, 484–91; marketing of women in, 325; organizing fantasy of, 484; racialized desire in, 77, 90, 231, 458, racialized maternal imaginary in, 481–83, 490–491; "Selvage" and, 470–71

—Faulkner's suppressed Introduction to *The Sound and the Fury,* 481, 483–91; Faulkner's ambivalence about, 483, 484; creative process revealed in, 483, 485, 487; erotic sources of creativity, 469–70; many extant drafts of, 483; mystery of, 484; private content of 480, 481, 484, 487, 488, 490, 491, 564n4, 568n12

South Carolina, slavery in, 40, 506n1; *See also* Barr, Caroline

Southern history: 238, 272, 357, 426

Southern Manhood: 8, 305, 349, 357; Maud Falkner's paintings of, 67–69; myths of, 8, 230; in Faulkner's fiction, 201–3, 222, 223, 230

Southern myths, 113; as communicated to Southern children, 292–93; and Fa(u)lkner family, 131, 140, 167, 170, 173; in Estelle Faulkner's fiction, 90, 272–73

Southern Womanhood: Maud Falkner's paintings of, 68–71, 138; in Estelle Faulkner's fiction, 80, 271–72, 275–76, 280, 284, 285, 286, 471; in William Faulkner's fiction, 201–2, 458; myths of, 65, 230–31; Victorian ideal of, 61, 84

Spillers, Hortense, 514n31

"Spotted Horses" (Faulkner), 459

Spratling, William, 244, 319, 321, 448, 451, 452, 459, 461, 462

Stainback, Ingrahm, 403

"Star Spangled Banner Stuff" (Estelle
Franklin [Faulkner]), 241, 246, 338, 344,
352–53, 387, 388–89, 417, 422, 423,
558n20; alcohol and alcoholism in,
431–32; American businessmen in, 419,
427, 430; as anti-romance, 435–36; caste
and class issues in, 431–32, 434–35,
546n11; as critique and parody of
American imperialism, 439; destabilizing
racial constructions in, 425, 426, 433, 437,
474; female agency in, 419, 426–27, 435,
436–37; figuring "Chinamen" in, 368,
418–19, 425, 428–29, 433; as imaginative
dialogue with Faulkner, 353, 377, 424–26,
429, 439; Emma Jane as parody of
Imperial Belle, 419, 433, 435; marketing
of women in, 419, 426–27; as precursor to
Cecily in Soldiers' Pay in "Hong Li," 444,
465; of the other, 426, 434; transgressive
desire in; 338, 368, 417–20, 425–428, 433,
434, 436, 439; racist hysteria critiqued in,
419, 420, 426, 427, 428–29, 434, 435–37,
438; structure of, 428
Stein, Gertrude, 139, 443, 446, 447, 450,
563n16
Stein, Jean, 11, 252, 563n22
Stevens, Wallace, 198
Stone, Jack, 389
Stone, James, 303, 388, 389
Stone, Phil, 303; alcoholism of, 286, 304,
314, as Faulkner's friend and early
mentor, 179, 193, 195, 242, 244, 286, 291,
298, 304–5, 309–22, 367, 391, 442–43,
446, 453, 459, 461, 465, 543n10,
544nn15,16,35; and Lem Oldham, 388,
389, 390–91; mental illness of, 543n10
Stone, Rosamond, 314
Summers, Jill Faulkner, 1, 69, 238, 336, 481;
and Callie Barr, 20, 26–27, 34, 38, 46,
47–48, 49, 78–79, 81–82, 83–84, 86,
87–88, 121–23; birth of, 481; on Estelle
Faulkner, 84, 245, 251, 277, 298, 299, 303,
397; on Maud Falkner, 81–82, 133;
Maud's painting of, 69; on Murry
Falkner, 29; on William Faulkner, 184,
542n38; Faulkner's photographs of, 122,
458, 470, 491–500; on Lem Oldham,
260–61; on Lida Oldham, 4; on her

parents' marriage, 15, 184, 246; on
parents' role-playing, 12–13, 246;
Summers, Paul D. ("Tad"), Maud's painting
of, 69
Suppressed Desires (Glaspell), 245, 368,
398–99, 400, 401, 556n40. See also
Faulkner, Estelle: in Hawaii
Swift, John R., 145, 148, 149, 150
Swift, John Tate, 143, 145, 148, 149–50
Swift, Lelia Dean. See Butler, Lelia Dean
Swift
Swift, Mahalah Pullen, 68, 70, 138, 141, 143,
145, 148, 149–50, 522–23n4
Swinburne, Algernon Charles, 203, 309;
Faulkner's thralldom to, 310–12, 321, 360,
543n6; same-sex desire in, 309–12

Taylor, Jeremy, 29
Tennyson, Alfred, Lord, 177, 321
"That Evening Sun" (Faulkner), 54–55, 62,
63, 72, 86, 459
theatricality: as aspect of Faulkner's fiction,
8–9, 11–13, 77–78, 203–4, 298
Their Eyes Were Watching God (Hurston),
53–54
"There Was a Queen" (Faulkner), 80
These 13 (Faulkner), 476
Thompson, Frank, 396
Thompson, Jacob, 154
Thompson, Sam, 155, 156–57
Three Lives (Stein), 443, 445, 447, 563n16
Tingle, Patricia, 20, 46, 125
Tomlinson, Edna Earl, 269, 336, 373. See
also A Crossing
Toomer, Jean, 443–44
Twain, Mark, 305

Uncle Tom's Cabin (Stowe), 276
University of Mississippi ("Ole Miss"), 151,
155, 195, 260; Cornell Franklin as student
at, 323–24; Estelle Oldham as student at,
296, 298, 542n26
Unvanquished, The (Faulkner), 103

Vardaman, James K., 54
violence: and the Falkner men, 179; racial,
53–54, 182–83; in Southern communities,
159

Virginia, Nottoway County: *see* Barr, Caroline: childhood of; origins of

Virginian, The (Wister), 177

Vision in Spring (Faulkner), 197, 231, 359, 362–64, 367, 400, 459, 464–65, 519n50; Estelle as muse for, 364–66

Volstead Act, 380

voodoo: in the South, 48

Wagner-Martin, Linda, 517n30

Wakefield, Dan, 553n35

Ward, Frances, 133

Ward, Rufus, 250

Wasson, Ben, 7, 11, 244, 321, 468, 476, 477, 479, 480, 481, 483, 506n35, 563n22

Watson, Elizabeth Otey, 349

Watson, James, 220

Watson, Judge, 338–39, 396

Watson, Lillie Moore, 339

Watson, Louise, 324, 339, 341–43, 346, 347, 394

Watson, Virginia Bradley, 339, 394

Wells, Dean Faulkner, 66, 72, 75, 81, 135, 136, 526–27n13; and Maud Falkner, 130, 133, 192, 512n3

"White Beaches" (Estelle Faulkner), 422, 461

White Supremacy, belief in: Faulkner's exposure to, 187–88, 205; as influence on Faulkner's fiction, 161, 182–83

Wilde, Meta Carpenter, 10, 11, 252, 301, 506n35, 563n22

Wilde, Oscar, 213

Wilkins, Mary Holland Falkner ("Auntee"), 132, 152, 158, 161–63, 189, 192, 264, 292, 293

Wilkins, Sallie Murry. *See* Williams, Sallie Murry Wilkins

Williams, Blanche Colton, 559n32

Williams, Joan, 11, 252

Williams, Sallie Murry Wilkins, 3, 132, 162, 163, 181, 189–90, 192, 193, 292, 389, 526n6

Williams, Tennessee, 333

Williamsburg District, South Carolina, 39

Williamson, Joel, 54, 114, 125, 132, 141, 171

Wilson, Woodrow, 323, 354, 390, 547–48n7

Winesburg, Ohio (Anderson), 445

Wishing Tree, The (Faulkner), 552n18

Wister, Owen, 177

women: exchanges of, as aspect of male homosocial bonding, 387–92, 554nn1–2; in Faulkner's fiction, 139–40; as influence on Faulkner's fiction, 1–2, 21–22, 93–95, 130, 140, 456; and the right to vote, 395. *See also* Barr, Caroline; Falkner, Maud Butler; Faulkner, Estelle Oldham Franklin

Women's Book Club, 132, 163, 177–78. *See also* Falkner, Sally Murry; Falkner, Maud; Oldham, Lida

Wood, John, 290

Woodward, C. Vann, 67

Woodward, Zaida, 467

Woolf, Virginia, 139

Wortham, Earl, 45–46, 541n9

Wortis, Bernard, 116, 117

Wright, Frederick G., 29

Wright, Willard Huntingon, 309

Yaeger, Patricia, 117, 520n12

Yale University: Phil Stone as student at, 310, 313. *See also* New Haven, Connecticut

Young, Stark, 7, 244, 302, 319, 321, 364, 366